Annual Review of

# INFORMATION SCIENCE AND TECHNOLOGY

# Annual Review of
# INFORMATION SCIENCE AND TECHNOLOGY

## Volume 44 • 2010
### Blaise Cronin, Editor

Published on behalf of the
American Society for Information Science and Technology
by Information Today, Inc.

Medford, New Jersey

ISBN: 978-1-57387-371-0
ISSN: 0066-4200
CODEN: ARISBC
LC No. 66-25096

*Published and distributed by*
Information Today, Inc.
143 Old Marlton Pike
Medford, NJ 08055-8750

*On behalf of*

The American Society for Information Science and Technology
1320 Fenwick Lane, Suite 510
Silver Spring, MD 20910-3602, U.S.A.

*Information Today, Inc. Staff*
President and CEO: Thomas H. Hogan, Sr.
Editor-in-Chief and Publisher: John B. Bryans
Managing Editor: Amy M. Reeve
Proofreader: Penelope Mathiesen
VP Graphics and Production:
 M. Heide Dengler
Cover Designer: Victoria Stover
Book Designer: Kara Mia Jalkowski

*ARIST Staff*
Editor: Blaise Cronin
Associate Editor: Debora Shaw
Copy Editors: Dorothy Pike,
 Victoria Johnson
Indexer: Becky Hornyak

**www.infotoday.com**

# Contents

## SECTION I
**Metrics**

## SECTION II
**Fundamentals**

# SECTION III
**Communication**

# SECTION IV
**Economics**

# SECTION V
**Practice**

# Introduction

*Blaise Cronin*

Metrics are *à la mode*. Once it was plain old bibliometrics, now we have scientometrics, informetrics, webometrics, cybermetrics, digimetrics, tagometrics. Neologisms abound. The widespread availability of Web log files affords unprecedented opportunity for assessing the visibility, productivity, and performance of individual scholars, research groups, institutions, and nation states. Illustrative of the general trend is the U.K. government's stated commitment to making the next Research Assessment Exercise (RAE) metrics-based. Of course, information science has long been concerned with the quantitative analysis of scholarly communication and publishing behaviors. Latterly, however, there has been a renaissance of sorts and we are witnessing spectacular growth in the volume and variety of bibliometric research and experimentation, not just within information science but also in other disciplines. As I observed some years ago, there "will soon be a critical mass of Web-based digital objects and usage statistics on which to model scholars' communication behaviors—publishing, posting, blogging, scanning, reading, downloading, glossing, linking, citing, recommending, acknowledging—and with which to track their scholarly influence and impact, broadly conceived and broadly felt" (Cronin, 2005, p. 196).

What, then, are the implications of these developments? Michael Kurtz and Johan Bollen show what digital data can tell us about the ways people access and use electronic information resources. Their primary focus in "Usage Bibliometrics" is the research literature of astrophysics, but the methods they describe and the points they make have general applicability. This chapter is a fine introduction to next-generation bibliometrics, in which citations will be just one of a battery of performance indicators upon which the RAE, for instance, will be able to draw. When Jorge Hirsch (2005) published his paper on the h-index—a novel technique for evaluating the impact of a scientist's work—it led almost immediatcly to a proliferation of follow-up studies within and well beyond the literature of information science. Some authors applied the h-index to specific populations or disciplines; others proposed modifications to, or elaborations of, Hirsch's original formulation. Leo Egghe, who has published extensively on the subject, here provides a very timely and thorough review of the literature on the h-index and related measures. The growing ubiquity and utility of metrics are illustrated in the chapter by Robert Schumaker, Osama Solieman, and Hsinchun Chen. A sporting event, be it a basketball game or a football/soccer match, routinely generates an enormous amount of potentially usable data on players' movements, scoring rates, assists, saves, tackles, blocks, and so forth. Often, a player's overall contribution to a game is not fully appreciated by either the coach or spectator; too much escapes the naked eye (see Lewis, 2008, on basketball). Often, too, fans and players alike hold assumptions that are at odds with the findings of empirical research (see Bray, 2006, on football/soccer). This is where sophisticated data mining and visualization software come into play. The application of such tools and techniques to professional sports management is a good illustration of how information technology, intelligently deployed, can create a competitive advantage—at least in the short term.

Jonathan Furner's chapter in Section II ("Fundamentals") is a crisp exposition of the various philosophical questions and positions that are to be found in the scholarly literature of information studies. He distinguishes at the outset between philosophical studies *about* information (meta questions relating to the nature of the field as a field) and questions that arise *in* the field (such as the influence philosophy has on information studies). Toward the end he flips the question and asks to what extent information studies has influenced philosophy. His answer is not terribly encouraging: "Hardly at all. ... Moreover, the status within the general philosophical community of philosophy of information studies sometimes seems to be roughly on a par with that of the philosophy of pasta." Fundamental philosophical questions underpin Hamid Ekbia's ambitious chapter, which reviews a half-century of research in artificial intelligence (AI). What, ultimately, differentiates a laughing cavalier from a social robot, Deep Blue from Kasparov? The frequently agonistic debate within the AI community continues with, as he puts it, "heavy traffic between philosophical and technical realms."

Just as bibliometrics experienced a revival with the advent of the Web, so, too, did faceted classification. In both cases, some reinventing of the wheel occurred, but that is not necessarily a bad thing. Recently, content developers, information architects, and others responsible for designing websites and large corporate databases seem to have discovered elements of the classical literature on facet analysis and faceted classification. Kathryn La Barre's chapter connects the then (Bliss, Ranganathan, the Classification Research Group, et al.) with the now (e.g., faceted search and browsing systems) and in so doing reminds us that, along with bibliometrics, classification remains one of the most important sub-fields of information science.

There are two chapters in the section on "Communication." Scholarly communication and publishing are familiar topics to *ARIST* readers, but Cecilia Brown's focus here is on how the evolving cyber-infrastructure is (or is not) altering the formal communication practices of scientists. (See, too, the chapter by Kurtz and Bollen in this volume.) Despite many significant developments in the last decade or so (e-preprints, digital repositories, open access, scientific blogging) she is adamant that peer review remains the lynchpin of the system. And, indeed, it does: Scientists are quite aware of the costliness and imperfections of peer review, but are not (yet) inclined to abandon the system, as a recent study demonstrated convincingly (Ware, 2008). Communication of a different kind is the subject of the wide-ranging chapter by Scott Robertson and Ravi Vatrapu. Digital government is a frequently used term, but, as the authors show, not one for which there is a universally agreed definition. Still, it is beyond dispute that there has been enormous recent growth in the amount of government information available online, in the number of services and functions that the average citizen can now perform digitally, and in the level of civic engagement made possible by interactive technologies. The Founders would surely be impressed.

Loet Leydesdorff has published extensively on social systems, knowledge creation, and innovation. "How," he asks here, "can an economy be based on something as volatile as knowledge?" and duly proceeds to take us on a highly theoretical journey in order to show the role codified knowledge plays in national innovation systems. The Triple Helix model—the principal components of which are universities, industry, and government—constitutes his analytic framework. Government, coincidentally, is the focus of Kirsti Nilsen's chapter on the application of economic theory to public sector information. She covers considerable ground, some of which will be familiar to regular *ARIST* readers; *ARIST*, as she notes, has a long tradition of commissioning chapters on the economics of information and related topics. Here Nilsen provides us with a tutorial on the economic, political, and social arguments relating to the provision of public sector information, in the process comparing prevailing practices and policies in Europe and the U.S.

Mass migration is one of the most challenging and politically contentious issues of the twenty-first century. Nadia Caidi, Danielle Allard, and Lisa Quirke note that the number of international migrants increased by 45 million between 1965 and 1990 and is currently growing annually at a rate of almost 3 percent. Countless studies of the "Information needs of *X*" have been published in the literature over the years, but relatively little attention has been given to the information needs, practices, and skills of those who have, for whatever reason, had to move to another country, adapt to an alien culture, and learn a new language. The authors "map out the general terrain that represents the information practices of immigrants" and in so doing make clear the need for thoughtful public policy making and effective professional intervention. Many of the aforementioned "Information needs of *X*" studies have used one or more of the three "confessional techniques" examined in detail by Elisabeth Davenport. Her careful review of the use of (a) the critical incident (CI) technique, (b) focus groups, and (c) micro moment time-line interviews in the so-called human information behavior (HIB) literature is both timely and disconcerting. Among other things, she describes Flanagan's development and meticulous application of the CI technique in studies of air crews more than fifty years ago and notes that his "caveats are rarely discussed, let alone heeded" in much contemporary HIB research. Reading her well-argued critique brought to mind Furner's "philosophy of pasta" remark. Let us hope that some lessons are learned from what she has to say.

# References

Bray, K. (2006). *How to score: Science and the beautiful game*. London: Granta.

Cronin, B. (2005). *The hand of science: Academic writing and its rewards*. Lanham, MD: Scarecrow Press.

Hirsch, J. E. (2005). An index to quantify an individual's scientific research output. *Proceedings of the National Academy of Sciences of the United States of America*, *102*(46), 16569–16572. Retrieved July 24, 2009, from www.pnas.org/content/102/46/16569

Lewis, M. (2008, February 15). The no-stats all-star. *New York Times Magazine*, 26–33, 63–64.

Ware, M. (2008). *Peer review: Benefits, perceptions and alternatives*. London: Publishing Research Consortium. Retrieved February 19, 2009, from www.publishingresearch.net/documents/PR Csummary4Warefinal.pdf

# Acknowledgments

Many individuals are involved in the production of *ARIST*. I gratefully acknowledge the contributions of our Advisory Board members and outside reviewers. Their names are listed in the pages that follow. Victoria Johnson and Dorothy Pike were enormously helpful with copy-editing and bibliographic checking. Becky Hornyak produced the thorough index. As always, Debora Shaw did what a first rate associate editor is supposed to do.

# *ARIST* Advisory Board

**Judit Bar-Ilan**
Hebrew University of Jerusalem, Israel

**Micheline Beaulieu**
University of Sheffield, UK

**Nicholas J. Belkin**
Rutgers University, New Brunswick, USA

**Christine L. Borgman**
University of California at Los Angeles, USA

**Terrence A. Brooks**
University of Washington, Seattle, USA

**Elisabeth Davenport**
Edinburgh Napier University, UK

**Susan Dumais**
Microsoft Research, Redmond, USA

**Abby Goodrum**
Ryerson University, Toronto, Canada

**E. Glynn Harmon**
University of Texas at Austin, USA

**Leah A. Lievrouw**
University of California at Los Angeles, USA

**Javed Mostafa**
University of North Carolina, Chapel Hill, USA

**Katherine W. McCain**
Drexel University, Philadelphia, USA

**Charles Oppenheim**
Loughborough University, UK

# Chapter Reviewers

Judit Bar-Illan
David Bawden
Clare Beghtol
John Carlo Bertot
Peter van den Besselaar
Lutz Bornmann
Sandra Braman
Kathy Buckner
Quentin Burrell
Donald Case
Clara Chu
Ian Cornelius
Elisabeth Davenport
Charles Davis
Ying Ding
Carl Drott
John Feather
Nigel Ford

Alan Gilchrist
Melissa Gross
Glynn Harmon
Stephen Hirtle
Birger Hjørland
Katherine McCain
Claire McInerney
Betsy Van der Veer Martens
Cheryl Metoyer
Javed Mostafa
Alice Robbin
Howard Rosenbaum
Ronald Rousseau
Reija Savolainen
Sanna Talja
Brian Vickery
Julian Warner
Howard White

# Contributors

**Danielle Allard** is a doctoral candidate at the Faculty of Information, University of Toronto. She has a B.A. (Hons.) in Women's Studies and Philosophy and an M.I.St. from the Faculty of Information Studies (Toronto). Her doctoral research examines the everyday information behavior of new immigrants to Toronto, with particular attention paid to newcomers' social networks and their use of both local and transnational ties to access settlement information. Danielle Allard can be reached at allard@fis.utoronto.ca.

**Johan Bollen** is a staff researcher at the Los Alamos National Laboratory, Research Library (Digital Library Research & Prototyping team). He was an Assistant Professor at the Department of Computer Science of Old Dominion University from 2002 to 2005. He obtained his Ph.D. in Experimental Psychology from the University of Brussels in 2001 on the subject of cognitive models of human hypertext navigation. His current research interests are usage data mining, computational sociometrics, informetrics, and digital libraries. Dr. Bollen has published extensively on these subjects as well as matters relating to adaptive information systems architecture. He is the Principal Investigator on the Andrew W. Mellon Foundation-funded MESUR project, which aims to expand the quantitative tools available for the assessment of scholarly impact. Johan Bollen can be reached at jbollen@lanl.gov.

**Cecelia Brown** is a Professor in the School of Library and Information Studies at the University of Oklahoma. She holds an M.L.I.S. from the University of Oklahoma and a Ph.D. in Nutritional Sciences from the University of Illinois. Her research focuses on the information behavior of physical and life scientists in the online environment. Also of interest is the promotion of information literacy among scientists and science students for the support of their research, teaching, and learning activities, as well as among health care professionals and the general public with an emphasis on nutrition and exercise information seeking and use. Cecelia Brown can be reached at cbrown@ou.edu.

**Nadia Caidi** is an Associate Professor at the Faculty of Information, University of Toronto. She holds an M.L.I.S. and a Ph.D. from the Department of Information Studies at UCLA, as well as an M.S.T. in Communication Studies from Grenoble 3,

France. Her primary research interests are information policy and community informatics. She received funding from the Social Sciences and Humanities Research Council (SSHRC) in Canada for her research on the state of information post 9/11. She has also researched and published on the information practices of ethno-cultural communities (funded by Citizenship and Immigration Canada) and on First Nations communities in rural and remote areas of Northern Ontario (through her involvement with the Canadian Research Alliance for Community Innovation and Networking). Nadia Caidi can be reached at nadia.caidi@gmail.com.

**Hsinchun Chen** is McClelland Professor of Management Information Systems at the University of Arizona and Director of the Artificial Intelligence Lab. He is a Fellow of the IEEE and AAAS. He received the IEEE Computer Society 2006 Technical Achievement Award and INFORMS 2008 Design Science Award. Dr. Chen is author/editor of 20 books, 180 *SCI* journal articles, and 120 refereed conference articles. He serves on ten editorial boards including *JASIST*, *ACM TOIS*, *IEEE Intelligent Systems*, *IEEE SMCA*, and *DSS*. Hsinchun Chen can be reached at hsinchunchen@gmail.com.

**Elisabeth Davenport** is Professor Emerita at the School of Computing, Edinburgh Napier University, and Visiting Scholar at the School of Library and Information Science, Indiana University, Bloomington. She has published widely in the areas of scholarly communication, information and knowledge management, and social informatics, and has presented her work extensively in Europe, Australia, and the Americas. Dr. Davenport's current research interests include information and documentary practices, the genealogy of ICTs, and the development of socio-technical theory and methodology. Elisabeth Davenport can be reached at e.davenport@napier.ac.uk.

**Leo Egghe** has a Ph.D. in Mathematics (University of Antwerp, Belgium, 1978), an habilitation in Mathematics (University of Antwerp, Belgium, 1985), and a Ph.D. in Information Science (City University London, UK, 1989). He has been Chief Librarian of the University of Hasselt, Belgium since 1979. He was the chairman of the first International Conference on Bibliometrics (now called the ISSI conference) and co-edited (with Ronald Rousseau) the first two proceedings. He was Professor in the Department of Library and Information Science of the University of Antwerp from 1983 to 2008 where he taught courses on informetrics and information retrieval. Together with Ronald Rousseau he wrote *Introduction to Informetrics* (Elsevier, 1990) and *Elementary Statistics for Effective Library and Information Service Management* (Aslib, 2001). Dr. Egghe also wrote *Power Laws in the Information Production Process: Lotkaian Informetrics* (Elsevier, 2005) and is the author of over 200 scientific articles in peer reviewed journals. He is the Founding Editor-in-Chief of the *Journal of Informetrics* (Elsevier), which was launched in 2007. In 2001 he received the Derek de Solla Price Award for Scientometrics and Informetrics. Leo Egghe can be reached at leo.egghe@uhasselt.be.

**Hamid R. Ekbia** is an Associate Professor of Information Science and Cognitive Science, and Director of the Center for Research on Mediated Interaction at the School of Library and Information Science, Indiana University, Bloomington.

His research is focused on mediation—that is, on how objects and meanings are transformed in hybrid networks of humans and non-humans. With this question in mind, Ekbia has written in the areas of knowledge management, network organizations, free/Open Source software, spatial decision making, and artificial intelligence (AI). His recent book *Artificial Dreams: The Quest for Non-Biological Intelligence* (Cambridge University Press, 2008) is a critical-technical analysis of AI. He teaches human-computer interaction, agent-based modeling, and geographic information systems. Hamid Ekbia can be reached at hekbia@indiana.edu.

**Jonathan Furner** is an Associate Professor at the Graduate School of Education and Information Studies at the University of California, Los Angeles. He has a Ph.D. in Information Studies from the University of Sheffield and an M.A. in Philosophy and Social Theory from the University of Cambridge. He works on cultural informatics and the history and philosophy of documentation. His current research includes studies of social tagging, art museum documentation, and the metaphysics of documents and their subjects. Jonathan Furner can be reached at furner@gseis.ucla.edu.

**Michael J. Kurtz** is an astronomer and computer scientist at the Harvard-Smithsonian Center for Astrophysics in Cambridge, Massachusetts, which he joined after receiving a Ph.D. in Physics from Dartmouth College in 1982. Kurtz is the author or co-author of over 250 technical articles and abstracts on subjects ranging from cosmology and extra-galactic astronomy, to data reduction and archiving techniques, to information systems and text retrieval algorithms. In 1988 Kurtz conceived what has now become the Smithsonian/NASA Astrophysics Data System, the core of the digital library in astronomy, perhaps the most sophisticated discipline-centered library extant. He has been associated with the project since that time, and was awarded the 2001 Van Biesbroeck Prize of the American Astronomical Society for his efforts. Michael Kurtz can be reached at kurtz@cfa.harvard.edu.

**Kathryn La Barre** is an Assistant Professor at the University of Illinois at Urbana-Champaign. Her research interests include information organization and access systems and structures, interactions between theoretical approaches and current practices in digital environments, and the historical and theoretical foundations of library and information science. Current research projects include the OCLC/ALISE LISRGP-funded Folktales and Facets and FRBR, which seeks to develop a next-generation catalog prototype implementation with enhanced records for access to a test-bed of folktales that gives special consideration to the shared and unique information seeking tasks of three distinct user group—scholars, practitioners, and laypeople. Kathryn La Barre can be reached at klabarre@illinois.edu.

**Loet Leydesdorff** (Ph.D. Sociology, M.A. Philosophy, M.Sc. Biochemistry) is Professor of Science and Technology Dynamics at the Amsterdam School of Communications Research (ASCoR) of the University of Amsterdam. He is Visiting Professor at the Institute of Scientific and Technical Information of China (ISTIC) in Beijing and Honorary Fellow of the Science and Technology Policy

Research Unit (SPRU) at the University of Sussex and at the Virtual Knowledge Studio of the Netherlands Royal Academy of Arts and Sciences. He has published extensively in systems theory, social network analysis, scientometrics, and the sociology of innovation. He received the Derek de Solla Price Award for Scientometrics and Informetrics in 2003 and held "The City of Lausanne" Honor Chair at the School of Economics, Université de Lausanne, in 2005. In 2007, he was vice president of the 8th International Conference on Computing Anticipatory Systems (CASYS'07, Liège). Loet Leydesdorff can be reached at loet@leydesdorff.net.

**Kirsti Nilsen** is an independent researcher and writer who, until retirement, was a faculty member in the University of Western Ontario's Faculty of Information and Media Studies; she has also taught at other universities in North America and Scandinavia. Author of *The Impact of Information Policy* (2001) and co-author of *Conducting the Reference Interview* (2001, 2009) and also *Constraining Public Libraries: The World Trade Organization's General Agreement on Trade in Services* (2006), she has published book chapters, articles, and conference papers on information policy, e-government, international trade policy, and reference. A past president of the Canadian Association for Information Science, she has degrees from Emerson College, Simmons College, and a Ph.D. from the University of Toronto. Kirsti Nilsen can be reached at knilsen@uwo.ca.

**Lisa Quirke** is a doctoral student at the Faculty of Information, University of Toronto. She received an M.A. in Immigration and Settlement Studies from Ryerson University (Toronto). Her current research examines the information practices and settlement experiences of immigrant and refugee youth in Canada, with a particular emphasis on the role that leisure plays in their acculturation. Lisa Quirke can be reached at lisa.quirke@utoronto.ca.

**Scott P. Robertson** is an Assistant Professor in the Information and Computer Sciences Department at the University of Hawaii at Manoa and Director of the Hawaii Computer-Human Interaction Lab (HI'CHI). He conducts research on information seeking behavior and social networking in the context of digital government. He is a Senior Member of the Association for Computing Machinery and a Fellow of the American Psychological Society. He serves on the editorial boards of the *ACM Transactions on Computer-Human Interaction* and *Interacting with Computers*. He received his Ph.D. in Cognitive Psychology, with a specialization in Cognitive Science, from Yale University. Scott Robertson can be reached at scottpr@hawaii.edu.

**Robert P. Schumaker** is an Associate Professor in Information Systems at Iona College. He received his undergraduate degree in Civil Engineering from the University of Cincinnati, an M.B.A. in Management and International Business from the University of Akron, and his Ph.D. degree in Management from the University of Arizona. His interests include sports data mining, stock price prediction, natural language systems, and textual analysis techniques. Robert Schumaker can be reached at rschumaker@iona.edu.

**Osama K. Solieman** attended the University of Arizona, graduating with a B.S. in Computer Science in 2003. In 2006, he received an M.S. in Management Information Systems and was the lead researcher on a database project for the Department of Electrical and Computer Engineering. Currently, he is an IT consultant regularly working with Fortune 500 companies. Osama Solieman can be reached at osolieman@googlemail.com.

**Ravi K. Vatrapu** is an Assistant Professor at the Center for Applied Information and Communication Technologies (CAICT) at the Copenhagen Business School. He received his Ph.D. in Communication and Information Sciences from the University of Hawaii, where he was also a researcher in the Hawaii Computer-Human Interaction Lab (HI'CHI) and the Laboratory for Interactive Learning Technologies (LILT). Dr. Vatrapu's doctoral research investigated cultural influences on the appropriation of affordances and technological intersubjectivity in computer-supported collaboration. His current research interests are in comparative informatics, which investigates the socio-technical intersections of computer science, cognitive science, consciousness studies, and cultural studies. Ravi Vatrapu can be reached at rv.caict@cbs.edu.

# About the Editor

**Blaise Cronin** is the Rudy Professor of Information Science at Indiana University, Bloomington, where he has been Dean of the School of Library and Information Science for eighteen years. From 1985 to 1991 he held the Chair of Information Science and was Head of the Department of Information Science at the University of Strathclyde in Glasgow. He is concurrently an Honorary Visiting Professor at City University, London, the University of Brighton, and Edinburgh Napier University. For six years he was the Talis Information Visiting Professor of Information Science at the Manchester Metropolitan University. Dr. Cronin is the author of numerous research articles, monographs, technical reports, conference papers, and other publications. Much of his research focuses on collaboration in science, scholarly communication, citation analysis, and the academic reward system— the intersection of information science and social studies of science. His books include *The Citation Process* (1984), *The Scholar's Courtesy* (1995), and *The Hand of Science* (2005). He has also published on topics such as information warfare, information and knowledge management, strategic intelligence, and digital pornography. Professor Cronin is Editor-in-Chief of the *Journal of the American Society for Information Science and Technology*.

He has extensive international experience, having taught, conducted research, or consulted in more than thirty countries: Clients have included the World Bank, NATO, Asian Development Bank, UNESCO, U.S. Department of Justice, Brazilian Ministry of Science & Technology, European Commission, British Council, Her Majesty's Treasury, Hewlett-Packard Ltd., British Library, Commonwealth Agricultural Bureaux, Chemical Abstracts Service, and Association for Information Management. He has been a keynote or invited speaker at scores of conferences, nationally and internationally. Dr. Cronin was a founding director of Crossaig, an electronic publishing start-up in Scotland, which was acquired in 1992 by Thomson Reuters. Professor Cronin was educated at Trinity College Dublin (M.A.) and the Queen's University of Belfast (Ph.D., D.S.Sc.) In 1997, he was awarded the degree Doctor of Letters (D.Litt., *honoris causa*) by Queen Margaret University,

Edinburgh for his scholarly contributions to information science. In 2006 he received the Award of Merit from the American Society for Information Science and Technology.

# About the Associate Editor

**Debora Shaw** is a Professor at the Indiana University, Bloomington, School of Library and Information Science. Her research focuses on information organization and information seeking and use. Her work has been published in the *Journal of the American Society for Information Science and Technology*, *Journal of Documentation*, *Library & Information Science Research*, and *First Monday*, among others. Dr. Shaw has served as President of the American Society for Information Science (1997) and has also served on ASIST's Board of Directors. She has been affiliated with *ARIST* as both a chapter author and as an indexer since 1986. Dr. Shaw received bachelor's and master's degrees from the University of Michigan and the Ph.D. from Indiana University. She was on the faculty at the University of Illinois before joining Indiana University.

# Metrics

# CHAPTER 1

# Usage Bibliometrics

*Michael J. Kurtz*
*Harvard-Smithsonian Center for Astrophysics, Cambridge, MA*

*Johan Bollen*
*Los Alamos National Laboratory, Los Alamos, NM*

## Introduction

How researchers access and read their technical literature has gone through a revolutionary change. Whereas fifteen years ago nearly all use was mediated by a paper copy, today nearly all use is mediated by an electronic copy. Within individual disciplines the change has been nearly instantaneous. As an example, in mid-1997 the number of papers downloaded from astronomy's digital library, the Smithsonian/NASA Astrophysics Data System (ADS; ads.harvard.edu) exceeded the sum of all the papers read in all of astronomy's print libraries, combined (Accomazzi, Eichhorn, Kurtz, Grant, & Murray, 2000; Eichhorn, Kurtz, Accomazzi, Grant, & Murray, 2000; Grant, Accomazzi, Eichhorn, Kurtz, & Murray, 2000; Kurtz, Karakashian, Grant, Eichhorn, Murray, Watson, et al., 1993; Kurtz, Eichhorn, Accomazzi, Grant, Demleitner, & Murray, 2005; Kurtz, Eichhorn, Accomazzi, Grant, Murray, & Watson, 2000). This was six months after two of astronomy's four largest journals became available electronically, and six months before the other two were available online.[1] Studies (Tenopir, King, Boyce, Grayson, & Paulson, 2005; Kurtz, Eichhorn, Accomazzi, Grant, Demleitner, & Murray, 2005) show that the ADS is used on a near-daily basis by a large majority of research astronomers. This rapid transformation took place across all scientific domains; in November 2006, Elsevier reported one billion downloads since the inception of its ScienceDirect service in 1999, a number that greatly exceeds the total number of citations published since the 1900s (www.info.sciencedirect.com/news/press_releases/archive/archive2006/one_billionths.asp).

A key difference between print and electronic libraries is the detailed records that electronic libraries keep of every transaction. In a paper library a typical researcher might browse a book of abstracts, find some articles of interest, retrieve them from the stacks, photocopy them, and return to her office to read them, leaving no trace, other, perhaps, than that captured by reshelving statistics. Today she would accomplish this

**3**

with a few commands to a search engine and a few clicks of the mouse, all from her desk, and all such actions would be recorded. Indeed, today, for every single use of an electronic resource, the system can record which resource was used, who used it, where that person was, when it was used, what type of request was issued, what type of record it was, and from where the article was used. Although these data do not include essentially unknowable quantities such as user motivations or goals, they do constitute a much more comprehensive record of usage than was previously available. When, in addition, these data are merged with bibliographic data, such as authors and citations, we have a very accurate record of user activity.

Methods have been and will be created to measure the flow of information among countries, disciplines, and groups of individuals, and to assess the productivity of a number of different entities on the basis of citations, number of publications, and other text-based data. These methods play an increasingly important role in the allocation of resources, but their present focus on citation and text data entails a number of distinct disadvantages. Citation data concern primarily journal articles and their authors, are subject to significant publication delays, and offer one particular perspective on scholarly activity that overlooks the activities of those not associated with the present publishing (and citation) system.

Large-scale usage data on the other hand are not subject to publication delays, not limited to journal articles and their authors, and offer a fairly comprehensive overview of activities within all phases and social layers of the scientific process. It is thus inevitable that this wealth of data will be increasingly integrated in bibliometrics. Indeed, following the success of usage data analysis in commercial environments, such as recommender systems employed by Amazon.com and Netflix.com, the past five years have seen a surge in bibliometric investigations of usage. The introduction of this new usage data environment is, however, both extremely powerful and extremely dangerous; it adds significant capabilities to the instrumentarium of bibliometric analysis, but does so on the basis of data whose characteristics and validity have only recently become the focus of scientific investigation.

The growing role of usage data necessitates an expanded definition of bibliometrics. Bibliometrics is generally defined (Broadus, 1987) as the quantitative study of published units on the basis of citation and text analysis, but can include studies based on usage data. Small-scale, institutionally bound studies of reshelving statistics have indeed played a minor role in traditional bibliometrics. However, this type of usage data is qualitatively and quantitatively different from that collected by modern electronic library services. Whereas well-vetted, large-scale databases have been available for bibliometric analysis for several decades, this has not been the case for usage data. Their limited scale, detail, and applicability have imposed strict limitations on their role in traditional bibliometrics.

In this chapter we are concerned with an expanded definition of bibliometrics that includes modern usage data that approximate or even surpass the scale, quality, and detail of citation and text databases. These usage data: are extremely large-scale; are sample significant and diverse portions of the scholarly community; are highly detailed in their request-metadata; allow reconstruction of user clickstreams; are recorded at the article level; and are now commonly recorded by the electronic services offered by publishers, aggregators, and institutional repositories. Present developments indicate an expanded role for this type of usage data that will revolutionize bibliometrics as we presently know it.

By our definition user-centric studies would come under the broader classification of user-based (scholarly) informetrics (Bar-Ilan, 2008; Wilson, 1999) and are beyond the scope of this review. For discussions of user behavior, the interested reader might consult the recent reviews by Jamali, Nicholas, and Huntington (2005), King and Tenopir (1999), Rowlands (2007), and Wang (1999). For discussions of searching behavior we suggest the papers by Borgman, Hirsh, and Hiller (1996), Hider, (2006), and Jansen (2005). Outside the realm of scholarly literature, user studies are an important component in the commercial world. Marketing, advertising, and product design are some obvious examples. In addition, the recent compendium "Usage Statistics of E-Serials" edited by Fowler (2007) contains 17 articles addressing various aspects of usage studies; this volume concentrates mainly on practical issues of immediate interest to practicing librarians; the present review is more concerned with theoretical and longer term issues; of particular interest here is the review of the MAXDATA project by Tenopir, Baker, Read, Manoff, McClanahan, Nicholas, and colleagues (2007). Luther (2000) reviewed the field a decade ago from the point of view of librarians.

This expanded notion of bibliometrics includes two general clusters of study. First, one focused on describing and modeling individual user behavior, for example, to improve user interfaces and to study user motivations. The second is to a greater degree concerned with the actors and units involved in the production of scholarly artifacts themselves, for example, ranking an article or an author as a function of usage. The latter does not require individual user identification and is therefore less affected by concerns of user privacy or user rights. We will not discuss these issues at length, but we note that user privacy remains an issue for all user studies; data sharing between researchers is a particular concern.

In this review we are principally concerned with how usage data may be defined and collected; we discuss some of the ways it has been used and combined with traditional bibliometric data; we also discuss some problems involved in collecting the data and obtaining fair or representative samples. Due to the exigencies of currently available data we restrict our discussion to (online) journal articles, leaving to another time the newer forms of scholarly communication, such as data archives, online databases, work flow systems, and blogs.

## Usage Data and Statistics

A review of the literature on usage-based bibliometrics shows that the notion of usage has been defined and operationalized in a variety of ways. Some authors have discussed usage in terms of "reads"; others have preferred "uses," "downloads," or "hits." A formal definition of usage must acknowledge the variety of contexts in which usage-based bibliometrics can take place but should not include unmeasurable quantities such as user motivations and intentions or context-specific issues such as interfaces and system configurations.

### A Request-Based Model of Usage

Usage data can be and have been recorded in a variety of contexts. However, when we examine the actors and entities that are typically involved, we find a number of common elements. First, we have the *user* who may or may not be personally identifiable but can be assumed to have an *interest or need* with regard to a particular resource. Second, we have the *information service*, which functions as a mediator between the *user* and the set of *resources*. Third, we have the *scholarly resources* themselves, which include books, journal articles, and e-science data sets.

When an agent has a particular interest or need for a particular resource, he or she issues a *request* to the information service. The information service processes the request and returns a *service* pertaining to the resource or some representation of the resource. The information service will have a vocabulary of requests to which it will respond and a set of services it can render. An overview of this model is shown in Figure 1.1.

We can now define the notion of usage in terms of these transactions:

> *Definition 1*: Usage occurs when a user issues a request for a service pertaining to a particular scholarly resource to a particular information service.

And consequently the notions of usage event and usage data:

> *Definition 2*: A usage event is the electronic record of a user-generated request for a particular resource, mediated by a particular information service, at a particular point in time. Usage log data are collections of individual usage events recorded for a given period of time.

Such requests generally result from some degree of user interest in the resource. However, they can serve as only a post hoc operationalization of user motivations, interests, needs, intentions, or post-request usage that led to the request. It is also assumed that different request

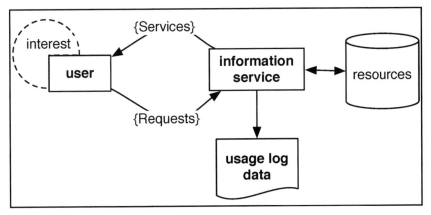

**Figure 1.1 Service request model underlying definition of usage**

types can express various degrees of user interest, for example, a request to view an article's abstract represents a lower degree of user interest in the article than a request for a full-text download. The relation between user motivations and requests, and the relation between the degree of interest to particular request types, are the subject of ongoing research.

Usage data can be recorded at any point in the processing of the request, but it is most commonly recorded by the information service at the time the request is fulfilled. This leads to usage data that generally capture the following information:

- *Event identifier* distinguishes individual events.

- *User or session identifier* distinguishes individual users or user sessions.

- *Request type identifier* indicates the type of user request issued, e.g., full-text download, abstract view, etc.

- *Resource identifier* or *resource metadata* provides a unique identifier of the resource for which the service was requested, or sufficient metadata (title, author name, etc.) to identify it.

- *Date and time of the request.*

We shall discuss how these information fields, although minimal in comparison with what is generally recorded, still provide sufficient information to support sophisticated bibliometric analysis.

## Usage Data versus Usage Statistics

It is quite common for usage data to be aggregated into usage statistics by an aggregation function. This function can be defined to perform any desired aggregation, for example, counting the number of events pertaining to a resource within a particular period of time. The result of this aggregation is referred to as a *usage statistic*. This process can be formally represented as follows:

$$S = \Sigma(U, R, P)$$

where $S$ is the usage statistic resulting from applying the aggregation function $\Sigma$ to the usage data $U$ with regard to resource $R$ using the set of parameters $P$ that controls the aggregation process, for example, a date range $d \in P$, $d = [d_1, d_2]$ so that $\Sigma$ is restricted to usage occurring at time $d_1 < t < d_2$ and $S$ will reflect cumulative usage rates for that period.

In contrast to usage data, usage statistics are generally characterized by the absence of all individual event information. However, the resource identifier $R$ will generally be retained because it is the referent of the usage statistic, in addition to the value of the usage statistic $S$, and possibly a period of time for which the aggregation was conducted as part of the parameter set $P$. Table 1.1 provides an overview of the main differences between usage data and usage statistics.

Table 1.1   **Comparison of features generally present or lacking in usage data and usage statistics**

| field | data | statistics |
|---|---|---|
| event ID | Yes | No |
| user ID | Yes | No |
| session ID | Yes | No |
| request type | Yes | Yes |
| resource ID | Yes | Yes |
| date-time | Yes | Yes |
| aggregate value | No | Yes |

Many usage-derived indicators of impact or status can be expressed as instances of the aggregation function $\Sigma$ wherein the parameter set $P$ is defined to yield a normalized or unnormalized impact metric over a particular period of time. The proposed Usage Impact Factor (Bollen &

Van de Sompel, 2008) or Usage Factor (Shepherd, 2007), defined as the average usage rate of a journal's articles over a two-year period, is an example of such a metric derived from aggregate usage statistics. The Metrics from Scholarly Usage of Resources (MESUR) project's (www.mesur.org) ontology (Rodriguez, Bollen, & Van de Sompel, 2007) represents an attempt to model the various relationships among resources, users, aggregation functions, and other metadata associated with such usage indicators.

## Usage Data: A Practical Overview

### Usage Data in the Pre-Electronic Era

Past technological limitations limited the recording of usage data to on-site library usage of printed matter. For example, Scales (1976), Galvin and Kent (1977), and more recently King, Tenopir, and Clarke (2006) operationalize usage in terms of reshelving and circulation statistics. Similarly, Tsay (1998b) determines journal usage from reshelving rates and has found statistically significant correlations between such journal usage and citation impact rankings.

We can frame these studies in terms of the request-based model. In this case a usage event is defined as the record of a user issuing a request to the information services of a physical library. The request can consist of physically retrieving a journal or book from the library's shelves, requesting that a hold be placed on a particular item, using interlibrary loan, or simply checking out the item. The fulfillment of the request consists of the physical transfer of the item from the library's collection to the user. The request and service are thus closely entangled because the physical library acts as the service provider (mediator) and as a collection of resources.

This yields usage data that share many features with usage statistics as listed in Table 1.1.

- *Absence of context*: Due to the physical entanglement of service and collection, little information can be recorded with regard to the context in which the request takes place, for example, types of user request, exact date and time of the request, and, therefore, the sequence or temporal relation of subsequent requests.

- *Loss of resource information*: Circulation and reshelving statistics generally do not distinguish between individual articles but are recorded at the journal and book level.

- *Scale*: Reshelving and circulation statistics are limited to particular library systems and their patrons.

This limits the role of circulation and reshelving statistics to that played by usage statistics, by contrast with usage data, which constitute a more detailed, contextual record of individual usage events.

## Usage Data from Web Server Logs

Since the early 1990s an increasing number of libraries and information services started to fulfill user requests via their Web servers. The resulting Web server "logs" record the parameters of the HTTP requests that were issued by users in their interactions with the particular service. This log thus reflects usage from the perspective of a Web server functioning as the mediator between users and the information service.

Given the prevalence of the Apache HTTP server, its Common Log Format (CLF) (httpd.apache.org/docs/logs.html) has become a *de facto* standard for usage data, shaping the log data recorded by other HTTP servers as well. The Apache CLF stores a number of fields pertaining to individual HTTP requests, such as the client's IP address, a user ID (if determined by HTTP authentication), the date and time at which the server processed the request, the actual HTTP request issued by the client, the request status code indicating whether the request was successfully fulfilled, and finally the byte size of the object returned to the client. In addition, it is possible to store the "Referrer," which corresponds to the site from which the client reports to have been referred. As such the Apache CLF conforms to the minimal requirements specified in our request-based model of usage.

A particular issue is the absence of reliable session information, which hampers the reconstruction of the sequences of individual user requests. Because many users do not have permanent IP addresses and access library services using proxies, the IP address does not adequately identify individual users or sequences of requests issued by the same user. The latter are crucially important to capture how users move from one resource to another in their usage "clickstreams." These are vital to modeling user traffic, determining resource relationships, and implementing personalized services. In addition, advanced social network impact indicators can be derived from resource relationships extracted from user clickstream data. The statistical reconstruction of session information from Web server logs is therefore a matter of considerable interest (He, Goker, & Harper, 2002; Heer & Chi, 2002; Pirolli & Pitkow, 1999).

Although the Apache CLF is frequently used to record usage data, the usage it records may be modulated by middleware applications such as EZproxy (www.oclc.org/ezproxy/about/default.htm) and other customized and ad hoc environments that control access and authentication. In such cases, the HTTP requests may contain additional information, for example, user identification code and session data, encoded in the HTTP request or request URL. In addition, EZproxy itself stores a record of user accesses that is recorded in a standard Web server log file format.

## Link Resolvers

In the past five years scholarly information services have started to support context-sensitive services (Van de Sompel & Beit-Arie, 2001a,

2001b) by implementing the OpenURL 0.1 specification. This development has been met by the widespread installation of linking servers by academic and research libraries to provide localized services. Link resolvers serve as a hub in the institutional information environment; they can therefore record usage across a variety of different scholarly information services.

Figure 1.2 provides an example of the pivotal role link resolvers play in allowing institutions to record their communities' usage across various information services. Each of the OpenURL-enabled information services, for example, Google Scholar, inserts an OpenURL into every reference to a scholarly work that is presented to a user. The OpenURL consists of an HTTP GET request to the institutional link resolver that contains metadata to identify the referenced work. Upon receiving the OpenURL, the institutional link resolver can offer a list of customized services pertaining to the referenced work, typically those of other information services that are available in the user's distributed information environment, such as full-text database systems.

Because user selections across a variety of OpenURL-enabled services are routed back to the institutional link resolver, it can track user

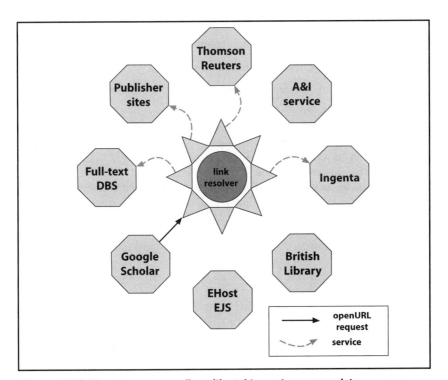

**Figure 1.2 Linking servers are well positioned to capture usage data.**

requests across various OpenURL-enabled services. The ability to collect institutional usage data that spans across many OpenURL-enabled information services and the reliance on a common standard to represent usage data have increased use of link-resolver-generated usage data in bibliometric research, for example, McDonald (2007) and Bollen and Van de Sompel (2008).

In addition to the unique capability to track user requests across different scholarly information services, link resolvers can rely on a common representation framework for usage data as provided by the ISO/ANSI Z39.88-2004 standard "The OpenURL Framework for Context-Sensitive Services" (library.caltech.edu/openurl/default.htm). The Z39.88-2004 standard rests on the notion of a ContextObject (shown in Figure 1.3) whose structure contains six different fields required to fulfill user requests and thus offers a representational framework for usage data as defined in our request-based model of usage.

- *Referent*: Subject of the service request that the ContextObject encodes

- *Requester*: Agent that requests the service pertaining to the *Referent*

- *ServiceType*: Type of service that is requested

- *ReferringEntity*: Entity that references the *Referent*

- *Resolver*: Target of a service request

- *Referrer*: The system that generated the ContextObject

The OpenURL ContextObject can as such express the relevant features of most usage events. Bollen and Van de Sompel (2006a) propose an eXtensible Markup Language (XML) serialization of the ContextObject in which the date-time stamp of the event is stored in the administrative element of the XML Context Object, namely the time-stamp attribute, as well as a globally unique event identifier in the form of a Universally Unique Identifier (UUID). The resulting usage data can then be exposed by Open Archives Initiative Protocol for Metadata Harvesting (OAI-PMH) repositories (Van de Sompel, Young, & Hickey, 2003) and harvested to form usage data aggregations across multiple institutional usage data repositories. Bollen and Van de Sompel (2006a) thus propose using linking servers as *intra-institutional* aggregators of usage information whereas the *inter-institutional* aggregation of usage data takes place by the OAI-PMH harvesting and aggregation of this data to a central location. The proposed system can create usage data aggregations with a global or regional reach.

A number of disadvantages of this approach have to be noted as well. First, linking servers cannot record user requests that do not pass through their services. No linking server usage logs thus will be available in cases where an institution does not employ a linking server or a

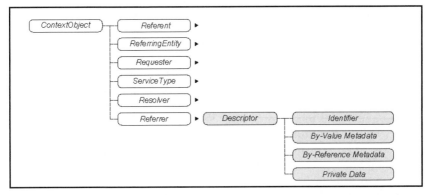

**Figure 1.3 Components of the OpenURL ContextObject (in Bekaert et al., 2005)**

user visits a service that is not OpenURL-enabled. Second, any fields or parameters associated with usage that are not captured by the OpenURL ContextObject will not be recorded. In other words, the standardized format of the OpenURL ContextObject limits the level of detail with which usage can be recorded. Third, although quite common, the use of linking servers is not universal. Many commercial products exist but may be outside the reach or requirements of many institutional library services. The architecture proposed by Bollen and Van de Sompel (2006a) to aggregate usage data recorded by multiple link resolvers cannot address this issue.

## Usage Statistics: Emerging Standards

The proposal by Bollen and Van de Sompel (2006a) concerns the construction of a standards-based infrastructure to aggregate the usage data recorded by link resolvers across multiple, different communities. In this sense it represents an attempt to standardize the recording, representation, and sharing of usage data.

The Metrics from Scholarly Usage of Resources (MESUR) project has continued this development. The project aims to expand the toolkit for scholarly evaluation by investigating the feasibility of numerous usage-based impact metrics calculated on the basis of large-scale usage data that were aggregated from some of the world's most significant publishers, aggregators, and institutional consortia. Its usage database now stands at approximately 1 billion ($1 \times 10^9$) usage events. Given the variety of formats and recording conditions across MESUR's providers of usage data, the project proposed an RDF/OWL ontology (Rodriguez et al., 2007) that formally describes the semantic relationships among various entities associated with citation and usage data.

Beyond that, very few efforts have focused on architectures and standards recording and aggregating usage data across institutional boundaries. However, considerable progress has been made with regard to the standardization and aggregation of usage *statistics*. In particular, the COUNTER initiative (Counting Online Usage of NeTworked Electronic Resources; www.projectcounter.org) has made significant inroads in recording and publishing *publisher*-generated usage statistics.

The COUNTER initiative has issued Codes of Practice that define standards and protocols with regard to the recording and sharing of vendor-generated usage statistics. Vendors can choose to comply with the COUNTER requirements that define how article and database usage is to be recorded and shared. A mechanism exists to audit the recording process and determine whether compliance has been achieved and maintained. Compliant vendors can issue various types of COUNTER reports that outline, for example, the "number of successful full-text article downloads" (Journal Reports 1 or JR1) or "Total Searches and Sessions by Month and Database" (Database 1 or DB1). COUNTER reports can be issued in a CSV-formatted document that includes the *journal title, publisher, platform, print and electronic journal ISSN, monthly totals,* and *year-to-date totals*. Furthermore, the Standardized Usage Statistics Harvesting Initiative (SUSHI; www.niso.org/workrooms/sushi) has defined a standard for the harvesting of electronic resource usage data that allows the exchange of XML-formatted COUNTER-compliant usage statistics.

A number of important distinctions should be noted between COUNTER-compliant usage statistics and usage data as described in our request-based model of usage: The former are journal-level, aggregate, monthly usage *statistics* whereas the latter contain the actual record of each unique user request, including the resources to which the request pertained, the time at which it occurred, and the user session of which it was a part.

## Usage Bibliometrics

Many bibliometric measures based on citations have direct analogs with usage. A citation is an action that refers to a document, as are all types of usage discussed here. Thus a paper, or group of papers (representing, say, an author) can have a citation rate and a usage rate (the number of citations or usage events per unit of time; other rates, such as the number of citations per usage event have also been studied), and these may be combined or analyzed in various ways. In addition to citation and usage rates, networks of related articles and journals can be extracted from citation and usage data and analyzed using methods developed in social network analysis.

Usage obviously has properties different from citation or article counts; it may be expected that measures derived from usage will have both similarities with and differences from these more traditional measures. As a first task it is necessary to demonstrate these similarities and differences, thus beginning to validate the domain where usage-based measures will be important.

## Direct Measures

What is the relation between an article's citation rate and its usage rate? Citations are normally referred to by their total, the integral of the rate over the time since publication; usage, although it is theoretically possible to measure it as a total integral over time, is normally measured as an approximately instantaneous usage rate. Systematics, such as the growth of the Internet and the development of new communication techniques—digital libraries, open access, mega-publishers—make the use of time-integrated total usage information problematic.

## Obsolescence

A convenient measure for comparing citations with usage is the obsolescence of articles—the description of how the passage of time affects the citation rate or usage rate for articles or aggregations of articles. Obsolescence based on citation and circulation information has a large literature, beginning with Gross and Gross (1927) and especially Gosnell (1944); White and McCain (1989) review it and Egghe and Rousseau (2000) discuss the mathematical issues. Obsolescence based on electronic usage has a much smaller literature; the first paper extensively exploring its properties and comparing them with citations was by Kurtz and colleagues (2000), which they later expanded substantially (Kurtz, Eichhorn, Accomazzi, Grant, Demleitner, Murray, et al., 2005).

Since then, Moed (2005) discussed the relation between usage and citations for articles within a single journal; Ladwig and Sommese (2005) tried to adjust usage statistics by using citation obsolescence measures to account for systematic differences in collected usage measures; the University College London (UCL) group studied usage obsolescence using the transaction logs of publishers (Nicholas, Huntington, Dobrowolski, Rowlands, Jamali, & Polydoratou, 2005) and using the transaction logs of a library consortium (Huntington, Nicholas, Jamali, & Tenopir, 2006); Duy and Vaughan (2006) looked into the possibility of replacing citation measures with usage measures; and McDonald (2007) used the logs of the CalTech library to examine the relation between usage and citations following the introduction of an OpenURL server (this paper also has an extensive bibliography). Tonta and Unal (2005) looked at use obsolescence via document delivery requests.

Figure 1.4, from the paper by Kurtz, Eichhorn, Accomazzi, Grant, Demleitner, Murray, et al. (2005), shows usage as a function of publication date, in terms of uses per article per year for the three principal U.S. astronomy journals (*Astronomical Journal, Astrophysical Journal, Publications of the Astronomical Society of the Pacific*); the publication dates range from 1889 to 2000. The data came from the transaction logs of the ADS (Kurtz et al., 1993, 2000; Kurtz, Eichhorn, Accomazzi, Grant,

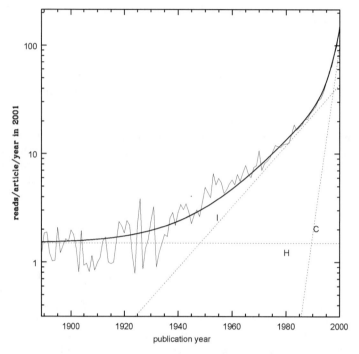

**Figure 1.4** Mean per article use (not differentiated by usage type) in 2001 of the three main U.S. astronomy journals, *Astronomical Journal*, *Astrophysical Journal*, and *Publications of the Astronomical Society of the Pacific*, as a function of publication date (1889–2000), compared with the readership model *R* in equation 1 (smooth solid line) and three of its components (I,C,H) (Kurtz, Eichhorn, Accomazzi, Grant, Demleitner, Murray, et al., 2005). Notice that the *R* model matches the data very well.

Demleitner, & Murray, 2005) for the first 7.66 months of the year 2001, and represent 1.8 million separate usage events.

These data may be (non-uniquely) modeled as the sum of three exponentials and a constant (Kurtz et al., 2000; Kurtz, Eichhorn, Accomazzi, Grant, Demleitner, Murray, et al., 2005):

$$R(t) = R_H + R_I + R_C + R_N \qquad \text{(1)}$$

where

$$R_H = H_0 e^{-k_H t}$$
$$R_I = I_0 e^{-k_I t}$$
$$R_C = C_0 e^{-k_C t}$$
$$R_N = N_0 e^{-k_N t}$$

and

$$H_0 = 1.5; k_H = 0$$
$$I_0 = 45; k_I = 0.065$$
$$C_0 = 110; k_C = 0.4$$
$$N_0 = 1600; k_N = 16$$

$t = $ time since publication in years

The four functions (three are represented in the figure) may be interpreted as four different modes of user behavior: $N$, New, represents the browse mode use of newly released articles, of which browsing the table of contents of the current issue of a journal would be an example; $C$, Current, represents non-specific searches for current articles, such as searches for recent papers on a subject or by an author; $I$, Interesting, represents searches for specific articles, such as from a reference list of another paper; $H$, Historical, is an approximately constant usage, nearly independent of the age of an article, and could perhaps be called random. There may well be other, more compelling interpretations of the shape of the obsolescence graph, in terms of user behavior, but that is outside the scope of this review.

Figure 1.5, also from the paper by Kurtz, Eichhorn, Accomazzi, Grant, Demleitner, Murray, et al. (2005), shows an expanded view of Figure 1.4 covering 25 years. Comparing the two figures makes clear that the data are well fit by the three components, $C$, $I$, and $H$, and that all three are necessary. The $N$ component of use is too short term to be visible on these graphs; Henneken, Kurtz, Eichhorn, Accomazzi, Grant, Thompson, and colleagues (2006, 2007), using access logs from arXiv (Ginsparg, 1994, 2001; Ginsparg, Houle, Joachims, & Sul, 2004), show the short term obsolescence of physics and astrophysics articles; the $N$ mode is clearly visible in the data from Henneken and colleagues.

Although they, perhaps wisely, do not attempt a parameterization, Huntington and colleagues (2006) confirm the four component usage model presented by Kurtz and colleagues (2000; Kurtz, Eichhorn, Accomazzi, Grant, Demleitner, Murray, et al., 2005). Using logs from a large university consortium (OHIOLINK) they noted the behavior of

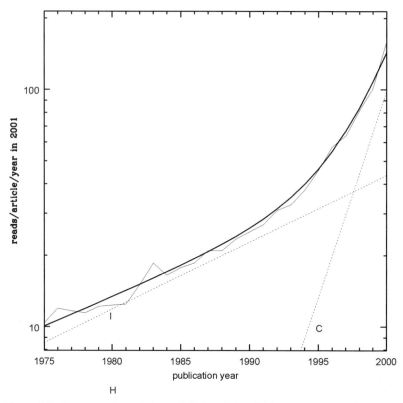

Figure 1.5   **An expansion of Figure 1.4 showing only the most recent 25 years, 1975–2000. Again the *R* model in equation 1 matches the data very well (Kurtz, Eichhorn, Accomazzi, Grant, Demleitner, Murray, et al., 2005).**

individuals viewing the table of contents "current awareness checkers" (the $R_N$ mode). They did not explicitly separate the $R_C$ and $R_I$ modes, but they note the characteristic shape of what they called "the sharp decline phase," which "spanned the first 8 to 9 years from publication date" (the $R_I$ mode); "decline was most evident in the first 2 to 3 years" (the $R_C$ mode). They then described the $R_H$ mode: "after the sharp decline period there followed a relatively stable or flat period of usage."

Work by Huntington and colleagues (2006) and the companion paper by Nicholas and colleagues (2005), which uses publisher logs, are the two papers from the UCL group that most closely correspond to our broad statistical (bibliometric) viewpoint, as presented in this review. David Nicholas and his very prolific (more than 100 papers) collaborators at UCL have created a large body of work looking at transaction log data similar to that discussed here; their viewpoint is, however, substantially more informetric, or user behavior centric than ours. This independent view stands on its own and deserves separate consideration; Rowlands (2007) and Jamali and colleagues (2005) present recent reviews.

## Sample Effects

Different sets of users have different patterns of use; whether physicists or physicians, astronomers or astrologers, groups have separate literatures and their own unique ways of using them. Bollen and Van de Sompel (2008) examined the usage patterns of an undergraduate university and found a substantial disparity between the actual use and that which might be predicted from the impact factor (Garfield, 1972, 2006). This disparity lessens substantially in areas where use is predominantly by post docs and professors. Huntington and colleagues (2006) found use could have an event-driven component, such as when students receive a reading assignment.

Figure 1.6 shows per article usage of papers from the four main astronomy journals (*Astronomical Journal*, *Astronomy and Astrophysics*, *Astrophysical Journal*, and *Monthly Notices of the Royal Astronomical Society*) as a function of publication date. The data come from the ADS logs for October 2007. The thick line represents the use by heavy (more than 10 queries per month) ADS users, essentially all astronomers; the thin line represents the use by individuals who enter ADS via a link from a Google query. The different sets of users yield very different obsolescence curves. The thick dotted line is the same model curve as in Figures 1.4 and 1.5. Save for the current year, which is strongly effected by $N$ mode behavior due to the introduction of the myADS notification service (Kurtz, Eichhorn, Accomazzi, Grant, Henneken, Thompson, et al., 2003), the model matches the data very well, suggesting that the usage obsolescence function attributable to professional astronomers has been very stable over the past six years.

The obsolescence obtained from Google users is very different in shape. The first five years after publication have slightly elevated usage, after which usage is lower and essentially constant, the $H$ component in equation 1. The obsolescence curve from Google Scholar use is even more different: It rises as a function of age (Figure 1.7); we examine this in the next section.

This example, as well as work by Bollen and Van de Sompel (2008), makes clear that usage obsolescence, as well as essentially any other usage statistic, is critically dependent on the nature of the users. Whereas citation obsolescence is caused by the actions of scholarly authors, usage obsolescence has no such a priori set of users. The fact that the universe of users of scholarly articles can be much broader and different from the universe of scholarly authors presents both substantial challenges and substantial opportunities.

## Comparison with Citations

The relation between usage and citations is complex (e.g., Line & Sandison, 1975); it depends on both the nature of the document being

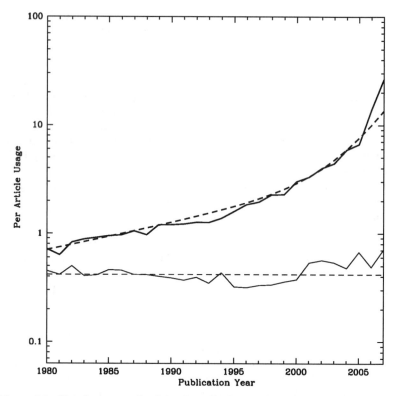

Figure 1.6 Obsolescence of articles from the four main astronomy journals
(*Astronomical Journal, Astronomy and Astrophysics, Astrophysical Journal*, and *Monthly Notices of the Royal Astronomical Society*) by
frequent ADS users and by Google users in terms of actual use as a
function of publication date. The top thick solid line represents use in
October 2007 by individuals who used the ADS query engine and
downloaded 10 or more articles during that month; typically these are
professional astronomers. The lower thin solid curve represents the
use by individuals who come directly from the Google search engine.
The top dashed curve is exactly the *R* model of equation 1 and
Figures 1.4 and 1.5; the bottom dotted line is a constant, independent
of publication date.

used/cited and the nature of the individuals performing these actions.
That different disciplines have different practices and mores concerning
citation behavior has been known for quite some time (Burton & Kebler,
1960; Krause, Lindqvist, & Mele, 2007; Moed, Van Leeuwen, & Reedijk,
1998); Figure 1.6 shows that different sets of users can exhibit substantially different behaviors even when accessing the same documents.
Indeed, comparing the obsolescence curves for the standard Google
interface in Figure 1.6 with the Google Scholar interface in Figure 1.7
demonstrates that the specific behavior of the search engine can have a

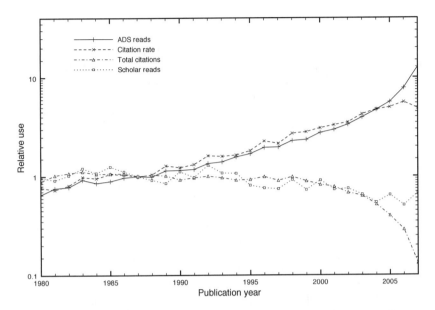

Figure 1.7  **Obsolescence of astronomy articles by frequent ADS users and by Google Scholar users. The top line (marked with X) shows use as a function of publication date for the main astronomy journals (*Astronomical Journal, Astronomy and Astrophysics, Astrophysical Journal*, and *Monthly Notices of the Royal Astronomical Society*) by heavy ADS users (mainly research astronomers). The thicker line (marked with +) is the citation rate to these articles. The line on the bottom (marked with boxes) shows the use of these articles by users who came to the ADS site via Google Scholar, and the line marked with triangles shows the total citations to these articles. All four functions are on a per article basis, and all four have been normalized to one for the publication year 1982 by dividing each function by its respective value for 1982; this normalization permits the shapes of the functions to be easily intercompared (Henneken et al., 2009).**

significant effect, as can the databases in which a paper is indexed (Hood & Wilson, 2005).

Of crucial importance to any comparison of usage with citations is the exact specification of the documents involved in the comparison. Garfield (1972) pointed out that newspapers are used a great deal but are almost never cited; thus it would make little sense to have a usage/citation study based on newspapers. Similarly, the *Bulletin of the American Astronomical Society* publishes mainly unrefereed conference abstracts; the *Astrophysical Journal* is the society's flagship journal, providing full length refereed papers. Papers in the *ApJ* are cited about 300 times more frequently than abstracts in the *BAAS*, but they are read only about six times as often. There is thus a factor of fifty difference in the usage to citation ratios for the two journals; clearly there are many measurements where it would not be appropriate to merge the two.

Kurtz, Eichhorn, Accomazzi, Grant, Demleitner, Murray, and colleagues (2005) pointed out that the series of papers by Trimble and colleagues: "Astrophysics in XXXX" (where XXXX is the immediate past year) each year is routinely the most used paper in astronomy, but is very rarely cited; for example, the most recent two, (Trimble, Aschwanden, & Hansen, 2006, 2007) have yet to be cited (as this is written). These papers are like newspapers in their usefulness. Clearly care must be taken, even for papers within a single journal, in not misconstruing effects.

An additional factor in determining the use of an article is that articles are read because they are cited. Kurtz, Eichhorn, Accomazzi, Grant, Demleitner, Murray, and colleagues (2005) showed the strong correlation between total citation and use for older papers, and Moed (2005) discussed the relationship for newer papers. Some search interfaces, such as Google Scholar, emphasize citation counts in their rankings. Figure 1.7, from Henneken, Kurtz, Accomazzi, Grant, Thompson, Bohlen, and colleagues (2009), shows how this affects the obsolescence curve. The top, solid line is the use of the main astronomy journals by heavy ADS users, the same curve as in Figure 1.6. The thick dotted line is the citation rate to these articles, measured during the three months following the measurement of use (November 2007–January 2008); the bottom thin solid line represents usage of the main astronomy journals by individuals who come to ADS via Google Scholar and the thin dotted line represents the total citations to these articles. The curves are normalized to the number of articles published and to the values for 1987, to emphasize the differences and similarities in shape.

We are thus justified in adding another, the fifth, independent function to the description of usage obsolescence $R_S$ to indicate the student's or learner's use:

$$R(t) = R_H + R_I + R_C + R_N + R_S \tag{2}$$

where $R_H$, $R_I$, $R_C$, and $R_N$ are as above and $R_S$ is proportional to the total citation count:

$$R_S = S_0 \int_{t_0}^{0} C dt$$

where $C$ is the citation rate and $S_0$ is a proportionality constant.

With the addition of the S mode we have a description of usage obsolescence that represents five different information seeking behaviors (and this is for only astrophysics journal articles). It may be assumed that the amplitudes and decay constants for these modes vary with a number of factors, including time, academic discipline, metadata composition, search engine performance, type of usage event, and mix of user types. Nicholas and colleagues (2005) list three types: practitioner, researcher, and undergraduate. We would add also the interested public. Eason, Richardson, and Yu (2000) identify eight user types.

As has been clear for some time (e.g., Gardner, 1990; Harnad, 1990) the advent of electronic research publication has had, and will continue to have, enormous influence on which articles are read, how they are read, and by whom. In the past, articles could be read only by researchers with access to scholarly libraries, more recently by those at subscribing scholarly institutions. Now, with changing cost and payment structures (such as Open Access [Drott, 2006]) an increasingly broad population of interested individuals can and does make use of the scholarly research literature.

With the accurate description of use being so complex, it is perhaps not surprising that the relation between use and citation has not been convincingly established. Parker (1982) first noticed that the use obsolescence function required the sum of two exponentials, similar to the citation obsolescence functions of Burton and Kebler (1960); matching parameterizations was impossible, because Parker needed to use a very broad selection of materials in order to achieve a significant result, whereas Burton and Kebler showed that the parameterization depended critically on the exact specification of research field.

Direct comparisons over the same set of input documents are rare; Line and Sandison (1975) were among the first to discuss the issue. Tsay (1998a) reviewed the pre-electronic results, essentially agreeing with the previous result of Broadus (1977, p. 319): "There do seem to be parallels between use of materials (not limited to journals) as indicated by citation patterns and as shown by requests to libraries." Stronger statements did not appear to be warranted. Scales (1976) correlated the top 50 journals according to use with their citation ranking and found a statistically significant correlation; however, the correlation of the top 50 journals according to citations with the ranked list of these journals by use was not significant. Brookes (1976) criticized Scales's work on methodological grounds; Bensman (2001) later confirmed Scales's findings; Meadows (2005) discusses this controversy. Pan (1978) and Rice (1979) found similar results. Stankus and Rice (1982) come to a key conclusion (quoting Tsay's [1998b, p. 32] paraphrase), stating that "a correlation will exist if the following conditions are met: (1) comparisons are made only among journals of fairly similar scope, purpose, and language; (2) with respect to the correlation between the citation data for a journal and the use of that journal, only if there is heavy journal use in that specialty or library."

Tsay's (1998a) results agree quite well with those of Stankus and Rice (1982): There is a significant correlation between the citations to medical journals and the use of these journals in a medical research library, but no significant correlation for the citations to other journals with use in a medical research library.

Past information comparing the actual shape of the obsolescence function for usage versus citations is very rare; again Tsay (1998b) summarizes and completes the pre-electronic results. Tsay found that use half-life was significantly shorter than citation half-life; Guitard in 1985 (discussed by Line, 1993) found use half-life longer than citation half-life, and Cooper and McGregor (1994) found use half-life shorter than citation half-life. King, McDonald, and Roderer (1981) found the data for various fields mostly not comparable.

Clearly usage and citations are not exactly correlated. Several studies have been done, and essentially each comes to a somewhat different conclusion. The difficulty in comparing usage information with citation histories is likely the underlying reason behind the controversy over the normative theory of citation, which would predict (MacRoberts & MacRoberts, 1987) that, in the aggregate, citations are proportional to use (e.g., Baldi, 1998; Cronin, 1984, 2001, 2005; Liu, 1993).

Toward the end of the twentieth century there was a rapid change in usage, as electronic media replaced paper. Kurtz and colleagues (2000) investigated use obsolescence in the ADS usage logs and found the four components of equation 1; they also compared use obsolescence with citation obsolescence, and found, for the period available, an exact match (Figure 1.8).

The data available to Kurtz and colleagues (2000), from mid 1998, were insufficient to examine any correlation between the very short term $R_N$ or the long term $R_H$ usage modes. By 2002 data became available to test the long term $R_H$ mode correlation (Kurtz, Eichhorn, Accomazzi, Grant, Demleitner, Murray, et al., 2005); no relation was found (Figure 1.9), leading to the equation relating use and citation obsolescence:

$$C(t) = c(R_C + R_I)(1 - e^{k_D})$$  (3)

where $R_C$ and $R_I$ are as in equation 1, $c$ is a proportionality constant (the mean number of times an article is cited per use) and $k_D$ parameterizes the citation latency (e.g., Egghe & Rousseau, 2000), which has been getting substantially shorter in the electronic era (Brody, Harnad, & Carr, 2006).

The relation between the $R_N$ usage mode and citations is more subtle and clearly cannot yield to the direct comparison of mean behaviors done by Kurtz and colleagues. Moed (2005, p. 1088) found a correlation coefficient between article downloads during the first two months and total citations after 25 months of only 0.11; he suggests that "initial downloads and citations relate to distinct phases in the process of collection and processing relevant scientific information." Brody and colleagues

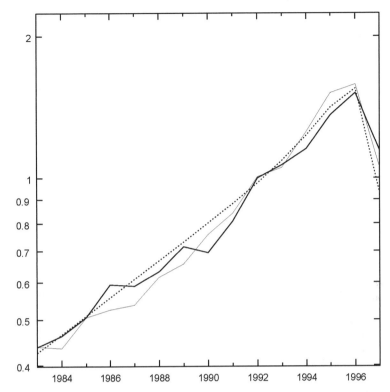

**Figure 1.8** Citation obsolescence of astronomy articles compared with actual use and the ($R_I + R_C$) model of equation 3. The thick solid line represents the actual citation rate to these articles for the first nine months of 1998 (shown on the y axis) as a function of publication date (shown on the x axis), on a per article basis. The thin solid line represents the actual use of these articles through the ADS interface during this same time period, times the exponential ramp up factor of equation 3. The dotted line is the model citation rate, C from equation 3 (Kurtz et al., 2000).

(2006) also examined the correlation of early downloads versus citations for individual articles and found significant correlations, but they looked at a substantially longer time interval; essentially mixing the $R_N$ mode with the $R_C$ mode. Moed's (2005) result also showed larger correlations for longer time windows.

Both Moed (2005) and Brody and colleagues (2006) examined the correlation between usage and citation rates to individual articles within the first few years after publication. Kurtz, Eichhorn, Accomazzi, Grant, Demleitner, Murray, and colleagues (2005) examined this correlation for two sets of data: All the usage of the entire ADS database in 2000 and the use in 2000 of *Astrophysical Journal* articles published from

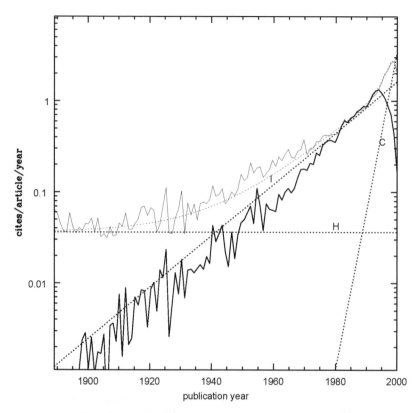

**Figure 1.9** Long term citation obsolescence of astronomy articles compared with actual use and the ($R_I$+$R_C$) model of equation 3. Notice that the long term constant, $R_H$ usage does not correspond to the citation behavior (Kurtz, Eichhorn, Accomazzi, Grant, Demleitner, Murray, et al., 2005).

1990–1997. For the larger sample they found that the citation rate was a good predictor of usage, but not the reverse (use did not predict citations). They attributed this to two main causes: Much of the use of the database is due to articles too new (the $R_N$ mode) to be cited, and to documents that are rarely cited. The *Astrophysical Journal* study showed a much stronger relationship between usage and citation. The time period covered is one where the $R_I$ mode dominates. There, use predicted citation just as well as citation predicted use. The relation in both directions was approximately log-normal, with a standard deviation of about a factor of two. Log-normal distributions have now been shown to be common in a number of similar social dynamic situations, such as multi-party voting (Castellano, Fortunato, & Loreto, 2009; Fortunato & Castellano, 2007).

## Summary

Although usage obsolescence (usage frequency as a function of publication date) is perhaps the most straightforward possible measure of use next only to total use, its interpretation is clearly quite complex. In the half century since Burton and Kebler (1960) and Price (1965a) demonstrated the need for a two component model to describe citation obsolescence it has not been necessary to add any additional complexity to the basic model; usage obsolescence, in contrast, has (at least) five components (equation 2). Citation measures are mediated by the actions of the researchers who write scholarly articles; usage measures are not due solely to the actions of the authors. Although writers are often users, users can often be non-writers. That the number of usage events vastly exceeds the number of citation events provides the basic information that will allow the complexity of the usage information to be understood; herein lies the future of the types of measurements and analyses discussed in this chapter.

## *Some Usage-Based Statistical Measures*

Like citation or publication counts, usage rate information can be used to measure the effectiveness and productivity of a number of entities, such as authors, journals, academic departments/universities, and countries. Unlike citation or publication count information, the use event records contain information not only about the entity (e.g., article) being used, but also about the user. This permits entirely new types of measures. Some general issues concerning these are discussed by Bertot, McClure, Moen, and Rubin (1997); Jansen (2006); Mayr (2006); Peters (2002); and Rowlands and Nicholas (2007).

By the nature of their time dependencies, usage data are sensitive to the recent publication record of an individual or organization but citation data are sensitive to the full integrated history.

Both traditional and usage bibliometrics can aggregate measures based in the properties of an article yielding, for example, number of citations or downloads to articles where country X is the address of the author; usage bibliometrics can also aggregate user based measures, such as downloads from users in country X. These techniques can, obviously, be merged.

Before describing some examples of how this is being done currently, we should make explicit some caveats about the use of these measures. As has been discussed, the populations that use articles can be very different from the populations that cite articles; this adds substantial complications to the understanding of the results of a usage based analysis, complications that should be understood before these measures are used in employment or funding decisions.

Also complicating the situation is the possibility of cheating, manipulating the data to influence a decision. As an example it would take only a couple of extra downloads per article per week for a tenure candidate to move from average to outstanding. Because use is mostly anonymous this may be impossible to detect.

## Individual Article

Per article use is a direct measure of the popularity of an article; co-use is often used as a measure of similar content. It has become a common feature in many digital libraries to show co-use statistics for an article, for example, "People who read this article also read ..." The ADS system has, since 1996, allowed the use of "second order operators" (Kurtz, 1992; Kurtz, Eichhorn, Accomazzi, Grant, & Murray, 1996, 2002; Kurtz, Eichhorn, Accomazzi, Grant, Demleitner, & Murray, 2005) that operate on the attributes of ensembles of articles. A common use is to begin with a collection of articles on a single subject and return a list of articles that are currently most popular with persons who "also-read" articles in the original list; this tends to yield the "hottest" papers on a subject.

As with any collaborative filter (e.g., Goldberg, Nichols, Oki, & Terry, 1992), one must decide exactly whose opinions should count. The ADS filters out infrequent users, thus following Nicholas and colleagues (2005) it might be better to include only those who download the full text.

## Authors

The main usage modes of researchers, $R_C + R_I$, are well correlated with citation counts for individual articles, as has been discussed. The two measurements, although both related to the usefulness of an article, have very different properties. Usage rates decrease monotonically with time following publication, even as citation counts increase monotonically. Usage rates are a measure of the current use; citation counts are a measure of all past use.

By taking the combined citation counts and usage rates for an aggregation of papers by a single author one obtains a two dimensional measure of that author's productivity or usefulness, which, in addition to the author's age, gives substantially more information than citation counts alone when evaluating performance.

Figure 1.10, from Kurtz, Eichhorn, Accomazzi, Grant, Demleitner, Murray, and colleagues (2005), shows how this works. The points represent individual research astronomers, and the positions of the points show the total citations to each author's papers and the amount of use those papers received (in the ADS system) between January 1999 and May 2000 (all measures normalized by number of authors in each paper).

The solid line in Figure 1.10 represents the locus of a very productive researcher's life in this diagram; the locus for less productive individuals would move to the left and would not reach as high. In addition to an

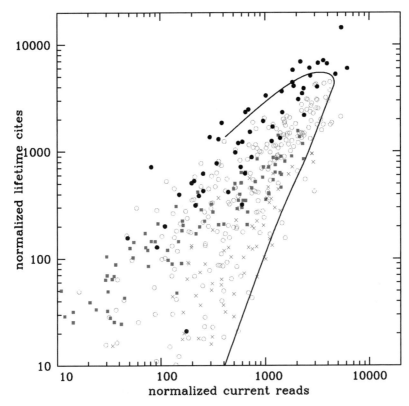

Figure 1.10  **Usage rate vs. total citations for individual astronomers; the solid line is a model for the most productive scientists at different ages (Kurtz, Eichhorn, Accomazzi, Grant, Demleitner, Murray, et al. [2005] fully describe the plot and the model).**

individual's productivity the model includes retirement and the growth in the number of papers published with time.

Figure 1.11 shows how, in addition to the length of time past the Ph.D. the "read-cite" diagram can be used to help evaluate an individual's performance. The solid dots represent the total usage rate and total citation counts for persons who received their Ph.D.s in astronomy from U.S. universities in 1980 and who published at least one item in the astronomy literature after 1990. The three sets of vectors represent models for these individuals for three different productivities (the lowest is ten times less productive than the highest), and the two vectors (for each productivity level) represent two life histories, where one individual stops publishing after ten years and the other continues publishing the entire twenty years.

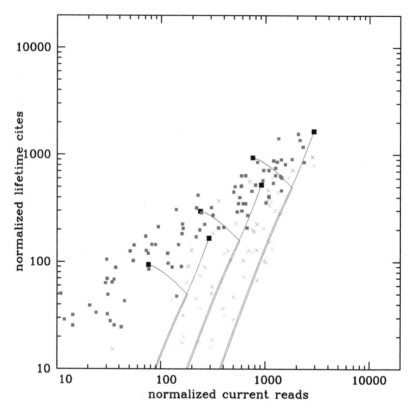

Figure 1.11 **The solid lines represent different productivity levels and work histories for astronomers in the usage rate total citation diagram (Kurtz, Eichhorn, Accomazzi, Grant, Demleitner, Murray, et al. [2005] fully describe the plot and the models).**

## Journals

Librarians have made purchase decisions on the basis of local usage data for a very long time (e.g., Gross & Gross, 1927; Walter & Darling, 1996). This has continued into the electronic era; for example, see articles by Darmoni, Roussel, and Benichou (2002); Davis (2002); and several papers in Fowler's (2007) book.

With the advent of electronic journals, usage studies have gone beyond the local use of journals. With all these studies the application and acceptance of the results depend crucially on the relevance of the sample. As with the rest of usage bibliometrics, studies involving journal use are in their infancy; there is no set of measures that is even remotely as complete or accepted as the journal citation impact factor (Garfield, 1972).

Kurtz, Eichhorn, Accomazzi, Grant, and Murray (1997) and Kurtz and colleagues (2000) studied differences in the shape of the usage obsolescence curves for several core astrophysics journals; they found indications of changes in editorial policy, differences in the relative currency of journals, and usage rate differences as a function of the user's country of origin.

Kaplan and Nelson (2000) looked into changes in the local citation rate as a function of the usage rate for documents that were included in an electronic library versus print-only documents; they found no effect. In a similar, much larger study McDonald (2007) was able to show significant increases in the local citation rate, correlated with the online availability and use of journals. In contrast, Kurtz, Eichhorn, Accomazzi, Grant, Demleitner, Henneken, and colleagues (2005) found no effect on the citation rate for older astronomy research articles after they had been digitized and posted, free, on the Internet.

Bollen, Luce, Vemulapalli, and Xu (2003) calculated centrality values for journals with a network where journals form the nodes and co-use forms the links. (Two journals would be linked to each other in the network if the same person downloaded an article from each of them.) In addition to finding obvious differences between the Thomson Reuters' citation impact factor for journals and the usage patterns for these journals in a physics research lab (Los Alamos National Laboratory was the source of the usage logs) they found they could show changes in research focus over short time scales (three years).

Davis and Price (2006) examined how usage statistics are affected by electronic journal design, making cross comparisons of different journals and publishers difficult. Blecic, Fiscella, and Wiberley (2007) similarly showed that the evolution of both interface and search methodologies is differentially changing the detailed meaning of usage statistics, again making cross comparisons difficult.

Bollen and Van de Sompel (2006a, 2008) have proposed a "Usage Impact Factor" similar to the Citation Impact Factor (Garfield, 1972). They have examined some of the sample biases that affect these measures; Bollen, Van de Sompel, and Rodriguez (2008) have analyzed and classified several different measures of journal quality or impact, both citation based and use based (see Figure 1.17).

## Departments

Universities and university departments may be viewed as collections of individuals; persons who are both creators and users of scholarly information. It is possible to measure both the use of articles written by members of a university faculty and the use of articles by members of a university faculty. The latter presents obvious problems of privacy.

Very little work has been published exploring these data. Kurtz, Eichhorn, Accomazzi, Grant, Demleitner, and Murray (2005) compared the number of heavy users of the astrophysics literature at a sample of major astronomical research centers with the number of members of the

American Astronomical Society at those centers to support their claim that nearly every astronomy researcher is a heavy ADS user; similar usage information is included in usage reports from publishers to libraries.

Kurtz, Eichhorn, Accomazzi, Grant, Demleitner, Murray, and colleagues (2005) examined the use of articles written by members of several prominent astronomy research faculties, both combining and contrasting usage measures with citation measures. Figure 1.12, for example, shows the number of authors in each of the highly ranked faculties who are in the top third (among all tenured faculty in the top departments) in terms of total citation (y-axis) and usage rate (using ADS log data) for articles published in the most recent ten years (x-axis, what Kurtz et al. call Read10). This is basically a prestige versus activity diagram.

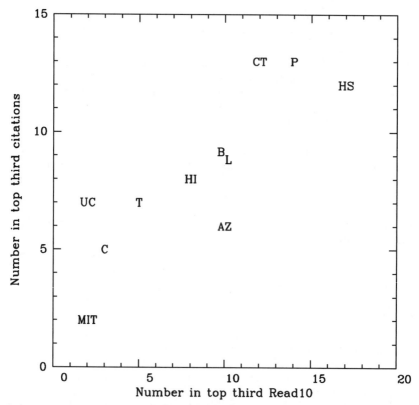

Figure 1.12 A prestige vs. activity diagram for the top U.S. astronomy faculties (Kurtz, Eichhorn, Accomazzi, Grant, Demleitner, Murray, et al. [2005] fully describe the plot and the symbols).

If the practical problems associated with gathering and interpreting usage event data can be solved, it may be expected that measures such as those shown in Figure 1.12 will become standard means for assessing the academic status of groups.

## Countries

Comparing the scholarly output of countries has been an important branch of bibliometrics for decades (e.g., Leydesdorff, 2008; May, 1997; Price, 1965b); the number of papers attributed to authors from a country, and citations to these papers are routinely tabulated in the Thomson Reuters Essential Science Indicators (sciencewatch.com).

To our knowledge, no systematic study to date has compared countries according to the usage of articles originating in them. A small number of studies has compared countries according to the number of scholarly usage events originating in them (Eichhorn et al., 2000; Henneken et al., 2009; Kurtz, Eichhorn, Accomazzi, Grant, Demleitner, & Murray, 2005).

Figure 1.13, from Kurtz, Eichhorn, Accomazzi, Grant, Demleitner, and Murray (2005), shows the relationship between per capita use of the astrophysics literature (from the ADS logs) and per capita Gross Domestic Product (GDP) for several countries. The straight line represents a quadratic relationship; per capita use is proportional to per capita GDP squared. King (2004) found a similar result, using citations.

Figure 1.14, from Henneken and colleagues (2009), shows the relative growth in use of the astrophysics literature by selected countries and regions as a function of per capita GDP; the factor of 30 total growth in global use over the ten years covered by the plot is divided out to show the relative growth. Interestingly, after very rapid comparative growth China is now growing at only the world average; India, on the other hand, continues to grow faster than the rest of the world (which is dominated by Europe and North America).

One property of usage information is that it is available in near real time; one can know the results of a usage data analysis, in some cases, essentially as the use happens. This is also true for data concerning the number of publications, but not for citation information. That the use of scholarly literature approximately scales with the number of scholars times the per capita GDP (Kurtz, Eichhorn, Accomazzi, Grant, Demleitner, & Murray, 2005) allows these effects to be removed, making it possible to analyze the effects of changes in science policy independent of changes due to increasing GDP.

The traditional bibliometric measures available immediately scale linearly with GDP. Taking astrophysics as an example: The number of astronomers is a constant times the GDP of a country (Kurtz, Eichhorn, Accomazzi, Grant, Demleitner, & Murray, 2005); the number of papers from a country is a linear function of the GDP of that country (Krause et al., 2007) for the closely related field of high energy physics; and the number of papers is a linear function of the number

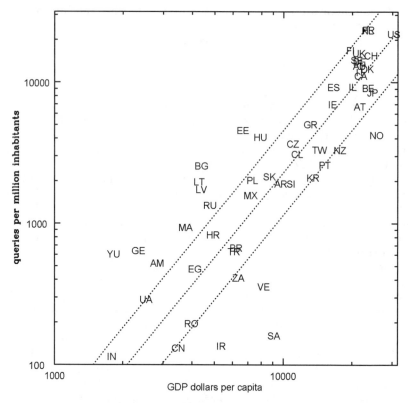

Figure 1.13 **The per capita use of the astrophysics literature vs. per capita GDP for several countries; the straight line represents a quadratic relationship (Kurtz, Eichhorn, Accomazzi, Grant, Demleitner, & Murray, 2005).**

of astronomers according to Abt (2007), who also showed the linearity for other disciplines.

That the use of scholarly articles by scholars in a country (Kurtz, Eichhorn, Accomazzi, Grant, Demleitner, & Murray, 2005) as well as citations to articles written by scholars in a country (King, 2004) both scale as a quadratic power law in GDP per capita suggests measurable differences that could, perhaps, be dubbed quality. If Kurtz, Eichhorn, Accomazzi, Grant, Demleitner, and Murray (2005), based on analyzing the outliers in Figure 1.13, are correct, GDP is a proxy for the infrastructure that supports research: Roads, universities, telecommunications systems, and so on. This leads to considering usage statistics as measures of the cumulative advantage of countries (Price, 1976) or, as Kurtz, Eichhorn, Accomazzi, Grant, Demleitner, and Murray (2005) point out, the Matthew effect for countries (Bonitz, 1997; Merton, 1968).

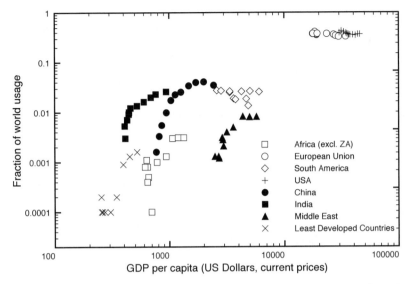

**Figure 1.14**  **The relative growth of use of the astrophysics literature by selected countries; each point is a single year's data (Henneken et al., 2009).**

## Social Network Measures

The results mentioned previously indicate that usage-based measures can be used to asses the impact of authors, articles, and journals. Usage rates furthermore predict future citation rates and show other interesting relationships to citation data. However, research also indicates that usage-based measures are sensitive to distribution parameters and sampling characteristics. In addition, questions can be raised with respect to their semantics. Do normalized usage and citation rates, such as the Usage Impact Factor and Citation Impact Factor, effectively express impact? Or do they rather express notoriety or popularity?

This situation is similar to that encountered in the study of social phenomena. To assess the status of individuals one could simply record the rates of their social interactions, for example, the number of e-mails, telephone calls, or endorsements received. However, such measures would be fraught with distribution and sampling biases and provide only very partial indications of individual status. The most common approach, therefore, is to consider social status a relational phenomenon that emerges from the structure of an individual's relationships. Social network analysis has generated numerous measures of individual status of this nature (Wasserman & Faust, 1994), for example, eigenvector centrality and betweenness centrality.

## Social Network Measures for Citation Data

Social network analysis has been applied sporadically to scholarly assessment. Various social network measures can be calculated on the basis of citation networks to assess journal and article impact. This approach has received considerable interest in recent years, but has not yet been expanded to usage bibliometrics. We provide an overview of its basic principles and measures, in particular in the context of the most commonly applied social network measures of node status, and subsequently discuss their applications to usage bibliometrics.

## Degree Centrality

Assume we collate all citations that pass from one journal's articles to another journal's articles in terms of the $n \times n$ matrix $A$. $n$ thus corresponds to the number of journals for which we have citation data. The entries of this matrix, $a_{i,j}$, are 1 if any number of citations point from journal $v_i$ to $v_j$ and 0 if no citations point from journal $v_i$ to $v_j$. A similar formulation can be developed for instances where

$$a_{i,j} \in \mathbb{N}^+$$

corresponds to the number of citations that point from journal $v_i$ to $v_j$.

Matrix $A$ now represents a citation network among $n$ journals. From this citation network we can define a set of social network measures of journal status.

The degree centrality measure follows the rationale of measures such as the Impact Factor, namely that the impact or status of a journal is defined by its rate of endorsement. However, because matrix $A$ is asymmetric, that is,

$$a_{i,j} \neq a_{j,i}$$

endorsements can be calculated as "incoming" or "outgoing" of a particular journal $v_i$. We thus define the in-degree centrality of journal $v_i$ according to matrix $A$ as

$$C_{\text{in}}(v_i, A) = \frac{\sum_j a_{j,i}}{\sum_i \sum_j a_{i,j}} \tag{4}$$

This definition can be modified to normalize

$$C_{\text{in}}(v_i, A)$$

by the maximum in-degree over matrix $A$ or other normalization factors. Note that this definition holds for either definition of $A$ where its entries are

$$a_{i,j} \in {0,1} \quad \text{or} \quad a_{i,j} \in \mathbb{N}$$

Likewise, we can define the out-degree of a journal $v_i$ according to matrix $A$ as

$$C_{\text{out}}(v_i, A) = \frac{\sum_j a_{i,j}}{\sum_i \sum_j a_{i,j}} \tag{5}$$

The definition of the Impact Factor is similar to that of in-degree centrality; with the exception that

$$\sum_i \sum_j a_{i,j}$$

is replaced by the number of articles published in journal $v_i$, hence an average per-article citation rate.

### Eigenvector Centrality, PageRank, and Random Walk Measures

In-degree and out-degree centrality, like all other rate-based measures of journal impact, suffer from one particular deficiency. They count the number of citations regardless of where they originate. As such they serve as an indicator of journal "popularity" but not necessarily of its impact, "influence," or "prestige." An example of this situation could be a journal whose articles receive numerous citations from lower-ranked journals (popular) in contrast with a journal whose articles receive few citations but from highly prestigious journals (prestigious).

The seminal work by Pinski and Narin (1976) first introduced the notion that journals should be ranked according to not only the number of citations they receive, but also whether these citations originate from influential journals. In particular, citations that originate from highly ranked journals should have a greater weight in determining the status of the cited journal. However, this introduces a circular reasoning; how, then, do we define the influence of the citing journals, and so on? The answer lies in the mathematically guaranteed convergence of an iterative recalculation of journal influence values.

Assume we define an influence vector $\vec{p}$ such that each entry $p_i$ corresponds to the influence of journal $v_i$. We can now define the influence value of each journal $v_i$ as the sum of the influence values of the journals by which it is cited, namely

$$p_i \simeq \lambda \sum_{v_j \in C(v_i)} \frac{p_j}{N(v_j)} \tag{6}$$

where $C(v_i)$ is the set of journals that cite journal $v_i$, $N(v_j)$ the number of journals cited by journal $v_j$, and $\lambda$ a linear scaling parameter. The $p_j$ values are normalized by $N(v_j)$ so that $v_i$ receives a portion of $p_j$ according to the total number of journals that $v_j$ cites; as $v_j$ cites more journals, each receives a lesser portion of its influence. This expression roughly corresponds to the definition of PageRank as originally proposed by Brin and Page (1998), namely

$$PR(v_i) = \frac{(1-\lambda)}{N} + \lambda \sum_j PR(v_j) \times \frac{1}{N(v_j)} \tag{7}$$

where $N$ represents the total number of journals. This definition simulates a random walk over the citation network wherein

$\frac{(1-\lambda)}{N}$

also referred to as "teleportation" factor, adds a probability of random teleportation.

We can reformulate equation 6 on the basis of matrix $A$ as:

$$p_i \simeq \lambda \sum_{j=1}^{n} \frac{p_j a_{j,i}}{N(a_{j,>0})} \tag{8}$$

where $N(a_{j,>0})$ corresponds to the number of non-zero entries of the row vector $a_j$.

We can reformulate the above expression in terms of the matrix-vector multiplication

$$\vec{p}_t = \lambda A \vec{p}_{t-1} \tag{9}$$

so that $\vec{p}_t$ gives the influence values of all journals at iteration $t$. Using the power iteration method $\vec{p}_t$ will converge to the primary eigenvector of $A$ such that

$$A\vec{p} = \lambda \vec{p} \tag{10}$$

redefining the issue as an eigenvector problem. Several different methods can be used to determine the primary eigenvector of *A*. However, the efficiency of the PageRank algorithm when calculated for very large, highly sparse graphs such as the Web's hyperlink network has caused it to become the preferred means to approximate the rankings of journals according to their citation eigenvector centrality.

The Eigenfactor project (www.eigenfactor.org) uses a principle similar to PageRank to produce journal rankings. Bollen, Rodriguez, and Van de Sompel (2006) propose using a weighted version of Google's PageRank algorithm to rank journals according to their prestige. Results indicate a significant, domain-dependent deviation of journal rankings according to Thomson Reuters' Impact Factor. The scatterplot in Figure 1.15 demonstrates how some journals, in particular review journals in medicine, receive high rankings according to their Impact Factors but receive low PageRank scores. This pattern is an indication of a journal receiving many citations, but from relatively unprestigious sources. Vice versa, journals characterized by low Impact Factor values but high PageRank values can be said to receive fewer citations but from more prestigious sources.

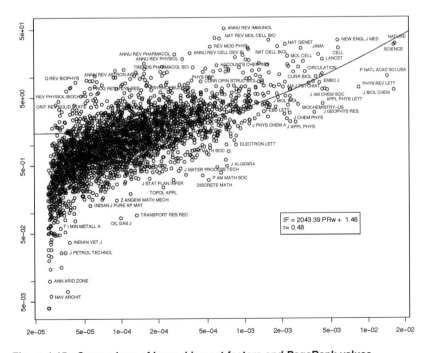

**Figure 1.15**  Comparison of journal impact factors and PageRank values calculated from 2003 *Journal Citation Reports* citation network (Bollen, Rodriguez, & Van de Sompel, 2006)

## Shortest Path Measures

Shortest path social network measures, including betweenness and closeness centrality, rely on the notion of a citation geodesic, that is, the shortest path connecting a pair of journals in a citation network. Bollen, Van de Sompel, Smith, and Luce (2005) apply betweenness and closeness centrality to a citation network to produce journal rankings, further explored by Bollen and colleagues (2005, 2008) and Leydesdorff (2007), who demonstrated that citation betweenness can serve as an indicator of journal interdisciplinarity.

We can formalize closeness and betweenness centrality as follows. We denote the geodesic between journals $v_i$ and $v_j$ in the network represented by the adjacency matrix $A$ as the ordered set

$$g_{i,j,A} = (v_i, \cdots, v_j) \tag{11}$$

The set of all geodesics in $A$ we denote

$$G(A) = \{\forall(v_i, v_j) | g_{i,j,A}\} \tag{12}$$

The length of a geodesic in $A$ is given by:

$$L(g_{i,j,A}) = ||g(v_i, \cdots, v_j)|| - 1 \tag{13}$$

In case the entries of matrix $A$ correspond to normalized citation counts, that is,

$$a_{i,j} \in \mathbb{R}^+ \quad \text{and} \quad \sum_i a_{i,j} = 1$$

we can define a geodesic weight that corresponds to the joint product of the normalized citation counts as

$$P(g_{i,j,A}) = \prod_{k=1}^{k=L(g_{i,j,A})} a_{v_k, v_{k+1}} \tag{14}$$

where $a_{v_k, v_{k+1}}$ represents the entry of $A$ that corresponds to the journal pair

$$v_k \in L(g_{i,j,A}) \text{ and } v_{k+1} \in L(g_{i,j,A}).$$

The journal closeness centrality of journal $v_i$, denoted $C(v_i,A)$, can now be defined as the mean length of all geodesics originating in $v_i$:

$$C(v_i, A) = \frac{\sum_{g \in G(A)} L(g_{i,j,A})}{||G(A)||} \tag{15}$$

In other words, closeness centrality expresses how far removed a journal is from all other journals in the citation network and thus how central and important it is to the network. Journal betweenness centrality of $v_i$, denoted $B(v_i, A)$, is then defined as a function of the number of times a particular journal sits on the geodesic of any pair of journals, that is,

$$B(v_i, A) \simeq \lambda ||\{v_m, v_n : v_i \in g_{m,n,A}\}|| \tag{16}$$

where $\lambda$ is a normalization factor. Betweenness centrality expresses how crucial the journal is in establishing the connections among other journals in the network and thus its interdisciplinary "power" position in network structure. Removing journals with high betweenness centrality from a citation network would break up and interrupt the paths that connect many pairs of journals.

## Social Network Measures for Usage Bibliometrics

Usage data consist of sequences of temporally ordered usage events that do not inherently contain journal to journal or article to article networks as citation data do. Therefore it is not possible to calculate network-based measures of impact from usage data without further processing. However, networks of resource relations can be extracted from usage data using methods that determine resource relationships by examining the degree to which pairs of resources occur within the same user sessions. Such methods are related to association rule learning in data mining (Aggarwal & Yu, 1998; Mobasher, Dai, Luo, & Nakagawa, 2001). They rest on the assumption that if users frequently issue requests for the same pairs of resources within the same session, referred to as co-usage, these resources may be statistically related. The degree of relationship is commensurate with the relative frequency by which the pair of resources is *co-used*.

Bollen and colleagues (2005) first proposed the extraction of resource networks from usage data and the subsequent calculation of network-based measures of journal or document status. This method can be summarized as shown in Figure 1.16.

Assume we have a log data set $R$ of $k$ requests $r \in R = \{r_1, r_2 ..., r_k\}$. Each request $r = \{d, t, s, q\}$ where $d$ is a document identifier, $t$ a request date-time, $s$ a session identifier, and $q$ a request type. We now assign each request $r$ within a session $s$ a rank order

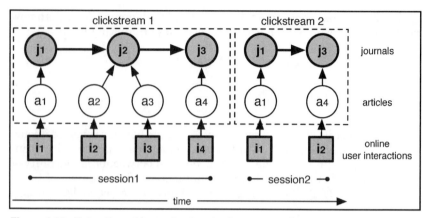

**Figure 1.16  Extraction of journal networks from usage data**

$$O(r, s) \in \mathbb{N}^+$$

according to its date-time stamp, so that we can order the requests in a session according to the sequence in which they took place. We extract a set of request pairs

$$T = \{(r_i, r_j) \in R \times R : O(r_i, s) = O(r_i, s) - 1\}.$$

We now define the function

$$F : F(d_i, d_j) \rightarrow \mathbb{N}^+$$

which returns the frequency by which each document pair $(d_i, d_j)$ occurs in $R$, so that $d_i \in r_i$ and $d_j \in r_j$ for the request pairs $(r_i, r_j) \in T$. $F(r_i,)$ returns the frequency of all pairs in which $r_i$ is the antecedent. This frequency can be normalized to determine the transition probability

$$p(r_i, r_j) = \frac{F(r_i, r_j)}{F(r_i, )} \tag{17}$$

$p(r_i, r_j) \in [0,1]$ and expresses the probability that users in their click-streams will move on to journal $r_j$. Note that, because the temporal sequence of requests is taken into account, the established document relationships are directional, that is, $(r_i, r_j) \neq (r_j, r_i)$ unlike other association learning approaches that disregard temporal sequence and rely on a bidirectional definition of *co-occurrence*. The resulting transition probabilities define a matrix $P$ whose entries $p_{i,j} \in [0,1]$ represent the transition probability between documents $d_i$ and $d_j$ according to the set of request sequences in $R$. The measures discussed in the section on social network measures for citation data are thus applicable to matrix $P$ and ranking of documents can be determined according to their relationships as indicated from usage.

Bollen and colleagues (2005, 2008) discuss a journal ranking on the basis of journal usage networks created from Los Alamos National Laboratory (LANL) link resolver logs and the MESUR reference data set. The rankings indicate the ability of a variety of social network measures to express various features of scholarly impact. Deviations between the resulting rankings and the Impact Factor point to how social network measures calculated from usage networks indicate various measures of scholarly impact. The MESUR project reports Spearman Rank Order correlations between the various social network metrics of impact and the Impact Factor that range from 0.28 to 0.80. These indicate that social network metrics can exhibit various degrees of congruence with existing citation-based measures of impact.

Bollen and colleagues (2008, 2009b) visualize the difference between rankings produced by a set of 43 measures of journal impact, including the Impact Factor, by a principal component analysis (PCA) of the set of measure correlations. The first two principal components cover nearly 85 percent of all variation. The resulting PCA mapping of measures (shown in Figure 1.17) reveals the two main clusters of measures: Those based on usage data and those based on citation data. However, the second component separates measures according to the facet of impact they represent, namely the degree to which they represent prestige or popularity. The Impact Factor is positioned among degree centrality and closeness centrality metrics that are indicative of a journal's number of relations to other journals and thus its general degree of endorsements or its popularity. Betweenness centrality and PageRank cluster strongly as well, in two usage- and citation-derived clusters. However, citation- and usage-based betweenness centrality and PageRank measures correlate more strongly to each other than either does to the Impact Factor. The latter is placed at a position removed from the main clusters of prestige-based measures.

## Open Access

A recent, interesting bibliometric controversy concerns the relationship between usage and citations. Are articles that have been posted on the Internet for all to freely read more read/cited than articles that can only be read by subscribers? There is an extensive literature on this issue; Hitchcock's online bibliography (opcit.eprints.org/oacitation-biblio.html) currently has more than 200 items.

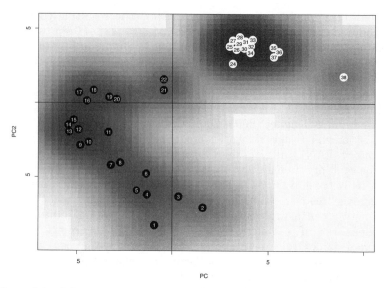

Figure 1.17    **Principal component analysis of the correlations between 39 impact measures calculated and retrieved by the MESUR project (Bollen et al., 2009b)**

Lawrence (2001) first showed that articles in computer science that had been posted on the Internet were cited at about twice the rate of similar articles that were not posted. Drott (2006) discussed some of the issues surrounding this observation. Harnad and Brody (2004) showed that the effect also existed, at about the same level, 2 to 1, in many of the subfields of physics covered by the arXiv e-print server (arxiv.org) (Ginsparg, 1994, 2001; Ginsparg et al., 2004). Combined with the strong correlation between usage and citation shown in Figure 1.8 and equation 1 from Kurtz and colleagues (2000; Kurtz, Eichhorn, Accomazzi, Grant, Demleitner, Murray, et al., 2005) and Kurtz (2004) showing that the ratio of full-text views to abstract views among astronomers is a strong function of ease of access to the full text, this led to the widely held assumption that the effect was causal: Because it is easier to access freely available articles than articles behind financial subscription barriers, more people read them and this *causes* them to be cited more frequently. This has been used as an argument in favor of open access (Eysenbach, 2006; Ginsparg, 2007) and is sometimes referred to as the "Open Access Advantage" (Harnad, 2005).

Kurtz, Eichhorn, Accomazzi, Grant, Demleitner, Henneken, and colleagues (2005) examined the question of causality more closely; their two main findings substantially undermined the causality postulate. First, they showed that older astrophysics articles that were posted on the Internet were not more frequently cited than they were before they were posted, in spite of substantially increased use; they did find evidence that very recent articles were more frequently cited following the founding of the arXiv e-print server. Second, they looked at astrophysics articles that were/were not posted on arXiv. They looked at three postulates explaining why arXiv posted articles were cited at roughly twice the rate of the articles not posted: The Open Access (OA) postulate, essentially the causal assumption of the previous paragraph; The Early Access (EA) postulate, articles are posted to arXiv several months (the median is four) before they appear in the journals, and this clearly gives them a head start in citation counts; and The Selection Bias (SB) postulate, more citable articles are more likely posted to the Internet than less citable articles, one possible reason (among many) for this being that authors preferentially post their better papers.

Kurtz, Eichhorn, Accomazzi, Grant, Demleitner, Henneken, and colleagues (2005) found that the distribution of highly cited papers was strongly inconsistent with the combined OA+EA postulates; this, combined with their historical analysis that showed no evidence for the OA postulate (but did show strong evidence for the EA postulate) led them to conclude that the increase in citations was due to a combination of EA+SB, with very small or no contribution from OA: That, in fact, the open access advantage did not exist.

Moed (2007) examined papers in condensed matter physics that were/were not posted on arXiv. He also found no evidence for the OA postulate and suggested that most of the effect was due to EA. Eysenbach (2006) showed that the effect existed in the "author choice" articles in the *Proceedings of the National Academy of Sciences*, where there could be no EA contribution. Henneken and colleagues (2006) showed that the use of the journal version of arXiv submitted articles vs. articles not submitted to arXiv in astrophysics closely parallels the citations and that amplitudes of the differences cannot be explained by EA alone. Davis and Fromerth (2007), looking at mathematics articles in arXiv, found no support for the OA or EA postulates, but found support for a quality bias (SB).

Craig, Plume, McVeigh, Pringle, and Amin (2007) reviewed the whole controversy, coming to the conclusion that the OA postulate was not necessary to explain the data and suggesting that a true randomized study be made. Kurtz and Henneken (2007) used the historical accident that the *Astrophysical Journal* switched from open access to closed access on January 1, 1998, to show that the arXiv/non-arXiv citation differential in astrophysics is associated only with arXiv submission, not with OA per se.

Subsequently, Davis, Lewenstein, Booth, and Connolly (2008), in collaboration with the journals of the American Physiological Society, conducted a true randomized statistical trial. Articles from APS journals were randomly assigned to be open access, or not, and their citation and usage were tracked. This experimental design totally eliminated any confusion from EA or SB factors. They found a significant increase in the full-text downloads for the open access articles but no difference in the citation rates between the open access and closed access articles, rejecting the OA postulate with high confidence. Note that both Harnad (2008) and Eysenbach (2008) have criticized this paper on methodological grounds.

Most recently, Norris, Oppenheim, and Rowland (2008, p. 1970) reviewed the controversy and found "the reasons why there is a citation advantage for OA articles still has not been satisfactorily explained"; Davis (2009), using methods similar to Eysenbach (2006), found that the effect could be explained by systematic differences between the OA/non-OA articles.

This change, from regarding the open access citation differential as causal to regarding it as a result of various biases, has not gone unchallenged. Stevan Harnad and his collaborators have provided the great bulk of the opposing view, primarily via online postings to the American Scientist Open Access Forum (amsci-forum.amsci.org/archives/American-Scientist-Open-Access-Forum.html) (Harnad is the moderator), the Sigmetrics listserver of the American Society for Information Science and Technology Special Interest Group on Metrics (listserv.utk.edu/archives/sigmetrics.html) (moderator: Eugene Garfield), and Harnad's own blog (openaccess.eprints.org).

These postings have provided a dialogue among the principals, often running for weeks. Representative postings, emphasizing the causal view, are by Harnad (2005; 2006a; 2006b; 2007a; 2007b; 2007c; 2007d). Perhaps the most complete exposition of their argument is in the paper by Hajjem and Harnad (2005).

Other important papers from this group include Hajjem, Harnad, and Gingras (2005) and Brody, Carr, Gingras, Hajjem, Harnad, and Swan (2007). Most recently Gargouri (2008), from an analysis of four mandated archives, found evidence for the causal hypothesis.

Although interesting, the importance of this issue is fleeting, as Ginsparg (2007, p. 16) points out:

> Studies have shown a correlation between openly accessible materials and citation impact, though a direct causal link is more difficult to establish, and other mechanisms accounting for the effect are easily imagined. It is worthwhile to note, however, that even if some articles currently receive more citations by virtue of being open access, it doesn't follow that the benefit would continue to accrue through widespread expansion of open access publication. Indeed, once the bulk of publication is moved to open access, then whatever relative boost might be enjoyed by early adopters would long since have disappeared, with relative numbers of citations once again determined by the usual independent mechanisms. Citation impact per se is consequently not a serious argument for encouraging more authors to adopt open access

publication. A different potential impact and benefit to the general public, on the other hand, is the greater ease with which science journalists and bloggers can write about and link to open access articles.

In addition, as discussed in the section "Some usage-based statistical measures," if measures of scholarly impact can be extracted from usage data, the issue is not whether the impact of openly accessible materials increases because increased usage leads to increased citations, but that increased usage (and derived measures) itself is a sufficient indicator of increased impact.

# Mapping of Science from Usage Data

Other than ranking journals, authors, departments, and countries, usage data can play an important role in another crucial aspect of bibliometrics, namely, the mapping and charting of science. Maps of science highlight the main distinctions and structural trends in science by visualizing the connections among articles, journals, and scholarly domains. These connections are most frequently derived from citation data, for example, co-citation data and journal citation similarities.

## Mapping Science from Citation Data

Although even earlier attempts exist, Garfield (1970) provides an example of the usefulness of visualizing citation networks by invalidating the common misconception that Gregor Mendel's paper on genetics was ignored by that community. It is shown that Mendel's paper was cited repeatedly and was in fact not ignored. The flow of citations surrounding Mendel's paper is used to assess the flow of ideas and influences from one publication to another.

Small (1999) provides an excellent historical overview of the literature in this domain and shows discipline mappings resulting from the analysis of the citation relations between 36,720 documents. More recent and more large-scale efforts include Boyack, Wylie, and Davidson's (2002) use of the VxInsight (www.cs.sandia.gov/~dkjohns/JIIS/Vx_Intro.html) package to create landscapes of related papers in microsystems technology and the physical sciences. Temporal trends in this domain are revealed by highlighting shifts and peaks in the resulting landscapes. Boyack, Klavans, and Börner (2005) maps the relations among 7,000 journals on the basis of journal similarities calculated from Science Citation Index (SCI) and Social Sciences Citation Index (SSCI) citation data. Five citation-based similarity measures are calculated and journals are placed in a map of science by VxOrd, a force-directed algorithm to optimize journal positions on the basis of their similarity. The resulting maps of science outline the major structure of science activity in terms of 212 clusters of related journals.

Leydesdorff (1994) produces maps of scholarly domains by positioning journals by means of multi-dimensional scaling on the basis of 1993 SCI data. The citation environments of specific journals, for example, the *Journal of Chemical Physics*, are mapped in terms of groupings resulting from a factor analysis. The results indicate that the relations between the specific journals do not correspond to "the administrative division of the natural sciences into disciplines like physics and chemistry" (p. 65). The resulting visualization highlights important distinctions in the influences of the publications of a particular journal (or domain).

Moya-Anegón, Vargas-Quesada, Chinchilla-Rodrìguez, Corera-Álvarez, Munoz-Fernández, and Herrero-Solana (2007) discuss a "scientogram" of world science that was generated from co-citation data calculated for 219 Journal Citation Report (JCR) categories. The maps visualize the relations among various scholarly disciplines as provided by Thomson Reuters' classification codes.

Chen (2006) does not so much produce maps of science as concept maps that delineate the important distinctions in scientific domains. These data can be visualized in terms of decision trees that outline which terms are most important in determining the citation context of items in the Sloan Digital Sky Survey (SDSS) or concept maps generated by CiteSpace.

Rosvall and Bergstrom (2008) generate maps of science that group more than 6,000 journals into scientific domains by means of a random walk simulation on the citation graph; frequent paths can be increasingly compressed to ever more succinct descriptions of network structure. The resulting citation maps of science highlight the connections among various scholarly domains in terms of their citation flow. Similar maps are used in the eigenfactor.org online service.

Saka and Igami (2007) discuss research maps generated from co-citation patterns of highly cited papers extracted from SCI data. Hot research areas are identified by means of average annual growth rates of citations over a six year period. A force-directed algorithm is used to create a discipline map of science in terms of 133 research areas.

A set of significant initiatives in this domain are provided by the Information Visualization Lab (ivl.slis.indiana.edu) and the Cyberinfrastructure for Network Science Center (cns.slis.indiana.edu) at Indiana University directed by Katy Börner, who has focused on creating tools and services for the visualization of knowledge domains (Börner, Chen, & Boyack, 2003; Börner, Sanyal, & Vespignani, 2007).

## The Potential for Science Mapping from Usage Data

As the literature review in the previous section indicates, citation data have held a dominant position in the mapping of science and knowledge domains. However, advances in applications of usage data, for example, social network metrics derived from usage graphs, may translate to the mapping of science and knowledge domains. This approach has not yet found widespread application although some examples have recently emerged in the literature. The general approach is similar to that outlined by Bollen and Van de Sompel (2006b) as shown in Figure 1.18.

Bollen and Van de Sompel (2006b) report on maps created from the flow of usage traffic recorded by the link resolvers of the Los Alamos National Laboratory. These maps are based not on journal or article citation similarities, but journal similarities derived from the flow of usage traffic from one journal to another as users interact with online information services as recorded by an institution's link resolver (Figure 1.19). The maps are based on a principal component analysis of journal usage-similarities that are overlaid with a k-means clustering of journals into particular knowledge domains. The resulting maps reveal the prominent dimensions according to which journals cluster in the online behavior of large groups of users.

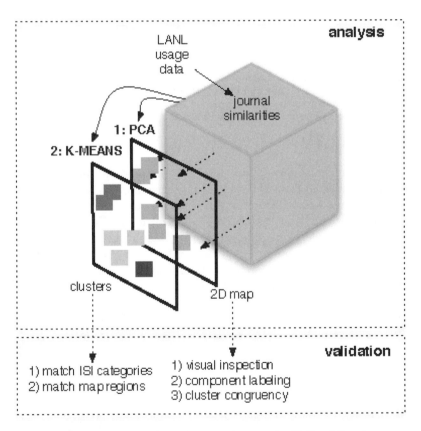

**Figure 1.18   Procedure used to map science from usage (Bollen & Van de Sompel, 2006a)**

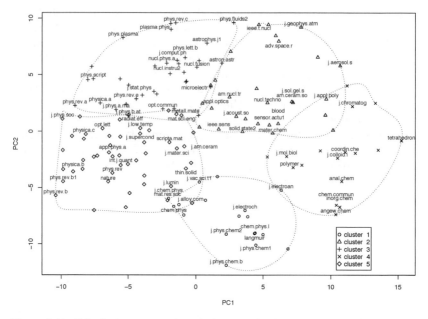

**Figure 1.19** Principal component analysis map of science generated from journal similarities derived from Los Alamos National Laboratory link resolver usage data recorded in 2004. Journal titles are abbreviated to reduce clutter (Bollen & Van de Sompel, 2006a).

Bollen and colleagues (2008) describe a map of journal clickstreams that was extracted from 200 million usage events that were part of the 1 billion usage events reference data set collected by the MESUR project. This work was later extended with an even larger clickstream data set and a more elaborate validation of the map structure using subject classification taxonomies in Bollen, Van de Sompel, Hagberg, Bettencourt, Chute, Rodriguez, and colleagues (2009a). Figure 1.20 shows a visualization of this network, illustrating the promise of this approach to map the most dominant patterns of traffic in the scholarly community and highlighting the important role of psychology and cognitive science in bridging the social sciences and natural sciences.

Although science mapping from usage has not yet achieved a prominent position in the domain of bibliometrics, the possibilities for tracking science as it takes place are quite promising if certain minimal requirements in terms of sampling and fidelity are met. Sample characterization—whose usage is being mapped—seems to be a crucial issue for attempts to map science and knowledge domains from usage. A particular interest exists in the identification of longitudinal trends in

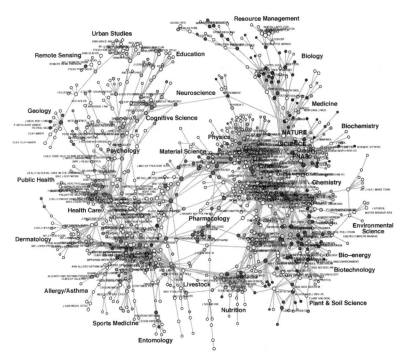

Figure 1.20 **Visualization of journal network extracted from user clickstreams in MESUR's usage data. Journals are represented by circles whose colors correspond to the journal's scientific domain. The lines that connect circles indicate a high probability of one journal following another in users' clickstreams (Bollen et al., 2009a).**

usage data that may inform funding agencies and policy makers of emerging innovation in science.

## Conclusion

Bibliometrics is undergoing a renaissance; novel types of data are being combined with powerful new mathematical techniques to create a substantial change. The new techniques are being developed across a wide range of scholarly disciplines, from evolutionary genetics to theoretical physics.

Central to the new bibliometrics is the study of usage and usage patterns. Collections of article level usage event records have existed for only about a decade and their applications are not yet at the level of commonplace acceptance that was long ago reached by article counts and citations. But as scholarly work increasingly moves online, this will change.

Considerable challenges still exist with regard to the standardization of recording and aggregation of usage data. In the present situation usage data are recorded in a plethora of different formats, each representing a different permutation of recording interfaces, data fields, data semantics, and data normalization. The commonalities expressed in the section "A request-based model of usage" can be translated to actual usage data in a variety of different and incompatible ways; this may make it impossible to create usage data sets aggregated across various communities and introduce "lowest-common denominator" limitations. Depending on the data fields that are being recorded and represented, various levels of data loss can take place. For example, privacy concerns can lead to the removal of Internet protocol (IP) addresses from usage data, but without a replacement in the form of an anonymous user ID or session ID, the temporal sequences of user requests are lost. This disables the structural analysis and mapping of the scholarly community, as well as the production of resource rankings such as the social network measures discussed in the section "Social network measures for usage bibliometrics." It is therefore of the utmost importance to consider issues of data loss and fidelity in the development of standards for usage data recording and representation.

Several projects are working to introduce standards to facilitate the recording and aggregation of usage data, for example, COUNTER and MESUR. Standards with regard to the recording and representation of usage data are a sine qua non for usage bibliometrics. However, aggregation of usage data is equally important but often overlooked; it is necessary to arrive at usage bibliometrics that can either exploit or negate the effects of sampling bias. The latter has been shown to greatly affect attempts to produce generalizable impact assessments and perform studies of the scholarly community on the basis of usage data. Bollen and Van de Sompel (2006b) propose an architecture that standardizes the recording, formatting, and aggregation of usage data across various resources and institutions. The proposed architecture presumes the existence of a trusted, third party that aggregates usage data across various participating providers and extracts useful services, for example, ranking and mapping, from the resulting, aggregated data set.

Privacy issues are ubiquitous in usage bibliometrics because the data can reveal the identity and behavior of individual users. However, privacy and confidentiality issues are relevant at three levels, namely that of individual users, their institutions, and the providers (or recorders) of usage data. Different privacy concerns can occur at each level. The protection of the privacy of individual users is not generally a matter of individually negotiated contracts (although stark differences exist in the treatment of individual privacy rights between the U.S. and the EU) but blanket measures can be employed to obscure the identities of users or prevent usage patterns from revealing a user's identity at the point of recording. The use of anonymous session identifiers has been advocated to maintain both temporal information on unique, individual usage patterns as well as user privacy. The protection of confidentiality and privacy at the institutional and provider levels remains within the realm of ad hoc crafted agreements. Usage data ownership presents a challenge as well. Overall the protection of user, institution, and provider privacy stands to benefit from well considered standards for the recording, representation, and aggregation of usage data.

The growth of electronic usage data is but one aspect of the rapid and profound changes affecting the scholarly communication process. For bibliometrics to maintain its traditional role of measuring and analyzing scholarly output, it must adapt and grow with these changes.

Many of the new forms of communication do not lend themselves easily to citation-based analysis. An example is the Sky Server system (Szalay & Gray, 2001, 2006), which provides access to billions of measurements from the Sloan Digital Sky Survey (York et al., 2000). The few thousand citations to the papers describing the dataset do not approach the information contained in the tens of millions of usage events. Singh, Gray, Thakar, Szalay, Raddick, Boroski, and colleagues (2007) have begun to investigate what information can be gleaned from these records. Bollen and colleagues (2008) discuss the discrepancy in scale between citation data and usage data sets by noting that the Web of Science database contains about 600 million article-to-article citations whereas Elsevier alone announced 1 billion full-text downloads in 2006. In other words, aggregations of usage data, such as that constructed by the MESUR project, can easily surpass the total number of citations in existence and thereby significantly enhance the reliability and span of bibliometric studies.

Printed articles are static, but Web services (such as the SDSS Sky Server) are dynamic. In addition to being directly used by individuals, they can be incorporated as part of a different Web service, which in turn can be part of another, and so on. Thus a scholarly Web service can be seen as a node in a complex intellectual infrastructure network. Evaluating the various nodes and links in such a network presents a great challenge for the future of information science. Managing sections of these networks is the task of so-called work flow or provenance systems (Freire, Silva, Callahan, Santos, Scheidegger, & Vo, 2006; Georgakopoulos, Hornick, & Sheth, 1995; Ludascher & Goble, 2005); the logs and audit trails of these systems will provide data to the information scientist, similar to the sets of usage events in today's access logs. Another issue is the meaningful grouping of online resources addressed by the OAI ORE project (www.openarchives.org/ore).

Considerable logistic challenges also lie ahead in applying usage data to scholarly assessment and the analysis of the structure and evolution of the scholarly landscape. Whereas institutional usage data are highly useful for institutional applications, for example, collections management and other services, aggregated usage data sets allow the creation of services and applications that are more generally applicable. Basic compilations, such as the Thomson Reuters' Essential Science Indicators for citation and article count data, can be created from usage data sets that are aggregated across a wide variety of representative institutions. It is an open issue how a representative sample of usage across the entire scholarly community can be achieved, lacking any reliable census data against which any sample can be validated. In addition, such compilations need to be created and maintained in a reliable manner that ensures continuity for extended time periods by parties that are generally trusted to act on behalf of the common good with due respect for privacy, confidentiality, and ownership. Various models can be adopted to support such efforts. However, an environment in which the resulting usage data sets and resulting analysis are least encumbered by rights and ownership issues would be most conducive to the scientific and pragmatic development of this field.

Given the widespread acceptance of *citation*-based measures of impact, such as for the Impact Factor, the final question after all scientific and logistic issues have been addressed will be the community acceptance of *usage*-based measures of article or journal impact. Citation-based measures are seemingly well understood and simple in their applications. Can we expect the same for usage-based measures? A better understanding of sampling issues (whom do the numbers represent?), the nature of usage-based measures of impact (what do the measures mean?), and how and where can they best be applied (what community do they best represent?) will be crucial in establishing usage bibliometrics as a viable complement to citation-based bibliometrics. However, an Albert Einstein quote may best sum up the present situation: "Make everything as simple as possible, but not simpler" (Shapiro, 2006, p. 231). The trade-off to achieve a more comprehensive and accurate usage bibliometrics may very well be one in which widely accepted, simple citation measures are replaced with more complex, but more accurate and reliable usage-based measures.

## Acknowledgments

Michael Kurtz would like to acknowledge the long term collaboration with the Astrophysics Data System (ADS) group at the Smithsonian Astrophysical Observatory, especially Guenther Eichhorn, Alberto Accomazzi, and Edwin Henneken. The ADS is supported by NASA grant NCC5-189. Johan Bollen would like to thank Herbert Van de Sompel and the Digital Library Research and Prototyping Team at the Research Library of the Los Alamos National Laboratory for their support in developing many of the ideas and much of the research presented in this paper. The Andrew W. Mellon Foundation supported the MESUR project to develop usage-based impact metrics from 2006 to 2008.

# Endnote

1. *The Astrophysical Journal* and *Astronomy and Astrophysics* became fully available online on January 1, 1997; *The Monthly Notices of the Royal Astronomical Society* and *The Astronomical Journal* followed on January 1, 1998, although test versions were available earlier.

# References

Abt, H. A. (2007). The publication rate of scientific papers depends only on the number of scientists. *Scientometrics, 73*(3), 281–288.

Accomazzi, A., Eichhorn, G., Kurtz, M., Grant, C., & Murray, S. (2000). The NASA Astrophysics Data System: Architecture. *Astronomy & Astrophysics Supplement Series, 143*(1), 85–109.

Aggarwal, C. C., & Yu, P. S. (1998). Mining large itemsets for association rules. *IEEE Data Engineering Bulletin, 21*(1), 23–31.

Baldi, S. (1998). Normative versus social constructivist processes in the allocation of citations: A network-analytic model. *American Sociological Review, 63*(6), 829–846.

Bar-Ilan, J. (2008). Informetrics at the beginning of the 21st century: A review. *Journal of Informetrics, 2*(1), 1–52.

Bekaert, J., & Van de Sompel, H. (2005). Access interfaces for open archival information systems based on the OAI-PMH and the OpenURL framework for context-sensitive services. *Symposium on ensuring long-term preservation and adding value to scientific and technical data* (PV 2005), Edinburgh, November 2005. Retrieved May 21, 2009, from www.ukoln.ac.uk/events/pv-2005/pv-2005-final-papers/032.pdf

Bensman, S. (2001). Urquhart's and Garfield's laws: The British controversy over their validity. *Journal of the American Society for Information Science and Technology, 52*(9), 714–724.

Bertot, J., McClure, C., Moen, W., & Rubin, J. (1997). Web usage statistics: Measurement issues and analytical techniques. *Government Information Quarterly, 14*(4), 373–395.

Blecic, D. D., Fiscella, J. B., & Wiberley, S. E., Jr. (2007). Measurement of use of electronic resources: Advances in use statistics and innovations in resource functionality. *College & Research Libraries, 68*(1), 26–44.

Bollen, J., Luce, R., Vemulapalli, S., & Xu, W. (2003). Usage analysis for the identification of research trends in digital libraries. *D-Lib Magazine, 9*(5). Retrieved March 1, 2009, from www.dlib.org/dlib/may03/bollen/05bollen.html

Bollen, J., Rodriguez, M. A., & Van de Sompel, H. (2006). Journal status. *Scientometrics, 69*, 669–687.

Bollen, J., & Van de Sompel, H. (2006a). An architecture for the aggregation and analysis of scholarly usage data. *Proceedings of the 6th ACM/IEEE-CS Joint Conference on Digital Libraries*, 298–307.

Bollen, J., & Van de Sompel, H. (2006b). Mapping the structure of science through usage. *Scientometrics, 69*(2), 227–258.

Bollen, J., & Van de Sompel, H. (2008). Usage impact factor: The effects of sample characteristics on usage-based impact metrics. *Journal of the American Society for Information Science and Technology, 59*(1), 136–149.

Bollen, J., Van de Sompel, H., Hagberg, A., Bettencourt, L., Chute, R., Rodriguez, M. A., et al. (2009a). Clickstream data yields high-resolution maps of science. *PLoS ONE, 4*(3), e4803. Retrieved March 1, 2009, from doi:10.1371/journal.pone.0004803

Bollen J., Van de Sompel, H., Hagberg, A., & Chute, R. (2009b). A principal component analysis of 39 scientific impact measures. *PLoS ONE, 4*(6), e6022. Retrieved June 30, 2009, from doi:10.1371/journal.pone.0006022

Bollen, J., Van de Sompel, H., & Rodriguez., M. A. (2008). Towards usage-based impact metrics: First results from the MESUR project. *Proceedings of the 8th ACM/IEEE-CS Joint Conference on Digital Libraries,* 231–240.

Bollen, J., Van de Sompel, H., Smith, J., & Luce, R. (2005). Toward alternative metrics of journal impact: A comparison of download and citation data. *Information Processing & Management, 41*(6), 1419–1440.

Bonitz, M. (1997). The scientific talents of nations. *Libri, 47*(4), 206–213.

Borgman, C., Hirsh, S., & Hiller, J. (1996). Rethinking online monitoring methods for information retrieval systems: From search product to search process. *Journal of the American Society for Information Science, 47*(7), 568–583.

Börner, K., Chen, C., & Boyack, K. W. (2003). Mapping science. *Annual Review of Information Science and Technology, 37,* 179–255.

Börner, K., Sanyal, S., & Vespignani, A. (2007). Network science. *Annual Review of Information Science and Technology, 41,* 537–607.

Boyack, K. W., Klavans, R., & Börner, K. (2005). Mapping the backbone of science. *Scientometrics, 64*(3), 351–374.

Boyack, K. W., Wylie, B. N., & Davidson, G. S. (2002). Domain visualization using vxinsight® for science and technology management. *Journal of the American Society for Information Science and Technology, 53*(9), 764–774.

Brin, S., & Page, L. (1998). The anatomy of a large-scale hypertextual Web search engine. *Computer Networks and ISDN Systems, 30*(1–7), 107–117.

Broadus, R. F. (1977). The application of citation analysis to library collection building. *Advances in Librarianship, 7,* 299–335.

Broadus, R. F. (1987). Toward a definition of bibliometrics. *Scientometrics, 12*(5–6), 373–379.

Brody, T., Carr, L., Gingras, Y., Hajjem, C., Harnad, S., & Swan, A. (2007). Incentivising the open access research Web: Publication-archiving, data-archiving, and scientometrics. *CTWatch Quarterly, 3*(3), 42–50.

Brody, T., Harnad, S., & Carr, L. (2006). Earlier Web usage statistics as predictors of later citation impact. *Journal of the American Society for Information Science and Technology, 57*(8), 1060–1072.

Brookes, B. C. (1976). Citation v. usage of serials. *Journal of Documentation, 32*(4), 320–322.

Burton, R., & Kebler, R. (1960). The half-life of some scientific and technical literatures. *American Documentation, 11*(1), 18–22.

Castellano, C., Fortunato, S., & Loreto, V. (2009). Statistical physics of social dynamics. *Reviews of Modern Physics, 81,* 591–646.

Chen, C. (2006). Citespace II: Detecting and visualizing emerging trends and transient patterns in scientific literature. *Journal of the American Society for Information Science and Technology, 57*(3), 359–377.

Cooper, M., & McGregor, G. (1994). Using article photocopy data in bibliographic models for journal collection management. *Library Quarterly, 64*(4), 386–413.

Craig, I. D., Plume, A. M., McVeigh, M. E., Pringle, J., & Amin, M. (2007). Do open access articles have greater citation impact? A critical review of the literature. *Journal of Informetrics, 1*(3), 239–248.

Cronin, B. (1984). *The citation process: The role and significance of citations in scientific communication.* London: Taylor Graham.

Cronin, B. (2001). Bibliometrics and beyond: Some thoughts on Web-based citation analysis. *Journal of Information Science, 27*(1), 1–7.

Cronin, B. (2005). A hundred million acts of whimsy? *Current Science, 89*(9), 1505–1509.

Darmoni, S., Roussel, F., & Benichou, J. (2002). Reading factor: A new bibliometric criterion for managing digital libraries. *Journal of the Medical Library Association, 90*(3), 323–327.

Davis, P. (2002). Patterns in electronic journal usage: Challenging the composition of geographic consortia. *College & Research Libraries, 63*(6), 484–497.

Davis, P. M. (2009). Author-choice open-access publishing in the biological and medical literature: A citation analysis. *Journal of the American Society for Information Science and Technology, 60*(1), 3–8.

Davis, P. M., & Fromerth, M. J. (2007). Does the arXiv lead to higher citations and reduced publisher downloads for mathematics articles? *Scientometrics, 71*(2), 203–215.

Davis, P. M., Lewenstein, B. V., Booth, J. G., & Connolly, M. J. (2008). Open access publishing, article downloads and citations: Randomised trial. *British Medical Journal, 337,* 586.

Davis, P. M., & Price, J. S. (2006). eJournal interface can influence usage statistics: Implications for libraries, publishers, and project COUNTER. *Journal of the American Society for Information Science and Technology, 57*(9), 1243–1248.

Drott, M. C. (2006). Open access. *Annual Review of Information Science and Technology, 40,* 79–109.

Duy, J., & Vaughan, L. (2006). Can electronic journal usage data replace citation data as a measure of journal use? An empirical examination. *Journal of Academic Librarianship, 32*(5), 512–517.

Eason, K., Richardson, S., & Yu, L. (2000). Patterns of use of electronic journals. *Journal of Documentation, 56*(5), 477–504.

Egghe, L., & Rousseau, R. (2000). Aging, obsolescence, impact, growth, and utilization: Definitions and relations. *Journal of the American Society for Information Science, 51*(11), 1004–1017.

Eichhorn, G., Kurtz, M., Accomazzi, A., Grant, C., & Murray, S. (2000). The NASA Astrophysics Data System: The search engine and its user interface. *Astronomy & Astrophysics Supplement Series, 143*(1), 61–83.

Eysenbach, G. (2006). Citation advantage of open access articles. *PLoS Biology, 4*(5), 692–698.

Eysenbach, G. (2008). Word is still out: Publication was premature. *British Medical Journal e-letters, 337.* Retrieved February 2, 2009, from www.bmj.com/cgi/eletters/337/jul31_1/a568#199926

Fortunato, S., & Castellano, C. (2007). Scaling and universality in proportional elections. *Physical Review Letters, 99*(13), 138701.

Fowler, D. C. (Ed.). (2007). *Usage statistics of e-serials*. Binghamton, NY: Hawthorn Press.

Freire, J., Silva, C. T., Callahan, S. P., Santos, E., Scheidegger, C. E., & Vo, H. T. (2006). Managing rapidly-evolving scientific workflows. *Provenance and Annotation of Data*, *4145*, 10–18.

Galvin, T. J., & Kent, A. (1977). Use of a university library collection: A progress report on a Pittsburgh study. *Library Journal*, *102*(20), 2317–2320.

Gardner, W. (1990). The electronic archive: Scientific publishing for the 1990s. *Psychological Science*, *1*(6), 333–341.

Garfield, E. (1970). Citation indexing for studying science. *Nature*, *227*, 669–671.

Garfield, E. (1972). Citation analysis as a tool in journal evaluation: Journals can be ranked by frequency and impact of citations for science policy studies. *Science*, *178*(4060), 471–479.

Garfield, E. (2006). The history and meaning of the journal impact factor. *JAMA: The Journal of the American Medical Association*, *295*(1), 90–93.

Gargouri, Y. (2008). *L'avantage de citations des articles auto-archivés mandatés*. Montreal, Quebec: Cognition and Communication Laboratory, Université de Quebec.

Georgakopoulos, D., Hornick, M., & Sheth, A. (1995). An overview of workflow management: From process modeling to workflow automation infrastructure. *Distributed and Parallel Databases*, *3*(2), 119–153.

Ginsparg, P. (1994). First steps towards electronic research communication. *Computers in Physics*, *8*(4), 390–396.

Ginsparg, P. (2001). Creating a global knowledge network. In *Electronic Publishing in Science II. Proceedings of the Joint ICSU Press/UNESCO Expert Conference* (pp. 99–104). Paris: UNESCO.

Ginsparg, P. (2007). Next generation implications of open access. *CTWatch Quarterly*, *3*(3), 11–18.

Ginsparg, P., Houle, P., Joachims, T., & Sul, J. H. (2004). Mapping subsets of scholarly information. *Proceedings of the National Academy of Sciences of the United States of America*, *101*(Suppl. 1), 5236–5240.

Goldberg, D., Nichols, D., Oki, B. M., & Terry, D. (1992). Using collaborative filtering to weave an information tapestry. *Communications of the ACM*, *35*(12), 61–70.

Gosnell, C. F. (1944). Obsolescence of books in college libraries. *College & Research Libraries*, *5*, 115–125.

Grant, C., Accomazzi, A., Eichhorn, G., Kurtz, M., & Murray, S. (2000). The NASA Astrophysics Data System: Data holdings. *Astronomy & Astrophysics Supplement Series*, *143*(1), 111–135.

Gross, P. L. K., & Gross, E. M. (1927). College libraries and chemical education. *Science*, *66*, 385–389.

Hajjem, C., & Harnad, S. (2005). The open access citation advantage: Quality advantage or quality bias? *On-Line Memorandum*. Retrieved February 2, 2009, from eprints.ecs.soton.ac.uk/13328

Hajjem, C., Harnad, S., & Gingras, Y. (2005). Ten-year cross-disciplinary comparison of the growth of open access and how it increases research citation impact. *IEEE Data Engineering Bulletin*, *29*(4), 39–47.

Harnad, S. (1990). Scholarly skywriting and the prepublication continuum of scientific inquiry. *Psychological Science*, *1*(6), 342–344.

Harnad, S. (2005). OA impact advantage = EA + (AA) + (QB) + QA + (CA) + UA. *On-Line Memorandum*. Retrieved February 2, 2009, from eprints.ecs.soton.ac.uk/12085

Harnad, S. (2006a). The self-archiving impact advantage: Quality advantage or quality bias? *On-Line Memorandum*. Retrieved February 2, 2009, from openaccess.eprints. org/index.php?%20/archives/168-The-Self-Archiving-Impact-Advantage-Quality-Advantage-or-Quality-Bias.html

Harnad, S. (2006b). The special case of astronomy. *On-Line Memorandum*. Retrieved February 2, 2009, from openaccess.eprints.org/index.php?%20/archives/145-The-Special-Case-of-Astronomy.html

Harnad, S. (2007a). Citation advantage for OA self-archiving is independent of journal impact factor, article age, and number of co-authors. *On-Line Memorandum*. Retrieved February 2, 2009, from openaccess.eprints.org/index.php?%20/archives/192-guid.html

Harnad, S. (2007b). Craig et al.'s review of studies on the OA citation advantage. *On-Line Memorandum*. Retrieved February 2, 2009, from openaccess.eprints.org/index.php? %20/archives/248-Craig-et-al.s-Review-of-Studies-on-the-OA-Citation-Advantage.html

Harnad, S. (2007c). The open access citation advantage: Quality advantage or quality bias? *On-Line Memorandum*. Retrieved February 2, 2009, from openaccess.eprints.org /index.php?%20/archives/191-The-Open-Access-Citation-Advantage-Quality-Advantage-Or-Quality-Bias.html

Harnad, S. (2007d). Where there's no access problem there's no open-access advantage. *On-Line Memorandum*. Retrieved February 2, 2009, from openaccess.eprints.org/index.php? %20/archives/289-Where-Theres-No-Access-Problem-Theres-No-Open-Access-Advantage.html

Harnad, S. (2008). Davis et al's 1-year study of self-selection bias: No self-archiving control, no OA effect, no conclusion. *British Medical Journal e-letters, 337*. Retrieved February 2, 2009, from www.bmj.com/cgi/eletters/337/jul31_1/a568#199775

Harnad, S., & Brody, T. (2004). Comparing the impact of open access (OA) vs. non-OA articles in the same journals. *D-Lib, 10*(6). Retrieved March 1, 2009, from www.dlib.org/dlib/june04/harnad/06harnad.html

He, D., Goker, A., & Harper, D. J. (2002). Combining evidence for automatic Web session identification. *Information Processing & Management, 38*(5), 727–742.

Heer, J., & Chi, E. H. (2002). Separating the swarm: Categorization methods for user sessions on the Web. *Proceedings of the SigChi Conference on Human Factors in Computing Systems*, 243–250.

Henneken, E. A., Kurtz, M. J., Accomazzi, A., Grant, C. S., Thompson, D., Bohlen, E., et al. (2009). Use of the astronomical literature: A report on usage patterns. *Journal of Informetrics, 3*, 1–8.

Henneken, E. A., Kurtz, M. J., Eichhorn, G., Accomazzi, A., Grant, C., Thompson, D., et al. (2006). Effect of e-printing on citation rates in astronomy and physics. *Journal of Electronic Publishing, 9*, 2. Retrieved March 1, 2009, from dx.doi.org/10.3998/3336451.0009.202

Henneken, E. A., Kurtz, M. J., Eichhorn, G., Accomazzi, A., Grant, C. S., Thompson, D., et al. (2007). E-prints and journal articles in astronomy: A productive co-existence. *Learned Publishing, 20*, 16–22.

Hider, P. (2006). Search goal revision in models of information retrieval. *Journal of Information Science, 32*(4), 352–361.

Hood, W., & Wilson, C. (2005). The relationship of records in multiple databases to their usage or citedness. *Journal of the American Society for Information Science and Technology, 56*(9), 1004–1007.

Huntington, P., Nicholas, D., Jamali, H. R., & Tenopir, C. (2006). Article decay in the digital environment: An analysis of usage of OhioLINK by date of publication, employing deep log methods. *Journal of the American Society for Information Science and Technology, 57*(13), 1840–1851.

Jamali, H., Nicholas, D., & Huntington, P. (2005). The use and users of scholarly e-journals: A review of log analysis studies. *ASLIB Proceedings, 57*(6), 554–571.

Jansen, B. (2005). Seeking and implementing automated assistance during the search process. *Information Processing & Management, 41*(4), 909–928.

Jansen, B. J. (2006). Search log analysis: What it is, what's been done, how to do it. *Library & Information Science Research, 28*(3), 407–432.

Kaplan, N., & Nelson, M. (2000). Determining the publication impact of a digital library. *Journal of the American Society for Information Science, 51*(4), 324–339.

King, D. (2004). The scientific impact of nations. *Nature, 430*(6997), 311–316.

King, D. W., McDonald, D. D., & Roderer, N. K. (1981). *Scientific journals in the United States: Their production, use, and economics.* Stroudsburg, PA: Hutchinson Ross Publishing (Academic Press).

King, D. W., & Tenopir, C. (1999). Using and reading scholarly literature. *Annual Review of Information Science and Technology, 34*, 423–477.

King, D. W., Tenopir, C., & Clarke, M. (2006). Measuring total reading of journal articles. *D-Lib Magazine, 12*(10). Retrieved March 1, 2009, from www.dlib.org/dlib/october06/king/10king.html

Krause, J., Lindqvist, C. M., & Mele, S. (2007). *Quantitative study of the geographical distribution of the authorship of high-energy physics journals. oai:cds.cern.ch:1033099* (Technical Report No. CERN-OPEN-2007-014). Geneva, Switzerland: CERN.

Kurtz, M. J. (1992). Second order knowledge: Information retrieval in the terabyte era. In A. Heck & F. Murtagh (Eds.), *Astronomy from large databases II* (pp. 85–92). Garching bei Muenchen, Germany: European Southwest Observatory.

Kurtz, M. J. (2004, February). *Restrictive access policies cut readership of electronic research journal articles by a factor of two.* Paper presented at National Policies on Open Access (OA) Provision for University Research Output: An International Meeting, Southampton, UK.

Kurtz, M. J., Eichhorn, G., Accomazzi, A., Grant, C., Demleitner, M., Henneken, E., et al. (2005). The effect of use and access on citations. *Information Processing & Management, 41*(6), 1395–1402.

Kurtz, M. J., Eichhorn, G., Accomazzi, A., Grant, C., Demleitner, M., & Murray, S. (2005). Worldwide use and impact of the NASA astrophysics data system digital library. *Journal of the American Society for Information Science and Technology, 56*(1), 36–45.

Kurtz, M. J., Eichhorn, G., Accomazzi, A., Grant, C., Demleitner, M., Murray, S., et al. (2005). The bibliometric properties of article readership information. *Journal of the American Society for Information Science and Technology, 56*(2), 111–128.

Kurtz, M. J., Eichhorn, G., Accomazzi, A., Grant, C. S., Henneken, E. A., Thompson, D. M., et al. (2003). The myADS update service. *Bulletin of the American Astronomical Society, 35*, 1241.

Kurtz, M. J., Eichhorn, G., Accomazzi, A., Grant, C. S., & Murray, S. S. (1996). Journal citations: An ADS-AAS collaboration. *Bulletin of the American Astronomical Society, 28,* 1281.

Kurtz, M. J., Eichhorn, G., Accomazzi, A., Grant, C. S., & Murray, S. S. (1997). The relative effectiveness of astronomy journals. *Bulletin of the American Astronomical Society, 29,* 1236.

Kurtz, M. J., Eichhorn, G., Accomazzi, A., Grant, C. S., & Murray, S. S. (2002). Second order bibliometric operators in the Astrophysics Data System. In J.-L. Starck & F. D. Murtagh (Eds.), *Astronomical Data Analysis II. Proceedings of the SPIE* (Vol. 4847, pp. 238–245). Bellingham, WA: International Society for Optical Engineering.

Kurtz, M. J., Eichhorn, G., Accomazzi, A., Grant, C., Murray, S. S., & Watson, J. (2000). The NASA astrophysics data system: Overview. *Astronomy & Astrophysics Supplement Series, 143*(1), 41–59.

Kurtz, M. J., & Henneken, E. A. (2007). Open access does not increase citations for research articles from the Astrophysical Journal. *ArXiv e-prints, 709.* Retrieved February 2, 2009, from arxiv.org/ftp/arxiv/papers/0709/0709.0896.pdf

Kurtz, M. J., Karakashian, T., Grant, C. S., Eichhorn, G., Murray, S. S., Watson, J. M., et al. (1993). Intelligent text retrieval in the NASA Astrophysics Data System. In R. J. Hanisch, R. J. V. Brissenden, & J. Barnes (Eds.), *Astronomical Data Analysis Software and Systems II* (Vol. 52, pp. 132–136). San Francisco: Astronomical Society of the Pacific.

Ladwig, J., & Sommese, A. (2005). Using cited half-life to adjust download statistics. *College & Research Libraries, 66*(6), 527–542.

Lawrence, S. (2001). Free online availability substantially increases a paper's impact. *Nature, 411*(6837), 521.

Leydesdorff, L. (1994). The generation of aggregated journal-journal citation maps on the basis of the CD-ROM version of the Science Citation Index. *Scientometrics, 31*(59–84).

Leydesdorff, L. (2007). Betweenness centrality as an indicator of the interdisciplinarity of scientific journals. *Journal of the American Society for Information Science and Technology, 58*(9), 1303–1319.

Leydesdorff, L. (2008). The delineation of nanoscience and nanotechnology in terms of journals and patents: A most recent update. *Scientometrics, 76*(1), 159–167.

Line, M. (1993). Changes in the use of literature with time: Obsolescence revisited. *Library Trends, 41*(4), 665–683.

Line, M., & Sandison, A. (1975). Practical interpretation of citation and library use studies. *College & Research Libraries, 36*(5), 393–396.

Liu, M. (1993). Progress in documentation: The complexities of citation practice: A review of citation studies. *Journal of Documentation, 49*(4), 370–408.

Ludascher, B., & Goble, C. (2005). Guest editors' introduction to the special section on scientific workflows. *SIGMOD Record, 34*(3), 3–4.

Luther, J. (2000). *White paper on electronic journal usage statistics.* Washington, DC: Council on Library and Information Resources.

MacRoberts, M. H., & MacRoberts, B. R. (1987). Another test of the normative theory of citing. *Journal of the American Society for Information Science, 38,* 305–306.

May, R. (1997). The scientific wealth of nations. *Science, 275*(5301), 793–796.

Mayr, P. (2006). Constructing experimental indicators for open access documents. *Research Evaluation, 15*(2), 127–132.

McDonald, J. D. (2007). Understanding journal usage: A statistical analysis of citation and use. *Journal of the American Society for Information Science and Technology, 58*(1), 39–50.

Meadows, J. (2005). A practical line in bibliometrics. *Interlending & Document Supply, 33*(2), 90–94.

Merton, R. (1968). The Matthew effect in science. *Science, 159*(3810), 56–63.

Mobasher, B., Dai, H., Luo, T., & Nakagawa, M. (2001). Effective personalization based on association rule discovery from Web usage data. *Proceedings of the Third International Workshop on Web Information and Data Management*, 9–15.

Moed, H. F. (2005). Statistical relationships between downloads and citations at the level of individual documents within a single journal. *Journal of the American Society for Information Science and Technology, 56*(10), 1088–1097.

Moed, H. F. (2007). The effect of "open access" on citation impact: An analysis of ArXiv's condensed matter section. *Journal of the American Society for Information Science and Technology, 58*(13), 2047–2054.

Moed, H. F., Van Leeuwen, T., & Reedijk, J. (1998). A new classification system to describe the ageing of scientific journals and their impact factors. *Journal of Documentation, 54*(4), 387–419.

Moya-Anegón, F. D., Vargas-Quesada, B., Chinchilla-Rodrìguez, Z., Corera-Álvarez, E., Munoz-Fernández, F. J., & Herrero-Solana, V. V. (2007). Visualizing the marrow of science. *Journal of the American Society for Information Science and Technology, 58*(14), 2167–2179.

Nicholas, D., Huntington, P., Dobrowolski, T., Rowlands, I., Jamali, M., & Polydoratou, P. (2005). Revisiting "obsolescence" and journal article "decay" through usage data: An analysis of digital journal use by year of publication. *Information Processing & Management, 41*(6), 1441–1461.

Norris, M., Oppenheim, C., & Rowland, F. (2008). The citation advantage of open-access articles. *Journal of the American Society for Information Science and Technology, 59*(12), 1963–1972.

Pan, E. (1978). Journal citation as a predictor of journal usage in libraries. *Collection Management, 2*, 29–38.

Parker, R. (1982). Bibliometric models for management of an information store 2: Use as a function of age of material. *Journal of the American Society for Information Science, 33*(3), 129–133.

Peters, T. A. (2002). What's the use? The value of e-resource usage statistics. *New Library World, 103*(1172/1173), 39–47.

Pinski, G., & Narin, F. (1976). Citation influence for journal aggregates of scientific publications: Theory, with application to the literature of physics. *Information Processing & Management, 12*(5), 297–312.

Pirolli, P., & Pitkow, J. E. (1999). Distributions of surfers' paths through the World Wide Web: Empirical characterization. *World Wide Web, 2*(1–2), 29–45.

Price, D. J. D. (1965a). Networks of scientific papers. *Science, 149*(3683), 510–515.

Price, D. J. D. (1965b). Scientific foundations of science policy. *Nature, 206*(4981), 233–238.

Price, D. J. D. (1976). General theory of bibliometric and other cumulative advantage processes. *Journal of the American Society for Information Science, 27*(5–6), 292–306.

Rice, B. A. (1979). Science periodicals use study. *Serials Librarian, 4*(1), 35–47.

Rodriguez, M. A., Bollen, J., & Van de Sompel, H. (2007). A practical ontology for the large-scale modeling of scholarly artifacts and their usage. *Proceedings of the 7th ACM / IEEE-CS Joint Conference on Digital Libraries*, 278–287.

Rosvall, M., & Bergstrom, C. T. (2008). Maps of random walks on complex networks reveal community structure. *Proceedings of the National Academy of Sciences of the USA, 105*, 1118–1123.

Rowlands, I. (2007). Electronic journals and user behavior: A review of recent research. *Library & Information Science Research, 29*(3), 369–396.

Rowlands, I., & Nicholas, D. (2007). The missing link: Journal usage metrics. *Aslib Proceedings, 59*(3), 222–228.

Saka, A., & Igami, M. (2007). Mapping modern science using co-citation analysis. *Proceedings of the 11th International Conference Information Visualization*, 453–458.

Scales, P. A. (1976). Citation analyses as indicators of use of serials: Comparison of ranked title lists produced by citation counting and from use data. *Journal of Documentation, 32*(1), 17–25.

Shapiro, F. R. (Ed.). (2006). *The Yale book of quotations*. New Haven, CT: Yale University Press.

Shepherd, P. T. (2007). The feasibility of developing and implementing journal usage factors: A research project sponsored by UKSG. *Serials, 20*(2), 117–123.

Singh, V., Gray, J., Thakar, A., Szalay, A. S., Raddick, J., Boroski, B., et al. (2007). SkyServer Traffic Report: The first five years. *ArXiv Computer Science e-prints*. Retrieved February 2, 2009, from arxiv.org/ftp/cs/papers/0701/0701173.pdf

Small, H. (1999). Visualizing science by citation mapping. *Journal of the American Society for Information Science, 50*(9), 799–813.

Stankus, T., & Rice, B. A. (1982). Handle with care: Use and citation data for science journal management. *Collection Management, 4*(1/2), 95–110.

Szalay, A., & Gray, J. (2001). The world-wide telescope. *Science, 293*, 2037–2040.

Szalay, A., & Gray, J. (2006). 2020 computing: Science in an exponential world. *Nature, 440*, 413–414.

Tenopir, C., Baker, G., Read, E., Manoff, M., McClanahan, K., Nicholas, D., et al. (2007). Maxdata: A project to help librarians maximize e-journals usage data. In D. C. Fowler (Ed.), *Usage statistics of e-serials* (pp. 59–82). Binghamton, NY: Hawthorn Information.

Tenopir, C., King, D. W., Boyce, P., Grayson, M., & Paulson, K. L. (2005). Relying on electronic journals: Reading patterns of astronomers. *Journal of the American Society for Information Science and Technology, 56*(8), 786–802.

Tonta, Y., & Unal, Y. (2005). Scatter of journals and literature obsolescence reflected in document delivery requests. *Journal of the American Society for Information Science and Technology, 56*(1), 84–94.

Trimble, V., Aschwanden, M. J., & Hansen, C. J. (2006). Astrophysics in 2005. *Publications of the Astronomical Society of the Pacific, 118*(845), 947–1047.

Trimble, V., Aschwanden, M. J., & Hansen, C. J. (2007). Astrophysics in 2006. *Space Science Reviews, 132*(1), 1–182.

Tsay, M. Y. (1998a). Library journal use and citation half-life in medical science. *Journal of the American Society for Information Science, 49*(14), 1283–1292.

Tsay, M. Y. (1998b). The relationship between journal use in a medical library and citation use. *Bulletin of the Medical Library Association, 86*(1), 31–39.

Van de Sompel, H., & Beit-Arie, O. (2001a). Generalizing the openURL framework beyond references to scholarly works: The Bison-Fute model. *D-Lib Magazine, 7*(7/8). Retrieved March 1, 2009, from www.dlib.org/dlib/july01/vandesompel/07vandesompel.html

Van de Sompel, H., & Beit-Arie, O. (2001b). Open linking in the scholarly information environment using the openURL framework. *D-Lib Magazine, 7*(3). Retrieved March 1, 2009, from www.dlib.org/dlib/march01/vandesompel/03vandesompel.html

Van de Sompel, H., Young, J. A., & Hickey, T. B. (2003). Using the OAI-PMH ... Differently. *D-Lib Magazine, 9*(7–8). Retrieved March 1, 2009, from www.dlib.org/dlib/july03/young/07young.html

Walter, P., & Darling, L. (1996). A journal use study: Checkouts and in house use. *Bulletin of the Medical Library Association, 84*(4), 461–467.

Wang, P. (1999). Methodologies and methods for user behavioral research. *Annual Review of Information Science and Technology, 34*, 53–99.

Wasserman, S., & Faust, K. (1994). *Social network analysis.* Cambridge, UK: Cambridge University Press.

White, H., & McCain, K. (1989). Bibliometrics. *Annual Review of Information Science and Technology, 24*, 119–186.

Wilson, C. (1999). Informetrics. *Annual Review of Information Science and Technology, 34*, 107–247.

York, D. G., Adelman, J., Anderson, J. E., Jr., Anderson, S. F., Annis, J., Bahcall, N. A., et al. (2000). The Sloan Digital Sky Survey: Technical summary. *Astronomical Journal, 120*, 1579–1587.

# CHAPTER 2

# The Hirsch Index and Related Impact Measures

*Leo Egghe*
*Universiteit Hasselt, Diepenbeek, Belgium*

## Introduction

The Hirsch index (or h-index), introduced in 2005 by Jorge Hirsch, is one of the most popular indicators in information science and in informetrics. Hundreds of articles have been written on the h-index or related h-type indices. To quote Ball (2007, p. 737), "the h-index does seem to be able to identify good scientists, and is becoming widely used informally, for example to rank applicants for research posts." A review of this important topic is thus warranted.

In the first section we define the h-index and lay out its advantages and disadvantages. To deal with some of the limitations of the h-index, several other "h-type" indices (also called impact measures) have been introduced. These are discussed in the next section. We then discuss the application of h-type indices to entities other than authors (e.g., journals or topics) and provide an overview of case studies. In the fourth section we consider the intrinsic properties impact factors have or should have. It is not possible to define exactly what a good impact measure is, but we can give axiomatic characterizations of some impact measures and look at the influence of production (i.e., number of articles and number of citations to these articles) on some impact measures.

In the fifth section we discuss some informetric models for these h-type measures (e.g., their dependence on the total number of articles and on the total number of citations). We also describe dynamical aspects of these indices—the influence of transformations on h-type indices—and study distributions of h-type indices, noting that these are of a different nature from the distributions of the impact factor. In the next section we study h-type indices as a function of time (e.g., the career of an author) and examine the possible shapes of these functions as well as case studies. We close with some conclusions and challenges.

This review does not describe many case studies (although an attempt is made to present a complete reference list up to the end of 2008) but focuses on the "philosophy" behind h-type indices as impact or performance measures and their potentialities as new informetric indicators.

## The Hirsch Index: Definition, Advantages, and Disadvantages

We start with an historical note, communicated to this author by R. Rousseau and reported by Edwards (2005). It appears that the Hirsch index (of course not with this name) was defined some 35 years earlier by the astrophysicist Sir Arthur Stanley Eddington as follows (in a communication to the geophysicist Harold Jeffreys). In order to record his cycling prowess, Eddington records $n$, being the highest number of days on which he had cycled $n$ or more miles. As will become clear, this is nothing other than Hirsch's index (but in cycling terminology).

Hirsch's (2005b) definition is: A scientist has index $h$ if $h$ of his/her $N_p$ papers have at least $h$ citations each, and the other $(N_p - h)$ papers have no more than $h$ citations each. It must be remarked, however, that the first formulation by Hirsch (2005a) in the arXiv paper of August 17, 2005 had the word "fewer" instead of "no more" in this definition. This was corrected in the arXiv paper on September 29, 2005 and subsequently published as Hirsch (2005b). This correction was indeed necessary because, in the formulation of August 17, the h-index does not always exist. Consider the following simple example: Say an author has 5 papers, 4 of them with 3 citations and the fifth with 1. Here ($h = 3$) but when, in this definition, "no more" is replaced by "fewer," the h-index does not exist (cf. remarks on this by Glänzel [2006a] and Rousseau [2006b]). Note that Hirsch's (2005b) correction was not mentioned by Anderson, Hankin, and Killworth (2008), by Lehman, Jackson, and Lautrup (2008), or by Sidiropoulos and Katsaros (2008).

Another, equivalent, definition is as follows: If we rank an author's papers in decreasing order by the number of citations they receive, then this author's h-index is the highest rank $r = h$ such that the papers at ranks 1, 2, ..., $h$, each have $h$ or more citations.

Although we do not like the term, the papers at ranks 1, ..., $h$ constitute the so-called h-core (introduced by Rousseau, 2006b). Note that this h-core is not really a core set of papers, although they are the $h$ most visible papers.

An example is presented based on this author's own publication and citation record (compiled October 22, 2008, using Web of Science [WoS]). Table 2.1 presents papers ranked in decreasing order of received citations. From this it is clear that $h = 17$ (this is clear from the table up to $r = 18$; for later use, we include authors with ranks up to 25).

What does the h-index measure? In itself the h-index does not give a value to an informetric unity. This is in contrast with other informetric indicators such as the impact factor, which, essentially, is an average number of citations per paper. The h-index is not an average,

**Table 2.1  Citation data for L. Egghe (Web of Science, October 22, 2008)**

| Rank | Number of citations |
|:---:|:---:|
| 1 | 58 |
| 2 | 52 |
| 3 | 45 |
| 4 | 37 |
| 5 | 37 |
| 6 | 33 |
| 7 | 27 |
| 8 | 25 |
| 9 | 22 |
| 10 | 19 |
| 11 | 18 |
| 12 | 18 |
| 13 | 18 |
| 14 | 18 |
| 15 | 17 |
| 16 | 17 |
| 17 | 17 |
| 18 | 17 |
| 19 | 16 |
| 20 | 15 |
| 21 | 14 |
| 22 | 14 |
| 23 | 13 |
| 24 | 13 |
| 25 | 12 |

not a percentile, not a fraction: It is a totally new way of measuring performance, impact, visibility, quality, ... (see also the fourth section of this chapter) for instance, of the career of a scientist (for other applications, see the third section). It is a simple measure without any threshold (e.g., for the Garfield-Sher impact factor one limits the citation period to two years, which is, as is well-known, not optimal in some fields). This should explain the popularity of the h-index. The h-index is so popular that Scopus and Web of Science, less than two years after its introduction, have decided to incorporate it as an indicator.

The h-index is a single, simple measure that combines papers (an indicator of quantity) and citations (an indicator of quality or impact). It is a robust measure in two ways: It is not influenced by a set of infrequently cited papers or by the (even severe) increase of citations to already highly cited papers. The first aspect is certainly an advantage of the h-index: A researcher should not be "punished" for writing some low-cited papers, as long as this researcher writes highly cited papers as well. The fact that the h-index does not count the actual citations to papers is, in our view, a disadvantage of the h-index: Once a paper belongs to the h-core, it does not matter how many more citations it will receive. We feel that very highly cited papers should contribute more to an impact measure than less cited papers. Other measures have, therefore, been introduced (see the next section). To illustrate the insensitivity of the h-index we compared in 2006 the citation data of E. Garfield and F. Narin (see Egghe, 2006c). The data can be found in Table 2.2.

As one readily sees, both scientists had h-index values of 27. But Garfield has no less than 14 papers with more than 100 citations (the top one has 625 citations) while Narin has only one paper with more than 100 citations. This clearly illustrates the insensitivity of the h-index.

Of course, like any citation indicator, the h-index is field dependent and thus h-indices of authors in different fields cannot be compared. Table 2.3 presents the top researchers in the fields of physics, chemistry, and computer science (Ball, 2005).

The differences are clear: The h-indices of the physicists are all lower than those of the chemists. The h-indices of the computer scientists are, in turn, low in comparison with those of the physicists. For more on this field-dependence, see the next section.

New researchers have a clear disadvantage because of the short length of their careers and they should not be compared with researchers with long careers. On the other hand, established researchers may rest on their laurels because the number of citations received may increase even if no new papers are published. In other words: The h-index can never decrease. In the next section we review measures that take career length into account.

In citation analysis there is the problem of how to treat self-citations (Egghe & Rousseau, 1990; Smith, 1981; Vinkler, 1986). It is no different for the h-index—see Schreiber (2007b) and Zhivotovsky and Krutovsky (2008). Another problem is how to deal with multi-authored papers (citing as well as cited). Several papers dealing with this issue are discussed in the next section. Burrell (2007e) also discusses both problems (self-citations and multi-authorship). Finally, one should also be aware that a researcher's h-index depends on the citation database that is used. One can use WoS, Scopus, or Google Scholar—see Bar-Ilan (2008c), Jacsó (2008a, 2008b, 2008c, 2008d, 2008e), Meho and Yang (2007), and Meho and Rogers (2008). Meho and Yang (2007) show that not only h-index values can change when one goes from one database to another but that, when comparing (ranking) h-indices for a set of researchers, the ranks can also change significantly. Bar-Ilan (2008c) and Jacsó (2008a, 2008e) compare the performance of WoS, Scopus, and Google Scholar in various respects. Meho and Rogers (2008) conducted a similar study showing the better coverage provided by Scopus. Note also that the website www.harzing.com/pop.htm offers software that retrieves and analyzes citation data based on Google Scholar: The h-index and several variants

**Table 2.2  Citation data and h-index for E. Garfield and F. Narin in 2006**

| E. Garfield | | F. Narin | |
|---|---|---|---|
| Total citations | Rank of paper | Total citations | Rank of paper |
| 625 | 1 | 112 | 1 |
| 149 | 2 | 95 | 2 |
| 138 | 3 | 86 | 3 |
| 132 | 4 | 82 | 4 |
| 132 | 5 | 73 | 5 |
| 129 | 6 | 71 | 6 |
| 127 | 7 | 70 | 7 |
| 111 | 8 | 63 | 8 |
| 109 | 9 | 59 | 9 |
| 108 | 10 | 55 | 10 |
| 107 | 11 | 55 | 11 |
| 105 | 12 | 53 | 12 |
| 104 | 13 | 52 | 13 |
| 101 | 14 | 52 | 14 |
| 96 | 15 | 44 | 15 |
| 91 | 16 | 41 | 16 |
| 89 | 17 | 38 | 17 |
| 88 | 18 | 37 | 18 |
| 87 | 19 | 35 | 19 |
| 85 | 20 | 33 | 20 |
| 80 | 21 | 33 | 21 |
| 67 | 22 | 29 | 22 |
| 63 | 23 | 28 | 23 |
| 41 | 24 | 28 | 24 |
| 29 | 25 | 28 | 25 |
| 28 | 26 | 27 | 26 |
| 27 | 27 | 27 | 27 |
| 26 | 28 | 26 | 28 |
| . | . | . | . |
| . | . | . | . |
| . | . | . | . |

(to be introduced in the next section) can be calculated. McKercher (2008) used this software.

As with any indicator, the h-index is a single number, thereby reducing a scientist's career to a one-dimensional measurement. In the last section we add a time dimension to the h-index (and other h-type indices).

The h-index is shown to be robust with regard to errors in citation lists (Vanclay, 2007) or missing publications (Rousseau, 2007b). Hirsch (2007) demonstrates that his h-index is a good indicator—better than total number of citations or papers or citations per paper (impact factor)—of future achievement.

More discussion of the (dis)advantages of the h-index can be found in works by Antonakis and Lalive (2008); Bar-Ilan (2006); Bornmann and Daniel (2005, 2007b); Braun, Glänzel, and Schubert (2005, 2006); Costas and Bordons (2007b); Egghe (2006a, 2006b, 2006c); Glänzel (2006b);

**Table 2.3   Top researchers in physics, chemistry, and computer science, by h-indices**

| Physics | | |
|---|---|---|
| 1. | Ed Witten, Institute for Advanced Study, Princeton | $h = 110$ |
| 2. | Marvin Cohen, University of California, Berkeley | $h = 94$ |
| 3. | Philip Anderson, Princeton University | $h = 91$ |
| 4. | Manuel Cardona, Max Planck Institute for Solid State Research, Stuttgart, Germany | $h = 86$ |
| 5. | Frank Wilczek, Massachusetts Institute of Technology | $h = 68$ |
| **Chemistry** | | |
| 1. | George Whitesides, Harvard University | $h = 135$ |
| 2. | Elias James Corey, Harvard University | $h = 132$ |
| 3. | Martin Karplus, Harvard University | $h = 129$ |
| 4. | Alan Heeger, University of California, Santa Barbara | $h = 114$ |
| 5. | Kurt Wüthrich, Swiss Federal Institute of Biology, Zurich | $h = 113$ |
| **Computer Science** | | |
| 1. | Hector Garcia-Molina, Stanford University | $h = 70$ |
| 2. | Deborah Estrin, University of California, Los Angeles | $h = 68$ |
| 3. | Ian Foster, Argonne National Laboratory, Illinois | $h = 67$ |
| 4. | Scott Shenker, International Computer Science Institute, Berkeley | $h = 65$ |
| 4. | Don Towsley, University of Massachusetts, Amherst | $h = 65$ |
| 4. | Jeffrey D. Ullman, Stanford University | $h = 65$ |

Glänzel and Persson (2005); Jin, Liang, Rousseau, and Egghe (2007); Kelly and Jennions (2007); Liu and Rousseau (2007); Popov (2005); Rousseau (2006b, 2008a); Sidiropoulos and Katsaros (2008); Thelwall (2008); van Leeuwen (2008); van Raan (2006); and Wendl (2007).

## Variants of the h-Index

As mentioned already, the h-index has some clear disadvantages such as its insensitivity to the actual number of citations to the articles in the h-core or the advantage that researchers with longer careers have (but it must be emphasized that it was Hirsch's explicit purpose to give an index that measures impact of "long" careers). Multiple authorship, self-citations and field-dependence are also issues that must be dealt with in connection with the h-index.

In fact, Hirsch himself introduced in the first defining article (Hirsch 2005b) a variant of the h-index: The m-quotient, which is simply the h-index divided by career length (time since the publication of the first paper). Burrell (2007a) gives a similar definition (in a time-dependent context—see also the last section), which he calls the h-rate. A variant is to divide the h-index not by time but by the total number of papers published by an author (called the normalized h-index). Sidiropoulos and Katsaros (2008) do this. Rousseau (personal communication) feels that this is a bad idea but thinks it is useful for journals (instead of authors) (see the next section for an application of the h-index to journals): In this way different years with different numbers of published articles can be compared, as Rousseau (2006a) has shown.

Iglesias and Pecharromán (2007) claim that dividing the h-index by the average number of citations per paper produces an index that can be used for inter-area comparisons. We are convinced that this index is more field independent than the h-index, but we do not think it is useable as a completely field-independent index. Batista, Campiteli, Kinouchi, and Martinez (2006) and Campiteli, Batista, and Martinez (2007) seem to prove that dividing the h-index by the total number of authors in the set of $h$ papers yields a relatively field-independent indicator. We are skeptical about the claim by Valentinuzzi, Laciar, and Atrio (2007) that they have found two discipline-independent h-type indices.

Radicchi, Fortunato, and Castellano (2008) also try to construct a field-independent h-index. They do not divide the h-index by the average number of citations per paper in the field (Iglesias & Pecharromán, 2007) but rather divide the actual number of citations to each of a researcher's papers by this average number. In addition, they divide the number of a researcher's publications by the average number of publications in the field. Using these "rescaled" numbers, they apply the definition of the h-index, thereby obtaining the "generalized h-index."

Qiu, Ma, and Cheng (2008) also mention the field-dependence of the h-index as well as the fact that the h-index is not very well suited to evaluating the outputs of young researchers. They introduce the Paper Quality Index (PQI), a relative index based on the impact factor of a field and the total number of citations in that field. This index is based on the impact factor and is, therefore, not of h-type.

Molinari and Molinari (2008a, 2008b) make a log-log plot of the h-index versus number of papers, yielding a regression line of the form $\ln h = A - \beta \ln N$ ($N$ = number of papers). Then $h_m$ is defined as

$$h_m = e^A = \frac{h}{N^\beta}$$

which is defined as the impact (or quality) index and which is claimed to be a correction for size. The name is not well chosen because all indices discussed here are impact indices (see also the fourth section).

Several papers deal with modifications of the h-index in connection with co-authors. Campiteli and colleagues (2007) and Batista and colleagues (2006) use the h-index, divided by the average number of authors per paper in the h-core. This index is denoted $h_I$ and equals $h / \overline{T}$ where $\overline{T} = T / h$, with T the total number of authors in the h-core, hence $h_I = h^2 / T$.

Independently, both Egghe (2008f) and Schreiber (2008c, 2008d) introduce the same measure $h_m$ (Schreiber) and $h_F$ ( Egghe) using fractional paper counts (thereby replacing entire ranks by fractional ranks being 1 divided by the number of co-authors of the paper). Egghe (2008f) also suggests the measure $h_f$ whereby one uses fractional citation counts instead of fractional paper counts. He presents a mathematical theory of $h_f$ and $h_F$, noting that, in practice, the corrections $h_f$ or $h_F$ on $h$ are not very large. Wan, Hua, and Rousseau (2007) and Chai, Hua, Rousseau, and Wan (2008) go even further and define the so-called "pure h-index" where one can even take into account a scientist's relative position in the byline of an article. In this connection see also Kim and Seo (2007).

Kosmulski (2006) introduces the $h^{(2)}$-index which is an h-type index that is easier to calculate than the h-index because one needs a shorter list of papers in decreasing order of number of citations: An author has Kosmulski's index $h^{(2)}$ if $r = h^{(2)}$ is the highest rank such that all papers at ranks 1, ..., $h^{(2)}$ have at least $(h^{(2)})^2$ citations. In Table 2.1, this would mean $h^{(2)} = 5$ for this author. The numbers $h^{(2)}$ are hence much smaller than the h-indices and we feel that, for this reason, $h^{(2)}$ does not discriminate very well among authors. In addition, the calculation of the h-index is not very time consuming and, as has been mentioned, can be calculated in both Web of Science and Scopus. Notwithstanding this criticism of the $h^{(2)}$-index, the Applications section of this chapter reviews an interesting application of the $h^{(2)}$-index to downloads.

Levitt and Thelwall (2007) give a generalization of the Kosmulski index. They define the Hirsch k-frequency $f(k)$ as the number of documents that are cited at least $kh$ times. Note that $f(h) = h^{(2)}$ is the Kosmulski index. The variable $k$ enables one to illustrate the distribution of the highly cited documents. They also introduce a "normalized" h-index:

$$h_{norm} = 100 \frac{h^2}{T}$$

where $T$ is equal to the number of documents of the set.

Hu and Chen (2009) introduce the so-called Major Contribution Index (MCI): An author's Hirsch index, based on his/her papers in which this author plays a major role (e.g., first or corresponding author). We do not see the value of this h-index variant: It is the number of citations that counts and this for any published paper of an author!

None of the variants of the h-index deals with the insensitivity of the h-index to the number of citations to the highly cited papers. This will be discussed now. Note that—in our opinion—we do not need variants of the h-index dealing with the lowly cited papers. Hence we think that the v-index, introduced by Riikonen and Vihinen (2008) (being $h$ divided by the total number of papers), does not make much sense as an impact measure.

First we introduce the g-index, as given by Egghe (2006a, 2006b, 2006c). Note that the actual number of citations to the first 17 papers of this author (Table 2.1) is in fact of no importance as long as this number is at least 17. The insensitivity of the h-index is also clear from Table 2.2 in the comparison of the careers of Garfield and Narin. Egghe notes that the h-index satisfies the property that the first $h$ papers, together, have at least $h^{(2)}$ citations (indeed, in the h-core we have $h$ papers each having at least $h$ citations). Then Egghe defines the g-index as the highest rank with this property. In other words, with the same ranking of papers in decreasing order of number of citations received, we define the g-index as the highest rank such that the first $g$ papers have at least $g^2$ citations together. In other words: The first $g$ papers have at least $g$ citations, on average. Note that, per definition, $g \geq h$.

In Table 2.1, the total number of citations to the first 24 papers equals $580 > 24^2$ and the total number of citations to the first 25 papers equals $592 < 25^2$ so that $g = 24$ for this author (as of October 22, 2008). Egghe (2006c) performs the same calculation on the (extended) citation data for Garfield and Narin (Table 2.2). Although their h-indices (in 2006) are equal ($h = 27$), Egghe finds that Garfield's g-index is 59 and Narin's is 40, demonstrating the g-index's greater discriminatory power. This is confirmed by Schreiber (2008a, 2008b) and Tol (2008). Costas and Bordons (2008) also confirm this finding, noting that for prolific scientists the ranks based on the g-index are lower than those based on the h-index, and their g-index/h-index ratios are, on average, higher. Burrell (2007c) compares the g-index with the h-index and finds that they are both proportional to career length (see also the section on time-dependent h-type sequences). Rosenstreich and Wooliscroft (2009) apply the g-index to the ranking of management journals.

Jin and colleagues (2007) introduce the R-index, another attempt to improve the sensitivity of the h-index to the number of citations to highly cited papers. It is defined as

$$R = \sqrt{\sum_{i=1}^{h} c_i} \tag{1}$$

where documents, as usual, are ranked in decreasing order of the number of received citations, $c_i$ is the number of citations to the $i^{\text{th}}$ paper, and $h$ is the h-index. So, as is also the case with the g-index, this measure takes into account the actual $c_i$-values in the h-core. It is an improvement of the A-index introduced by Jin (2006) (the name was suggested by Rousseau [2006b]; see also Jin et al. [2007]), which defined as the average number of citations to papers in the h-core:

$$A = \frac{1}{h} \sum_{i=1}^{h} c_i \qquad (2)$$

This measure has the undesirable property that an increase in the number of citations might lead to a decrease in the A-index (see the section on desirable properties of impact measures). Consider a situation where four papers have 6, 5, 4, and 3 citations respectively: $h = 3$ and $A = \frac{1}{3}(6 + 5 + 4) = 5$. Add one citation to the fourth paper: 6, 5, 4, 4; now $h = 4$ and $A = \frac{1}{4}(6 + 5 + 4 + 4) = \frac{19}{4} < 5$, which is not desirable: More citations should not lead to a strict decrease in an impact measure. Note that the g- and R-indices do not suffer from this deficiency. The square root in (1) is necessary to conform with the h-index in case all $c_i = h$, $i = 1, ..., h$. Then $R = h$, as is readily seen.

Glänzel (2008c, p. 66) compares the h-index and A-index with so-called characteristic scores and scales (CSS), which are mean citation rates of subsets of an author's papers. One example of a CSS is the average number of citations to those papers that have at least a number of citations larger than or equal to the overall average number of citations.

Sezer and Gokceoglu (2009) define the so-called "fuzzy academic performance index," which is built around three indicators—total number of publications, total number of citations, and academic life span—and one notes a high correlation of this index with the h-index. It can be seen from Table 2.1 that the R-index of this author is 21.86, the square root of the sum of the number of citations to the $h = 17$ most highly cited articles. In order to normalize for the age of an article (which is more advantageous for attracting more citations), Jin and colleagues (2007) introduce the AR-index:

$$AR = \sqrt{\sum_{i=1}^{h} \frac{c_i}{a_i}} \qquad (3)$$

where $h$ and $c_i$ are as given and $a_i$ is the age of article $i$. The AR-index is an approach to define an h-type index that can actually decrease. In this way authors cannot "rest on their laurels." Rousseau and Jin (2008), Jin (2007), and Jin and Rousseau (2007) discuss the AR-index further; Glänzel (2007a) provides comments on the R- and AR-indices. Järvelin and Persson (2008) criticize the AR approach and propose another way of taking age into account (their proposal, however, is not an h-type index).

Rousseau and Jin (2008) present an alternative for (3). Instead of the square of (3):

$$\sum_{i=1}^{h} \frac{c_i}{a_i} \tag{4}$$

one could also define

$$AR_1^2 = \frac{\sum_{i=1}^{h} c_i}{\sum_{i=1}^{h} a_i} \tag{5}$$

similar in form to the meta-journal average impact factor and the meta-journal global impact factor, respectively. Egghe and Rousseau (1996a, 1996b) discuss their difference—and hence, indirectly, the difference between (4) and (5). However, Rousseau and Jin (2008) indicate some deficiencies with the index defined in (5).

Another way to take the citation scores of the (highly cited) papers into account is to weight the articles according to their citations: This is the weighted h-index denoted $h_w$ (Egghe & Rousseau, 2008). The discrete $h_w$-index suffers from the same problem as the A-index but Egghe and Rousseau show that the continuous model does not suffer from this aberration.

Anderson and colleagues (2008) present another attempt to solve the problem of the insensitivity of the h-index to the number of citations to the highest cited articles. Although it is not a practical solution (they have to take into account all citations to all papers), there is some theoretical interest in their proposal. Their inspiration comes from a theory of partitions, described by Andrews (1998). A table (called a Ferrers graph) is constructed as follows: Papers are vertically ranked in decreasing order of citations received. Instead of writing the number of received citations, dots (equal to this number) are shown horizontally, for each paper. From the upper left corner, squares of side length 1, 2, 3, … are made. First the square of side-length 1 (consisting of the first citation dot to the first paper) is made and this point receives a weight of 1. The square of side-length 2 is made by adding to this square of side-length 1 the second citation (dot) to the first paper and the first two citations (dots) to the second paper. So we add three citations each receiving a weight of ⅓. The next square with side-length 3 consists of the square of length 2, extended with five citations (each receiving a weight of ⅕): The third citation (dot) to the first paper and to the second paper and the first three citations (dots) to the third paper, and so on. We can continue like this until all citations to all papers are covered. Figure 2.1 provides an example.

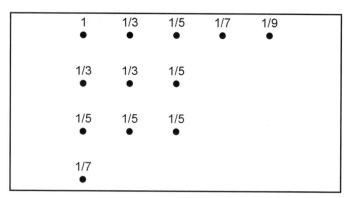

**Figure 2.1** **Ferrers graph of (5,3,3,1): four papers with respectively 5, 3, 3 and 1 citation(s)**

The sum of all the weights of given citations is the so-called tapered h-index; it is denoted $h_T$ and is a (theoretical) natural extension of the h-index $h$. Indeed, the h-index $h$ equals the side-length of the largest completed (filled in) square of points, being also equal to the sum of all the scores in this square (called the Durfee square) (in Figure 2.1, $h = 3$). Hence, clearly $h £ h_T$ (in Figure 2.1, $h_T = 3 + \frac{3}{4} + \frac{1}{9}$) but $h_T$ takes into account ("in an h-type way") all citations to all papers (as said, this is not practical and hence a disadvantage of the tapered h-index $h_T$).

Egghe (2008a) shows how these Ferrers graphs can be transformed to yield the g-index in a natural (theoretical) way. He considers the so-called conjugate sequence of a partition (decreasing sequence of coordinates of a vector) and shows that its h-index is the same as the h-index of the original partition. Egghe (2005) studies Lorenz curves for partitions, and their conjugates are studied in both discrete and continuous (introduced by Egghe [2008a]) ways.

Van Eck and Waltman's (2008) study of generalizations of the h-index and the g-index involves an extra parameter $\alpha$. The generalized h-index $h_\alpha$ is the highest rank such that all the papers at this rank (and lower ranks) have at least $\alpha h$ citations. Note that $h_1 = h$. Similarly, the generalized g-index $g_\alpha$ is defined as the highest rank such that the first $g_\alpha$ papers have, together, at least $\alpha g^2$ citations. Note again that $g_1 = g$. The authors demonstrate properties for varying $\alpha$. Independently, Levitt and Thelwall (2007) also define $h_\alpha$, but in another notation: They define the Hirsch-frequency $f(k)$ as the number of documents in the collection that are cited at least $kh$ times. Hence $f(k) = h_\alpha$ for $\alpha = k$.

Deineko and Woeginger (in press) and Woeginger (2008d) even generalize this by replacing $\alpha h$ and $\alpha g^2$ by general functions $s(k)$, $k = 1, 2, \ldots$ . Subsequent sections of this chapter discuss axiomatic characterizations of these indices (including the h-index and g-index) and their informetric properties.

Bornmann, Mutz, and Daniel (2008) compare nine of these indices (h, m quotient of Hirsch, g, $h^{(2)}$, A, R, AR, $h_w$, and a new m-index). The m-index is the median number of citations received by papers in the h-core. They classify (using factor analysis) indices as:

- Describing the most productive core of a scientist's output (such as h, m quotient, g, and $h^{(2)}$)

- Depicting the impact of the papers in the core (such as A, m-index, R, AR, and $h_w$)

(See also Bornmann, Mutz, Daniel, Wallon, & Ledin, 2008.)

Furthermore, Bornmann, Mutz, and Daniel (2009) argue, the classical bibliometric indicators "number of publications" and "total citation counts" load so high on these two factors that, in this (statistical) vision, h-type indices are not necessarily required. Several papers discussed in the next section report similar conclusions.

Bornmann, Mutz, and Daniel (2007) introduce the b-index of a scientist as the number of his papers that belong to the top 10 percent of papers in a field. Because this index uses a threshold value, we consider this as a non-h-type measure.

Leydesdorff (in press) compares the h-index statistically (using principal component analysis) with non-h-type indices (such as PageRank, impact factor, Scimago Journal Ranking, and network centrality measures). He finds that the h-index combines the dimensions of size and impact.

Ruane and Tol (2008) introduce rational interpolations of the h-index (i.e., between $h$ and $h + 1$); see also Tol (2008) and Guns and Rousseau (2009a) (who also study the g-index). Rousseau (2008d) introduces real-valued h-indices and g-indices, which receive further attention from Guns and Rousseau (2009a). These real-valued indices are based on the piecewise linearly interpolated citation curve. Researchers who have investigated other h-type indices include Sidiropoulos and Katsaros (2008); Rousseau, Guns, and Liu (2008); Kosmulski (2007); Boell and Wilson (2008); and Ruane and Tol (2008).

## Applications

It is clear from Hirsch's (2005b) original definition that the h-index (and hence also the other h-type indices) has been defined in order to have a simple informetric indicator of the impact of a researcher's career. Worldwide the h-index (and some of its variants) is used for this purpose and we have mentioned that the h-index is available in WoS and Scopus. Researchers in the same field (and with equally long careers) can be compared using the h-index. The h-index can also be used to predict future achievements and for deciding on tenure positions or grants (Hirsch, 2005b).

Soon after the introduction of the h-index, Braun and colleagues (2005, 2006) noticed the important fact that the h-index can also be applied to journals: The same definition applies to a ranked set of articles (in decreasing order of the number of citations they received) of a journal (e.g., for a certain period or for all articles of the journal). The same goes, of course, for the other h-type indices. This leads to the constatation that the journal impact factor (IF) has a serious competitor, especially because the IF is dependent on the defined citing and publication period: This arbitrariness in the definition of IF does not apply to the h-index and derivatives. Miller (2006) claims the superiority of the h-index over the IF for physics and Vanclay (2007) expresses a similar preference, although Vanclay (2008b) subsequently reports high correlation between journal rankings based on IF and rankings based on the h-index. Harzing and van der Wal (2009) find the h-index for journals, based on Google Scholar, to be a better measure of journal impact than the IF itself. Vanclay (2006) comments on the work by Braun and colleagues (2005).

In general, one finds comparisons of the h-index with other bibliometric indicators such as total number of publications, total number of citations, average number of citations per publication (IF), and even peer review for authors, journals, or groups of authors in papers by Bornmann and Daniel (2007a); Bornmann, Wallon, and Ledin (2008); Costas and Bordons (2007b); and van Raan (2006). Wan, Hua, Rousseau, and Sun (2009) compare the h-index for journals with a new indicator, the "download immediacy index" (DII) defined as the number of downloads of a journal's articles within one publication year, divided by the number of articles published in that journal during that year (this measure was introduced by Wan, Hua, Du, & Song, 2007). The conclusions are, in general, the same: All these rankings correlate strongly. From this point of view, research evaluation does not need the h-index, although all authors agree that the h-index is a valuable, simple tool that, due to the previously mentioned correlation, can to a certain extent, replace the other indicators. Bornmann, Marx, and Schier (2009) reach a similar conclusion: h-type indices correlate highly with IF and hence, from a statistical point of view, are empirically redundant. Coincidentally Reedijk and Moed (2008) come to the conclusion that the "impact" of impact factors is decreasing, which indirectly leads to a higher importance of the h-index for journals. However, Honekopp and Kleber (2008) reach an opposite conclusion as far as the prediction of future success of an article is concerned.

In addition to applications to authors, groups of authors (e.g., institutes), and journals there are possible applications to all source-item relations in an information production process (IPP) (cf. Egghe, 2005). An IPP is a set of sources (e.g., authors, journals) that produce items (e.g., articles) where one indicates which sources produce which items (see Egghe [2005] or Egghe & Rousseau [1990] for many more examples). These sources can be ranked in decreasing order of the number of items and hence the h-index (or any h-type measure) of this IPP can be calculated—see also Egghe (in press c).

In this sense the paper by Banks (2006) is very interesting because it defines the h-index for (scientific) topics and compounds. Thus "hot" topics can be detected in diverse research areas. Bar-Ilan (2007, 2008a) applies this idea to the h-index of the topic "h-index." Egghe and Rao (2008a), Jin and Rousseau (2008), Minasny, Hartemink, and McBratney (2007), Rousseau (2007a), and The STIMULATE6 Group (2007) undertake similar investigations.

Csajbók, Berhidi, Vasas, and Schubert (2007) study the h-index for countries (by various science fields). Liu and Rousseau (2007, 2009) calculate the h-index for book classifications and the number of times the books in these classifications are borrowed, an example of how the h-index can be used in library management. Guan and Gao (2009) apply the h-index to citations to patents.

Because the h-index can be applied in any IPP, Egghe and Rao (2008b) studied different h-indices for groups of authors. If we look at a group of authors (e.g., in an institute or field) we can arrange these authors in decreasing order of number of publications. The corresponding h-index is denoted $h_p$. If we arrange these authors in decreasing order of the total number of citations received, we arrive at the h-index $h_C$. Rousseau and Rons (2008) propose a similar h-index, but using the total number of different citing papers (instead of all received citations). If we consider the group of authors as one meta-author and if we arrange the papers of this meta-author in decreasing order of the number of citations received we have the global h-index $h_G$, also studied by van Raan (2006) and mentioned by Prathap (2006). Egghe and Rao (2008b) prove interrelations among these h-indices; they also examine the successive h-index, $h_2$. This successive h-index was introduced, independently, by Prathap (2006) and Schubert (2007) and we define it now.

Suppose we have a group of authors, for example, at an institute, and that each author has an h-index. If we arrange these authors in decreasing order of their h-indices then we can define the h-index of this list (denoted $h_2$) as the highest rank such that the first $h_2$ authors have an h-index of at least $h_2$. This is called the successive h-index because it was derived from the h-indices of the authors. Schubert (2007) offers a slightly different example, replacing authors by journals (e.g., of a publisher); with this approach the h-indices of these journals determine the successive h-index, $h_2$, of this publisher (see also Braun et al., 2005, 2006). One can even go to a higher aggregation level, using the $h_2$-indices to determine the successive h-index, $h_3$, of a country. Egghe and Rao (2008b) also study the successive h-index $h_2$ in comparison with the previously defined $h_p$, $h_C$, and $h_G$ for a group of authors. Egghe (2008g) provides a description of the modeling of successive h-indices; see also the section on informetric models.

Ruane and Tol (2008) apply successive h-indices to the field of economics in the Republic of Ireland; Tol (2008) introduces the successive g-index and applies it to the same topic. As has been mentioned, Tol (2008, p. 153) finds that "the successive g-index has greater discriminatory power than the successive h-index." Arencibia-Jorge and Rousseau (in press) apply successive h-indices to Cuban institutions. Arencibia-Jorge, Barrios-Almaguer, Fernández-Hernández, and Carvajal-Espino (2008) undertake a similar study. Rousseau and colleagues (2008) investigate the (successive) h-index in the generalized framework of a conglomerate (which is a slight extension of an IPP). Da Silva, Palazzo de Oliveira, Valdeni de Lima, Warpechowski, Hannel, Medianeira Denardi, and colleagues (2009) use successive h-indices in the construction of a relative h-index for groups (among a set of groups). They combine this relative h-index for groups with the Gini index (Gini, 1909) of the group (based on its members' h-indices) to yield the $\alpha$-index. This index measures the quality of a group and is independent of the size of the group. Jacsó (2007) addresses the problem of recognizing author names for h-index calculations.

H-indices have numerous applications. They can be used not only with citations but also with download data (O'Leary, 2008). Hua, Rousseau, Sun, and Wan (2009) find that, in general, downloads yield higher numbers than citations and, therefore, one does not use the h-index but the Kosmulski $h^{(2)}$-index. We consider this an interesting use and advantage of the $h^{(2)}$-index.

One could determine h-indices of websites (based on their in- or out-links). We even feel (although there are apparently no references yet) that the h-index (and h-type indices) could be used in econometrics and other -metrics fields as a new assessment indicator, for example, of wealth or income.

We talk nowadays of a "3-tier" evaluation system (peer review, citations, downloads) in a "2-tier" communication system (pre-publication in a repository [e-print server], publication in a [e-]journal). The British government has announced that, after 2008, it will base funding assessments for universities on h-type indicators (Ball, 2007).

We have mentioned applications of the h-index to researchers, journals, institutes, and topics. Additional application areas are mentioned here, grouped by broad topic.

- **Authors, Career Assessment**: Aguayo-Albasini and Campillo-Soto (2008); Bar-Ilan (2006); Batista and colleagues (2006); Bornmann, Wallon, and Ledin (2008); Brahler and Decker (2005); Costas and Bordons (2007a); Cronin and Meho (2006); de Araujo (2008); Dodson (2008); Dorta-Contreras, Arencibia-Jorge, Marti-Lahera, and Araujo-Ruiz (2008); Engqvist and Frommen (2008); Ferrand (2007); Frangopol (2005); Glänzel and Persson (2005); Harnad (2007); Heaney (2007); Hermes-Lima, Alencastro, Santos, Navas, and Beleboni (2007); Humberto Romero, Garcia, and Kiwi (2009); Imperial and Rodriguez-Navarro (2007); Jones (2008); Kellner (2008); Kellner and Ponciano (2008); Kelly and Jennions (2006, 2007); Levitt and Thelwall (2009); Lovegrove and

Johnson (2008); Lufrano and Staiti (2008); Machacek and Kolcunova (2008); McKercher (2008); Minasny and colleagues (2007); Mugnaini, Packer, and Meneghini (2008); Oppenheim (2007); Purvis (2006—a 20-line note); Rao (2007); Rau (2007); Rodriguez, Janssens, Debackere, and De Moor (2007, 2008); Romero, Cortés, Escudero, Lopez, and Moreno (2007); Saad (2006); Salgado and Paez (2007); Sanderson (2008); Sangam and Girji (2008); Schreiber (2007a); Sebire (2008); Sidiropoulos and Katsaros (2008); Sidiropoulos, Katsaros, and Manolopoulos (2007); Timofieiev, Snásel, and Dvorský (2008); Torro-Alves, Herculano, Tercariol, Filho, and Graeff (2007); Ursprung and Zimmer (2007); van Haselen (2007); van Leeuwen (2008); Vanclay (2007); Vinkler (2007).

- **Journals**: Barendse (2007); Gracza and Somoskovi (2008); Harzing and van der Wal (2009); Jeang (2007); Krauskopf and Krauskopf (2008); Levitt and Thelwall (2008); Liu, Rao, and Rousseau (in press); Olden (2007); Orbay and Karamustafaolu (2008); Rousseau (2006a); Rousseau and Small (2005); Saad (2006); Satyanarayana and Sharma (2008); Sebire (2008); Sidiropoulos, Katsaros, and Manolopoulos (2007); Vanclay (2007, 2008a, 2008b).

- **Research Groups and Institutions**: de Araujo (2008); Grothkopf and Stevens-Rayburn (2007); Kinney (2007); Molinari and Molinari (2008a, 2008b); Mugnaini and colleagues (2008); Pires da Luz, Marques-Portella, Mendlowicz, Gleiser, Silva Freire Coutinho, and Figueira (2008); Torro-Alves and colleagues (2007); van Raan (2006).

- **Countries**: Lufrano and Staiti (2008); Mahbuba and Rousseau (2008), Pilc (2008).

- **Topics**: Marx and Barth (2008); Minasny and colleagues (2007); Rousseau (2007a); The STIMULATE6 Group (2007).

- **Library Management**: Liu and Rousseau (2007, 2009).

It is clear that the majority of case studies on h-type indices focuses on authors (researchers) and/or career assessment, which is in line with the original purpose of the h-index as defined by Hirsch (2005a, 2005b).

We end this section with an intriguing question: If we consider "all" publications of all authors as if they were written by one meta-author M, what is the h-index of M? This h-index could then be considered as the h-index of "humanity." We know that, in essence, the answer to this problem has no real value because we mix all scientific disciplines, which is not allowed when dealing with citation analysis (and by extension when dealing with the h-index), so the question should be considered as merely an intriguing challenge.

Of course one has to define what "all" publications means. We have limited ourselves to WoS. Henry Small (personal communication, May 2007) reported (and this information was published by Egghe and Rao [2008a] with Small's permission) that, depending on the time period used (up to 1955 or up to 1972), the h-index of WoS (standing for "all" publications) is between 1,500 and 2,000. Note that in May 2007, WoS (up to 1972) contained a little more than $33.10^6$ documents of which about 80 percent have received at least one citation (Small, personal communication, May 2007).

## Theories of Impact and Performance Measurement

Glänzel (1996), supported by Rousseau (2002), explains the need for standards in informetric research. This is certainly an issue when introducing a new topic like h-type indices.

In this section we examine theoretical properties of h-type indices so that we can learn to "understand" their true nature. But first, what do we want? In other words what do we expect from an impact or performance measure (the terms should be standardized, so we suggest, from now on, using the term "impact measure")?

Let us compare this with concentration measures (i.e., those capable of measuring concentration or inequality) (Egghe, 2005, chapter 4), which were introduced in econometrics, 100 or so years ago. Concentration measures have little to do with impact measures but act, like impact measures, on a decreasing sequence $x_1, x_2, ..., x_N$ of positive numbers. We will show that the g-index has a concentration property. Here we introduce briefly the notion of a concentration measure and show that we can define, in an exact way, what we expect from a concentration measure. Then we go back to impact measures and investigate whether such an exact "wish list" can also be given for impact measures.

Lorenz (1905) invented concentration theory in econometrics in 1905. It has also found its way into informetrics because, as in econometrics, many phenomena in informetrics are very concentrated in the sense that few sources have many items and many sources have few items (e.g., few papers receive many citations and many papers receive few [or no] citations [Egghe, 2005]).

Lorenz concentration theory goes as follows. Let $X = (x_1, x_2, ..., x_N)$ be a decreasing vector with positive coordinates $x_i$, $i = 1, ..., N$. The Lorenz curve $L(X)$ of $X$ is the polygonal curve connecting $(0,0)$ with the points

$$\left( \frac{i}{N}, \sum_{j=1}^{i} a_j \right), \quad i = 1, ..., N$$

where

$$a_i = \frac{x_i}{\sum\limits_{j=1}^{N} x_j}$$

(6)

Note that for $i = N$ we have (1,1) as end point of $L(X)$. Let $X$ and $Y = (y_1, y_2, \ldots, y_N)$ be two such vectors. We say that $X$ is more concentrated than $Y$ if $L(X) > L(Y)$, that is, if the Lorenz curve of $X$ is strictly above that of $Y$ (except, of course, in the common points (0,0) and (1,1)). We also say that the coordinates of $X$ are more unequal than those of $Y$.

That Lorenz curves are the right tool to measure concentration (or inequality) is seen in Muirhead's (1903) results, stating[1] $L(X) > L(Y)$ if and only if $X$ is constructed, starting from $Y$, by a finite number of applications of elementary transfers. An elementary transfer (e.g., on $Y = (y_1, \ldots, y_N)$) changes $Y$ into the vector

$$\left( y_1, \ldots, y_i + a, \ldots, y_j - a, \ldots, y_N \right)$$

(7)

where $1 \leq i < j \leq N$ and $a > 0$. Because $Y$ is decreasing, this means, in econometric terms that "we take away ($a > 0$) from the poor ($j$) and give it to the rich ($i$)," producing a more unequal (concentrated) situation, which is applied repeatedly to yield $X$ out of $Y$.

Now we define a function $f$, acting on $N$-dimensional vectors $X = (x_1, \ldots, x_N)$ with values $f(X) = f(x_1, \ldots, x_N) \geq 0$ to be a good concentration measure if

$$L(X) > L(Y) \text{ implies } f(X) > f(Y)$$

(8)

Well-known, good concentration measures are the variation coefficient (i.e., the standard deviation of $X$ divided by its average) and the Gini index (Gini, 1909; or see Egghe, 2005, Chapter 4).

So we were able to define in a mathematically exact and unique way what we expect from a concentration measure. We are, at this time, unable to do the same for impact measures. Indeed, each of the different impact measures we have defined so far has different impact properties, and it can be proved (see later) that there does not exist a measure that satisfies all of these impact properties. Let us start with the work of Woeginger (2008b), who defines an impact measure (therein called a scientific impact index) as a function $f$, acting on vectors (we assume that the vectors $X, Y, \ldots$ are decreasing, i.e., their coordinates are in decreasing order) $X = (x_1, \ldots, x_M)$ and $Y = (y_1, \ldots, y_N)$ (note that now $M$ can be different from $N$) such that

(i) $f(0, \ldots, 0) = 0$ (in any dimension, including 0)

(ii) $X \leq Y$ implies $f(X) \leq f(Y)$. Here $X \leq Y$ is defined as follows: $X \leq Y$ if $N \leq M$ and $x_i \leq y_i$ for $i = 1, ..., N$.

It is clear that (i) and (ii) are necessary conditions for an impact measure but that they are far from sufficient: A zero vector has no impact.
In other words, if an author has no papers with citations or has no
papers at all, the impact of this author is zero and if on every common
coordinate (say rank) of two authors $X$ and $Y$ the paper (at that rank) of
$Y$ has more $\geq$ citations than the paper (at that rank) of $X$, then $Y$ has
more impact than $X$. These requirements for an impact measure are
non-controversial but are not enough to call $f$ a good impact measure; in
fact it might have been better had Woeginger chosen another name for $f$
satisfying (i) and (ii) (cf. the requested standardization in informetrics
mentioned previously) but we will keep the name in order not to confuse
the reader.

Woeginger (2008b, p. 227) then continues his search for "desired elementary properties," other than (i) and (ii), for impact measures. He formulates five "fairly natural axioms" (p. 227) that are desired for impact
measures f (a so-called wish-list, as Cater and Kraft [1989] suggested in the
context of information retrieval). Again the vectors $X$, $Y$ are decreasing.

A1. If the $(N + 1)$-dimensional vector $Y$ results from the $N$-
dimensional vector $X$ by adding a new article with $f(X)$
citations, then $f(Y) \leq f(X)$.

A2. If the $(N + 1)$-dimensional vector $Y$ results from the $N$-
dimensional vector $X$ by adding a new article with $f(X) + 1$
citations, then $f(Y) > f(X)$.

B. If the $N$-dimensional vector $Y$ results from the $N$-dimen-
sional vector $X$ by increasing the number of citations of a
single article, then $f(Y) \leq f(X) + 1$.

C. If the $N$-dimensional vector $Y$ results from the $N$-dimen-
sional vector $X$ by increasing the number of citations of
every article by at most 1, then $f(Y) \leq f(X) + 1$.

D. If the $(N + 1)$-dimensional vector $Y$ results from the $N$-
dimensional vector $X$ by first adding an article with $f(X)$
citations and then increasing the number of citations of
every article by at least 1, then $f(Y) > f(X)$.

Although somewhat artificial, these are all "desirable" properties of a
good impact measure. Only A1 looks controversial but this axiom shows
the robustness required of an impact measure. It is better understood as:
Adding an article with $f(X)$ citations will not increase $f(X)$. In fact A1 and
(ii) together imply $f(X) = f(Y)$. Also, axioms B and C are not completely
natural: Why should $f(Y)$ be maximally one unit larger than $f(X)$? These
axioms clearly are meant to describe the h-index and certainly not other
h-type indices such as the g-index or R-index.

Woeginger (2008b) shows A2 => D but also that A1 and A2 => not B, so that there is no impact measure that can satisfy all these axioms. He goes on to prove that an impact measure $f$ is the h-index if and only if $f$ satisfies A1, B, and D. This reveals much about the true nature of the h-index as an impact measure. Other, less important measures are also characterized using some of the axioms. Quesada (2009) gives a similar characterization of the h-index (but now for the real-valued version of it, i.e., with values in the positive real numbers).

Woeginger (2008d) provides another characterization of the h-index. First we introduce a new axiom.

S. For every decreasing vector $X$, we have $f(X) = f(R(X))$ where $R(X)$ is the mirrored vector $X = (x_1,...,x_N)$ (depicted in the plane with the indices [papers] as abscissa and the $x_i$ [citations] as ordinates) over the first bissectrix (the 45° line).

Then Woeginger proves that an impact measure $f$ is the h-index if and only if $f$ satisfies A1, S, and D.

In all these characterizations it is easy to show that $h$ satisfies these axioms; the difficult part is the reverse (if) part. Axiom S is logical as regards the definition of the h-index.

Characterizing the g-index is an even more difficult task that was also performed by Woeginger (2008a). He adds to (i) and (ii) the trivial requirement that an impact measure should also satisfy: If $X = (x_1,...,x_N)$ and $Y = (x_1,...,x_N, 0)$ , then $f(X) = f(Y)$. This is indeed logical: Adding a new paper without citations cannot increase (or decrease) the impact. It is slightly strange that Woeginger keeps the same name for a measure $f$ satisfying these three axioms as one that satisfies only (i) and (ii) (the standardization problem again). Woeginger needs other "desirable" properties to characterize the g-index than those for the h-index, showing the different nature of the g-index. The three axioms needed are (for $X$, $Y$ decreasing)

E. If the $(N + 1)$-dimensional vector $Y$ results from the $N$-dimensional vector $X$ by first adding an article with $f(X)$ or $f(X) + 1$ citations and then increasing the number of citations of every article by one, then $f(Y) = f(X) + 1$.

Axiom E is of the same nature as axiom D. The difference is needed for technical reasons. Of a completely different nature are the following two axioms (again for decreasing vectors $X$ and $Y$).

$T_1$. Let $X = (x_1, ..., x_N)$ and let $1 \leq i < j \leq N$. If the vector $Y$ results from $X$ by setting $x_k = y_k$ for all $k = 1, ..., N$ but $k \neq i, k \neq j, y_i = x_i + 1$, and $y_j = x_j - 1$, then $f(Y) \geq f(X)$.

$T_2$. Let $X = (x_1,...,x_N)$ and let $1 \leq i < j \leq f(X)$. If the vector $Y$ results from $X$ by setting $x_k = y_k$ for all $k = 1, ..., N$ but $k \neq i, k \neq j, y_i = x_i - 1$, and $y_j = x_j + 1$, then $f(Y) = f(X)$.

Next Woeginger proves that an impact measure $f$ is the g-index if and only if $f$ satisfies E, $T_1$, and $T_2$. Axiom $T_2$ is merely a technical item in order to obtain the characterization of the g-index. Axiom $T_1$ is very interesting: In view of Muirhead's theorem, we see that $T_1$ (called the transfer property) is nothing else than property (8), except for the inequality sign. This is strict in (8) (>) but in $T_1$ it is not (≥). Due to the requirement that impact measures should be robust with respect to a change of citation quantities, we think that the non-strict inequality is a good property in this context. So the g-index (and essentially only the g-index) satisfies this econometric concentration property. What does this mean from the point of view of impact measures? Essentially it says that, if we have two situations (e.g., two authors) with the same number of papers and the same number of citations in total, then the author for whom the citations are more concentrated over the papers has the higher impact. In other words, it is better to write one paper with 100 citations (and nine papers without a citation) than to write 10 papers with 10 citations each. That is a good property of the g-index. Lehmann and colleagues (2008) and Leydesdorff (in press) also recognize a desired property for good impact (performance) measures. Woeginger's theorem, characterizing the g-index, is not trivial but it is trivial to see that the g-index satisfies axiom $T_1$.

Note also that the h-index does not satisfy $T_1$: For $x = (3,3,3)$ we have $h(X) = 3$ but for $Y = (4,3,2)$ we have $h(Y) = 2 < h(X)$.

Egghe (2008b) discusses the "econometric" aspects of the g-index and also defines the Kosmulski variant $h^{(2)}$ of the h-index for the g-index. He shows that this variant satisfies $T_1$. Egghe further discusses the case that $L(X) = L(Y)$: Then we require that

$$\sum_{i=1}^{N} x_i > \sum_{i=1}^{N} y_i$$

should imply that $X$ has the highest impact, which is proved to be true for most impact measures.

Gagolewski and Grzegorzewski's (2009) work is similar to Woeginger's. Several h-type indices such as the h-index, Woeginger's w-index, and Kosmulski's MAXPROD index are characterized by the maximal generalized circles or ellipses that are still dominated by the citation function, that is the step function on unit intervals having the decreasing citation scores as ordinates.

Deineko and Woeginger (in press) study a new family of impact measures that generalize the Kosmulski index and provide axiomatic characterizations of these measures. Woeginger (2008c) does the same for a family of generalizations of the g-index. Van Eck and Waltman (2008) study similar generalizations of the h-index and the g-index. Rousseau (2008d) checks some of Woeginger's axioms on the g-index, the $h^{(2)}$-index, and the R-index.

Marchant (2009a) characterizes some impact measures (impact in a broad sense): total number of publications, total number of citations, maximal number of citations, number of papers with at least $\alpha$ citations ($\alpha$ = a threshold), and the h-index. All these measures are ranking devices (e.g., of authors) and Marchant characterizes them according to their ranking properties. Most ranking properties are technical and sometimes cumbersome (as Marchant himself indicates). It takes no fewer than six ranking properties to characterize the h-index; Rousseau (2008a) remarks that one other important ranking property defined by Marchant (2009a) is not a property of the h-index: The weak independence property. This ranking property is defined as follows. Consider two scientists $A$ and $B$ (represented by their total publications and all the citations received by these publications) and suppose we have a ranking device that gives a lower rank to $B$ than to $A$ (i.e., $B$ is preferred to $A$ or states otherwise, according to a certain impact measure, $B$ has more impact than $A$). Assume that one adds the same publications (each with their citations) to the publication lists of scientists $A$ and $B$. Then $B$ should still be preferred over $A$: The impact measure of $B$ should still be larger than $A$'s. This apparently logical requirement is, strangely enough, not satisfied by the impact measure $h$. Indeed, as Rousseau (2008a) argues, let $A$ be represented by the vector (5,5) and $B$ by the vector (5,3,3): $A$ has two publications with each receiving 5 citations and $B$ has three publications with 5, 3, and 3 citations. Hence $A$ has h-index 2 and $B$ has h-index 3. Suppose we add to both authors two publications with 4 citations each. Then $A$ and $B$ are now represented as: $A$ = (5,5,4,4), $B$ = (5,4,4,3,3). Now $A$'s h-index is 4 (up from 2 to 4) and $B$'s h-index still is 3, now smaller than $A$'s.

Neither Rousseau nor Marchant argues that ranking according to the h-index is bad, but they underline that, whatever method one uses, one must know the properties of the ranking method. Marchant (2009a) presents a good inventory.

We underscore Rousseau's comments that the g-index and the R-index also lack this property. For the R-index we can take the example (which is a slight modification of Rousseau's examples so that it can also be used for the R-index). In the first case we have

$$R_A = \sqrt{10} < R_B = \sqrt{11}$$

and in the second case we have

$$R_A = \sqrt{18} > R_B = \sqrt{13}$$

For the g-index we offer an example. Let first $A = (6,2)$ and $B = (5,2,2)$. We have $g_A = 2$ (even adding a zero to $A$ does not yield a $g_A$-value of 3) and $g_B = 3$. Now add two articles with 4 citations each to $A$ and $B$: $A = (6,4,4,2)$, $B = (5,4,4,2,2)$. Now $g_A = 4$ and $g_B = 3$.

Impact measures are examples of scoring rules. Marchant (2009b) characterizes general scoring rules.

This section has made it clear that it is not easy to define exactly what we mean by a "good" impact measure. Furthermore there is the intriguing problem of the influence of productivity on impact measures. Productivity can be defined as an author's total number of publications, but what is its influence on impact measures? Egghe (in press c) has studied impact measures of the h-type (h, g, R, $h_w$) and non-h-type (average number of citations per paper) [i.e., general IF], median citation, or fraction of the papers with at least a certain number of citations). Relations, such as an increasing relation between an impact measure and productivity, cannot be proved in general although, intuitively, we feel that such a relationship is plausible. Egghe, Goovaerts, and Kretschmer (2007) indicate this in connection with productivity versus collaboration (in the sense of "fraction of co-authored papers"), at least in fields in the exact sciences.

The study of the general relation between productivity and impact measures has not yet been undertaken and, hence, is flagged here as a research challenge.

Lehman and colleagues (2008) (see also Lehmann, Jackson, & Lautrup, 2005) also study impact measures of the h- and non-h-types (similar to those Egghe [in press c] studied) and conclude, for instance that the average number of citations per paper is a superior indicator of scientific quality (based on statistical arguments). This is, however, disproved by Hirsch (2007).

## Informetric Models for h-Type Indices

Most models for impact measures follow the simple framework of Lotka's law. This law is used in two ways. We assume that the number of authors $f(n)$ with $n = 1, 2, 3 \dots$ publications equals

$$f(n) = \frac{C}{n^\alpha} \tag{9}$$

where $C > 0$, $\alpha > 1$. This is the classical Lotka's law (Lotka, 1926); it is not controversial. Theoretically it applies in every IPP where sources have (or produce) items: The number of sources with $n$ items is given by formula 9. A second application used in this text is the paper-citation relation (say for an author): The number of papers with $n$ citations (received) is given by formula 9. Of course, each application requires its dedicated $C$ and $\alpha$ and can be obtained via a fitting procedure (see Rousseau & Rousseau, 2000; or Egghe, 2005, appendix).

Applying formula 9 to the paper-citation relation is somewhat controversial because we can see from van Raan (2001a, 2001b) as well as Brantle and Fallah (2007), Lehmann and colleagues (2008), Radicchi and colleagues (2008), and Molinari and Molinari (2008a using the rank-frequency version of formula 9—see formula 10) that formula 9 does not completely apply. For formula 9 to apply one needs a linearly decreasing data set in a log-log, scale which is not completely true: In practice we see a concavely decreasing graph in a log-log scale, modeled by van Raan (2001a, 2001b) by Bessel functions—see also earlier work of Glänzel, Burrell, and Sichel and the recent article in which Burrell (2008a) extends Lotkaian informetrics using a Pareto type II distribution. All these functions are difficult to use in calculations and using such a model would prevent us from creating informetric models for impact measures.

Using Lotka's law in the past (e.g., Egghe, 2005) we have obtained good approximations of reality and this turns out to be the case with impact measures.

Of course, for calculatory reasons we take $n \geq 1$ as a continuous variable. In this framework it is well known (Egghe, 2005) that Lotka's law (9) is equivalent to Zipf's law: In the first application, if we rank the authors in decreasing order of their number of publications, then the number of publications $g(r)$ of the author on rank r equals

$$g(r) = \frac{D}{r^{\beta}}$$

(10)

$D > 0$ and where $\beta$, is given by

$$\beta = \frac{1}{\alpha - 1}$$

(11)

The notation $r \rightarrow g(r)$ is classical and used by Egghe (2005). We use this notation here but note that one should not confuse this function $g(.)$ with the g-index.

In the second application we rank the papers (of an author) in decreasing order of the number of citations received. Then the number $g(r)$ of citations to the paper at rank $r$ is given by (10), where (11) is always valid.

Having the rank-frequency function $g(r)$ at our disposition (in the papers-citations context as has been described), we can give an elegant variant of the definition of the h-index: The h-index is simply the side of the square determined by the function $g(r)$ and its intersection with the first bissectrix. In other words, if we intersect the curve $r \rightarrow g(r)$ in the plane with the first bissectrix, then the point of intersection has

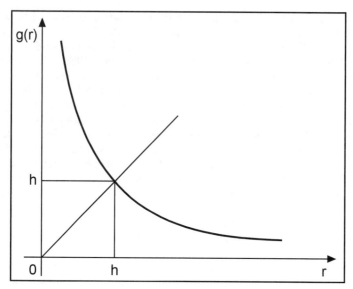

**Figure 2.2  Geometric illustration of the determination of the h-index**

coordinates (h,h), thereby determining the Hirsch index $h$ (hence also the equation $g(h) = h$ defines the h-index). Figure 2.2 provides a graphical illustration. Hirsch (2005a, 2005b) presents this definition, which also appears in papers by Miller (2006), Valentinuzzi and colleagues (2007), Woeginger (2008d), and, indirectly, Woeginger (2008b).

The exponent $\alpha$ is called Lotka's exponent; it is very important in informetrics and will play a similarly important role in the modeling of impact measures. A classical value is $\alpha = 2$; this value is a turning point of informetric properties.

So much for this short introduction to Lotkaian informetrics; Egghe (2005) provides more detail. Egghe and Rousseau (2006) have obtained the simplest model for the impact for the h-index. Because the result is basic and its proof simple we present it here. Suppose (9) is valid for the paper-citation relation (of an author or of a journal). Let there be $T$ cited papers in total. Then the h-index of this author or journal is given by

$$h = T^{\frac{1}{\alpha}} \tag{12}$$

Proof: By definition of $f$ is the total number of papers given by

$$T = \int_1^\infty f(n)\,dn = \frac{C}{\alpha - 1} \tag{13}$$

because $\alpha > 1$. The total number of papers with $n$ or more citations is given by

$$\int_{n}^{\infty} f(n') dn' = \frac{C}{\alpha - 1} n^{1-\alpha}$$

(14)

So (13) and (14) imply that the total number of papers with $n$ or more citations is given by $Tn^{1-\alpha}$. For $n = h$ (the h-index) we need, by definition of $h$

$$Th^{1-\alpha} = h$$

(14a)

whence (12).

Result (12) shows that, because $\alpha > 1$, the h-index is a concavely increasing function of $T$, the total number of papers. We will use (12) in the next section (in a time-dependent context) to model h-index sequences. Here we restrict ourselves to fixed time.

Glänzel (2006a) obtained an approximation of (12) via an argument with discrete values of $n$ (see also Glänzel, 2007b, 2008b). Egghe and Rousseau (2006) also proved the Zipf variant of (12) and it is confirmed by Molinari and Molinari (2008a) (reference to Egghe and Rousseau 2006 is given but, surprisingly, not mentioned in the text); see also Kinney (2007). Kinney is apparently not aware of formula (12) but it seems—experimentally—that (12) is valid for $1/_{\alpha} \approx 0.4$ (there called the "master-curve"). Given the prevalent view that citation analysis is highly dependent on the field under study, we doubt that these experimental findings are universal and in fact they are not confirmed by Molinari and Molinari (2008a). Formula (12) was experimentally verified by Egghe and Rao (2008a) on papers containing $N$-grams of variable length. Egghe and Rousseau (2006) also found a relation between $h$ and $A$ = the total number of citations: If $\alpha > 2$ we have, by definition of $f$ that

$$A = \int_{1}^{\infty} nf(n) dn = \frac{C}{\alpha - 2}$$

(15)

Hence (13) and (15) yield

$$A = T \frac{\alpha - 1}{\alpha - 2}$$

(15a)

and hence, by (12):

$$h = \left( \frac{\alpha - 2}{\alpha - 1} A \right)^{\frac{1}{\alpha}} \tag{16}$$

, also a concavely increasing function of $A$.

Both formulae (12) and (16) are confirmed in the experimental work of van Raan (2006): On a log-log scale, (12) and (16) are linear functions of $T$ and $A$ respectively, meaning log $h$ is a linear function of log $T$ and log $A$. Van Raan (2006) finds a linearly correlated cloud of points. Similar correlations are studied in Ball and Ruch (2008); Barendse (2007); Bornmann and Daniel (2007a); Bornmann, Wallon, and Ledin (2008); Costas and Bordons (2007b); Iglesias and Pecharromán (2007); Saad (2006); and Schubert and Glänzel (2007). Minasny and colleagues (2007) also report the concave relation (16).

Schubert and Glänzel (2007) and Glänzel (2008b; see also 2007a) study statistical relations between the h-index and so-called composite indicators (combining publication output and mean citation rate). They report strong linear statistical relations. It must, however, be noted that these composite indicators have one factor equaling (in our notation) $T^{\%}$, which is $h$ itself according to (12), the other factor being a power of the mean citation rate. Glänzel (2008b) proposes using z-statistics to analyze the tail of citation distributions in light of the h-index.

Other h-type indices can, likewise, be modeled (if $\alpha > 2$). For the g-index (Egghe, 2006c)

$$g = \left( \frac{\alpha - 1}{\alpha - 2} \right)^{\frac{\alpha - 1}{\alpha}} T^{\frac{1}{\alpha}} \tag{17}$$

$$g = \left( \frac{\alpha - 1}{\alpha - 2} \right)^{\frac{\alpha - 1}{\alpha}} h \tag{18}$$

by (12); for the R-index

$$R = \sqrt{\frac{\alpha - 1}{\alpha - 2}} \, T^{\frac{1}{\alpha}} \tag{19}$$

$$R = \sqrt{\frac{\alpha - 1}{\alpha - 2}} \, h \tag{20}$$

by (12) (see Jin et al., 2007) and similarly for the weighted h-index $h_w$ (Egghe & Rousseau, 2008). One might conclude, based on (18) and (20), that $g$ and $R$ are linear functions of $h$. This is not really true: If $h$ varies, then, by (12) and (13), it is likely that $\alpha$ varies and hence not only $h$ varies in (18) and (20). Only when $\alpha$ is constant and when $C$ varies in (13) we find that $h$ varies (by (12)) and that $g$ and $R$ are linear in $h$ (by (18) and (20)).

Beirlant, Glänzel, Carbonez, and Leemans (2007) propose an alternative for T-dependent indices:

$$\frac{1}{\alpha - 1}$$

(incidentally equal to Zipf's exponent $\beta$,—see formula 11) is called the extreme value index. Rousseau (2008c) calculates (and compares) the h-index and the g-index in some simple distribution models.

Let us further study the simple formula (12) for the h-index: $h = T^{1/\alpha}$. This allows us to see how $h$ will change if the publication-citation relation changes. Egghe (2008c) does this using results obtained previously (Egghe 2007c, 2008e). If we apply a power law transformation to the paper rank r: $\psi$ (r) and to the citation density n: $\varphi$ (n) of the form

$$\psi\left(r\right) = Ar^{b} \tag{21}$$

$$\varphi\left(j\right) = Bj^{c} \tag{22}$$

(A,B,b,c > 0) then we prove that the h-index of the transformed system, denoted $h^{*}$, is given by

$$h^{*} = B^{\frac{\delta-1}{\delta}} A^{\frac{1}{\delta}} T^{\frac{b}{\delta}} \tag{23}$$

where $T$ is the total number of papers before the transformation and where

$$\delta = 1 + \frac{b\left(\alpha - 1\right)}{c} \tag{24}$$

the Lotka exponent of the transformed system. Egghe (2008c) considers the simple case, $b = c = 1$ which gives, by (23) and (24):

$$h^{*} = B^{\frac{\alpha-1}{\alpha}} A^{\frac{1}{\alpha}} h \tag{25}$$

This has the following simple application:

(i) $\psi(r) = r$, $\varphi(j) = 2j$: Papers remain the same but they double their number of citations. Then

$$h^* = 2^{\frac{\alpha-1}{\alpha}} h \tag{26}$$

which yields

$$h < h^* < 2h \tag{27}$$

: Doubling of citations does not multiply $h$ by 2, a logical fact.

(ii) $\psi(r) = 2r$, $\varphi(j) = j$: Double the number of papers with the same number of citations. Now we have

$$h^* = 2^{\frac{1}{\alpha}} h \tag{28}$$

and again we have

$$h < h^* < 2h \tag{29}$$

, again a logical fact.

(iii) $\psi(r) = 2r$, $\varphi(j) = 2j$: If we double papers and citations then we have

$$h^* = 2h \tag{30}$$

which is logical.

(iv) $\psi(r) = r$, $\varphi(j) = \frac{j}{2}$. Double the number of papers but divide their number of citations by 2. This principle occurs (approximately) in uncontrolled lists where the same paper occurs twice and where the citations to this paper are divided over the two occurrences of the paper. This also occurs (approximately) when an author has "publicities," i.e., where an author publishes "the least publishable unit" and where, therefore, fewer citations per paper are obtained. Now we have

$$h^* = 2^{\frac{2}{\alpha}-1} h \tag{31}$$

Does this practice raise the h-index? We have from (31) that $h^* > h$ if and only if $\alpha < 2$, so for low values of $\alpha$. By (12) this means high values of $h$, that is, for prolific authors this practice pays off.

The next problem to be addressed is that of the distribution of the h-index (given a group of authors). First we deal with the size-frequency function $\varphi(h)$, that is, the number of authors with h-index $h$. As discussed in the beginning of this section, we assume that both the paper-citation relation and the author-paper relation conform with Lotka's law. Let $f(n) = \%_{n^a}$ be the number of papers with $n$ citations and

$$\varphi(T) = \frac{C^*}{T^{\alpha^*}}$$

the number of authors with $T$ papers. If there are $T$ papers and because $f(n) = \%_{n^a}$ we find that this author has h-index

$$h = T^{\frac{1}{\alpha}}$$

(see formula 12) hence $T = h^{\alpha}$. If we put this in the formula for $\varphi$ we have that

$$\varphi(h) = \frac{C^*}{h^{\alpha\alpha^*}} \qquad\qquad (32)$$

Hence the h-index is distributed according to Lotka's law with exponent $\alpha\alpha^*$, which Egghe (2007a) has proved. A similar result was proved for the g-index. Rao (2007) gives empirical evidence for the high degree of skewness of (32) (because the Lotka exponent is $\alpha\alpha^*$ with $\alpha > 1$ and $\alpha^* > 1$).

We have two applications of this result. First we can model successive h-indices. If there are $S$ authors it follows from (32) and (12) that

$$h_2 = S^{\frac{1}{\alpha\alpha^*}} \qquad\qquad (33)$$

is the h-index of the group of authors (e.g., an institute). Egghe (2008g) obtained this result. Further successive h-indices can be modeled in like fashion.

Egghe (2008h) gives the second application. Because we have result (32) we find that the rank-frequency distribution $h(r)$ is Zipf's law, as remarked in the beginning of this section, hence is convexly decreasing.

Because Zipf's is a power law on a log-log scale, the function $h(r)$ is a decreasing straight line. This result was also experimentally confirmed based on the h-indices of the mathematics journals in WoS. Pyykkö (2008) provides confirmation where most $h(r)$-curves in a log-log scale are linear. This also shows that $h(r)$ has a totally different shape from IF($r$), the impact factor rank distribution. Based on the Central Limit Theorem, Egghe (in press b) proved that IF($r$) has an S-shape, first convexly decreasing and then concavely decreasing, hence completely different from the shape of $h(r)$—although Beirlant and Einmahl (2008) show the asymptotic normality of the h-index (as $T \to \infty$).

Several researchers have studied merging aspects of the h-index. Glänzel (2008a) discusses the merging of disjoint sets. The stochastic proof essentially boils down to the following observation. Let us have two sets of papers consisting of $T_1$ and $T_2$ papers, respectively. If both paper-citation systems satisfy Lotka's law (9) with the same $\alpha$ then their h-indices are (see formula 12):

$$h_1 = T_1^{\frac{1}{\alpha}}$$

and

$$h_2 = T_2^{\frac{1}{\alpha}}$$

, respectively. Hence $T_1 = h_1^{\alpha}$ and $T_2 = h_2^{\alpha}$. So $T_1 + T_2 = h_1^{\alpha} + h_2^{\alpha}$, hence

$$h = \left(T_1 + T_2\right)^{\frac{1}{\alpha}} = \left(h_1^{\alpha} + h_2^{\alpha}\right)^{\frac{1}{\alpha}}$$

is the h-index of the merged system. A similar result can be found in work by Molinari and Molinari (2008a). Egghe (2008d) discusses more general merging models, where the merged sets are not necessarily disjoint. Only inequalities between the h-indices of the sets and the h-index of the merged set can be given. Two merging devices are given: In the merging one can add the citation scores or one can take the maximum of the citation scores. Examples of both scoring systems are given. Vanclay (2007) provides an example of merging, using the max-device.

Rousseau (2007b) and Vanclay (2007) discuss the robustness of the h-index. Rousseau shows its robustness with respect to missing publications and Vanclay with respect to citation errors.

We conclude with some references on different topics. Basu (2007) compares the Random Hierarchical Model (see Basu, 1992) with a formula derived by Hirsch (2005b) under unexplained assumptions on the rank-order citation distribution of papers. We refer to Egghe (2008f) for the mathematical derivation of some inequalities between the h-index $h$ (where authorship is counted in the total way) and the fractional h-indices $h_f$ and $h_F$ (described previously) and to Egghe (in press c) for some mathematical results on the influence of productivity on some impact measures. Finally Torra and Narukawa (2008) interpret the h-index and the total number of citations as fuzzy integrals.

## Time Series of h-Type Indices

All h-type indices are single numbers—as is the case for any indicator. We can add (literally) an extra dimension by looking at h-type indices over time $t$. In case of, for example, an author, we can let $t$ vary over the career (or any other time span). This yields a much stronger evaluation tool than just one number and can also indicate (by extrapolation) what the value of this index will be in the (near) future.

Much of this section is devoted to h-index sequences, but most theoretical results are also valid for other impact measures (because they are the h-index multiplied by a number dependent only on Lotka's exponent $\alpha$; see formulae 17–20, for example).

The h-type measures can be calculated only when we know the publication period and the citation period. So it is clear that different h-index sequences are possible. Liu and Rousseau (2008) defined not less than 10 different h-index sequences, using dedicated tables indicating which publication and citation periods are used. Egghe (in press a) studies four different h-index sequences, including the "real career h-index sequence" which, we think, is the most important h-index sequence: For every year $t = 1, 2, \ldots, t_m$ ($t_m$ is, e.g., the present [or last] year of the career) we calculate the h-index $h(t)$ based on the papers published in the years $1, 2, \ldots, t$ and on the number of citations that these papers received in the same period. Such an h-index sequence is, obviously, increasing. Further in this section we will indicate when such a sequence increases concavely, linearly, or convexly. Hirsch (2005a, 2005b) originated the real career h-index sequence, but see also Burrell (2007b).

It is best that $h(t)$ in this real career h-index sequence is calculated at every present year $t$ (i.e., calculate $h(t)$ from year to year, say each time at the end of the year). In this way one does not have to truncate for citation years in the past. Such truncations are very tedious to execute, for example, in WoS where citation data are presented up to now. Of course, because the h-index was defined in 2005, this is not possible for most authors, whose careers began (long) before that date. So, for example, in the case of this author (whose publication career started in 1978) we truncated citation from that year onward (Egghe, 2009a), which produces a linearly increasing h-index sequence.

This problem led Liang (2006) to study another h-index sequence, one going backward in time: So the h-index at time $t$, denoted $h^*(t)$, uses papers and citations to these papers in the years $t_m$ - $t$, ... , $t_m$. Note that for this h-index sequence one always has a citation period up to now, so that truncation in WoS is not necessary. Liang was the first to study h-index sequences; Burrell (2007a) noticed that Liang's h-index sequence used time going backward. He remarks that the real career h-index sequence, as introduced previously, is the more natural, which is true. Burrell further remarks that, for a theoretical model, the difference between the two h-index sequences will not be large. This is, however, not true as the mathematical theory, as Egghe's (2009a) development shows. It is proved there that, for every $t$ in the interval $[0, t_m]$ (continuous time model),

$$h^{*}\left(t\right)=\left(T\left(t_{m}\right)-h\left(t_{m}-t\right)^{\alpha}\right)^{\frac{1}{\alpha}}$$ (34)

in the Lotkaian model (12) and where $T(t_m)$ is the total number of (cited) publications at time $t_m$ (e.g., now). Based on (34) one can show that the sequences $h(t)$ and $h^*(t)$ are very different. For example, if $h(t)$ is convex (including the linear case) then $h^*(t)$ is strictly concave. Within the Lotkaian model it is shown that both sequences are equal if and only if the researcher has a constant production of publications per time unit.

Another h-index sequence, where time goes forward (the normal case) but where one does not have to execute tedious citation truncation actions is the so-called total career h-index sequence. Here, as in the real career h-index sequence, the h-index at time $t$ is calculated based on publications of years 1, ..., t but one considers, for every $t$, the total citation period 1, ..., $t_m$. Ye and Rousseau (2008) perform several fitting exercises for this total career h-index sequence (for authors, journals, universities, and companies).

Let us go back to the real career h-index sequence $h(t)$, which is the most important. Egghe (2009a) gives a simple mathematical model for $h(t)$, based on (12). Denote by $T(t)$ the total number of cited publications at time t. Then (12), applied to $T(t)$ gives

$$h\left(t\right)=T\left(t\right)^{\frac{1}{\alpha}}$$ (35)

Assume that the author has a constant number b of publications per year. Hence at time $t$ there are $T(t) = bt$ publications yielding, by (35)

$$h\left(t\right)=b^{\frac{1}{\alpha}}t^{\frac{1}{\alpha}}$$ (36)

which is a concavely increasing sequence (because $\alpha > 1$). As has been mentioned, this author's real career h-index sequence is increasing linearly. This can be modeled by assuming that the author produces more papers as $t$ increases: Assume that the author produces at year $t$, $bt^\beta$ papers ($\beta > 0$; the case $\beta = 0$ corresponds to the case of constant production). Egghe (2009a) then finds that

$$h(t) = ct^{\frac{\beta+1}{\alpha}} \tag{37}$$

where $c$ is a constant. We now have that $h(t)$ is strictly concave if $\beta + 1 < \alpha$, is linear if $\beta + 1 = \alpha$, and is convex if $\beta + 1 > \alpha$. Because this author's $h(t)$ is linear we can conclude that, for this author, $\beta + 1 \approx \alpha$ (e.g., for $\alpha \approx 2$ we have $\beta \approx 1$, yielding also a linear increase in the number of publications for this author, which is confirmed in practice).

Burrell (2007b, 2007d) studies the time dependence of the h-index using a different model for the publication and citation process: In each case a Poisson process is assumed (of course, with different rates). In this model Burrell (2007b) proves that the h-index is approximately linear in career length and in the logarithm of the publication rate and citation rate. Burrell (2007d) shows that Jin's A-index (formula (2)) is approximately a linear function of time and of $h$; and the total number of citations to the papers in the h-core has, approximately, a square-law relationship with time and hence also with Jin's $A$ and the h-index. Burrell (2007a, 2007c) also confirmed the linear dependence of the h-index on career length (see also Burrell [2008b] for a case study). Hirsch (2005b) presents a simple model. Burrell (2007c) also notes that the g-index is proportional to career length and hence to the h-index. This follows from (18) proved by Egghe (2006c). Da Fontoura Costa (2006) finds linear as well as concave h-index sequences for authors.

Anderson and colleagues (2008) compare authors' h-index sequences and $h_T$-index sequences ($h_T$ is the tapered h-index, described previously). They show that there is an essentially linear relationship between $h$ and $h_T$. This requires an explanation. The result, however, shows that the "trouble" of calculating the more difficult-to-obtain $h_T$-index is not really worth the effort (but, as has been mentioned, there is some theoretical interest in the tapered h-index, $h_T$).

Egghe (2009b) proposes a general Lotkaian growth model for sources and for items. Based on this model, he derives a time-dependent growth model for the h-index $h(t)$ and the g-index $g(t)$. He also has presented special cases of this result (Egghe, 2007b, 2007d).

Rousseau and Ye (2008) define a dynamic h-type index based on the R-index at time $t$ multiplied by $h'(t)$, the derivative of the h-index sequence. This is a difficult calculation to execute. Using computer simulations, Guns and Rousseau (2009b) generate h-index sequences. For these simulations they use peak models (fast linear increase followed by a slow linear decrease) for the distribution of the number of received citations. They find that many simulations yield a linear h-index sequence, although convex as well as concave cases occurred.

Finally we mention the case studies of journal h-index sequences by Liu, Rao, and Rousseau (in press) and Rousseau (2006a) and of h-index sequences of countries by Mahbuba and Rousseau (2008).

## Conclusions and Challenges

As is clear from this review, the h-index and its variants are extensively studied in informetrics, experimentally and theoretically, although its introduction was by Hirsch (2005b), a physicist. Outside informetrics, h-type indices are mostly used in case studies.

We have described advantages and disadvantages of the h-index and variants of the h-index (such as the g-index and R-index) that try to avoid some of the h-index's limitations.

The h-index, originally conceived of as a way to measure the citation impact of a researcher and to predict future performance, was soon applied to other sources. An important application of the h-index (or its variants) is to journals, as proposed by Braun and colleagues (2005, 2006). One is then immediately interested in comparing the performance of the h-index for a journal with the (classical) impact factor (IF). Although there is some disagreement on the matter, we are inclined to say that the h-index will challenge the impact factor. One reason is that the IF has time thresholds for both the publication period (2 years) and the citation period (1 year), which is not optimal in several fields; the h-index does not impose such time limitations. Also, both Scopus and WoS allow one to calculate the h-index for any set of articles, hence not only for the publication set of an author but also of a journal (for a particular year or all years).

As mentioned, the application of h-type indices to topics and compounds (Banks, 2006) is a potentially very interesting (determining "hot" topics) area for research. The study of h-type indices related to downloads (of articles in an e-journal or a repository) or even outside our field (e.g., in econometrics) is another challenging area.

Further study is needed on "the real nature" of impact measures. Not all given "desirable properties" for impact measures, presented in the fourth section (mainly by Marchant and Woeginger) are so natural, because they are—simply—needed to characterize some h-type indices (such as the h-index and g-index) and hence were not formulated based on a philosophy on "desired properties" for impact measures. More standardized properties are needed as is the case, for example, in concentration theory using Lorenz curves.

More studies are needed on informetric models for h-type indices. We would recommend extending informetric models to some non-Lotkaian cases of the paper-citation relation.

Finally, time series of h-type indices are very important. They add, literally, an extra dimension to this assessment tool, describing the evolution of a researcher's career (to take one example). We have noted that many different time series can be studied (different publication and citation periods), but they are also dependent on the source used (e.g., Scopus, WoS, Google Scholar).

The shapes of these time series still have to be determined in many research areas, not only for authors but also for institutes and topics.

More research-funding bodies can be expected to use h-type indices (and their sequences) for assessment purposes and consequent funding (cf. Ball, 2007). More e-literature sources will add such indicators to their information products (Scopus, WoS, but also institutional repositories), and thereby become readily available to governments, universities, and research centers.

We also note that the long-standing controversy surrounding citation analysis is diminishing thanks to the creation of objective indicators such as the h-index. This is certainly the case in the exact, applied, and medical sciences (every researcher wants to know his/her h-index). Just as it is a challenge for citation analysis in general, it is a challenge to apply h-type indices to the human and social sciences in an appropriate way.

## Endnote

1. Muirhead's (1903) theorem was published two years before Lorenz (1905) introduced the Lorenz curve. Therefore, Muirhead did not use the Lorenz terminology but a combinatorial variant of it. Here we present the Lorenz variant of Muirhead's theorem. Hardy, Littlewood, and Pólya (1952) and Egghe and Rousseau (1991) also discuss Muirhead's theorem.

## References

Aguayo-Albasini, J. L., & Campillo-Soto, A. (2008). Evaluation of research activity by means of the Hirsch h index. *Medica Clinica*, *131*(6), 239.

Anderson, T. R., Hankin, R. K., & Killworth, P. D. (2008). Beyond the Durfee square: Enhancing the h-index to score total publication output. *Scientometrics*, *76*(3), 577–588.

Andrews, G. E. (1998). *The theory of partitions*. Cambridge, UK: Cambridge University Press.

Antonakis, J., & Lalive, R. (2008). Quantifying scholarly impact: IQp versus the Hirsch h. *Journal of the American Society for Information Science and Technology*, *59*(6), 956–969.

Arencibia-Jorge, R., Barrios-Almaguer, I., Fernández-Hernández, S., & Carvajal-Espino, R. (2008). Applying successive H indices in the institutional evaluation: A case study. *Journal of the American Society for Information Science and Technology*, *59*(1), 155–157.

Arencibia-Jorge, R., & Rousseau, R. (in press). Influence of individual researchers' visibility on institutional impact: An example of Prathap's approach to successive h-indices. *Scientometrics*. Retrieved February 2, 2009, from dx.doi.org/10.1007/s11192-007-2025-0

Ball, P. (2005). Index aims for fair ranking of scientists. *Nature*, *436*, 900.

Ball, P. (2007). Achievement index climbs the ranks. *Nature, 448*, 737.

Ball, R., & Ruch, S. (2008). New correlations between the h-index, citation rate (CPP) and number of papers (NP) in neuroscience and quantum physics: The new S-index. In J. Gorraiz & E. Schiebel (Eds.), *Book of abstracts. 10^{th} International Conference on Science and Technology Indicators*, 262–263.

Banks, M. G. (2006). An extension of the Hirsch index: Indexing scientific topics and compounds. *Scientometrics, 69*(1), 161–168.

Bar-Ilan, J. (2006). H-index for Price medalists revisited. *ISSI Newsletter, 2*(1), 3–5.

Bar-Ilan, J. (2007). The h-index of h-index and of other informetric topics. In D. Torres-Salinas & H. F. Moed (Eds.), *Proceedings of the 11th International Conference of the International Society for Scientometrics and Informetrics*, 826–827.

Bar-Ilan, J. (2008a). The h-index of h-index and of other informetric topics. *Scientometrics, 75*(3), 591–605.

Bar-Ilan, J. (2008b). Informetrics at the beginning of the 21st century: A review. *Journal of Informetrics, 2*(1), 1–52.

Bar-Ilan, J. (2008c). Which h-index? A comparison of WoS, Scopus and Google Scholar. *Scientometrics, 74*(2), 257–271.

Barendse, W. (2007). The strike rate index: A new index for journal quality based on journal size and the h-index of citations. *Biomedical Digital Libraries, 4*(3). Retrieved January 28, 2009, from dx.doi.org/10.1186/1742-5581-4-3

Basu, A. (1992). Hierarchical distributions and Bradford's law. *Journal of the American Society for Information Science, 43*(7), 494–500.

Basu, A. (2007). A note on the connection between the Hirsch index and the random hierarchical model. *ISSI Newsletter, 3*(2), 24–27.

Batista, P. D., Campiteli, M. G., Kinouchi, O., & Martinez, A. S. (2006). Is it possible to compare researchers with different scientific interests? *Scientometrics, 68*(1), 179–189.

Beirlant, J., & Einmahl, J. H. J. (2008). Asymptotics for the Hirsch index. *CentER Discussion Paper Series*, 2007–2086.

Beirlant, J., Glänzel, W., Carbonez, A., & Leemans, H. (2007). Scoring research output using statistical quantile plotting. *Journal of Informetrics, 1*(3), 185–192.

Boell, S. K., & Wilson, C. S. (2008). Use of h-like indicators based on journal impact factors for evaluating scientific performance: Australian cancer research case study. In J. Gorraiz & E. Schiebel (Eds.), *Book of Abstracts. 10th International Conference on Science and Technology Indicators*, 253–255.

Bornmann, L., & Daniel, H.-D. (2005). Does the h-index for ranking of scientists really work? *Scientometrics, 65*(3), 391–392.

Bornmann, L., & Daniel, H.-D. (2007a). Convergent validation of peer review decisions using the h-index: Extent of and reasons for type I and type II errors. *Journal of Informetrics, 1*(3), 204–213.

Bornmann, L., & Daniel, H.-D. (2007b). What do we know about the h index? *Journal of the American Society for Information Science and Technology, 58*(9), 1381–1385.

Bornmann, L., & Daniel, H.-D. (2009). The state of h index research: Is the h index the ideal way to measure research performance? *EMBO reports, 10*(1), 2–6.

Bornmann, L., Marx, W., & Schier, H. (2009). Hirsch-type index values for organic chemistry journals: A comparison of new metrics with the Journal Impact Factor. *European Journal of Organic Chemistry, 2009*(10), 1471–1476.

Bornmann, L., Mutz, R., & Daniel, H.-D. (2007). The b index as a measure of scientific excellence. A promising supplement to the h index. *Cybermetrics*, *11*(1), Paper 6. Retrieved January 31, 2009, from www.cindoc.csic.es/cybermetrics/articles/v11i1p6.html

Bornmann, L., Mutz, R., & Daniel, H.-D. (2008). Are there better indices for evaluation purposes than the h index? A comparison of nine different variants of the h index using data from biomedicine. *Journal of the American Society for Information Science and Technology*, *59*(5), 830–837.

Bornmann, L., Mutz, R., & Daniel, H. D. (2009). Do we need the h index and its variants besides standard bibliometric measures? *Journal of the American Society for Information Science and Technology*, *60*(6), 1286–1289.

Bornmann, L., Mutz, R., Daniel, H.-D., Wallon, G., & Ledin, A. (2008). Are there really two types of h index variants? A validation study by using molecular life sciences data. In J. Gorraiz & E. Schiebel (Eds.), *Book of Abstracts. 10th International Conference on Science and Technology Indicators*, 256–258.

Bornmann, L., Wallon, G., & Ledin, A. (2008). Is the h index related to (standard) bibliometric measures and to the assessments by peers? An investigation of the h index by using molecular life sciences data. *Research Evaluation*, *17*(2), 149–156.

Brahler, E., & Decker, O. (2005). The H-index. *Psycotherapie Psychosomatik Medizinische Psychologie*, *55*(11), 451.

Brantle, T. F., & Fallah, M. H. (2007). Complex innovation networks, patent citations and power laws. *Portland International Center for Management of Engineering and Technology, PICMET 2007 Proceedings*, 540–549.

Braun, T., Glänzel, W., & Schubert, A. (2005). A Hirsch-type index for journals. *The Scientist*, *19*(22), 8–10.

Braun, T., Glänzel, W., & Schubert, A. (2006). A Hirsch-type index for journals. *Scientometrics*, *69*(1), 169–173.

Burrell, Q. L. (2007a). Hirsch index or Hirsch rate? Some thoughts arising from Liang's data. *Scientometrics*, *73*(1), 19–28.

Burrell, Q. L. (2007b). Hirsch's h-index: A stochastic model. *Journal of Informetrics*, *1*(1), 16–25.

Burrell, Q. L. (2007c). Hirsch's h-index and Egghe's g-index. *Proceedings of the 11th International Conference of the International Society for Scientometrics and Informetrics*, 162–169.

Burrell, Q. L. (2007d). On the h-index, the size of the Hirsch core and Jin's A-index. *Journal of Informetrics*, *1*(2), 170–177.

Burrell, Q. L. (2007e). Should the h-index be discounted? In W. Glänzel, A. Schubert, & B. Schlemmer (Eds.), *The multidimensional world of Tibor Braun: A multidisciplinary encomium for his 75th birthday* (pp. 65–68). Leuven, Belgium: ISSI.

Burrell, Q. L. (2008a). Extending Lotkaian informetrics. *Information Processing & Management*, *44*(5), 1794–1807.

Burrell, Q. L. (2008b). The publication/citation process at the micro level: A case study. In H. Kretschmer & F. Havemann (Eds.), *Proceedings of the Fourth International Conference on Webometrics, Informetrics and Scientometrics & Ninth COLLNET Meeting*. Retrieved February 2, 2009, from www.collnet.de/Berlin-2008/BurrellWI S2008tpc.pdf

Campiteli, M. G., Batista, P. D., & Martinez, A. S. (2007). A research productivity index to account for different scientific disciplines. *Proceedings of the 11th International Conference of the International Society for Scientometrics and Informetrics*, 184–188.

Cater, S. C., & Kraft, D. H. (1989). A generalization and clarification of the Waller-Kraft wish list. *Information Processing & Management, 25*(1), 15–25.

Chai, J., Hua, P., Rousseau, R., & Wan, J. (2008). The adapted pure h-index. *Proceedings of the Fourth International Conference on Webometrics, Informetrics and Scientometrics & Ninth COLLNET Meeting*. Retrieved February 2, 2009, from www.collnet.de/Berlin-2008/ChaiWIS2008aph.pdf

Costas, R., & Bordons, M. (2007a). A critical view of the h-index: Observations based on a practical application. *Profesional de la Informacion, 16*, 427–432.

Costas, R., & Bordons, M. (2007b). The h-index: Advantages, limitations and its relation with other bibliometric indicators at the micro level. *Journal of Informetrics, 1*(3), 193–203.

Costas, R., & Bordons, M. (2008). Is g-index better than h-index? An exploratory study at the individual level. *Scientometrics, 77*(2), 267–288.

Cronin, B., & Meho, L. (2006). Using the h-index to rank influential information scientists. *Journal of the American Society for Information Science and Technology, 57*(9), 1275–1278.

Csajbók, E., Berhidi, A., Vasas, L., & Schubert, A. (2007). Hirsch-index for countries based on Essential Science Indicators data. *Scientometrics, 73*(1), 91–117.

da Fontoura Costa, L. (2006). *On the dynamics of the h-index in complex networks with coexisting communities*. Retrieved January 31, 2009, from arxiv.org/PS_cache/physics/pdf/0609/0609116v1.pdf

da Silva, R., Palazzo de Oliveira, J., Valdeni de Lima, J., Warpechowski, M., Hannel, K., Medianeira Denardi, R., et al. (2009). *Statistics for ranking program committees and editorial boards*. Unpublished work.

de Araujo, A. F. P. (2008). Increasing discrepancy between absolute and effective indexes of research output in a Brazilian academic department. *Scientometrics, 74*(3), 425–437.

Deineko, V. G., & Woeginger, G. J. (in press). A new family of scientific impact measures: The generalized Kosmulski-indices. *Scientometrics*.

Dodson, M. V. (2008). Research paper citation record keeping: It is not for wimps. *Journal of Animal Science, 86*(10), 2795–2796.

Dorta-Contreras, A. J., Arencibia-Jorge, R., Marti-Lahera, Y., & Araujo-Ruiz, J. A. (2008). Productivity and visibility of Cuban neuroscientists: Bibliometric study of the period 2001–2005. *Revista de Neurologia, 47*, 355–360.

Edwards, A. W. F. (2005). System to rank scientists was pedalled by Jeffreys. *Nature, 437*, 951.

Egghe, L. (2005). *Power laws in the information production process: Lotkaian informetrics*. Oxford: Elsevier.

Egghe, L. (2006a). How to improve the h-index. *The Scientist, 20*(3), 14.

Egghe, L. (2006b). An improvement of the h-index: The g-index. *ISSI Newsletter, 2*(1), 8–9.

Egghe, L. (2006c). Theory and practice of the g-index. *Scientometrics, 69*(1), 131–152.

Egghe, L. (2007a). Distributions of the h-index and the g-index. *Proceedings of the 11th International Conference of the International Society for Scientometrics and Informetrics*, 245–253.

Egghe, L. (2007b). Dynamic h-index: The Hirsch index in function of time. *Journal of the American Society for Information Science and Technology, 58*(3), 452–454.

Egghe, L. (2007c). General evolutionary theory of IPPs and applications to the evolution of networks. *Journal of Informetrics, 1*(2), 115–122.

Egghe, L. (2007d). Item-time-dependent Lotkaian informetrics and applications to the time-dependent h- and g-index. *Mathematical and Computer Modelling, 45*(7–8), 864–872.

Egghe, L. (2008a). *Conjugate partitions in informetrics: Lorenz-curves, h-type indices, Ferrers graphs and Durfee squares in a discrete and continuous setting*. Unpublished work.

Egghe, L. (2008b). *An econometric property of the g-index*. Unpublished work.

Egghe, L. (2008c). Examples of simple transformations of the h-index: Qualitative and quantitative conclusions and consequences for other indices. *Journal of Informetrics, 2*(2), 136–148.

Egghe, L. (2008d). The influence of merging on h-type indices. *Journal of Informetrics, 2*(3), 252–262.

Egghe, L. (2008e). The influence of transformations on the h-index and the g-index. *Journal of the American Society for Information Science and Technology, 59*(8), 1304–1312.

Egghe, L. (2008f). Mathematical theory of the h-index and g-index in case of fractional counting of authorship. *Journal of the American Society for Information Science and Technology, 59*(10), 1608–1616.

Egghe, L. (2008g). Modelling successive h-indices. *Scientometrics, 77*(3), 377–387.

Egghe, L. (2008h). *A rationale for the Hirsch-index rank-order distribution and a comparison with the impact factor rank-order distribution*. Unpublished work.

Egghe, L. (2009a). Mathematical study of h-index sequences. *Information Processing & Management, 45*(2), 288–297.

Egghe, L. (2009b). Time-dependent Lotkaian informetrics incorporating growth of sources and items. *Mathematical and Computer Modelling, 49*(1–2), 31–37.

Egghe, L. (in press a). Comparative study of h-index sequences. *Scientometrics*.

Egghe, L. (in press b). Mathematical derivation of the impact factor distribution. *Journal of Informetrics*.

Egghe, L. (in press c). Performance and its relation with productivity in Lotkaian systems. *Scientometrics*.

Egghe, L., Goovaerts, M., & Kretschmer, H. (2007). Collaboration and productivity: An investigation into "Scientometrics" journal and "Uhasselt" repository. *COLLNET Journal of Scientometrics and Information Management, 1*(2), 33–40.

Egghe, L., & Rao, I. K. R. (2008a). The influence of the broadness of a query of a topic on its h-index: Models and examples of the h-index of N-grams. *Journal of the American Society for Information Science and Technology, 59*(10), 1688–1693.

Egghe, L., & Rao, I. K. R. (2008b). Study of different h-indices for groups of authors. *Journal of the American Society for Information Science and Technology, 59*(8), 1276–1281.

Egghe, L., & Rousseau, R. (1990). *Introduction to informetrics*. Amsterdam, The Netherlands: Elsevier.

Egghe, L., & Rousseau, R. (1991). Transfer principles and a classification of concentration measures. *Journal of the American Society for Information Science, 42*(7), 479–489.

Egghe, L., & Rousseau, R. (1996a). Average and global impact of a set of journals. *Scientometrics, 36*(1), 97–107.

Egghe, L., & Rousseau, R. (1996b). Averaging and globalising quotients of informetric and scientometric data. *Journal of Information Science, 22*(3), 165–170.

Egghe, L., & Rousseau, R. (2006). An informetric model for the Hirsch-index. *Scientometrics, 69*(1), 121–129.

Egghe, L., & Rousseau, R. (2008). An h-index weighted by citation impact. *Information Processing & Management, 44*(2), 770–780.

Engqvist, L., & Frommen, J. G. (2008). The h-index and self-citations. *Trends in Ecology & Evolution, 23*(5), 250–252.

Ferrand, L. (2007). Hirsch's h index: A new measure to quantify the research output of individual scientists. *Année Psychologique, 107*, 531–536.

Frangopol, P. T. (2005). The Hirsch index: A new scientometric indicator for the evaluation of the results of a scientific researcher. *Revista de Chimie, 56*(12), 1279–1281.

Gagolewski, M., & Grzegorzewski, P. (2009). *A geometric approach to scientific impact indices construction*. Unpublished work.

Gini, C. (1909). Il diverso accrescimento delle classi sociali e la concentrazione della richezza. *Giornale degli Economisti*, serie *11*, 37.

Glänzel, W. (1996). The need for standards in bibliometric research and technology. *Scientometrics, 35*, 167–176.

Glänzel, W. (2006a). On the h-index: A mathematical approach to a new measure of publication activity and citation impact. *Scientometrics, 67*(2), 315–321.

Glänzel, W. (2006b). On the opportunities and limitations of the H-index. *Science Focus, 1*(1), 10–11.

Glänzel, W. (2007a). The R- and AR-indices: Complementing the h-index: Comments. *Chinese Science Bulletin, 52*(6), 863.

Glänzel, W. (2007b). Some new applications of the h-index. *ISSI Newsletter, 3*(2), 28–31.

Glänzel, W. (2008a). H-index concatenation. *Scientometrics, 77*(2), 369–372.

Glänzel, W. (2008b). On some new bibliometric applications of statistics related to the h-index. *Scientometrics, 77*(1), 187–196.

Glänzel, W. (2008c). What are your best papers? *ISSI Newsletter, 4*(4), 64–67.

Glänzel, W., & Persson, O. (2005). H-index for Price medalists. *ISSI Newsletter, 1*(4), 15–18.

Gracza, T., & Somoskovi, E. (2008). Research papers in the crosshairs: Newer viewpoints on the development of library resources. *Library Collections Acquisitions & Technical Services, 32*(1), 42–45.

Grothkopf, U., & Stevens-Rayburn, S. (2007). Introducing the h-index in telescope statistics. *Proceedings of the 5th Library and Information Services in Astronomy Conference*, 86–92.

Guan, J. C., & Gao, X. (2009). Exploring the h-index at patent level. *Journal of the American Society for Information Science and Technology, 60*(1), 35–40.

Guns, R., & Rousseau, R. (2009a). Real and rational variants of the h-index and the g-index. *Journal of Informetrics, 3*(1), 64–71.

Guns, R., & Rousseau, R. (2009b). Simulating growth of the h-index. *Journal of the American Society for Information Science and Technology, 60*(2), 410–417.

Hardy, G., Littlewood, J. E., & Pólya, G. (1952). *Inequalities.* Cambridge, UK: Cambridge University Press.

Harnad, S. (2007). Open access scientometrics and the UK research assessment exercise. *Proceedings of the 11th International Conference of the International Society for Scientometrics and Informetrics,* 27–33.

Harzing, A.-W., & van der Wal, R. (2009). A Google Scholar h-index for journals: An alternative metric to measure journal impact in economics and business. *Journal of the American Society for Information Science and Technology, 60*(1), 41–46.

Heaney, P. J. (2007). What's your h-index? *Elements, 3*(4), 229–230.

Hermes-Lima, M., Alencastro, A. C. R., Santos, N. C. F., Navas, C. A., & Beleboni, R. O. (2007). The relevance and recognition of Latin American science: Introduction to the fourth issue of CBP-Latin America. *Comparative Biochemistry and Physiology C-Toxicology & Pharmacology, 146,* 1–9.

Hirsch, J. E. (2005a). *An index to quantify an individual's scientific research output.* Retrieved January 31, 2009, from arxiv1.library.cornell.edu/PS_cache/physics/pdf/0508/0508025v1.pdf

Hirsch, J. E. (2005b). An index to quantify an individual's scientific research output. *Proceedings of the National Academy of Sciences of the United States of America, 102*(46), 16569–16572.

Hirsch, J. E. (2007). Does the h-index have predictive power? *Proceedings of the National Academy of Sciences of the United States of America, 104*(49), 19193–19198.

Honekopp, J., & Kleber, J. (2008). Sometimes the impact factor outshines the H index. *Retrovirology, 5,* 88.

Hu, X., & Chen, J. (2009). *An exploration of the Major Contribution Index for leading scientists in the field of health sciences in China.* Unpublished work.

Hua, P.-H., Rousseau, R., Sun, X.-K., & Wan, J.-K. (2009). *A download $h^{(2)}$-index as a meaningful indicator of Web impact of academic journals.* Manuscript submitted for publication.

Humberto Romero, A., Garcia, A., & Kiwi, M. (2009). *Evaluation of the scientific impact and biological age based upon the H-index in three Latin American countries: The material science case.* Unpublished work.

Iglesias, J. E., & Pecharromán, C. (2007). Scaling the h-index for different scientific ISI fields. *Scientometrics, 73*(3), 303–320.

Imperial, J., & Rodriguez-Navarro, A. (2007). Usefulness of Hirsch's h-index to evaluate scientific research in Spain. *Scientometrics, 71*(2), 271–282.

Jacsó, P. (2007). Software issues related to cited references. *Online Information Review, 31*(6), 892–905.

Jacsó, P. (2008a). The plausibility of computing the h-index of scholarly productivity and impact using reference-enhanced databases. *Online Information Review, 32*(2), 266–283.

Jacsó, P. (2008b). The pros and cons of computing the h-index using Google Scholar. *Online Information Review, 32*(3), 437–452.

Jacsó, P. (2008c). The pros and cons of computing the h-index using Scopus. *Online Information Review, 32*(4), 524–535.

Jacsó, P. (2008d). The pros and cons of computing the h-index using Web of Science. *Online Information Review, 32*(5), 673–688.

Jacsó, P. (2008e). Testing the calculation of a realistic h-index in Google Scholar, Scopus and Web of Science for F. W. Lancaster. *Library Trends, 56*(4), 784–815.

Järvelin, K., & Persson, O. (2008). The DCI-index: Discounted impact-based research evaluation. *Journal of the American Society for Information Science and Technology, 59*(9), 1433–1440. Erratum. *Journal of the American Society for Information Science and Technology, 59*(14), 2350–2351.

Jeang, K. T. (2007). Impact factor, H index, peer comparisons, and Retrovirology: Is it time to individualize citation metrics? *Retrovirology, 4*(42). Retrieved January 31, 2009, from doi:10.1186/1742-4690-4-42

Jin, B. (2006). H-index: An evaluation indicator proposed by scientist. *Science Focus, 1*(1), 8–9.

Jin, B. (2007). The AR-index: Complementing the h-index. *ISSI Newsletter, 3*(1), 6.

Jin, B., Liang, L., Rousseau, R., & Egghe, L. (2007). The R- and AR-indices: Complementing the h-index. *Chinese Science Bulletin, 52*(6), 855–863.

Jin, B., & Rousseau, R. (2007). R-index and AR-index: Complementing indicators to h-index. *Science Focus, 2*(3), 1–8.

Jin, B., & Rousseau, R. (2008). Dust storms. *E-LIS*, ID 14592. Retrieved January 31, 2009, from eprints.rclis.org/14592/1/Dust_storms.pdf

Jones, A. W. (2008). Hirsch-index for winners of TIAFT's mid-career achievement award. *Journal of Analytical Toxicology, 32*(4), 327–328.

Kellner, A. W. A. (2008). Critical review of radiopharmaceutical-drug interactions, unexpected new age for a Tupiguarani settlement and the h-index in the Brazilian Academy of Sciences. *Anais da Academia Brasileira de Ciencias, 80*(4), 595.

Kellner, A. W. A., & Ponciano, L. C. M. O. (2008). H-index in the Brazilian Academy of Sciences: Comments and concerns. *Anais da Academia Brasileira de Ciencias, 80*(4), 771–781.

Kelly, C. D., & Jennions, M. D. (2006). The h index and career assessment by numbers. *TRENDS in Ecology and Evolution, 21*(4), 167–170.

Kelly, C. D., & Jennions, M. D. (2007). H-index: Age and sex make it unreliable. *Nature, 449*, 403.

Kim, W. J., & Seo, J. (2007). Evaluation of an individual's scientific productivity using author rank. *Information: An International Interdisciplinary Journal, 10*(3), 365–372.

Kinney, A. L. (2007). National scientific facilities and their impact on nonbiomedical research. *Proceedings of the National Academy of Sciences of the United States of America, 104*, 17943–17947.

Kosmulski, M. (2006). A new Hirsch-type index saves time and works equally well as the original h-index. *ISSI Newsletter, 2*(3), 4–6.

Kosmulski, M. (2007). MAXPROD: A new index for assessment of the scientific output of an individual, and a comparison with the h-index. *Cybermetrics, 11*(1), Paper 5. Retrieved February 2, 2009, from www.cindoc.csic.es/cybermetrics/articles/v11i1p5.html

Krauskopf, M., & Krauskopf, E. (2008). A scientometric view of Revista Medica de Chile. *Revista Medica de Chile, 136*(8), 1065–1072.

Lehmann, S., Jackson, A. D., & Lautrup, B. E. (2005). *Measures and mismeasures of scientific quality.* Retrieved January 31, 2009, from arxiv.org/PS_cache/physics/pdf/0512/0512238v2.pdf

Lehmann, S., Jackson, A. D., & Lautrup, B. E. (2008). A qualitative analysis of indicators of scientific performance. *Scientometrics, 76*(2), 369–390.

Levitt, J. M., & Thelwall, M. (2007). Two new indicators derived from the h-index for comparing citation impact: Hirsch frequencies and the normalized Hirsch index. *Proceedings of the 11th International Conference of the International Society for Scientometrics and Informetrics*, 876–877.

Levitt, J. M., & Thelwall, M. (2008). Is multidisciplinary research more highly cited? A macrolevel study. *Journal of the American Society for Information Science and Technology, 59*(12), 1973–1984.

Levitt, J. M., & Thelwall, M. (2009). The most highly cited library and information science articles: Interdisciplinarity, first authors and citation patterns. *Scientometrics, 78*(1), 45–67.

Leydesdorff, L. (in press). How are new citation-based journal indicators adding to the bibliometrics toolbox? *Journal of the American Society for Information Science and Technology*. Retrieved February 2, 2009, from dx.doi.org/10.1002/asi.21024

Liang, L. (2006). h-index sequence and h-index matrix: Constructions and applications. *Scientometrics, 69*(1), 153–159.

Liu, Y., Rao, I. K. R., & Rousseau, R. (in press). Empirical series of journal h-indices: The JCR category Horticulture as a case study. *Scientometrics*. Retrieved February 2, 2009, from dx.doi.org/10.1007/s11192-009-0415-1

Liu, Y., & Rousseau, R. (2007). Hirsch-type indices and library management: The case of Tongji University Library. *Proceedings of the 11th International Conference of the International Society for Scientometrics and Informetrics*, 514–522.

Liu, Y., & Rousseau, R. (2008). Definitions of time series in citation analysis with special attention to the h-index. *Journal of Informetrics, 2*(3), 202–210.

Liu, Y., & Rousseau, R. (2009). Properties of Hirsch-type indices: The case of library classification categories. *Scientometrics, 79*(2), 235–248.

Lorenz, M. O. (1905). Methods of measuring concentration of wealth. *Journal of the American Statistical Association, 9*, 209–219.

Lotka, A. J. (1926). The frequency distribution of scientific productivity. *Journal of the Washington Academy of Sciences, 16*(12), 317–324.

Lovegrove, B. G., & Johnson, S. D. (2008). Assessment of research performance in biology: How well do peer review and bibliometry correlate? *Bioscience, 58*, 160–164.

Lufrano, F., & Staiti, P. (2008). *A bibliometric analysis of the international literature in supercapacitors*. Unpublished work.

Machacek, M., & Kolcunova, E. (2008). Hirsch index and rankings of Czech economists. *Politicka Ekonomie, 56*(2), 229–241.

Mahbuba, D., & Rousseau, R. (2008). Scientific research in Bangladesh and a comparison with India and Pakistan. *Proceedings of the Fourth International Conference on Webometrics, Informetrics and Scientometrics & Ninth COLLNET Meeting*. Retrieved February 2, 2009, from www.collnet.de/Berlin-2008/MahbubaWIS2008srb.pdf

Marchant, T. (2009a). An axiomatic characterization of the ranking based on the h-index and some other bibliometric rankings of authors. *Scientometrics, 79*(2), 311–327.

Marchant, T. (2009b). Score-based bibliometric rankings of authors. *Journal of the American Society for Information Science and Technology, 60*(6), 1132–1137.

Marx, W., & Barth, A. (2008). Carbon nanotubes: A scientometric study. *Physica Status Solidi B: Solid State Physics, 245*(10), 2347–2351.

McKercher, B. (2008). A citation analysis of tourism scholars. *Tourism Management, 29*(6), 1226–1232.

Meho, L. I., & Rogers, Y. (2008). Citation counting, citation ranking, and h-index of human-computer interaction researchers: A comparison of Scopus and Web of Science. *Journal of the American Society for Information Science and Technology, 59*(11), 1711–1726.

Meho, L. I., & Yang, K. (2007). Impact of data sources on citation counts and rankings of LIS faculty: Web of Science versus Scopus and Google Scholar. *Journal of the American Society for Information Science and Technology, 58*(13), 2105–2125.

Miller, C. W. (2006). *Superiority of the h-index over the impact factor for physics.* arXiv. Retrieved January 31, 2009, from arxiv.org/PS_cache/physics/pdf/0608/0608183v1.pdf

Minasny, B., Hartemink, A. E., & McBratney, A. (2007). Soil science and the h index. *Scientometrics, 73*(3), 257–264.

Molinari, A., & Molinari, J.-F. (2008a). Mathematical aspects of a new criterion for ranking scientific institutions based on the h-index. *Scientometrics, 75*(2), 339–356.

Molinari, J.-F., & Molinari, A. (2008b). A new methodology for ranking scientific institutions. *Scientometrics, 75*(1), 163–174.

Mugnaini, R., Packer, A. L., & Meneghini, R. (2008). Comparison of scientists of the Brazilian Academy of Sciences and of the National Academy of Sciences of the USA on the basis of the h-index. *Brazilian Journal of Medical and Biological Research, 41*(4), 258–262.

Muirhead, R. F. (1903). Some methods applicable to identities and inequalities of symmetric algebraic functions of n letters. *Proceedings of the Edinburgh Mathematical Society, 21*, 144–157.

O'Leary, D. E. (2008). The relationship between citations and number of downloads in Decision Support Systems. *Decision Support Systems, 45*(4), 972–980.

Olden, J. D. (2007). How do ecological journals stack-up? Ranking of scientific quality according to the h index. *Ecoscience, 14*(3), 370–376.

Oppenheim, C. (2007). Using the h-index to rank influential British researchers in information science and librarianship. *Journal of the American Society for Information Science and Technology, 58*(2), 297–301.

Orbay, M., & Karamustafaolu, O. (2008). Chinese Journal of Chemistry's Hirsch index: A case study of 1995–2005. *Chinese librarianship, 24.* Retrieved February 2, 2009, from www.white-clouds.com/iclc/cliej/cl24OK.htm

Pilc, A. (2008). The use of citation indicators to identify and support high-quality research in Poland. *Archivum Immunologiae et Therapiae Experimentalis, 56*(6), 381–384.

Pires Da Luz, M., Marques-Portella, C., Mendlowicz, M., Gleiser, S., Silva Freire Coutinho, E., & Figueira, I. (2008). Institutional h-index: The performance of a new metric in the evaluation of Brazilian psychiatric post-graduation programs. *Scientometrics, 77*(2), 361–368.

Popov, S. B. (2005). *A parameter to quantify dynamics of a researcher's scientific activity.* arXiv:physics/0508113v1. Retrieved January 31, 2009, from arxiv.org/PS_cache/physics/pdf/0508/0508113v1.pdf

Prathap, G. (2006). Hirsch-type indices for ranking institutions' scientific research output. *Current Science, 91*(11), 1439.

Purvis, A. (2006). The h index: Playing the numbers game. *TRENDS in Ecology and Evolution, 21*(8), 422.

Pyykkö, P. (2008). *Power-law distribution of individual Hirsch indices, the comparison of merits in different fields, and the relation to a Pareto distribution.* arXiv:physics/0608282 v1. Retrieved January 31, 2009, from www.chem.helsinki.fi/~pyykko/pekka/0608282.pdf

Qiu, J., Ma, R., & Cheng, N. (2008). New exploratory work of evaluating a researcher's output. *Scientometrics, 77*(2), 335–344.

Quesada, A. (2009). Monotonicity and the Hirsch index. *Journal of Informetrics, 3*(2), 158–160. Retrieved February 2, 2009, from gandalf.fcee.urv.es/professors/Antonio Quesada/152.2.pdf

Radicchi, F., Fortunato, S., & Castellano, C. (2008). Universality of citation distributions: Toward an objective measure of scientific impact. *Proceedings of the National Academy of Sciences of the United States of America, 105*(45), 17268–17272.

Rao, I. K. R. (2007). Distributions of Hirsch-index and g-index: An empirical study. *Proceedings of the 11th International Conference of the International Society for Scientometrics and Informetrics,* 655–658.

Rau, J. R. (2007). h-index (2000–2004) of the most cited environmental researchers based at Chilean institutions. *Revista Chilena de Historia Natural, 80,* 381–383.

Reedijk, J., & Moed, H. F. (2008). Is the impact of journal impact factors decreasing? *Journal of Documentation, 64*(2), 183–192.

Riikonen, P., & Vihinen, M. (2008). National research contributions: A case study on Finnish biomedical research. *Scientometrics, 77*(2), 207–222.

Rodriguez, V., Janssens, F., Debackere, K., & De Moor, B. (2007). On material transfer agreements and visibility of researchers in biotechnology. *Proceedings of the 11th International Conference of the International Society for Scientometrics and Informetrics,* 659–671.

Rodriguez, V., Janssens, F., Debackere, K., & De Moor, B. (2008). On material transfer agreements and visibility of researchers in biotechnology. *Journal of Informetrics, 2*(1), 89–100.

Romero, A. G., Cortes, J. N., Escudero, C., Lopez, J. A. F., & Moreno, J. A. C. (2007). Measuring the contribution of clinical trials to bibliometric indicators: Citations and journal impact factor. *Proceedings of the 11th International Conference of the International Society for Scientometrics and Informetrics,* 300–304.

Rosenstreich, D., & Wooliscroft, B. (2009). *An improved method for ranking management journals using the g-index and Google Scholar.* Unpublished work.

Rousseau, B., & Rousseau, R. (2000). LOTKA: A program to fit a power law distribution to observed frequency data. *Cybermetrics, 4*(1), paper 4. Retrieved February 2, 2009, from www.cindoc.csic.es/cybermetrics/articles/v4i1p4.html

Rousseau, R. (2002). Lack of standardisation in informetric research: Comments on "Power laws of research output: Evidence for journals of economics" by Matthias Sutter and Martin G. Kocher. *Scientometrics, 55*(2), 317–327.

Rousseau, R. (2006a). A case study: Evolution of JASIS' h-index. *Science Focus, 1*(1), 16–17.

Rousseau, R. (2006b). New developments related to the Hirsch index. *Science Focus, 1*(4), 23–25.

Rousseau, R. (2007a). Hungary—and Tibor Braun—on top. In W. Glänzel, A. Schubert, & B. Schlemmer (Eds.), *The multidimensional world of Tibor Braun: A multidisciplinary encomium for his 75th birthday* (pp. 25–28). Leuven, Belgium: ISSI.

Rousseau, R. (2007b). The influence of missing publications on the Hirsch index. *Journal of Informetrics, 1*(1), 2–7.

Rousseau, R. (2008a). Luckily, science focuses on achievements: Some thoughts related to the h-index. *ISSI Newsletter, 4*(3), 49–50.

Rousseau, R. (2008b). Reflections on recent developments of the h-index and h-type indices. In H. Kretschmer & F. Havemann (Eds.), *Proceedings of WIS 2008. COLLNET Journal of Scientometrics and Information Management, 2*(1), 1–8.

Rousseau, R. (2008c). *Simple models and the corresponding h- and g-index.* Retrieved February 2, 2009, from eprints.rclis.org/archive/00006153

Rousseau, R. (2008d). Woeginger's axiomatization of the h-index and its relation to the g-index, the $h^{(2)}$-index and the $R^2$-index. *Journal of Informetrics, 2*(4), 335–340.

Rousseau, R., Guns, R., & Liu, Y. (2008). The h-index of a conglomerate. *Cybermetrics, 12*(1), Paper 2. Retrieved February 2, 2009, from www.cindoc.csic.es/cybermetrics/articles/v12i1p2.html

Rousseau, R., & Jin, B. (2008). The age-dependent h-type $AR^2$-index: Basic properties and a case study. *Journal of the American Society for Information Science and Technology, 59*(14), 2305–2311.

Rousseau, R., & Rons, N. (2008). Another h-type index for institutional evaluation. *Current Science, 95*(9), 1103.

Rousseau, R., & Small, H. (2005). Escher staircases dwarfed. *ISSI Newsletter, 1*(4), 8–10.

Rousseau, R., & Ye, F. Y. (2008). A proposal for a dynamic h-type index. *Journal of the American Society for Information Science and Technology, 59*(11), 1853–1855.

Ruane, F., & Tol, R. S. J. (2008). Rational (successive) h-indices: An application to economics in the Republic of Ireland. *Scientometrics, 75*(2), 395–405.

Saad, G. (2006). Exploring the h-index at the author and journal levels using bibliometric data of productive consumer scholars and business-related journals respectively. *Scientometrics, 69*(1), 117–120.

Salgado, J. F., & Paez, D. (2007). Scientific productivity and Hirsch's h index of Spanish social psychology: Convergence between productivity indexes and comparison with other areas. *Psicothema, 19*(2), 179–189.

Sanderson, M. (2008). Revisiting h measured on UK LIS and IR academics. *Journal of the American Society for Information Science and Technology, 59*(7), 1184–1190.

Sangam, S. L., & Girji, R. M. (2008). Hirsch index: A new measure for assessing scientific productivity of an individual researcher. *Current Science, 94*, 291.

Satyanarayana, K., & Sharma, A. (2008). Impact factor: Time to move on. *Indian Journal of Medical Research, 127*(1), 4–6.

Schreiber, M. (2007a). A case study of the Hirsch index for 26 non-prominent physicists. *Annalen der Physik, 16*, 640–652.

Schreiber, M. (2007b). Self-citation corrections for the Hirsch index. *Europhysics Letters, 78*(3). Retrieved February 2, 2009, from dx.doi.org/10.1209/0295-5075/78/30002

Schreiber, M. (2008a). An empirical investigation of the g-index for 26 physicists in comparison with the h-index, the A-index, and the R-index. *Journal of the American Society for Information Science and Technology, 59*(9), 1513–1522.

Schreiber, M. (2008b). The influence of self-citation corrections on Egghe's g index. *Scientometrics, 76*(1), 187–200.

Schreiber, M. (2008c). A modification of the h-index: The $h_m$-index accounts for multi-authored manuscripts. *Journal of Informetrics, 2*(3), 211–216.

Schreiber, M. (2008d). To share the fame in a fair way, h(m) modifies h for multi-authored manuscripts. *New Journal of Physics, 10*. Retrieved February 2, 2009, from dx.doi.org/10.1088/1367-2630/10/4/040201

Schubert, A. (2007). Successive h-indices. *Scientometrics, 70*(1), 201–205.

Schubert, A., & Glänzel, W. (2007). A systematic analysis of Hirsch-type indices for journals. *Journal of Informetrics, 1*(3), 179–184.

Sebire, N. J. (2008). H-index and impact factors: Assessing the clinical impact of researchers and specialist journals. *Ultrasound in Obstetrics & Gynecology, 32*(7), 843–845.

Sezer, E., & Gokceoglu, C. (2009). *A fuzzy approach for the assessment of academic performance.* Unpublished work.

Sidiropoulos, A., & Katsaros, D. (2008). *Unfolding the full potentials of H-index for bibliographic ranking.* Unpublished work.

Sidiropoulos, A., Katsaros, D., & Manolopoulos, Y. (2007). Generalized Hirsch h-index for disclosing latent facts in citation networks. *Scientometrics, 72*(2), 253–280.

Smith, L. (1981). Citation analysis. *Library Trends, 30*, 83–106.

The STIMULATE6 Group. (2007). The Hirsch index applied to topics of interest to developing countries. *First Monday, 12*(2). Retrieved February 2, 2009, from firstmonday.org/htbin/cgiwrap/bin/ojs/index.php/fm/article/view/1622

Thelwall, M. (2008). Bibliometrics to webometrics. *Journal of Information Science, 34*(4), 605–621.

Timofieiev, A., Snásel, V., & Dvorský, J. (2008). h-index calculation in Enron corpus. *ICSOFT 2008: Proceedings of the Third International Conference on Software and Data Technologies*, Vol. ISDM/ABF, 206–211.

Tol, R. S. J. (2008). A rational, successive g-index applied to economics departments in Ireland. *Journal of Informetrics, 2*(2), 149–155.

Torra, V., & Narukawa, Y. (2008). The h-index and the number of citations: Two fuzzy integrals. *IEEE Transactions on Fuzzy Systems, 16*(3), 795–797.

Torro-Alves, N., Herculano, R. D., Tercariol, C. A. S., Filho, O. K., & Graeff, C. F. O. (2007). Hirsch's index: A case study conducted at the Faculdade de Filosofia, Ciencias e letras de Ribeirao Preto, Universidade de Sao Paulo. *Brazilian Journal of Medical and Biological Research, 40*, 1529–1536.

Ursprung, H. W., & Zimmer, M. (2007). Who is the "Platz-Hirsch" of the German economics profession? A citation analysis. *Jahrbücher für Nationalökonomie und Statistik, 227*(2), 187–208.

Valentinuzzi, M. E., Laciar, E., & Atrio, J. L. (2007). Two new discipline-independent indices to quantify individual's scientific research output. *Journal of Physics: Conference Series, 90*, 012018.

van Eck, N. J., & Waltman, L. (2008). Generalizing the h- and g-indices. *Journal of Informetrics, 2*(4), 263–271.

van Haselen, R. (2007). The h-index: A new way of assessing the scientific impact of individual CAM authors. *Complementary Therapies in Medicine, 15*, 225–227.

van Leeuwen, T. (2008). Testing the validity of the Hirsch-index for research assessment purposes. *Research Evaluation, 17*(2), 157–160.

van Raan, A. F. J. (2001a). Competition amongst scientists for publication status: Toward a model of scientific publication and citation distributions. *Scientometrics, 51*(1), 347–357.

van Raan, A. F. J. (2001b). Two-step competition process leads to quasi power-law income distributions. Application to scientific publication and citation distributions. *Physica A, 298*, 530–536.

van Raan, A. F. J. (2006). Comparison of the Hirsch-index with standard bibliometric indicators and with peer judgment for 147 chemistry groups. *Scientometrics, 67*(3), 491–502.

Vanclay, J. K. (2006). Refining the h-index. *The Scientist, 20*(7), 14–15.

Vanclay, J. K. (2007). On the robustness of the h-index. *Journal of the American Society for Information Science and Technology, 58*(10), 1547–1550.

Vanclay, J. K. (2008a). Gauging the impact of journals. *Forest Ecology and Management, 256*(4), 507–509.

Vanclay, J. K. (2008b). Ranking forestry journals using the h-index. *Journal of Informetrics, 2*(4), 326–334.

Vinkler, P. (1986). Evaluation of some methods for the relative assessment of scientific publications. *Scientometrics, 10*, 157–177.

Vinkler, P. (2007). Eminence of scientists in the light of the h-index and other scientometric indicators. *Journal of Information Science, 33*(4), 481–491.

Wan, J.-K., Hua, P.-H., Du, J., & Song, H.-M. (2007). Focus on the front of scientific evaluation, putting new indicators into practice: Three new bibliometric indicators adopted by China Academic Journals Comprehensive Citation Report. *Digital Library Forum, 3*, 36–41.

Wan, J.-K., Hua, P., & Rousseau, R. (2007). The pure h-index: Calculating an author's h-index by taking co-authors into account. *COLLNET Journal of Scientometrics and Information Management, 1*(2), 1–5.

Wan, J.-K., Hua, P.-H., Rousseau, R., & Sun, X.-K. (2009). *The downloaded immediacy index (DII): Experiences using the CNKI full-text database.* Unpublished work.

Wendl, M. C. (2007). H-index: However ranked, citations need context. *Nature, 449*(7161), 403.

Woeginger, G. J. (2008a). An axiomatic analysis of Egghe's g-index. *Journal of Informetrics, 2*(4), 364–368.

Woeginger, G. J. (2008b). An axiomatic characterization of the Hirsch-index. *Mathematical Social Sciences, 56*(2), 224–232.

Woeginger, G. J. (2008c). Generalizations of Egghe's g-index. *Journal of the American Society for Information Science and Technology, 60*(6), 1267–1273.

Woeginger, G. J. (2008d). A symmetry axiom for scientific impact indices. *Journal of Informetrics, 2*(4), 298–303.

Ye, F. Y., & Rousseau, R. (2008). The power law model and total career h-index sequences. *Journal of Informetrics, 2*(4), 288–297.

Zhivotovsky, L. A., & Krutovsky, K. V. (2008). Self-citation can inflate h-index. *Scientometrics, 77*(2), 373–375.

# CHAPTER 3

# Sports Knowledge Management and Data Mining

*Robert P. Schumaker*
*Iona College, New Rochelle, NY*

*Osama K. Solieman*
*Information Technology Consultant, Tucson, AZ*

*Hsinchun Chen*
*University of Arizona, Tucson, AZ*

## Introduction

Vast amounts of sports data are routinely collected about players, coaching decisions, and game events. Making sense of such data is important to those seeking a competitive edge. By transforming data into actionable information, scouts, managers, and coaches have a better idea of what to expect from opponents and how to use a player draft more effectively. With millions of dollars riding on the many decisions made within a sports franchise (Lewis, 2003), the sports environment is ideally suited to data mining and knowledge management approaches. Although the application of these methods to the world of sports may be novel, the topics of data mining and knowledge management are familiar to *ARIST* readers.

### Background and Motivation

Before the advent of data mining and knowledge management techniques, sports organizations relied almost exclusively on human expertise. It was believed that domain experts (coaches, managers, scouts) could effectively convert collected data into usable knowledge. As the different types of data being collected grew, sporting organizations sought more practical methods to make sense of what they had. This led to the employment of in-house statisticians who created better measures of performance and refined decision-making criteria. One way that these measures were used was to augment domain experts' decision making with additional information that could provide a competitive advantage. Armed with this knowledge, sporting organizations and fans alike began to develop more practical methods of extracting knowledge using data mining techniques. These new techniques allowed organizations to predict particular player matchups and/or forecast how a player might perform under specific conditions. Sports organizations were sitting on a wealth of data and needed ways to harness those data.

The knowledge management and data mining techniques that can be used by sports organizations include statistical analysis, pattern discovery, and outcome prediction. A variety of non-typical sports data can also be monitored. One such example is a biomedical tool piloted by AC Milan, an Italian soccer club, which uses software to monitor workouts and help to predict player injuries (Flinders, 2002). Another example is software used to monitor unusual betting patterns that may signal corrupt officiating or players who are compromised (Audi & Thompson, 2007). Similarly, data mining researchers have found that physical aptitude correlates with anticipated physical performance (Fieltz & Scott, 2003). Every year the National Football League (NFL) conducts a Combine where prospective college draft players are run through a series of physical drills in front of team scouts and coaches. The Combine also includes a mental evaluation of players called the Wonderlic Personnel Test, which assesses the prospects' intellectual capacity. The NFL has developed expected Wonderlic scores based on the level of intelligence required to play in a particular position; for example, a quarterback who has to make myriad on-field decisions should have a higher Wonderlic score (24) than a halfback (16) whose job is to run the ball (Zimmerman, 1985).

Sport statistics by themselves can be misleading without an understanding of their fundamental meaning. This may be a result of either imprecise measurement of an event or the sports community's misuse of, or over reliance on, particular statistics. As evidence, consider the fact that certain players can build impressive individual statistics yet have little impact on the performance of the team. The imprecision of sports statistics can be best illustrated by baseball's runs batted in (RBI) metric, which has long been considered a cornerstone of player evaluation. Developed by British-born journalist Henry Chadwick during the mid-1800s, the RBI was an attempt to quantify game events and attribute them to particular players (Lewis, 2003). Although Chadwick was more familiar with cricket than baseball and had an incomplete understanding of the game, he managed to popularize his statistics, which were never seriously questioned until the latter half of the 20th century. The RBI's imprecise measurement can be summed up in the following thought experiment. Suppose two players have the same batting average, meaning that they hit the ball with the same percentage of success. Further suppose that both players are not power hitters but routinely hit for singles, advancing themselves and their teammates one base at a time. The RBI is then dependent upon the actions of those who batted before them. If team members were routinely able to get on base for one of these players and not for the other, then the first of our hypothetical players would be credited with RBIs when his teammates crossed home plate as a consequence of the player's hits. The second of our hypothetical players would not receive any RBIs, even though both players performed the same actions. Basing a player's value on RBI statistics alone would be a misleading indicator of performance. The sports community has also overvalued the RBI as a measure of performance in contract negotiations and player comparisons. It was not until pioneering baseball statistician Bill James began questioning the RBI that better measurements emerged, such as the on-base percentage (OBP), which measures how often a player gets on base.

A difficulty with the use of sports statistics is how to measure risk. In American football, a defensive back can either stay in mid-field and attempt to intercept the ball or play solid cover defense. In the first instance, the player is taking a risk that can quickly change the momentum of the game whereas in the second instance he is playing it safe. However, by being successful at taking risks and making interceptions, the player has a greater perceived value. Quantifying risk-taking behavior is a challenging problem.

Another example of statistical imprecision is the measurement of defensive rebounds off missed free-throws in basketball. In order to get a defensive rebound, teammates must block out opposing players and in so doing they typically cannot get the rebound themselves (Ballard, 2005). However, because of the way in which rebounds are measured, only the player who gets the ball is credited with the rebound.

In this chapter, we outline a sports knowledge management framework to categorize the different methods sports organizations use to uncover new knowledge and better evaluate player contributions. We highlight measurement inadequacies and showcase techniques to make better use of data collected in a wide range of sport and sport-related specialties. Properly leveraging sports knowledge management techniques can result in better team performance by matching players to certain situations, identifying individual player contributions, evaluating the tendencies of the opposition, and exploiting any weaknesses.

For these reasons, it is hardly surprising that many sports organizations are revolutionizing old practices. The traditional decision-making approach of relying on intuition or gut instinct is falling out of favor. Instead, assessments are being made on the basis of robust analysis and scientific exploration. With more and more sports organizations embracing digital technologies, it may soon become be a battle of algorithms, where back-office analysts become just as important as the players on the field.

### Significance of This Survey

The knowledge management revolution in organized sports began with the book *Moneyball*, a case study of the successes enjoyed by the Oakland Athletics professional baseball team (Lewis, 2003). The

Oakland Athletics, commonly known as the A's, had long been at the low end of major league baseball's payroll with salaries well below the league average. This made it difficult for the A's to acquire talented players from other teams and impossible for them to retain their good players. Rather than accepting the situation, team management adopted a radical approach. By carefully selecting players in the 2002 draft, the A's could lock players that were often overlooked by other clubs into long-term contracts that did not pay much money and thus develop a strategy to compete with wealthier teams. When the players became good and their contracts were about to expire, the A's would then have the option of trading or selling them to larger market teams and securing a return on their investment. The trick was to pick the "right" players.

Until that time, the player draft was seen as something of a gamble because teams never really knew what they were going to acquire. Teams generally did not spend much time on the draft and left the bulk of the work to scouting departments, whose staff would travel the country to view new talent and make recommendations. Billy Beane, the general manager of the Oakland A's, questioned this approach and began to use a systematic method of statistically analyzing draft picks by the numbers they generated throughout their careers. It was reasoned that if the A's were careful in the selection process, they could extract a few productive years from the players before the higher salary teams would take them.

As a result of this strategy, the Oakland A's began to field a competitive team that differed from those of all other low salary ball clubs. Relying on computers and algorithms to pick talent, the A's produced star players such as Barry Zito, Mark Mulder, Tim Hudson, Jason Giambi, Miguel Tejada, Eric Chavez, Nick Swisher, and Mark Teahan. The first step in their selection process was to eliminate all high school players from consideration. This was a significant departure from the old way of doing things, where high school players were seen as valuable commodities. However, stars at the high school level rarely lived up to expectations and making comparisons between high school players and leagues at that level was difficult. Instead, Beane focused on the statistics generated for college players, adopting different evaluative metrics. For example, the RBI does not measure the ability of a player to get on base, so he tested different formulae and found that on-base and slugging percentages were the most influential predictors of run production. Beane and his colleagues would then use these metrics to rank order the draft players. Most of the players who were rated highly using these methods were overlooked by other clubs, who would even tease Oakland for picking players whom they saw as worthless, especially so high in the draft.

The results soon became clear when Oakland fielded successful teams year after year in spite of its low payroll. Competitors and commentators alike did not understand how Oakland was able to win consistently. Even Major League Baseball's Blue Ribbon Panel of economic experts, which was investigating the salary inequities in baseball, concluded that Oakland's performance was a statistical anomaly (Levin, Mitchell, Volcker, & Will, 2000). At that time, knowledge management techniques were not widely used in sports.

Baseball was not the only sport undergoing transformation. During the 1980s and 1990s, Dean Oliver was applying statistical analysis techniques to basketball, many years before the *Moneyball* revolution. A contemporary of baseball's Bill James, Oliver (2005) focused more on creating statistics that would showcase team behavior rather than individual performance and began to publish his thoughts for the rest of community. Oliver and James were eventually both hired as statistical consultants to the Seattle Supersonics and Boston Red Sox, respectively, cementing data analysts in the new foundation of sports competitiveness.

Sports organizations are big business. Advancing to playoffs and winning championships can result in lucrative television revenues and vast marketing opportunities. The key is winning. With so many competitive forces confronting professional sports organizations, such as larger salaried teams, salary caps, and revenue sharing schemes, it is of paramount importance that the right decisions are made in order to maintain a competitive advantage. These decisions can be influenced by the hard facts and data already acquired. The challenge is finding ways to discover knowledge buried in the available data.

## Chapter Scope and Structure

This chapter investigates a number of sports knowledge management techniques and related research about data mining methods, with a special emphasis on those sports with the most interesting applications. However, novel and insightful techniques from lesser known sports and sports outside the U.S. are also included in our survey of trends.

Although the scope is broad, covering a multitude of organizations, sports research centers, academia, and private industry, readers are encouraged to consult prior *ARIST* chapters on data mining and knowledge management topics (e.g., Benoit, 2002).

This chapter is arranged as follows. We begin with an analytic framework for knowledge management and locate sports data mining within it. Then we review the data sources that fans and organizations can access. The next section examines the use of statistical analyses as methods of knowledge extraction. We next provide an overview of the systems and tools that are used to gather both data and knowledge and then detail the predictive aspects of sports knowledge systems. The next section considers multimedia and video analysis as means of obtaining competitive advantage; the final section presents our conclusions and a brief discussion of future research directions.

## Analytic Framework for Knowledge Management and Data Mining in Sports

Knowledge management first announced itself in 1975 as a way to harness a range of tools, technologies, and human expertise (Davenport & Prusak, 1998) that can provide an organization with a competitive advantage (Lahti & Beyerlein, 2000). By retaining and sharing organizational knowledge (Serenko & Bontis, 2004), businesses can increase productivity and innovation (O'Reilly & Knight, 2007). First, however, we should consider the different levels represented by the data-information-knowledge-wisdom (DIKW) hierarchy (Ackoff, 1989). The DIKW hierarchy is widely accepted in the knowledge management community as a way to represent the different levels of what can be seen and what can be known (Cleveland, 1982; Zeleny, 1987). Each successive level—data, information, knowledge, wisdom—builds upon preceding levels and provides an increased awareness of surroundings (Carlisle, 2006) where meaning can be found (Chen, 2001, 2006).

Data are the observable differences in physical states (Boisot & Canals, 2004) that are acquired from stimuli and examination of the world around us. By themselves, data can be overwhelming and not always useable. In the framework we propose here, data can be thought of as all the individual events that occur in the sporting arena. If applied to baseball, these data would contain a record of pitch sequences, at-bat events, and defensive moves, which by themselves provide little of interest or value.

In order to be of practical value, data have to be transformed by identifying relationships (Barlas, Ginart, & Dorrity, 2005) or limited to only those elements relevant to the problem at hand (Carlisle, 2006). This transformation results in information, or meaningful, actionable data (Bierly, Kessler, Christensen, 2000). Using the baseball example, information could be focused on only the pitch sequences by a particular pitcher. Although of limited use at this stage, abstracting the information to the next level of the hierarchy, knowledge, can provide additional meaning by identifying underlying patterns within the data.

Knowledge is the aggregation of related information (Barlas et al., 2005) that forms a set of expectations or rules (Boisot & Canals, 2004) and provides a clearer understanding of the aggregated information (Bierly et al., 2000). At this level of the hierarchy, rule-based systems are developed that can allow individuals to expand their own knowledge while also benefitting the organization (Alavi & Leidner, 2001). Returning to the baseball example, analysts can evaluate pitching information and look for tendencies or expectations as to the types of pitches batters will encounter. Data mining is the search for latent knowledge within data.

Although the precise definitions of data, information, and knowledge are still a matter of debate, wisdom can be viewed as a holistic appreciation of the situation (Barlas et al., 2005) that uses knowledge alone

(Carlisle, 2006) to achieve goals (Bierly et al., 2000; Hastie, Tibshirani, & Friedman, 2001). In our baseball example, we have: (1) knowledge of the types of pitches to be encountered; (2) knowledge of effective strategies to combat specific types of pitches; and (3) knowledge that a successful at-bat can help win a game. Fusing this knowledge with a player's experience results in wisdom; the batter has a chance to influence the game in his favor.

Data mining involves procedures for uncovering hidden trends and developing new data and information from data sources. These sources can include well-structured and defined databases, such as statistical compilations, or unstructured data in the form of multimedia sources. The DIKW framework sets the stage for disambiguating data from knowledge and sets loose, definitional boundaries for what data, information, and knowledge are. Applying this to the sports domain, certain activities and techniques serve at the data level (i.e., data collection, data mining, and basic statistics). Other techniques and algorithms are more suited to the knowledge end of the spectrum, such as strategies and simulations. Throughout this chapter, the DIKW framework is used to identify the set of relevant tools that can be used depending on whether the focus is data or knowledge.

## Sports Knowledge Management Framework

Sports data come from myriad structured and unstructured sources. The process of transforming these data into useful and interesting sports knowledge can be categorized by the techniques used: expert examination, statistics, and machine learning techniques, as shown in Figure 3.1.

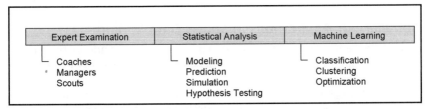

**Figure 3.1 A sports knowledge framework**

Human domain experts (i.e., coaches, general managers, scouts) make decisions based upon their experience and the data presented to them. Sometimes these decisions are shaped by gut reaction and instinct that may run counter to the available data (Lewis, 2003; Page, 2005). The use of sports experts as the sole repository of knowledge has been declining with the advent of computational knowledge acquisition techniques in sports. Such systems can give an organization an analytical edge that few domain experts can match.

Statistical techniques are often used in sports knowledge discovery. Although statistics in sports are not new, there has been a recent overhaul in the way performance is measured. Newer and more sophisticated algorithms are being used to find patterns in player tendencies and team strengths and weaknesses (Dong & Calvo, 2007). Sub-areas such as prediction, simulation, and hypothesis testing can be used as augmentation tools (Hirotsu & Wright, 2003) by players, coaches, and general managers to make better decisions. Statistical techniques lie at the heart of data mining, allowing researchers to distinguish between something interesting and random noise and also allowing them to test hypotheses and make predictions (Piatetsky-Shapiro, 2008).

The third area of sports knowledge gathering is machine learning. Machine learning techniques differ from statistics by allowing an algorithm to learn patterns from the data and apply that knowledge in real time to previously unseen data. Leveraging pattern-matching algorithms can uncover hidden trends that domain experts and statisticians may not have thought of pursuing. Sub-areas such as classification, clustering, and optimization allow analysts to maximize their team's effectiveness by conducting a series of what-if analyses on the data by changing one or more variables (Berry, 2005; Chen & Chau, 2004).

Although expert examination can suffer from biases and unquantifiable gut instincts, statistical and machine learning methods also have weaknesses in generalizing from results to future activity. Each study should take account of these limitations.

Taken together, these knowledge discovery methods offer a powerful set of tools to sports organizations. For more details about machine learning algorithms, readers are referred to the *ARIST* chapter by Chen and Chau (2004).

## Summary of Applications in Sports Data Mining

Until recently sports knowledge was believed to reside in the minds of scouts, coaches, and managers. These experts were solely responsible for translating the relevant data into actionable knowledge. However, faced with large volumes of technology-generated data, the experts were quickly overwhelmed, which led to the hiring of technologically sophisticated analysts to make sense of the data. Their focus was on discovering better methods of performance measurement, and they soon created new formulae such as baseball's on-base plus slugging (OPS) (Thorn & Palmer, 1984) and basketball's player efficiency rating (PER) (Hollinger, 2002), to name but two. Similarly, progress was made in the area of event prediction using tools such as neural networks.

Scouting has been the backbone of sports organizations' knowledge collection for nearly a century. Scouts serve two primary roles: first to seek out and evaluate new talent and second to prepare assessments of opposing teams. To seek out new pools of talent, scouts often travel to the locations of potential draft picks and evaluate their skills during practice and regular games. The reports generated usually focus on the potential draft pick's strengths and weaknesses as well as the overall impression of the draftee's potential to the organization. These reports are important because they affect a player's draft position and indicate the organization's expectations for that player (Page, 2005).

The second type of scout, an advance scout, observes competing teams, compiles reports on player weaknesses and opposing teams' strategies, and gathers other useful tidbits that may generate a competitive advantage. Traditional scouting involves the collection of hard data and expert opinions about the potential of draftees and also opponents' strategies and performances. However, these opinions sometimes result in biases when a scout "falls in love" with a certain player's skills or overlooks others, which can lead to questionable recommendations (Lewis, 2003).

Following the recent *Moneyball* (Lewis, 2003) revolution, scouting has witnessed two fundamental changes. The first was to adopt a more scientific and statistically based strategy to compare players against one another in an unbiased manner. Applying data mining tools to the data already gathered, players and opponents could be evaluated without the usual scouting biases. From there, scouting moved away from simply identifying strengths and weaknesses to providing in-depth study of situations and tendencies (White, 2006). The second major change was the advent of more automated and fine-grained data gathering and analysis techniques, including multimedia and video analysis.

## Data Sources for Sports

Data on sport performance can come from a variety of sources, most commonly in-house statisticians. Statistics are generally gathered for team-level and individual player performances. However, most organizations keep such information to themselves, which has opened the door to professional societies and application-specific companies to fill gaps in sports data provision.

### *Professional Societies*

Several professional societies are dedicated to exploring new facets of knowledge management within their particular sports. They serve as centralized repositories where members can share insights and undertake further research. Many of these societies collect, evaluate, store, and disseminate sport-related data for members and maintain newsletters and journals. Their main activities involve discovering and sharing knowledge within the sporting community.

The Society for American Baseball Research (SABR) was formed in baseball's Hall of Fame Library in 1971 (Society for American Baseball Research, 2008). Its purpose is to foster research about baseball and create a repository of baseball knowledge not captured in the box scores, which contain both teams' runs, hits, and errors for each game. In 1974 SABR founded the Statistical Analysis Committee (SAC) with the goal of carefully studying both the historical and modern game of baseball from an analytical point of view. Its research has become known as sabermetrics, and the SAC Committee publishes its research on a quarterly basis (Birnbaum, 2008).

The Professional Football Researchers Association (PFRA) was started in 1979 with the goal of preserving and reconstructing historical game-day events (Professional Football Researchers Association, 2008). The PFRA also publishes bi-monthly articles that cover statistical analyses as well as new methods of performance measurement.

The Association for Professional Basketball Research (APBR) was formed in 1997 with the objective of promoting the history of professional basketball (Solieman, 2006). Although its research concentrates on NBA-related statistics, the Association also includes rival basketball leagues, many of which are now defunct (Association for Professional Basketball Research, 2008). Similar to baseball's sabermetrics, the APBR has developed the APBRmetrics, which are used to create better measurements and statistical yardsticks for comparison purposes.

The International Association on Computer Science in Sport (IACSS) was founded in 1997 to improve cooperation among researchers interested in applying techniques and technologies from the field of computer science to sport-related challenges (International Association on Computer Science in Sport, 2008). The IACSS focuses on disseminating the research of their members through periodic newsletters, journals, and organized conferences.

The International Association for Sports Information (IASI) was founded in 1960 with the goal of standardizing and archiving the world's sports libraries (International Association for Sports Information, 2008). The IASI is a worldwide network of sport experts, librarians, and document repositories. The association's information dissemination comes in the form of a tri-annual newsletter and an organized world congress every four years.

### Special Interest Sources

Other organizations, in addition to professional sport-related societies, collect and analyze sport-related statistics. Often these sources offer traditional statistics as well as augmented data in the form of player biographies, records, and awards. Examples of these sources include Baseball-Reference.com (2008), which portrays itself as a one-stop shop for all basic statistics, current standings, player and team rankings by various categories, draft picks, and historical box score data. Pro-Football-Reference.com (2008) compiles player, team, and league statistics along with historical game data, and 82games.com (2008) positions itself as Basketball's innovative data source for fans, coaches, and the media.

## Statistical Analysis Research in Sports

Once the data have been gathered, the next steps involve finding the knowledge locked within. Statistical analyses of many types can be applied to data from statistically intense sports such as baseball and basketball to less data-intense sports such as curling. Other types of analysis can be used to measure player performance, team balance, opposition weaknesses, and even the possibility of a debilitating injury. Although statistical records of sporting events have been kept for nearly a century, the statistics themselves have not been called into question. The basic question became, "are we measuring what we think we are measuring?" Early pioneers of statistical analysis such as Bill James and Dean Oliver not only asked these questions, but also began to offer new statistics and insights.

### *History and Inherent Problems of Statistics in Sports*

As already noted, the origins of early baseball statistics are often traced to Henry Chadwick, the nineteenth-century sportswriter and statistician (Lewis, 2003). Chadwick created many of today's familiar statistics, for example, batting average and earned run average, based on his experience with the game of cricket. This is one of the reasons walks (advancing to a base without a hit) are not included in these formulae; the walk has no equivalent in cricket.

Batting average, defined as the number of hits a player collects divided by the number of times at bat, is an example of a statistic that ignores walks. If a player manages to draw a walk during a time at bat, then the at-bat is not counted. This leads to imprecision when rating players, because if the goal is to get on base, hits and walks should be both counted. Players who walk often may have lower batting averages; therefore using batting average as the sole measurement of performance will lead to an unfair comparison and may underestimate a player's contribution to team performance.

The earned run average (ERA) is another bedrock of baseball's performance metrics. The ERA is the number of earned runs against a pitcher per nine innings. The term "earned run" is important because it is a run that is achieved through a hit. Other means of getting on base and scoring, such as getting hit by a pitch (when the batter is awarded first base after being hit by the ball during an at-bat), a balk (an illegal motion by the pitcher, which results in base runners being awarded the next base), a dropped third strike (normally a batter strikes out after a third strike but can attempt to run to first base if the catcher drops the pitch), fielding errors, and walks do not count toward the ERA. Again the overemphasis on hitting tends to skew ERA values. These two statistics alone, batting average and ERA, were used as the primary performance indicators by scouts, coaches, and general managers for well over a century.

American football also has some imprecision in its measurements, such as the number of receptions and yards per carry. Defining the number of receptions as the number of times a player catches a forward pass is misleading. Receptions do not indicate success in terms of touchdowns, but may instead indicate a preference for a particular player by a quarterback and thus inflate the reception total of the preferred receiver. Yards per carry is another example of success not being predicated on scoring points. Should one player who ran for 40 yards in one play be valued more than another who runs an average of three yards per play? Although one obvious solution would be to compare only those players with a minimum number of carries, the process of setting arbitrary thresholds ignores the issue that yards per carry does not take into account the points scored; thus the statistic leads to inexact comparisons.

Basketball uses similarly imprecise statistics, such as field goal percentage and rebounds. The field goal percentage is the number of field goals made divided by the number attempted. A player who scores a high number of points yet has a low field goal percentage may be rated as unsuccessful. Likewise the rebound statistic, or the number of times a player gets the ball after a missed shot attempt, does not imply that points will be scored. Nevertheless, basketball experts have long valued these statistics as adequate measures of performance.

The problem with these traditional formulae lies in what the statistic is intended to measure. Often, data are gathered and used in ways that cannot be meaningfully interpreted. The data are not at fault; the problem is the methods that are used for comparing player performances. This also leads to the realization that some questions cannot be answered through statistical examination alone. The questioning of statistics that were once held as truths, the very foundations of modern sports, led to the adoption of new techniques and measures within sports organizations.

### Bill James

The fundamental shift from traditional statistics to knowledge management can be credited to Bill James. In 1977, James published the first of many "Bill James Baseball Abstracts" in which he began to openly question traditional statistics and to offer remedies. Although selling only 50 copies at the outset, James was not deterred and continued to publish his annual compendium of insights, new statistical measures—which he called *sabermetrics*—and strange ranking formulae. Readers of the "Abstracts" became interested in the new way of computing performance and began to make their own contributions. Soon sporting enthusiasts and fantasy baseball team owners began applying this newfound knowledge with considerable success. In spite of great fan excitement for this revolution in thinking, sports organizations resisted these new ideas for several decades because scouting was so entrenched within organizations as the principal source of knowledge (Lewis, 2003).

In 2002, Oakland A's General Manager Billy Beane became the first Bill James disciple in Major League Baseball to adopt sabermetrics when selecting draft picks. Beane's use of data mining and knowledge extraction tools landed the A's in either the playoffs or playoff contention for five consecutive years (Lewis, 2003). That same year, the Boston Red Sox hired another Bill James disciple, Theo Epstein. Epstein, a Yale graduate, similarly appreciated the hard facts that could be gleaned from reams of data. He hired Bill James as a consultant in 2003 and went on to engineer the Red Sox World Championships in 2004 and 2007.

### Dean Oliver

Dean Oliver is to basketball what Bill James is to baseball. Asking some of the same types of questions throughout the 1990s, Oliver sought to quantify player contribution more accurately and began popularizing *APBRmetrics*, basketball's answer to sabermetrics. Oliver focused attention on the proper use of the possession statistic, the amount of time a team has the ball. Part of Oliver's contribution was to evaluate team performance on the basis of the number of points they scored or allowed opponents to score per 100 possessions. In 2004 the Seattle Supersonics hired Dean Oliver as a consultant, ushering basketball into the *Moneyball* era. Seattle went on to win the division title in 2005.

Also in 2005, the Houston Rockets hired Daryl Morey as assistant general manager. Morey, an MIT graduate and believer in knowledge management principles, had previously worked with the Boston Celtics and STATS Inc., where he invented and refined several new basketball statistics (*MIT Sloan Alumni Profile*, 2008).

### Baseball Research

Baseball has been called the "national pastime" and has been a part of American culture for nearly two centuries. The first professional baseball team, the Cincinnati Red Stockings, was founded in 1869 and played amateur teams across the country, amassing an impressive 81-game winning streak (Voigt, 1969). Baseball was further organized into sustainable leagues in 1876, with the creation of the National League. The National League, which quickly became the premier baseball league, withstood competition from startup leagues, including the Players' League, the American Association, and the Federal League; Wrigley Field in Chicago was originally built as a Federal League ballpark (Fetter, 2003). However, in 1901 a startup called the American League was not so easy to brush aside. The leagues competed intensely with one another and poached talent to the detriment of the game until 1903, when both sides agreed to recognize each other as major league and also began the tradition of World Series competitions between the two (New York Times Staff, 2004).

## Building Blocks

Statistics by themselves should not be the primary means by which player performance is determined, but rather the beginning of a process during which useful knowledge is discovered. For instance, one of baseball's fundamental statistics has been hits. As discussed earlier, this statistic does not take account of the other ways by which a player can get on base and these additional means do not count in either the batting average or hits total. Because of this, OBP, which does include these methods, was developed as a better measure of a player's ability. Another statistic that can better measure offensive player productivity is slugging percentage. Here the number of bases reached is divided by the number of at-bats. This rewards players who hit doubles, triples, or home runs. In contrast the hits statistic treats these as equivalent to singles.

Building upon both of the fundamental statistics of OBP and slugging percentage, we can derive the OPS statistic, the summation of these two statistics, which provides a better representation of a player's ability to get on base and hit with power. OPS is considered one of the most effective measures of a player's offensive capabilities.

## Runs Created

In his third *Baseball Abstract*, James (1979) reasons that players' performances should be measured in relation to what they are trying to accomplish, scoring runs, rather than baseball's predominant indicator of the day, batting average. James recognized the disconnect between the two concepts and questioned how run production could be better measured. To this end he developed the runs created (RC) formula, which was ((Hits + Walks) * Total Bases) / (At-Bats + Walks) (James, 1982). The RC formula reflected a team's ability to get on base as a proportion of its opportunities through at-bats and walks. James then evaluated historical baseball data using his model and found that RC was better than other models for predicting the number of runs that a major league team would score (Lewis, 2003). This formula was found to be a better measure of a player's offensive contribution than batting average because wins are achieved by the team with the highest number of runs, not the highest batting average.

Further instantiations of RC led to runs created above average (RCAA) (Sinins, 2007), which compares runs created to the league average (Woolner, 2006) and runs created per 27 outs (RC/27) (James & Henzler, 2002), which takes into account sacrifice flies (where the player hits the ball to the outfield with the expectation that the ball will be caught by the opposition in order to advance one of the base runners to the next base) and sacrifice hits (where the batter hits the ball to the infield with the expectation that he will be thrown out at first base in order to advance one of the base runners to the next base). RC/27 is simply RC / (At-Bats − Hits + Number of times caught stealing + Number of times a player hits into a double play + Sacrifice Flies + Sacrifice Hits). The RC/27 models complete offensive player performance over the course of an entire game (27 outs). Further analysis revealed that bench players (i.e., players who do not start but come into the game later) typically have 80 percent of the offensive capability of the starter, with the exception of catchers at 85 percent and first basemen at 75 percent (Woolner, 2006).

## Win Shares

In 2001's *Baseball Abstract*, James introduced the concept of win shares, where players are assigned a portion of the win based upon their offensive and defensive contributions; the concept was further explained in a follow-up book with that title (James & Henzler, 2002). Win shares is a complicated formula that takes into account many constants and educated guesses, including measures that were never captured in the historical data. Although still a subject of debate within the sabermetric community, win shares attempts to assign players credit for winning a game based upon their performance. Assuming a team has equal offensive and defensive capabilities, defense is credited with 52 percent of a win and offense is granted only 48 percent. This seemingly arbitrary division is justified as a way to even out the public's perception that offense is the more important component of a win. Although the formula itself is still being refined within the sabermetric community, the results are difficult to ignore. Players with seasonal win shares of around 20 are typically all-stars. A win share of 30 indicates a most valuable player (MVP) season and a win share of 40+ points to an historic season. For example, Barry Bonds had a win share of 54 in 2001 when he set the record of 73 home runs in a single season.

## Linear Weights and Total Player Rating

The linear weights formula calculates runs based on the actions of the offensive player. George Lindsey used the formula $0.47(1B) + 0.78(2B) + 1.09(3B) + 1.40(HR) + 0.33(BB + HBP) + 0.30(SB) − 0.60(CS) − 0.25(AB − H) − 0.5(\text{Outs on Base})$ as an alternative to simple batting average (Albert, 1997). Recognizing that there were three ways to get on base, hits (1B, 2B, 3B, and HR), walks (BB), and being hit by a pitch (HBP), Lindsey extended his model to reward players who advanced through base stealing (SB), punish players caught stealing (CS), and punish those called out on the base paths (outs on base).

Pursuing the idea of linear weights further, total player rating (TPR) is a little more complicated and includes comparisons for the position played and the ballpark (Schell, 1999). This allows statisticians to compare performance (above or below average) based on the player's defensive position and the ballpark in which he is playing; some ballparks may be more difficult for a particular position than others. TPR has ratings of batting runs, pitching runs, and fielding runs, which are (1) summed, (2) adjusted for player position and ballpark, and (3) divided by 10 so that players can be compared against league averages. However, this statistic has come in for some criticism (James & Henzler, 2002).

## Pitching Measures

So far we have analyzed measures meant to capture the value of a player's offensive performance. Pitching is another important staple of baseball, and the performance of pitchers is closely watched by fans and sports organizations alike. Earned run average (ERA), which measures pitching performance as the number of earned runs (runs that come from hits over nine innings), is one of the most relied upon pitching statistics. It is usually coupled with a win/loss record and can be deceptive. Take for instance a poorly performing pitcher who plays on a team with a high-powered offense. The pitcher will have a high ERA but also a deceptively high win/loss record. Similarly, an excellent pitcher playing on a team without run support will have a good ERA but a poor win/loss record. In order to adjust to these situations, the pitching runs statistic was developed to compare pitches more directly with league performance. In pitching runs, the number of innings pitched is divided by nine, then multiplied by the league's ERA, and then the earned runs allowed is subtracted. The result gives the anticipated number of runs a pitcher would allow over the course of a complete game. Average pitchers would have a pitching runs score of zero, and the pitching runs for poorly performing pitchers would be negative.

Another pitching measure recently put forth by James is the component ERA (ERC), which breaks out the different components of pitching outcomes and combines them with the ERA. ERC is $(((H + BB + HBP) * PTB) / (BFP * IP)) * 9 - 0.56$ where BFP is number of batters faced by the pitcher, IP is number of innings pitched, and PTB is $0.89(1.255(H - HR) + 4 * HR) + 0.56(BB + HBP - IBB)$ (IBB is intentional walks) (Baseball Info Solutions, 2003). However, the ERC can be more complicated under certain conditions and other organizations offer different models.

## *Football Research*

Advances in statistical techniques in football have not reached the levels of those in baseball and basketball. For this reason, statistical data exist on individual players. Although some basic statistics are collected, such as number of touchdowns, receptions, and interceptions, these aggregate counts do not rise to the level of their sabermetric counterparts. The paucity of data stems also from the number of games played. The NFL plays 16 regular-season games compared to baseball's 162 and basketball's 82 games. Nevertheless, several metrics are in use.

### Defense-Adjusted Value Over Average

The defense-adjusted value over average (DVOA) is a comparative measure of success for a particular play (Schatz, 2006). This statistic treats each play as a discrete event and measures the potential for success against the average in the league. Certain variables are taken into account, such as time remaining, the down, distance to the next down, field position, score, and quality of opponent. These variables carry different rewards if met and can be used to measure a particular player's contribution or aggregated to highlight team-based performance. A DVOA of zero indicates that the defense is performing on par with the league average; positive and negative DVOA values indicate that the defense is performing either above or below league averages.

In football, possession is broken into four downs (or plays) with a sub-goal of exceeding a set number of yards before the expiration of downs. DVOA considers that in order to meet this sub-goal, 45 percent of the required yards should be gained on the first down, 60 percent by the second down, and 100 percent by the third or fourth down (Carroll, Palmer, Thorn, & Pietrusza, 1998). If the play is deemed successful, DVOA assigns it one point. If the play is successful early (e.g., attaining the sub-goal in the early downs), more points are awarded.

### Defense-Adjusted Points Above Replacement

Defense-adjusted points above replacement (DPAR) is a player-based statistic compiled over the course of a season (Schatz, 2006). DPAR is used to determine the point-based contribution of a player as compared with the performance of a replacement player. If a player has a +2.7 DPAR, it means that the team should score 2.7 points because of the player's presence in the lineup and that 2.7 points would be lost if a typical replacement were substituted for the player.

### Adjusted Line Yards

Adjusted line yards (ALY) is a statistic to assign credit or responsibility to an offensive line in relation to the distance the ball is carried (Schatz, 2006). This statistic attempts to separate the running back from the contribution of the offensive line. If a running back is brought down behind the line of scrimmage (i.e., takes a loss of yards), the offensive line will be penalized heavily for the failure. If the running back manages to break free and make a long gain (i.e., picks up many more yards than usual), the offensive line is given minimal credit because the offensive line can contribute only a certain amount and much of the gain is attributable to the running back. The ALY is also adjusted to league averages.

## Basketball Research

Basketball experienced its own sabermetric revolution shortly after the book *Moneyball* began to circulate among baseball enthusiasts (Pelton, 2005). With their own wealth and depth of statistics, several pioneers of basketball statistics attempted to better quantify and assign credit through the creation of APBRmetrics, named for the Association of Professional Basketball Research (APBR). APBRmetrics is fundamentally different from sabermetrics in that APBRmetrics attempts to view statistics in terms of team rather than individual performance. An example of this is team possession and how effective the team is at scoring points. The thinking is that because teams must function as cohesive units, they should be analyzed as such; quantifying team chemistry (how well players perform with one another) at the individual level is currently infeasible.

To underscore this point, players can have either a positive or negative impact on team performance. As an example, during the 2004–2005 season, Stephon Marbury of the New York Knicks had a –0.4 point impact on the team while he was on the court. At the outset, this statistic would indicate that Marbury was performing at or slightly below average. However, when Marbury was off the court and not helping his team, the team had a –12.0 point deficit. This 11.6 point differential when Marbury was on rather than off the court illustrates that Marbury could improve his team's performance when he was on court.

### Shot Zones

The basketball court can be divided into 16 areas from which a player on offense might shoot a basket. By analyzing the percentage of player success from each of these zones, defensive adjustments can be made to limit scoring while, offensively, coaches may try to maximize these types of shots (Beech, 2008). Figure 3.2 illustrates the shot zone locations.

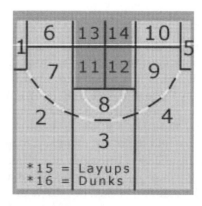

Figure 3.2   Shot zone layout (82games.com)

Analyzing the 2004–2005 season, 82games.com found that for three-point shots from the corner (zones 1 and 5), Golden State's Dunleavy had the highest accuracy of 0.571 from the left corner and Sacramento's Mobley had 0.600 accuracy from the right corner. Shot zones can also portray player tendencies. For example, under the basket (zones 13 and 14), Miami's Shaquille O'Neal made the most attempts in the league but was not very successful, 0.416 from the left and 0.424 from the right. Knowing where players are successful and comfortable can lead to better strategies.

### Player Efficiency Rating

Player efficiency rating (PER) is a per-minute rating of a player's effectiveness that rewards positive contributions and punishes negative ones (Hollinger, 2002). This formula incorporates many variables including assists, blocked shots, fouls, free throws, made shots, missed shots, rebounds, steals, and turnovers and tries to quantify a player's performance throughout the game and the average performance level of the league. However, PER is still a matter of debate as Hollinger (2002) admits that it does not take into account all performance related criteria, such as hustle and desire.

### Plus/Minus Rating

Another method of calculating performance is through the plus/minus rating system, in which each player is evaluated by calculating the number of points the team makes with that player on the field minus the number of points the opposing team receives. This calculation is done for each team player while he is on court and also while he is on the bench. Player contribution can then be measured as the differential between his on- and off-court presence (Rosenbaum, 2004). Positive values indicate the player is making a positive point-based contribution to the team and negative values would suggest counterproductivity. Take the case of Dwight Howard (Orlando Magic) during the 2004–2005 season. Howard had a plus/minus rating of –2 when he was on the court versus an even rating when not (Rosenbaum, 2005). This would seem to indicate that the team was better off without Howard's presence. However, the plus/minus rating system is not without quirks of its own. Critics of the system point to its over-valuing of players who take a high number of shots and commit a large number of turnovers, which is not a beneficial team activity.

### Measuring Player Contribution to Winning

A further metric for evaluating player contribution versus a substitute player is to adjust the plus/minus rating system to account for the talent level of teammates (Rosenbaum, 2004). The reasoning is that player performance does not occur within a vacuum but is a function of the overall team effort. The adjusted plus/minus is a regression estimate where the constant is the home court advantage against all teams, the $k^{th}$ order constants are the plus/minus differences between player $K$ and the players of interest, holding all others constant. The $x$ values, $x_1$ through $x_{14}$, refer to game-level statistics per 40 minutes of play: points, field goal attempts at home, field goal attempts on the road, three-point attempts, free throw attempts, assists, offensive rebounds, defensive rebounds, turnovers, steals, blocks, personal fouls, (points * assists * rebounds)$^{1/3}$, and minutes per game. Regressing these 14 values together creates the adjusted plus/minus rating.

### Rating Clutch Performances

The analysis typically focuses on 40 minutes, rather than the standard game time of 48 minutes, because of the belief that the final minutes are completely different from the rest of the game (Ilardi, 2007). In instances where one team is ahead by several points, the lagging team may institute fouling in order to retrieve possession of the ball. This behavior tends to skew the statistics from normal game behavior. The final eight minutes of game time and any overtime, in cases where the scores of the two teams are within five points of one another, is referred to as the clutch. Some players tend to excel during this period, leading APBRmetricians to study the clutch performances of players. Some would argue that player contribution during the clutch is more important than during the rest of regulation play because the prospect of winning or losing hangs in the balance. Others point toward legends of the game who defined themselves with clutch performances (e.g., Bill Walton, Michael Jordan). Using PER during this period can generate new insights into offensive capability. To test the defensive match-up in man-to-man coverage, it assumed that one player's PER (i.e., looking at PERs of opposing positions) will be superior to that of his counterpart if a clutch performance is occurring. Although PER is limited to man-to-man coverage and cannot be used in other types of defenses such as zone (where the defensive player is confined to a specific area of space), this method can still provide valuable insight into player performance.

Another strategy for measuring clutch performance is to evaluate the performance of the team as a whole by using the plus/minus rating system and aggregating clutch points among the entire squad on the court during the last eight minutes of the game. This provides additional insight into a player's clutch abilities by showing both on-court and off-court results in terms of point contribution.

### *Emerging Research in Other Fields*

In addition to baseball, football, and basketball, many other sports are experiencing a statistical renaissance. Soccer is pioneering work in predicting the likelihood of injury based on biomedical monitoring as well as isolating the features that lead to tournament wins. NCAA college basketball researchers are predicting tournament matchups and victories with impressive accuracy. Teams in other sports, Olympic curling and cricket, are similarly gathering data on their opponents and analyzing the factors that contribute to winning.

## Soccer

Soccer attracts the most passionate fans worldwide. With such devotion to the sport, it is understandable that researchers and fans alike have an interest in predicting prestigious tournament outcomes. Although one study found that the amount of possession is an important factor in game outcomes (Papahristoulou, 2006), others have noted that country of origin and home field advantage are sizable factors in predicting team success (Barros & Leach, 2006). From Barros and Leach's study of the teams comprising the Union of European Football Associations (UEFA) Tournament, researchers used myriad factors—including league win/loss records, tournament win/loss records, shots, team record at home and on the road, and past tournament performance—to predict not only who the strongest teams will be, but also which team should win the tournament.

Another important contribution is the ability to forecast when a player may be experiencing the onset of athletic impairment through injury prediction. Often a player, regardless of the sport, will try to play in spite of the injury or performance degradation. AC Milan has piloted predictive software that monitors the workouts of their players (Flinders, 2002). This software compares an athlete's workout performance against a baseline; drops in performance may indicate that the player may be more susceptible to injury. Other biomedical methods employ a series of weighted variables including injury rate, odds of injury, and history of injury to compile a risk likelihood measure (Hopkins, Marshall, Quarrie, & Hume, 2007). Another method looked at 17 risk factors—such as previous injuries, playing characteristics, endurance, and game-time preparation—and found that inadequate warm-ups were a common factor in injury-related events (Dvorak, Junge, Chomiak, Graf-Baumann, Peterson, Rosch, et al., 2000).

## NCAA Basketball

College basketball has its own share of research. One notable figure is Jeff Sagarin, who publishes his basketball rating system based on a team's win/loss record and the strength of their schedule (*USA Today*, 2008). However, more research exists concerning the NCAA men's basketball tournament. Every March, college basketball enters into March Madness—a tournament where 64 Division I teams compete for the title of National Champion. Although the exact selection process for the 64 teams is not made public, a selection committee makes the determinations and the 64 teams are selected on a "dance card." Two researchers who were interested in this process developed a method of predicting the at-large bids with a 93.3 percent success rate over the past 14 years

(Coleman & Lynch, 2008a). This would seem to indicate that the selection committee uses similar techniques over time, even though the membership of the committee changes from year to year (SAS, 2005). The technique weights 42 pieces of information on each team—including its RPI ranking (or relative strength against other teams), win/loss record, and conference win/loss record—and forms a rank order score called the "dance card score" (Coleman & Lynch, 2001).

Once the teams have been selected, this same team of researchers uses a second algorithm, "Score Card," to predict the winners (Coleman & Lynch, 2008b). Using data from the 2007 tournament, their system was able to predict correctly the winners for 51 of the 64 games, an accuracy level of 79.7 percent. The Score Card algorithm is much simpler than its counterpart dance card because only four variables are necessary: the team's RPI value, RPI value of the team against non-conference opponents, whether the team won the conference title, and the number of wins in their previous ten games.

### NCAA Football

NCAA football also uses data mining and knowledge management techniques to rank collegiate teams. Because NCAA football does not enter into a tournament style of play as basketball does, disputes routinely break out regarding which two teams should compete for the National Championship. The Bowl Championship Series, or BCS, was created to address these problems. However, it became part of the controversy in 2004 when the University of Southern California (USC) was rated number one by the Associated Press poll and number three by the BCS. The BCS algorithm was subsequently rewritten.

The BCS is a fairness type algorithm in which various polls are taken into account and weighted accordingly. In particular, the BCS uses the Harris Interactive College Football poll, the Coaches poll (the rankings football coaches believe are fair) and computer polls including Jeff Sagarin's NCAA football poll at *USA Today* and the *Seattle Times*. Each team is assigned points based on their poll ranking in all of the component polls. Teams are then rank ordered based on their score.

### Olympic Curling

The curling event in the 1998 Winter Olympics might appear to be an unusual place to find data mining and knowledge management tools at work. During the eight days of curling competition at the Nagano Olympics, IBM was collecting data on players, strategy, the precise paths the stones took, and outcomes (Taggart, 1998). Although the collected data were not extensively used at the time, the potential exists to isolate a curling player's tendencies and weaknesses (Cox & Stasko, 2002).

## Cricket

The game of cricket has an extensive store of data recorded in the Wisden Cricketers' Almanack going back to 1864 (CricInfo, 2008). This archive has also been exploited using data mining and knowledge management tools with some success. A study of One Day Test matches found that a mix of left/right batsmen and a high runs-to-overs ratio were both highly correlated with winning (Allsopp & Clarke, 2004). The usage of alternating left- and right-handed batsmen is believed to keep the opposing team's bowlers out of their typical rhythm and render them less effective (Allsopp & Clarke, 2004). The high number of runs-to-overs ratio, (e.g., number of runs scored as a proportion to the number of offensive periods) indicated that a faster paced game (i.e., more runs) was also a factor in determining a winning team. These factors can be used to assess team effectiveness and also tournament play.

# Tools and Systems for Sports Data Mining and Knowledge Management

The adoption of systematic data mining and knowledge management tools has been limited largely to in-house analyses by sports organizations. However, simpler tools using the theories of Bill James and his contemporaries have been used by fantasy team managers and rotisserie leagues since before the *Moneyball* revolution. These individuals found success in using data mining and knowledge management tools leading to further development of measurement techniques and knowledge-based tools. There is a growing trend of third-party vendors using data mining and knowledge management tools to sell niche services to individuals and sporting organizations to isolate player tendencies, provide more in-depth scouting reports, and uncover fraudulent activity within the sports arena.

### Data Mining and Knowledge Management Tools

One aspect of this third-party development has been the design of tools that do not fit the traditional data mining mold. Incorporating elements of game footage that can be broken into component pieces and queried is one of the ways that companies such as Virtual Gold are filling the gap. Other distinctive methods include simple graphical analysis of existing statistics, allowing domain experts to identify more readily patterns within the data. Information visualization has long been recognized as an effective tool for knowledge management (Zhu & Chen, 2005).

### Advanced Scout

Advanced Scout was developed by IBM during the mid-1990s as a data mining and knowledge management program. Its purpose is to glean hidden patterns within NBA game data and provide insights to coaches and other officials. Advanced Scout collects not only the structured game-based statistics during play, but also unstructured multimedia footage. With the entire NBA league having access to Advanced Scout, coaches and players can use this tool to prepare for upcoming opponents and study their own game-level performance (Shulman, 1996).

The multimedia aspect of Advanced Scout functions by collecting raw game-time footage, processing and error-checking the content, and finally segmenting it into a series of time-stamped events such as shots, rebounds, and steals (Bhandari, Colet, Parker, Pines, Pratap, & Ramanujam, 1997). The processing and error-checking stage is a rule-based series of steps to verify the consistency and accuracy of the data. This includes removing impossible events (events tagged incorrectly), looking for missing events, and attributing plays to particular players. In cases where the rule-based strategy is unable to identify key elements, a domain-expert can use game footage to label the event manually.

Advanced Scout also possesses a knowledge management component called Attribute Focusing, where a particular attribute can be evaluated over the entire distribution of data and both textual and graphical descriptions of the anomalous subsets (i.e., those with a distinctly different statistical distribution) set aside for further analysis by players or coaches (Bhandari, 1995). Consider the following textual description from Advanced Scout:

> When Price was Point-Guard, J. Williams missed 0 percent (0) of his jump field-goal-attempts and made 100 percent (4) of his jump field-goal-attempts. The total number of such field-goal attempts was 4. This is a different pattern than the norm which shows that: Cavaliers players missed 50.70 percent of their total field-goal-attempts. Cavaliers players scored 49.30 percent of their total field-goal-attempts. (Bhandari et al., 1997, p. 123)

This description illustrates an easy to read analysis of the anomalous behavior of Williams when Mark Price was the Cavaliers point guard. Once a coach or player receives this information, it is up to him to determine why this is the case. With respect to this example, it was determined that when Price was double-teamed, he would pass the ball to Williams for wide-open jump shots. Aside from the anomaly detection facet of Attribute Focusing, Advanced Scout can also be queried to find relevant game-time events such as particular shots and rebounds. Players and coaches alike can use this information to hone skills and better understand player dynamics.

## Visualization Tools

Another way of finding interesting data is to do so graphically. SportsVis is a tool that allows users to view a plethora of data over a

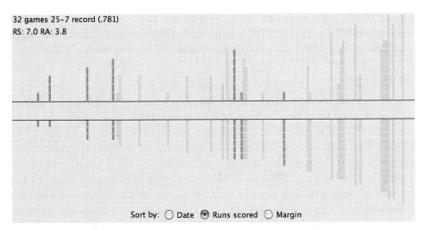

**Figure 3.3  Curt Schilling runs scored over 32 games (Cox & Stasko, 2002, online)**

selected period of time (Cox & Stasko, 2002). The data could include team runs over an entire season or player-specific data such as the runs scored off professional baseball pitcher Curt Schilling over a 32 game period, as shown in Figure 3.3.

This pictorial description may indicate trends or reveal potential problems such as injuries. Other interesting visualization techniques can be found in *Baseball Hacks*, where author Joseph Adler (2006) walks users through the process of using Excel and Access databases to view various baseball statistics. These techniques include batter spray diagrams, demonstrating that a hitter may favor hitting the ball to certain portions of the field under certain situations, and frequency distributions using many of the sabermetric statistics.

## Scouting Tools

Scouts used to rely on manual methods to keep track of player performance. Today that power is being placed in the hands of fans and next generation scouts. Game statistics can be captured on the fly and complete game reports and individual attributes can be analyzed for later player improvement.

### Digital Scout

Digital Scout is the electronic answer to collecting statistics or filling out score cards. Fans and sports organizations alike can use this software on a palmtop, laptop, or desktop machine to collect and analyze game statistics. The software can be adapted for all the major sports, including volleyball. Digital Scout also allows users to print box score results and create custom reports on particular attributes, such as baseball hits, basketball shots, and football formation strengths (Digital

Scout, 2008). This software has been found to be very useful and has been adopted by Baseball's Team USA (Petro, 2001), Little League Baseball (Petro, 2003), and basketball tournaments (Weeks, 2006).

## Inside Edge

Another scouting tool is Inside Edge, which was created by Randy Istre and Jay Donchetz in 1984 and provides pitch charting and hitting zone statistics for college and professional baseball teams (Inside Edge, 2008a). Coupled with a professional scouting department, Inside Edge has been used by many MLB ball clubs including all of the World Series champions between 1996 and 2001. The strength of Inside Edge lies in its easy to read scouting reports that employ a host of textual and graphical elements. Reports on strengths, weaknesses, and tendencies are all backed by statistical data. A spray chart for Rafael Furcal of the Atlanta Braves is shown in Figure 3.4. Note the density of infield hits shown for the second baseman.

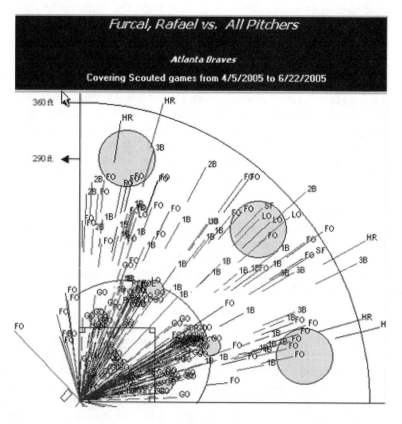

**Figure 3.4   Spray report of Rafael Furcal (Inside Edge, 2008b, online)**

Another more complete report is the Pitcher Postgame, as shown in Figure 3.5. From this output one can easily see the increase in the velocity of pitches as the game progresses (from 92 to 95 mph for fastballs) as well as pitch effectiveness (opposing left-handed batters, LHBs, perform poorly against Bartolo Colon's fastball pitch with a 0.167 batting average).

The graphical representation of pitcher performance in the strike zone, based on individual statistical performance, allows pitchers to grasp visually the areas of the strike zone in which they are most effective.

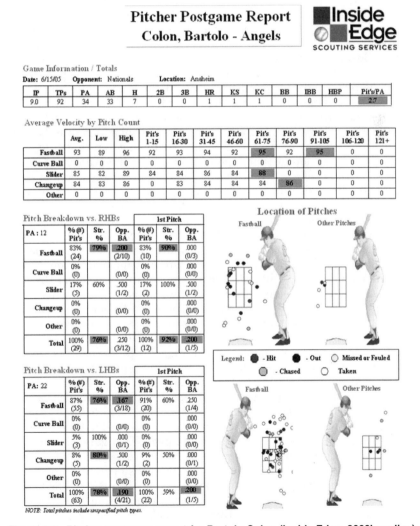

Figure 3.5   Pitcher postgame report for Bartolo Colon (Inside Edge, 2008b, online)

## Fraud Detection

Fraud in sports is nothing new. The 1919 White Sox's throwing of the World Series resulted in eight players being banned from organized baseball for life. Pete Rose's alleged betting on the team he was managing resulted in his being banned from the game. Recent scandals include the use of performance-enhancing drugs. Fraudulent activity in sports generally falls into one of three categories: poor player performance, a pattern of unusual calls from the referee, and lopsided wagering (Audi & Thompson, 2007).

Poor player performance, or point shaving, is one way game integrity can be compromised. This involves a player or group of players purposefully under-performing in order to affect the game's betting line. Before two teams physically meet for a match, sportsbooks set a betting line that will draw an equal dollar amount of wagers for the two teams. That way the losing side of the wager pays the winning side minus the sportsbook's commission. Should the line become unbalanced, the sportsbooks would be responsible for the difference and would either lose money or lose business. If one team is heavily favored, then the line will be more pronounced with one team having to achieve a larger victory in order to win the wager. Point shaving involves a player trying to manipulate the outcome of the game by not meeting the betting line. A recent study into NCAA basketball found that 1 percent of games involve some form of point shaving (Wolfers, 2006). Being able to discover instances of point shaving is extremely difficult (Dobra, Cargill, & Meyer, 1990), especially when there is no serial correlation in betting markets from game to game (Oorlog, 1995).

A pattern of unusual calls from the referee can also influence the game outcome. As with point shaving, compromised referees can manipulate the betting line. Referees have the power to make the game easier or harder for a team, thus influencing the betting line (Igloo Dreams, 2007). A recent example of this was in the summer of 2007 when NBA referee Tim Donaghy was investigated by the FBI for compromising games to pay off his gambling debts.

Both point shaving and questionable referee calls have the same goal in mind: making money. Thus, lopsided wagering can be used as an indicator of a potentially compromised game. This type of wagering could involve betting in excess of what is normally expected or betting heavily against the favorite. In one case, a gambler from Detroit made repeated bets against the University of Toledo versus Temple in football (Audi & Thompson, 2007). One of the wagers, $20,000, was four times greater than a typical large wager for that conference. This gambler correctly picked that Toledo would be unable to make the required number of points and suspicions were raised from sportsbook operators. In the following game, more atypical wagers began coming in against Toledo forcing one of the sportsbooks to cancel Toledo events from their boards; Sportsbooks make their money through evenly positioning the wagers, one side hands its money over to the other, minus a commission. When games are compromised and the wagers uneven, the sportsbook will lose money on the event. So it is in the sportsbooks' best interests to maintain integrity within sports and to set unbiased betting lines (Paul & Weinbach, 2005).

### Las Vegas Sports Consultants

Las Vegas Sports Consultants Inc. (LVSC) is one of the organizations that actively looks for fraudulent sports activity. This group sets betting lines for 90 percent of Las Vegas casinos. The LVSC statistically analyzes both betting lines and player performance, looking for any unusual activity. Player performance is judged on a letter-grade scale (i.e., A–F) and takes into account variables such as weather, luck, and player health (Audi & Thompson, 2007). Taken together, games are rated on a 15-point scale of seriousness. A game rated at four or five points may undergo an in-house review; eight to nine point games will involve contact with the responsible league. Leagues are similarly eager to use the services of LVSC to maintain game honesty. The LVSC counts several NCAA conferences, the NBA, NFL, and NHL, among its clients.

### Offshore Betting

Las Vegas Sportbooks are not the only gambling institutions with an interest in honest and fair sports events; offshore betting operations are starting to fill this role as well. One offshore gambling site, Betfair.com, has signed an agreement with UEFA to help monitor games for match-fixing, unusual results, or suspicious activity (Jimmy, 2007). Although it is difficult to detect all instances of gambler-tainted matches, these beginning steps can assure fans and bettors alike that vigilance is the order of the day and that player and referee activity is being scrutinized.

## Predictive Modeling for Sports and Gaming

The ability to predict events has long been a goal for both researchers and gamblers. This has led to many developments in the sports world, including statistical simulations and machine learning techniques. Using these approaches, trends in the data can be identified and exploited for personal, competitive, or economic advantage.

One area of predictive research that has been comprehensively explored is that of streaky performance. This phenomenon includes players with the supposed "hot-hand" effect, where performance is elevated above average for an extended period of time. Research on the hot-hand effect in basketball has argued that, if the hot-hand effect existed, making a shot would increase the probability of making another (Tversky & Gilovich, 2004). However, empirical study showed that the success of a shot was independent of previous shot outcomes. Baseball still has those who believe in streaky behavior. An interesting piece of research that sought to model streaky player performance found that certain players do exhibit significant streakiness, greater than chance would allow (Albert, 2008). This is where simulation and machine learning come into play.

## Statistical Simulations

Statistical simulations involve the imitation of game data using historical data as a reference. Once these imitation data have been constructed, they can be compared against actual game play to see the accuracy of the model's predictive power. Simulations can be performed for a wide variety of sports, including baseball, basketball, football, and hockey.

### Baseball

Baseball has long been an enthusiastic adopter of simulation, with fantasy and rotisserie leagues. Simulations can identify the optimal pinch hitters using Markov chains, where matrices of players, inning states (top or bottom of the inning), number of outs, and the on-base possibilities are all taken into account and multiplied by substitution matrices using pinch hitters (Hirotsu & Wright, 2003). This method can determine the optimal pattern of player substitutions given the prevailing situation.

A player-focused simulation method developed at Loyola Marymount uses historical player data to predict future home run totals by analyzing the frequency distributions of home runs, where top performances (i.e., record-breaking seasons) are considered "large" events and then relating those large event frequencies to the frequencies of smaller events (e.g., individual home runs) (Kelley, Mureika, & Phillips, 2006). To put it colloquially, if the ball is flying out of the park more than usual during a season, the potential exists for someone to have a terrific year, leading to the observation that such historical performances follow this frequency distribution pattern.

Another study that investigated the prediction of division winners, those who finish first within their respective divisions, used a two-stage Bayesian mode. This model was based on a team's relative strength, measured by winning percentage, batting averages, starting pitcher ERAs, and home field advantage (the belief that teams playing at home possess an advantage) (Yang & Swartz, 2004). This study simulated MLB baseball's entire 2001 season and the method was found to be surprisingly accurate in predicting five of the six division winners by July 30. Other Bayesian models such as predicting Cy Young winners (best pitcher in the league that season) have also produced results with similar accuracy (Smith, Lipscomb, & Simkins, 2007).

## B-BALL

B-Ball is a popular basketball simulator. It was developed by Bob Chaikin, a consultant to the Miami Heat (Solieman, 2006). The software uses historical data and APBRmetrics to simulate a game or an entire season. Developed for NBA coaches, scouts, and general managers, B-Ball can determine a team's optimum substitution pattern over the course of a season (e.g., the pattern that produces the most simulated wins), the effect a player trade may have on the team's performance, the effect of losing one or more players to injury, and the identification of the factors necessary to improve team performance (rebounds, assists, scoring, etc.).

### Other Sports Simulations

Other sports can benefit from using simulated data as well. In yacht racing, a variety of factors related to boat design can be tested and winning designs can be put into practice (Philpott, Henderson, & Teirney, 2004). In boxing, an array of both physical and psychological characteristics can be used to determine match winners 81 percent of the time (Lee, 1997).

Hockey game simulation research involves using hidden Markov chains to pattern expected outcomes based on where the puck is located and the team holding possession (Thomas, 2006).

Football games can be simulated using both regressive and autoregressive techniques to determine the factors most responsible for scoring events (Glickman & Stern, 1998; Willoughby, 1997) in addition to Bayesian learning (Stern, 1991). Soccer has taken advantage of simulating game play by using Monte Carlo methods (Koning, 2000; Rue & Salvensen, 2000).

Historical data can often provide clues as to future performance. If the right algorithms are used, historical data can yield accurate predictions.

## *Machine Learning*

In addition to statistical prediction, machine learning techniques are another means of providing sport-related predictions. Neural networks are one of the most popular machine learning approaches used in sports. Within neural networks, data sets are learned by the system and hidden trends in the data can be exploited for a competitive or financial advantage. Other machine learning techniques include genetic algorithms, the ID3 decision tree algorithm, and a regression-based variant of the Support Vector Machine (SVM) classifier called Support Vector Regression (SVR).

### Soccer

In a predictive study of Finland's soccer championships, Rotshtein, Posner, and Rakityanskaya (2005) compared the forecasting ability of both genetic algorithms and neural networks. They first set about classifying the wins into one of five categories: big loss, small loss, draw, small win, and big win, where a big loss would be in the range of a 3 to 5 point deficit and a small loss would be a 1 to 2 point deficit. From there, they fed past tournament data (the tournament win/loss performance of each team over the prior 10 years) into both a genetic algorithm and a neural network for training on data for the most recent seven years. The results showed that the neural network performed significantly better than the genetic algorithm in all five categories. Overall, the neural network had 86.9 percent accuracy in selecting winners compared to the genetic algorithm's 79.4 percent accuracy level. The other finding was that the neural network required less time for training, as the genetic algorithm was attempting to optimize the solution set and did not satisfy the study's stopping conditions.

### Greyhound and Thoroughbred Racing

Predictive algorithms can be applied to other sports, such as greyhound and thoroughbred racing. This generally involves machine learning techniques first to train the system on the various data components and second to feed new data and extract predictions from them.

Neural networks have been used with success in greyhound racing. Feeding a back-propagation neural network (BPNN) ten parameters that greyhound racing experts identified as the most important variables, Chen et al. evaluated simulation results in two ways: accuracy of predicting a winner and payout if a bet was placed on the predicted winner (Chen, Rinde, She, Sutjahjo, Sommer, & Neely, 1994). They found the BPNN operating with 20 percent accuracy and a $124.80 payout as compared to track experts who managed 18 percent accuracy and a payout loss of $67.60. Using the same data on the ID3 algorithm, Chen and colleagues found better accuracy, 34 percent, but lower payout (than BPNN), $69.20. They posited that the BPNN was better equipped to find and capitalize on the races with higher odds, which led to better payout in spite of lower accuracy.

A follow-up study that built upon this work examined the influence of predicting wins, quiniela (selecting the first two dogs to finish in any order) and exacta (selecting the first two dogs to finish in order). The researchers tested a 4-layer BPNN with 18 parameters instead of 10, and found similarly accurate results (24.9 percent win, 8.8 percent quiniela, 6.1 percent exacta) but differing payouts ($6.60 loss for win, $20.30 gain for quiniela, $114.10 gain for exacta) (Johansson & Sonstrod, 2003). It was suspected that the extra parameters used had a substantial impact on predicting long-shot races.

Another follow-up study to Chen and colleagues' pioneering work used the SVR machine learning algorithm instead of BPNN. This variant of SVM takes the hyperplane that is used to separate the classes maximally and performs regression estimates against it (Schumaker & Chen, 2008). This study was more interested in determining the factors that go into predicting long shots: It would vary its bets from just strong dogs (those that are predicted to finish first) to betting on all dogs (those that will finish above eighth place). From this simulation strategy and a study of all the exotic wagers, it was found that the system achieved a peak of 17.39 percent accuracy on superfecta box wagers (betting on the first four dogs in any order) when betting on dogs expected to finish between first and second place or better, as compared to random probability at 2.79 percent (Schumaker, 2007).

Predictive measures have also been applied to thoroughbred racing. A study of the factors that lead to racing success found that the motion of a two-year-old thoroughbred's foreleg had a direct relation to its future earnings potential (Seder & Vickery, 2005). Horses that were determined by veterinary experts as having good foreleg motion (e.g., a lack of extraneous activity), earned 83 percent more than those with bad foreleg motion. This has a direct impact on the racing industry, as thoroughbred investments can now be screened and thereby the chances of selecting a winning steed improved.

Another important factor in thoroughbred racing is the career length of the horse. Thoroughbreds with longer careers will understandably have better earning potential than those with shorter careers. Using simulation techniques on a pool of potential genetic parents, theoretical offspring can be modeled and their career lengths approximated (Burns, Enns, & Garrick, 2006). Using these techniques, thoroughbred owners can attempt to maximize the revenue potential of their investments.

## Multimedia and Video Analysis

Within recent years, video capture and the isolating of particular events for later analysis have become common. Baseball players can go to the locker room and study a pitcher's delivery or their own motions either to prepare before the game or to make adjustments during play (Lewis, 2003). Advanced Media is a leader in video content management (Ortiz, 2007). The company handles the digital content of Major League Baseball, including video streaming games to fans, and the innovative MLB Game Day tool, which allows fans to watch an abstraction of an actual game—the basic information without video. MLB's Advanced Media has proved such a success that substantial revenues are distributed to all 30 teams.

Basketball players can use similar video services to query the system for particular shots or defensive moves (Sandoval, 2006). Before this technology became available, teams would often have to wait several days to receive game footage; but now footage is almost instantaneously streamed to players, coaches, and scouts alike. The formerly tedious process of retrieving particular video sequences has been replaced, for example, by soccer queries such as "corner kicks resulting in a goal in the final two minutes," which will return the appropriate footage for immediate analysis.

## Searchable Video

The process of automated video searching may appear to be a daunting task. However, sports events generally follow a particular sequence of actions (Roach, Mason, Xu, & Stentiford, 2002). For example, when it comes to finding a particular baseball player's at-bat sequence, many facts about the game such as the batting order are known in advance. Similarly, when transitioning from one batter to the next, the first batter will either get on base or head for the dugout, both of which actions can be identified as separate events by a multimedia system and tagged. The process of retrieving specific video sequences then becomes a matter of querying the tagged material.

Tagging sports events in real-time can be done manually by domain experts or automatically by identifying a sequence of events (e.g., a basketball appearing near the rim can be tagged as a shot). Automatic tagging typically takes advantage of changes in the video, such as pans, zooms, fades, and cuts that signal when a new video segment has begun (Truong & Dorai, 2000).

Tags can be metadata or a simple descriptor of events. Consider the following metadata tagging using XML (Babaguchi, Ohara, & Ogura, 2007):

```
<AudioVisualSegment>
    <StructuralUnit>
        <Name>at-bat</Name>
    </StructuralUnit>
    <TextAnnotation>
        <FreeTextAnnotation>Arias</FreeTextAnnotation>
        <StructuredAnnotation>
            <Who>
                <Name>Arias</Name>
                <Name>Kudou</Name>
            </Who>
        </StructuredAnnotation>
        <KeywordAnnotation>
            <Keyword>SoloHomeRun</Keyword>
            <Keyword>OpenTheScoring</Keyword>
        </KeywordAnnotation>
    </TextAnnotation>
</AudioVisualSequence>
```

In this sequence, one can easily understand that the event is a solo home run by Arias, which led to the team's first score of the game.

A notable multimedia tool is SoccerQ, which allows users to store, manage, and retrieve soccer game video sequences (Chen, Shyu, & Zhao, 2005). This program supports basic queries such as: select video/shot/variable from search_space [where condition]. The "variable"

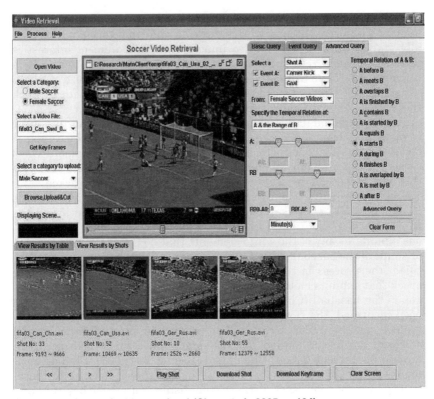

**Figure 3.6    SoccerQ video retrieval (Chen et al., 2005, p. 134)**

term can refer to a particular team, where "search_space" can be limited to certain sub-categories, such as men's or women's soccer. As an example, a query could be "select all corner kick shots from all female soccer videos where the corner kick resulted in a goal event occurring in 2 minutes," as shown in Figure 3.6.

From Figure 3.6, the left side of the SoccerQ application has only "female soccer" selected to limit the search space. The right side shows two events selected, "Corner Kick" and "Goal." To the far right, the temporal precedence of Event A (corner kick) starts Event B (goal) is selected. At the right center, 2 minutes is selected. The far bottom shows the four scenes that match the criteria.

The field of searchable sports video is fast developing. Tools that link multimedia retrieval to data mining are promising, but as yet few.

## *Motion Analysis*

Motion analysis in sports research is generally concerned with object tracking and trajectory. Baseball analyses consider not only pitching mechanics and ball trajectory but also the motion of batters as they approach different pitches. Object tracking and trajectory analysis usually start with a baseline video image where the item of interest is selected or some reference point of known size is recognized (e.g., a human can be of an estimated size for comparison with the size of a ball) (Chang & Lee, 1997). Once the system has been calibrated, it can track the motion of the intended target.

Another method in motion analysis is to break down videos into three component parts: the background or camera motion, the foreground object motion, and shot or scene changes (i.e., a different camera view) as a result of an external edit (Roach, Mason, & Pawlewski, 2001). In this way, videos can be segmented and foreground motion tracked.

One technique for identifying trajectory is to filter the video frames. Using baseball as an example, one filters the video to identify all the white objects in the frames, white being the color of the ball. From there, one eliminates any of the white elements that do not conform to the size or shape of the baseball. Now that a candidate list of balls has been identified, the process is repeated on the following frames and the white speck that exhibits motion between the pitcher's mound and the batter's box is the baseball (Chu, Wang, & Wu, 2006). Once the trajectory has been identified, the type of pitch can be extracted as well. Curve balls typically exhibit a high arcing motion in contrast to a slider with lateral or sharp downward motion. These systems have fairly high accuracy, around 90 percent (Chen, Chen, Tsai, Lee, & Yu, 2007). Similar techniques are being used in other sports, such as soccer, to track ball location, player location, shot distance, the distance a player has run, and ball speed (Bialik, 2007; TRACAB, 2007; Yow, Yeo, Yeung, & Liu, 1995); in football (Ding & Fan, 2007); and even tennis (Takagi and Hattori, 2003).

## Challenges and Future Directions

Several challenges within the domain of sports knowledge management and data mining need to be addressed. First, not many organizations are taking full advantage of advanced sports knowledge management and data mining techniques. Resistance to change is firmly ingrained in older sports, such as baseball. However, it should be realized that those who do embrace these sophisticated instruments generally perform better (e.g., Oakland Athletics, Toronto Blue Jays, Boston Red Sox, and Cleveland Indians).

Second, the clubs that have recognized the potential competitive advantages of knowledge management and data mining systems typically hold results in-house and do not share technologies or lessons learned with either their fans or peer organizations. Some sports organizations take a different approach and house all data in a central sport-related repository where individuals and teams all can have equal access. What is missing are hybrid approaches in which a significant amount of material is housed collectively and teams are still free to exploit any advantages found therein. We see the beginning of such a hybrid approach for various sport-related interest groups.

The Australian Institute of Sport (AIS) has unveiled two initiatives designed to house data from various sports (Lyons, 2005). The first is the creation of a digital repository to store various sport-related video, audio, and data files. This centralized repository will allow players and teams to access data. The second initiative provides data mining techniques to apply to the data repository in order to gather new insight into underlying patterns. We would suggest that further knowledge could be extracted from such a repository and that individual teams and players could take advantage by implementing their own proprietary tools in the pursuit of competitive advantage.

The full application of sports knowledge management and data mining is still in its infancy. Advances such as distributed Artificial Intelligence that uses multiple agents or new applications of existing algorithms borrowed from computer science or physics may revolutionize sports data mining. Although several pioneering organizations are beginning to harness their data through advanced statistical/predictive analyses, many are struggling with the prospect of adopting such systems, let alone using them to achieve a competitive edge. As larger market professional sports organizations increase payrolls to meet demands for talent, knowledge management and data mining can be leveraged by smaller market teams in an effort to remain competitive. This trend has begun to return competitive parity to sports leagues. It will not be long before an arms race of sorts develops, with two teams in action: the players on the field and the analysts in the back office.

# References

82games.com. (2008). *A visitor's guide to 82games.com*. Retrieved February 20, 2008, from 82games.com/newuser.htm

Ackoff, R. (1989). From data to wisdom. *Journal of Applied Systems Analysis, 16*, 3–9.

Adler, J. (2006). *Baseball hacks*. Beijing: O'Reilly.

Alavi, M., & Leidner, D. E. (2001). [Review of the book] *Knowledge management and knowledge management systems: Conceptual foundations and research issues. MIS Quarterly, 25*(1), 107–136.

Albert, J. (1997). *An introduction to sabermetrics*. Retrieved January 30, 2008, from www-math.bgsu.edu/~albert/papers/saber.html

Albert, J. (2008). Streaky hitting in baseball. *Journal of Quantitative Analysis in Sports, 4*(1). Retrieved November 1, 2008, from www.bepress.com/jqas/vol4/iss1/3

Allsopp, P. E., & Clarke, S. R. (2004). Rating teams and analysing outcomes in one-day and test cricket. *Journal of the Royal Statistical Society: Series A, 167*(4), 657–667.

Association for Professional Basketball Research. (2008). Apbr.Org. Retrieved February 16, 2008, from apbr.org.

Audi, T., & Thompson, A. (2007, October 3). Oddsmakers in Vegas play new sports role. *The Wall Street Journal*, A1.

Babaguchi, N., Ohara, J., & Ogura, T. (2007). Learning personal preference from viewer's operations for browsing and its application to baseball video retrieval and summarization. *IEEE Transactions on Multimedia*, *9*(5), 1016–1025.

Ballard, C. (2005, October). Measure of success. *Sports Illustrated*. Retrieved November 1, 2008, from vault.sportsillustrated.cnn.com/vault/article/magazine/MAG1105478/ index.htm

Barlas, I., Ginart, A., & Dorrity, J. (2005). Self-evolution in knowledgebases. *IEEE Aerospace and Electronics Systems and Instrumentation and Measurement Conference*, 325–331.

Barros, C. P., & Leach, S. (2006). Performance evaluation of the English premier football league with data envelopment analysis. *Applied Economics*, *38*(12), 1449–1458.

Baseball Info Solutions. (2003). *The Bill James handbook*. Chicago: ACTA Publications.

Baseball-Reference.com. (2008). *Baseball-reference*. Retrieved February 20, 2008, from www.baseball-reference.com

Beech, R. (2008). *NBA player shot zones*. Retrieved January 30, 2008, from www.82games.com/shotzones.htm

Benoit, G. (2002). Data mining. *Annual Review of Information Science and Technology*, *36*, 265–310.

Berry, S. (2005). Introduction to the methodologies and multiple sports articles. In J. Albert, J. Bennett, & J. Cochran (Eds.), *Anthology of statistics in sports* (pp. 205–208). Alexandria, VA: Cambridge University Press.

Bhandari, I. S. (1995). *Attribute focusing: Data mining for the layman* (Research Report RC 20136). Yorktown Heights, NY: IBM TJ Watson Research Center.

Bhandari, I. S., Colet, E., Parker, J., Pines, Z., Pratap, R., & Ramanujam, K. (1997). Advanced scout: Data mining and knowledge discovery in NBA data. *Data Mining and Knowledge Discovery*, *1*(1), 121–125.

Bialik, C. (2007, May 23). Tracking how far soccer players run. *The Wall Street Journal*. Retrieved November 1, 2008, from blogs.wsj.com/numbersguy/tracking-how-far-soccer-players-run-112

Bierly, P. E., Kessler, E. H., & Christensen, E. (2000). Organizational learning, knowledge and wisdom. *Journal of Organizational Change Management*, *13*(6), 595–618.

Birnbaum, P. (2008). *Sabermetrics*. Retrieved February 16, 2008, from philbirnbaum.com

Boisot, M., & Canals, A. (2004). Data, information and knowledge: Have we got it right? *Journal of Evolutionary Economics*, *14*(1), 43–67.

Burns, E., Enns, R., & Garrick, D. (2006). The effect of simulated censored data on estimates of heritability of longevity in the thoroughbred racing industry. *Genetic Molecular Research*, *5*(1), 7–15.

Carlisle, J. P. (2006). Escaping the veil of Maya: Wisdom and the organization. *39th Hawaii International Conference on System Sciences*, 162.

Carroll, B., Palmer, P., Thorn, J., & Pietrusza, D. (1998). *The hidden game of football: The next edition*. New York: Total Sports.

Chang, C.-W., & Lee, S.-Y. (1997). A video information system for sport motion analysis. *Journal of Visual Languages and Computing*, *8*(3), 265–287.

Chen, H. (2001). *Knowledge management systems: A text mining perspective.* Tucson: University of Arizona Department of Management Information Systems.

Chen, H. (2006). *Intelligence and security informatics for international security: Information sharing and data mining.* New York: Springer.

Chen, H., & Chau, M. (2004). Web mining: Machine learning for Web applications. *Annual Review of Information Science and Technology, 38,* 289–329.

Chen, H., Rinde, P., She, L., Sutjahjo, S., Sommer, C., & Neely, D. (1994). Expert prediction, symbolic learning, and neural networks: An experiment in greyhound racing. *IEEE Expert, 9*(6), 21–27.

Chen, H.-S., Chen, H.-T., Tsai, W., Lee, S., & Yu, J. (2007). Pitch by pitch extraction from single view baseball video sequences. *IEEE International Conference on Multimedia and Expo,* 1423–1426.

Chen, S.-C., Shyu, M.-L., & Zhao, N. (2005). An enhanced query model for soccer video retrieval using temporal relationships. *International Conference on Data Engineering,* 1133–1134.

Chu, W.-T., Wang, C.-W., & Wu, J. (2006). Extraction of baseball trajectory and physics-based validation for single-view baseball. *IEEE International Conference on Multimedia and Expo,* 1813–1816.

Cleveland, H. (1982). Information as a resource. *The Futurist, 16*(6), 34–39.

Coleman, J., & Lynch, A. (2001). Identifying the NCAA tournament "Dance card." *Interfaces, 31*(3), 76–86.

Coleman, J., & Lynch, A. (2008a). *Dance card rankings for 2008.* Retrieved February 19, 2008, from www.unf.edu/~jcoleman/dance.htm

Coleman, J., & Lynch, A. (2008b). *Score card rankings for 2008.* Retrieved January 30, 2008, from www.unf.edu/~jcoleman/score.htm

Cox, A., & Stasko, J. (2002). Sportsvis: Discovering meaning in sports statistics through information visualization. *IEEE Symposium on Information Visualization,* 114–115.

CricInfo. (2008). *Wisden.* Retrieved June 19, 2008, from content-www.cricinfo.com/wisden almanack/content/current/story/almanack

Davenport, T., & Prusak, L. (1998). *Working knowledge.* Cambridge, MA: Harvard Business School Press.

Digital Scout. (2008). *Digital scout.* Retrieved February 20, 2008, from www.digitals cout.com

Ding, Y., & Fan, G. (2007). Segmental hidden Markov models for view-based sport video analysis. *IEEE Conference on Computer Vision and Pattern Recognition,* 1–8.

Dobra, J., Cargill, T., & Meyer, R. (1990). Efficient markets for wagers: The case of professional basketball wagering. In B. Goff & R. Tollison (Eds.), *Sportometrics* (pp. 215–249). College Station: Texas A&M University Press.

Dong, D., & Calvo, R. (2007). Integrating data mining processes within the Web environment for the sports community. *IEEE International Conference on Integration Technology,* 658–662.

Dvorak, J., Junge, A., Chomiak, J., Graf-Baumann, T., Peterson, L., Rosch, D., et al. (2000). Risk factor analysis for injuries in football players: Possibilities for a prevention program. *American Journal of Sports Medicine, 28*(5), 69–74.

Fetter, H. (2003). *Taking on the Yankees: Winning and losing in the business of baseball 1903–2003.* New York: W. W. Norton.

Fieltz, L., & Scott, D. (2003). Prediction of physical performance using data mining. *Research Quarterly for Exercise and Sport, 74*(1), 1–25.

Flinders, K. (2002). *Football injuries are rocket science.* London: Vnunet.com.

Glickman, M., & Stern, H. (1998). A state-space model for national football league scores. *Journal of American Statistics Association, 93*, 25–35.

Hastie, T., Tibshirani, R., & Friedman, J. (2001). *The elements of statistical learning: Data mining, inference, and prediction.* New York: Springer-Verlag.

Hirotsu, N., & Wright, M. (2003). A Markov chain approach to optimal pinch hitting strategies in a designated hitter rule baseball game. *Journal of Operations Research, 46*(3), 353–371.

Hollinger, J. (2002). *Pro basketball prospectus: 2002 edition.* Dulles, VA: Brassey's.

Hopkins, W., Marshall, S., Quarrie, K., & Hume, P. (2007). Risk factors and risk statistics for sports injuries. *Clinical Journal of Sports Medicine, 17*(3), 208–210.

Igloo Dreams. (2007). *Data mining: The referees.* Retrieved February 6, 2008, from igloo dreams.blogspot.com/2007/08/data-mining-referees.html

Ilardi, S. (2007). Adjusted plus-minus: An idea whose time has come. Retrieved September 25, 2008 from www.82games.com/ilardi1.htm

Inside Edge. (2008a). *About us.* Retrieved February 20, 2008, from www.inside-edge.com/Aboutus.aspx

Inside Edge. (2008b). *Sample reports.* Retrieved February 20, 2008, from www.inside-edge.com/palmscout/PalmScout_packager.aspx

International Association for Sports Information. (2008). *About IASI.* Retrieved February 16, 2008, from www.iasi.org/.html

International Association on Computer Science in Sport. (2008). *IACSS— objectives.* Retrieved February 16, 2008, from www.iacss.org/index.php?id=31

James, B. (1979). *The Bill James baseball abstract.* Lawrence, KS: The author.

James, B. (1982). *The Bill James baseball abstract.* New York: Ballantine Books.

James, B., & Henzler, J. (2002). *Win shares.* Morton Grove, IL: STATS Publishing.

Jimmy, D. (2007). *Point-shaving ref: NBA betting scandal borne [sic] of hypocritical anti-betting stance.* Retrieved February 22, 2008, from jimmydsports.com/fantasy-sports-columns/nba-point-shaving-ref-july242007.aspx

Johansson, U., & Sonstrod, C. (2003). Neural networks mine for gold at the greyhound track. *International Joint Conference on Neural Networks,* 1798–1801.

Kelley, D., Mureika, J., & Phillips, J. (2006). *Predicting baseball home run records using exponential frequency distributions.* Retrieved January 15, 2008, from arxiv.org/abs/physics/0608228v1

Koning, R. (2000). Balance in competition in Dutch soccer. *The Statistician, 49*, 419–431.

Lahti, R., & Beyerlein, M. (2000). Knowledge transfer and management consulting: A look at the firm. *Business Horizons, 43*(1), 65–74.

Lee, C. (1997). *An empirical study of boxing match prediction using a logistic regression analysis.* Paper presented at the Section Statistics Sports, American Statistical Association, Joint Statistical Meeting, Anaheim, CA.

Levin, R., Mitchell, G., Volcker, P., & Will, G. (2000). *The report of the independent members of the Commissioner's Blue Ribbon Panel on Baseball Economics.* New York: Major League Baseball.

Lewis, M. (2003). *Moneyball: The Art of Winning an Unfair Game*. New York: Norton.

Lyons, K. (2005). Data mining and knowledge discovery. *Australian Sports Commission Journals*, *2*(4), 20.

*MIT Sloan Alumni Profile*. (2008). Daryl Morey, MBA '00. Retrieved January 30, 2008, from mitsloan.mit.edu/mba/alumni/morey.php

New York Times Staff. (2004). *The New York Times guide to essential knowledge: A desk reference for the curious mind*. New York: St. Martin's Press.

O'Reilly, N., & Knight, P. (2007). Knowledge management best practices in national sport organizations. *International Journal of Sport Management and Marketing*, *2*(3), 264–280.

Oliver, D. (2005). *Basketball on paper: Rules and tools for performance analysis*. Dulles, VA: Brassey's.

Oorlog, D. (1995). Serial correlation in the wagering market for professional basketball. *Quarterly Journal of Business and Economics*, *34*(2), 96–109.

Ortiz, J. L. (2007, December 5). MLB's online venture is big hit. *USA Today*, 5C.

Page, G. (2005). *Using box scores to determine a position's contribution to winning basketball games*. Provo, UT: Brigham Young University Department of Statistics.

Papahristoulou, C. (2006). *Team performance in UEFA champions league 2005–2006*. Munich Personal RePEc Archive (Paper No. 138). Munich, Germany: The Archive. Retrieved November 1, 2008, from mpra.ub.uni-muenchen.de/138

Paul, R., & Weinbach, A. (2005). Bettor misconceptions in the NBA: The overbetting of large favorites and the hot hand. *Journal of Sports Economics*, *6*(4), 390–400.

Pelton, D. (2005). *The Sonics play moneyball: Part one*. Retrieved January 30, 2008, from www.nba.com/sonics/news/moneyball050119.html

Petro, N. (2001). *Digital Scout to provide statistical analysis for USA baseball tournament*. Retrieved February 20, 2008, from www.digitalscout.com/news/news_tournament.php

Petro, N. (2003). *Digital Scout signs two-year agreement with little league baseball*. Retrieved February 20, 2008, from www.digitalscout.com/news/news_littleleague.php

Philpott, A., Henderson, S., & Teirney, D. (2004). A simulation model for predicting yacht match race outcomes. *Operations Research*, *52*(1), 1–16.

Piatetsky-Shapiro, G. (2008). *Difference between data mining and statistics*. Retrieved October 2, 2008, from www.kdnuggets.com/faq/difference-data-mining-statistics.html

Pro-Football-Reference.com. (2008). *Pro-football-reference*. Retrieved February 20, 2008, from www.pro-football-reference.com

Professional Football Researchers Association. (2008). *Welcome!!* Retrieved February 16, 2008, from www.profootballresearchers.org/index.htm

Roach, M., Mason, J., & Pawlewski, M. (2001). Video genre classification using dynamics. *IEEE International Conference on Acoustics, Speech, and Signal Processing*, 1557–1560.

Roach, M., Mason, J., Xu, L., & Stentiford, F. (2002). Recent trends in video analysis: A taxonomy of video classification problems. *International Conference on Internet and Multimedia Systems and Applications*, 348–354.

Rosenbaum, D. (2004). *Measuring how NBA players help their teams*. Retrieved January 30, 2008, from www.82games.com/comm30.htm

Rosenbaum, D. (2005, April 10). A statistical holy grail: The search for the winner within. *New York Times*. Retrieved November 1, 2008, from query.nytimes.com/gst/fullpage.htm l?res=9B05E4DE153EF933A25757C0A9639C8B63

Rotshtein, A., Posner, M., & Rakityanskaya, A. (2005). Football predictions based on a fuzzy model with genetic and neural tuning. *Cybernetics and Systems Analysis, 41*(4), 619–630.

Rue, H., & Salvensen, O. (2000). Prediction and retrospective analysis of soccer matches in a league. *The Statistician, 49*, 399–418.

Sandoval, G. (2006). *A video slam dunk for the NBA*. Retrieved January 30, 2008, from www.news.com/A-video-slam-dunk-for-the-NBA/2100-1008_3-6034908.html

SAS. (2005). *A method to March madness*. Retrieved January 30, 2008, from www.sas.com/news/feature/01mar05/dancecard.html

Schatz, A. (2006). *Pro football prospectus 2006: Statistics, analysis, and insight for the information age*. New York: Workman.

Schell, M. J. (1999). *Baseball's all-time best hitters: How statistics can level the playing field*. Princeton, NJ: Princeton University Press.

Schumaker, R. P. (2007). *Using SVM regression to predict greyhound races*. Paper presented at the Information Systems Department Research Seminar, Iona College, New Rochelle, NY.

Schumaker, R. P., & Chen, H. (2008). Evaluating a news-aware quantitative trader: The effects of momentum and contrarian stock selection strategies. *Journal of the American Society for Information Science and Technology, 59*(1), 1–9.

Seder, J., & Vickery, C. (2005). The relationship of subsequent racing performance to fore-leg flight patterns during race speed workouts of unraced 2-yr-old thoroughbred race-horses at auctions. *Journal of Equine Veterinary Science, 25*(12), 505–522.

Serenko, A., & Bontis, N. (2004). Meta-review of knowledge management and intellectual capital literature: Citation impact and research productivity rankings. *Knowledge and Process Management, 11*(3), 185–198.

Shulman, K. (1996). *Data mining in the backcourt: Advanced scout gives coaches an assist*. Retrieved February 6, 2008, from www.dciexpo.com/news/archives/scout.htm

Sinins, L. (2007). *Complete baseball encyclopedia* (version 8.0). Retrieved November 1, 2008, from www.baseball-encyclopedia.com

Smith, L., Lipscomb, B., & Simkins, A. (2007). Data mining in sports: Predicting Cy Young award winners. *Journal of Computing Sciences in Colleges, 22*(4), 115–121.

Society for American Baseball Research. (2008). *About SABR*. Retrieved February 16, 2008, from www.sabr.org/sabr.cfm?a=cms,c,110,39,156

Solieman, O. (2006). *Data mining in sports: A research overview*. Tucson: University of Arizona Department of Management Information Systems.

Stern, H. (1991). On probability of winning a football game. *Journal of American Statistics Association, 45*, 179–183.

Taggart, S. (1998). *Olympic data crunching*. Retrieved February 6, 2008, from www.wired.com/science/discoveries/news/1998/08/14175

Takagi, S., & Hattori, S. (2003). Sports video categorizing method using camera motion parameters. *International Conference on Multimedia and Expo*, Baltimore, MD, 461–464.

Thomas, A. (2006). The impact of puck possession and location on ice hockey strategy. *Journal of Quantitative Analysis in Sports*, 2(1). Retrieved November 1, 2008, from www.hockeyanalytics.com/Research_files/Impact%20of%20Puck%20Possession%20and %20Location%20on%20Strategy.pdf

Thorn, J., & Palmer, P. (1984). *The hidden game of baseball*. Garden City, NJ: Doubleday.

TRACAB. (2007). *Tracab in champions league*. Retrieved April 4, 2008, from www.tracab.com/news.asp?id=25

Truong, B. T., & Dorai, C. (2000). Automatic genre identification for content-based video categorization. *International Conference on Pattern Recognition*, Barcelona, Spain, 230–233.

Tversky, A., & Gilovich, T. (2004). The cold facts about the "hot hand" in basketball. In A. Tversky & E. Shafir (Eds.), *Preference, belief, and similarity: Selected writings* (pp. 257–266). Cambridge, MA: MIT Press.

USA Today. (2008, September 27). Jeff Sagarin NCAA basketball ratings. Retrieved September 27, 2008, from www.usatoday.com/sports/sagarin/bkt0708.htm

Voigt, D. (1969). America's first red scare: The Cincinnati Reds of 1869. *Ohio History*, 78, 13–24.

Weeks, C. (2006). Digital scout software powers the stats for the inaugural Arizona Cactus Classic. Retrieved February 20, 2008, from www.digitalscout.com/news/news_az_cactus_ classic_06.php

White, P. (2006, March 3). Scouts uncover a winning edge. *USA Today*, 7E.

Willoughby, K. (1997). Determinants of success in the CFL: A logistic regression analysis. *National Annual Meeting to the Decision Sciences Institute*, 1026–1028.

Wolfers, J. (2006). Point shaving: Corruption in NCAA basketball. *AEA Papers and Proceedings*, 96(2), 279–283.

Woolner, K. (2006). Why is Mario Mendoza so important? In J. Keri (Ed.), *Baseball between the numbers* (pp. 157–173). New York: Basic Books.

Yang, T. Y., & Swartz, T. (2004). A two-stage Bayesian model for predicting winners in major league baseball. *Journal of Data Science*, 2(1), 61–73.

Yow, D., Yeo, B.-L., Yeung, M., & Liu, B. (1995). Analysis and presentation of soccer highlights from digital video. *Asian Conference on Computer Vision*, Singapore, 499–503.

Zeleny, M. (1987). Management support systems: Towards integrated knowledge management. *Human Systems Management*, 7(1), 59–70.

Zhu, B., & Chen, H. (2005). Information visualization. *Annual Review of Information Science and Technology*, 39, 139–178.

Zimmerman, P. (1985). *The new thinking man's guide to pro football*. New York: Simon and Schuster.

# Fundamentals

# CHAPTER 4

# Philosophy and Information Studies

*Jonathan Furner*
*University of California, Los Angeles*

## Introduction

Several scholarly activities and practices coalesce at the intersection of, on one hand, the interdisciplinary field that is sometimes known as information studies, and on the other, the discipline of philosophy. This chapter aims to distinguish among some of these practices, to identify and review some of the most interesting products of those practices, and to point to ways of assessing the significance of those products—for information studies, for philosophy, and for our general understanding of the world.

In the first section following this introduction, an attempt is made to characterize, in a few paragraphs, the subject matter, methods, and goals of philosophy. Suffice it to say, any such attempt runs the risk of gross oversimplification as well as of inappropriate prioritization. That such an attempt be made is nevertheless a necessary adjunct to the short statement of scope that concludes this introduction. In succeeding sections, a distinction is drawn between philosophical questions asked *about* information studies and philosophical questions asked *in* information studies (cf. Floridi, 2002c, pp. 136–137) and the goals and subject matter of *philosophy of information studies* and *philosophy of information* are respectively described. This distinction is made in the spirit of conceptual clarity, rather than to reflect a division that is rigorously respected in actual scholarly practice: people interested in philosophy (or, indeed, in information studies) are likely to be interested in questions of both of these kinds. A concluding section poses questions about the reciprocal impact of each field.

Notwithstanding the publication in recent *ARIST* volumes of reviews of specific areas of philosophical interest (e.g., M. M. Smith [1997] on information ethics; Cornelius [2002] and Capurro & Hjørland [2003] on conceptions of information; Blair [2003] on information retrieval and the philosophy of language; Day [2005] on poststructuralism and information studies; and Fallis [2006] on social epistemology and information science), the present chapter is the first general review of its kind to appear in these pages. Consequently, its scope is not deliberately limited to a review of the work done in any particular time period; but an emphasis is nevertheless placed on contributions to the literature of the twenty-first century. No attempt has been made to be comprehensive in coverage; the bibliography is rather a selective one that represents the author's personal judgments as to which are some of the more interesting, illuminating, or insightful contributions. The bias is toward work that is informed by what is often characterized as the "analytic" tradition in western philosophy—with the caveat that it has become increasingly difficult and (some would say) in any case misguided and unhelpful to distinguish between "analytic" and "continental" philosophy as currently practiced (cf. Moran, 2008b, pp. 13–16). Otherwise, some additional care has been taken to avoid covering too much of the same ground as the recent *ARIST* chapters by David Blair and Don Fallis. A shorter, earlier version of some of this chapter's material appears as the entry on "Philosophy and the information sciences" in the *Encyclopedia of Library and Information Sciences* (Furner, in press b).

## Philosophy

The question "What is philosophy?" is a meta-question about philosophy that arises in philosophy of philosophy (a.k.a. *metaphilosophy*; see, e.g., Williamson, 2007). Answers of many different kinds have been proposed since the original identification of philosophy as a discrete field in the ancient era. These proposals may be categorized on the basis of the kinds of criteria on which each proposal distinguishes philosophy from other fields. For example, one proposal might be to distinguish philosophy from other fields by pointing to differences between the kinds of *phenomena* that form the subject matter of philosophy and those of other fields; another might point to differences in the kinds of *questions* that are asked in philosophy and in the other fields; another might point to differences in the kinds of *methods* that are used to answer the questions that arise in philosophy and in the other fields; yet another might point to differences in the kinds of *goals* or purposes that motivate people to engage in philosophy and in the other fields.

Different kinds of proposals have attracted varying levels of consensus at different times and in different places. It is important, yet difficult, to avoid misleading overgeneralization when characterizing the state of philosophy, even when the scope of the exercise is deliberately restricted to whatever is called "philosophy" by those who claim to practice it in a particular culture, such as the academy in the "western" world of the early twenty-first century. A simple caricature of the nature of philosophy at this point in its history might emphasize its concern with the most basic, fundamental, or foundational of phenomena (such as action, beauty, belief, being, causation, consciousness, evidence, existence, experience, goodness, identity, intentionality, knowledge, meaning, necessity, rationality, reality, representation, responsibility, rightness, thought, time, truth, value, and virtue); its concern to ask the most basic of questions (such as "What is $x$?," "How do we know that $p$?," and "Why ought we do $a$?"); its promotion of, and reliance upon, the most basic of methods in answering such questions (such as analysis of the very concepts that are used in expressing the questions, analysis of the logical form of arguments, and analysis of the mental processes by which we interpret our worlds); and its pursuit of the most basic of goals (such as happiness, justice, peace, authenticity, consistency, power, and an understanding of the meaning of life).

Such a caricature would fail to represent several significant respects in which metaphilosophy inspires ongoing debate: (1) the ways in which contemporary "western" philosophy is similar to and different from philosophy as practiced in "other" contemporary cultures and from philosophy as practiced in earlier eras; (2)

the ways in which philosophy as traditionally practiced may be infected with systemic biases deriving from its domination by old, white, middle-class, heterosexual males; (3) the ways in which twentieth-century "analytic" philosophy (also known, somewhat misleadingly, as Anglo-American philosophy) is similar to and different from twentieth-century "continental" philosophy (also known, again somewhat misleadingly, as European philosophy); (4) the ways in which several historically specific "turns" or transdisciplinary shifts in emphasis (such as "the cognitive turn," "the linguistic turn," "the pragmatic turn," "the cultural turn," "the naturalistic turn," and even [cf. Adams, 2003] "the informational turn") have affected different groups' understanding of the nature of inquiry in general and the proper purpose of philosophy in particular; (5) the extent to which philosophy is conceived as having a normative or prescriptive rather than merely descriptive purpose, on account of which conclusions are drawn about how the world *ought* to be, as well as or instead of about how the world *is*; (6) the extent to which philosophy is conceived as having an "applied" as well as a "pure" function, in which real-world decision making is informed by insights derived from philosophical analysis; (7) the ways in which different communities of philosophical practice emphasize different criteria for evaluating the results of philosophical analysis: e.g., truth, correspondence with external reality, internal coherence, power, utility for producing testable theory, utility for controlling future events, richness of coverage, simplicity, elegance; (8) the ways in which the methods and goals of philosophy are similar to and different from those of the empirical or natural sciences and the ways in which, historically, the pendulum of dominant opinion has swung between *rationalism* (very roughly, the view that a priori knowledge is possible) and *empiricism* (which denies the possibility of any kind of justification for knowledge other than experience); and (9) the ways in which philosophy may be divided into discrete branches or subfields.

At the most general level, it has become conventional to distinguish between, on one hand, a small number of long-standing subfields such as *metaphysics* (which focuses on questions to do with being and existence), *epistemology* (knowledge and belief), *ethics* (goodness), *aesthetics* (beauty), *phenomenology* (experience), and *philosophical logic* (truth) and on the other, a much larger number of subfields with (in most cases) shorter histories, whose names typically take the form "philosophy of *x*." There are branches of philosophy that are concerned with the fundamental ways in which human beings relate to their selves, to one another, and to their environments: *philosophy of mind, philosophy of language, philosophy of action*. And there are branches of philosophy that are concerned with particular intellectual, creative, spiritual, social, and physical pursuits: *philosophy of education, philosophy of art, philosophy of technology, philosophy of religion, political philosophy, philosophy of sport*. There are branches of philosophy that are concerned with particular disciplines, fields, professions, and practices: *philosophy of science* (including philosophy of physics, of mathematics, of psychology, of the social sciences, of information studies, etc.), *philosophy of history, philosophy of law*. And there are branches of philosophy concerned with particular phenomena: *philosophy of time, philosophy of race, philosophy of information*. Of course, the boundaries of these branches of philosophy are themselves social constructs that are historically and culturally specific (see, e.g., R. Collins, 1998). Such boundaries are entirely arbitrary and far from definite.

Insights derived from work that is characterized as contributing to any one branch are regularly applied in (or, just as regularly, contradicted by) work done in another.

In philosophy, the standard encyclopedic sources are the ten-volume *Routledge Encyclopedia of Philosophy* (Craig, 1998), and the continuously updated, online *Stanford Encyclopedia of Philosophy* (Zalta, 1997–). The standard bibliographic database is *The Philosopher's Index* (1967–). Leading publishers include Blackwell, Cambridge University Press, Oxford University Press, Routledge, and Springer. Useful series of collections of introductory essays to various branches of philosophy include the Blackwell Philosophy Guides, the Oxford Handbooks in Philosophy, and the Routledge Philosophy Companions. A recent volume in the third of these series, *The Routledge Companion to Twentieth Century Philosophy* (Moran, 2008a), is particularly useful for those wishing to become rapidly oriented to a wide range of branches of the field. *The Blackwell Guide to the Philosophy of Computing and Information* (Floridi, 2003a) is the standard introduction to philosophy of computing; Luciano Floridi's earlier monograph, *Philosophy and Computing* (Floridi, 1999b) covers similar ground. *The Handbook of Information and Computer Ethics* (Himma & Tavani, 2008) is a comprehensive introduction to information ethics. No single text provides a comprehensive overview of philosophical concerns in information studies, but monographs by Blair (2006), Budd (2001), Cornelius (1996), Day (2001), Dick (2002), Frohmann (2004), Hjørland (1997), Svenonius (2000), and Wilson (1968) serve as philosophically sophisticated introductions to their respective areas, as do the *ARIST* chapters by Blair (2003), Capurro and Hjørland (2003), Cornelius (2002), Day (2005), and Fallis (2006) mentioned earlier. *The Epistemological Lifeboat* (Hjørland & Nicolaisen, 2005) is a valuable Web-based resource. Special issues of information-studies journals devoted to philosophical themes include those guest edited by Ken Herold (2004) and by Birger Hjørland (2005b). Another important source is the special issue on "Social epistemology and information science" of *Social Epistemology*, guest edited by Don Fallis (2002).

The leading general journals in philosophy include *Analysis*, *Journal of Philosophy*, *Mind*, *Noûs*, *Philosophical Quarterly*, *Philosophical Review*, and *Philosophical Studies*. Other highly ranked philosophy journals that have published information-related papers include *Erkenntnis*, *Metaphilosophy*, *Minds and Machines*, and *Synthese*. There is no journal that is devoted exclusively to philosophy and information, but several titles cover areas of specialist interest, for example: *Episteme* and *Social Epistemology* in epistemology; *Applied Ontology* and *Axiomathes* in ontology; and *Ethics and Information Technology*, *International Review of Information Ethics*, *Journal of Information, Communication and Ethics in Society*, and *Journal of Information Ethics* in ethics. Journals in the information studies that carry philosophically informed articles on more than a very occasional basis include *Archival Science*, *Archivaria*, *Journal of the American Society for Information Science and Technology*, *Journal of Documentation*, *Library Quarterly*, and *Library Trends*. The Special Interest Group on the History and Foundations of Information Science (SIG/HFIS) of the American Society for Information Science and Technology (ASIST) regularly sponsors sessions of philosophical interest at annual meetings of ASIST, and the Conceptions of Library and

Information Science (CoLIS) conference series is similarly receptive to philosophically themed papers.

## Philosophy of Information Studies

We may distinguish questions that are raised *by* or *in* a discipline, field of inquiry, or group of fields—for example, philosophical questions raised in information studies—from questions that are *about* that field or group of fields—for example, philosophical questions raised about information studies (cf. Floridi, 2002c, pp. 136–137). Questions of the second kind might include questions about the subject matter of the field, its scope, its purposes and/or goals, its methods, its relationships to other fields and to other activities, and its usefulness, worth, or value. These are meta-questions about the field *as a field*: that is, questions that are raised by studies *of* the field, rather than by studies *in* the field.

Sometimes it is considered that it is worth keeping the second-order questions that relate to a given field separate from their first-order cousins and treating the second-order questions collectively as a discrete "meta-field." Sometimes such meta-questions are identified as being philosophical questions simply by virtue of their second-order status and the aggregate of such questions is what is construed as the philosophy of field *x*—even though it might be unclear as to what is strictly *philosophical* about any given meta-question. More commonly, however, the history, sociology, and politics of any given field *x* are identified as meta-fields that are distinguishable from the philosophy of field *x*. Meta-questions about the who, what, where, when, and why of information studies are the kinds of questions that are asked by sociologists, historians, and political theorists: What is the subject matter of information studies as it has been practiced at different points in history, and in different social contexts? What are the characteristics of the social groups whose members work on information studies? What motivations have people had for devoting time and other resources to the study of information and related phenomena? Why ought people to be interested in information?

*Philosophy of information studies* may then be distinguished from the history, sociology, and politics of information studies as the meta-field in which distinctively *philosophical* questions are posed (and philosophical answers attempted) *about* information studies *as a field*. We might ask, for example, what is the nature of information studies? What kinds of metatheoretical assumptions serve to orient and ground research in information studies (see, e.g., Bates, 2005b; Hjørland, 1998)? What kinds of methods are used in the pursuit of knowledge in information studies? In what essential respects does information studies differ from other areas of inquiry? The goals of philosophy of information studies may be stated as follows: (1) to locate and illuminate the position of information studies as an interdisciplinary field in the universe of inquiry: that is, to understand its role in interpreting and changing the world, its internal structure, and its relationships with other fields; (2) to provide justifications for any decision to engage in research in information studies; and (3) to provide orientations toward and directions for scholarly practice in information studies by identifying the kinds of problems that are most significant, the kinds of questions that are most relevant, the kinds of research methods that are most reliable, and the kinds of answers that are most acceptable.

## The Nature of Information Studies

On this basis, it might be argued that making any attempt to define a field—perhaps by specifying the necessary and sufficient conditions that must be satisfied before identifying any given work as a contribution to that field—would itself be to engage in philosophy. Maybe if we briefly indulge in an attempt to define information studies, it will become partially clear, through example, what philosophy of information studies is.

The goals of people engaged in any field of inquiry typically include not just fame, fortune, and happiness, but also the production of knowledge about (or, perhaps, the shedding of light on, or the making sense of) a particular part or aspect of the world. This is accomplished through the construction of theories and explanations, the interpretation of meanings and understandings, and the application of that knowledge in a way that changes the world for the better in some respect. What is the particular part or aspect of the world with which information studies, especially, is concerned? What is its subject matter? What is it *about*?

The simplest answer, of course, would be that information studies is about information. Perhaps this answer could be extended relatively uncontroversially to include, as the subject matter of information studies, certain phenomena that are thought to be closely related to information and the ways in which people interact with information and with information-related phenomena. Even taking this short step, however, would likely dismay some who would prefer to treat an emphasis on people's interactions with information as merely one example of a range of approaches that may possibly be taken to the study of information, each of which is associated with a number of presuppositions about the nature of information and its role in the world. In any case, such a barely extended answer would require augmentation in several respects before it could provide real insight into the nature of information studies. Helpful additions would include: (1) a definition of "information"; (2) enumeration and description of information-related phenomena, and indication of the respects in which and strengths with which they are related; and (3) enumeration and description of ways in which people interact with information and with information-related phenomena.

Some possible approaches to the task of defining "information" are reviewed in the section on Conceptions of Information. It should be clear that the aggregate scope of the group of fields collectively labeled "information studies" is very broad and that any precise delineation of that scope will depend partly on the sense in which "information" is understood. Different authors, working with different conceptions of information, continue to define the scope of information studies and/or the information sciences—and the relationships among that broad category and its various overlapping subfields and related professions, such as library and information science, archival studies, social informatics, information retrieval, knowledge organization, information management, documentation, librarianship, bibliography—in very different ways (see, e.g., Bates, 1999, 2007; Case, 2007; Cronin, 2008; Hjørland, 2000; Raber, 2003; Rayward, 1983; Vakkari & Cronin, 1992; Warner, 2001; and, applying a distinctive method, White & McCain, 1998).

Different kinds of phenomena may be considered to be "related" to information (howsoever information is defined) in different ways. Authors, indexers, and searchers are related to information in respect of their being agents that are involved in the creation, representation, and seeking of information resources; libraries, archives, and museums are related to information in respect of their being institutions that are involved in the preservation and provision of access to collections of information resources; aboutness (see, e.g., Wilson, 1968, pp. 69–92), relevance (see, e.g., Wilson, 1968, pp. 41–54), and work instantiation (see, e.g., Wilson, 1968, pp. 6–19) are related to information in respect of their being relations that structure networks of information resources; and so on. Lists of information-related phenomena are necessarily endless and of limited utility; what is potentially more interesting from a philosophical perspective is the structure of fundamental categories of phenomena (e.g., objects, properties, relations, agents) developed by the listmaker. Similarly, no list of the kinds of things that we might imagine people wanting to do to, with, or through information could be exhaustive, no matter what definition of information is accepted. But taxonomists of information-related actions or events commonly adopt a framework that is loosely based on the notion of an information life-cycle, whereby information resources or *documents* (if not the meanings attributed to those resources) are assumed to have a concrete existence in space-time, and to be subject to change and to processes of cause and effect (cf. Buckland, 1991, 1996). Within such a framework, distinctions are often made among the following categories of actions or events: production, creation, and generation; reproduction; preservation and storage; representation, description, cataloging, registration, and documentation; organization, arrangement, and classification; transfer, communication, retrieval, and provision of access; search, discovery, and seeking; evaluation and appraisal; use and application; and destruction.

There thus appears to be a reasonably stable consensus about the identity of those areas of concern that collectively form the central core of the field of information studies, in contrast to other areas that are typically recognized as more peripheral. One formulation of the goals of projects associated with this core might run as follows: (1) understanding the nature of information, of information-related phenomena, and of human–information interaction; (2) understanding the identities, purposes, motivations, intentions, needs, desires, and actions of people engaged in interaction with information; (3) designing and building systems, services, and structures that help people to meet their goals when interacting with information; and (4) developing and administering policies and institutions that enable and/or constrain people's interactions with information.

Within this framework, it is possible also to distinguish between a conception of information studies (or of some of its components) as itself essentially *descriptive*, devoted to the construction of theories that explain how information-related events actually do occur in the real world and why real people actually do act and think in the ways that they do, and a conception of the field as essentially prescriptive or *normative*, devoted to the specification of the ways in which things should happen and the ways in which people should act.

In pursuing projects of these kinds, scholars in information studies draw on theories and practices developed in many overlapping fields of inquiry, not least of which is philosophy and its various branches. Understandings of the nature of information and of information-related phenomena are constructed in the light of developments in metaphysics, epistemology, ethics, and logic, as well as in the humanistic fields of art theory, literary theory, semiotics, linguistics, and history.

Understandings of the activities of information users build on behavioral and cognitive models developed in the life sciences: biology, psychology, and cognitive science. Information systems design is informed by work done in engineering, technology, and design fields including computer science; information policy development and institutional management rely on insights generated by the social sciences and related applied fields: sociology, anthropology, political science, economics, public policy, business administration, and law. Notwithstanding one's readiness to accept the particular formulation of the core of information studies presented here, the general extent to which the content of information studies overlaps with that of "other" fields (if not the particular geography of any individual case of overlap) should be clear.

## Approaches to Philosophy of Information Studies

Just as we may distinguish approaches of two general kinds—descriptive and normative—taken by information-studies scholars, we may correspondingly distinguish two general approaches to philosophy of information studies. One is more descriptive, passive, and socio-historical: the emphasis is on giving an explanatory account of what scholars of information studies actually do, and what they have actually done, to locate themselves in the academic universe, justify their decisions, and orient their practices. Another flavor of philosophy of information studies is more prescriptive, active, normative, and (it might be argued) genuinely philosophical: The assumption is that philosophy of information studies should determine what information studies *should* be about, now and in the future.

Some of the questions asked in philosophy of information studies are questions about the *metaphysics* of information studies. For example: Does information studies propose a distinctive ontology, or a distinctive view of the kinds of things that exist in the world? The short answer here appears to be "No." Different theories in information studies, constructed by scholars working in different subfields, have different ontological commitments. (An ontological commitment is any acceptance, explicit or implicit, of a proposition that a given category of things exists.) Often, however, the precise nature of a theory's ontological commitments will not be made clear at the time of the theory's presentation, even though it may well be recognized that any evaluation of the theory will depend partly on an evaluation of those commitments.

Many of the philosophical questions that are asked about information studies are questions about the *epistemology* of information studies, in that they are motivated by a concern to understand the various kinds of knowledge that are produced, and the various processes by which knowledge is producible, by research in information studies. Even more specifically, such questions are normative, methodological questions about the ways in which research in information studies ought to be carried out—about how hypotheses should be tested, results interpreted, and theories constructed. Again, we might ask: Does information studies have a distinctive methodology, or a distinctive view of how knowledge claims might be generated and defended? And again the answer appears to be "No."

One common way of distinguishing among fields of inquiry or communities of inquirers is to locate the fields or communities somewhere between two opposite poles according to their methodological assumptions. Thomas Kuhn (1962), for instance, distinguishes between those academic communities whose members generally find themselves in agreement about the kinds of question that they ought to be asking (and about the kinds of method that they ought to be using to arrive at answers), and those preparadigmatic communities that presently lack such consensus (but that continue to strive toward it). Tony Becher (1994, p. 152) develops a two-dimensional model that distinguishes between the "hard pure" (natural sciences and mathematics), "hard applied" (science-based professions, such as engineering), "soft applied" (social professions, such as education and law), and "soft pure" (social sciences and humanities). In Becher's model and others like it, the hard–soft dimension roughly corresponds to a scientific–humanistic distinction. "Hard" fields are restricted in scope, studying a clearly delineated range of physical phenomena with a limited range of tried-and-tested methods, with the positivist goal of establishing general, deterministic laws of cause and effect that can each be used to explain the occurrence of large numbers of discrete events. Members of "hard" communities tend to make objectivist assumptions about the nature of reality, of truth, and of knowledge: scientists typically proceed, for example, on the basis that it is possible to acquire knowledge of "the" truth about "the" real world. "Soft" fields, in contrast, are more open to the study of complex, messy, lumpy problems, using a wide range of exploratory methods to come to interpretative understandings, both of the unique constellations of factors that produce particular events, and of the meanings those events have for individuals and for groups. Members of "soft" communities typically allow that our knowledge of the world (if not the world itself) is both socially constructed, in the sense that our beliefs are shaped not only by the ways in which we interpret others' beliefs about the world, and perspectival or relative, in the sense that the "truth" (or goodness) of our beliefs may be evaluated differently depending on the evaluator's present point of view.

Several communities of inquirers who have self-identified with a focus on information and information-related phenomena have a long tradition of soul-searching when it comes to locating themselves among the four quadrants of the Becherian model. Many commentators have drawn attention, in more or less exasperated tones, to the positivist nature of much of the research in the information sciences (see, e.g., Ellis, 1984; Harris, 1986), and such observations have usually been accompanied by impassioned calls for a "softening" (in the Becherian sense) of information research. These days, we are more likely to read about information studies' hospitality to a plurality of approaches, the implication being that each of its different subfields can be comfortably located in different quadrants, or even that each of its topics or problem sets can be explored using multiple methods originating in different quadrants. Marcia Bates (2005b), for instance, distinguishes nomothetic (hard, scientific, universal) from idiographic (soft, humanistic, particular) approaches and describes thirteen separate approaches to library and information science that can be located along the nomothetic–idiographic spectrum.

Humanistically oriented scholars are more likely to emphasize questions about the relations between information and the following (among other phenomena): conscious experience and the human condition; interpretation and sensemaking; meaning, language, and discourse; ideology, race, class, and gender; identity and diversity; preservation and cultural heritage; remembering and forgetting; narratives and stories; and aesthetic and moral value. Several attempts have been made to develop complete epistemological frameworks for such research, based variously on phenomenology (Budd, 2005), hermeneutics (Budd, 1995; Cornelius, 1996; Hansson, 2005), critical theory (Benoît, 2002; Day, 2001, 2005), feminist and standpoint epistemology (Olson, 1997; Trosow, 2001), and discourse analysis (Buschman, 2007; Frohmann, 2004; Radford, 2003). An understanding of philosophy of representation, itself a diffuse area, would appear to be a quality shared by proponents of the emergent view that information studies is properly about the relation between people and (not technology, nor even information, but) *reality* (see, e.g., Borgmann, 1999).

Comparative evaluation of the propriety of rival approaches to information studies is a difficult task. We could choose to ignore that the issue exists, or at least to deny that it is important (other than perhaps from a socio-historical perspective), given that the bundling up of questions and methods to form more-or-less distinct fields is essentially arbitrary and varies historically and culturally according to how phenomena are perceived rather than according to how the phenomena change in themselves. A more productive approach might be to focus on establishing the *values* or criteria (e.g., truth, power, utility) upon which different approaches may be evaluated and the methods by which an approach's "performance" against such criteria may be measured.

## *Floridi's PI*

Luciano Floridi is currently the most prolific and most widely celebrated scholar working on problems of philosophy and information. In his contribution to a 2002 special issue of the journal *Metaphilosophy* on "Cyberphilosophy: The Intersection of Philosophy and Computing," Floridi (2002c, pp. 123–124) provides a systematic description of the origins and characteristics of the field that he names "*philosophy of information* (PI)," summarizing work that he began for a lecture series on "Epistemology and Information Technology" in 1996–1997. In a companion piece (Floridi, 2004b, p. 559), he enumerates and categorizes eighteen "open problems" in PI, in the manner of David Hilbert's review in 1900 of twenty-three open problems in mathematics. Floridi expressly characterizes PI as a branch of philosophy that "combin[es] phenomenological and metatheoretical interests" (Floridi, 2002c, p. 136); and in that sense it should be regarded as encompassing *both* philosophy of information *and* philosophy of information studies as defined.

At first blush, Floridi's emphasis in the 2002 paper seems to be squarely on the intersection of philosophy and computing. The prehistory of PI is discussed with reference to its "earlier appearance" as philosophy of artificial intelligence (Floridi, 2002c, p. 126); and Floridi dates the emergence of PI as an "area of research" to the mid-1980s, when committees, conferences, and special issues of journals began to appear on "philosophy and computers," "computing and philosophy," and "computers and ethics" (p. 128). The "topics investigated by PI" at that time included "concepts or process[es] like algorithm, automatic control, complexity, computation, distributed network, dynamic system, implementation, information, feedback, and symbolic representation; phenomena such as human-computer interaction (HCI), computer-mediated communication (CMC), computer crimes, electronic communities, and digital art; disciplines like AI and Information Theory; issues like the nature of artificial agents, the definition of personal identity in a disembodied environment, and the nature of virtual realities; models like those provided by Turing machines, artificial neural networks, and artificial life systems" (p. 128). Floridi highlights the importance of "computational and information-theoretic research" in philosophy (p. 123), of the application of "information-theoretic and computational methodologies" to philosophical problems (p. 137), and of so-called computational/informational turns and shifts in philosophical paradigms (p. 125), citing Bynum and Moor's (1998) edited collection (on the new philosophical paradigm provided by computing) as evidence of "the emergence of PI as a new force" (Floridi, 2002c, p. 129). The relevance (actual or potential) of branches of information studies such as library and information science is not examined in detail here.

A perceived lack of engagement with prior work of philosophical significance in information studies, in contrast to a deep engagement with relevant work in computer science; a tendency to emphasize those potential applications of PI that relate to computation; and a choice of publication venues (notably *Metaphilosophy* and *Minds and Machines*) that are not especially well-read by information studies scholars may be factors contributing to the relative infrequency with which Floridi's work has been cited in the LIS literature. It would be a gross error, however, to conclude that Floridi's version of philosophy of information is somehow tangential to the primary concerns of information studies. Such a conclusion could be drawn only from a surface reading of the relevant works. Reasons (if any should yet be needed) for promoting awareness and appreciation of Floridi's PI within information studies include the following:

1. *PI's broadness of scope*. Floridi's conception of PI is such that it is concerned both with phenomenological examinations of "specific classes of first-order phenomena," such as information, and with metatheoretical analysis of "specific classes of second-order theoretical statements," such as the methodologies and theories developed in what Floridi (2002c, pp. 136–137) calls "ICS" (i.e., the "information and computational sciences." He defines PI precisely yet inclusively as "the philosophical field concerned with (a) the critical investigation of the conceptual nature and basic principles of information, including its dynamics, utilisation, and sciences, and (b) the elaboration and application of information-theoretic and computational methodologies to philosophical problems" (p. 137). By the "dynamics" of information, Floridi means to refer to "(i) *the constitution and modelling of information environments* ...; (ii) *information life cycles*, that is, the series of various stages in form and functional activity through which information can pass ...; and (iii) *computation*, both in the Turing-machine sense of *algorithmic processing* and in the wider sense of *information processing*" (p. 138, all emphases in original). Floridi (p. 138) notes that topics in the third of these categories have "attracted much philosophical attention in recent years," but points out that PI explicitly privileges information over computation as "the pivotal topic" of the new field: "PI treats computation as only one ... of the processes in which information can be involved. Thus, the field should be interpreted as a philosophy of information rather than just of computation, in the same sense in which epistemology is the philosophy of knowledge, not just of perception."

Moreover, Floridi recognizes that PI is characterized not just by a unique subject matter (which in itself would be sufficient to mark PI out as an autonomous field) but additionally by an innovative methodology that can be applied in many philosophical areas that amount to branches or subfields of PI. The methodology that Floridi has in mind is that comprising "information-theoretic and computational methods, concepts, tools, and techniques" (Floridi, 2002c, p. 139); some of the branches he lists as beneficiaries are information-theoretic semantics, information-theoretic epistemology, information-flow logic, situation logic, artificial life, cybernetics, game theory, formal ontology, virtual reality, computer and information ethics, and research on "psychological, anthropological, and social phenomena characterising the information society and human behavior in digital environments" (p. 139). It is this last group of areas of application that will be of most interest to library and information scientists. That Floridi casts the net much wider than this last group should not be taken to indicate a lack of relevance for information studies.

2. *PI's embeddedness in social theory.* Floridi sees PI as a timely response to the emergence of the information society—which he characterizes both as a stage in the development of society in which information resources and computer technologies are of "culturally defining" importance (Floridi, 2002c, p. 127) and a stage in a broader process of "semanticization" by which the mental world, that is, the "conceptual environment designed ... by the mind," becomes "*the* environment in which more and more people tend to live" (p. 131, emphasis in original). In this environment—the *infosphere*—ideas, values, emotions, and personal identities are reified as information objects that "quietly acquir[e] an ontological status comparable to that of ordinary things like clothes, cars, and buildings" (p. 131). Floridi's conception of the infosphere is itself an original contribution to our understanding of the development of the information society; and his realist view of information objects is a distinctive metaphysical position that has ramifications well beyond the traditional confines of metaphysics.

3. *PI's utility for ethical analysis.* Floridi is optimistic about the potential for PI to provide nothing less than the conceptual framework and roadmap that are required for making sense of contemporary society. He envisages PI being used to "guide the *purposeful* construction of our intellectual environment," thus enabling us "to make sense of the world and construct it *responsibly*" (both emphases added), ushering in a "new stage" in the ongoing process of semanticization (Floridi, 2002c, p. 141). The ethical concerns indicated here are echoed in Floridi's characterization of PI as a field that "is *prescriptive* about, and legislates on, what may count as information, and how information *should* be adequately created, processed, managed, and used" (p. 138, emphases added). In fact, Floridi has developed a sophisticated framework for applying the methods of PI to the analysis of problems in information ethics (see, e.g., Floridi, 1999a; 2002b; 2008a; 2008b).

4. *PI's foundational position at the heart of contemporary philosophy.* For Floridi (2002c, p. 141), the concept of information is as fundamental and important as the concepts of being, knowledge, truth, meaning, goodness, and even life itself. He traces the development of philosophers' interests in the modern period at first from metaphysics to epistemology (i.e., "from the nature of the knowable object to the epistemic relation between it and the knowing subject"), then from epistemology to philosophy of language and logic (i.e., to "the instruments whereby the

infosphere is managed"), and finally to philosophy of information (i.e., the infosphere's "very fabric and essence"). In this way, PI should thus be recognized as the *"philosophia prima"*—or, at the very least, "one of the most exciting and fruitful areas of philosophical research"—of our time (Floridi, 2002c, p. 141).

With regard to the second of the three categories of topics relating to information dynamics that he enumerates in his definition of PI, Floridi catalogs the phases that make up a "typical" information life cycle in a footnote (Floridi, 2002c, p. 138, note 11): "occurring (discovering, designing, authoring, etc.), processing and managing (collecting, validating, modifying, organising, indexing, classifying, filtering, updating, sorting, storing, networking, distributing, accessing, retrieving, transmitting, etc.), and using (monitoring, modelling, analysing, explaining, planning, forecasting, decision making, instructing, educating, learning, etc.)." The broad scope of this list closely matches that of descriptions of the concerns of information scientists and information management professionals. Floridi emphasizes the "natural relation" between PI and library and information science (LIS) in a pair of papers that attracted attention as much for their downgrading of the special relationship that, thanks to Jesse Shera's advocacy, LIS has enjoyed for so long with social epistemology, as they did for their promotion of PI as the most productive conceptual foundation for LIS (Floridi, 2002a, 2004a). It is to be hoped that projects in which PI is applied to topics in Floridi's broad category of information dynamics continue to attract willing volunteers. There is much to be done.

## Philosophy of Information

Some of the questions asked *in* information studies are philosophical questions, and it is in this sense that philosophy and information studies most clearly overlap. Encountering information studies for the first time, we might wonder, for example, what is this thing they call "information"? In what way does it exist? Of what fundamental category of things is it an instance? What are its properties? What are the necessary and the sufficient conditions some thing must satisfy for it to be counted as information?

The questions just listed are questions about a phenomenon that is clearly a core component of the subject matter of information studies; and they are questions that are commonly addressed both in introductory texts (e.g., Case, 2007) and in more advanced treatises (e.g., Bates, 2006) in information studies. Their philosophical nature (of which more will be said) and their focus on the phenomenon of information are individually necessary and jointly sufficient conditions of their also being considered part of the branch of philosophy known as *philosophy of information*; and they are questions that are commonly addressed both in introductory (e.g., Floridi, 2003b) and more advanced texts (e.g., Floridi, 2005a) in that field, too. The simple form of questions of this sort belies the difficulty of providing answers that survive all challenges. Similar kinds of questions may be asked about various information-related phenomena and about various kinds of human-information interaction.

## Conceptions of Information

Different conceptions of information have attracted consensus to different degrees in different communities; and there seem to be almost as many surveys and histories of those different conceptions—and of the relationship of conceptions of information to conceptions of data, knowledge, content, meaning, and wisdom—as there are interested parties (see, e.g., Capurro & Hjørland, 2003; A. Collins, 2007; Cornelius, 2002; Floridi, 2005b; Furner, 2004c; Machlup, 1983; Mingers, 1995; Rowley, 2007). The multiplicity of current conceptions partly reflects the lack of agreement among communities on a prioritization of the desiderata that a conception should satisfy. In particular, the outlook for those who would hold out for a "one size fits all," transdisciplinary definition of information is not promising (cf. Floridi, 2003b, pp. 40–42). It is possible, nevertheless, to identify a number of general categories or families of conceptions of information that have proven useful in relatively broad ranges of contexts.

1. A *semiotic* family. In conceptions in this group, distinctions are typically made on one hand among (a) real-world states, facts, or situations, (b) mental representations of those situations, and (c) linguistic expressions of those representations, and on the other between (a) tokens, and (b) types, of situations, representations, and expressions—forming a model (of the relationships between reality, thought, and language) of the kind roughly depicted in Figure 4.1 (Furner, 2004c). Each distinct conception of information in this family equates information with the content of a different cell in the model. For many, the crucial decision will be to choose between a conception of information-as-signal (Michael Buckland's [1991] "information-as-thing") and one of information-as-message (Buckland's "information-as-knowledge"), but conceptions of information as the very stuff of which real-world states are actually composed are not rare (cf. Bates, 2005a, 2006; Bawden, 2007; Floridi, 2003b, p. 44). *Objectivist* versions of the popular view of information-as-message assert that information resources (texts, sentences, words, characters, bits) "contain" information, that information resources "have" meanings, that "the" meaning of an information resource is discoverable by all, and that whether a given information resource has a given meaning is an objective matter. *Subjectivist* versions recognize, in contrast, that information resources do not "have" meanings, but that different meanings are assigned to the same resource by different people at different times, and that "the" conventional meaning of a given resource is a matter of intersubjective consensus (Hjørland, 1992, 2007).

| | Real-world situations: Information as reality | Mental representations: Information as message, meaning, knowledge, image | Linguistic expressions: Information as signal, vehicle, data, document, thing |
|---|---|---|---|
| Tokens/Particulars | States of affairs | Thoughts | Utterances |
| Types/Universals | | Propositions | Sentences |

Figure 4.1 **A semiotic model of the relationships between reality, thought, and language**

2. A *socio-cognitive* family. In conceptions in this group (see, e.g., Belkin, 1990; Boulding, 1956; Brookes, 1980; Pratt, 1977; Shera, 1970), the emphasis is on action and process, and especially on processes by which people become informed or inform others. Information is conceived either as the act that causes a change in a person's mental state, internal "knowledge structure," or "image" of the world, or as the event in which such change takes place. Different theorists have different views about the respective strengths of different kinds of influence on the effects of the informing act (Talja, Tuominen, & Savolainen, 2005). Adherents to a *physical*, systems-oriented paradigm that is based on a literal reading of Claude Shannon's (1948) mathematical theory of communication ascribe no role to the intentions of the individual person, whereas proponents of the *cognitive*, user-oriented viewpoint allow that the nature of the change wrought on an individual's mental model or image of the world by a given informative act depends at least in part on the prior state of that individual's model. The main theme of the *sociological*, community-oriented paradigm is that individuals' images of the world are shaped at least partly by those individuals' understandings of others' views; the *cultural*, discourse-oriented paradigm derives from a recognition that the world itself is socially con-structed in a strong sense, that is, as a direct result of people talking about it.

3. An *epistemic* family. Conceptions of information in this group are developed with the aim of providing an account of the properties that an information resource must have if the beliefs that are generated upon interpreting the content of that resource are seen to be justified. These are conceptions of information-as-*evidence* (see also Furner, 2004b). On the relatively few occasions on which information is taken seriously in the philosophical literature as a category to be distinguished care-fully from knowledge, it is typical for "information" to be equated roughly with "evidence." The primary question about information is understood as the question about what the evidence must be like to justify a given belief-that-*p*, and thus to qualify that belief (if it is one that is true) as knowledge. Theories of *informational semantics* (cf. Floridi, 2003b, pp. 53–56) have been developed that propose proba-bilistic methods of evaluating the informativeness of evidence as the degree to which it provides warrant or grounds for believing-that-*p*. Such methods typically involve calculating the unexpectedness of the observed evidence given the proba-bilities of occurrence of all the possible alternatives. In this sense, they derive from Shannon's (1948) mathematical theory of communication and form the core of the branch of philosophy of knowledge known as *information-theoretic epistemology* (Dretske, 1981; Harms, 1998).

## The Information-Theoretic Tradition

The *mathematical theory of communication* (MTC), popularized by Shannon's development of the work of Hartley and others (Hartley, 1928; see also Cherry, 1951), is sometimes known as *information theory*. It has become a commonplace remark that the use of this alternate name is unfortunate, given the lack of concern of MTC with information in any ordinary sense of the word. The problem that the architects of MTC hoped to solve is an *engineering* problem: how to design com-munication systems that allow data to be transferred with maximal efficiency across channels of finite capacity. MTC emerged as an outcome of the application of probability theory in this domain, providing a method of calculating the average *informativeness* (or "amount of information") of messages sent and received across a particular channel. The informativeness of a message is the extent to which other possible messages are eliminated (i.e., the extent to which "uncertainty is reduced") in the process of message selection; it is measured in binary units (i.e., bits): the larger the number $n$ of messages in the population $s$ from which individual selections are made, the larger the average value of informativeness $I(s) = \log_2 n$ of those selections (cf. Dretske, 1981, pp. 3–26; Floridi, 2003b, pp. 46–51).

MTC in its classical form has nothing to say about the nature of messages or about the nature of the data that make them up, let alone about the nature of information. It identifies and accounts for no properties of data or of information, beyond that of informativeness in one distinctively quantifiable sense. Since the publication of Shannon's original presentation of MTC in 1948, many attempts have been made to build theories that provide authentic analyses of *information* on the foundations he supplied. In some cases (e.g., Dretske, 1981), the probabilistic approach distinctive to MTC is preserved, to a greater or lesser degree; in others (e.g., Israel & Perry, 1990), alternative frameworks derived from philosophical logic have been applied. Following the lead of Bar-Hillel and Carnap (1953), these are sometimes known as theories of *semantic information*, in virtue of the nature of the distinction that their advocates commonly draw between, on one hand, containers, carriers, or vehicles of meaning, and on the other, the meaning(s) borne. When considered in isolation, the vehicles of meaning—for example, sequences of sounds, strings of characters, patterns of differences—are merely *data*; it is only when such signals are considered as phenomena that have meaning for their creators and/or for their audiences that they are considered as information.

As a rhetorical device in his book *Knowledge and the Flow of Information* (Dretske, 1981; summarized with peer commentary, Dretske, Alston, Arbib, Armstrong, Barwise, Bogdan, et al., 1983), Fred Dretske initially adopts the conceptual framework of MTC, complete with its talk of signals, channels, noise, and entropy. Dretske and others have pointed toward a plausible merger of such a framework with that of philosophy of language, where the focus is on such things as utterances, sentences, propositions, and meaning. It remains to be seen precisely how such a combined framework may be reconciled with the traditional concern of document-oriented information studies involving works, texts, editions, and copies (see, e.g., Svenonius, 2000, pp. 31–51; Wilson, 1968, pp. 6–19).

Imagine it is June 1984, and the Boston Celtics have just beaten the Los Angeles Lakers in Game 7 of the National Basketball Association Finals. Bob missed the game and wants to know which team won. Andy says to Bob "The Celtics are champions." The Celtics' winning the championship is a real-world event that is both datable (in time) and locatable (in space), as is Andy's utterance of the sentence "The Celtics are champions." Many philosophers of logic and language find it useful to treat utterances not only as tokens of sentences but also as tokens of propositions (or, at least, to distinguish between an utterance's syntactic form and its semantic content). Andy's utterance, in this particular context, of the sentence $s$ "The Celtics are champions" is also an expression of the proposition $p$ that the Celtics are champions. Proposition $p$ is a proposition about what is actually the case—about the state of affairs that actually obtains—in the real world. Does proposition $p$ itself also exist in the real world? Those philosophers who are realists about abstract objects such as propositions are wont to assert that propositions (rather than, e.g., sentences) are the things that have truth value. According to one theory of truth, a proposition is true if it corresponds to reality. If it is actually the case that the Celtics are champions, then proposition $p$, that the Celtics are champions, is true.

Is semantic or propositional content the same kind of thing as meaning, and/or indeed the same kind of thing as information? Given that any particular sentence can be uttered at any particular time by any particular speaker with any of a variety of different propositional intentions, many theorists of meaning follow Grice (1968) in distinguishing between the occasion meaning (a.k.a. speaker meaning) of an individual utterance and the timeless meaning (a.k.a. conventional meaning) of a sentence or utterance-type. Dretske's position is to equate semantic content with occasion meaning but to distinguish between meaning and information. For Dretske, information is content of a certain kind—viz., that content which is true. Suppose that Andy has not watched the game, has misheard the result, and, instead of telling Bob that the Celtics have won, says "The Lakers are champions." Andy believes that the proposition he intends to express is true, but in fact it is false. In Dretske's view, Andy fails to inform Bob that the Lakers are champions, even if Bob takes Andy at his word, simply because it is not the case that the Lakers are champions. For Dretske, the proposition $q$, that the Lakers are champions, is not information.

The theoretical ramifications of Dretske's development of this distinctive conception of information are wide-ranging, substantial, and complex; his project is a major contribution to several of the classical branches of philosophy, including philosophy of mind and epistemology, in particular the analysis of knowledge. In one traditional account, knowledge is analyzed as justified true belief: $S$ knows that $p$ if and only if (1) $p$ is true, (2) $S$ believes that $p$, and (3) $S$ is justified in believing that $p$ (see, e.g., Steup, 2006). The challenges faced by this conventional analysis include certain problematic scenarios in which the three conditions of truth, belief, and justification appear to be insufficient (Gettier, 1963). Dretske's response to such challenges is an instance of an alternative approach to the analysis of knowledge known as *reliabilism*. In the reliabilist's view, true beliefs are counted as knowledge if and only if they are produced by a reliable cognitive process (i.e., by a cognitive process—sense experience, say—that has consistently produced knowledge in the past). Dretske's reliabilism is encapsulated in his analysis of knowledge as information-caused belief: $S$ knows that $p$ if and only if $S$'s belief that $p$ is caused by the information that $p$ (Dretske, 1981, p. 86).

Notwithstanding the considerable influence of Dretske's information-theoretic analysis of knowledge on epistemology, we may wish to ask: In what ways are Dretske's conception of information, and information-theoretic analyses of knowledge in general, useful for information studies? For example, if such a conception or analysis were accepted, could our understanding regarding how information services might satisfy the desires of their users be improved (cf. Fallis, 2006, pp. 493–494)? Pending further examination, it should be noted that Dretskean conceptions of information are decidedly not the norm in information studies.

Floridi (2003b, pp. 42–46) clarifies this by developing a hierarchy of categories of phenomena that includes (1) data; (2) (semantic) information, a.k.a. (semantic) content—that is, *meaningful*, well-formed data; and (3) factual information, a.k.a.

"epistemically-oriented" semantic information—that is, *truthful*, meaningful, well-formed data. Floridi's "general" definition of information (GDI) specifies three conditions (data-ness, well-formedness, and meaningfulness) that must be satisfied for an *x* to qualify as an instance of information; his "specific" definition of information (SDI) adds a fourth (truthfulness). Floridi (2003b, p. 45) cites Dretske (1981, p. 45) and Grice (1989, p. 371) as authoritative advocates of the "specific" definition and of the concomitant view that what is called "false [i.e., nonfactual] information" is in fact not information (in the same way that a rubber duck is not a duck). He notes that the general sense in which information is understood simply as semantic content is "trivial" (Floridi, 2003b, p. 46) and that, in the context of communication, "the most important type of semantic information is *factual information*" (p. 45, emphasis in original). Floridi (p. 42) asserts that the general definition has nonetheless become the "operational standard" in fields such as information science.

Why should this be so? For what reasons have scholars working in information studies come to adopt the general definition rather than the specific definition? Floridi points in the direction of a possible answer with his identification, among a set of "very important" concepts of information that he elects not to consider further, of "*pragmatic information* ... [which] includes *useful information*, a key concept in ... information management theory, ... where characteristics such as relevance, timeliness, updatedness, cost, significance, and so forth are crucial" (Floridi, 2003b, p. 57). This list of values—alternatives, in a way, to truth—serves to remind us that, even though advocates within information science of the conception of information characterized by Floridi as the GDI are prone to making statements that appear to be versions of the Dretske-esque slogan "Information is what is informative" (i.e., what yields or causes knowledge), their conceptions of informativeness and knowledge itself are quite different from those traditionally acceptable to epistemologists (cf. Capurro & Hjørland, 2003, p. 350; Dretske, 1981, p. 44). Information scientists in the socio-cognitive tradition tend to be interested in changes in personal cognitive structures or "images" of the world, in how such changes are produced, and in how personal needs and desires are thus met, rather than in matters of "truth."

## Bates's Evolutionary Model of Information

One of the most controversial of recent contributions to the literature on conceptions of information is Marcia Bates's (2005a, 2006) development of an "evolutionary" framework for the analysis of information and related concepts. This framework is based on Bates's interpretations of work done in the field of evolutionary psychology, which provides "an understanding of evolution and its impact on the cognitive, linguistic and social structures of human beings" (Bates, 2005a, "Objectives of this essay") and of Susantha Goonatilake's (1991) model of "lineages" of information flow (see also Bates, 2006).

Bates's framework includes a complex taxonomy of different "forms" (i.e., kinds) of information, in which she distinguishes (1) between "represented" information—which is generated by (or at least "associated with") living organisms, and which exists either in "encoded" form as sequences of symbols or in "embodied" form as the physical manifestation of such sequences—and other kinds of information existing in the natural world; (2) between "genetic" information, "neural-cultural" information that is generated by humans and animals, and "exosomatic" information that is stored outside people's bodies; (3) within the class of embodied, neural-cultural information, between "experienced," "enacted," and "expressed" information; and (4) within the class of exosomatic information, between "embedded" and "recorded" information (Bates, 2006, pp. 1035–1036). Some of the things that Bates calls information are: every individual person's internal experience and memory of his or her life, thoughts, and activities (experienced information); every person's actions in the external world (enacted information); every person's acts of communication with others (expressed information, "technically a subset of enacted information" [Bates, 2006, p. 1039]); all physical evidence of the actions of people in the world, such as footprints and vases (embedded information); and all durable results of people's acts of communication, such as pictures and writings (recorded information).

Bates (2005a, "Is the definition too inclusive?") admits that, in the early stages of the peer-review process, her model drew criticism in part for its all-encompassing ambitions. Reviewers found it difficult to see the value of a model that seems to include so much of the universe in a category called "information" and may additionally have been distracted by Bates's accompanying presentation of a separate framework for distinguishing between information, data, meaning, and knowledge. Bates distinguishes between what she calls "Information 1," "Information 2," "Knowledge," "Data 1," and "Data 2," providing definitions of each as follows: Information 1: "the pattern of organization of matter and energy"; Information 2: "some pattern of organization of matter and energy given meaning by a living being"; Knowledge: "information given meaning and integrated with other contents of understanding" (Bates, 2006, p. 1042); Data 1: "that portion of the entire information environment available to a sensing organism that is taken in, or processed, by that organism"; and Data 2: "information selected or generated by human beings for social purposes" (Bates, 2005a, "Finally, what are data?"). Bates's intention seems to be that Information 2 is a subset of Information 1; that Knowledge is a subset of Information 2; that Data 1 is another subset of Information 1, overlapping with Information 1; and that Data 2 is another subset of Information 2, overlapping with Knowledge. One thing that is clear is that any instance of any one of the latter four categories should simultaneously be understood as an instance of Information 1. All information is Information 1; some Information is Knowledge, some is Data 1, and so on.

Bates's definition of Information 1 is derived from Edwin Parker (1974, p. 10): "Information is the pattern of organization of matter and energy." She takes several opportunities to point out that this definition should *not* be taken to imply that instances of information are composed of matter or of energy, but rather that they are made up of something else. She claims that information "resides in" physical reality, but that "to say this … is not to say that information is *identical* with the physical materials or waves that make up the pattern of organization. *The information is the pattern of organization of the material, not the material itself*" (Bates, 2005a, emphases in original). For Bates, instances of information are instances of "pattern of organization," which is a *property* of matter and of energy: "Information … is the pattern of organization *to be found in* any matter or energy" (Bates, 2005a, emphasis added). She cites Wiener (1961, p. 132) as an authority: "Information is information, not matter or energy."

In lieu of a formal definition of "pattern of organization," Bates uses a number of semi-synonymic and related terms to build a picture of what she is referring to: differentiation, configuration, arrangement, regularity, bunching, and clustering. She also gives numerous examples of instances of this property, including the following: the particular pattern exhibited by the set of ice crystals that have settled on a particular window pane; the particular pattern exhibited by the series of actions taken by a particular teenager; the particular pattern exhibited by the set of atoms that make up a particular chair; and the particular pattern exhibited by the set of objects that a particular person calls "chairs," i.e., that we identify as instances of the class "chair." Here Bates (2005a, "*Whose* pattern of organization?") is recognizing that the universe is not a uniform, undifferentiated, indivisible monad. In any slice of space-time, there are "differences, distinctions, differentiations." It is possible to differentiate, to distinguish between, any one member of any set of objects or events (e.g., the set of ice crystals on window pane $x$, the set of teenager $y$'s actions, the set of chair $z$'s atoms, the set of things that person $a$ calls chairs) and the background context (i.e., the rest of the universe). Differences of this kind are what constitute the particular "pattern of organization" of any set of entities. And it is the ability of people (and animals) to recognize the existence of these differences in their environment, to recognize the patterns formed by these differences, and to recognize the meta-patterns formed by similarities and differences among patterns, that allows people (and animals) to form concepts—to individuate, or identify as discrete individuals, particular sets of objects and events (such as the set of atoms making up chair $z$) and to categorize objects and events as instances of classes (such as the class "chair").

It is clear that Bates is a realist about instances of Information 1. That is, she believes that the existence of instances of Information 1 is not dependent on the mental activity of any person, that any proposition of the form "Phenomenon $x$ is an instance of Information 1" has the truth value that it has (i.e., is true or false) as a matter of objective fact and that (given an appropriate means of obtaining knowledge about matters of objective fact) it is logically possible to obtain an answer to any question of the form "Is phenomenon $x$ an instance of Information 1?" by accessing the facts of the matter. It is almost as clear that Bates is a realist about instances of Information 2, in the same senses as previously outlined. Whether an instance of Information 1 has been "given meaning by a living being" is also, for Bates, a matter of objective fact. This is not to say, however, that any proposition of the form "Instance-of-Information-2 $x$ has particular meaning $y$" is true or false as a matter of objective fact, or that there are any "facts" to access when attempting to answer any question of the form "Does instance-of-Information-2 $x$ have particular meaning $y$?" This is because the attribution of meaning to instances of Information 1 is a mental act undertaken by individual persons. The existence of a relationship between any given instance of Information 1 and any given meaning is dependent on the mental activity of a given person; we can know about it only by asking that person. The existence of instances of Information 2 is not in question; what is at issue here is whether a given instance of Information 2 has a given property (or, to put it another way, whether it is a member of a given class). Because the semantic properties of instances of Information 2 (or the semantic classes to which they are perceived to belong) are matters of subjective belief rather than of objective fact, one rough-and-ready way of capturing the distinction between the metaphysical status of Information 1 and that of Information 2 is to refer to Information 1 as "objective" and Information 2 as "subjective." Hjørland (2007) takes Bates to task for, as he sees it, her failure to clarify this distinction; in her rejoinder, Bates (2008) heads off any further misinterpretation of her views.

The central distinction that Bates makes between her "Information 1" and "Information 2" is what one is left with, once one strips away the layers of the taxonomy of "forms" of information. At this foundational level, one is struck by the concordance between Bates's fundamental understanding of information and the idea encapsulated in Floridi's specification of the "general" definition of information that he sees as characteristic of the information sciences. Given Bates's idiosyncratic usage of "Information 1" and "Information 2," however, there is a possibility that the similarity may be obscured by discrepancies in terminology. We may recall Floridi's general definition of information as meaningful, well-formed data. Floridi's (2003b, p. 43) conception of a datum—a "lack of uniformity" or a difference—corresponds roughly to Bates's conception of Information 1; his conception of information ("data + meaning"; Floridi, 2003b, p. 42) corresponds roughly to Bates's Information 2. In this sense, Bates's model seems not to break new ground.

What is more compelling is the creativity with which Bates grounds a theory of living organisms' responses to the environment in information-scientific terms. Bates's model amounts to a theory of concept formation; ideally, it should be evaluated from the perspective of cognitive psychology (or, given Bates's further claims about the evolutionary development of concept-forming abilities, from the perspective of evolutionary psychology). One element of the model that, if widely accepted, could substantially raise the profile of information studies among the cognitive sciences is the claim that access to instances of information—to the ways in which particular sets of entities are different from their contexts—is an essential prerequisite to any individual concept-forming act.

## Metaphysics, Philosophy of Logic, and Information

As we have seen, the scope of information studies is wide; and correspondingly there are fundamental "What-is-$x$?"-type questions to ask about information-related phenomena and activities of many different kinds. In addition to the basic question about the nature of information itself, we may ask: What are information sources, information services, information structures? What are collections, libraries, archives, museums? What are documents, data, records, metadata? How do documents correspond to inscriptions, sentences, propositions? What do documents do? How do they "mean"? How do they inform? What are works, texts, editions, versions, copies? What is the nature of the relationship between a document and the work that it instantiates? What is the nature of the relationships between a document and the classes of similar documents of which it is a member? What are representations, reproductions, images? What is aboutness? What kinds of things are subjects? How do we determine what a document is about? How do documents serve as evidence? How does the informational value of a document relate to its evidential value? What is authorship? What are authors, indexers, searchers? What are people doing when they are generating, looking for, or using information? How do we evaluate these interactions? What is the nature of people's conscious experience of interacting with documents, with information, with information services? What is the difference between information, education, and entertainment? What kinds of motivation do people have for choosing to engage with information, education, and entertainment services? What is relevance? How does relevance relate to other epistemic values? How do we determine how relevant a document is? What is effectiveness? How do we determine how effective information services are? What is access? How does access relate to other socially important objectives, such as preservation? In what ways are information services socially valuable? How should access to information resources be distributed among members of a given social group? How should resources be represented and organized so that access is optimized? How can the power relations among information institutions and groups of information producers and users be changed?

In search of answers to questions of these kinds, branches of philosophy upon which work in information studies has touched more than momentarily include philosophies of action, art, communication, education, history, language, law, logic, mathematics, mind, representation, science, and technology, as well as epistemology, ethics, critical theory, hermeneutics, and phenomenology (cf. Herold, 2001). Questions that are specifically about the mode of existence and the basic nature of different kinds of things are questions of the sort that are asked in the branch of philosophy known as *metaphysics*, that is, philosophy of being. Many of the philosophical questions asked in philosophy of information are metaphysical questions, in that they are motivated by a desire to understand the essential nature of information-related phenomena and the roles or positions of those phenomena within the totality of phenomena. The basic motivation for attending to questions of these kinds is the prediction that our answers—developed by carrying out careful analysis of the concepts or categories that we construct and use to think about real-world substances and properties—will help us to clarify our thoughts, strengthen our arguments, and improve the quality of the decisions and actions taken on the basis of the conclusions of those arguments.

In turn, many metaphysical questions can be construed as *ontological* questions. Ontology is the branch of metaphysics that is concerned to identify and understand the fundamental categories or kinds of things that exist in the world. For any information-related phenomenon, we may ask, What kind of thing is it? A concrete thing (existing in space-time as a datable, locatable object or event that is capable of undergoing change and/or of causing effects), or an abstract thing? A universal (that is instantiable or exemplifiable), or a particular? A substance (that is characterizable), or a property? An object or an event? A set or an element? One of the tasks of ontology is to identify, characterize, and relate these different categories in a coherent framework (see, e.g., Lowe, 2006). It may sometimes be helpful to distinguish between "pure" ontology in that sense and the "applied" ontology that is being done when information-related phenomena are being fitted into any predefined categorical structure (see, e.g., B. Smith, 2003). Another sense of applied ontology is that which is used to encompass work on modeling the kinds of entities and relationships about which information is to be stored in databases (see, e.g., Delsey, 2005; Furner, 2006b; International Federation of Library Associations and Institutions, Study Group on the Functional Requirements for Bibliographic Records, 1998; Le Boeuf, 2005; Renear & Dubin, 2007). In virtue of its focus on human-created artifacts that are the objects of human interpretation, ontology of information is closely related to both ontology of art (including ontology of literature) and projects with metaphysical ramifications in philosophy of language and representation and in semiotics (see, e.g., Furner, 2006a; Thomasson, 2003).

Different thinkers have different views on the existence (i.e., the reality) or otherwise of entities in various categories—in other words, they have different ontological commitments and may be regarded as realists or anti-realists with respect to the entities in any given category. In the philosophical literature, authors typically make their ontological assumptions well known, especially if those assumptions form the foundations on which are built understandings of the concepts under analysis. In information studies, on the other hand, such views are not frequently made explicit, notwithstanding their equal importance for the development of cohesive and powerful conceptual frameworks. One consequence of the tendency for metaphysical assumptions to be left unstated is a general perception that contributions to the literature of metaphysics are of limited relevance to debates in information studies. Any review of philosophical contributions to information studies whose coverage was restricted to works that include explicit discussion of philosophical topics would not be well equipped to alter that perception.

As we have seen, one of the tasks of philosophy of information is to carry out the "proper" (i.e., epistemically valuable) analysis of concepts that are central to information studies. One such concept is that of *aboutness* (see, e.g., Hjørland, 1992; Maron, 1977; Wilson, 1968, pp. 69–92); others are *relevance* (see, e.g., Borlund, 2003; Floridi, 2008c; Harter, 1992; Wilson, 1968, pp. 41–54; Wilson, 1973) and *work-instantiation* (see, e.g., Smiraglia, 2001; Svenonius, 2000, pp. 31–51; Wilson, 1968, pp. 6–19). In each of these three cases, a substantial and relevant body of literature exists in mainstream philosophy, resulting from the efforts to understand these concepts made by philosophers of logic, language, and being. And in each of these cases, the extent to which the philosophical literature has received attention in the literature of information studies is small, despite the importance of these concepts and the corresponding extent to which they have been the object of analysis in information studies.

Taking aboutness as an example, the primary question about that concept that has attracted the attention of analytic philosophers since the early part of the twentieth century may be paraphrased as follows: What do we really mean when we say that a given sentence, statement, or proposition *s* is *about* a given thing *z*? In other words, what do we really mean when we say that a given sentence *s* has a given *subject* or topic *z*? Consider the simple *sentence*, or sequence of words, *s*: "Lubetzky is wise." By speaking or writing down these words, it seems that we are saying something *about* Lubetzky (viz., that he is wise). Indeed, we might express our judgment on that matter—in response, say, to a question such as "What is sentence *s* about?" or "What is the (semantic) subject (i.e., the topic) of sentence *s*?"—with a sentence such as *t*: "'Lubetzky is wise' is about Lubetzky" or "The topic of 'Lubetzky is wise' is Lubetzky." In determining how we might make sense of sentences such as *t*, a number of subsidiary philosophical questions, both onto-logical and *logical*, arise.

For example: Would it be appropriate or useful to conclude that the pair made up of (1) the sentence "Lubetzky is wise" and (2) the person Lubetzky, is an instance of a *relation* called "aboutness"? At the same time, would it be appropriate or useful to conclude, independently of any answer that we might give to the previous question, that sentence *s*'s being about Lubetzky is an instance of a *property* called "aboutness"? Are sentences really the kinds of things that can be about other things? Are there any other kinds of things (e.g., propositions, documents, works) that can be about things? Must every instance of any of these kinds of things always be about something? Are people really the kinds of things that other things can be about? Are there any other kinds of things (e.g., classes, concepts, works) that things can be about? Must things *exist* in order to be capable of entering into an aboutness relation, or can things that no longer exist (e.g., Lubetzky) or things that have never existed (e.g., Harry Potter) be topics? Must topics be *concreta* (i.e., things that exist in time-space), or can they be *abstracta*? Must topics be *particulars* (i.e., things that are not instantiable), or can they be *universals*? Are the elements of an aboutness instance (e.g., "Lubetzky is wise," and Lubetzky) related *necessarily*, or *contingently*? Is it impossible that the pairing could ever be different, or not? Are statements of aboutness instances (e.g., statements such as "The topic of 'Lubetzky is wise' is Lubetzky") *analytic*, or *synthetic*? In other words, are such statements true by definition or by logical form (and therefore analytic), or not? Is our knowledge of the topics of sentences *a priori*, or *empirical*? In other words, is such knowledge justifiable without appealing to experience, or not? Are sentences such as "*s* is about *z*" true or false *objectively*, that is, independently of any of our beliefs about their truth? And is there a way of determining their truth value objectively, that is, independently of any examination of people's beliefs about their truth? Is the relation of aboutness most appropriately conceived as a two-place relation or are more than two places involved? For example, does aboutness vary in accordance with (1) the identity of the agents who speak the sentences that express the aboutness instances, and/or (2) the dates on which such sentences are spoken? Is Lubetzky the only thing that "Lubetzky is wise" is about? Or is it possible that sentence *s* is simultaneously about wisdom, or wise things in general? Could it be about the class of non-wise things as well as about Lubetzky (because "Lubetzky is wise" is logically equivalent to "Non-wise things are non-Lubetzkies")? Or about the class of non-Lubetzkies as well as about the class of non-wise things? Is it equally about librarians, and catalogers, and professors in general (given the truth of the additional proposition that Lubetzky is an instance of each of those classes of things)? Is it also about these things but about them to some lesser extent than it is about Lubetzky? Is it about the class of non-librarians (given the logical equivalence of "Lubetzky is a librarian" and "Non-librarians are non-Lubetzkies")? Would that mean that sentence *s*, like every sentence, is about everything? Or is it only about Lubetzky's being wise and nothing else, not Lubetzky, nor even "Lubetzky"? In general: What is the *logical* nature of the relationship between a sentence *s* and the thing *z* that *s* is said to be about? Finally, what method of or procedure for identifying instances of aboutness (i.e., for determining the topics of, e.g., sentences) is most reliable or most useful?

Questions of these kinds have been addressed in several contributions to philosophy of logic since the 1930s and different philosophers have answered such questions in different ways (see, e.g., Goodman, 1961; Putnam, 1958; Ryle, 1933). These answers involve several technical concepts that have historically received much additional attention in philosophy of logic, philosophy of language, and ontology. One prerequisite for understanding and evaluating candidate answers is an appreciation of a number of distinctions that are commonly made in philosophical discourse—distinctions, for example, between linguistic things and non-linguistic things; among linguistic things, between utterances and sentences, and between sentences and expressions; among expressions, between subject-terms and predicate-terms; among non-linguistic things, between mental and material things; among mental things, between concepts and propositions; among material things, between objects and situations; between substances and properties, properties and relations, objects and concepts, classes and instances, sets and members, types and tokens, abstracta and concreta, universals and particulars. The list is long. Other distinctions that are commonly made in the presentation and development of theoretical frameworks in logic, metaphysics, and epistemology include those between analytic and synthetic propositions, between necessary and contingent truths, between a priori and empirical knowledge, and so on. Different philosophers have different ideas about the reality and importance of, and relations among, such distinctions. Much of the history of twentieth- (and now twenty-first-) century philosophy of logic and language is the history of debates about the nature of the relations between words, concepts, and objects (see, e.g., Stanley, 2008).

Given a conventional understanding of documents as sequences or aggregates of sentences, or of works as sequences or aggregates of propositions, it requires little imagination to see these questions as having direct analogs in information studies. Instead of asking them about sentences such as "Lubetzky is wise," we might ask them about documents such as Svenonius and McGarry's (2001) introduction to *Seymour Lubetzky: Writings on the Classical Art of Cataloging*. Of course, it is possible that answers to questions of the kind "What is document *d* (or work *w*) about?" may be different in form from those of the kind "What is sentence *s* (or proposition *p*) about?" Or indeed that such answers may be arrived at only if approaches of correspondingly different kinds are taken. It might be considered surprising, nevertheless, that the topic of document-aboutness or work-aboutness (as distinct from sentence-aboutness or proposition-aboutness) does not seem to have captured the imagination of many working in philosophy of logic or indeed in philosophy of literature. For scholars working in information studies, of course, document-aboutness is of far more immediate concern; but few have taken a philosophical approach, noted the analogy between document- and sentence-aboutness, or cited the philosophical literature on the latter.

The author in information studies who has engaged most productively with philosophical analyses of aboutness is Patrick Wilson (1968, pp. 69–92), in his chapter titled "Subjects and the Sense of Position." Wilson's (p. 89) general conclusion is that "the notion of the subject of a writing is indeterminate." He (Wilson, p. 90) contrasts works (which he calls here "writings") with physical objects that are "determinate in every respect" and that "must have some definite shape and size and so on, at any moment," regardless of whether we are able to discover the values of those variables. For Wilson, works are not like physical objects and the subjects of works are not like the shapes or sizes of physical objects. Not only is it the case that different methods of determining the subjects of a work produce different results: There is no way in principle of deciding which of two equally specific or equally exhaustive subject statements is the "correct" statement because (for Wilson) works do not "have" subjects in the same way that physical objects have shapes. Wilson (p. 92) claims that "being on a given subject" contains a "quasi-technical term which is nowhere explained" in libraries or in the literature of librarianship. The claim is that, "to the librarian, 'being on a given subject' means [nothing more nor less than] 'being the sort of writing which our methods of assigning single locations assign to the positions with such and such a name'" (p. 92).

Wilson's position exemplifies a family of views on the nature of document/work-aboutness and semantic subjecthood that may be placed at one of the two ends of a spectrum of such kinds of view. At this pole—which might conveniently be called *nominalist* or (following Hjørland, 1992) "idealist"—we may locate views that comprise some or all of the following component claims: aboutness cannot sensibly be conceived as a property of works, but rather as a relation among sets of works, subjects, agents, and dates; what we call subjects are merely linguistic expressions that serve as labels or names for sets of works or for positions within a sequence or hierarchical structure; subjects do not exist independently of the thoughts and actions of humans; the sets of documents designated by subject labels are nominal kinds, not natural kinds: It is not possible to specify an intentional definition of such a set; it makes no sense to speak of documents "having" subjects, of subjects "inhering in" documents, or of "the" subject of a document (unless the intention is to designate the expression that happens to be attributed to the document by a particular agent on a particular date); and it is not possible to determine the truth of the sentence "Document $d$ is about subject $z$" objectively (i.e., without reference to the thoughts or actions of humans), either on an a priori basis or empirically: It is not possible to specify any regular procedure by which document $d$ may be analyzed in order to discover or generate "the" subject of $d$.

Conversely, at the opposite pole—which (again following Hjørland, 1992), we might call *realist*—lie views made up of some or all of the following elements: aboutness is a property class whose instances are predicated of classes of works; what we call subjects are the things designated by the linguistic expressions that comprise subject statements: Such things may be concrete (existing in space-time) or abstract and they may be particulars (not instantiable) or universals; subjects exist independently of the thoughts and actions of humans; the classes of works of which aboutness instances are predicated are natural kinds that may be defined intentionally; we may speak sensibly of works "having" subjects, and of "the" subject(s) of any given work; and it is possible to determine the truth of the proposition that work $w$ is about subject $z$ objectively, by specifying a regular procedure by which work $w$ may be analyzed in order to discover its subject.

The fact that, at this point in the history of theory in information studies, the nature of aboutness continues to be the subject of such debate in the field is a result not primarily of the inability of proponents of views at the two poles to persuade their opponents of the merits of those views, but rather of the largely unacknowledged influence of the realist view on the activity of designers and users of knowledge organization systems. It is difficult to find well-reasoned defenses of the realist view in the literature, yet most of us who are actively engaged in the tasks of designing bibliographic classification schemes, indexing documents in accordance with such schemes, and using those schemes as tools for finding documents of the kinds that we want, continue to *act* as if we accept the realist view as the correct one.

Establishing the *ontological* nature of the thing $z$ that a given sentence $s$ or sentence-aggregate $d$ (or proposition $p$ or proposition-aggregate $w$) is said to be about is not only of purely academic interest, but has a bearing on very practical matters such as the design of library catalogs. Any sentence $t$ of the form "Work $w$ is about subject $z$" is an example of a kind of statement—a subject statement—that is found in millions of catalog records around the world. One of the aims of the designers of data models such as the one presented in the *Final Report* of the International Federation of Library Associations and Institutions, Study Group on the Functional Requirements for Bibliographic Records (FRBR) (1998, p. 12) is to identify the fundamental categories or classes of entities that are of interest to users of bibliographic data, including not only "the products of intellectual or artistic endeavour that are named or described in bibliographic records" (such as works) but also those entities that are capable of serving as "the subjects" of works.

The original FRBR model allows for the following classes of entities to serve as subjects: Concept (each of whose instances is "an abstract notion or idea"), Object ("a material thing"), Event ("an action or occurrence"), and Place ("a location"), as well as Work, Manifestation, Expression, Item, Person, and Corporate Body (International Federation of Library Associations and Institutions, Study Group on the Functional Requirements for Bibliographic Records, 1998, p. 16). In this sense, the FRBR model amounts to an ontology of subjects: The claim that is being made is that anything that is an instance of one of these entity classes can sensibly be treated as the subject $z$ of a given work $w$. Tom Delsey (2005, p. 50) identifies three "broad objectives" to be met by re-examination of the ways in which the FRBR model analyzes data relevant to subject access, the first of which is "to ensure that the scope of the entities [i.e., the entity classes] ... is sufficient to cover everything that a user of a library catalogue might view as a 'subject'." He goes on (p. 50) to pose two "key questions" that arise in the context of this first objective: "The first [of the key questions] is whether the entities are defined in sufficiently broad terms to cover fully what we might characterize as the 'subject' universe. The second is whether the categorizations represented by the entities defined in the models are appropriate and meaningful for the purposes of clarifying the bibliographic conventions through which that 'subject' universe is reflected." In other words: (1) Are the entity classes collectively exhaustive? Does the model cover the whole universe of subject-related entity classes? (2) Are the entity classes individually appropriate? Does the model carve up the universe of subject-related entity classes in the "right" way?

Furner (2006a) notes that the entities listed in the FRBR *Final Report* as examples of instances of Object, Event, and Place are similar in that they are all individual named things—they are concrete particulars that exist in space-time (i.e., they are datable and locatable), and that are not themselves instantiable but that instantiate universals. The examples given of instances of Concept do not include kinds of objects, events, and places, but the implication is that such universals (i.e., kinds of concrete particulars) are to be considered as concepts, along with "abstract notions or ideas" such as "Economics," whose status as universal or particular, or indeed as abstract or concrete, is as ambiguous in the FRBR context as is the ontological status of any instance of Work.

## Epistemology and Information

Some of the philosophical questions that are asked in information studies are *epistemological* questions, in that they are motivated by a desire to understand the ways in which information and other information-related phenomena are involved in the processes by which belief can become knowledge (see, e.g., Steup, 2005).

In information studies, just as there is no standard conception of information, there is no standard conception of knowledge. The two main rival views are those of knowledge as true information (or information about the facts, i.e., information about the way the world really is) and knowledge as internalized information (i.e., the content of individuals' mental images or representations of the world). These both differ from the theory of knowledge that is traditionally provided by epistemology, which is that knowledge is justified true belief. In other words, for any one of our beliefs to count as knowledge, it must be both (1) one that is true and (2) one for which justification can be provided. Different forms of the traditional theory give different accounts of what it means for a belief to be evaluated as true, how the truth-value of a belief may be determined, how justifications of different kinds may be supplied, what degree of certainty is required of a justification, and so on.

For the scholar of information studies, there is a dual motivation for studying and contributing to epistemology. In the first place, we may learn about some of the epistemological assumptions underlying the scholarly practice of information studies (see, e.g., Hjørland, 2005a) and about potentially productive methods of generating knowledge in information studies. In the second place, if we accept the idea that there is some sort of conceptual relationship between information and knowledge, we are only a short step away from accepting that what we say about the nature of knowledge and about how it is acquired will influence what we say both about the nature of information and about how we collect, organize, and provide access to the content of information sources, that is, recorded knowledge (Budd, 2001). An understanding of epistemology thus helps us to determine what our information structures, systems, services, policies, and institutions ought to be like, and what they ought to do, if the processes by which we interact with information are to result in the satisfaction of our "epistemic objectives"—for example, the rapid, cheap, and easy acquisition of all and only those beliefs that are justified, true, and relevant (Fallis, 2006).

Historically, there have been two main points of intersection between epistemology and information studies. First, and as already mentioned, some accounts of justification and/or knowledge rely on a particular conception of *information as evidence* (e.g., Dretske, 1981). Second, librarians and information scientists were among the first to express and address the idea that the processes by which knowledge is acquired are significantly *social* in several respects. Margaret Egan and Jesse Shera were the first authors to use the term "social epistemology" in print; they focused on demonstrating how an understanding of the ways in which social groups (as well as individuals) acquire knowledge can be applied in the design of information services to those groups (Budd, 2002; Egan & Shera, 1952; Furner, 2002b, 2004a). More recently, epistemologists such as Alvin Goldman (1999, 2006; see also Wilson, 1983) have been concerned to give an account of the conditions under which social processes such as the provision and receipt of testimony can result in the acquisition of knowledge; and a number of conceptual analyses have been undertaken of trust, reputation, authority, reliability, credibility, and other criteria for evaluating the likelihood that information sources of various kinds will be productive of epistemically valuable beliefs (cf. Rieh & Danielson, 2007).

In a series of papers, Don Fallis (2006; 2007b; 2008; Fallis & Whitcomb, in press) demonstrates how the methods and results of epistemology may be applied in attempts to improve the quality of decision making in information management, information policy, and information use. Some of the areas of activity that may benefit from applied epistemological analysis of this kind are knowledge organization (where decisions must be made about how to organize documents in such a way that knowledge acquisition is maximized; see, e.g., Andersen, 2002), reference service and information retrieval (which involve decisions about which documents to recommend [Furner, 2002a]), collection development (which involves decisions about which documents to collect [Fallis & Whitcomb, in press]), resource discovery and evaluation (which involves decisions about which sources to trust [Fallis, 2008]), and information policymaking and legislation (which involve decisions about which rights to respect [Fallis, 2007b]).

Fallis and Whitcomb (in press) outline a general method of identifying the kinds of goals, values, or criteria, and the kinds of relationships among those criteria, that should be considered when choosing among alternative courses of action such as the acquisition of, provision of access to, or use of document $x$ rather than document $y$. Fallis and Whitcomb recognize that, in any given context, such values may include financial criteria, legal criteria, ethical criteria, aesthetic criteria, and so on; but, they argue, we create, provide access to, and seek information primarily because we believe that information is what allows us to *acquire knowledge*: "Our typical reason for seeking information is to acquire knowledge, or at least beliefs with knowledge-making properties like truth and justification" (Fallis & Whitcomb, in press, "Focusing on epistemic values"; cf. Dretske's [1981, p. 86] conception of information as that which yields knowledge). In other words, we do not value information as an end in itself but rather for its instrumental quality as a means to the ends of knowledge acquisition. Fallis and Whitcomb consequently focus on *epistemic* goals such as the maximization of knowledge acquisition; they draw on epistemology to identify ways of breaking down such general objectives into more specific components (e.g., maximization of acquisition of *true* belief and maximization of acquisition of *justified* belief) and ways of identifying, categorizing, and weighting the relationships and trade-offs among those components.

If the objective of an information-management decision is to promote the acquisition of knowledge in the form of certain kinds of "good" or epistemically valuable beliefs (at the same time as obstructing the acquisition of certain kinds of "bad" beliefs), how might "goodness" be interpreted in this context? Contributions to the ongoing debate in epistemology about the conditions for knowledge can help us sift among candidate values such as truth and justification. But in many contexts (as Fallis and Whitcomb note), the ulterior motivation for engaging in a search for information is not so much the prospect simply of acquiring knowledge but the prospect of putting acquired knowledge to some practical *use*, in the course (for example) of carrying out a task (see, e.g., Byström & Hansen, 2005), solving a problem, understanding an explanation, becoming wise, achieving happiness, or living purposefully (cf. Floridi's [2003b, p. 57] conception of pragmatic information).

In order to understand and improve decision making in contexts of those kinds, ideally we would consider the non-epistemic criteria on which beliefs may be valued highly—criteria such as the *relevance* of beliefs to a given ulterior goal, or the *utility* of beliefs for achieving that goal. There are connections waiting to be made between the work being done by applied epistemologists such as Fallis and an existing body of work in information studies on criteria for evaluating library and information services in general (see, e.g., Saracevic & Kantor [1997], cited by Fallis & Whitcomb [in press]) and resource discovery systems in particular (see, e.g., Harter & Hert, 1998). In this latter tradition, an analytical distinction is commonly made between (1) criteria for evaluating the average success with which a system fulfills its dual function of finding resources that are relevant (useful, interesting) and avoiding resources that are irrelevant (useless, uninteresting) to searcher *s* at time *t*, and (2) criteria for judging the actual relevance (usefulness, interest level) to searcher *s* at time *t* of individual resources (Borlund, 2003; see also Floridi, 2008c). In this literature, some care is usually applied in taking into account the subjective (i.e., mind-dependent) and contextual nature of the relationship (between resource and searcher) of *relevance*, which contrasts with the objective (i.e., mind-independent) nature of the relationship (between belief and reality) of *truth*. Whether, or to what degree, a proposition *p* believed by searcher *s* at time *t* is true or justified is something that can, in principle, be determined independently of any input from the searcher. In contrast, whether, or to what degree, a document *d* is actually relevant to searcher *s* at time *t* is something that can be determined only (if ever) by asking the searcher. It will be interesting to see how future applications of epistemic value theory can be extended similarly to take into account the pragmatic nature of much decision making in information-management contexts.

## Ethics and Information

One sense of "philosophy" that has not been covered in this chapter is the one that people mean when they talk about their (or their institution's) personal or professional "philosophy" of information work, scholarship, or research. It is in this sense that people sometimes talk about *having* a philosophy, which is different from the sense in which philosophers *do* philosophy. Talk about the philosophy that one has, in this sense, is typically equivalent to a state of one's long-term or fundamental goals or mission, or a statement of one's basic or most strongly held values. Having a knowledge of professional ethics is not a necessary prerequisite for making statements of goals or values. Nevertheless, study of professional ethics can provide suggestions of values to hold that are in line with others' and can provide knowledge of ethical principles that can aid choice among values (see, e.g., Callahan, 1988). *Information ethics* is commonly construed as a branch of philosophy of information, but mere statements of values (which may or may not result from the study of information ethics) are not usually conceived as contributions to philosophy—at least, not in the strict sense of "philosophy" used by most philosophers.

Several branches of philosophy deal with questions of value or goodness and with claims about the kinds of things that ought to be done in given situations. Social and political philosophy, for example, are concerned with the evaluation of public policy, governmental activity, and group interaction and with the analysis of socially valuable states such as justice and freedom. Aesthetics is concerned to establish criteria upon which works of art may be evaluated. Ethics is concerned with the rightness of actions in general. Within ethics, some fairly fuzzy boundaries may be drawn between ethical theory, meta-ethics, and applied ethics. Ethical theories propose criteria for distinguishing between right and wrong actions; meta-ethics categorizes ethical theories (e.g., as consequence-based, duty-based, rights-based, or virtue-based [Fallis, 2007a; Spinello, 1995, pp. 14–42]) and analyzes the concepts and assumptions on which they are based; and projects in applied ethics demonstrate the consequences of applying particular ethical theories as guides to action in particular situations.

As we approach the end of the first decade of the twenty-first century, information ethics (see, e.g., Himma, 2007) is the most visible of subfields of philosophy of information. This is a field that already has its own international association, its own journals, and its own handbooks and readers (see, e.g., Himma & Tavani, 2008; Moore, 2005). "Information ethics" is typically understood to include "computer ethics" (Bynum, 2008) and to emphasize questions about the ethical implementation and use of information technologies but rarely to the exclusion of more general questions about the ethical provision and use of information services (online or offline; computerized or not; see, e.g., Hauptman, 2002). For the information policymaker, systems developer, or service provider, the fundamental ethical question is "Who should have [what level of] access to what information?" (Fallis, 2007a, p. 24). The issues that tend to arise in the evaluation of rival answers to this question include equity of access to information, intellectual freedom, information privacy and confidentiality, and intellectual property. The literature on each of these issues is large and straddles the boundaries between ethical theory, meta-ethics, and applied ethics, paying close attention to the problems that arise when criteria or principles for ethical action conflict. Kay Mathiesen and Don Fallis (2008), for example, discuss the ethical dilemmas facing librarians that arise from challenges to intellectual freedom; Mathiesen (2008) reviews concepts of censorship and justifications for limiting access to information; Adam Moore (2007, 2008a) and Herman Tavani (2008) review concepts of privacy and justifications of information privacy rights; Moore (2008b) and Kenneth Einar Himma (2008) analyze justifications for the legal protection of intellectual property rights; Rafael Capurro (2008) assesses the significance of intercultural information ethics. Hope Olson (2002) uncovers the causes and effects of bias in the construction of bibliographic classification and subject indexing schemes, and Clare Beghtol (2002, 2005) explores strategies for creating and maintaining knowledge organization systems that are ethically acceptable. Jonathan Furner (2007; in press a) draws on critical theories of race, social justice, and social identity to develop a conception of the just knowledge organization system.

Mathiesen (2004) proposes a theory of information ethics that distinguishes between the subjective (contextual) and objective (intrinsic) value of the information access states in which particular people find themselves with respect to particular information resources. Floridi (e.g., 2008a) develops an interpretation of an information macroethics that is intended to encompass and supersede information-as-resource approaches such as Mathiesen's (which focus on the values of availability, accessibility, and accuracy), information-as-product approaches (focusing on issues of, for example, plagiarism, libel, and propaganda), and information-as-target approaches (focusing on intellectual freedom, intellectual property, privacy, confidentiality, and security, etc.). Further research on meta-ethical categories and concepts can only raise the profile of information ethics within mainstream philosophy circles even higher. Early contributions to this subfield were covered in an *ARIST* chapter by Martha Montague Smith (1997), and Leah Lievrouw and Sharon Farb (2003) dealt with ethical issues in their discussion of inequities of access to information. A true successor to Smith's chapter that comprehensively covers work in information ethics published in the interim is well overdue.

## Conclusion

Just as there are meta-questions (philosophical, historical, sociological, and political) to be asked about information studies, there are meta-questions that may be asked both about philosophy of information studies and about philosophy of information. These include questions about when, where, and how philosophy of these kinds has been done, by whom it has been done, and what motivations people have had for doing it. Such questions are asked by historians and sociologists of philosophy (see, e.g., R. Collins, 1998).

It is relatively easy to trace the histories of a few well-defined branches of philosophy of information: information ethics, information-theoretic epistemology, and social epistemology come to mind. But, taken as wholes, both philosophy of information and philosophy of information studies are diffuse, unbounded fields that lack scholarly associations, journals, textbooks, and reputations. The high-quality work that exists remains scattered, infrequently cited, and (one sometimes suspects) unread. The appearance in the early 2000s of several special issues of journals devoted to topics in philosophy of information demonstrates that the field is gradually attaining some degree of respectability within information studies; but, given the field's lack of a clearly expressed identity, it is probably too early to expect any significant contributions to an understanding of its historical development. When that history is written, it will assuredly be of great interest to scholars wishing to see how the kinds of philosophical questions asked in information studies, and the kinds of answers offered, have changed over the years, which long-standing assumptions and beliefs (if any) have been challenged by the various paradigm shifts that have been identified in the broader academy, and how social factors have played a role in those developments.

Much of the intent of this review has been to examine the influence of philosophy on information studies. As part of any general quest to understand the interdisciplinary nature of information studies (see, e.g., L. C. Smith, 1992), we may well wish to look in the opposite direction and ask, To what extent does information studies contribute to "mainstream" philosophy? The short answer here is "Hardly at all." The "trade deficit" produced by the imbalance between intellectual imports (from philosophy to information studies) and exports (to philosophy from information studies) could doubtless be demonstrated bibliometrically (see, e.g., Cronin & Meho, 2008, for a description of the kinds of methods that could be used). Certainly, the frequency with which contributions to the literature of information studies are cited in the literature of philosophy is vanishingly low. Moreover, the status within the general philosophical community of philosophy of information studies sometimes seems to be roughly on a par with that of the philosophy of pasta. Things may change in the future as increasing numbers of philosophers first find inspiration in information-related phenomena and subsequently become aware of the existence of an entire field that, for one reason and another, has often struggled to attract the academic respect for which it has yearned.

## Acknowledgments

The author would like to thank the three anonymous reviewers of an earlier draft of this chapter for their very helpful comments.

## References

Adams, F. (2003). The informational turn in philosophy. *Minds and Machines, 13*, 471–501.

Andersen, J. (2002). The role of subject literature in scholarly communication: An interpretation based on social epistemology. *Journal of Documentation, 58*(4), 463–481.

Bar-Hillel, Y., & Carnap, R. (1953). Semantic information. *British Journal for the Philosophy of Science, 4*(14), 147–157.

Bates, M. J. (1999). The invisible substrate of information science. *Journal of the American Society for Information Science, 50*(12), 1043–1050.

Bates, M. J. (2005a). Information and knowledge: An evolutionary framework for information. Retrieved January 9, 2009, from informationr.net/ir/10-4/paper239.html

Bates, M. J. (2005b). An introduction to metatheories, theories, and models. In K. E. Fisher, S. Erdelez, & L. McKechnie (Eds.), *Theories of information behavior* (pp. 1–24). Medford, NJ: Information Today.

Bates, M. J. (2006). Fundamental forms of information. *Journal of the American Society for Information Science and Technology, 57*(8), 1033–1045.

Bates, M. J. (2007). Defining the information disciplines in encyclopedia development. *Information Research, 12*(4), paper 29. Retrieved September 28, 2008, from informationr.net/ir/12-4/colis/colis29.html

Bates, M. J. (2008). Hjørland's critique of Bates' work on defining information. *Journal of the American Society for Information Science and Technology, 59*(5), 842–844.

Bawden, D. (2007). Organised complexity, meaning and understanding: An approach to a unified view of information for information science. *Aslib Proceedings, 59*(4/5), 307–327.

Becher, T. (1994). The significance of disciplinary differences. *Studies in Higher Education, 19*(2), 151–161.

Beghtol, C. (2002). A proposed ethical warrant for global knowledge representation and organization systems. *Journal of Documentation, 58*(5), 507–532.

Beghtol, C. (2005). Ethical decision-making for knowledge representation and organization systems for global use. *Journal of the American Society for Information Science and Technology, 56*(9), 903–912.

Belkin, N. J. (1990). The cognitive viewpoint in information science. *Journal of Information Science, 16*(1), 11–15.

Benoît, G. (2002). Toward a critical theoretic perspective in information systems. *Library Quarterly, 72*(4), 441–471.

Blair, D. C. (1990). *Language and representation in information retrieval.* Amsterdam: Elsevier.

Blair, D. C. (2003). Information retrieval and the philosophy of language. *Annual Review of Information Science and Technology, 37,* 3–50.

Blair, D. C. (2006). *Wittgenstein, language, and information: "Back to the rough ground!"* Dordrecht, The Netherlands: Springer.

Borgmann, A. (1999). *Holding on to reality: The nature of information at the turn of the millennium.* Chicago: University of Chicago Press.

Borlund, P. (2003). The concept of relevance in IR. *Journal of the American Society for Information Science and Technology, 54*(10), 913–925.

Boulding, K. E. (1956). *The image: Knowledge in life and society.* Ann Arbor: University of Michigan Press.

Brookes, B. C. (1980). The foundations of information science, Part I: Philosophical aspects. *Journal of Information Science, 2*(3/4), 125–133.

Buckland, M. K. (1991). Information as thing. *Journal of the American Society for Information Science, 42*(5), 351–360.

Buckland, M. K. (1996). What is a "document"? *Journal of the American Society for Information Science, 48*(9), 804–809.

Budd, J. M. (1995). An epistemological foundation for library and information science. *Library Quarterly, 65*(3), 295–318.

Budd, J. M. (2001). *Knowledge and knowing in library and information science: A philosophical framework.* Lanham, MD: Scarecrow.

Budd, J. M. (2002). Jesse Shera, sociologist of knowledge? *Library Quarterly, 72*(4), 423–440.

Budd, J. M. (2005). Phenomenology and information studies. *Journal of Documentation, 61*(1), 44–59.

Buschman, J. (2007). Transgression or stasis? Challenging Foucault in LIS theory. *Library Quarterly, 77*(1), 21–44.

Bynum, T. W. (2008). Computer and information ethics. In E. N. Zalta (Ed.), *Stanford encyclopedia of philosophy.* Stanford, CA: Metaphysics Research Lab, Center for the Study of Language and Information, Stanford University. Retrieved December 16, 2008, from plato.stanford.edu/entries/ethics-computer

Bynum, T. W., & Moor, J. H. (Eds.). (1998). *The digital phoenix: How computers are changing philosophy.* Oxford, UK: Blackwell.

Byström, K., & Hansen, P. (2005). Conceptual framework for tasks in information studies. *Journal of the American Society for Information Science and Technology, 56*(10), 1050–1061.

Callahan, J. C. (Ed.). (1988). *Ethical issues in professional life.* New York: Oxford University Press.

Capurro, R. (2008). Intercultural information ethics. In K. E. Himma & H. T. Tavani (Eds.), *The handbook of information and computer ethics* (pp. 639–665). Hoboken, NJ: Wiley.

Capurro, R., & Hjørland, B. (2003). The concept of information. *Annual Review of Information Science and Technology, 37,* 343–411.

Case, D. O. (2007). The concept of information. In *Looking for information: A survey of research on information seeking, needs, and behavior* (2nd ed., pp. 40–67). London: Academic Press.

Cherry, E. C. (1951). A history of the theory of information. *Proceedings of the Institution of Electrical Engineers, 98*, 383–393.

Collins, A. (2007). From H=log s$^n$ to conceptual framework: A short history of information. *History of Psychology, 10*(1), 44–72.

Collins, R. (1998). *The sociology of philosophies: A global theory of intellectual change.* Cambridge, MA: Harvard University Press.

Cornelius, I. V. (1996). *Meaning and method in information studies.* Norwood, NJ: Ablex.

Cornelius, I. V. (2002). Theorizing information for information science. *Annual Review of Information Science and Technology, 36*, 393–425.

Craig, E. (Ed.). (1998). *Routledge encyclopedia of philosophy* (10 vols.). London: Routledge.

Cronin, B. (2008). The sociological turn in information science. *Journal of Information Science, 34*(4), 465–475.

Cronin, B., & Meho, L. I. (2008). The shifting balance of trade in information studies. *Journal of the American Society for Information Science and Technology, 59*(4), 551–564.

Day, R. E. (2001). *The modern invention of information: Discourse, history, and power.* Carbondale: Southern Illinois University Press.

Day, R. E. (2005). Poststructuralism and information studies. *Annual Review of Information Science and Technology, 39*, 575–609.

Delsey, T. (2005). Modeling subject access: Extending the FRBR and FRANAR conceptual models. *Cataloging & Classification Quarterly, 39*(3/4), 49–61.

Dick, A. L. (2002). *The philosophy, politics and economics of information.* Pretoria, South Africa: Unisa Press.

Dretske, F. I. (1981). *Knowledge and the flow of information.* Cambridge, MA: MIT Press.

Dretske, F. I., Alston, W. P., Arbib, M.A., Armstrong, D. M., Barwise, J., Bogdan, R. J., et al. (1983). Précis of *Knowledge and the flow of information*; with Open peer commentary, and Author's response. *Behavioral and Brain Sciences, 6*(1), 55–90.

Egan, M. E., & Shera, J. H. (1952). Foundations of a theory of bibliography. *Library Quarterly, 22*(2), 125–137.

Ellis, D. (1984). Theory and explanation in information retrieval research. *Journal of Information Science, 8*(1), 25–38.

Fallis, D. (Ed.). (2002). Social epistemology and information science [special issue]. *Social Epistemology, 16*(1).

Fallis, D. (2006). Social epistemology and information science. *Annual Review of Information Science and Technology, 40*, 475–519.

Fallis, D. (2007a). Information ethics for 21st century library professionals. *Library Hi Tech, 25*(1), 23–36.

Fallis, D. (2007b). Toward an epistemology of intellectual property. *Journal of Information Ethics, 16*(2), 34–51.

Fallis, D. (2008). Toward an epistemology of Wikipedia. *Journal of the American Society for Information Science and Technology, 59*(10), 1662–1674.

Fallis, D., & Whitcomb, D. (in press). Epistemic values and information management. *The Information Society.*

Floridi, L. (1999a). Information ethics: On the theoretical foundations of computer ethics. *Ethics and Information Technology, 1*(1), 37–56.

Floridi, L. (1999b). *Philosophy and computing*. London: Routledge.

Floridi, L. (2002a). On defining library and information science as applied philosophy of information. *Social Epistemology, 16*(1), 37–49.

Floridi, L. (2002b). On the intrinsic value of information objects and the infosphere. *Ethics and Information Technology, 4*(4), 287–304.

Floridi, L. (2002c). What is the philosophy of information? *Metaphilosophy, 33*(1/2), 123–145.

Floridi, L. (Ed.). (2003a). *The Blackwell guide to the philosophy of computing and information*. Oxford, UK: Blackwell.

Floridi, L. (2003b). Information. In L. Floridi (Ed.), *The Blackwell guide to the philosophy of computing and information* (pp. 40–61). Oxford, UK: Blackwell.

Floridi, L. (2004a). LIS as applied philosophy of information: A reappraisal. *Library Trends, 52*(3), 658–665.

Floridi, L. (2004b). Open problems in the philosophy of information. *Metaphilosophy, 35*(4), 554–582.

Floridi, L. (2005a). Is information meaningful data? *Philosophy and Phenomenological Research, 70*(2), 351–370.

Floridi, L. (2005b). Semantic conceptions of information. In E. N. Zalta (Ed.), *Stanford encyclopedia of philosophy*. Stanford, CA: Metaphysics Research Lab, Center for the Study of Language and Information, Stanford University. Retrieved December 16, 2008, from plato.stanford.edu /entries/information-semantic

Floridi, L. (2008a). Foundations of information ethics. In K. E. Himma & H. T. Tavani (Eds.), *The handbook of information and computer ethics* (pp. 3–23). Hoboken, NJ: Wiley.

Floridi, L. (2008b). Information ethics: Its nature and scope. In J. van den Hoven & J. Weckert (Eds.), *Moral philosophy and information technology* (pp. 40–65). Cambridge, UK: Cambridge University Press.

Floridi, L. (2008c). Understanding epistemic relevance. *Erkenntnis, 69*(1), 69–92.

Frohmann, B. (2004). *Deflating information: From science studies to documentation*. Toronto: University of Toronto Press.

Furner, J. (2002a). On recommending. *Journal of the American Society for Information Science and Technology, 53*(9), 747–763.

Furner, J. (2002b). Shera's social epistemology recast as psychological bibliology. *Social Epistemology, 16*(1), 5–22.

Furner, J. (2004a). "A brilliant mind": Margaret Egan and social epistemology. *Library Trends, 52*(4), 792–809.

Furner, J. (2004b). Conceptual analysis: A method for understanding information as evidence, and evidence as information. *Archival Science, 4*(3/4), 233–265.

Furner, J. (2004c). Information studies without information. *Library Trends, 52*(3), 427–446.

Furner, J. (2006a, November). *The ontology of subjects of works*. Paper presented at the 69th Annual Meeting of the American Society for Information Science and Technology, Austin, TX. Retrieved December 23, 2008, from polaris.gseis.ucla.edu/jfurner/papers/furner-06asist-b-ppt.pdf

Furner, J. (2006b, November). *The ontology of works*. Paper presented at the 69th Annual Meeting of the American Society for Information Science and Technology, Austin, TX. Retrieved December 23, 2008, from polaris.gseis.ucla.edu/jfurner/papers/furner-06asist-c-ppt.pdf

Furner, J. (2007). Dewey deracialized: A critical race-theoretic perspective. *Knowledge Organization*, *34*(3), 144–168.

Furner, J. (in press a). Interrogating "identity": A philosophical approach to an enduring issue in knowledge organization. *Knowledge Organization*.

Furner, J. (in press b). Philosophy and the information sciences. In M. J. Bates (Ed.), *Encyclopedia of library and information sciences*. New York: Taylor and Francis.

Gettier, E. (1963). Is justified true belief knowledge? *Analysis*, *23*(6), 121–123.

Goldman, A. I. (1999). *Knowledge in a social world*. Oxford, UK: Oxford University Press.

Goldman, A. I. (2006). Social epistemology. In E. N. Zalta (Ed.), *Stanford encyclopedia of philosophy*. Stanford, CA: Metaphysics Research Lab, Center for the Study of Language and Information, Stanford University. Retrieved September 28, 2008, from plato.stanford.edu/entries/epistemology-social

Goodman, N. (1961). About. *Mind*, *70*(277), 1–24.

Goonatilake, S. (1991). *The evolution of information: Lineages in gene, culture, and artefact*. London: Pinter.

Grice, P. (1968). Utterer's meaning, sentence meaning, and word-meaning. *Foundations of Language*, *4*, 225–242.

Grice, P. (1989). *Studies in the way of words*. Cambridge, MA: Harvard University Press.

Hansson, J. (2005). Hermeneutics as a bridge between the modern and the postmodern in library and information science. *Journal of Documentation*, *61*(1), 102–113.

Harms, W. F. (1998). The use of information theory in epistemology. *Philosophy of Science*, *65*(3), 472–501.

Harris, M. J. (1986). The dialectic of defeat: Antimonies [sic] in research in library and information science. *Library Trends*, *34*(3), 515–531.

Harter, S. P. (1992). Psychological relevance and information science. *Journal of the American Society for Information Science*, *43*(9), 602–615.

Harter, S. P., & Hert, C. A. (1998). Evaluation of information retrieval systems: Approaches, issues, and methods. *Annual Review of Information Science and Technology*, *32*, 3–94.

Hartley, R. V. L. (1928). Transmission of information. *Bell System Technical Journal*, *7*, 535–563.

Hauptman, R. (2002). *Ethics and librarianship*. Jefferson, NC: McFarland.

Herold, K. R. (2001). Librarianship and the philosophy of information. *Library Philosophy and Practice*, *3*(2). Retrieved December 23, 2008, from www.webpages.uidaho.edu/~mbolin/herold.pdf

Herold, K. (Ed.). (2004). The philosophy of information [special issue]. *Library Trends*, *52*(3).

Himma, K. E. (2007). Foundational issues in information ethics. *Library Hi Tech*, *25*(1), 79–94.

Himma, K. E. (2008). The justification of intellectual property: Contemporary philosophical disputes. *Journal of the American Society for Information Science and Technology*, *59*(7), 1143–1161.

Himma, K. E., & Tavani, H. T. (Eds.). (2008). *The handbook of information and computer ethics*. Hoboken, NJ: Wiley.

Hjørland, B. (1992). The concept of "subject" in information science. *Journal of Documentation*, *48*(2), 172–200.

Hjørland, B. (1997). *Information seeking and subject representation: An activity-theoretical approach to information science*. Westport, CT: Greenwood.

Hjørland, B. (1998). Theory and metatheory of information science: A new interpretation. *Journal of Documentation*, *54*(5), 606–621.

Hjørland, B. (2000). Library and information science: Practice, theory and philosophical basis. *Information Processing & Management, 36*(3), 501–531.

Hjørland, B. (2005a). Empiricism, rationalism and positivism in library and information science. *Journal of Documentation, 61*(1), 130–155.

Hjørland, B. (Ed.). (2005b). Library and information science and the philosophy of science [special issue]. *Journal of Documentation, 61*(1).

Hjørland, B. (2007). Information: Objective or subjective/situational? *Journal of the American Society for Information Science and Technology, 58*(10), 1448–1456.

Hjørland, B., & Nicolaisen, J. (Eds.). (2005). *The epistemological lifeboat: Epistemology and philosophy of science for information scientists.* Copenhagen, Denmark: Royal School of Library and Information Science. Retrieved December 23, 2008, from www.db.dk/jni/lifeboat

International Federation of Library Associations and Institutions, Study Group on the Functional Requirements for Bibliographic Records. (1998). *Functional requirements for bibliographic records: Final report.* München, Germany: K. G. Saur.

Israel, D., & Perry, J. (1990). What is information? In P. P. Hanson (Ed.), *Information, language, and cognition* (pp. 1–19). Vancouver: University of British Columbia Press.

Kuhn, T. S. (1962). *The structure of scientific revolutions.* Chicago: University of Chicago Press.

Le Boeuf, P. (2005). FRBR: Hype or cure-all? Introduction. *Cataloging & Classification Quarterly, 39*(3/4), 1–13.

Lievrouw, L. A., & Farb, S. E. (2003). Information and equity. *Annual Review of Information Science and Technology, 37*, 499–540.

Lowe, E. J. (2006). *The four-category ontology: A metaphysical foundation for natural science.* Oxford, UK: Oxford University Press.

Machlup, F. (1983). Semantic quirks in studies of information. In F. Machlup & U. Mansfield (Eds.), *The study of information: Interdisciplinary messages* (pp. 641–671). New York: John Wiley.

Maron, M. E. (1977). On indexing, retrieval and the meaning of about. *Journal of the American Society for Information Science, 28*(1), 38–43.

Mathiesen, K. K. (2004). What is information ethics? *Computers and Society, 34*(1). Retrieved January 8, 2009, from doi.acm.org/10.1145/1050305.1050312

Mathiesen, K. K. (2008). Censorship and access to expression. In K. E. Himma & H. T. Tavani (Eds.), *The handbook of information and computer ethics* (pp. 573–588). Hoboken, NJ: Wiley.

Mathiesen, K. K., & Fallis, D. (2008). Information ethics and the library profession. In K. E. Himma & H. T. Tavani (Eds.), *The handbook of information and computer ethics* (pp. 221–244). Hoboken, NJ: Wiley.

Mingers, J. C. (1995). Information and meaning: Foundations for an intersubjective account. *Information Systems Journal, 5*, 285–306.

Moore, A. D. (Ed.). (2005). *Information ethics: Privacy, property, and power.* Seattle: University of Washington Press.

Moore, A. D. (2007). Toward informational privacy rights. *San Diego Law Review, 44*(4), 809–845.

Moore, A. D. (2008a). Defining privacy. *Journal of Social Philosophy, 39*, 411–428.

Moore, A. D. (2008b). Personality-based, rule-utilitarian, and Lockean justifications of intellectual property. In K. E. Himma & H. T. Tavani (Eds.), *The handbook of information and computer ethics* (pp. 105–130). Hoboken, NJ: Wiley.

Moran, D. (Ed.). (2008a). *The Routledge companion to twentieth century philosophy.* London: Routledge.

Moran, D. (2008b). Towards an assessment of twentieth century philosophy. In D. Moran (Ed.), *The Routledge companion to twentieth century philosophy* (pp. 1–40). London: Routledge.

Olson, H. A. (1997). The feminist and the emperor's new clothes: Feminist deconstruction as a critical methodology for library and information studies. *Library & Information Science Research, 19*(2), 181–198.

Olson, H. A. (2002). *The power to name: Locating the limits of subject representation in libraries.* Dordrecht, The Netherlands: Kluwer Academic.

Parker, E. B. (1974). Information and society. In C. A. Cuadra & M. J. Bates (Eds.), Library and information service needs of the nation: Proceedings of a Conference on the Needs of Occupational, Ethnic, and other Groups in the United States (pp. 9–50). Washington, DC: U.S. Government Printing Office.

*Philosopher's Index.* (1967–). Bowling Green, OH: Philosopher's Information Center.

Pratt, A. D. (1977). The information of the image: A model of the communications process. *Libri, 27*, 204–220.

Putnam, H. (1958). Formalization of the concept "about." *Philosophy of Science, 25*(2), 125–130.

Raber, D. (2003). *The problem of information: An introduction to information science.* Lanham, MD: Scarecrow.

Radford, G. P. (2003). Trapped in our own discursive formations: Toward an archaeology of library and information science. *Library Quarterly, 73*(1), 1–18.

Rayward, W. B. (1983). Library and information sciences: Disciplinary differentiation, competition, and convergence. In F. Machlup & U. Mansfield (Eds.), *The study of information: Interdisciplinary messages* (pp. 343–363). New York: John Wiley.

Renear, A. H., & Dubin, D. (2007). Three of the four FRBR Group 1 entity types are roles, not types. *Proceedings of the 70th Annual Meeting of the American Society for Information Science.* CD-ROM published by the Society.

Rieh, S. Y., & Danielson, D. R. (2007). Credibility: A multidisciplinary framework. *Annual Review of Information Science and Technology, 41*, 307–364.

Rowley, J. (2007). The wisdom hierarchy: Representations of the DIKW hierarchy. *Journal of Information Science, 33*(2), 163–180.

Ryle, G. (1933). "About." *Analysis, 1*(1): 10–12.

Shannon, C. E. (1948). A mathematical theory of communication. *Bell System Technical Journal, 27*, 379–423, 623–656.

Shera, J. H. (1970). *Sociological foundations of librarianship.* New York: Asia Publishing House.

Smiraglia, R. P. (2001). *The nature of "a work": Implications for the organization of knowledge.* Lanham, MD: Scarecrow.

Smith, B. (2003). Ontology. In L. Floridi (Ed.), *The Blackwell guide to the philosophy of computing and information* (pp. 155–166). Oxford, UK: Blackwell.

Smith, L. C. (1992). Interdisciplinarity: Approaches to understanding library and information science as an interdisciplinary field. In P. Vakkari & B. Cronin (Eds.), *Conceptions of library and information science: Historical, empirical and theoretical perspectives* (pp. 253–267). London: Taylor Graham.

Smith, M. M. (1997). Information ethics. *Annual Review of Information Science and Technology, 32*, 339–366.

Spinello, R. A. (1995). *Ethical aspects of information technology.* Upper Saddle River, NJ: Prentice Hall.

Stanley, J. (2008). Philosophy of language. In D. Moran (Ed.), *The Routledge companion to twentieth century philosophy* (pp. 382–437). London: Routledge.

Steup, M. (2005). Epistemology. In E. N. Zalta (Ed.), *Stanford encyclopedia of philosophy*. Stanford, CA: Metaphysics Research Lab, Center for the Study of Language and Information, Stanford University. Retrieved December 23, 2008, from plato.stanford.edu/entries/epistemology

Steup, M. (2006). The analysis of knowledge. In E. N. Zalta (Ed.), *Stanford encyclopedia of philosophy*. Stanford, CA: Metaphysics Research Lab, Center for the Study of Language and Information, Stanford University. Retrieved December 23, 2008, from plato.stanford.edu/entries/knowledge-analysis

Svenonius, E. (2000). *The intellectual foundation of information organization*. Cambridge, MA: MIT Press.

Svenonius, E., & McGarry, D. (2001). Introduction. In E. Svenonius & D. McGarry (Eds.), *Seymour Lubetzky: Writings on the classical art of cataloging* (pp. xi–xxiii). Englewood, CO: Libraries Unlimited.

Talja, S., Tuominen, K., & Savolainen, R. (2005). "Isms" in information science: Constructivism, collectivism and constructionism. *Journal of Documentation*, *61*(1), 79–101.

Tavani, H. T. (2008). Informational privacy: Concepts, theories, and controversies. In K. E. Himma & H. T. Tavani (Eds.), *The handbook of information and computer ethics* (pp. 131–164). Hoboken, NJ: Wiley.

Thomasson, A. I. (2003). The ontology of art. In P. Kivy (Ed.), *The Blackwell guide to aesthetics* (pp. 78–92). Oxford, UK: Blackwell.

Trosow, S. E. (2001). Standpoint epistemology as an alternative methodology for library and information science. *Library Quarterly*, *71*(3), 360–382.

Vakkari, P., & Cronin, B. (Eds.). (1992). *Conceptions of library and information science: Historical, empirical and theoretical perspectives*. London: Taylor Graham.

Warner, J. (2001). W(h)ither information science?/! *Library Quarterly*, *71*(2), 243–255.

White, H. D., & McCain, K. W. (1998). Visualizing a discipline: An author co-citation analysis of information science, 1972–1995. *Journal of the American Society for Information Science*, *49*(4), 327–355.

Wiener, N. (1961). *Cybernetics: Or, control and communication in the animal and the machine* (2nd ed.). Cambridge, MA: MIT Press.

Williamson, T. (2007). *The philosophy of philosophy*. Oxford, UK: Blackwell.

Wilson, P. (1968). *Two kinds of power: An essay on bibliographic control*. Berkeley: University of California Press.

Wilson, P. (1973). Situational relevance. *Information Processing & Management*, *9*(8), 457–471.

Wilson, P. (1983). *Second-hand knowledge: An inquiry into cognitive authority*. Westport, CT: Greenwood.

Zalta, E. N. (Ed.). (1997–). *Stanford encyclopedia of philosophy*. Stanford, CA: Metaphysics Research Lab, Center for the Study of Language and Information, Stanford University. Retrieved September 28, 2008, from plato.stanford.edu

# CHAPTER 5

# Fifty Years of Research in Artificial Intelligence

*Hamid R. Ekbia*
*Indiana University, Bloomington, IN*

## Introduction

Artificial Intelligence (AI) has come of age. Two thousand and six marked the fiftieth anniversary of the Dartmouth Conference, where the term Artificial Intelligence was accepted as the official label for a new discipline that seemed to hold great promise in the pursuit of understanding the human mind. AI, as the nascent discipline came to be known in public and academic discourse, has accomplished a lot during this period, breaking new ground and providing deep insights into our minds, our technologies, and the relationship between them. But AI has also failed significantly, making false promises and often manifesting a kind of unbridled enthusiasm that is emblematic of Hollywood-style projects. This chapter seeks to capture both of these aspects: AI's successes, accomplishments, and contributions to science, technology, and intellectual inquiry, on one hand, and its failures, fallacies, and shortcomings, on the other.

The history of AI can, furthermore, be reviewed from different perspectives—humanistic, cognitive, sociological, and philosophical, among others. This review examines AI from two key perspectives—scientific and engineering. The former represents AI claims about the human mind and the nature of intelligence; the latter embodies the wide array of computer systems that are built by AI practitioners or by others who have, or claim to have, taken inspiration from ideas in AI in order to solve a practical problem in an area of application. Ideally, the scientific face should guide the engineering one and the engineering face would provide support and substance to its scientific counterpart. In reality, however, that relationship is not as straightforward as it should be, turning AI into a schizophrenic Janus. The way AI practitioners "talk" about these two faces complicates the situation even further, as we shall see. This review seeks to provide a balanced portrait of the two faces. Currently, we are witnessing a resurgence of interest in, and application of, AI in areas such as education, video gaming, financial forecasting, medical diagnosis, health and elderly care, data mining, self-aware computing, and the Semantic Web. The list is illustrative, but it clearly indicates the broad range of application domains that draw on AI techniques for ideas and solutions. As a general heuristic, whenever one encounters something qualified as "smart" or "intelligent"—as in "smart phones," "smart homes," "smart bombs," "intelligent tutoring systems," or "intelligent decision support"—an association with AI is implied.

How best to review a field with such apparent complexity—dual aspects, dual faces, numerous applications, and so on—is a question with no best answer. One reasonable way to do this would be to treat these dimensions separately, pointing out links where they exist, and maintaining a critical perspective throughout. This is the tack that we follow here. We navigate the terrain from the perspective of the various *approaches* that practitioners have adopted in implementing AI applications and systems. The notion of "approach" is used here in the sense typically understood in AI to refer to research programs with common conceptual frameworks—that is, with a common set of intuitions, metaphors, and philosophies together with their accompanying tools and formalisms. On this basis, people in AI divide the field into different approaches—mainly symbolic, connectionist, and situated. I follow a more fine-grained classification that respects this division, but that is more useful for our purposes here (see Table 5.1). Central to each of these approaches is a basic understanding of intelligence as comprising a particular property or capability—for example, symbol manipulation, computational speed, knowledge. Classifying AI according to these approaches provides a useful organizing principle for present purposes.

The chapter consists of four major sections: The first provides the historical background of AI developments, including the history of its relationships to information science; the second gives an overview of the major AI approaches listed in Table 5.1; the third reviews a subset of AI applications in domains that have

Table 5.1  **Main approaches in AI and their basic understanding of intelligence**

| The Approach | The Basic Idea |
|---|---|
| Symbolic | Token Manipulation |
| Brute-Force | Speed of Computation |
| Knowledge-Intensive | Knowledge |
| Case-Based | Reminiscence |
| Creative | Analogy-Making |
| Biocomputational | Architecture |
| Dynamical | Continuous State Change |
| Situated | Physical and Social Interaction |

attracted the most attention; and the last section presents an overall assessment of the current state of the art in AI and its future potentials.

## Historical Background

AI has a short but intriguing history. Since its inception half a century ago, the discipline has gone through many periods of unbridled optimism followed by periods permeated by a spirit of despair and failure. As Crevier (1993, p. 1) aptly put it, this is indeed a "tumultuous history." One general pattern that has emerged in these years is that every so often a new paradigm appears on the scene with the explicit claim of overthrowing the previous ones and replacing them with new ideas, methods, and models that will entirely overcome or bypass existing problems. Although this kind of punctuated development is not unfamiliar in the history of science, it takes an unusually "revolutionary" character in the history of AI, in the form of all-or-nothing statements about the essence of intelligence, cognition, and mind. Most commonly, such statements take one or both of the following forms:

- Intelligence is nothing but $X$

- Intelligence has nothing to do with $Y$

where $x$ and $y$ vary depending, respectively, on the specific approach that is being advocated and on the approach(es) against which it has been launched. Three practices are common to all of AI:

1.  As an engineering practice, AI seeks to build precise working systems.

2.  As a scientific practice, it seeks to explain the human mind and human behavior.

3.  As a discursive practice, it seeks to use psychological terms (derived from its scientific practice) to describe what its artifacts (built through the engineering practice) do.

The first two practices highlight the fact that AI, as a way of *knowing* and a way of *doing*, straddles the boundary between science and engineering. On one hand, its object is typically the building of artifacts that perform specific tasks. On the other hand, those same artifacts are intended as media to model and explain an aspect of human behavior. These dual objectives have been present in AI since its beginnings. AI pioneer Herbert Simon (1995, p. 100) argued, "far from striving to separate science and engineering, we need not distinguish them at all. ... We can stop debating whether AI is science or engineering; it is both."

The engineering principle of "understanding by building" is a strong driving force in AI and accounts for a good deal of its appeal among its advocates. In the eyes of these practitioners, the fact that AI theories and models of cognition are physically instantiated in computer systems provides them with an aura of being "real"—a quality that was, by and large, absent from previous psychological theories. In fact, the role of technology is what distinguishes AI from any previous attempt to study human behavior (Varela, Thompson, & Rosch, 1991). It is what, according to some accounts, generates within AI (and cognitive science) a potential for rigor, clarity, and controlled experimentation (Crevier, 1993), as well as a certain degree of honesty, which is acknowledged even by the staunchest of AI's critics (Dreyfus, 1992). However, engineering and scientific principles often clash with each other, generating a gap that needs to be filled by discursive practice (Ekbia, 2008a).

In sum, AI seeks to be three things at the same time: A way of doing, a way of knowing, and a way of talking (Ekbia, 2008b). These practices pull the field in different directions, generating a body of models, metaphors, and techniques that, judging by AI's history, keeps moving in cycles of fads and fashions (Ekbia, 2001; Shanker, 1987). This happens because the discursive practice simply cannot fulfill the role expected of it: Not only does it fail to bridge the gap between engineering and scientific practices, it widens the gap by introducing ever more layers of anthropomorphic language, metaphorical imagery, and technical jargon. This pattern is discernible in all the approaches examined here, but also in its long relationship with information science, as we see next.

## AI and Information Science

AI and the information field (information science and information systems) have had an active, albeit cautious, relationship from the early stages of their history. In particular, information scientists found in AI a rich source of ideas for thinking about theoretical questions as well as a repertoire of tools and techniques for dealing with practical applications. As Smith (1980) points out, information systems practitioners had already recognized the relevance of research in AI to information processing in the early 1970s—as reflected, for instance, in the UNISIST (World Science Information System) 1971 report, published by the United Nations Educational, Scientific, and Cultural Organization. Indeed, Smith traces the origins of this relationship back to the pioneering works of Alan Turing and Vannevar Bush in the 1940s on, respectively, machine intelligence and information retrieval (Houston & Harman, 2007). Later work by Licklider (1965, p. 36) focused explicitly on the "precognitive system" as a possible library of the future. This work, as we shall see later, foreshadows much of the current research on ontologies and the Semantic Web.

Smith's (1980) review represents the first stand-alone review of AI published in *ARIST*; she developed a conceptual framework using four key ideas in AI relevant to information systems: Pattern recognition, representation, problem solving, and learning. She related these concepts to topics in information retrieval such as query selection, document representation, and reference retrieval, anticipating the future growth of AI applications in information systems with a shift of focus toward "intelligent" online assistants and tutors (p. 94). She also proposed computer-assisted instruction as a potential application area of AI. Smith (1987) explored the further development of these ideas, with an emphasis on the application of AI expert systems in reference, cataloging, and search (see also Clarke & Cronin, 1983). Smith's (1987, p. 62) updated review ended with a cautionary note on why discussions of intelligent information retrieval should "avoid false optimism and unrealistic expectation or risk disenchantment." These cautions echoed similar concerns by other information scientists about the broader implications of AI applications in information systems (e.g., Obermeier, 1983; Sowizral, 1985).

Information retrieval may be the oldest and the most significant application of AI in information science. However, numerous other application areas have been explored—e.g., machine learning (Chen, 1995), natural language processing (Chowdhury, 2003), human-computer interaction (Rogers, 2004), and, more recently, ontologies and the Semantic Web (Legg, 2007). This last area is interesting in that it reintroduces many of the same issues and questions that were at the core of information retrieval. We revisit the Semantic Web in more detail later in the review.

# AI in Theory

The history of AI includes a number of "revolutions" that were launched against a governing paradigm (e.g., logic, computation, representations), but that in the end only reinforced some of that paradigm's fundamental assumptions in a more disguised form. Various intellectual, institutional, cultural, and socio-economic threads have contributed to the entrenchment of this situation, as has the interdisciplinary character of the field that brings together people from different disciplines with various intuitions, assumptions, and widely disparate understandings of AI's concepts and practices (Ekbia, 2008a). Differences can begin even at the most basic level— for example, the characterization of "intelligence," which is the most fundamental notion in the field. These differences are clearly manifested in the various AI approaches that we explore now.

## Symbolic AI: Intelligence as Token Manipulation

The convergence of a number of intellectual traditions of the last few centuries (mainly Descartes's dualism and Hobbes's logicism) found a dramatic culmination in the idea of the mind as a computer: "The view that mental states and processes are *computational*" (Fodor, 1997, p. 468). (The exact meaning of "computational" could be a bone of contention, but we can disregard that here.) Technically, this view is closely linked to modern digital computers, but it has deeper historical roots, famously captured in Hobbes's dictum that "Reasoning is reckoning" and instantiated in Leibniz's wheel, Babbage's Analytic Engine, and so on.

The development of digital computers followed a series of important findings in mathematical logic during the first half of the twentieth century. These historical lineages are accounted for in numerous studies, both as formal commentaries (e.g., Davis, 1988; Hayes, 1973; Kowalski, 1977) and as broad studies of the modern intellectual scene (e.g., Bolter, 1984; Hofstadter, 1979). I wish here to highlight (what seem to be) three major contributions of computational views to AI: The idea of a universal machine, the idea of computers as intelligent machines, and the idea of intelligence as problem solving.

### Computers as Universal Machines

The idea of "thinking machines" is not entirely novel. As early as the 1830s, Charles Babbage conceived of an all-purpose automatic calculating machine and remarked glibly that his engine "could do everything but compose country dances" (Huskey & Huskey [1980, p. 300]; Babbage would probably have been gleefully surprised to learn that computers do, in fact, compose country dances nowadays; see Cope [2001]). What *is* novel is the concrete implementation of the idea on electronic computers, which started almost a hundred years ago. Alan Turing (1936) captured this novelty in a famous proposition:

> It is possible to invent a single machine which can be used to compute any computable sequence.

Turing was arguably the first person to theorize this proposition, which he did in roughly three major strokes. What was needed, according to Turing, was:

- The analysis, in an intuitive fashion, of what *human* computers do when they calculate with paper and pencil

- The development of an abstract model of this human activity by breaking it up into simple mechanical steps, based on other simplifying assumptions (e.g., the use of one- instead of two-dimensional paper, limiting the types and number of symbols that the computer observes at any given moment)

- The detailed design of a machine that implements this abstract model

The first of these steps is straightforward and falls in line with the atomistic tradition in science. The second step gave birth to the notion of a universal machine—a machine that could perform all conceivable computations. As this was a rather unexpected consequence, however—nothing in the prior history of technology had such a strong feature—the third step was taken as "a significant vindication" of the prior two (Davis, 1988, p. 157).

This threefold scheme reveals a pattern that seems to have set a precedent for the later practice of AI—namely, the stages of observing and decomposing some aspect of human behavior into small, functional steps; throwing away superfluous aspects and maintaining only those that are deemed relevant; and constructing an abstract model that can be implemented on an actual machine. Most important, it explains the prevalent belief among AI researchers in the idea of *explaining by building*, which was alluded to earlier.

## Computers as Intelligent Artifacts

The cognitivist approach—as opposed to, for instance, the behaviorist approach (Skinner, 1985)—to the study of human psychology is based on the idea that people's behavior is determined by the (representational) content of their minds—namely, by their beliefs, goals, and desires. The intentional stance or strategy, famously elaborated by the philosopher Daniel Dennett (1997, p. 70), posits:

> There *are* patterns in human affairs that impose themselves, not quite inexorably but with great vigor, absorbing physical perturbations and variations that might as well be considered random; there are the patterns that we characterize in terms of beliefs, desires, and intentions of rational agents. (emphasis in the original)

To think that Dullsburg is a boring town, according to this strategy, is to have a representation of it as boring and to be in a special relation—that is, belief—to that representation. To want to leave Dullsburg and reside in Joyville, similarly, is to have some representation of these places, the desire to leave one, and the intention to live in the other. This is the crux of the "belief-desire-intention" model of human psychology, which underlies the cognitivist approach.

Intuitively, this might sound like a (if not the only) plausible viewpoint to us half a century after the rise of cognitivism; but it was not so appealing less than a hundred years ago, when behaviorism sanctioned only those theories of psychology that dealt with observable behaviors and rejected as unscientific those that invoked "nonobservable" mental processes. The shift of focus from directly observable behavior to mental phenomena that are not directly observable marks a serious change of attitude that has much to do with the emergence of digital computers and theories thereof. Pylyshyn (1984, p. xiii) articulates this link as follows:

> What makes it possible for humans … to act on the basis of representations is that they instantiate such representations physically as cognitive codes and that their behavior is a causal consequence of operations carried out on these codes. Since this is precisely what computers do, [it] amounts to a claim that cognition *is* a type of computation.

This radical computational view of cognitivism is based on the idea that the brain, like the computer, has distinct classes of physical states that *cause* behaviors that are meaningfully distinct. In our example, there is a physically distinct state of your brain that represents your belief in the boringness of Dullsburg, there is another physically distinct state that represents the attractiveness of Joyville. These states are not only physically distinct, they can cause distinct behaviors such as interest in one town and repulsion from another. In other words, semantically distinct behaviors—that is, behaviors that bear different relations to the outside world—are causally enabled by physically distinct states of the brain. Because this physically driven and semantically distinct behavior is also what computers display, the argument goes, then cognition is a type of computation.

On the basis of intuitions such as this, computers have acquired a central role in cognitive science—not merely as tools and instruments for studying human behavior, but also, and more importantly, as *instantiations* of such behavior. Pylyshyn (1984, pp. 74–75) highlights the role of the computer implementation of psychological theories in three major respects: The representation of cognitive states in terms of symbolic expressions that can be interpreted as describing aspects of the outside world, the representation of rules that apply to these symbols, and the mapping of this system of symbols and rules onto causal physical laws so as to preserve a coherent semantic relationship between the symbols and the outside world. These principles found explicit realization in some of the earliest models of AI, such as the General Problem Solver (Newell, Shaw, & Simon, 1960).

## Intelligence as Problem Solving

The notion that human life is comprised of a set of problems, and human intelligence at its core is the capability to solve problems, is deeply rooted in modern sensibilities. In AI, similarly, the idea of an *agent* trying to change its internal *state* in order to come up with a sequence of *actions* as a possible *solution to a problem* or as a means to achieve a *goal* pervades traditional AI and its view of the nature of intelligence. According to this view, an intelligent agent "moves" in a space of problems ("problem space") of varying difficulties and types that, most often, also makes the means and tools for solving those problems available, and the task of the agent is to discover those tools and to figure out the least costly or most efficient way to achieve its preset goals. In chess, for example, the problem is to find the best next move and the tools are the legal moves of the game. This picture accurately portrays a chess-playing machine whose preset, given goal is to win a game—or more precisely, to put the opponent's king in a checkmate position on the (virtual) board—by taking a finite number of discrete steps according to prescribed rules. The question is, does this picture also accurately portray how human beings behave and conduct their lives in real situations?

Early approaches in AI took this to be the case—for example, logic systems, rational agents, and general problem solvers, all of which use search as their key design technique. For the builders of these systems, search is not only a technique and method; it is the royal road to intelligence. An influential version of this view is the *physical symbol system hypothesis* proposed by AI pioneers Newell and Simon (1976). Taking AI as an empirical science, they seek to devise for it "laws of qualitative structure" on a par with the cell doctrine in biology, plate tectonics in geology, or atomism in physical chemistry (p. 116). The physical symbol system hypothesis, according to these authors, is such a law. Symbols are, in their view, physical patterns (neural activity in the brain or electrical pulses in a computer) and many interrelated symbols taken together constitute a *symbol structure;* a physical symbol system is, therefore, "a machine that produces through time an evolving collection of symbol structures" (p. 116). The thesis is that such a machine (whether a human being or a digital computer) "has the necessary and sufficient conditions for general intelligent action" (p. 116).

Although this principled way of studying human thought offered certain advances with respect to previous methods of doing psychology, its the-world-in-the-mind character is evident on different dimensions: from the characterization of problems in an abstract mental space to the search for solutions in the same space (Agre, 1997). This particular view of mind dominated AI for more than three decades. Early AI systems that used heuristic search included the General Problem Solver (Newell & Simon, 1961), a checker program (Samuel, 1959), and Dendral (Lindsay et al., 1980), as well as a few applications in scheduling and linear programming. However, chess provides the best known domain area where these ideas have been applied in combination with the computational capabilities of supercomputers.

## *Brute-Force AI: Intelligence as Fast Computation*

With the advent of computers in the 1950s, chess turned into a litmus test for assessing the capabilities of these machines. The interest in chess and other similar games on the part of computer scientists derives from various considerations, including the "formal" character of these games—roughly, the discreteness and determinateness of the moves and pieces (Haugeland, 1981). This property of games aligns with the early AI notion of thinking as a purely mental activity, of planning in the head and executing in the outside world, and of problem solving as search in a problem space (cf. Agre, 1997). In the case of chess, this interest is further enhanced by its manageable complexity and by a decomposability that allows techniques of parallel computing to be brought to bear. Soon after the appearance of von Neumann computers, Claude Shannon (1950) published a paper entitled "Programming a Computer for Playing Chess," and the next year Turing (1953) proposed a chess-playing program and hand-simulated it. The first running chess programs appeared in the late 1950s. Early optimism was buoyed by modest success. The challenge, however, proved to be much greater than originally estimated.

At the core of early chess-playing programs are data structures called "trees." The conception of a chess game as a tree structure makes it possible to break up the search space into separate parts, each of which can be evaluated by a separate processor. Although this is very different from the types of parallel processing attributed to the human brain, the technique works well in parallel computing environments. A psychologically realistic model, by contrast, would not depend so much on heavy computing and search. Rather, it would focus on perceptual aspects of playing chess, at which humans seem to excel. Considerable evidence supports this difference. The Dutch psychologist de Groot, for instance, showed that experts, unlike novices, perceive the chessboard not as an arrangement of individual pieces but in terms of groups or *chunks*. That there is a strong perceptual dimension to human chess playing is also shown in the mistakes that are committed by human players but not by computers—for example, paying too much attention to the center of the board at the expense of the periphery (Newborn, 1997, p. 85).

These considerations, in fact, gave rise to a project designed in the 1970s at Carnegie-Mellon University by Hans Berliner, a computer scientist and top-notch chess player himself—a project that never achieved spectacular success in terms of victories, and that eventually petered out, leaving the domain wide open to its brute-force competitors. Brute-force methods typically use a *search method* to enumerate all legal moves at any given point in the game, as well as a *pruning algorithm* to eliminate some of the (unpromising) moves early on. They also use a *scoring function* (also known as "static evaluation") as a quick-and-dirty measure of the desirability of a position from the point of view of one of the players.

Once software techniques have been thoroughly explored and exploited, the obvious next step is to look at hardware. Two main possibilities arise in this realm: The development of special-purpose hardware and the use of many processors at the same time. Both of these strategies are motivated by the idea that speed is a crucial component of intelligence. For decades, this observation has motivated a quest for achieving ever more efficient performance; this holds not only in computer chess but also elsewhere in AI. The idea of multiple processors, however, has proved to work effectively only in special domains such as chess. For technical reasons that are not germane to this review, the ideal of attaining an $N$-fold speedup when using $N$ processors is never reached in other domains. Problems of communication, coherence, consistency, and synchronization among processors are some of the main reasons (Hennessy & Patterson, 1996). However, if the task is broken down in an optimal way, a considerable improvement is attainable. For instance, in 1996, in an historical match against Kasparov, the world chess champion, the supercomputer Deep Blue employed 192 processors. Work on chess provides one example of a broader approach to AI, which focuses on parallel computing techniques. This approach, which gained some momentum in the 1990s under the rubric of "massively parallel AI" (e.g., Kitano, 1994), is currently pursued in models of biological computation, as we discuss later.

## Knowledge-Intensive AI: Intelligence as Large Quantities of Knowledge

The next approach in AI is motivated by the idea that a vast amount of knowledge is the key to intelligence. What we need in order to achieve human-level intelligence, the advocates of this approach argue, is to provide a machine with enough *commonsense knowledge* for it to be able to continue the process of knowledge acquisition on its own. Cyc ("from encyclopedia") is the major project built on this premise. Launched in 1984, it was originally envisaged as a three-decade research program that would proceed in three distinct stages, ending in 2001 (Lenat, 1997). By going through these stages, Cyc was intended to break out of AI's so-called knowledge acquisition bottleneck. According to initial estimates, the critical mass for passing through the first stage of hand-coding was on the order of one million facts. Putting such a large number of facts together with the heuristics necessary to apply them under the right circumstances was a daunting task that called for a "large, high-risk, high-payoff, decade-sized project" (Lenat & Guha, 1990, Preface). Cyc was supposed to be exactly such a system—a $50 million project that in its first decade would require two person-centuries for data entry.

What drove the creation of Cyc were the limitations and failures of earlier expert systems such as Dendral. Developed by Edward Feigenbaum and his colleagues over a period of ten years, Dendral was an expert system for the analysis of the molecular structure of chemical compounds—a tedious task traditionally performed by chemists taking educated guesses on the data obtained from mass spectroscopy. Dendral consisted of a set of IF-THEN rules like the following, together with the logic required to combine them (Feigenbaum & Barr, 1982; cited by Crevier, 1993, p. 149):

IF
  the spectrum for the molecule has two peaks at masses $x_1$ and $x_2$ such that
  $x_1 + x_2$ = Molecular Weight + 28, AND
  $x_1$ - 28 is a high peak, AND
  $x_2$ - 28 is a high peak, AND
  at least one of $x_1$ or $x_2$ is high,
THEN
  the molecule contains a ketone group.

In this way, Dendral drastically reduced the effort needed to determine the structure of a chemical substance, narrowing the search in some cases better than chemists could and demonstrating the possibility of capturing expert knowledge as a set of rules in a machine. The integration of the rules and meta-rules (i.e., the rules that determine which rules to apply) was, however, a major weakness of Dendral and prevented its expansion beyond a certain point. The Cyc group's approach was motivated by the belief that the problem with expert systems was one of *brittleness*—that is, the inability of these systems to handle novel and unexpected situations. They believed that expert systems had fallen into what they called "the representation trap," which they defined as:

> choosing a set of long, complex primitives (predicate names) that have a lot of knowledge compiled within them, and writing rules that are also tailored to the program's domain (omitting premises that needn't be worried about in that particular task). The bait in the trap is the fact that it works—at least within the narrow domain for which that particular program was designed. The catch is that the resultant system is isolated and brittle. (Lenat & Guha, 1990, p. 17)

Or, as Lenat and Feigenbaum (1991, p. 240) more concisely put it, the system uses "variable names pregnant with meaning—pregnant to the user, but barren to the system." (This should remind the reader of current debates on the potentials and challenges of the Semantic Web, which we discuss later.) The remedy, according to Lenat and Feigenbaum, was to provide AI systems with commonsense knowledge consisting of both general facts and methods (heuristics) for applying those facts. The basic theoretical claim is that knowledge, especially of the commonsense variety, is all we need for intelligence and that formal systems such as Cyc can acquire this knowledge first by spoon feeding and eventually on their own. According to this view, knowledge—vast amounts of it—is the key to intelligence; and so little else is required, in that the Cyc group considers the current generation of personal computers as possible candidates for the realization of human-level intelligence race—as long as they are provided with sufficient amounts of commonsense knowledge.

To the best of my knowledge, no one in AI or cognitive science has tried to provide an account of the term *commonsense,* even though it is widespread. The ambiguity of this term is consequential for a project such as Cyc. In fact, the meaning of the term *commonsense* has changed drastically for the Cyc group members since they launched the project in 1984. Originally, they deemed commonsense knowledge to be "real world factual knowledge, the sort found in an encyclopedia"—hence the project's name (Lenat, Prakash, & Shepherd, 1985, p. 65). Later, the term's meaning changed to "the knowledge that an encyclopedia would assume the reader knows without being told (e.g., an object can't be in two places at once)" (p. 65). Even with this new conception in mind, Lenat and Guha (1990, p. 29) admit that they include "some of that [encyclopedic knowledge] as well." Given the central role that this notion plays in their project, this uncertainty and ambiguity might be one of the reasons for the difficulties that Cyc has faced in practice. Pratt (1994) and Ekbia (2008a) report some of these difficulties as observed through their direct interactions with Cyc.

## Case-Based AI: Intelligence as Reminiscence of Past Experience

Case-based reasoning (CBR) is a prolific research program in AI and cognitive science. Originally motivated by the study of natural language processing, it has been applied to computer models of story understanding, learning, and planning, as well as a host of commercial, manufacturing, legal, and educational areas such as multimedia instruction and design.

As its name implies, case-based reasoning involves the interplay of two major themes: A (positive) theme about "cases" and a (negative) theme about "reasoning." The core intuition in CBR is that people reason and learn from experience and that the knowledge acquired from experience, captured in *cases*, is central to their understanding of the world. In the domain of language, this intuition gives primacy to meaning and "semantics," as opposed to form and "syntax," which were of prime concern in the logicist approach. As a negative claim, therefore, CBR presents a challenge to (formal) logic. It promotes a kind of reasoning different from deductive inference and emphasizes the role of memory in human cognition. CBR can be understood in part as a project countering the logicist tradition, as exemplified in AI by Cyc.

Striving for psychological realism has been a strong guiding force in the development of CBR; it is motivated by the belief that "the best way to approach the problem of building an intelligent machine is to emulate human cognition" (Schank & Kass, 1988, p. 181). Human intelligence has to do with getting the "right information at the right time," according to the proponents of CBR; and information, in their view, has mainly to do with world knowledge. Therefore, the main challenges to those who would design and implement a computational model of mind are "what data structures are useful for representing knowledge and what algorithms operate on those knowledge structures to produce intelligent behavior?" (p. 181).

The philosopher Ludwig Wittgenstein also challenged the idea that human language derives its meaning from an objective world, arguing that the meaning of any utterance depends on the human and cultural context of its use. In contemporary AI terminology, this amounts to the claim that language is "scruffy" and not "neat" (Crevier, 1993, p. 168). CBR could perhaps be thought of as an attempt to realize Wittgenstein's view in computer systems (through the use of "scripts" and other data structures), but it fails to take into account the other side of this view—namely, the difficulty, if not the impossibility, of capturing life forms in fixed, rule based structures (Neumaier, 1987; Woolgar, 1995).

The origins of CBR lie in the early work of Roger Schank and his students. What differentiated their work from most other work on natural language processing in those days was the "integrated knowledge hypothesis"—namely, "that meaning and processing knowledge are often crucial at even the earliest points in the process of understanding language" (Schank & Birnbaum, 1984, p. 212; cf. Schank & Leake, 2001). Schank's first step in modeling this view of language was his development of the theory of *conceptual dependency* (CD), which sought to formulate "a conceptual base into which utterances in natural language are mapped during understanding" (Schank, 1973, p. 188). It assumes, in other words, that underneath any linguistic utterance (sentence) are nonlinguistic representations. These representations are "image-like in nature, in that each concept is processed with respect to the whole picture that is created" (p. 241) and they are governed by a set of rules that maps the inputs into a "predefined representation scheme" (Schank & Riesbeck, 1981, p. 13). CD seeks to find these rules and representations.

CBR workers tried to enrich their models by introducing new structures such as "scripts" and "memory organization packets" to the original CD scheme. The main function of these is to bring world knowledge to bear in processing and understanding language. Scripts, like frames, are data structures for representing stereotyped sequences of events such as a football play (come to the line of scrimmage in a given formation, hike the ball, hand off the ball, run toward the goal, etc.). The idea behind scripts is to provide automatic contexts by generating stereotyped sets of expectations. Thus, expectations help us fill in the gaps in hearing a story—for example, that the quarterback has the ball and that a tackle takes place:

> The quarterback received the hike, ran toward the line of scrimmage, and was stopped five seconds later.

But we do not seem to keep every detail of every event in memory. In football, for example, there are different types of run—a run to the line of scrimmage, a run toward a specific player, a run toward the goal, and so on. Each of these may constitute a distinct concept, but the common features among them can all be captured in a single, higher level (i.e., abstract) memory structure for "run." In other words, the theory is that memories are organized in hierarchies of stereotyped structures that vary in their degree of detail. The theory of memory organization packets (MOPs) was devised to implement this vision in a computational fashion.

In summary, the CBR approach to memory and reminding can be summarized as follows:

1. Experience, as a replay or adaptation of daily routines, is captured in discrete representations such as cases and scripts.

2. Memory is a storehouse or library of cases, indexed so as to make appropriate subsequent retrieval possible.

3. Understanding a situation, text, or story is achieved by explaining it, which in turn involves calling upon the right script.

These principles have greatly influenced the technical work in CBR, as is evident in the following passage:

> Human memory depends upon good methods of labeling cases so that they can be retrieved when needed. Human experts are not systems of rules, they are libraries of experiences. (Riesbeck & Schank, 1989, p. 7)

It is in this "storage" view of memory that CBR comes closest to the computer metaphor of mind. In particular, the emphasis on cases or scripts in CBR has turned the problem of remembering into a search paradigm based on efficient *indexing*— in other words, the strategy is to label and index cases as they occur so that, much later, they can be remembered and efficiently retrieved in "similar" situations. This scheme, however, has one major problem: It often employs surface similarities that are rarely useful in classifying interesting situations. The question, then, is, "How do the relevant features emerge and come to light when one is dealing with a situation?" Taking note of this problem, Kolodner (1996, p. 355) suggested that "indexing" might have been the wrong term and "accessibility" might be more appropriate. Wills and Kolodner (1996, pp. 83–85), in fact, point out an alternative solution that partly solves the problem. This consists of "a flexible and highly opportunistic manner" of redescribing new situations in terms of old ones. Rather than first saving (a description of) an experience in memory with the "right" labels and then using those labels to assess other situations, this alternative view lumps the two stages together, trying to make sense of a new situation by *seeing it as* a previous one, ideally somewhat in the manner of models of analogy making such as Copycat and Metacat (Hofstadter & Fluid Analogies Research Group, 1995), which we discuss next.

## Creative AI: Intelligence as Analogy Making

Creativity, in art and music but also in daily activities, is considered a mark of intelligence. Studying creativity might indeed provide an acid test for AI and cognitive science: "Cognitive science cannot succeed if it cannot model creativity, and it is here that it is most likely to fail" (Dartnall, 2002, p. 14). Psychologically speaking, traditional accounts of creativity—from the inspirational view that considers creativity as essentially mysterious to the romantic view that attributes creativity to exceptional gifts such as insight or intuition—are inadequate because they beg the question by simply replacing one name (creativity) with another (divine gift, insight, etc.). Arthur Koestler (1964) recognized this shortcoming and tried to give a more principled account of *how* creativity works but, as Boden (1990, p. 5) points out, his own view was no more than suggestive. Henri Poincaré (1982) adopted a more systematic approach and formulated a four-phase process of creative thinking—roughly, conscious preparation, subconscious incubation, abrupt insight, and evaluation. Like Koestler, his account highlights the significance of long, unconscious prior work preceding the creative act. The key question for AI is, What does this "work" consist of? And how could it be best studied? In their attempt to answer these questions, studies in AI and cognitive science focus on mental *processes* that give rise to creativity. We introduce a few examples of such studies here.

### Emmy: The Computer Composer

Experiments with computer composition in music abound (Loy, 1989; see Cope, 1991, Chapter 1 for a brief history). One of the most interesting and celebrated of these is David Cope's Experiments in Musical Intelligence, EMI or Emmy. Imagine feeding Beethoven's nine symphonies into a machine and it producing Beethoven's Tenth. That is almost what Emmy is all about. Initially conceived in 1981, Emmy has produced music in the styles of such revered musicians as Bach, Brahms, Chopin, and Mozart, with a quality that the most sophisticated musicians find impressive and deceitful. Hofstadter (2002) reports a set of auditions in which students and faculty at reputable schools such as Indiana, Julliard, and Eastman listened to the music composed either by these great composers or by Emmy working in *their* style and were unable to guess the provenance with better than a chance probability.

Very briefly, the basic idea behind Emmy is what Cope calls "recombinant music" (Dartnall, 2002, pp. 21, 74)—finding recurrent structures of various kinds in a composer's music and reusing those structures in new arrangements, so as to construct a new piece *in the same style* (Hofstadter, 2002, p. 74). Given a set of input pieces (usually by a single composer and belonging to the same general form, such as mazurka), Emmy chops up and reassembles them in a principled and coherent way. The guiding principles in this process are very similar to those followed by someone solving a jigsaw puzzle—namely, to observe simultaneously the local fit of each piece with other pieces and the global pattern of the whole picture. Hofstadter calls these syntactic and semantic meshing, as they deal, respectively, with form and content. In addition, in each composition Emmy incorporates *signatures*—a characteristic intervallic pattern that recurs throughout a composer's oeuvre—as well as another sophisticated mechanism that captures and manipulates repeated motifs at different levels of the input pieces.

## Aaron: The Figurative Painter

In art, too, people have tried to test computers in terms of creativity. One of the first experiments in computer generated art is Harold Cohen's *Aaron*, a computer artist whose products have enjoyed the approval of the art world, being exhibited in respected museums around the world. A well established painter himself, Cohen was originally interested in abstract, nonrepresentational art. Cohen's early view, which is sometimes referred to as "abstract symbolism," was influenced by both the Modernists' denial of meaning in art and by Abstract Expressionists' fascination with universal themes; he adhered to neither, however, arguing that art should be a "meaning generator not a meaning communicator" (Cohen, 1995; cf. McCorduck, 1992, p. 5). In other words, rather than receiving a specific meaning codified in the artwork, the viewer of art should create meaning *de novo*—a feat at which human beings seem to excel in various degrees. This propensity of humans to assign meaning became a central theme for Cohen, who wanted to answer the question "How is it that the marks you make take on certain kinds of meaning?" (McCorduck, 1991, p. 16).

Cohen experimented with these ideas first by creating map-like paintings produced by splattering a canvas with paint and then drawing lines between the dots of paint according to certain rules; he later generated child-like paintings from ink and crumpled Dacron cloth. The desire to exclude himself from execution led Cohen to computers on the presumption that this "would permit a rigorous test of ideas about art making and would demonstrate their validity if their execution produced art objects" (McCorduck, 1991, p. 16). Aaron's drawings continued to improve in terms of balance, perspective, and accuracy, acquiring a rough resemblance in subject and treatment (although not style) to primitivist paintings of Gauguin and Rousseau (see Figure 5.1). Although Cohen views Aaron as merely a means of producing his art on a par with other machines that artists use to make art, he makes an argument for the significance of Aaron to cognitive science. He claims that the reason Aaron's paintings function as art is deeply buried in how humans see the world—we skew what we see in the direction of what we know" (p. 104). Aaron's

**Figure 5.1  An example of Aaron's primitivist paintings**

productions might have more to say about what humans bring to the experience of art than about computers acquiring human abilities.

## Copycat: A Model of Analogy Making

A major strand of ideas in AI and cognitive science invokes analogy making as the key process behind creativity. One way to be creative is to look at new situations as similar to previous, more familiar situations—that is, to make analogies between situations. Analogies have reportedly played a key role in the creation of new scientific theories (Boden, 1990; Koestler, 1964). But in the context of everyday thinking, scientific discoveries might just be the tip of an iceberg. That is, analogies might indeed be at work at a much more mundane level than examples of scientific creativity suggest. This is the view held by many cognitive scientists (e.g., Forbus, Gentner, Markman, & Ferguson, 1998; Gentner, 1983; Hofstadter, 2001; Holyoak & Thagard, 1995; Hummel & Holyoak, 1997).

Copycat is a computer model of analogy making in the domain of letter-string puzzles. Given an analogy problem such as "**abc** →**abd**; **iijjkk** →," for example, it comes up with a set of various answers such as **iijjll**, **iijjdd**, **iijjkl**, **iijjkd**, **iijjkk**, **iikjkk**, **iidjkk**, or even **abd** or **aabbdd**. Puzzles such as these are common in aptitude tests because they apparently provide useful measures of people's intelligence and creativity. Copycat, by the same token, is believed to have some degree of creativity, albeit a minute one. An interesting feature of the domain of Copycat analogies is that there is no single "right" answer for any given problem; rather, a range of answers is always possible. In the example just discussed, as we saw at the outset, there are about eight possible answers. People often make consistent judgments about the quality of some of these answers, but the ones judged "best" are not at all the most obvious answers. Copycat has a feature that allows it to evaluate its answers to particular problems. Called *temperature*, this is a simple numerical measure of overall structural "coherence" of the program, which reflects, at any given moment, the amount and quality of structures built so far—the lower the temperature the higher the organization and the higher the quality of the relevant answer.

However, the concept of temperature, in spite of its usefulness, is crude because Copycat is still unable to explain *why* it considers particular answers to be good or bad; it cannot explain its choices. In other words, the program does not have the capability to *watch* and evaluate its own processing. This shortcoming is the main motivation behind Metacat, the successor to Copycat that has a "self-watching" capability as well as a memory to retain answers to a given problem for the purpose of comparing and contrasting them. For example, given the problem "**abc** → **abd**; **xyz** →?," two possible answers are **xyd** and **wyz**. The second answer derives from the observation that **abc** and **xyz** start at the opposite ends of the alphabet, with **abc** going to the right based on successorship and **xyz** going to the left based on predecessorship. In other words, this answer is associated with the notion of symmetry between the "opposite" letters **a** and **z**, which makes it qualitatively superior, in most people's minds, to the literal-minded answer **xyd**. People who make such a judgment are often also able to explain it in terms of the notion of symmetry, as does Metacat. In addition, people also see the contrast between this problem and "**rst** → **rsu**; **xyz** →?," in which the notion of symmetry is absent, making the literal-minded **xyu** superior to the alternative **wyz** in this case. In other words, **xyd** and **xyu** play essentially identical roles in their respective problems and are thus of comparative quality, whereas the two **wyz** answers are quite different, even though on the surface they appear to be identical. Metacat is also capable of making similar judgments, demonstrating its ability to "see" similarities and differences between problems as well as answers.

## *Biocomputational AI: Intelligence as an Architectural Property*

A large set of models and techniques in AI is inspired by natural mechanisms, such as those studied in biology. These biologically motivated attempts have led to different techniques and approaches in AI—for instance, neural networks, machine learning (mimicking human learning), and genetic algorithms (simulating biological evolution). One recent class of such attempts is identified as biologically inspired cognitive architectures (BICA) (Samsonovich & Mueller, 2008). Most of these involve computationally intensive techniques, which in turn call for new technologies and paradigms such as quantum computing. We briefly discuss these here.

### Connectionism and Artificial Neural Networks

Connectionism is rooted in long-standing views about the human mind. As a philosophy, it goes back to Hume's view that mental activity consists mainly in associations among ideas. As a scientific theory, it originates in the works of McCulloch and Pitts (1943), Hebb (1949), and Rosenblatt (1958), who developed theories of neural circuitry based on mutual activations and inhibitions among neurons. And as an approach in AI and cognitive science, it was instigated by a number of independent researchers during the 1970s and 1980s—for example, Dell (1986), Grossberg (1976), and McClelland and Rumelhart (1986). Most notably, the publication of

*Parallel Distributed Processing* by the PDP Research Group in 1986 marks a resurgence of interest in connectionist approaches, which has persisted until now.

Unlike the symbolic approach of early AI, the connectionist approach is motivated by the low level architecture of the brain—whence the term "artificial neural networks" applied to connectionist models. Like the brain, which is a network consisting of a huge number of tightly connected neurons, artificial networks are composed of a large number of interconnected "nodes" (usually indicated by circles in diagrams), some of which serve as "input" nodes, some as "output" nodes, and others as "hidden" nodes (without direct connection to the outside world; the simplest models do not have hidden nodes; see Figure 5.2).

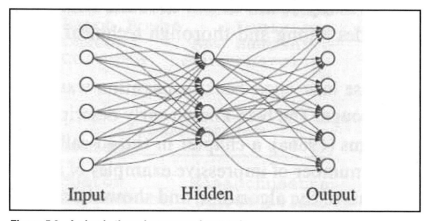

**Figure 5.2** **A simple three-layer neural network**

The nodes of a neural network are interconnected in ways that depend on the specific architecture. The *strength* of the connection between any two nodes is indicated by a numerical value, its *weight*, and the set of all connection values constitutes a pattern of connectivity. The *training* of the network, which takes place in discrete steps, proceeds by presenting the system with a set of input values and letting it modify and adjust its pattern of connectivity until it produces a desired output. At each step, each node has an *activation* level, also indicated by a numerical value. The activation is computed by using the *activation rule* (a function that combines the inputs) and it produces an output according to the *output function*. In most models, the activation rule is linear (the input values are simply added algebraically), and the output function is quasi-linear (the output is linearly proportional to the input up to a certain threshold, where it is cut off). For training, the network follows a prespecified *learning rule*—for example, *backpropagation of error*, in which the output of the network is compared, at each step, with reference values delivered by a "teacher" and the error, if any, is fed back to the network in order to adjust the connection weights (Rumelhart, Hinton, & Williams, 1986).

What is distinctive about the connectionist style of work (in comparison to the work of knowledge engineers, for instance) is that it takes place in a relatively opaque environment where there is no possibility to play around with explicit rules or instructions; instead, all one can do is tweak numerical values of various features and parameters. Of course, such tweaking can be repeated indefinitely in pursuit of ever better simulation of human behavior. This is indicative less of a discrepancy in goals between symbolic and connectionist approaches than of a discrepancy in method and style of work. In the hands of a connectionist, the computer is, as Turkle (1995, p. 61) has suggested, "still a tool but less like a hammer and more like a harpsichord."

Probably the most important aspect of connectionist models (of the PDP type) is the *distributed* character of their representations. These networks are quasidemocratic systems, where all nodes participate in all stages of processing and for all input combinations, so that no single node has a decisive role in the performance of the model. Instead, the pattern of activity of the nodes constitutes an implicit encoding of the input features, which the network sometimes even breaks into a set of *microfeatures* (in nonlocalist encoding schemes, where an input such as a word, for instance, is represented not as one unit, but as a collection of phonemes). Eventually, in an unpreprogrammed way, certain nodes may become so closely associated with certain features that they can be thought of as *encoding* those features. However, given the typically large number of hidden units in a system, it is not realistic to hope to determine how this takes place and which nodes encode which features (or microfeatures). However, a successful implementation of the division of labor among nodes is the key to the success of neural networks. The distributed character of representations in connectionist models allows learning and the emergence of novel behavior.

The capability of connectionist models in learning, dealing with ambiguity, and degrading gracefully underscores their advantages, but the relatively opaque style of functioning constitutes a major shortcoming of these models. "Neural network mysticism," as James Anderson (1995, p. 277) dubbed it, represents a rebellious rejection of the traditional scientific commitment to tractable analysis and this, according to some authors, resonates well with the so-called postmodern sensibilities of our times (Turkle, 1995). W. Daniel Hillis, the inventor of the Connection Machine, refers to this mysterious quality as "the appealing inscrutability of emergent systems" (Turkle, 1995, p. 134). NETtalk provides a classic illustration of this point. This model takes English text as input and produces a coding for speech at the output. The encoded output could be then fed to a standard speech synthesizer that transforms it into real speech sounds (Sejnowski & Rosenberg, 1987). Anyone who listens to a session in which NETtalk progresses from initial babbling sounds to semirecognizable words, and then to a fair simulacrum of human speech, cannot help being mightily impressed (Clark, 2001). However, this level of performance is accomplished at the expense of biological realism, which was one of the driving motivations behind the connectionist movement. NETtalk, for instance, produces language before comprehending it, in sharp contrast with language learning in human beings where comprehension precedes production. Seen in this light, connectionist models are more like demonstrations (or, in the language of computer professionals, "proof of concept") of the kinds of performance that tinkering with networks can achieve, rather than models of mental activity, brain architecture, or human cognition as such. For this reason, no "lifesize chunk of behavior" has been exhibited by connectionists (Harnad, 1990, p. 338).

## Genetic Algorithms

One of the first biologically inspired techniques, genetic algorithms, was originally proposed by John Holland (1975). As their name implies, these techniques were inspired by certain mechanisms of evolutionary biology—mutation, crossover, and inversion—which are universally utilized by organisms to alter or shuffle segments of their DNA. The key idea of genetic algorithms is to think of strings of bits (ones and zeros) as genes and to apply the operators to transform the gene pool from generation to generation. Long bit-strings consisting of many genes are thus analogous to individual genomes in a population. In nature, evolutionary (or natural) selection accounts for the survival of the fittest genomes. In genetic algorithms, this role of selector is played by the programmer, who devises both the selection criteria and the mechanism by which such selection takes place. As Mitchell (1996) points out, success with this technique often requires both computational parallelism—many processors evaluating many bit-strings at the same time—and an intelligent strategy for choosing which bit-strings should survive and which should die. The first is a matter of computational hardware and the second one of programming skill. Together, the two give rise to a highly effective parallelism for simultaneous searching for solutions through a large number of possibilities.

Carrying out genetic algorithms normally involves a huge amount of computation. In order to do this efficiently, the process requires increasingly cheap and fast machinery. The empirical observation known as "Moore's Law" suggests this will be the case for the foreseeable future.

## Moore's Law and Quantum Computing

In 1965 Gordon Moore, a former chair of Intel Corporation and one of the inventors of the integrated circuit, captured this trend in computer technology in what has come to be known as Moore's Law of Integrated Circuits. According to this law, the surface area of a state-of-the-art transistor is reduced by approximately 50 percent every twenty-four months. Over the last four decades, this rate has been largely maintained within the computer industry. Experts have even expressed confidence that the rate will be maintained for another fifteen years through techniques such as high-resolution optical lithography. Of course, there is a limit to how compact the components on a chip can be: In the current technological paradigm of discrete electronic elements we cannot shrink below the size of an atom.

This, in turn, implies a limit to the extent of progress achievable through sheer computing power (except for making ever bigger machines, which is not a realistic alternative for most applications). Although the limit is impressively large, its mere existence seems to imply that purely computational approaches can go only so far, and no further. At this point, another alternative suggests itself. Quantum computing, as its name suggests, is rooted in quantum mechanics and works on the basis of quantum logic. Instead of *bits*, it deals with *qubits* (quantum bits). Like a bit, a qubit can be in one of two states; but unlike bits, qubits can also exist in *superpositions* of those states. Furthermore, they also can be *entangled* with other qubits. Roughly speaking, entanglement is the result of nonlocal correlations among the parts of a quantum system. What this means is that we cannot fully understand the state of the system by dividing it into parts and studying the states of the separate parts. Information can be encoded in nonlocal correlations among the parts of the system. Preskill (1997) points out that much of the art of designing quantum algorithms involves finding ways to make efficient use of the nonlocal correlations. Superposition and entanglement are the sources of power of quantum computing because, unlike the classical case, a qubit is equivalent to a vector in a two-dimensional space of real numbers. The state of a system with $N$ qubits would thus involve $2^N$ such vectors (each of which is equivalent to one complex number). A system with a mere 100 qubits, for instance, is equivalent to $2^{100} = 10^{30}$ complex numbers—a magnitude far too big for any classical computer to handle.

In spite of the enormous potential that might, theoretically, be created by quantum computing, the idea has serious limitations (Meglicki, 2008). Difficulties associated with these limitations make the design and manufacturing of real quantum computers a daunting task. With the current state of the art, researchers would be content if they managed to build a quantum computer with as many as just two or three qubits. Meglicki speculates that quantum computing is now where classical computing was 70 years ago. Many questions about how a practical quantum computer could be built or what might be done with it are still completely open. In short, quantum computing remains extremely speculative. No one yet has a clear idea as to how quantum computers could be constructed.

## Nanotechnology

The other major technology contributing to biocomputational approaches that should be mentioned is nanotechnology. Broadly speaking, this term refers to the use of materials with dimensions from one nanometer (one billionth of a meter) to one hundred nanometers. This scale includes collections of a few atoms, semiconductor wafers (as small as twenty nanometers), and protein based "motors." The enterprise has engaged physicists and chemists as much as it has attracted biologists and computer engineers. One intriguing idea that originated in science fiction but has nonetheless attracted serious attention is the notion of miniature "assemblers" that can presumably build anything atom by atom from the ground up. Such assemblers might, for example, produce self-replicating molecules, such as peptides. Generally speaking, however, nanotechnology is no less embryonic than quantum computing.

This is just a small sample of burgeoning technologies currently under investigation in AI and related fields. Many other technologies, especially interface technologies such as augmented reality, wearable computers, and tangible user interfaces, have been enabled by AI theories and techniques (Lester, 2001) or can potentially grow out of these (Grosz, 2005).

## *Dynamical AI: Intelligence as Complexity*

Three centuries ago, philosopher David Hume proposed putting mathematical garb on psychology, as Newton had done for physics. This project has been pursued under different rubrics ever since. What is called the dynamical approach in AI and cognitive science is one of the latest examples. Mathematically, a dynamical system is defined as a set of time-dependent variables that collectively constitute the system's "state." The focus in such approaches is on the change of the state with time, which is generally expressed in the form of *differential equations*. A differential equation formulates the change in time of system *variables* in terms of system *parameters*. The formula $m\, d^2x/dt^2 = -kx$ for a spring-mass oscillator, for instance, is a differential equation that relates the oscillator's position ($x$) in time ($t$) to its mass ($m$) and the spring's stiffness ($k$). Simple variations of this formula are also used to model various muscle and limb movements in humans and animals (Latash, 1993). The challenge for mathematical accounts is to develop similar equations that would govern more complex bodily and mental behaviors.

The dynamical systems approach offers a viewpoint that, at least superficially, is in sharp contrast with how traditional AI and cognitive science view things. For example, in contrast to the "filing-cabinet view" of the brain as a repository of text-style information (Clark, 1997, p. 67), a dynamical view portrays it in the following way:

> The human brain is *fundamentally* a pattern-forming, self-organized system governed by nonlinear dynamical laws. Rather than compute, our brain "dwells" (at least for short times) in metastable states: It is poised on the brink of instability where it can switch flexibly and quickly. By living near criticality, the brain is able to anticipate the future, not simply react to the present. (Kelso, 1995, p. 26)

The more radical interpretations of the dynamical approach advocate the wholesale replacement of all talk of computation and representation by the language of geometry and dynamical systems (van Gelder, 1998; cf. Clark, 1997, p. 101). Van Gelder (1998, p. 615), for instance, introduces what he calls the "Dynamical Hypothesis in Cognitive Science" as a contender for "the status of the 'law of quantitative structure' concerning the nature of cognition." He compares and contrasts his Dynamical Hypothesis with what he calls the "Computational Hypothesis," which he characterizes as having four major components: Digital variables and states, discrete and ordered time, algorithmic behavior, and semantic interpretation. Although the emphasis in computational approaches, van Gelder claims, is on structures that transform according to rules, the dynamical perspective emphasizes change, geometry, timing, and so on, as well as the quantitative nature of these features. In his conception, a system is dynamical to the extent that it is quantitative in terms of state, time, or the rate of change of state with time (p. 619). These radical interpretations have come under criticism on various grounds, most starkly because of their emphasis on the quantification of cognitive behavior. The ensuing debate between proponents and opponents is met with conciliatory efforts at a kind of compromise according to which "the dynamical approach is best for *some* of the sensory and motor functions, especially those with tight feedback loops, whereas the computational approach is best for higher cognitive processes as well as some perceptual-motor processes" (Dietrich & Markman, 1998, p. 637).

More recent interpretations of the dynamical approach draw on the extensive work that is done under the rubric of complex adaptive systems (Holland, 1995).

The objective of work on complex adaptive systems, Holland (p. 38) believes, is "to uncover general principles that will enable us to synthesize complex adaptive systems' behaviors from simple laws." One such principle, in Holland's view, is "diversity" of the components, as opposed to the homogeneity of, for instance, the atoms in a gas or the nodes in today's connectionist networks. One implication of this principle is that systems with heterogeneous components may not be easily amenable to mathematical formalisms such as differential equations. Holland (p. 125), in fact, considers the use of partial differential equations unnecessary and believes that "a move toward computer-based models that are directly described, rather than PDE-derived, will give handsome results in the study of complex adaptive systems." Such models, he further notes, "offer the possibility of controlled experiments that can suggest both guidelines for examining real organizational processes and guidelines for mathematical abstractions of organizational dynamics" (pp. 124–125).

## Situated AI: Intelligence as Embedded Interaction

Most of the approaches we have reviewed so far (except certain interpretations of the dynamical approach) view cognition as *abstract* (physical embodiment is irrelevant), *individual* (the solitary mind is the essential locus of intelligence), *rational* (reasoning is paradigmatic of intelligence), and *detached* (thinking is separated from perception and action) (Smith, 1999). The situated approach reverses these premises by taking cognition to be embodied, embedded, and distributed. The AI lab at MIT is one of the pioneering sites for the situated approach. In the mid-1980s, vexed by the dilemma that AI tries to build expert physicians and engineers while at the same time failing to build a machine that can, so to speak, tie its own shoes, Rodney Brooks (1986, 1991/1997), the then-director of the lab, suggested that AI should aim for the more modest goal of insect-level intelligence. Following what he called an "engineering methodology," Brooks (1991/1997, p. 42) proposed the building of "creatures" that are let loose in the world, learn to cope with the environment, and pursue multiple goals. Taking natural evolution as a guide, Brooks (p. 140) argued that high-level behaviors such as language and reasoning "are all pretty simple once the essence of acting and reacting are available." Building on this evolutionary trope, Brooks made an argument that appealed to contemporary sensibilities: It took natural evolution much longer (billions of years) to perfect behaviors having to do with perception and mobility than to develop the capacities of abstract thought and reasoning (millions of years). He even postulated that 97 percent of human activity (whatever such a figure might mean) is concept-free—that is, does not involve concepts of the kind assumed in traditional AI (cf. Kirsh, 1991).

Therefore the first step, according to Brooks, was to turn the tables on the central tenet of both classical and connectionist AI—namely, the idea of representation. Based on the idea of "using the world as the best model," Brooks (1991/1997, p. 144) argued that an intelligent being would be better served by taking direct advantage of the information available in the environment than trying to compute and reason using a mental model of the world. Driven by this intuition, the focus of research in many AI labs shifted to a set of new ideas and principles, the most important of which are the following (Brooks 1991/1997, p. 417; 1999, pp. 165–170):

1. *Situatedness*: A situated creature or robot is embedded in the world and deals not with abstract descriptions (such as logical sentences, plans of action), but with the here and now of the world (through its sensors), which directly influences the behavior of the creature.

2. *Embodiment*: An embodied creature or robot has a physical body and experiences the world, at least in part, directly through the influence of the world on that body.

3. *Intelligence*: Although vague, this is intended to highlight the point that "Intelligence is determined by the dynamics of interaction with the world" (Brooks, 1999, p. 169). In imitation of natural evolution, AI should focus its efforts on "low-level" intelligence.

4. *Emergence*: Complex behavior should emerge as a result of interactions among simple and primitive tasks and modules: "Intelligence is in the eye of the observer" (Brooks, 1999, p. 170).

This line of research has resulted in interesting outcomes, mostly in the form of humanoid robots that mimic certain aspects of human behavior—for example, the robots Cog and Kismet developed at MIT (see Figure 5.3). Kismet, the baby robot, is said to have capabilities for emotive facial expressions indicative of anger, fatigue, fear, disgust, excitement, happiness, interest, sadness, and surprise. For this purpose, Kismet's face is embellished with what might have otherwise seemed like rather frivolous or superfluous features: Eyebrows (each one with two degrees of freedom: lift and arc), ears (each with two degrees of freedom: lift and rotate), eyelids and a mouth (each with one degree of freedom: open/close). Kismet in its current incarnation exhibits novel interactive behaviors. For instance, using the face- and eye-finding routines discussed earlier, it can establish "eye contact" with a human being. In addition to eye contact, Kismet can also imitate the head-nodding of a human being who stands in front of it. (Curiously, the Cog group calls a researcher who interacts with Kismet a "caretaker," not an "observer" or "experimenter," and not even a "trainer," as is usually said of people who interact with animals in a similar fashion.) That is, if the experimenter nods yes, the robot responds by nodding yes, and similarly for shaking one's head in denial. This is achieved by adding a tracking mechanism to the output of the face detector. By keeping track of the location of a salient feature on the face (such as the mouth or the eyebrows), this mechanism provides information about the direction of movement (roughly, horizontal and vertical), which is further classified as *yes*, *no*, or *no-motion*. Because the nodding and shaking mechanisms get their input from the face detection module, the robot reacts to the movement of only a face-like object (human or doll), not other objects.

Other similar projects are under development in other research labs and other parts of the world, giving rise to a new area called Epigenetic Robotics (Metta & Berthouze, 2006). The RobotCub developed in Europe, for instance, aims to build a fully fledged humanoid robotic platform shaped like a two-year-old child. The dual goals of research in this area are to understand the brain by constructing embodied systems and to build better systems by learning from human studies. Researchers at Osaka University in Japan have also developed a toddler robot to study child development. Called CB2, for Child-Robot with Biomimetic Body, this

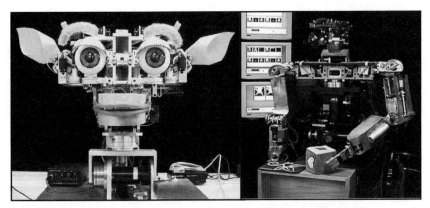

**Figure 5.3   Humanoid robots Cog and Kismet developed at MIT's AI lab**

robot rolls over, crawls, and spurts out something similar to a child voice. The strange but natural-looking character of these behaviors has aroused a certain sense of disbelief and discomfort in observers, who often describe the robot as "creepy," "disturbing," and "freakish" (Noyes, 2007, online).

The psychological significance of these projects is not yet clear (Ekbia, 2008a; Suchman, 2007). For instance, one aim of projects such as Kismet and RobotCub is to explain the differences between autistic and so-called "normal" children on the basis of the difference in their abilities to replicate the actions of others. Autistic children are known to have difficulties early on in following the direction of gaze of others. If you turn your face toward a doll or point your finger in its direction, a normal child would usually do the same but an autistic child would not. Building a robot on these principles can demonstrate this difference in action and potentially provide ideas about treatment. In other words, there might be some value in explaining the difference in terms of bodily capabilities instead of innate mental capabilities. However, the reductionist approach of most of this research and the desire to understand the difference in terms of "a single parameter" (Metta & Berthouze, 2006, p. 129) undermine the potential contribution of the research.

Furthermore, Kismet and other robots built on similar principles are unlikely to overcome the semantic barrier—that is, to reach out to those parts of the environment that are spatially or temporally distant. Think of things that a normal human being can do easily but that Kismet, Cog, or any enhanced version of them built on the four principles (embodiment, embeddedness, development, social interaction) would fail to perform, even if it could freely walk around and presumably converse in natural language (Smith, 2000):

- Deal with hypotheticals: "Are you going to be sad if I leave you right away?" Or, "If you take that route, do you think you'll get through before they shut the last section at 5:00?"

- Report on what one did: "Before I came in, were you talking to someone else?" Or, "When you came by the door, did you see a backpack on the floor next to the door?"

- Plan sensibly: For example, pick up something that one should know one is going to need in the near future.

- Make deliberate adjustments to one's behavior: For example, realize that even though some route is geometrically shorter, there are usually so many obstacles along it that it would take less time to travel by a longer but less crowded route.

These are serious challenges facing situated AI (and, for that matter, all of AI). Meeting them requires the kind of systematic, communal, and skeptical effort that is believed to be the mark of scientific inquiry (Merton, 1973).

# AI in Practice

The review so far has covered the theoretical or "scientific" face of AI. The theories and approaches discussed have inspired extensive engineering work in different application areas. Today, the business and popular press credit and praise AI systems for filtering spam in electronic mail (Kantor, 2006), searching for information on the Web (Kantor, 2006), saving energy and protecting the environment (Levinson, 2006), securing financial transactions (Cohn, 2006), fighting terrorism (Gordon, 2007), and so forth. Although some of these claims might be inflated and should be received cautiously, the impact of AI on how business is conducted in these various areas is hardly disputable (Reddy, 2006). We briefly review five major application areas: Games, business and finance, medicine, education, the military, and the Semantic Web.

## AI in Games

In 1950, Shannon published his seminal work on how to program a computer to play chess. Since then, developing game-playing programs that can compete with (and even exceed) the abilities of the human world champions has been a long sought goal of the AI research community. Today, there are computer programs that are claimed to play world class backgammon, checkers, chess, *Othello*, and *Scrabble*. These achievements are the result of a better understanding of the problems being solved, major algorithmic insights, and tremendous advances in hardware technology (Schaeffer, 2001). According to Schaeffer, computer games research is one of the important success stories of AI.

An example was the victory of Deep Blue over the world chess champion, Garry Kasparov, in 1997. In August 1996, after a long series of preparatory steps, the chess playing program Deep Blue confronted Kasparov in a six-game regulated and timed match under the auspices of the International Computer Chess Association in Philadelphia. Deep Blue was the last link in a chain of programs that started as a graduate student project at Carnegie Mellon University in 1985 and ended as a major project at International Business Machines (IBM). In a rematch that took place nine months later, Kasparov, having won the first game and lost the second, reached three consecutive draws with Deep Blue. The outcome of the match thus hinged on the sixth and final game. On May 11, in a shocking finale that lasted barely more than an hour, the World Champion resigned after only nineteen moves, handing a historic match victory to Deep Blue. Subsequent attempts by the chess world to reverse this milestone have ended in failure. Kasparov's successor, Vladimir Kramnik, for example, could only draw an eight-game match against one of Deep Blue's successors, Fritz. AI's success in the realm of chess, however, seems to be an exception rather than the norm, as similar attempts at other games such as bridge, *Go*, and *Scrabble* have not been as successful (Levy, 2002).

The confrontation between machines and humans is one area of AI applications in games. The other is in simulating intelligent behavior in computer games. Game developers and programmers increasingly draw on AI techniques such as neural networks and genetic algorithms to simulate certain behaviors, for example, chasing, evading, and flocking in a realistic manner (Bourg & Seemann, 2004; Millington, 2006).

## AI in Business and Finance

The business world has devised many applications of AI in areas such as marketing, finance, and investing. An early application of AI in business was Business Process Reengineering (BPR) (Hamscher, 1994), where insights from AI were reportedly used in both reengineering business and organizational processes and in supporting the change process itself. For many years, investment analysts have used neural networks, genetic algorithms, and machine learning techniques in stock and portfolio selection, risk analysis, and modeling market behavior (Trippi & Lee, 1996). Financial engineering, the most computationally intense subfield of finance, has used AI techniques in the following areas: Analysis of financial condition, business failure prediction, debt risk assessment, security market applications, financial forecasting, portfolio management, fraud detection and insurance, mining of financial and economic databases, and other (e.g., macroeconomics) applications (Monostori, 1999). In finance today, traders draw on expert systems for real-time, market-level advice, as well as time-series analysis and portfolio generation. Ward and Sherald (2006) describe a neural network system used in optimization, prediction, and portfolio management. Kelly (2007, online) reports on a project to build an AI system that would "think like a Wall Street trader." As commentators point out, however, these systems perform better in areas such as data mining than in those where judgment is required.

As with other application areas, there has been a great deal of hype about what can be achieved through AI. The business and popular press contributes heavily to the promotion and distribution of inflated claims. A neural network model is claimed to use earnings estimates and other metrics to determine whether stocks are trading above or below their fair value (Andrews, 2006). Another model is claimed to know "what many [mutual fund] managers don't" (Jelveh, 2006, online). Yet another computer program called Asset Allocation Neural Network (AANN) is claimed to outperform money managers in financial forecasting (Benjamin, 2007). In light of the current financial downturn, however, it is sobering to know that in December 2007 the same program had predicted that the *Standard and Poor's 500* stock index would climb as much as 18 percent by the middle of 2008 (Benjamin, 2007).

## AI in Medicine

Medical practice represents one of the earliest practical applications of AI. In reviewing this area in 1984, Clancey and Shortliffe (1984, p. 4) provided the following definition:

> Medical artificial intelligence is primarily concerned with the construction of AI programs that perform diagnosis and make therapy recommendations. Unlike medical applications based on other programming methods, such as purely statistical and probabilistic methods, medical AI programs are based on symbolic models of disease entities and their relationship to patient factors and clinical manifestations.

Today there is less emphasis on diagnosis as a task requiring computer support in routine clinical situations; the strict focus on the medical setting has broadened across the healthcare spectrum (Durinck, Coiera, Baud, Console, Cruz, Frutiger, et al., 1994). As such, it is more typical to describe AI systems in medicine as *clinical decision support systems* (CDSS). Intelligent systems today are thus found supporting the prescription of medication, in clinical laboratories and educational settings, for clinical surveillance, or in data-rich areas such as intensive care (Coiera, 2003). A wide variety of expert systems can be found in routine clinical use; Table 5.2 provides an exemplary subset of such systems, including alerts and reminders, diagnostic assistance, therapy critiquing and planning, prescribing decision support, information retrieval, and image recognition and interpretation. Applications of case-based reasoning in medicine have also been reported (Xiong & Funk, 2006), as have Web-based diagnosis systems (Ishak & Siraj, 2006).

**Table 5.2  Examples of expert systems in medicine (from Coiera, 2003)**

| SYSTEM | DESCRIPTION |
| --- | --- |
| *ACUTE CARE SYSTEMS* | |
| (Dugas et al., 2002) | Decision support in hepatic surgery |
| POEMS (Sawar et al., 1992) | Post-operative care decision support |
| VIE-PNN (Miksch et al., 1993) | Parenteral nutrition planning for neonatal ICU |
| NéoGanesh (Dojat et al., 1996) | ICU ventilator management |
| SETH (Darmoni, 1993) | Clinical toxicology advisor |

| LABORATORY SYSTEMS | |
|---|---|
| GERMWATCHER (Kahn et al., 1993) | Analysis of nosocomial infections |
| HEPAXPERT I, II (Adlassnig et al., 1991) | Interprets tests for hepatitis A and B |
| Acid-base expert system (Pince et al., 1990) | Interpretation of acid-base disorders |
| MICROBIOLOGY/PHARMACY (Morrell et al., 1993) | Monitors renal active antibiotic dosing |
| PEIRS (Edwards et al., 1993) | Chemical pathology expert system |
| PUFF (Snow et al., 1988) | Interprets pulmonary function tests |
| Pro.M.D. – CSF Diagnostics (Trendelenburg, 1994) | Interpretation of CSF findings |
| EDUCATIONAL SYSTEMS | |
| DXPLAIN (Barnett et al., 1987) | Internal medicine expert system |
| ILLIAD (Warner et al., 1988) | Internal medicine expert system |
| HELP (Kuperman et al., 1991) | Knowledge-based hospital information system |
| QUALITY ASSURANCE AND ADMINISTRATION | |
| COLORADO MEDICAID UTILIZATION REVIEW SYSTEM | Quality review of drug prescribing practices |
| MANAGED SECOND SURGICAL OPINION SYSTEM | Aetna Life and Casualty assessor system |
| MEDICAL IMAGING | |
| PERFEX (Ezquerra et al., 1992) | Interprets cardiac SPECT data |
| (Lindahl et al., 1999). | Classification of scintigrams |

As these examples illustrate, the medical application area is thriving, having many dedicated publication venues such as *Artificial Intelligence in Medicine (AIM)*, *Journal of the American Medical Informatics Association (JAMIA),* and *the International Journal of Applied Expert Systems*. One recent addition to this area is elder care. Longstanding issues such as chronic diseases, high risk of falling, physical and cognitive deterioration, and memory loss have attracted increased attention because of the growing population of the elderly. AI research on computer vision, planning, reasoning, and robotics may provide solutions in the form of smart homes, reminder systems, wearable sensors, fall detection, and so on (Association for the Advancement of Artificial Intelligence, 2008).

## AI in Education

AI is applied in education in at least three different ways (Shapiro, 1992):

1. To model tutors teaching and students learning in different domains

2. To explain learning and teaching as parts of human cognitive processes

3. To explore the use of intelligent instructional systems in training and class-room situations

Summarizing these applications as of 1997, Molnar (1997) mentions, as early pioneers of computers in education, John Kemeny and Thomas Kurtz's work at Dartmouth College on BASIC programming language, Seymour Papert's work at MIT on LOGO programming language, and John Seely Brown's work on SOPHIE (a SOPHisticated Instructional Environment) as a new kind of learning environment. This last system provides an early example of what has come to be known as Intelligent Tutoring Systems, which assist learners in articulating their ideas and strategies in solving domain-specific problems. Tutoring systems are part of a broader category of AI systems in education—the so-called intelligent tools, which allow the learner to focus on the problem-solving activity rather than manipulative skills. For instance, the Assistment program, a software tool designed at Carnegie Mellon University, "breaks a larger problem down into step-by-step questions, trying to tease out exactly where the students got off track" (Marek, 2005, online). It also saves teachers' time by administering and automatically scoring quizzes that are similar to Massachusetts' state achievement test. Intelligent tutors are now in 4 percent of schools in the United States and attracting wide interest among government agencies. By some estimates, the application of these systems at the college level has resulted in enhanced learning as well as an average reduction of 37 percent in instructional costs (Silverstein, 2006). This came about by deemphasizing lectures and relying more on online tutorials and discussion forums, along with computerized grading to give students speedier assessments of what they were learning well and where they were making mistakes.

One recent area of development, called Education Informatics, seeks to employ architectures for content-delivery systems, content development and markup, pedagogical strategies, educational data mining, assessment, and classroom deployment in order to "provide free access to primary and secondary school curricula, aligned with national, state, and local standards, delivered by our best AI tutoring technologies" (Association for the Advancement of Artificial Intelligence, 2008, online).

The education area of AI application has also generated special venues such as the *International Journal of Artificial Intelligence in Education* (aied.inf.ed.ac.uk) and *Journal of Interactive Learning Research* (www.aace.org/pubs/jilr/

default.htm). Forbus and Feltovich's (2001) account of AI contributions to education and learning, in spite of its overly optimistic assessment, remains a useful resource.

## AI in the Military

The military establishment, particularly in the United States, has been a major proponent and the key financial resource for AI throughout its history. Although this support is not necessarily translated into the military's direct influence on AI research, the dynamics of the relationship is an interesting issue that has been discussed by various authors (Agre, 1997; Edwards, 1996; Ekbia, 2008a). One outcome of this relationship is a large number of military applications that are either in use or under development. These have ranged over a wide variety of areas and topics, including combat simulation (Campbell, Lotmin, DeRico, & Ray, 1997; Heinze, Goss, Josefsson, Bennett, Waugh, Lloyd, et al., 2002); pattern recognition (Rhea, 2000); decision making (Rasch, Kott, & Forbus, 2003); autonomous agents, unmanned vehicles, and air systems (Brzezinski, 2003; Cahlink, 2004); translation and second-language learning (Lamb, 2004); and tutoring (Chisholm, 2003).

During the last decade or so, the military's focus has shifted toward robots that are intended to replace human warriors (see Figure 5.4). A *New Scientist* article speculates that weapon-toting robots may eventually help the infantry decide who is friend and who is foe on the battlefield (Marks, 2006). Singer (2009) examines the legal and ethical issues that arise with the deployment of robots in the battlefield. The following excerpt from a *New York Times* report captures the trend quite well (Weiner, 2005):

> The American military is working on a new generation of soldiers, far different from the army it has. "They don't get hungry," said Gordon Johnson of the Joint Forces Command at the Pentagon. "They're not afraid. They don't forget their orders. They don't care if the guy next to them has just been shot. Will they do a better job than humans? Yes." The robot soldier is coming. The Pentagon predicts that robots will be a major fighting force in the American military in less than a decade, hunting and killing enemies in combat. Robots are a crucial part of the Army's effort to rebuild itself as a 21st century fighting force, and a $127 billion project called Future Combat Systems is the biggest military contract in American history. … Military planners say robot soldiers will think, see, and react increasingly like humans. In the beginning, they will be remote-controlled, looking and acting like lethal toy trucks. As the technology develops, they may take many shapes. And as their intelligence grows, so will their autonomy.

## AI and the Semantic Web

As has been discussed, AI and information science deal with similar questions and issues, especially in the area of information retrieval. Licklider's (1965) work on precognitive systems, for instance, foreshadows much of current research on

**Figure 5.4  A military robotic vehicle (courtesy of Mike Derer, Associated Press)**

ontologies and the Semantic Web, which also deals with many of the same questions that have engaged IR researchers for decades. One key question is how "to develop technology to facilitate the retrieval of information via *meanings*, not just *spellings*" (Legg, 2007, p. 407). The World Wide Web, despite its stunning success, is severely limited in this respect, and the Semantic Web is seen as a way to overcome this limitation by giving information "well-defined meaning, better enabling computers and people to work in cooperation" (Berners-Lee, Hendler, & Lassila, 2001, p. 35). According to prevailing thinking, this will happen by drawing on "some kind of shared, structured, machine-readable *conceptual scheme*" (Legg, 2007, p. 407). In other words, the ultimate vision behind the Semantic Web is to standardize or *canonicalize* the process of information retrieval and integration across an arbitrary range of sources through a ubiquitous and invisible "web of meaning" (Heflin, Hendler, & Luke, 2003, p. 29; see also Guha & McCool, 2003). And this is where the work in AI on *formal ontologies* comes in (Goble, 2002). However, given the decentralized character of the development of the World Wide Web, and (it is hoped) of the Semantic Web as well, a key issue for the implementation of this vision is how to standardize while maintaining informational democracy. Furthermore, numerous other challenges have also to be met in order to realize the vision (Legg, 2007)—for example, inferential tractability (given a task or problem, how to handle it within a reasonable amount of time), logical consistency (how to deal with contradictions across various information sources), rapid changeability (how to keep track of changes in the real world effectively), and a host of socio-political issues such as trust (of information sources), power (who should provide the markup, the metadata scheme, etc.), relationships (between producers and consumers of data), incentives (to develop applications), and so on.

AI, it turns out, is less equipped to tackle some challenges than others, and for a number of reasons. First, there is no shared understanding in the AI community of what ontologies are, how best to implement them, which representations to use, or what theory of meaning to adopt (Welty, 2003). Furthermore, the notion of "semantics" itself has multiple meanings, especially as it pertains to the Semantic Web. Uschold (2003), for instance, identifies four such meanings or types of semantics: Implicit, explicit and informal, explicit and formal for human processing, and explicit and formal for machine processing. Third, many of the ideas borrowed from AI in the development of the Semantic Web are based on traditional or so-called classical approaches to AI—for example, in their emphasis on representations, formal ontologies, and logical inference. Given the limited success of these approaches and models such as Cyc (as has been discussed), it is not clear how effective these ideas could be when imported to the realm of the Web. Lastly, socio-political issues alluded to earlier are well beyond the scope of AI.

Given that AI practitioners have for a long time dealt with conceptual questions similar to those facing the Semantic Web community, they should be able to make potentially significant contributions to the future development of the Web, although caution is advised (Berners-Lee, 2006). Moreover, the Semantic Web may also be the most fertile ground for the AI and information science communities to cultivate their shared interests.

## The Future of AI

AI, as suggested at the outset, has at least two faces: a scientific face and an engineering one. We have seen both of these at work in the current review. Practically, we have examined numerous examples of AI applications in different areas. Although progress across applications has not been uniform and consistent, the outlook is promising. On the intellectual front, we have seen how the AI community has striven to accomplish the ultimate goal of building intelligent artifacts in a unique and *novel* manner. I emphasize "novel" here because many of these goals could be attained only through AI models, approaches, and techniques. As Smith (1996, p. 20) points out, "Midway between matter and mind, computation stands in excellent stead as a supply of concrete cases of middling complexity ... against which to test specific metaphysical hypotheses." AI models occupy a unique place in this middle realm, as they face the mind-matter question head-on. The models and approaches discussed here illustrate this point clearly. From the issues of knowledge, language, and representation to those of experience, emergence, and embodiment, AI confronts longstanding questions of ontology, epistemology, and metaphysics, which have eluded scholars and philosophers for centuries. AI docs this with a kind of rigor and doggedness that is affordable only with the material and generative character of its artifacts. In so doing, AI and computing in general provide novel ways for rethinking entrenched conceptions of what it means to be human (Hayles, 1999; Suchman, 2007), raise interesting questions about the relationship between humans and nonhumans, introduce new concepts and vocabularies for thinking about these questions, and enrich the current intellectual landscape in unprecedented ways. The path has not, of course, been smooth and straight. There has been exaggeration, digression, and deviation, which complicate the overall assessment of the field and some of its theoretical and practical claims.

For decades now, researchers in AI have been talking about programs that understand stories, news reports, humor, or even poetry; systems that have commonsense knowledge of the world, that can create cooking recipes, that can engage in meaningful conversation; or robots that can be your servants, friends, companions, or even lovers. The fact is that these claims are far from real; in other words, people in AI, advertently or inadvertently, tend to exaggerate the capabilities of their systems. There are many reasons for this, but one is a tendency to exploit what is called the Eliza Effect. This refers to a program that was developed in the 1970s by Weizenbaum at MIT. Eliza gave the verbal appearance of a psychotherapist, but in reality it had a very limited set of canned sentences (about 100) that it used in a smart way. For instance, if you say, "I'm feeling sad," Eliza may respond: "Tell me about your day." (There are various versions of Eliza available on the Web, and you can interact with them.) Many people were led to believe that there was much more happening behind the scene—that they were indeed interacting with a really intelligent program. Weizenbaum was an honest intellectual; these reactions made him realize how susceptible we are to over-attributing intelligence, and he basically revolted against his own creation and became an ardent alarmist of this phenomenon—hence, the term Eliza Effect in AI (Ekbia, 2008a).

Now, many people in AI did not follow Weizenbaum; they did the opposite, instead. AI has a tendency to exploit the Eliza Effect by smoothly conflating the real world events that are being modeled with the tiny, stripped-down versions found in the models. A program that was claimed to understand news reports, for instance, was nothing more than a string-matching program, similar to Google but much weaker in its capabilities. We do not see anyone claiming that Google can understand stories. This was roughly the situation in the 1970s and 1980s; it has survived even in radical reinterpretations of AI that were supposed to correct the fallacies of the early stripped-down models. At MIT, as we saw, in the early 1990s a healthy shift took place toward systems and robots that interact with the world in a physical and embodied manner, and hence would have a much richer interaction with the world than those early models. The idea was to mimic natural evolution, starting with very simple creatures such as cockroaches and moving up the evolutionary ladder to, say, mice, rabbits, and monkeys. In other words, researchers proposed a program that made sense, at least in principle. However, very soon they abandoned the idea, and leapfrogged from cockroaches to humanoid robots such as Kismet that are claimed to have social capabilities and experience emotions such as happiness, sadness, and surprise. In short, the in-principle possibility of developing social robots was soon turned into claims about human-level intelligence. Or, to take another example, the futurist Ray Kurzweil cunningly builds a whole philosophical edifice on the basis of purely engineering evidence such as Moore's Law. Moore's Law, as we noted, suggests that computers will be able to perform certain types of calculations faster than we do (actually, they already do that in certain areas). But Kurzweil goes much further, claiming that computers *will* inevitably surpass us in *all* respects in the not-so-distant future. This heavy traffic between philosophical and technical realms makes AI a fascinating but also delicate and risky enterprise, where in-principle arguments turn into grandiose scientific claims.

The dual—scientific and engineering—aspirations of AI are still discernible today and will probably persist for the foreseeable future. They can be identified, for instance, in two current trends in the field, one represented by the Association for the Advancement of Artificial Intelligence (AAAI) community and the other by a group that identifies itself with "singularity." The latter is characterized by its proponents in the following fashion (Kurzweil, n.d., online):

> "The Singularity" is a phrase borrowed from the astrophysics of black holes. The phrase has varied meanings. As used by Vernor Vinge and Raymond Kurzweil, it refers to the idea that accelerating technology will lead to superhuman machine intelligence that will soon exceed human intelligence, probably by the year 2030. The results on the other side of the "event horizon," they say, are unpredictable. We'll try anyway.

This statement captures well the entrepreneurial, adventurist, and futurist aspirations of some AI practitioners. At the same time, however, it has generated a great deal of enthusiasm and activity among a new generation of practitioners who work under the rubric of Artificial General Intelligence (AGI) (see, for instance, Goertzel, 2007; Goertzel & Pennachin, 2007; Goertzel & Wang, 2006).

The other trend, which is embodied in the work of those researchers affiliated with the AAAI, shows a much stronger engineering and practical bent. The 2008 and 2009 symposia of this group, for instance, include topics such as "Adaptive Agents in Cultural Contexts," "AI in Eldercare," "Education Informatics," "Multimedia Information Extraction," "Experimental Design for Real-World Systems," and "Agents that Learn from Human Teachers" (Association for the Advancement of Artificial Intelligence, 2008, 2009).

The claims made by enthusiasts in both groups may show, to different degrees, similar patterns of hype and hope in earlier developments, but their contrastive focus is obvious. It would be premature to discard the premises and aspirations of either group at this point. One can only wait and see how the intellectual and practical outcomes of these attempts fare in comparison with what AI has hitherto accomplished.

# References

Agre, P. E. (1997). *Computation and human experience*. Cambridge, UK: Cambridge University Press.

Anderson, J. A. (1995). *An introduction to neural networks*. Cambridge, MA: MIT Press.

Andrews, W. (2006, May 3). A "neural" approach to the market. *Business Week Online*. Retrieved February 21, 2009, from www.businessweek.com/investor/content/may2006/pi20060508_776926.htm

Association for the Advancement of Artificial Intelligence. (2008). *Fall Symposium Series*, Arlington, VA. Retrieved December 24, 2008, from www.aaai.org/Symposia/Fall/fss08symposia.php

Association for the Advancement of Artificial Intelligence. (2009). *Spring Symposium Series*, Stanford, CA. Retrieved December 24, 2008, from www.aaai.org/Symposia/Spring/sss09.php

Benjamin, J. (2007, December 3). Man vs. machine. *Investment News*. Retrieved January 4, 2009, from www.investmentnews.com/apps/pbcs.dll/article?AID=/20071203/FREE/712030324/1017/TOC&ht=

Berners-Lee, T. (2006). *Artificial Intelligence and the Semantic Web*. Retrieved December 24, 2008, from www.w3.org/2006/Talks/0718-aaai-tbl

Berners-Lee, T., Hendler, J., & Lassila, O. (2001). The Semantic Web. *Scientific American 284*(5), 34–43.

Boden, M. A. (Ed.). (1990). *The creative mind: Myths and mechanisms*. New York: Basic Books.

Bolter, D. (1984). *Turing's man: Western culture in the computer age*. Chapel Hill: University of North Carolina Press.

Bourg, D. M., & Seemann, G. (2004). *AI for game developers: Creating intelligent behavior in games*. Sebastopol, CA: O'Reilly Press.

Brooks, R. A. (1986). A robust layered control system for a mobile robot. *IEEE Transactions on Robotics and Automation, 2*(1), 14–23.

Brooks, R. A. (1991/1997). Intelligence without representation. In J. Haugeland (Ed.), *Mind design II* (pp. 395–420). Cambridge, MA: MIT Press.

Brooks, R. A. (1999). *Cambrian intelligence: The early history of the new AI*. Cambridge, MA: MIT Press.

Brzezinski, M. (2003, April 20). The unmanned army. *New York Times*. Retrieved February 21, 2009, from query.nytimes.com/gst/fullpage.html?res=9C03EFDF103BF933A15757C0A9659C8B63

Cahlink, G. (2004). War of machines. *GovernmentExecutive.com*. Retrieved December 24, 2009, from www.govexec.com/features/0704-15/0704-15s5.htm

Campbell, L., Lotmin, A., DeRico, M. M. G., & Ray, C. (1997). The use of artificial intelligence in military simulations. *IEEE International Conference on Systems, Man, and Cybernetics*, 2607–2612.

Chen, H. (1995). Machine learning for information retrieval: Neural networks, symbolic learning, and genetic algorithms. *Journal of the American Society for Information Science, 46*(3), 194–216.

Chisholm, P. (2003). Tutoring for future combat. *Military Training Technology, 8*(3). Retrieved February 21, 2009, from www.mt2-kmi.com/archive_article.cfm?DocID=219

Chowdhury, G. G. (2003). Natural language processing. *Annual Review of Information Science and Technology, 37*, 51–89.

Clancey, W. J., & Shortliffe, E. H. (1984). *Readings in medical artificial intelligence: The first decade*. Reading, MA: Addison-Wesley.

Clark, A. (1997). *Being there: Putting brain, body, and world together again*. Cambridge, MA: MIT Press.

Clark, A. (2001). *Mindware*. Cambridge, MA: MIT Press.

Clarke, A., & Cronin, B. (1983). Expert systems and library/information work. *Journal of Librarianship and Information Science, 15*(4), 277–292.

Cohen, H. (1995). The further exploits of AARON, painter. *Stanford Humanities Review, 4*(2), 141–158.

Cohn, D. (2006). AI reaches the golden years. *Wired News*. Retrieved February 14, 2009, from www.wired.com/science/discoveries/news/2006/07/71389

Coiera, E. (2003). *Guide to health informatics*. Oxford, UK: Oxford University Press.

Cope, D. (1991). *Computers and musical style*. Madison: WI: A-R Editions, Inc.

Cope, D. (2001). *Virtual music: Computer synthesis of musical style*. Cambridge, MA: MIT Press.

Crevier, D. (1993). *The tumultuous history of the search for artificial intelligence.* New York: Basic Books.

Dartnall, T. (Ed.). (2002). *Creativity, cognition, and knowledge.* Westport, CT: Praeger.

Davis, M. (1988). Mathematical logic and the origin of modern computers. In R. Herken (Ed.), *The universal Turing machine: A half-century survey* (pp. 149–174). Oxford, UK: Oxford University Press.

Dell, G. S. (1986). A spreading-activation theory of retrieval in sentence production. *Psychological Review, 93,* 283–321.

Dennett, D. C. (1997). True believers: The intentional strategy and why it works. In J. Haugeland (Ed.), *Mind design II: Philosophy, psychology, artificial intelligence* (pp. 57–79). Cambridge, MA: MIT Press.

Dietrich, E., & Markman, A. B. (1998). All information processing entails computation. *Behavioral and Brain Sciences, 21*(5), 637–638.

Dreyfus, H. L. (1992). *What computers still can't do? A critique of artificial reason.* Cambridge, MA: MIT Press.

Durinck, J., Coiera, E., Baud, R., Console, L., Cruz, J., Frutiger, P., et al. (1994). The role of knowledge based systems in clinical practice. In P. Barahona & J. P. Christensen (Eds.), *Knowledge and decisions in health telematics: The next decade* (pp. 199–203). Amsterdam, The Netherlands: IOS Press.

Edwards, P. N. (1996). *The closed world: Computers and the politics of discourse in cold war America.* Cambridge, MA: MIT Press.

Ekbia, H. R. (2001, November). *Once again, artificial intelligence at a crossroads.* Paper presented at the Annual Meeting of the Society for Social Studies of Science, Boston.

Ekbia, H. R. (2008a). *Artificial dreams: The quest for non-biological intelligence.* Cambridge, UK: Cambridge University Press.

Ekbia, H. R. (2008b, July). *Knowing, doing, and talking: The inherent tension of artificial intelligence.* Paper presented at the 2008 North American Conference on Computing and Philosophy, Bloomington, IN.

Feigenbaum, E. A., & Barr, A. (Eds.). (1982). *The handbook of artificial intelligence.* Reading, MA: Addison-Wesley.

Fodor, J. A. (1997). Selections from "Methodological solipsism considered as a research strategy in cognitive psychology." In P. A. Morton (Ed.), *A historical introduction to the philosophy of mind: Readings with commentary* (pp. 468–477). Peterborough, ON: Broadview Press.

Forbus, K. D., & Feltovich, P. J. (2001). *Smart machines in education.* Menlo Park, CA: AAAI Press.

Forbus, K. D., Gentner, D., Markman, A. B., & Ferguson, R. W. (1998). Analogy just looks like high level perception: Why a domain-general approach to analogical mapping is right. *Journal of Experimental and Theoretical Artificial Intelligence, 10,* 231–257.

Gentner, D. (1983). Structure-mapping: A theoretical framework for analogy. *Cognitive Science, 7*(2), 155–170.

Goble, C. (2002). The Semantic Web: A killer app for AI? *Proceedings of the 10th International Conference on Artificial Intelligence: Methodology, Systems, Applications,* 274–278.

Goertzel, B. (2007). Artificial general intelligence: Now is the time. *KurzweilAI.net.* Retrieved February 14, 2009, from www.kurzweilai.net/meme/frame.html?main=/articles/art0701.html

Goertzel, B., & Pennachin, C. (2007). *Artificial general intelligence.* New York: Springer.

Goertzel, B., & Wang, P. (2006). *Advances in artificial general intelligence: Concepts, architectures and algorithms.* Amsterdam, The Netherlands: IOS Press.

Gordon, L. (2007, October 1). USC student's computer program enlisted in security efforts at LAX. *Los Angeles Times*. Retrieved February 12, 2009, from teamcore.usc.edu/ARMOR/LATIMES.pdf

Grossberg, S. (1976). Adaptive pattern classification and universal recoding: Part I. Parallel development and coding of neural feature detectors. *Biological Cybernetics, 21*, 121–134.

Grosz, B. J. (2005). Beyond mice and menus. *Proceedings of the American Philosophical Society, 149*(4), 529–542.

Guha, R., & McCool, R. (2003). TAP: A Semantic Web platform. *Journal of Network Computing, 42*, 557–577.

Hamscher, W. (1994). AI in business-process reengineering. *AI Magazine, 15*(4), 71–72.

Harnad, S. (1990). The symbol grounding problem. *Physica D, 42*, 335–346.

Haugeland, J. (Ed.). (1981). *Mind design I*. Cambridge, MA: MIT Press.

Hayes, P. J. (1973). Computation and deduction. *Proceedings of the 2nd Mathematical Foundations of Computer Science Symposium, Czechoslovakian Academy of Sciences*, 105–117.

Hayles, N. K. (1999). *How we became posthuman: Virtual bodies in cybernetics, literature, and informatics*. Chicago: University of Chicago Press.

Hebb, D. (1949). *Organization of behavior*. New York: Wiley.

Heflin, J., Hendler, J., & Luke, S. (2003). SHOE: A blueprint for the Semantic Web. In D. Fensel, J. Hendler, H. Lieberman, & W. Wahlster (Eds.), *Spinning the Semantic Web: Bringing the World Wide Web to its full potential* (pp. 29–63). Cambridge, MA: MIT Press.

Heinze, C., Goss, S., Josefsson, T., Bennett, K., Waugh, S., Lloyd, I., et al. (2002). Interchanging agents and humans in military simulation. *AI Magazine, 23*(2), 37–47.

Hennessy, J. L., & Patterson, D. A. (1996). *Computer architecture: A quantitative approach* (2nd ed.). San Francisco: Morgan Kaufmann.

Hofstadter, D. R. (1979). *Gödel, Escher, Bach: An eternal golden braid*. New York: Basic Books.

Hofstadter, D. R. (2001). Analogy as the core of cognition. In K. J. Holyoak, D. Gentner, & B. Kokinov (Eds.), *Integration of theory and data from the cognitive, computational, and neural sciences* (pp. 499–537). Cambridge, MA: MIT Press.

Hofstadter, D. R. (2002). Staring Emmy straight in the eye, and doing my best not to flinch. In T. Dartnall (Ed.), *Creativity, cognition, and knowledge* (pp. 67–100). Westport: CT: Praeger.

Hofstadter, D. R., & Fluid Analogies Research Group. (1995). *Fluid concepts and creative analogies*. New York: Basic Books.

Holland, J. (1975). *Adaptation in natural and artificial systems*. Ann Arbor: University of Michigan Press.

Holland, J. (1995). *Hidden order: How adaptation builds complexity*. Reading, MA: Addison-Wesley.

Holyoak, K. J., & Thagard, P. (1995). *Mental leaps: Analogy in creative thought*. Cambridge, MA: MIT Press.

Houston, R. D., & Harmon, G. (2007). Vannevar Bush and Memex. *Annual Review of Information Science and Technology, 41*, 55–92.

Hummel, J. E., & Holyoak, K. J. (1997). Distributed representations of structure: A theory of analogical access and mapping. *Psychological Review, 104*, 427–466.

Huskey, V. R., & Huskey, H. D. (1980). Lady Lovelace and Charles Babbage. *Annals of History of Computing, 2*, 299–329.

Ishak, W. H. W., & Siraj, F. (2006). Artificial intelligence in medical applications: An exploration. *Health Informatics Europe*. Retrieved February 12, 2009, from www.hi-europe.info/files/2002/9980.htm

Jelveh, Z. (2006, July 9). How a computer knows what many managers don't. *New York Times*. Retrieved January 12, 2009, from www.nytimes.com/2006/07/09/business/mutfund/09quant.html?adxnnl=1&adxnnlx=1235346966

Kantor, A. (2006, June 1). Take a moment and a [*sic*] raise a glass to the wonderful, underappreciated AI. *USA Today*. Retrieved February 12, 2009, from www.usatoday.com/tech/columnist/andrewkantor/2006-06-01-wonder-ai_x.htm

Kelly, J. (2007). HAL 9000-style machines, Kubric's fantasy, outwit traders. *Bloomberg.com*. Retrieved December 22, 2008, from www.bloomberg.com/apps/news?pid=20601109&sid=amK25dKbMrhQ&refer=news

Kelso, J. A. S. (1995). *Dynamic patterns: The self-organization of brain and behavior*. Cambridge, MA: MIT Press.

Kirsh, D. (1991). Today the earwig, tomorrow man? *Artificial Intelligence, 47*, 161–184.

Kitano, H. (1994). *Massively parallel artificial intelligence*. Menlo Park, CA: AAAI Press.

Koestler, A. (1964). *The act of creation*. New York: Macmillan.

Kolodner, J. L. (1996). Making the implicit explicit: Clarifying the principles of case-based reasoning. In D. B. Leake (Ed.), *Case-based reasoning: Experiences, lessons, and future directions* (pp. 349–370). Cambridge, MA: MIT Press.

Kowalski, R. A. (1977). *Algorithm = logic + control* [unpublished manuscript]. London.

Kurzweil, R. (2005). *The singularity is near: When humans transcend biology*. New York: Viking.

Kurzweil, R. (n.d.). *The singularity*. Retrieved March 9, 2009, from www.kurzweilai.net/meme/frame.html?m=1

Lamb, G. M. (2004, April 22). E-translators: The more you say, the better. *The Christian Science Monitor, 96*(103), 15.

Latash, M. L. (1993). *Control of human movement*. Champaign, IL: Human Kinetics.

Legg, C. (2007). Ontologies on the Semantic Web. *Annual Review of Information Science and Technology, 41*(1), 407–451.

Lenat, D. B. (1997). *The dimensions of context space*. Retrieved April 25, 2008, from www.cyc.com/doc/context-space.pdf

Lenat, D. B., & Feigenbaum, E. A. (1991). On the thresholds of knowledge. *Artificial Intelligence, 47*(1–3), 185–250.

Lenat, D. B., & Guha, R. V. (1990). *Building large knowledge-based systems*. Reading, MA: Addison Wesley.

Lenat, D. B., Prakash, M., & Shepherd, M. (1985). Using common-sense knowledge to overcome brittleness and knowledge acquisition bottlenecks. *AI Magazine, 7*, 65–85.

Lester, J. (2001). Introduction to the special issue on intelligent user interfaces. *AI Magazine, 22*(4), 13–14.

Levinson, M. (2006). IT innovation: Robots, supercomputers, AI and more. *CIO*. Retrieved February 12, 2009, from www.cio.com/article/23921/IT_Innovation_Robots_Supercomputers_AI_and_More?contentId=23921&slug=&

Levy, D. (2002, October 24). Do not pass go. *The Guardian*. Retrieved February 12, 2009, from www.guardian.co.uk/technology/2002/oct/24/games.onlinesupplement2

Licklider, J. C. R. (1965). *Libraries of the future*. Cambridge, MA: MIT Press.

Lindsay, R. K., Bruce, G. B., Feigenbaum, E. A., & Lederberg, J. (1980). *Applications of artificial intelligence for organic chemistry: The Dendral Project*. New York: McGraw-Hill.

Loy, G. (1989). Composing with computers: A survey of some compositional formalisms and music programming languages. In M. Mathews & J. R. Pierce (Eds.), *Current directions in computer music research* (pp. 291–396). Cambridge, MA: MIT Press.

Marek, A. C. (2005). Enter the computer tutor: PCs can help kids pass No Child Left Behind tests. *USNews.com's E-Learning Guide.* Retrieved February 21, 2009, from www.vantagelearning.com/docs/articles/MA_UT_USNewsWR_20070427.pdf

Marks, P. (2006). Robot infantry get ready for the battlefield. *New Scientist, 2570,* 28.

McClelland, J., & Rumelhart, D. (1986). *Parallel distributed processing* (Vol. 2). Cambridge, MA: MIT Press.

McCorduck, P. (1991). *Aaron's code: Meta-art, artificial intelligence and the work of Harold Cohen.* New York: Freeman.

McCorduck, P. (1992). Art and artificial intelligence. In J. Belzer, A. Kent, A. G. Holzman, & J. G. Williams (Eds.), *Encyclopedia of computer science and technology* (Vol. 26, pp. 1–8). New York: Dekker.

McCulloch, W. S., & Pitts, W. H. (1943). A logical calculus of the ideas immanent in nervous activity. *Bulletin of Mathematical Biophysics, 5,* 115–133.

Meglicki, Z. (2008). *Quantum computing without magic.* Cambridge, MA: MIT Press.

Merton, R. K. (1973). *The sociology of science: Theoretical and empirical investigations.* Chicago: University of Chicago Press.

Metta, G., & Berthouze, L. (2006). Epigenetic robotics: Modelling cognitive development in robotic systems. *Interaction Studies, 7*(2), 129–134.

Millington, I. (2006). *Artificial intelligence for games.* San Francisco: Elsevier.

Mitchell, M. (1996). *An introduction to genetic algorithms.* Cambridge, MA: MIT Press.

Molnar, A. (1997). Computers in education: A brief history. *THE Journal (Technological Horizons in Education), 24*(11), 63.

Monostori, L. (1999). Subsymbolic and hybrid artificial intelligence techniques in financial engineering. *ERCIM News (the European Research Consortium for Informatics and Mathematics), 38.* Retrieved February 12, 2009, from www.ercim.org/publication/Ercim_News/enw38/monostori2.html

Neumaier, O. (1987). A Wittgensteinian view of artificial intelligence. In R. Born (Ed.), *Artificial intelligence: The case against* (pp. 132–174). London: Croom Helm.

Newborn, M. (1997). *Kasparov versus Deep Blue: Computer chess comes of age.* New York: Springer.

Newell, A., Shaw, J. C., & Simon, H. A. (1960). Report on a general problem-solving program for a computer. *Proceedings of the International Conference on Information Processing,* 256–264.

Newell, A. & Simon, H. A. (1961). GPS: A program that simulates human thought. In H. Billing (Ed.), *Lernende Automaten* (pp. 109–124). Munich, Germany: Oldenbourg.

Newell, A., & Simon, H. A. (1976). Computer science as empirical inquiry. *Communications of the ACM, 19*(3), 113–126.

Noyes, K. (2007). Researchers create "creepy" child robot. *TechNewsWorld.* Retrieved February 14, 2009, from www.technewsworld.com/story/57763.html

Obermeier, K. K. (1983). Expert systems: Enhancement of productivity? *Proceedings of the 46th Annual Meeting of the American Society for Information Science,* 9–13.

Poincaré, H. (1982). *The foundations of science: Science and hypothesis, the value of science, science and method.* Washington, DC: University Press of America.

Pratt, V. (1994). *Visit to Cyc.* Retrieved July 24, 2008, from boole.stanford.edu/pratt.html

Preskill, J. (1997). *Lecture notes for physics 229: Quantum information and computation.* Retrieved October 4, 2008, from www.theory.caltech.edu/people/preskill/ph229

Pylyshyn, Z. W. (1984). *Computation and cognition: Toward a foundation for cognitive science.* Cambridge, MA: MIT Press.

Rasch, R., Kott, A., & Forbus, K. D. (2003). Incorporating AI into military decision making: An experiment. *IEEE Intelligent Systems, 18*(4), 18–26.

Reddy, R. (2006). Robotics and intelligent systems in support of society. *IEEE Intelligent Systems, 21*(3), 24–31.

Rhea, J. (2000). The next "new frontier" of artificial intelligence. *Military & Aerospace Electronics Magazine, 11*(11). Retrieved February 21, 2009, from mae.pennnet.com/Articles/Article_Display. cfm?Section=Archives&Subsection=Display&ARTICLE_ID=86890

Riesbeck, C., & Schank, R. C. (1989). *Inside case-based reasoning.* Hillsdale, NJ: Erlbaum.

Rogers, Y. (2004). New theoretical approaches for human-computer interaction. *Annual Review of Information Science and Technology, 38,* 87–143.

Rosenblatt, P. (1958). The perceptron: A probabilistic model for information storage and organization in the brain. *Psychological Review, 65,* 386–408.

Rumelhart, D. E., Hinton, G. E., & Williams, R. J. (1986). Learning internal representations by error propagation. In D. E. Rumelhart & J. L. McClelland (Eds.), *Parallel distributed processing* (Vol. 2, pp. 318–362). Cambridge, MA: MIT Press.

Samsonovich, A. V., & Mueller, S. T. (2008). Toward a growing computational replica of the human mind. In A. V. Samsonovich (Ed.), *Biologically inspired cognitive architectures: Papers from the AAAI Fall Symposium* (pp. 1–3). Menlo Park, CA: AAAI Press.

Samuel, A. (1959). Some studies in machine learning using the game of checkers. *IBM Journal, 3*(3), 210–229.

Schaeffer, J. (2001). A gamut of games. *AI Magazine, 22*(3), 29–46.

Schank, R. C. (1973). Identification of conceptualizations underlying natural language: Models of belief systems. In R. C. Schank & K. M. Colby (Eds.), *Computer models of thought and language* (pp. 187–247). San Francisco, CA: W. H. Freeman.

Schank, R. C., & Birnbaum, L. (1984). Memory, meaning, and syntax. In *Talking minds: The study of language in cognitive science* (pp. 209–251). Cambridge, MA: MIT Press.

Schank, R. C., & Kass, A. (1988). Knowledge representation in people and machines. In U. Eco, M. Santambrogio, & P. Violi (Eds.), *Meaning and mental representations* (pp. 181–200). Bloomington: Indiana University Press.

Schank, R. C., & Leake, D. B. (2001). Natural language processing: Models of Roger Schank and his students. In *Encyclopedia of cognitive science* (pp. 592–594). Cambridge, MA: MIT Press.

Schank, R. C., & Riesbeck, C. K. (1981). *Inside computer understanding: Five programs plus miniatures.* New Haven, CT: Yale University Computer Science Department.

Sejnowski, T., & Rosenberg, C. (1987). *NETtalk: A parallel network that learns to read aloud* (Technical Report No. JHU/EECS-86/01). Baltimore, MD: Johns Hopkins University.

Shanker, S. G. (1987). AI at the crossroads. In B. Bloomfield (Ed.), *The question of artificial intelligence* (pp. 1–58). London: Croom Helm.

Shannon, C. (1950). Programming a computer for playing chess. *Philosophical Magazine, 41,* 256–275.

Shapiro, S. C. (1992). *Encyclopedia of artificial intelligence* (2nd ed., Vol. 1). New York: Wiley.

Silverstein, S. (2006, September 12). Colleges see the future in technology. *Los Angeles Times.* Retrieved February 12, 2009, from articles.latimes.com/2006/sep/12/local/mc-125future12

Simon, H. A. (1995). Artificial intelligence: An empirical science. *Artificial Intelligence, 77*(1), 95–127.

Singer, P. W. (2009). *Wired for war: The robotics revolution and conflict in the 21st century.* New York: Penguin.

Skinner, B. F. (1985). Cognitive science and behaviourism. *British Journal of Psychology, 76,* 33–43.

Smith, B. C. (1996). *The origin of objects.* Cambridge, MA: MIT Press.

Smith, B. C. (1999). Situatedness. In R. A. Wilson & F. C. Keil (Eds.), *MIT encyclopedia of cognitive science* (pp. 769–770). Cambridge, MA: MIT Press.

Smith, B. C. (2000). *Indiscrete affairs.* [unpublished manuscript].

Smith, L. C. (1980). Artificial intelligence applications in information systems. *Annual Review of Information Science and Technology, 15,* 67–105.

Smith, L. C. (1987). Artificial intelligence and information retrieval. *Annual Review of Information Science and Technology, 22,* 41–77.

Sowizral, H. A. (1985). Expert systems. *Annual Review of Information Science and Technology, 20,* 179–199.

Suchman, L. A. (2007). *Human-machine reconfigurations.* Cambridge, UK: Cambridge University Press.

Trippi, R. R., & Lee, J. K. (1996). *Artificial intelligence in finance and investing: State-of-the-art technologies for securities selection and portfolio management.* Scarborough, Canada: Irwin Professional Publishing.

Turing, A. M. (1936). On computable numbers, with an application to the Entscheidungsproblem. *Proceedings of the London Mathematical Society, 2*(42), 230–265.

Turing, A. M. (1953). Digital computers applied to games. In B. V. Bowden (Ed.), *Faster than thought.* London: Pitman Publishing. Retrieved July 26, 2009, from www.turingarchive. org/browse.php/B/7

Turkle, S. (1995). *Life on the screen: Identity in the age of the Internet.* New York: Simon & Schuster.

United Nations. Educational, Scientific and Cultural Organization; International Council of Scientific Unions. (1971). *UNISIST: Study report on the feasibility of a world science information system.* Paris: UNESCO.

Uschold, M. (2003). Where are the semantics in the Semantic Web? *AI Magazine, 24*(3), 25–36.

van Gelder, T. (1998). The dynamical hypothesis in cognitive science. *Behavioral and Brain Sciences, 21*(5), 615–628.

Varela, F. J., Thompson, E., & Rosch, E. (1991). *The embodied mind: Cognitive science and human experience.* Cambridge, MA: MIT Press.

Ward, S., & Sherald, M. (2006). *Successful trading using artificial intelligence.* Frederick, MD: Ward Systems Group.

Weiner, T. (2005, February 16). A new model army soldier rolls closer to the battlefield. New York Times. Retrieved February 21, 2009, from query.nytimes.com/gst/fullpage.html?res=9900E7DD133 AF935A25751C0A9639C8B63

Welty, C. (2003). Ontology research [Guest Editorial, Special Issue]. *AI Magazine, 24*(3), 11–12.

Wills, L. A., & Kolodner, J. L. (1996). Toward more creative case-based design systems. In D. B. Leake (Ed.), *Case-based reasoning: Experiences, lessons, and future directions* (pp. 81–91). Menlo Park, CA: AAAI Press/MIT Press.

Woolgar, S. (1995). Representation, cognition, and self: What hope for the integration of psychology and sociology? In S. L. Star (Ed.), *Ecologies of knowledge: Work and politics in science and technology* (pp. 154–179). Albany: State University of New York Press.

Xiong, N., & Funk, P. (2006). Case-based reasoning and knowledge discovery in medical applications with time series. *Computational Intelligence, 22*(3/4), 238–253.

# CHAPTER 6

# Facet Analysis

*Kathryn La Barre*
*University of Illinois, Urbana-Champaign*

## Overview

In 2001, a group of information architects and knowledge management professionals, charged with designing websites and access to corporate knowledge bases, seemingly rediscovered faceted classification (FC), a form of information organization and access deeply situated in the intersections of information retrieval and knowledge organization. These professionals have been instrumental in creating new and different ways for people to engage with digital content on the Web and in libraries' online public access catalogs (OPACs) (Adkisson, 2003; Antelman, Pace & Lynema, 2006; La Barre, 2006).

This rediscovery becomes more intriguing because FC is essentially a legacy form of information organization. Its roots trace back to the Universal Decimal Classification (UDC) (International Institute of Bibliography, 1905–1907), which was adapted from the Dewey Decimal Classification, devised for organizing library books and pamphlets. Another predecessor is the Bliss Classification, a scientific, logical, and adaptable system with fourteen rules of classification and a classificatory structure that relies on the relation and interrelation of concepts (Bliss, 1931), notions that are still central to ongoing work on the second revised edition (BC2) (Mills & Broughton, 1977).

Faceted classification is commonly associated with S. R. Ranganathan, an Indian mathematician who became the first head librarian at the University of Madras in 1924. His frustrations with then-extant classifications were similar to those that gave rise to the UDC, namely the restricted access imposed by these classifications on the rapidly growing universe of knowledge. Ranganathan's source of inspiration illustrates why this system has contemporary appeal and can be difficult to comprehend fully. (Note: Throughout the text, terms with specialized definitions are indicated by ***bold italic typeface*** at first appearance and refer the reader to Appendix 1: Glossary of Terms.)

> I happened to visit one of the shops of Selfridge. There, I saw, for the first time, a Meccano Set. It consisted of only a few metal strips, small metal plates, a few wheels and axles, some screws and nuts, hooks and pieces of strings. With this set, the shop-keeper would make all the kinds of toys. I decided that a Classification Scheme should be like a

> Meccano Set. It should consist only of perhaps two or three dozen short lists each of a page or two of *isolate*s (basic subjects) and not of compound subjects. The classifier should analyse a subject into its isolates or *facet*s and then pick out the correct facet numbers from the appropriate short lists and synthesize them into a Class Number. (Ranganathan, 1998, p. 199)

This chapter situates contemporary discussions and future directions for facets in the context of heritage principles and practices. Legacy aspects such as the rapid spread of facet theory through the work of several classification groups in Britain, India, and the United States, and the inclusion of facet theory in various applications and standards for controlled vocabularies, will permit a long view of facet theory (British Standards Institution, 2005; National Information Standards Organization, 2005). Also included is a small but representative subset of facet applications that represents the sweep of the heritage of facet theory. These will be compared and contrasted with contemporary and other cognate developments outside library and information science in diverse areas including philosophy, psychology, linguistics, and computer science. Criticisms of facet theory, and observations of weaknesses as well as strengths, will be explored throughout to demonstrate the challenges facing this theory as it offers a robust set of access and discovery tools to the Semantic Web and other networked *knowledge organization system*s (Tudhope, 2003).

Before this discussion can proceed, terms central to *facet theory* must be defined and two central but frequently misunderstood features must be disambiguated:

1. *Facet analysis* (FA) and its relation to *faceted classification*

2. The role of *fundamental categories* in the technique of facet analysis

In order to understand fully contemporary faceted discovery and access applications, it is critical to make a distinction between the *structure* of a faceted classification and the *technique* of facet analysis (Broughton & Slavic, 2004). Faceted classification and facet analysis are not synonymous, as many current references seem to suggest. Together, facet analysis and faceted classification form facet theory, an umbrella term for *facet analytical approach (FAA), facet analytico-synthetic theory (FAST),* and *facet analytical theory (FAT)*.

The technique of facet analysis depends upon the use of provisional lists of fundamental categories that are composed of *concept*s, *subject*s or terms that support the analysis of a given topic or set of objects into *facet*s or basic components, *attribute*s, *characteristic*s or functions. These are clustered into categories to create a 'bottom-up' map of knowledge. Facet analysis relies on various forms of system syntax, "links and rules for ordering and combination between categories," many "based on natural language models. The method used in 'classical' U.K. facet theory depends on a formulaic inter-category order" (Broughton & Slavic, 2004, online). This example is drawn from the Bliss Classification second edition (Mills & Broughton, 1977; Broughton, 2004a, p. 266). In Class H (Medicine) the fundamental categories and their constituent terms are shown in Table 6.1.

Table 6.1   Fundamental categories and their constituent terms in the Bliss
Classification, class H (Medicine)

| CATEGORY | Term(s) | Facet of subject |
|---|---|---|
| THING | human | patient |
| KIND | women, children, etc. | age or gender |
| PART | head, legs, muscle, etc. | anatomy |
| PROCESS | respiration, reproduction | specialization |
| OPERATION | surgery, drug therapy, etc. | treatment or therapy |
| AGENT | doctors, nurses, equipment | people, organizations, mode |

Many different lists of fundamental categories exist. Each listing is intended to serve as a preliminary (not prescriptive) starting point for the application of facet analysis to a set of entities in a given domain. Any such listing of fundamental categories must be tailored to reflect user interests, domain knowledge, and the characteristics of the entities being analyzed. Most often these lists have resulted from the analysis of scientific or technological subject fields. (See section on Fundamental Categories: Role in Facet Analysis.)

## Facet Theory: Language and Definition

Clear definition of the central concepts that comprise facet theory is desirable but, in spite of multiple attempts, has been difficult to achieve in practice. The preferred meaning of each term in this discussion, whenever possible, has been taken from the canonical literature, a set of full-length treatises and journal articles by founding experts that provide full description of the principles and practices of facet theory. (See Appendix II for a listing.) This approach offers a return to terra firma, in stark contrast to the welter of contemporary definitions. Ranganathan's (1967b) most complete description of facet theory consists of a series of seven normative principles, forty-two canons, thirteen postulates, twenty-two principles, and nine devices; and is written in often inscrutable language. Several scholarly articles knit together the various definitions of central concepts and attempt to provide more approachable descriptions (to list a few: Atherton, 1965c; Broughton, 2002, 2003; Broughton & Lane, 2000; Crowston & Kwasnik, 2004; Kwasnik, 1999; Mills, 2004; Palmer, 1971; Poli & Gnoli, 2008; Spiteri, 1998).

### Definition: Facet

Facet, the term most central to facet theory, is variously defined. Terms that are often thought to be interchangeable with facet include category, attribute, class, group, concept, and dimension. Much confusion has resulted from such a loose assemblage of equivalent terms. Instead of the term facet, Ranganathan (1937,

p. 122; 1951, p. 2; 1963, p. 71) initially used the phrase "train of characteristics" to emphasize that facets, "inhere in the subject [*entity*] themselves, whether we sense them or not." In describing a facet, he also stated that faceted classification "of a particular universe [of entities] is made on the basis of *characteristics*" (Ranganathan, 1967b, pp. 81–82). Ranganathan's use of the term characteristic reflects his mathematical background. Here, *characteristic* is equivalent to a mathematical *parameter* presenting a range of possible factors, aspects, or elements that assist in the identification of a collection of distinct cases. In facet theory, each parameter creates a *dimension*, or small number of *group*ings, and each grouping represents a *facet*. Each facet has potentially multiple dimensions (Ranganathan, 1967b). A facet can be a recursive or linguistically nested structure. Such a structure can exist in a *system* that dynamically generates facets that are independent but specific to a particular discipline. Figure 6.1 shows a website with dynamic presentation of facets, such as product type or brand, to assist browsing.

Mills (2004), an original member of the Classification Research Group (CRG) and editor of the second now fully faceted version of the Bliss Bibliographic Classification, notes two general types of facets: basic (geographical location, chronological time, material of composition) or relational (kind, part, property).

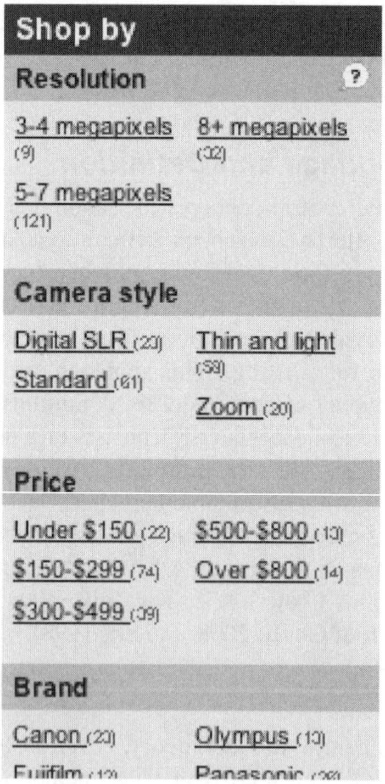

**Figure 6.1  Circuit City e-commerce website, www.circuitcity.com, demonstrating camera facets: resolution, camera style, brand, price**

This draws on Ranganathan's postulate of the basic facet: All compound subjects have a basic facet and may have at least one isolate facet. For example, the subject *coal washing* has *mining* as its basic facet; the subject *X-ray diagnosis of cows* has *animal husbandry* as its basic facet. *Coal washing* has two isolate facets: coal, and washing. *X-ray diagnosis of cows* has four isolate facets: X-ray, diagnosis, disease, and cow (Ranganathan, 1998, p. 405). Mills's (2004) reference to relational facets is a recognition of the central role of semantic relations between concepts in access and retrieval systems. In facet theory, concepts are represented by the words describing the entities to be classified and also by the relations between concepts.

## Definition: Facet Analysis

Facet theory is iterative. The technique of facet analysis results in a set of facets that is used to create the structure of a faceted classification. Facet analysis is used to verify the resulting classification structure as it is applied to the items for which the faceted classification was constructed (Mills, 2004, p. 550).

Facet analysis has been used with great success in a variety of settings to create a series of different applications for information retrieval. One example is the seven facet hierarchy used by the *Art and Architecture Thesaurus* (*AAT*). It is intended for use in "cataloguing, as data value standards; research tools; and search assistants in database retrieval systems" (Petersen, 1994, p. 26; see also *Art and Architecture Thesaurus*, 2002). AAT facets include **Associated concepts** (e.g., Marxism), **Physical attributes** (e.g., surface texture), **Styles and Period** (e.g., European Neolithic period), **Agents** (e.g., national organizations), **Activities** (e.g., bowling), **Materials** (e.g., gold), and **Objects** (e.g., installations [visual works]).

During the late 1950s, members of the CRG in London worked intensively with Ranganathan's facet theory. They rejected the use of conventional disciplines as the only starting point for a universal classification and attempted to locate a more robust framework for facet analysis (Spiteri, 1995; T. D. Wilson, 1972) by investigating the theory of integrative levels (Feibleman, 1965), which proposes:

> The world of things develops from the simple towards the complex by accumulation of new and divergent properties. Changes occur which transform the "entity" from a member of one group or class into a member of a new group. The new entity has properties of its own, characteristic of the new level of organization within it, and behaves in a similarly new and characteristic manner. (Foskett, 1962, p. 136)

The theory of integrative levels was not as fruitful as the CRG expected. Dahlberg (1978) has speculated that this failure resulted from how disciplines were treated. Today researchers are revisiting the intersection of integrative levels and facets (Dahlberg, 2008; Gnoli, 2008; Gnoli & Poli, 2004).

## Distinction Between Facet Analysis and Faceted Classification

As has been mentioned, facet analysis and faceted classification are not synonymous although these terms are often used in this manner. Facet analysis together with faceted classification offers "a simple and consistent method for analysis"

(Vickery, 1960, p. 79; 1966, p. 21), and "more than one way to view the world" (Kwasnik, 1999, p. 40). They "may provide multi-dimensional and structured access points to collections [of entities]" (Ingwersen & Wormell, 1992, p. 189). Facet analysis is described as, "the mental process by which the possible trains of characteristics which can form the basis of classification of a subject are enumerated" (Ranganathan, 1951, p. 2).

In contrast, Vickery (1960, p. 17) describes a faceted classification as, "a schedule of standard terms to be used in document subject description" and in the assignment of **notation**. Broughton and Slavic (2004, online) advise that, "Although *faceted classification* is regarded by many as a *structure* with specific characteristics, essentially *facet analysis* is a *technique*, and different models of the same universe of discourse can be derived to meet different local or subject-specific needs using different categories and variations on the syntax" [emphasis added]. Unfortunately the term "faceted classification is often used to mean any system of subject organization in which analytico-synthesis is used" (Broughton, 2002, p. 135). Ranganathan (1967b, pp. 94–110) distinguished among five kinds of subject classification, which he viewed on a continuum from Enumerative to Analytico-Synthetic (Ranganathan, 1967b, p. 94).

1. *Enumerative* classification consists of a single schedule enumerating all subjects—of the past, the present, and the anticipatable future.

2. *Almost-Enumerative* classification consists of a large schedule enumerating most of the subjects and a few schedules of common isolates.

3. *Almost-Faceted* classification consists of a large schedule enumerating most of the subjects of the past, the present and anticipatable future; a few schedules of common isolates; and some schedules of special *isolate*s.

4. *Rigidly-Faceted* is a classification in which the facets and their sequence are predetermined for all subjects in a basic class.

5. *Freely Faceted* classification has no rigid pre-determined facet formulae for the compound subjects which belong to a basic subject.

All types of bibliographical classification share common purposes: *language normalization* by harmonizing differing terminology, *indexing support* for the indexer *characterizing the subject contents* of the document, and s*earch and access* as tools for searchers to analyze and define questions. Each type of classification tends to emphasize one technique over another (Vickery, 1966, p. 22).

Vickery (1966, pp. 44–45) notes that faceted classification, although "partly analogous to the traditional rules of logical division on which classification has always been based" results in a system which differs in three important ways:

1. By strict application of rules and facet analysis such that: "every distinctive logical category should be isolated, every characteristic should be clearly formulated, and each new relation should be recognized."

2. Facets are not locked into "rigid enumerative schedules, but are left free to combine with each other in fullest freedom, so that every type of relation between terms and between subjects may be expressed."

3. Such a system "breaks free from the restriction of traditional classification to the hierarchical, genus-species relations. By combining terms in compound subjects, it introduces new logical relations between them, thus better reflecting the complexity of knowledge."

## Primer for Facet Analysis and Faceted Classification

This section will articulate the basic principles and techniques of facet analysis. FA is a form of conceptual analysis that collects commonly used terms in a given domain and uses these terms as raw material for analysis (Vickery, 1960, pp. 12–13). During analysis, each term is examined and a series of questions asked: What concept does this represent? In what conceptual category should this concept be included? What are the class relations between this concept and other concepts included in the same category? In sum, a faceted classification schedule consists of a set of clearly defined, terminologically expressed concepts along with their semantic relations that have been defined and identified through the process of facet analysis (Vickery, 1966).

## Basic Steps in Facet Analysis

Vickery (1960, 1966) provides instructions for constructing a faceted classification through the technique of facet analysis. The following outline defines and describes basic procedures, demonstrating the iterative interplay of facet analysis and faceted classification (Vickery, 1960, 1966). It is not possible to create a faceted classification without conducting facet analysis because the analysis facilitates choice of terms, assignment of subject access points (subject analysis), and assignment of notation.

Facet Analysis:

1. Define the subject field: This is accomplished by first asking, "what *entities* are of interest to the user group, what *aspects* of those entities are of interest" (Vickery, 1966, p. 11).

2. Facet formulation: Examine a representative range of material that directly expresses the interests of the user group: reports, papers, comprehensive texts, glossaries, subject heading lists, etc. This provides a list of candidate terms to use.

   A. Sort these terms into homogeneous groups known as facets.

   B. Each group is derived by "taking each term and defining it with respect to the terms that are the center of interest in the classification." (Vickery, 1966, p. 45).

Facet Analysis and Faceted Classification:

3. Facet amplification and structuring: It is helpful at this stage to construct a hierarchical order for the terms collected within each facet. Even if no well developed hierarchy results, the procedure

helps to coalesce synonyms, eliminate terms that are collated with the wrong facet, and to indicate gaps in the system.

4. Creation of scope notes: These notes will define terms that are unclear and provide instructions to users and indexers as to the meaning and use of each facet.

5. Facet arrangement: Decide how the facets are to be arranged among themselves. This is use dependent, i.e., for post-coordinate use (as a thesaurus), arrange in categories, for pre-coordinate use (in a catalog), more thought must be given to the sequence of facets in the schedule and placing them in citation order. The order chosen should be that of greatest utility to the person using the system.

Faceted Classification:

6. Notation: Vickery devotes ten pages to the construction of notation, or call numbers, for materials in a system classified using faceted classification. Once analysis is complete, it is possible to create a classification with filing and citation order, notation, and index.

7. Fitting a notation: This is the final result of facet analysis and one of the ways in which the full sequence of structured facets may be displayed (items may be sorted according to notation—see suggestions for thesaurus in step 5 for alternate arrangements). This arrangement should provide for helpful display of the structure of a given subject field.

## Fundamental Categories: Role in Facet Analysis

A list of fundamental or frequently occurring categories is essential to the successful completion of facet analysis by preventing omissions and ensuring more complete analysis of a given domain. Ranganathan (1933) originally proposed five fundamental categories—Personality, Matter, Energy, Space, and Time (PMEST)—as universally sufficient to analyze any domain. The role of fundamental categories was not fully discussed until the fourth edition of the *Colon Classification* was published in 1952.

Throughout the 1950s, in the course of practical experience with the construction of special faceted schemes, CRG members found that the component features of such a list might be more varied in scope than five. New lists of provisional categories were proposed that greatly extended the PMEST formula. These resulted from the creation of faceted schemes for special collections by CRG members and each stands as an exemplar of best practice (Vickery, 1966, p. 24):

Substance, Organ, Constituent, Structure, Shape, Property, Object of action (patient, raw material), Action, Operation, Process, Agent, Space, and Time

As a member of the CRG, Vickery (1960, p. 29) also proposed his own list:

> Things; Entities (naturally occurring, products, mental constructs); Parts, components, structure (organs); Materials; Constituents; Attributes (qualities, properties, processes, behavior); Operations (experimental, mental); Operating agents; Place; Condition

Vickery (1966, p. 24) compiled other extant lists of fundamental categories including those proposed by Jesse Shera and Margaret Egan (agent, act, tools, object of action, time, space, and product), Barbara Kyle (natural phenomena, artifacts, activities, and "purposes, aims, *ideas*, and abstracts"), and Eric de Grolier ("constant categories": time, space, action, and "variables": substance, organ, analytic, synthetic, property, form, and organization). Contemporary lists of facets exist. One appropriate for use in classifying software components for reuse was created by Prieto-Díaz and Freeman (1987) and included function, objects, medium, system-type, functional area, and setting. Provisional lists of "standard categories" retain great value for contemporary researchers. Aitchison [née Binns], Gilchrist, and Bawden (2002, p. 71) have collocated these into a list with five main categories:

1. Entities, things, and objects subdivided by characteristics and function

2. Actions and activities

3. Space, place, location, and environment

4. Time

5. Kinds or types; systems and assemblies; applications and purposes

## Fundamental Categories: Criticisms

The purpose and role of fundamental categories in facet analysis is subject to frequent criticism (Hjørland, 2008, p. 90; La Barre, 2006, pp. 200–207). Moss (1964) observed that PMEST was based on Aristotle's own formulation without explicit acknowledgement, and discredits their use by leveraging Russell's (1946) criticism of Aristotelian categories as syllogistic, lacking principles of construction, and therefore false. Moss (1964, p. 297) states, "it is difficult to see how any consistent scheme of classification could ever be developed on a basis so precariously poised." This extends earlier criticisms by John Metcalfe (1959, p. 247), who considered facet analysis to be "new jargon" for a previously existing concept, subject analysis. Metcalfe found the iterative development of facet theory—responsive as it was to extension and refinement through practical discussion, testing, and challenges—grounds for outright dismissal. Deeply troubling was Ranganathan's minimal acknowledgment of Otlet and the Universal Decimal Classification: "he really is the most complete plagiarist of ideas, devices, and terms in the whole history of bibliographical classification" (Metcalfe, 1959, p. 248). Metcalfe's most devastating criticism was the lack of "wide and impartial comparative study in any detail" of facet theory (p. 248). Although Metcalfe's writings may seem like vitriolic hyperbole, his call for critical and impartial study for all organization and access systems, especially in the context of faceted systems, warrants close attention.

Contemporary and earlier critics, as summarized by Tyaganatarajan (1961), protest the restrictive limitations and the impossibility of fitting all concepts into Ranganathan's five universal categories. Such criticism is more nuanced and challenges the basic assumption that "all subjects can be analyzed in a way that fits these [Ranganathan's] five categories" (Hjørland, 2008, p. 90). This goes to the heart of a perennial philosophical question—whether fundamental categories are provisional and dynamically developed (Vickery, 1966, p. 24) or pre-existing and prescriptive.

Misunderstanding or confusion often arises when attempting to understand the nature of several of the original PMEST categories (La Barre, 2006, pp. 200–207; Moss, 1964, p. 296–297). Vickery (1966, p. 25) offers clarification: "*Space and Time* are relatively straightforward geographical and chronological schedules. *Energy* covers categories such as problem, method, process, operation, handling and technique. *Matter* comprises constituent materials of all kinds. *Personalities* (the most difficult for many to grasp) include libraries, numbers, equations, wavelengths of radiation, engineering works, organisms, crops, religions, art styles, literary works, languages, social groups, communities and states." Many have observed that these vague terms offer a robust framework for the creation of more precise categories.

Hjørland (2008, p. 90) asserts that facets are logical a priori categories and thus embody a problematic philosophical assumption: that the notational elements assigned to each facet (category) maintain the same meaning throughout use and without regard to changing contexts. In the same vein, Miksa (1998, p. 73) observes that facet theory "may well have represented [Ranganathan's] need to find more order and regularity in the realm of subjects than actually exist."

Vickery (1959a, p. 18) counters that fundamental facets rely instead on the concept of warrant: "our grouping of terms in a newly approaching field cannot be carried out a priori. New associations are continually being discovered and recovered in the literature. … Classification must be based—as far as raw material is concerned—on literary warrant." In another, more contemporary view, Kwasnik (1999) states that Ranganathan's greatest contribution is his recognition of the provisional nature of systems of access and order. Ranganathan (1967a, p. 401) recognized the existence of a "two-fold infinity" in the universe of knowledge due to the multiplicity of individual worldviews and information seeking purposes and the infinitely complex and dynamic nature of the universe of knowledge. This duality imposes the requisite features of flexibility and responsiveness as a measure of the success of any system (Ranganathan, 1998, p. 67).

In the fourth edition of the *Colon Classification*, Ranganathan (1952a) introduced phase analysis and a schedule of semantic relations designed to capture and emphasize the dynamic, inherently provisional, and contextual nature of facets. These devices support notation that indicates bias or viewpoint by inclusion of aspects such as influence/influencing, stimulating/stimulated by, suppressing/suppressed by, and comparison. Similar devices occur in editions of the UDC that predate these. Examples of the relational symbols in the UDC include (+) to indicate addition, (/) to indicate extension, (:) to indicate a basic relation, ( [ ] ) to indicate an algebraic sub grouping, and (=) to indicate language (International Federation for

Documentation, 1981; McIlwaine, 1997). These devices continue to evolve throughout subsequent editions of both schemes.

Hjørland (2008) correctly observes scarce critical engagement about the nature of fundamental facets and the philosophical underpinning of facet theory. This is indicative of underdeveloped understanding and predominantly superficial application of facets in many current system designs (La Barre, 2006). Theoretically engaged exemplars of facet applications exist and will be discussed in a later section. This underscores the need for sustained and critical engagement with facet theory as potentially fruitful in digital environments. What should not be forgotten is that over time, regardless of discipline or subject area, the technique of facet analysis has proven successful in the construction of a variety of cultural heritage information retrieval tools.

# Heritage of Facet Analysis

Tracing the parameters of facet theory heritage involves three main periods of increased activity, at once technical, institutional, and intellectual. The intellectual and theoretical heritage that informs the present work began at the inception of the European documentalist movement and the creation of the UDC. A strong line of continuity runs through the efforts of European documentalists to early information retrieval experimentation in the United States and elsewhere. That European and later American documentalists created innovative means to disseminate scientific information is clear; however, their motivations were different. Increased awareness of the importance of theoretically grounded development undergirds these innovations.

## *Facet Heritage: Early Development*

Facet analysis heralded the dawn of a new era in information organization systems by capturing the imaginations of a generation of practitioners and researchers. Earlier thinkers, including Paul Otlet, co-creator of the UDC, and Henry Evelyn Bliss (1929, 1931), author of the Bliss Classification, had explored the basic theoretical tenets; but S. R. Ranganathan (1937, 1957b) provided preliminary descriptions of facet analysis (FA) and faceted classification (FC) in the first two editions of the *Prolegomena to Library Classification*, with full articulation of the theory, postulates, and principles of facet analysis in the 1967 edition.

Facet theory continued to develop over the years through intensive effort by three groups, the Library Research Circle (LRC), the Classification Research Group, and the Classification Research Study Group (CRSG). Each challenged, strengthened, and extended Ranganathan's contributions. Until his death in 1972, Ranganathan was supportive and encouraging of these efforts.

### Facet Heritage: Library Research Circle—India

Members of the LRC, which formed in India in 1951, worked closely with Ranganathan on the development and continuing revision of facet theory and engaged in general discussion of the problems facing library science. This group met informally each Sunday on the veranda at Ranganathan's house and openly discussed pragmatic problems (Ranganathan personal correspondence, 1952b). Inspired by Russell and Whitehead's work in mathematics, the aim of the group was to "tidy up" and promulgate definitions, axioms, and postulates of classificatory technique and principles for integration into *Depth Classification* (Ranganathan, 1953) and the second edition of the *Prolegomena* (Ranganathan, 1957b; Parthasarathy, 1952, pp. 153–159; Ranganathan, 1963, pp. 88–89). In 1962 the work of the LRC moved to the Documentation Research and Training Centre (DRTC; drtc.isibang.ac.in/DRTC.html) at the Indian Statistical Institute in Bangalore, where special classification work was continued (Bhattacharyya, 1967, 1969; Chakraborty, 1967; Kumedan & Parkhi, 1967; Sangameswaran, 1967).

## Facet Heritage: Classification Research Group—Britain

Meanwhile, in England, instigated by J. D. Bernal and formally organized in 1952 under the leadership of A. J. Wells, B. I. Palmer, D. J. Foskett, and B. C. Vickery, the CRG formed as a sister group to the LRC (Classification Research Group, 1955; Foskett, 1962, 1969; Foskett & Palmer, 1961; McIlwaine, 2003). This prolific and well-documented group still meets monthly in London.

In 1955 the CRG issued a manifesto, *The Need for a Faceted Classification as the Basis for all Methods of Information Retrieval*, rejecting all "existing classification schemes as unsatisfactory, in one way or another, for the demands of modern documentation" (Classification Research Group, 1955, p. 263). In 1957, the CRG facilitated an international conference for practitioners and researchers in Dorking, England. The proceedings of this conference (Association of Special Libraries and Information Bureaux, 1957), attended by Jesse Shera, Eugene Garfield, S. R. Ranganathan, and N. T. Ball of the National Science Foundation, are still critical reading.

Members of the CRG created a number of special schemes for subject classifications at their places of employment, including the *Occupational Safety and Health Documents Classification Scheme* (Foskett, 1957, pp. 115–136), the *English Electric Scheme* (Binns & Bagley, 1958, 1961), Langridge's 1956 *Classification of Enterprise Activities* (Vickery, 1966, p. 19), and the *British Catalogue of Music* (Wells, 1960). Three manuals of practice provide assistance in creating special classifications in various subjects: science (Vickery, 1959a), social science (Foskett, 1963), and the humanities (Langridge, 1976). Many of these classifications are still in use.

## Facet Heritage: Classification Research Study Group—North America

The CRSG was modeled after the British CRG and formed in the United States and Canada in 1957. Spearheaded by two women, Phyllis Richmond, then a librarian at Rochester University, and Pauline Atherton Cochrane, then assistant director of the Documentation Research Project at the American Institute of Physics (AIP), the group was actively supported by Jesse Shera, then dean at the Baxter Graduate School of Library Science at Western Reserve University, home to the Center for Documentation and Communication Research (CDCR).

Richmond considered the activities of the three groups essential in filling the gap between theory and practice. "The members [of the CRG] produced original well-organized logical systems, applicable to new or revised needs of the communities which they served ... [and] have managed to close the gap between universal classification systems and highly specialized ones" (Richmond, 1988, pp. 247–248).

Throughout the mid-1960s the CRSG, "informally organized, with an open program, with no visible means of support," held sessions in empty rooms at odd hours at the annual meetings of professional societies such as the American Library Association, the Special Libraries Association, and the American Documentation Institute (Richmond, 1963a, p. 58). The group was composed of members from academia, business, and government (Cochrane interview, 2001, p. 27). The contributions of this group are difficult to measure because few publications bear the CRSG imprimatur. The group promoted activities that introduced facet analysis to North American researchers and provided practical engagement with facet theory. The 1965 volume, *Classification Research: Proceedings of the Second International Study Conference* edited by one of the co-founders of the CRSG (Atherton, 1965b), remains a valuable companion to the proceedings of the Dorking Conference that was organized by CRG, their British counterparts, in concert with other British library groups.

This was also a time of conferences that brought together researchers interested in the development and extension of facet theory in Europe and North America. The most notable of these occurred at such places as Dorking, England (Association of Special Libraries and Information Bureaux, 1957), with its focus on "Classification for Information Retrieval" and Elsinore, Copenhagen, which hosted the Second International Study Conference for Classification Research and brought together many luminaries in the field (Atherton, 1965b). North American conferences were held throughout the 1960s at Case Western University in Cleveland, Ohio. In New Jersey, the *Rutgers Series on Systems for the Intellectual Organization of Information* provided a forum for the open discussion of many organization and access systems including the Colon Classification (Ranganathan, 1998), the Universal Decimal Classification (Mills, 1964), and Vickery's (1966) discussion of the faceted classification schemes then being created and utilized in Great Britain. Facet theory has undergone extension and modification from the early days of the UDC and Bliss classification to the complete explication in Ranganathan's (1957b, 1967b) *Prolegomena* through practical application by three groups: the LRC, CRG, and CRSG.

## Chronological Overview of Developments: 1950–1999

This section presents a chronological overview of the development of facet theory. Even those who accept similar definitions of central concepts have created systems that often seem remarkably dissimilar, whether a thesaurus, special classification, universal classification, or Web application. Given the variability of resultant practices, a survey of applications and research provides an idea of trends, novel approaches, and strands of continuing research. This is not an attempt to cover each system or theoretical development in existence. Several comprehensive sources discuss research in this area at this time and include: Taube's (1953–1959)

*Studies in Coordinate Indexing*, Garfield (1955), Lancaster and Fayen (1973), Doyle (1975), and Bourne and Hahn (2003). Broad trends and representative developments are highlighted using time increments of one to two decades as approximate and artificial groupings.

## Early Information Retrieval Experimentation: 1950–1968

This was a period of intense activity in early information retrieval experimentation with design and testing of faceted classification schemes or the use of facet analysis to create indexing systems (Atherton, 1962; Ranganathan, 1965, p. 275). In many cases CRG and CRSG members were at work behind the scenes: in a consulting capacity, by constructing faceted classifications for testing as in the Aslib Cranfield Research Project (Cleverdon, 1960a, 1960b, 1962; Vickery, 1959b), by using faceted schemes in mechanized information retrieval systems as in the American Institute of Physics projects to test the application of the UDC in the Documentation Research Project (DRP) and Audacious Projects (Atherton, 1965a; Freeman, 1966a, 1966b; Freeman & Atherton, 1967, 1968a, 1968b). CRSG members also organized informational seminars (Freeman & Atherton, 1969) and criticized the design of system tests or the interpretation of results (Richmond, 1963b). Projects at three institutes represent the full sweep of this research: the CDCR, the Aslib Cranfield studies, and the American Institute of Physics.

### Center for Documentation and Communication Research

In 1955, Western Reserve University's (WRU) newly established Center for Documentation and Communication Research served as a testing center for coordinate indexing systems created by Allen Kent and James Perry, such as the semantic code and the telegraphic abstract. The semantic code, or "WRU system," utilized *semantic factoring* (a process of conceptual analysis that results in a set of independent and *mutually exclusive* categories), role indicators, and special punctuation (Aspray, 1999, p. 6; Kent, 1960; Melton, 1958). The American Society for Metals sponsored a program that oversaw application of the WRU system to the literature of metallurgy (Melton, 1960, p. 1). The WRU system was also tested as part of the Aslib Cranfield Research Project.

Many contemporaries noted similarity between the WRU system to facet theory; one observed: "the Semantic Code, which was highly structured, is basically the Colon Classification scheme, the principal difference being the *notation* employed—the difference in notation being from the requirement for a machine system, rather than a manual system" (Taulbee & House, 1965, p. 124). References to Ranganathan are veiled by observations of common motivations as explanation for common features (Melton, 1960, p. 1). These observations may overstate the similarities and dependence of the WRU system upon the Colon Classification. The WRU system used relational indicators to link terms explicitly, in a fashion similar to the work of the CRG. The Colon Classification utilized term juxtaposition rather than explicit indicators to imply term relations.

## Aslib Cranfield Studies

In 1957 Cyril Cleverdon received a National Science Foundation (NSF) grant to conduct comparative testing of indexing systems. This came to be known as the Aslib Cranfield Research Project and consisted of two phases. This overview concerns the three studies that comprised the first phase (or Cranfield I). Study 1 (1958) tested four indexing systems. The UDC was chosen for its widespread use in England and because it was primarily an enumerative system with some principles of synthesis. Two of the systems were created for the test itself: an alphabetical subject catalog of a type uncommon except in North America and a faceted classification of aeronautics. The final system tested was Taube's Uniterm system, chosen for its use of coordination (Cleverdon, 1960a, 1960b, 1962; Gull, 1956). The second Cranfield study tested a faceted classification for electrical engineering created by CRG member Jean Binns and D. Bagley (Aitchison & Cleverdon, 1962; Binns, undated manuscript, 1961; Binns & Bagley, 1958, 1961). The final study in this phase of the project involved a comparative test of two faceted indexing models: the WRU system and the model faceted classification of aeronautics that was tested in the first Cranfield study (Aitchison & Cleverdon, 1962, 1963; Cleverdon & Mills, 1963; Melton, 1960).

## American Institute of Physics

Also of interest are three projects at the American Institute of Physics that were directed by Robert Freeman and Pauline Atherton. The first was the Documentation Research Project (AIP/DRP) conducted between 1961 and 1966 (Atherton, 1961, 1963; Atherton & Borko, 1965; Atherton & Keenan, 1965; Freeman 1965). This project involved translating the extant English, French, and German schedules of the UDC; some experimentation with automatic alphabetic indexing of the UDC schedules; and initial steps toward creating a retrieval system for testing and evaluation. Next, the AIP/UDC project from 1965 through 1968 (Freeman, 1966a; Freeman & Atherton, 1968a) resulted in the creation of a prototype file management system for the UDC. The CDCR hosted some testing of the mechanization of UDC for retrieval in the *American Meteorological Society Index of Literature* (Freeman & Atherton, 1969). Lastly, the AUDACIOUS project used the UDC as an indexing language for nuclear science literature (Freeman & Atherton, 1967, 1968b).

## Thesaural Developments and Classificatory Extensions: 1969–1979

Early discussions of the applicability of facet analysis to thesaurus construction began in the mid-1960s (for example, Brenner, 1966). Aitchison's work on *Thesaurofacet*, a faceted classification and controlled vocabulary for engineering and related subjects, was among the first to utilize facet analysis explicitly (Aitchison, Gomersall, & Ireland, 1969). Originally designed as the faceted *English Electric Scheme*, *Thesaurofacet* provided classification schedules as well as controlled vocabulary for scientific and technical subjects. *Thesaurofacet* proved equally adaptable for use in computerized indexing and information retrieval systems and traditional library and documentation centers (Aitchison, 1970).

Aitchison was also instrumental in the development of the faceted *UNESCO Thesaurus* for use in indexing and information retrieval (Aitchison, 1975). She describes the strengths of facet analysis in support of analyzing complex subjects into simple groupings with combinatorial capability in a thesaurus for post-coordinate use, or in class marks for a pre-coordinate system (Aitchison & Clarke, 2004, pp. 10–11). Following Aitchison's lead, Anderson (1979) completed a faceted classification and indexing system to provide access to the *Modern Language Association* bibliographic database.

Other special thesauri developed or extended through the use of facet analysis include the *British Technology Index* (Coates, 1963), the *London Education Classification* (Foskett, 1974) and the *London Classification of Business Studies* (Vernon & Lang, 1979/2001). Members of the CRG pledged to maintain and continually revise the schedules of the fully faceted *Bliss Bibliographic Classification* (BC2). In a retrospective article, Coates (1978) reviewed developments in facet theory in the twenty years after the Dorking conference and found that updating of the Universal Decimal and Colon (third edition) classifications continued, but only the second edition of the Bliss Bibliographic Classification (Mills & Broughton, 1977) came close to a working model of facet theory. Another exemplar was Austin's (1974, 1984) work on PRECIS (PREserved Content Indexing System) for use in the British National Bibliography with general facets such as location, key entity or system, modifier, action, and agent or instrument. Another exemplar was Neelameghan, Gopinath, and Bhattacharyya's work on POPSI (POstulate based Permuted Subject Index) (Bhattacharyya, 1979; Coates, 1978; Neelameghan & Gopinath, 1975; Rajanand & Guha, 1975) with basic elementary categories of discipline, entity, property, and action as indexing devices. Also of note, the Broad System of Ordering (BSO) (Coates, Lloyd, & Simandl, 1979) was created to serve as a general faceted classification, search and retrieval mechanism, information exchange, and a switching language to enable search across vocabularies. It makes use of the following facets:

1. Tools or equipment for carrying out operations

2. Operations (purposive activities)

3. Parts and/or subsystems of objects of action

    A. Or: parts and/or sub-systems of study

    B. Or: parts and/or subsystems of products

4. Objects of action or study

    A. Or products

    B. Or total systems

In spite of these developments, in North America few American Library Association (ALA)-accredited schools included instruction in the Colon Classification and facet analysis. Instruction outside North America was far more comprehensive (Thomas, 1977). Fewer special schemes were created and most were used as access devices in information retrieval. Examples of this include methods for the automatic encoding of chemical reactions (Osinga, 1977) and for faceted retrieval of linguistics information (B. Harris, 1976).

## Revision, Criticism, and Automation: 1980–1989

The 1980s were a time of revision and criticism of existing schemes. Attention turned from creation of thesauri to new attempts to integrate thesauri into a master thesaurus to serve as a switching language for search across databases (Aitchison, 1981; Anderson, 1980). Similar work continued at the DRTC in India, where researchers began to experiment with the creation of computer-generated thesauri, such as *Classaurus*, using the postulates and principles of facet analysis (Devadason, 1985; Devadason & Balasubramanian, 1981) while still paying close attention to the creation of schemes of depth classification (Gopinath, 1986). Batty (1981) captured this shift in the use of facet analysis as the basis of index language construction in his book *Life Begins at Forty: The Resurgence of Facet Analysis*.

The Bliss Classification (BC2) attracted renewed attention at this time as a "rich source of structure and terminology for thesauri covering different subject fields," even as its limitations were also being discussed (Aitchison, 1986, p. 160). Some new special faceted schemes were created, such as the Dickens House Classification to assist in the creation of finding aids (K. Harris, 1986). The 7th and final edition of the Colon Classification was also published (Satija, 1989). Discussions of a faceted approach to hypertext on the Web began during this period (Duncan, 1989).

As noted earlier, facet theory attracted the attention of software engineer Reuben Prieto-Díaz, with a groundbreaking faceted classification of software components that marked the first use of facet analysis in the construction of databases for the reuse of software components. Facet analysis yielded the following facets: function, objects, medium, system-type, functional area, and setting (Prieto-Díaz 1989, 1990; Prieto-Díaz & Freeman, 1987). This classification did not meet with universal approval and by 1997 its demise was announced by at least one set of researchers (Mili, Ah-Ki, Godin, & Mcheick, 1997), but it did serve as an exemplar that enhanced understanding of the provisional nature of facets.

## Databases, Interfaces, and Retrieval Systems: 1990–1999

Focus on the applicability of facets to database construction and in the design of information retrieval interfaces and systems continued. The *Art and Architecture Thesaurus* appeared (Petersen, 1994). Originally designed to classify terminology and to present faceted hierarchies of terms, it also functions as a classified system for subject cataloging (Whitehead, 1989). *AAT* is currently in its second edition (2002) and is available on the Web (www.getty.edu/research/conducting_research/vocabularies/aat).

Beginning in the 1990s, the UDC underwent extensive revision as the editors explored the potential for converting it into a fully faceted system and began the task of conversion to an automated format (McIlwaine & Williamson, 1995; Williamson, 1994; Williamson & McIlwaine, 1993). That same year Gerard Riesthuis and David Strachan created CDS/ISIS, a database for the UDC Master Reference file consisting of the 60,000 newly updated classes of the UDC. Through the use of facet analysis, UDC notation is now more expressive and some classes of the UDC were completely restructured (Riesthuis, 2003; Slavic, Cordeiro & Riesthuis, 2008). Riesthuis and others conducted thesaurisation work to explore the possibility of turning the UDC index into a thesaurus (Riesthuis, 1997).

Facet-directed research throughout the 1990s continued a long tradition of testing retrieval efficacy in online environments and knowledge bases (Lancaster, 1992). The potential of facets in the creation of multiple access points and in dynamic search procedures was explored. Facets were found to improve access and facilitate information retrieval by providing physical access through notational devices (such as call numbers for books), while also providing intellectual access on a deep conceptual level (Ingwersen & Wormell, 1992, pp. 184, 191). Facet analysis was also used by many researchers to increase user friendliness in online environments through improved search interfaces (Anderson, 1990; Foskett, 1992; Hearst, 1999; Pollitt, 1998; Pollitt, Ellis, & Smith, 1994; Pollitt, Smith, Braekevelt, & Treglown, 1996; Priss & Jacob, 1999; Vickery, 1990, 2008) and to provide search assistance through faceted query formation (Drabenstott, 2000; Iyer, 1995; Pomerantz, 2003). Applicability of facets to the design of databases continues as a prominent theme following research initiated by Anderson in the 1970s (Neelameghan, 1992; Prieto-Díaz & Freeman, 1987; Priss & Jacob, 1999).

## Facet Theory on the Web: 2000–Present

This section covers recent developments in facet theory. Over the years it is notable that researchers continue to refer to the historical impact of facet analysis and its potential in digital environments, especially on the Web. Foskett (2004) remarked on the timeless influence of Ranganathan in the creation of special classification schemes. Foskett favored the technique of facet analysis because it allows the uncovering of previously hidden or uncoordinated concepts in such a way that possible areas for future research are brought to light. Ellis and Vasconcelos (1999, p. 3) also attest to "the portability of [Ranganathan's] ideas across time, technology, and cultures, simply because they address the very foundations of the business of effective information storage and retrieval." They predicted that contemporary Web developers would do well to pay attention to Ranganathan's facet theory, which has been largely ignored by contemporary information retrieval research in favor of algorithmic approaches.

As in the 1980s, facet theory continues to be widely discussed (see, for example, Broughton, 2006; La Barre, 2006; La Barre & Cochrane, 2006; Poli & Gnoli, 2008; Vickery, 2008). Earlier discussions of facet theory seemed to focus on faceted classification; current discussion is beginning to appreciate the distinction between the structure of a faceted classification and the technique of facet analysis. Today, it would seem that facet theory has broad crossover appeal among knowledge management (KM) specialists and information architecture (IA) firms. Often, attempts to find common ground are hampered by the task of translating practice into understandable language. Statements such as these are seductive: "Faceted classification [is] one of the most powerful, yet least understood, methods of organizing information" (Merholz, 2001, online). "Faceted classification serves up multiple 'pure' classification schemes rather than single 'motley' taxonomy" (Rosenfeld & Morville, 2002, p. 506). Those interested in building faceted systems often have difficulty locating useful guidelines or exemplars. Top sources include Peter Merholz's (2001) extensive discussion of "Innovation in Classification" at peterme.com; and the Faceted Classification Discussion List (www.poorbuthappy.com/fcd) moderated by Peter Van Dijck, creator of XFML (eXchangeable Faceted Metadata Language) and Phil Murray, founder of KMConnection. References to scholarly articles about facet analysis and faceted classification in the library and information science (LIS) literature are slowly beginning to appear in lists of Web links and Web logs. One of the standard handbooks of information architecture (Rosenfeld & Morville, 2002, pp. 204–207) devotes a section to Ranganathan and how to use facets as website organizational devices.

At recent American Society for Information Science and Technology (ASIST) Information Architecture summits, facet analysis has been a frequent topic. Many applications and presentations claim to be implementations of faceted classification. This underscores Broughton's earlier caution about care in terminology and points to a broad gulf that remains between researchers in LIS and those outside the field. Clear standards for determining what constitutes a facet are critical to evaluation and testing in this area. Empirical research into the effectiveness and validity of facet use in contemporary systems is long overdue. Faceted applications typically fall into three general categories: (1) faceted metadata, (2) software-based data modeling or data management applications, (3) and faceted search (FS) or browsing (FB).

### Faceted Metadata

*Faceted metadata* is a common application. Peter Van Dijck's (2002, online) XFML (xfml.org) provides "an open XML format for publishing and sharing hierarchical faceted metadata and indexing efforts between websites." The main idea behind XFML is to provide support for automatic links between websites with related content (see Mark Pilgrim's [2002] excellent tutorial [diveintomark.org/archives/2002/12/03/this_is_xfml]).

The Flamenco project (FLexible information Access using MEtadata in Novel Combinations) (bailando.sims.berkeley.edu/flamenco.html) uses hierarchical faceted metadata, or HFM, to support query expansion in digital collections of art and architectural images.

Hearst's research culminated in the Flamenco testbed, one of the best known contemporary implementations of facets (Hearst, Smalley, & Chandler, 2006). Flamenco software is Open Source; its code has been freely available to researchers since 2006 (flamenco.berkeley.edu). Figure 6.2 is the entry screen for Flamenco. Unlike most commercial implementations, Hearst provides usability data and full disclosure. Her work always provides A to B comparisons between search systems and the system interface designs she has tested. Regardless of the data used for the experiments, whether recipes, architectural designs, or fine art images, Hearst's research indicates that users prefer the HFM interface to those interfaces that use keyword searching or category clustering. Hearst's work also seems to indicate increasing acceptance of tightly integrated browsing and searching systems on websites (Hearst, 2006; Hearst, Smalley, & Chandler, 2006).

Hearst's work recently inspired the Science Education Resource Center (SERC) at Carleton College. This group "builds educational portals" for digital libraries.

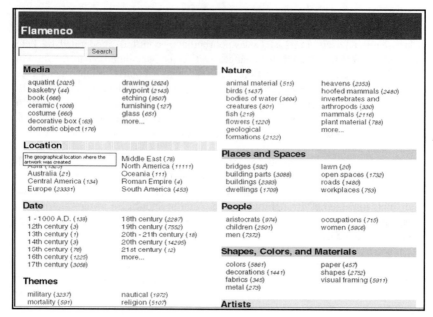

**Figure 6.2 Flamenco entry screen**

They created a faceted search interface modeled on Flamenco expressly to "provide both a full text search interface and a browse interface over multiple controlled vocabularies" (Fox, Manduca, & Iverson, 2005, online). A similar project provides access to a database of archaeological artifacts through faceted query expansion and browsing (Ross, Janevski, & Stovanovich, 2005).

### Faceted Data Modeling

Other facet applications support *data modeling or management* such as Travis Wilson's Facetmap (facetmap.com), have been "created to let users browse complex metadata while retaining a simple, familiar, menu interface" (Wilson, 2009, online). Facetmap consists of software that supports browsing by facets or conceptual categories. Figure 6.3 is a screenshot of facetmap that shows one of several possible displays that can be generated using the software with XML encoded data.

Facetmap, unlike traditional faceted applications, does not permit assignment of multiple headings from a single facet to a given resource. Wilson (2006) argues for a strict faceted classification model. By far the most common question asked of Facetmap is, "Why can't I assign multiple headings, from a single facet, to one of my resources? Isn't that the whole point of faceted classification?" The brief answer is, that is not the point of faceted classification. That is what tags are for.

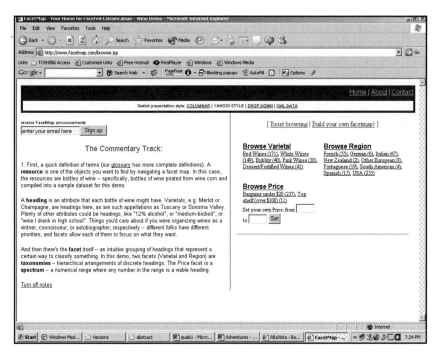

**Figure 6.3   Visual display from Facetmap (facetmap.com)**

### Faceted Search and Browsing Systems

Similar to Facetmap but lacking visualization and modeling features are *search and browsing systems* that provide faceted search and browsing capabilities in the form of site search and/or site architecture. Two commercial examples are Endeca (endeca.com) and Siderean (siderean.com). Work is progressing quickly in this area. Examples include the recent (2005) deployment of FAST search (www.fast search.com) in Elsevier's Engineering Village 2. Users can browse by facets such as author affiliation, treatment, or expertise. In January 2006, Endeca's ProFind software with guided (or faceted) navigation was deployed in the North Carolina State University (NCSU) online catalog (North Carolina State University, 2006). Figure 6.4 is a screenshot of the NCSU catalog. This was simply the first of many OPAC implementations that use faceted navigation or faceted browsing. Others include VuFind, Koha Zoom, and the University of Virginia's Blacklight project. Facets in these implementations are selected through use of existing MARC metadata, not through rigorous application of traditional facet analysis prior to system implementation. Because of these systems, library interest in facets has resumed with a vigor not seen since 1981, when Richmond (1981) published her book about PRECIS.

Websites often cited as exemplars of faceted design include Epicurious, the "world's greatest recipe collection" (www.epicurious.com), and Wine.com (wine.com). The following screenshots (Figures 6.5 and 6.6) are the entry screens for each website.

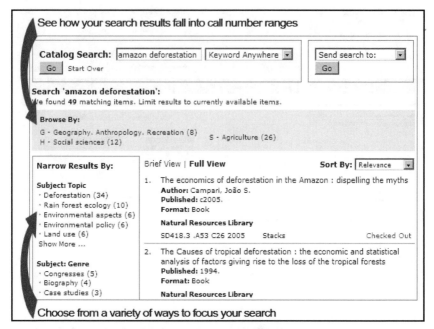

Figure 6.4   **From the North Carolina State University OPAC instruction page: The library is introducing a new guided navigation system to improve access to the collection. This approach facilitates browsing within your catalog search results. This is a sample results screen (www.lib.ncsu.edu/catalog/index_arrows.html).**

Although the reasoning is unclear, these two sites are the most frequent illustrations of facets mentioned on KM and IA lists and weblogs; both have made frequent appearances in presentations during the last few years of the ASIST IA Summit (Denton, 2003; Merholz, 2001; Morville, 2001; Rayborn, 2004; Rosenfeld & Morville, 2002).

### Traditional Applications of Facet Theory

Traditional implementations of facet theory exist alongside these other applications. FATKS: Facet analytical theory in managing knowledge structure for humanities (www.ucl.ac.uk/fatks) is an automated faceted classification and indexing tool for the humanities (Broughton, 2001, 2003, 2004b). The Facet Project is another exemplar that tested the efficacy of faceted thesauri for retrieval of multimedia collections (Binding & Tudhope, 2004; Tudhope & Koch, 2004). Prieto-Díaz continues to discuss the power of facet analysis in building ontologies and generating descriptors for software reuse communities, through use of the DARE tool for semi-automated building of thesauri and faceted classifications (Frakes, Prieto-Díaz, & Fox, 1998; Tudhope & Koch, 2004).

**Figure 6.5    Entry browsing screen for Epicurious.com; facets noted by most demonstrations include: ingredient, cuisine, preparation, occasion, meal, dish type.**

Pollitt's work with Interactive Information Retrieval was based on facet analysis and used a faceted thesaurus to enhance post-coordinated searching. It gave users the ability to generate different faceted views of search results. Following his death in 2006, work continues at View-Based Systems Ltd. (www.view-based-systems. com) (Pollitt, 1998; Pollitt, Ellis, & Smith, 1994). Pollitt's work is echoed in several ongoing projects. One of the most representative involves creating a system for searching a large e-mail corpus that "supports the user ... by providing multiple facets or viewpoints to the corpus" (Tuulos, Perkiö, & Tirri, 2005, p. 683). The authors describe this work as tightly coupled data mining and information retrieval methods.

Inspired by the revolutionary work, *Thesaurofacet*, by Aitchison and colleagues (1969), many have used the technique of facet analysis in the construction of controlled vocabularies. The use of facets and facet analysis as tools for vocabulary

**Figure 6.6 Screenshot of Wine.com with facets highlighted**

construction has recently been incorporated into the ANSI/NISO (American National Standards Institute/National Information Standards Organization) Standards for Controlled Vocabularies Z39.19-2005 (National Information Standards Organization, 2005), as well as the British Standard BS8723-2 (British Standards Institution, 2005). Ongoing facet analytical work by the Gruppo di Ricerca sull'Indicizzazione per Soggetto to transform the *Nuovo Soggettario*, an Italian subject heading list, into a general vocabulary builds on lessons learned in the construction of Austin's PRECIS vocabulary (Cheti & Paradisi, 2008).

Broughton (2008) describes the potential challenges that face those who attempt to derive faceted thesauri from the schedules of a faceted classification. Tudhope and Binding (2008) describe the basic elements and prominent features of faceted thesauri derived from faceted classification schedules. These research projects provide hope that it may be possible to leverage semantic relations evident in faceted thesauri such as the *Art and Architecture Thesaurus* or *Thesaurofacet* for use in Semantic Web applications that assist in query expansion and knowledge discovery. In order to enhance use of existing faceted systems, Slavic (2008) advocates that all existing faceted classifications be published in machine readable format for wider adoption and repurposing by automated systems throughout the Web in furtherance of the goals of Tudhope and Binding (2008).

Cochrane and others issue words of warning that not all faceting efforts are equally well considered (La Barre & Cochrane, 2006; Gnoli, 2008). OCLC's FAST (Faceted Access to Subject Terms), the best known implementation of facets until the implementation of Endeca in the NCSU online catalog, needs further explication, implementation, and testing if it is to be viewed as more than a superficial approach to faceting by simple decomposition of Library of Congress Subject Heading strings (Mann, 2006). Some evaluative frameworks for FAST exist (Mitchell & Hsieh-Yee, 2007; Qiang, 2008) but need further testing and expansion. With the recent recommendations of the Library of Congress Working Group (2007) to pursue decoupling of subject strings through the use of FAST and other faceted discovery tools, continuing interest in faceted implementations heightens the need for critical and evaluative frameworks.

## Facets or Facet-Like Structures in Cognate Areas

Over time, many researchers have noted the existence of facets in cognate areas that bear striking similarities to facets in LIS (among them Beghtol, 2008; Gnoli, 2008; Hjørland, 2008; Priss, 2008). Some simply ascribe these similarities to evidence of "faceted thinking," not actual facet use. This section briefly compares and contrasts these developments chiefly to bring them to the attention of researchers.

### Psychology and Guttman's Facet Theory

Beghtol (1995, 2006) has noted that facet theory simultaneously arose in the disciplines of LIS and psychology. The psychologist Lois Guttman (1954) was unfamiliar with Ranganathan's work in LIS, yet both researchers adopted *facet* as the central construct in their formulations of facet theory. Both theories are currently enjoying a resurgence of interest, with Guttman's theory widely used in both psychology and education (Dancer, 2008).

The two conceptualizations are similar. Guttman's facet theory provided a model for conceptual analysis that would result in a classification sequence for mapping the structure of psychological theories. Central to facet theory in psychology is the technique of defining observations through a mapping sentence that "contains a variety of facets" (Bergling, 1999, p. 32). Each facet has a specific role in the classification of research issues and also in the analysis of systematic relationships within the empirical data. Facets allow a researcher to map the correspondence between the definition and one aspect of collected empirical data. Facet theory in psychology seeks to integrate practice and theory systematically within a framework that is especially valuable for instrument development and validation (Bergling, 1999). The Facet Theory Association maintains a comprehensive bibliography of research in this area (Cohen, 2005) and has published a manual of best practice (Shye, 1995).

### *Linguistic Notions and Facet-Like Conceptualizations*

A number of authors, among them Hjørland (2008) and Spärck Jones (2007) have remarked on the similarity of semantic factoring to the linguistic and semiotic notion of semantic primitives (Soergel, 1985). Others have found that the technique of facet analysis is similar to Fillmore's (1968) deep case grammar, in that "a facet plays a function in subject strings very similar to that played by cases or prepositions in languages" (Gnoli, 2008). Both Richmond (1988) and Gnoli (2008) note that the PRECIS indexing system drew heavily on Chomsky's generative grammar.

### *Computer Science and Facet-Like Structures*

Several researchers have proposed algebraic formulae for facet operators for a software module interconnection language (Streich, 1999) or for generating faceted taxonomies through an algebraic equation that can specify the set of valid compound terms (Tzitzikas, Analyti, Spyratos, & Constantopoulos, 2007). Priss (2006, 2008) provides a comprehensive treatment of this subject from an interdisciplinary standpoint by comparing and contrasting LIS facets with structures that appear in relational database structures, ontologies, and artificial intelligence, among others. The common conception of facets as equivalent to fields in a relational database fails to grasp "the more subtle aspects of the idea of facets" (Priss, 2008, p. 245). Formal concept analysis (Ganter & Wille, 1999) is introduced as a cognate development and an appropriate mathematical model for facets (Priss, 2008, p. 251). Priss observes that facet-like techniques have been invented to structure complex class hierarchies in many computer science applications and finds that facet-like structures are commonplace features of knowledge representations and information processing.

## Future Challenges for Facet Theory

This discussion has defined the terms central to facet theory and clarified frequently misunderstood aspects: (1) how to conduct facet analysis, (2) the role of fundamental categories in the technique of facet analysis, and (3) the relation between facet analysis and faceted classification. Broad trends and representative early developments with traditional facet applications were compared and contrasted with contemporary and other cognate developments outside library and information science in areas as diverse as philosophy, psychology, linguistics, and computer science. Criticisms, observations of weaknesses as well as strengths, and areas that are ripe for inquiry were identified.

It remains to be seen whether facet implementations in digital environments will engage more deeply with facet theory and if this will result in more robust faceted applications. Empirical testing is critical, as is evaluative review of ongoing work in this area. Evaluation and empirical testing require attention to research frameworks drawn from the heritage of facet theory. Clear and comprehensive definition of what constitutes a facet will allow meaningful comparisons across implementations and applications.

Facet theory should be challenged through practice, but perhaps the greatest challenge is the extent to which facet analysis will be adopted and adapted for use in rapidly developing digital environments, such as the Semantic Web. Without a serious commitment to Web-enabled controlled vocabularies, there is little hope that the Semantic Web can succeed. Vocabularies constructed through the use of facet analysis may well prove to be the backbone of the future Web. What is most exciting about these developments is that work on the standards for these vocabularies, whether NISO Z39.19-2005 or BS 8723-2, has been highly integrated through the cooperative efforts of many participants working across international boundaries and agencies, with interoperability as the foremost goal (Clarke, 2007, 2008). Each of the current standards has reiterated a commitment to facet analysis as an important tool in the creation of knowledge organization systems, part of the quiet revolution initiated by the pioneering efforts of Jean Aitchison, principal author of *Thesaurofacet*. Many in the Semantic Web community look to the structure and syntax provided by existing vocabularies, whether in the form of traditional thesauri, website taxonomies, or ontologies, as scaffolding for Semantic Web applications (British Standards Institution, 2008). Because facet theory provides guidance for the creation of highly principled syntactical structures, it has special appeal and is receiving renewed attention. In this way, the Web of the future may well serve as the final proving ground for facet theory.

## Appendix I: Glossary of Terms

Definitions have been drawn from literature that forms the canon of facet theory. (See Appendix II for a bibliography of canonical literature.) It is provided here for reference and as an overview of the specialized vocabulary of facet theory.

**Array:** The classes derived from a universe on the basis of a single characteristic at any one step in the progress toward its complete assortment and arranged in the preferred sequence (Ranganathan, 1998, p. 61). *See also chain.*

**Attribute:** Any property or quality or quantitative measure of an entity. Example: In the case of a boy attributes can be—height, strength, character, date of birth (Ranganathan, 1998, p. 62).

**Basic class:** Generic name for a main or a canonical class in a scheme of classification for the universe of knowledge (which consists of the universe of entities and ideas) (Ranganathan, 1998, p. 290).

**Basic facet:** See Ranganathan's (1967b, p. 402-RC) Postulate of the basic facet, which states that every compound subject has a basic facet. A subject may have one or more basic facets. To identify the basic facet of a compound subject, a general knowledge of the schedule of basic subjects is necessary. Most schemes of classification give roughly similar schedules of basic facets. *See also subject.*

**Category:** A form or class of concepts, varying from subject to subject, into which isolates can be grouped, e.g., matter or material, energy or action, organ, property, space, or time. Ranganathan postulates five fundamental categories: Personality, Matter, Energy, Space, and Time (Campbell, 1957, p. 13).

**Chain:** A sequence of classes made up of any given class and its universe (Ranganathan, 1998, p. 63).

**Characteristic:** Characteristics (or attributes) often function as the basis of division in classification. Language form and period are common characteristics in the classification of literature (Campbell, 1957, p. 14).

**Classification:** A scheme of classes fitted with terminology [names for the classes] and notation [ordinal numbers representing the classes] (Ranganathan, 1998, p. 72). A classification schedule is a dictionary of each class number and its components in a natural language or a jargon [index] (Ranganathan, 1998, p. 73).

**Concept:** A formation deposited in memory as a result of association with percepts already deposited in the memory (Ranganathan, 1998, p. 81).

**Dimension:** In mathematics, the term means the degree of manifoldness of an aggregate as fixed by the number of parameters necessary and sufficient to identify any one of its members—that is to distinguish it from all the others. The physical space surrounding us has three dimensions (Ranganathan, 1967b, p. 377). *See also parameter.*

**Division of a universe:** Process of sorting entities of a universe into groups on the basis of a preferred characteristic, or putting like entities into the same group and unlike entities into different groups (Ranganathan, 1998, p. 56).

**Entity:** Any existent: concrete or conceptual—that is a thing or an idea (Ranganathan, 1967b, p. 53), which can have attributes, some of which can serve as a characteristic for division of the main class into groups. Any object or group of objects which has or may have existed, or which can be held to exist (Palmer, 1971, p. 20).

**Facet:** (1) A generic term used to denote any component of a compound subject—be it a basic subject or an isolate—and also its ranked forms, terms, and numbers (Ranganathan, 1967b, p. 88). (2) A general manifestation of a subject (Ranganathan, 1967b, p. 82). (3) Groups of terms derived by taking each term and defining it, *per genus et differentiam,* with respect for its parent class (Vickery, 1960, p. 12). *See also focus.*

**Facet analysis:** The essence of facet analysis is the sorting of terms in a given field of knowledge into homogeneous, mutually exclusive facets, each derived from the parent universe by a single characteristic of division (Vickery, 1960, p. 12). *Note:* Ranganathan made a distinction between *facet analysis, faceted classification*, and *analytico-synthetic classification.* Analytico-synthetic is the most highly developed of the three approaches, in that system construction follows a set of postulates and principles.

**Facet analytical approach (FAA):** Proper and rigorous practice of facet analysis by observing the rules of logical division (Broughton, 2001, p. 67; Mills, 2004, p. 268).

**Facet analytical theory (FAT):** Broughton's (2004b) terminology refers to the use of the technique of facet analysis to create the structure of a faceted classification.

**Facet analytico-synthetic theory, and facet analytico-synthetic technique (FAST)** These two terms embody Ranganathan's theory most completely and are synonymous with **Facet analytical theory (FAT)** because the use of either of these terms indicates the existence of guiding principles and is in keeping with CRG understanding.

**Facet synthesis:** Synthesis of the focal numbers of a subject into class numbers according to the postulates and principles stated for that purpose (Ranganathan, 1998, p. 292).

**Facet theory:** This is used as the superordinate term for similar conceptualizations of Ranganathan's facet theory. Other terms used include: Facet analytical approach (FAA), Facet analytical theory (FAT), Facet analytico-synthetic theory (FAST).

**Faceted classification (FC):** A faceted scheme for classification consists of schedules of basic classes, common *isolate*s, and special isolates only. In a faceted classification scheme, facet analysis is used to identify which facets occur in a compound subject. Vickery (1960, p. 17) describes FC as "a schedule of standard terms to be used in document subject description" (and assignment of notation).

**Faceted notation:** Also known as "synthetic notation." The facets of a classification system are conceptually linked through the use of explicit "facet indicators" as in UDC and Colon (e.g., arbitrary symbols such as ()." ", :, -.) (Mills, 2004, p. 550). Blocks of digits connected by a meaningful connecting digit, analogous to punctuation marks, indicating the distinctive character of the idea represented by the succeeding block of digits (Ranganathan, 1967b, pp. 236–237). For example: 338.11(410) "195" is a notation with five facets that are represented by bold text:

> **33** is the basic facet number for (Economics);
> **338** is the facet for (Industry).
> 338.**11** represents (Productivity)
> 338.11**(410)** represents (United Kingdom)
> 338.11(410) **"195"** represents (1950s)

**Focus:** A generic term used to denote any isolate or any subject and also the number of any of them as well as the name denoting any of them (Ranganathan, 1967b, p. 88). A particular manifestation of the basic class or of the fundamental categories concerned (Ranganathan, 1965, p. 82). *See also facet.* For example, notice the progression of increased focus through notational change in the following subjects:

> [*J38*] agriculture of *cereal*
> [*J381*] agriculture of *rice*
> [*J38*.**44**] agriculture of *cereal* **in India**
> [*J381*.**44**] agriculture of *rice* **in India** (Ranganathan, 1967b, p. 89).

**Fundamental categories:** There are only five fundamental categories according to Ranganathan: Time, Space, Energy, Matter, and Personality (Ranganathan, 1967b, p. 401). Fundamental categories are useful as a provisional guide in approaching the analysis of a new field … provid[ing] an outline framework … and giv[ing] guidance in suggesting possible characteristics that should not be overlooked (Vickery, 1960, pp. 23, 27).

**Group:** Any sub-aggregate of entities formed by the division of the entities in a universe (Ranganathan, 1967b, p. 56).

**Idea:** Product of thinking, reflecting, imagining. It is a process of the intellect and logic (Ranganathan, 1998, p. 81).

**Information:** That which is communicated by others (idea) or obtained by study or investigation (Ranganathan, 1998, p. 81).

**Isolate:** Any idea or idea-complex fit to form a component of a subject but not sufficiently independent to be deemed a subject. Example: Structure is a component of many different subjects such as: Physical Structure, Chemical Structure. Subjects that do not have isolate ideas as a component are considered basic *subject*s. Example: Mathematics (Ranganathan, 1967b, p. 83). Isolates are distinctly different objects that may be associated; some are merely distinguishable, although separable by various means such as quality, consistency, operations.

**Knowledge:** The totality of ideas conserved by humans. Knowledge = *Universe of Ideas* (Ranganathan, 1998, p. 81).

**Knowledge Organization System (KOS):** Knowledge organization systems include classification and categorization schemes, subject headings, authority files that control variant versions of key information such as geographic names and personal names; KOSs also include highly structured vocabularies, such as thesauri, and less traditional schemes, such as semantic networks and ontologies (Hodge, 2000).

**Logical division:** (1) Only one characteristic of division should be applied at a time [conceptual analysis]. (2) Division should not make a leap; steps should be proximate. (3) Division should be exhaustive (Mills, 2004, p. 550).

**Mutually exclusive:** In the practice of mathematics, two events are mutually exclusive if it is not possible for both of them to occur at the same time. In the case of *division of a universe*, it is the characteristics that must be mutually exclusive in that "no two headings shall overlap" (Sayers, 1915, p. 42).

**Notation:** "In definition, the notation is a series of symbols or shorthand signs … composed of characters which can be easily understood, are brief, are expansive and adjustable and which in their arrangement show the arrangement of the classification" (Sayers, 1915, p. 51). *See also faceted notation*.

**Parameter:** In mathematics this is an arbitrary constant, each particular value of which characterizes some particular member of a system of functions, curves, or surfaces. In the classification of a universe of isolate ideas, each of the successive characteristics used in arriving at an isolate idea is, therefore, sometimes referred to as the *parameter* of its classification (Ranganathan, 1967b, p. 377).

**Semantic factoring:** Conceptual decomposition of compound concepts according to their meaning. It renders explicit all essential aspects of a concept (Soergel, 1985). "A scheme of facets is very helpful for semantic factoring and for organizing elemental concepts into a coherent structure" (Soergel, 1985, p. 285).

**Subject:** The organization or systematized body of ideas whose extension and intension are likely to fall coherently within a field of interest and comfortably within the intellectual competence and field of inevitable specialization of a normal person (Ranganathan, 1998, p. 82).

**System:** The term system refers to methods for carrying out any part of the complete information cycle directly concerned with the organization of materials for the effective retrieval of the information contained in those materials. (Ranganathan, 1998, pp. 5–7).

**Universe of entities:** A collection of entities, without any special arrangement, that is under consideration in a given context (Ranganathan, 1998, p. 54).

**Universe of ideas:** Consists of the universe of subjects and the universe of isolates. These are composed of the (1) universe of basic subjects, (2) the universe of compound subjects, and (3) the universe of complex subjects (Ranganathan, 1998, p. 54).

# Appendix II: Canonical Literature

## *Full-Length Treatises*

Foskett, D. J. (1970). *Classification for a general index language: A review of recent research by the Classification Research Group.* London: Library Association.

Mills, J., & Broughton, V. (Eds.). (1977). *Bliss bibliographic classification.* London: Butterworth.

Palmer, B., & Wells, A. (1951). *The fundamentals of library classification.* London: Allen & Unwin.

Ranganathan, S. R. (1962). *Elements of library classification.* Bombay: Asia Publishing House.

Ranganathan, S. R. (1965). *The Colon Classification* (Rutgers series on systems for the intellectual organization of information, Vol. 4). New Brunswick, NJ: Graduate School of Library Science, Rutgers University.

Ranganathan, S. R. (1967b). *Prolegomena to library classification.* (3rd ed.). New York: Asia Publishing House.

Vickery, B. C. (1960). *Faceted classification: A guide to the construction and use of special schemes.* London: Aslib.

Vickery, B. C. (1966). *Faceted classification schemes.* New Brunswick, NJ: Graduate School Library Science, Rutgers, The State University.

## *Article-Length Treatments*

Atherton, P. (1965). Ranganathan's classification ideas: An analytico-synthetic discussion. *Library Resources and Technical Services, 9*(4), 462–473.

Broughton, V. (2006). The need for faceted classification as the basis of all methods of information retrieval. *Aslib Proceedings, 58*(2), 49–72.

Classification Research Group. (1955). The need for a faceted classification as the basis for all methods of information retrieval. *Library Association Record, 57*(7), 262–268. Also available in L. M. Chan, P. Richmond, & E. Svenonius (Eds.). (1985). *Theory of subject analysis: A sourcebook.* Littleton, CO: Libraries Unlimited.

Mills, J. (2004). Faceted classification and logical division in information retrieval. *Library Trends, 52*(3), 541–570.

Spiteri, L. (1998). A simplified model for facet analysis. *Canadian Journal of Information and Library Science, 23,* 1–30.

# References

Adkisson, H. (2003). *Use of faceted classification: Web design practices.* Retrieved February 2, 2004, from www.webdesignpractices.com/navigation/facets.html

Aitchison, J. (1970). The *Thesaurofacet*: a multipurpose retrieval language tool. *Journal of Documentation, 26*(3), 187–203.

Aitchison, J. (1975). *Unesco thesaurus.* Paris: UNESCO.

Aitchison, J. (1981). Integration of thesauri in the social sciences. *International Classification, 8*(2), 75–85.

Aitchison, J. (1986). Classification of H.E. Bliss as a source of thesaurus terms and structure. *Journal of Documentation, 42*(3), 160–181.

Aitchison, J., & Clarke, S. D. (2004). The thesaurus: A historical viewpoint, with a look to the future. *Cataloging & Classification Quarterly, 37*(3/4), 5–21.

Aitchison, J., & Cleverdon, C. (1962). *A report on the testing and analysis of an investigation into the comparative efficiency of indexing systems.* Cranfield, UK: College of Aeronautics.

Aitchison, J., & Cleverdon, C. (1963). *A report on a test of the index of metallurgical literature of Western Reserve University.* Cranfield, UK: College of Aeronautics.

Aitchison, J., Gilchrist, A., & Bawden, E. (2002). *Thesaurus construction and use: A practical manual.* London: Fitzroy Dearborn.

Aitchison, J., Gomersall, A., & Ireland, R. (1969). *Thesaurofacet: A thesaurus and faceted classification for engineering and related subjects.* Whetstone, UK: English Electric Company.

Anderson, J. D. (1979). Contextual indexing and faceted classification for databases in the humanities. *Proceedings of the 42nd Annual Meeting of the American Society for Information Science,* 194–201.

Anderson, J. D. (1980). Prototype designs for subject access to the Modern Language Association's bibliographic database. In J. Raben & G. Marks (Eds.), *Data bases in the humanities and social sciences: Proceedings of the IFIP Working Conference* (pp. 291–295). Amsterdam: North-Holland.

Anderson, J. D. (1990). Ad hoc, user-determined classified displays based on faceted indexing. In S. M. Humphrey & B. H. Kwasnik (Eds.), *Advances in classification research* (pp. 1–7). Medford, NJ: Learned Information, for the American Society for Information Science.

Antelman, K., Pace, A., & Lynema, E. (2006). Toward a 21st century library catalog. *Information Technology & Libraries, 25*(3), 128–139.

*Art and architecture thesaurus.* (2002). Los Angeles: Getty Research Institute. Retrieved March 6, 2006, from www.getty.edu/research/conducting_research/vocabularies/aat

Aspray, W. (1999). Command and control, documentation, and library science: The origins of information science at the University of Pittsburgh. *Annals of the History of Computing, 21*(4), 4–20.

Association of Special Libraries and Information Bureaux. (1957). *Proceedings of the International Study Conference on Classification for Information Retrieval.* London: The Association.

Atherton, P. (1961). *A project for the development of a reference retrieval system for physicists* (AIP/DRP 62-1). New York: American Institute of Physics.

Atherton, P. (1962). Indexing requirements of physicists: The literature of nuclear science: Its management and use. In: *Proceedings of the Conference held at the Division of Technical Information Extension* (TID-7674). Oak Ridge, TN: Atomic Energy Commission, Division of Technical Information Extension.

Atherton, P. (1963). *Aid-to-indexing forms: A progress report* (AIP/DRP 63-2). New York: American Institute of Physics.

Atherton, P. (1965a). *American Institute of Physics Documentation Research Project: A review of work completed and in progress, 1961–1965*. New York: American Institute of Physics.

Atherton, P. (1965b). *Classification research: Proceedings of the Second International Study Conference.* Copenhagen, Denmark: Munksgaard.

Atherton, P. (1965c). Ranganathan's classification ideas: An analytico-synthetic discussion. *Library Resources & Technical Services, 9*(4), 462–473.

Atherton, P., & Borko, H. (1965). *A test of the factor-analytically derived automated classification method applied to descriptions of work and search requests of nuclear physicists* (Report no. AIP/DRP 65-1; SDC/SP 1905). New York: American Institute of Physics.

Atherton, P., & Keenan, S. (1965). *Review of AIP/Documentation Research Project Studies.* (Report No. AIPDRP-65-2). New York: American Institute of Physics. Retrieved March 6, 2006, from www.lib sci.sc.edu/bob/ISP/cochrane2.htm

Austin, D. (1974). The development of PRECIS: A theoretical and technical history. *Journal of Documentation, 30*(1), 47–102.

Austin, D. (1984). *PRECIS: A manual of concept analysis and subject indexing.* London: The British Library Bibliographic Services Division.

Batty, C. D. (1981). *Life begins at forty: The resurgence of facet analysis.* Silver Spring, MD: Alpha Omega Group.

Beghtol, C. (1995). Facets as interdisciplinary undiscovered public knowledge: S. R. Ranganathan in India and L. Guttman in Israel. *Journal of Documentation, 51*(3), 194–234.

Beghtol, C. (2006). The facet concept as a universal principle of subdivision. In K. S. Raghavan & K. N. Prasad (Eds.), *Knowledge organization, information systems and other essays: Professor A. Neelameghan Festschrift* (pp. 41–52). New Delhi, India: Ess Ess Publications.

Beghtol, C. (2008). From the universe of knowledge to the universe of concepts: The structural revolution in classification for information retrieval. *Axiomathes, 18*(2), 131–144.

Bergling, B. M. (1999). Extending facet design to such complex psychological structures as Piaget's theory. *Quality and Quantity, 12*(3), 22–46.

Bhattacharyya, G. (1967). Library cataloguing: Depth classification. In *Annual Seminar 5* (pp. 92–106). Bangalore, India: Documentation Research and Training Centre.

Bhattacharyya, G. (1969). Vital role of depth classification in a system for documents-finding: A trend report. *Library Science with a Slant to Documentation, 6*, 23–52.

Bhattacharyya, G. (1979). POPSI: Its fundamentals and procedure based on a general theory of subject indexing languages. *Library Science with a Slant to Documentation, 16*(1), 1–34.

Binding, C., & Tudhope, D. (2004). KOS at your service: Programmatic access to knowledge organization systems. *Journal of Digital Information, 4*(4), 265. Retrieved January 1, 2009, from jodi.tamu.edu/Articles/v04/i04/Binding/#TUDHOPE2003

Binns, J. (undated, unpublished manuscript). *A faceted classification scheme: Construction and operation.* Held as part of the Cochrane papers at Syracuse University archives. Notation indicates "Classification Research Study Group holdings."

Binns, J. (1961). *Operating experience with a facet system in the English Electric Company.* Unpublished manuscript held as part of the Cochrane papers at Syracuse University Archives.

Binns, J., & Bagley, D. (1958). *A faceted classification for engineering* (2nd ed.). Whetstone, UK: English Electric Company.

Binns, J., & Bagley, D. (1961). *A faceted classification for engineering* (3rd ed.). Whetstone, UK: English Electric Company.

Bliss, H. E. (1929). *The organization of knowledge and the system of the sciences.* New York: Henry Holt.

Bliss, H. E. (1931). Scientific is not philosophic classification. *Library Association Record*, *9*(5), 174–175.

Bourne, C., & Hahn, T. B. (2003). *A history of online information services, 1963–1976*. Cambridge, MA: MIT Press.

Brenner, E. (1966). Faceted organization of a thesaurus vocabulary. *Proceedings of the Annual Meeting of the American Documentation Institute*, *3*, 175–183.

British Standards Institution. (2005). *Structured vocabularies for information retrieval: Guide: Thesauri* (BS 8723-2:2005). London: The Institution.

British Standards Institution. (2008). *Structured vocabularies for information retrieval: Guide: Formats and protocols for data exchange* (BS-DD 8723-5:2008 ). London: The Institution.

Broughton, V. (2001). Faceted classification as a basis for knowledge organisation in a digital environment: The Bliss Bibliographic Classification as a model for vocabulary management and the creation of multidimensional knowledge structures. *New Review of Hypermedia and Multimedia*, *7*, 67–102.

Broughton, V. (2002). Faceted classification as a basis for knowledge organization in a digital environment: The Bliss Bibliographic Classification as a model for vocabulary management and the creation of multidimensional knowledge structures. In M. J. López-Huertas, & F. J. Muñoz-Fernández (Eds.), *Advances in knowledge organization* (pp. 135–142). Würzburg, Germany: Ergon Verlag.

Broughton, V. (2003). Facet analytical theory. *Facet analytical theory in managing knowledge structure for humanities*. Retrieved February 2, 2004, from www.ucl.ac.uk/fatks/fat.htm

Broughton, V. (2004a). *Essential classification*. New York: Neal Schuman.

Broughton, V. (2004b). Faceted classification: A tool for subject access in the twenty first century. *Signum*, *8*, 5–18.

Broughton, V. (2006). The need for faceted classification as the basis of all methods of information retrieval. *Aslib Proceedings*, *58*(2), 49–72.

Broughton, V. (2008). A faceted classification as the basis of a faceted terminology: Conversion of a classified structure to thesaurus format in the Bliss Bibliographic Classification, 2nd edition. *Axiomathes*, *18*(2), 193–210.

Broughton, V., & Lane, H. (2000). Classification schemes revisited: Applications to Web indexing and searching. *Journal of Internet Cataloguing*, *2*(3/4), 143–155.

Broughton, V., & Slavic, A. (2004). *Facet analytical theory in managing knowledge structures for the humanities*. Retrieved May 1, 2004, from www.ucl.ac.uk/fatks/fat.htm

Campbell, D. J. (1957). Glossary to Dr. Ranganathan's paper. *Proceedings of the International Study Conference on Classification for Information Retrieval* (pp. 13–14). London: Aslib.

Chakraborty, A. (1967). Furnace production engineering. Depth classification. In *Annual Seminar 5* (pp. 107–122). Bangalore, India: Documentation Research and Training Centre.

Cheti, A., & Paradisi, F. (2008). Facet analysis in the development of a general controlled vocabulary. *Axiomathes*, *18*(2), 223–241.

Clarke, S. G. D. (2007). Evolution towards ISO 25964: An international standard with guidelines for thesauri and other types of controlled vocabulary. *Information Wissenschaft & Praxis*, *58*(8), 441–444.

Clarke, S. G. D. (2008). ISO 2788 + ISO 5964 + Much Energy = ISO 25964. *Bulletin of the American Society for Information Science and Technology*, *35*(1), 31–34. Retrieved January 1, 2009, from www.asis.org/Bulletin/Oct-08/Bulletin_OctNov08_Final.pdf

Classification Research Group. (1955). The need for a faceted classification as the basis for all methods of information retrieval. *Library Association Record*, *57*(7), 262–268.

Cleverdon, C. (1960a). *Interim report on the test programme into the comparative efficiency of indexing systems*. Cranfield, UK: The College of Aeronautics.

Cleverdon, C. (1960b). *Report on the first stages of an investigation into the comparative efficiency of indexing systems.* Cranfield, UK: The College of Aeronautics.

Cleverdon, C. (1962). *Report on the testing and analysis of an investigation into the comparative efficiency of indexing systems.* Cranfield, UK: Aslib/Cranfield Research Project.

Cleverdon, C., & Mills, J. (1963). The testing of index language devices. *Aslib Proceedings, 15*(4), 106–130.

Coates, E. (1963). Aims and methods of the British Technology Index. *The Indexer, 5*(1), 27–34.

Coates, E. (1978). Classification in information retrieval: The twenty years following Dorking. *Journal of Documentation, 34*(4), 288–298.

Coates, E., Lloyd, G., & Simandl, D. (1979). *The BSO manual: The development, rationale and use of the Broad System of Ordering.* The Hague, Netherlands: FID. Retrieved January 1, 2009, from www.ucl.ac.uk/fatks/bso/index.htm

Cochrane interview by Kathryn La Barre. (2001). Transcripts and tapes. Pauline Atherton Cochrane papers, Box 23587, Syracuse University, New York.

Cohen, E. (2005). *Facet theory bibliography.* Rome: Facet Theory Association. Retrieved January 1, 2009, from www.facet-theory.org/files/Facet%20Theory%20Bibliography_edited%20by%20Erik%20Cohen.pdf

Crowston, K., & Kwasnik, B. (2004). A framework for creating a faceted classification for genres: Addressing issues of multidimensionality. *Proceedings of the Hawai'i International Conference on System Sciences,* 1–7. Retrieved February 20, 2004, from csdl.computer.org/comp/proceeding s/hicss/2004/2056/04/205640100aabs.htm

Dahlberg, I. (1978). *Ontical structures and universal classification.* Bangalore, India: Sarada Ranganathan Endowment for Library Science.

Dahlberg, I. (2008). The Information Coding Classification (ICC): A modern, theory-based fully-faceted, universal system of knowledge fields. *Axiomathes, 18*(2), 161–176.

Dancer, S. (2008). Introduction to facet theory and its applications. *Applied Psychology, 39*(4), 365–377.

Denton, W. (2003). *Putting facets on the Web: Annotated bibliography.* Retrieved June 1, 2004, from www.miskatonic.org/library/facet-biblio.html

Devadason, F. J. (1985). Online construction of alphabetic classaurus: A vocabulary control and indexing tool. *Information Processing & Management, 21*(1), 11–26. Retrieved January 1, 2009, from www.geocities.com/devadason.geo/OnlineClassaurus.htm

Devadason, F. J., & Balasubramanian, V. (1981). Computer generation of thesaurus from structured subject-propositions. *Information Processing & Management, 17*(1), 1–11.

Doyle, L. B. (1975). *Information retrieval and processing.* Los Angeles: Melville.

Drabenstott, K. M. (2000). Web search strategies. In William J. Wheeler (Ed.), *Saving the user's time through subject access innovation* (pp. 56–72). Champaign: Graduate School of Library and Information Science, University of Illinois.

Duncan, E. (1989). A faceted approach to hypertext? In R. McAleese (Ed.), *Hypertext: Theory into practice* (pp. 157–163). Oxford, UK: Intellect Press.

Ellis, D., & Vasconcelos, A. (1999). Ranganathan and the Net: Using facet analysis to search and organize the World Wide Web. *Aslib Proceedings, 51*(1), 3–10.

Feibleman, J. (1965). The integrative levels in nature. In B. Kyle (Ed.), *Focus on information and communication* (pp. 27–41). London: Aslib.

Fillmore, C. J. (1968). The case for case. In E. Bach & R. T. Harms (Eds.), *Universals in linguistic theory* (pp. 1–88). New York: Holt, Rinehart & Winston.

Foskett, D. J. (1957). Appendix I: Occupational safety and health documents classification scheme. In *Proceedings of the International Study Conference on Classification for Information Retrieval* (pp. 115–136). London: Aslib.

Foskett, D. J. (1962). The Classification Research Group, 1952–1962. *Libri, 12*(2), 127–138.

Foskett, D. J. (1963). *Classification and indexing in the social sciences.* London: Butterworth.

Foskett, D. J. (1969). The Classification Research Group, 1952–1968. In A. Kent & J. O. Williams (Eds.), *Encyclopedia of library and information science* (vol. 5, pp. 141–145). New York: Marcel-Dekker.

Foskett, D. J. (1974). *The London education classification: A thesaurus/classification of British educational terms.* London: University of London Institute of Education Library.

Foskett, D. J. (1992). Ranganathan and "user-friendliness." *Libri, 42*(3), 227–234.

Foskett, D. J. (2004). *From librarianship to information science: Pioneers of information science.* Retrieved February 2, 2004, from www.libsci.sc.edu/bob/ISP/foskett2.htm

Foskett, D. J., & Palmer, B. (Eds.). (1961). *The Sayers memorial volume.* London: Library Association.

Fox, S., Manduca, C., & Iverson, E. (2005). Building educational portals atop digital libraries. *D-Lib Magazine, 11*(1). Retrieved April 1, 2008, from www.dlib.org/dlib/january05/fox/01fox.html

Frakes, W., Prieto-Díaz, R., & Fox C. (1998). DARE: Domain analysis and reuse environment. *Annals of Software Engineering, 5*, 125–141.

Freeman, R. (1965). *Research project for the evaluation of the UDC as the indexing language for a mechanized information retrieval system: Progress report.* (AIP/DRP UDC-2). New York: American Institute of Physics.

Freeman, R. (1966a). *Modern approaches to the management of a classification.* AIP/UDC-3. New York: American Institute of Physics.

Freeman, R. (1966b). *Research project for the evaluation of the UDC as the indexing language for a mechanized reference retrieval system: Progress report for the period July 1, 1965– January 31, 1966* (AIP/DRP UDC-2). New York: American Institute of Physics.

Freeman, R. R., & Atherton, P. (1967). *File organization and search strategy using the Universal Decimal Classification in mechanized reference retrieval systems* (AIP/UDC-5). New York: American Institute of Physics, UDC Project.

Freeman, R. R., & Atherton, P. (1968a). *Audacious: An experiment with online, interactive reference retrieval system using the Universal Decimal Classification as the index language in the field of nuclear science* (AIP.UDC-7). New York: American Institute of Physics, UDC Project.

Freeman, R. R., & Atherton, P. (1968b). *Final report of the research project for the evaluation of the UDC as the indexing language for a mechanized reference retrieval system.* Springfield, VA: American Institute of Physics.

Freeman, R. R., & Atherton, P. (1969). Report on use of the UDC in a mechanized information retrieval system. In R. Mölgaard-Hansen & M. Rigby (Eds.), *Proceedings of a First Seminar on UDC in a Mechanized Retrieval System* (pp. 22–41). Copenhagen, Denmark: Danish Center for Documentation.

Ganter, B., & Wille, R. (1999). *Formal concept analysis: Mathematical foundations.* Berlin, Germany: Springer.

Garfield, E. (1955). Citation indexes for science. *Science, 122*(3159), 108–111.

Gnoli, C. (2008). Categories and facets in integrative levels. *Axiomathes, 18*(2), 177–192.

Gnoli, C., & Poli, R. (2004). Levels of reality and levels of representation. *Knowledge Organization, 31*(3), 151–160.

Gopinath, M. (1986). *Construction of depth version of Colon Classification: A manual.* New Delhi, India: Wiley Eastern.

Gull, D. (1956). Seven years of work on the organization of materials in the special library. *American Documentation, 12,* 320–329.

Guttman, L. (1954). A new approach to factor analysis: The Radex. In P. F. Lazarsfield (Ed.), *Mathematical thinking in the social sciences* (pp. 258–348). Glencoe, IL: The Free Press.

Harris, B. (1976). Faceting. *TA Informations, 17*(2), 44–50.

Harris, K. (1986). *Dickens House classification.* London: Polytechnic of North London.

Hearst, M. (1999). User interfaces and visualization. In R. Baeza-Yates & B. Ribeiro-Neto (Eds.), *Modern information retrieval* (pp. 257–323). New York: ACM Press.

Hearst, M. (2006). Clustering versus faceted categories for information exploration. *Communications of the ACM, 49*(4), 59–61.

Hearst, M., Smalley, P., & Chandler, C. (2006). *Faceted metadata for information architecture and search.* CHI 2006 course. Retrieved January 1, 2006, from bailando.sims.berkeley.edu/talks/chi_course06.pdf

Hjørland, B. (2008). What is knowledge organization? *Knowledge Organization, 35*(2), 86–101.

Hodge, G. (2000). *Systems of knowledge organization for digital libraries: Beyond traditional authority files.* Washington, DC: Council on Library and Information Resources. Retrieved January 1, 2009, from www.clir.org/pubs/reports/pub91/contents.html

Ingwersen, P., & Wormell, I. (1992). Ranganathan in the perspective of advanced information retrieval. *Libri, 42*(3), 184–201.

International Federation for Documentation. (1981). *Principles of the Universal Decimal Classification* (FID Publ. 598).The Hague, The Netherlands: The Federation.

International Institute of Bibliography. (1905–1907). *Manuel du repertoire bibliographique universel.* Brussels, Belgium: The Institute.

Iyer, H. (1995). *Classificatory structures: Concepts, relations and representation* (Text books for knowledge organization, 2). Frankfurt, Germany: Indeks Verlag.

Kent, A. (1960). Machine literature searching and translation: An analytical review. *Advances in Documentation and Library Sciences, 3,* 13–36.

Kumedan, B., & Parkhi, R. (1967). Schedule of commodities in food technology. In *Annual Seminar 5* (pp. 153–171). Bangalore, India: Documentation Research and Training Centre.

Kwasnik, B. (1999). The role of classification in knowledge representation and discovery. *Library Trends, 48*(1), 22–47.

La Barre, K. (2006). The use of faceted analytico-synthetic theory as revealed in the practice of website construction and design. Unpublished doctoral dissertation, Indiana University, Bloomington.

La Barre, K., Cochrane, P. (2006). Facet analysis as a knowledge management tool on the Internet. In K. S. Raghavan & S. K. Prasad (Eds.), *Knowledge organization, information systems, and other essays: Professor A. Neelameghan Festschrift* (pp. 53–70). New Delhi, India: Ess Ess Publications.

Lancaster, F. W. (1992). *Indexing and abstracting in theory and practice.* Champaign: University of Illinois, Graduate School of Library and Information Science.

Lancaster, F. W., & Fayen, E. G. (1973). *Information retrieval on-line.* New York: Wiley.

Langridge, D. W. (1976). *Classification and indexing in the humanities.* London: Butterworth.

Library of Congress Working Group. (2007). *Report on the future of bibliographic control.* Retrieved December 5, 2007, from www.loc.gov/bibliographic-future/news/lcwg-report-draft-11-30-07-final.pdf

Mann, T. (2006). *The changing nature of the catalog and its integration with other discovery tools: A critical review of the final report prepared for the Library of Congress by Karen Calhoun.* Retrieved January 1, 2009, from www.guild2910.org/AFSCMECalhounReviewREV.pdf

McIlwaine, I. (1997). The Universal Decimal Classification: Some factors concerning its origins, development, and influence. *Journal of the American Society for Information Science, 48*(4), 331–339.

McIlwaine, I. (2003). Indexing and the Classification Research Group. *Indexer, 23*(4), 204–208.

McIlwaine, I., & Williamson, N. (1995). Restructuring of Class 61—medical sciences. *Extensions and corrections to the UDC* (pp. 11–66). The Hague, The Netherlands: UDC Consortium.

Melton, J. L. (1958). The semantic code. In A. Kent & J. Perry (Eds.), *Centralized information services, opportunities and problems* (pp. 221–279). New York: Interscience Publishers.

Melton, J. S. (1960). *Note on the compatibility of two information systems: Colon classification and Western Reserve University encoded telegraphic abstracts and the feasibility of interchanging their notations.* (Technical Note 13 AFOSR). Cleveland, OH: The Center for Documentation and Communications Research, Western Reserve University.

Metcalfe, J. W. (1959). *Subject classifying and indexing of libraries and literature.* New York: Scarecrow Press.

Merholz, P. (2001). *Innovation in classification.* peterme.com. Retrieved June 1, 2004, from www.peterme.com/archives/00000063.html

Miksa, F. (1998). *The DDC, the universe of knowledge, and the post-modern library.* Albany, NY: Forest Press.

Mili, H., Ah-Ki, E., Godin, R., & Mcheick, H. (1997). *Another nail to the coffin of faceted controlled-vocabulary component classification and retrieval.* In *Proceedings of the Symposium on Software Reuse* (pp. 89–98). New York: ACM Press.

Mills, J. (1960). *A modern outline of library classification.* London: Chapman & Hall.

Mills, J. (1964). *The Universal Decimal Classification* (Rutgers series on systems for the intellectual organization of information, Vol 1). New Brunswick, NJ: Graduate School of Library Science, Rutgers, The State University.

Mills, J. (2004). Faceted classification and logical division in information retrieval. *Library Trends, 52*(3), 541–570.

Mills, J., & Broughton, V. (Eds.). (1977). *Bliss bibliographic classification* (2nd ed.). London: Butterworth.

Mitchell, V., & Hsieh-Yee, I. (2007). Converting Ulrich's subject headings to FAST headings: A feasibility study. *Cataloging and Classification Quarterly, 45*(1), 59–85.

Morville, P. (2001). *The speed of information architecture.* Ann Arbor, MI: Semantic Studios. Retrieved, June 1, 2004, from semanticstudios.com/publications/semantics/000003.php

Moss, R. (1964). Categories and relations: Origins of two classification theories. *American Documentation, 15*(4), 296–301.

National Information Standards Organization. (2005). *NISO Z39.19 Guidelines for the construction, format, and management of monolingual controlled vocabularies.* Retrieved May 6, 2006, from www.niso.org/kst/reports/standards?step=2&gid=&project_key=7cc9b583cb5a62e8c15d3099e0bb46bbae9cf38a

Neelameghan, A. (1992). Application of Ranganathan's general theory of knowledge classification in designing specialized databases. *Libri, 42*(3), 202–226.

Neelameghan, A., & Gopinath, M. A. (1975). Postulate-based permuted subject indexing (POPSI). *Library Science with a Slant to Documentation, 12*(3), 79–87.

North Carolina State University. (2006). OPAC implementation of Endeca's Profind. NCSU / Endeca Profind implementation: Retrieved March 5, 2006, from www2.lib.ncsu.edu/catalog/?view=full&Ntt=ranganathan&Ntk=Keyword&N=206305&Nty=1

Osinga, M. (1977). Automatic encoding of chemical reactions. In W. E. Batten (Ed.), *Eurim II: A European conference on the application of research in information services and libraries* (pp. 122–125). London: Aslib.

Palmer, B. I. (1971). *Itself an education: Six lectures on classification.* London: Library Association. (Original work published in 1962)

Parthasarathy, S. (1952). Memoirs of the Library Research Circle. *Abgila, 2,* 153–159.

Petersen, T. (1994). *Art & architecture thesaurus.* New York: Oxford University Press.

Pilgrim, M. (2002). *This is XFML.* Retrieved. February 1, 2005 from diveintomark.org/archives/2002/12/03/this_is_xfml

Poli, A., & Gnoli, C. (Eds.). (2008). Facet analysis [Special issue]. *Axiomathes, 18*(2).

Pollitt, S. (1998). The essential role of dynamic faceted classification in improving access to online information, *Proceedings of the 22nd International Online Information Meeting,* 17–21.

Pollitt, S., Ellis, G., & Smith, M. (1994). HIBROWSE for bibliographic databases. *Journal of Information Science, 20*(6), 413–426.

Pollitt, S., Smith, M., Braekevelt, J., & Treglown, M. (1996, May). HIGHBROWSE for EMBASE: The application of view-based searching techniques to Europe's most important biomedical database. Paper presented at INFO 96: 11th Annual Information Meeting, Tel Aviv, Israel.

Pomerantz, J. (2003). *Question taxonomies for digital reference.* Unpublished doctoral dissertation, Syracuse University, New York.

Prieto-Díaz, R. (1989). Classification of reusable modules. *Software reusability: Concepts and models* (Vol. 1, pp. 99–123). New York: ACM Press.

Prieto-Díaz, R. (1990). Implementing faceted classification for software reuse (experience report). *Proceedings of the 12th International Conference on Software Engineering,* 88–99.

Prieto-Díaz, R., & Freeman, P. (1987). Classifying software for reusability. *IEEE Software, 4*(1), 6–16.

Priss, U. (2006). Formal concept analysis in information science. *Annual Review of Information Science and Technology, 40,* 521–543.

Priss, U. (2008). Facet-like structures in computer science. *Axiomathes, 18*(2), 243–255.

Priss, U., & Jacob, E. (1999). Utilizing faceted structures for information systems design. *Proceedings of the 62nd Annual Meeting of the American Society for Information Science,* 203–212.

Qiang, J. (2008). Is FAST the right direction for a new system of subject cataloging and metadata? *Cataloging and Classification Quarterly, 45*(3), 91–110.

Rajanand, T. N., & Guha, B. (1975). A comparative study of subject heading structuring according to POPSI and PRECIS. *Proceedings of the 3rd International Study Conference on Classification Research,* pp. 369–382.

Ranganathan, S. R. (1933). *Colon Classification.* Madras, India: Madras Library Association.

Ranganathan, S. R. (1937). *Prolegomena to library classification.* New York: Asia Publishing House.

Ranganathan, S. R. (1951). *Classification and communication.* Delhi, India: University of Delhi.

Ranganathan, S. R. (1952a). *Colon Classification* (4th ed.). Madras, India: Madras Library Association.

Ranganathan, S. R. (1952b). Personal correspondence to Jesse Shera, and Margaret Egan, January 26, 1952. Papers of Jesse Hauk Shera. Case Western Reserve University Archives. 27DD5 10:3.

Ranganathan, S. R. (1953). *Depth classification: Reference services and reference materials.* Madras, India: Indian Library Association.

Ranganathan, S. R. (1957a). *Colon Classification* (5th ed.). Madras, India: Madras Library Association.

Ranganathan, S. R. (1957b). *Prolegomena to library classification* (2nd ed.). New York: Asia Publishing House.

Ranganathan, S. R. (1963). Classification research, no longer a toddler. *Annals of Library Science*, *10*(3–4), 82–96.

Ranganathan, S. R. (1965). *The Colon Classification* (Rutgers series on systems for the intellectual organization of information, Vol. 4). New Brunswick, NJ: Graduate School of Library Science, Rutgers University.

Ranganathan, S. R. (1967a). Hidden roots of classification. *Information Storage & Retrieval*, *3*(4), 399–410.

Ranganathan, S. R. (1967b). *Prolegomena to library classification* (3rd ed.). New York: Asia Publishing House.

Ranganathan, S. R. (1998). *A descriptive account of the Colon Classification*. Bangalore, India: Sarada Ranganathan Endowment for Library Science. (Original work published in 1967)

Rayborn, T. (2004). *Field notes from the IA Summit: Drinking game (2 shots for screenshots of Epicurious or Wine.com)*. Retrieved June 1, 2004, from www.pixelcharmer.com/fieldnotes/archives/process_living/2004/000386.html#000386

Richmond, P. (1963a). Classification Research Study Group in the United States and Canada: 1959–1962. *Libri*, *13*(1), 55–60.

Richmond, P. (1963b). Review of the Cranfield project. *American Documentation*, *14*, 307–311.

Richmond, P. (1981). *Introduction to PRECIS for North American usage*. Littleton, CO: Libraries Unlimited.

Richmond, P. (1988). Precedent-setting contributions to modern classification. *Journal of Documentation*, *44*(3), 242–249.

Riesthuis, G. (2003). A revised format for the master reference file. *Extensions and Corrections to the UDC*, *23*, 11–18.

Riesthuis, G. J. A. (1997). Decomposition of complex UDC notation. *Knowledge Organization for Information Retrieval: Proceedings of the Sixth International Study Conference on Classification Research*, 139–143.

Rosenfeld, L., & Morville, P. (2002). *Information architecture for the World Wide Web* (2nd ed.). Cambridge, MA: O'Reilly.

Ross, K., Janevski, A., & Stovanovich, J. (2005). A faceted query engine applied to archaeology. *Proceedings of the 31st International Conference on Very Large Databases*, 1334–1337.

Russell, B. (1946). *History of Western philosophy*. New York: Allen & Unwin.

Sangameswaran, S. (1967). Social work: Depth classification. In *Annual Seminar 5* (pp. 242–268). Bangalore, India: Documentation Research and Training Centre.

Satija, M. P. (1989). *Colon classification: A practical introduction* (7th ed.). New Delhi, India: Ess Ess Publications.

Sayers, W. C. B. (1915). *Canons of classification: Applied to "The Subject," "The Expansive," "The Decimal" and "The Library of Congress" classifications: A study in bibliographical classification method*. London: Grafton.

Shye, S. (1995). *Facet theory: Form and content*. Newbury Park, CA: Sage.

Slavic, A. (2008). Faceted classification: Management and use. *Axiomathes*, *18*(2), 257–271.

Slavic, A., Cordeiro, M. I., & Riesthuis, G. (2008). Maintenance of the Universal Decimal Classification: Overview of the past and preparations for the future. *International Cataloguing and Bibliographic Control*, *37*(2), 23–29.

Soergel, D. (1985). *Organizing information: Principles of database and retrieval systems.* New York: Academic Press.

Spärck Jones, K. (2007). Semantic primitives: The tip of the iceberg. In K. Ahmad, C. Brewster, & M. Stevenson (Eds.), *Words and intelligence: Part II: Essays in honour of Yorick Wilks* (pp. 235–253). Dordrecht, The Netherlands: Springer-Verlag.

Spiteri, L. (1995). The Classification Research Group and the theory of integrative levels. *Katharine Sharp Review, 1*(1), 1–6. Retrieved June 10, 2009, from mirrored.ukoln.ae.uk/lis-journals/review/review

Spiteri, L. (1998). A simplified model for facet analysis. *Canadian Journal of Information and Library Science, 23,* 1–30.

Streich, R. (1999). Documents are software: A focus on reuse. *Markup languages: Theory and practice, 1*(2), 77–93.

Taube, M. (1953–1959). *Studies in coordinate indexing* (Vols. 1–5). Washington, DC: Documentation Incorporated.

Taulbee, O., & House, R. W. (1965). Classification in information storage and retrieval. *Proceedings of the 1965, 20th National ACM Conference,* 119–137.

Thomas, A. (1977). The influence of S. R. Ranganathan on basic instruction in subject analysis at ALA-accredited library schools. *Indian Librarian, 32*(2), 51–53.

Tudhope, D. (2003). ECDL 2003 workshop report: Networked knowledge organization systems/services (NKOS): Evolving standards. *D-Lib Magazine, 9,* 9. Retrieved January 1, 2009, from dlib.ejournal.ascc.net/dlib/september03/09inbrief.html#TUDHOPE

Tudhope, D., & Binding, C. (2008). Faceted thesauri. *Axiomathes, 18*(2), 211–222.

Tudhope, D., & Koch, T. (2004). Editorial: New applications of knowledge organization systems: Introduction to a special issue. *Journal of Digital Information, 4*(4). Retrieved June 10, 2009, from journals.tdl.org/jodi/issue/view/20

Tuulos, V., Perkiö, J., & Tirri, H. (2005). Multi-faceted information retrieval system for large scale email archives. *Proceedings of the 28th Annual ACM SIGIR Conference on Research and Development in Information Retrieval,* 683.

Tyaganatarajan, T. (1961). A study in the developments of the Colon Classification. *American Documentation, 12*(4), 270–278.

Tzitzikas, Y., Analyti, A., Spyratos, N., & Constantopoulos, P. (2007). An algebra for specifying valid compound terms in faceted taxonomies. *Journal on Data and Knowledge Engineering, 62*(1), 1–40.

Van Dijck, P. (2002). *eXchangeable faceted metadata language.* Retrieved July 26, 2009, from peter vandijck.com/xfml

Vernon, K., & Lang, V. (1979/ 2001). *The London Classification of Business Studies: A classification and thesaurus for business libraries.* London: London Graduate School of Business Studies. Retrieved January 3, 2001, from www.london.edu/theschool/ourfacilities/library/londonclassificationofbusiness studies.html

Vickery, B. C. (1959a). *Classification and indexing in science.* London: Butterworths.

Vickery, B. C. (1959b). CRG Bulletin 5: Construction of a classification scheme for aeronautics Cranfield. *Journal of Documentation, 15,* 39–57.

Vickery, B. C. (1960). *Faceted classification: A guide to construction and use of special schemes.* London: Aslib.

Vickery, B. C. (1966). *Faceted classification schemes* (Rutgers Series on Systems for the Intellectual Organization of Information, Vol. 5). New Brunswick, NJ: Graduate School of Library Science at Rutgers University.

Vickery, B. C. (1990). Classificatory principles in intelligent interfaces. Tools for knowledge organization and the human interface. *Proceedings of the 1st International ISKO Conference*, 14–20.

Vickery, B. C. (2008). Facet analysis for the Web. *Axiomathes*, *18*(2), 145–160.

Wells, A. J. (1960). *British catalogue of music*. London: Council of the British National Bibliography. Retrieved January 1, 2009, from www.archive.org/stream/britishcatalogue001781mbp

Whitehead, C. (1989). Faceted classification in the Art and Architecture Thesaurus. *Art Documentation*, *8*(4), 175–177.

Williamson, N. (1994). Future revision of UDC: Second progress report on a feasibility study for restructuring. *Extensions and Corrections to the UDC*, *16*, 19–27.

Williamson, N., & McIlwaine, I. (1993). Future revision of UDC: Progress report on a feasibility study for restructuring. *Extensions and Corrections to the UDC*, *15*, 11–17.

Wilson, T. (2006, March). *Strict faceted classification*. Presentation at the ASIST IA Summit, Vancouver, BC. Retrieved April 5, 2006, from www.facetmap.com/pub/strict_faceted_classification.pdf

Wilson, T. (2009). *About Facetmap*. Retrieved July 26, 2009, from facetmap.com/contact.jsp

Wilson, T. D. (1972). The work of the British Classification Research Group. In H. Wellisch & T. D. Wilson (Eds.), *Subject retrieval in the seventies* (pp. 62–71).Westport, CT: Greenwood.

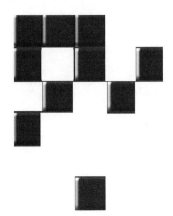

# Communication

# CHAPTER 7

# Communication in the Sciences

*Cecelia Brown*
*University of Oklahoma*

## Introduction

The digital infrastructure has the potential to alter traditional modes of scientific communication that revolve around publication in a peer-reviewed journal. The ability to access scientific instruments, research related data, and interact with colleagues virtually across space and time may also change how scientists communicate. However, studies of scientists' communication behaviors—including their citation practices, reading habits, downloading activities, dissemination of online information, and collaborative activities—indicate that, although the digital infrastructure facilitates new kinds of interaction, it has not altered the essential nature of scholarly communication.

Science is social enterprise in which innovation and advancement depend upon the ability of scientists to communicate their research findings to the wider community. The axial form of scientific communication is the peer-reviewed journal article. Journal articles advance scientific knowledge by translating complex theories and data into compact yet meaningful information packages. Review by peers prior to publication provides a measure of assurance that the work is ethical and scientifically valid. Although outwardly straightforward, a scientific publication is the result of an intricate web of formal and informal communication processes occurring in a variety of contexts and formats. Prior to publication scientists discuss their results with colleagues locally, nationally, and internationally during casual interactions and at professional conferences. Scientists may also disseminate their research via technical reports and preprints to receive feedback and to stake their claims before officially submitting their work to a journal. In short, scientists spend most of their time preparing and writing articles for publication (Hyland & Salager-Meyer, 2008; Latour, 1987).

In spite of the lynchpin nature of the peer-reviewed journal article, publication does not mark the end point of the scientific communication process. Once an article appears, indexing and abstracting services make it possible for other scientists to engage in the communication process as they read, discuss, and, ideally, cite the work. Garvey and Griffith (1972) describe this now traditional model of scientific communication in their classic work on the communication patterns of psychologists. A model incorporating electronic information dissemination was subsequently proposed by Lancaster (1978) and further modified by Hurd (1996, 2000). Hurd (2000) speculates that advances in digital information sharing capabilities will fundamentally transform the way scientists communicate by the year 2020, yet acknowledges that several behavioral, economic, and social pressures may prevent scientific communication from becoming fully electronic. Those pressures were at work over 60 years ago when Vannevar Bush, Director of the Office of Scientific Research and Development, was charged by President Roosevelt to make recommendations for continuing the high level of scientific research and development generated during World War II (Bush, 1945a, 1945c). Believing that the methods available for disseminating and accessing scientific information were inadequate, Bush advocated the development of technology to mechanize the storage of books, reports, and other records of scientific communication. Scientists did not embrace Bush's (1945b) forward thinking "Memex" system, in spite of its potential to facilitate scientific communication.

Scientific productivity continued to flourish over the next two decades, leading Derek Price (1963) to coin the term "Big Science" to describe the shift from the paradigm of the lone scientist toiling independently on "Little Science" projects to large, capital-intensive collaborative experiments. The advent of "Big Science" resulted in an increase in the number of multi-authored papers as well as an overall increase in the number of papers published, thereby further compounding scientists' difficulty in finding the information they needed to engage effectively in the exchange of ideas. At the end of the twentieth century, Bush's early vision was finally being realized with the creation of online repositories containing not only millions of peer-reviewed papers but also terabytes of data generated from research in genomics, proteomics, particle physics, astronomy, and meteorology, thus signaling the emergence of networked, data-driven science, or "e-Science" (Hey & Hey, 2006, p. 515). The rapid development and disparate nature of the many initiatives undertaken to handle large volumes of data led to the convening of a Blue Ribbon Panel in 2003 by the Assistant Director for Computer and Information Science and Engineering of the National Science Foundation (Atkins, Droegemeier, Stuart, Feldman, Garcia-Molina, Klein, et al., 2003). Not unlike Roosevelt's request of Bush in 1945, the Panel was asked to identify and explore trends in digital data collection and warehousing and to make strategic recommendations on the creation, dissemination, and preservation of scientific and engineering knowledge. The Panel recommended the creation of a coordinated cyberinfrastructure for the support and sharing of digital collections of literature, data, instruments, and software to facilitate collaborations among scientists around the world. Although the cyberinfrastructure has yet to be fully realized (Lynch, 2008), there have been enormous technological advances, not only since the time of Garvey and Griffith (1972), but also since Hurd's (1996, 2000) proposal for a totally electronic model of scientific communication. Another recent development is the National Institute of Health's (NIH) Public Access Policy, signed by President Bush in late 2007, requiring all NIH funded researchers to submit an electronic version of their final, peer-reviewed manuscripts to the National Library of Medicine's openly accessible repository, *PubMed Central*; this policy, approved in spite of fervent opposition from the American Chemical Society (ACS) and the Association of American Publishers, creates the potential for a shift in how scientists communicate their research results (Suber, 2008; Trager, 2008). It is therefore an opportune moment to consider how the developments in the digital infrastructure have affected the traditional and modern modes of scientific communication.

The topic of scientific communication has been addressed previously in *ARIST*. Hyland and Salager-Meyer (2008) review the literature on scientific writing; both Finholt (2002) and Sonnenwald (2007) provide insights into scientific collaboration. The relationship of science and technology studies to information science is the topic of Van House's (2004) chapter; King and Tenopir (1999) survey research about the use and reading of the scientific literature. Borgman and Furner's (2002) chapter discusses the use of bibliometrics for the study of the influences of electronic media on scholarly communication structures and processes. The issue of open access electronic publishing and its influence on scholarly communication has been the topic of chapters by Drott (2006), Kling (2004), Kling and Callahan (2003), and Peek and Pomerantz (1998). This chapter complements and builds upon previous reviews by examining the current research literature on the influence of the digital infrastructure on the formal communicative practices of reading, citing, and disseminating journal articles and research-related information as modeled by Garvey and Griffith (1972) and Hurd (1996, 2000). Also considered are the influences of digital information sharing technologies on scientists' informal and collaborative communication activities. The communication processes of physical and life scientists studying both pure and applied scientific problems are considered, and comparisons and contrasts drawn as appropriate. The communication patterns of medical and health care practitioners and professional engineers are not emphasized here. However, pertinent studies are incorporated when there is a direct and illustrative connection to the communication behaviors of research scientists. The majority of the literature reviewed focuses on the communication behaviors of American scientists, although international perspectives are incorporated where possible.

## Journal Article Reading Behavior

The way scientists read journal articles is changing as more and more articles become available online. In the year 2000, university scientists spent on average 182 hours reading 188 journal articles, whereas non-university scientists spent 88 hours reading 106 articles (Tenopir & King, 2000). Sixty percent of the article readings occurred within six months of publication and 75 percent of the readings were to support research, 50 percent for current awareness, 41 percent to support teaching, and 32 percent to prepare talks or presentations (Tenopir & King, 2000). These findings show the pivotal role of journal articles in scientific communication at a time when electronic publishing in the sciences was in its early stages. To understand how the digital delivery of information influences scientists' communication behaviors, Tenopir and colleagues (Tenopir, King, Boyce, Grayson, Zhang, & Ebuen, 2003) investigated the electronic journal readership behaviors of over 1,600 scientists from the University of Tennessee, Drexel University, and Oak Ridge National Laboratory, as well as members of the American Astronomical Society (AAS). As the capabilities of electronic scientific journal systems became more advanced, the number of articles read more than doubled, while the time spent reading increased approximately 60 percent. A shift is seen in the proportion of readings from library print collections in the early 1990s (99 percent) to library electronic subscriptions a decade later (87 percent). Current articles continue to represent the highest percentage of readings (65 versus 64 percent). Even though more articles were discovered by browsing in 1990 than 12 years later (58 versus 21 percent), scientists continue to learn about articles of interest from their colleagues (16 versus 21 percent). The researchers also report a decrease in use of personal journal subscriptions in favor of copies of individual articles (13 versus 36 percent) due primarily to increased reading of single papers from electronic preprint (eprint), and other online article archives. This raises questions about the effectiveness of bundling articles into journal volumes for delivery on a fixed schedule when it is now possible to post articles individually on the Internet as soon as they are available.

To better understand the effects of unbundled electronic article delivery on the communication practices of scientists, Tenopir, King, Boyce, Grayson, and Paulson (2005) surveyed astronomers about their reading habits as well as their opinions about electronic journals and databases. Questionnaires were sent to two separate random samples of 2,200 members of the AAS and generated 512 (Survey 1) and 491 (Survey 2) responses. The primary purpose of reading articles for 47 percent of the astronomers is to support their research by: inspiring new thinking (38 percent), improving experimental results (33 percent), and changing research focus (20 percent). These findings are similar to those of an earlier study by Tenopir and colleagues (2003). Most of the readings were from unbundled electronic versions of articles from both the AAS electronic suite (84 percent) as well as non-AAS electronic journals (67 percent). Some 58 percent of the astronomers download and print articles before reading; only 22 percent of the readings are done on screen. This habit had been noted seven years earlier in a survey of astronomers who typically accessed journals electronically yet printed them for reading (Brown, 1999). Finally, Tenopir and colleagues (2005) note that astronomers are unique among scientists in their information behavior as they are less likely than other scientists to find articles by browsing (21 versus 46 percent) and more likely to discover articles by searching electronic databases (39 versus 16 percent). Disciplinary differences also influence the communication patterns of scientists (Kling & McKim, 2000).

Bar-Ilan and Fink's (2005) survey of 201 faculty members and 238 doctoral candidates in physics, chemistry, life, and applied sciences at the Hebrew University in Jerusalem similarly indicates a preference for electronic delivery of journal articles. Eighty percent of the respondents are considered habitual users, using electronic journals at least once a week (13 percent), several times a week (47 percent) or daily (34 percent). Eighty-seven percent do not regularly use print journals. In fact, for 64 percent of the respondents, 76 to 100 percent of their scientific reading is accounted for by electronic journals. When surveyed about the reasons for preferring electronic journals to print, the primary responses (81 percent) are: searching and retrieval are easier and more effective, accessibility any time and place, no need to photocopy, and accelerated publication schedules. The preference for electronic journals is maintained in spite of the fact that reading from a computer screen is deemed difficult. Furthermore, many online journal archives are incomplete and some journals are not available online. The small number of scientists favoring print are aged 20-29 and 60+, raising an intriguing question about generational differences in scientific information use. If the younger generation is as adept at using technology as is commonly supposed, why is this group of young Israeli scientists (20 percent of the survey population) less likely to use electronic journals than their mentors? Bar-Ilan and Fink suggest that it has to do with younger scientists' habit of reading articles from print journals or from their personal subscriptions. Perhaps, as Covi's (2000) interviews with 10 doctoral students in molecular biology from a diverse set of eight Carnegie-classified Research I Universities in the U. S. suggest, even though graduate students are often instrumental in introducing novel electronic communication practices into the laboratory, they still mimic the communication patterns of their advisors. Bar-Ilan and Fink caution that their results apply only to the users of the Harmann Science Library at the Hebrew University. However, the patterns they described match the results of a survey of 96 science faculty members at nine Dutch universities (Voorbij & Ongering, 2006). A survey of 775 physicists, 494 chemists, and 521 pathologists working in universities and other research institutes across Japan (Kurata, Matsubayashi, Mine, Muranushi, & Ueda, 2007) also reports an overall preference for electronic journals.

These studies indicate both the enduring role of the peer-reviewed journal in scientific communication and the growing importance of electronic reading. As Smith (2003) suggests, scientists are not actually changing their communication patterns with regard to journal articles, but their preferred form of delivery is changing. The increasing importance of the open access literature in scientific communication, as discussed in the next section, further supports Smith's suggestion.

## Communication Using Open Access Literature

Drott's (2006) review of the economical, technological, and sociological aspects of the open access literature captures the complex and potentially transformative nature of the issue. The significance of open access for scientific communication has captured the attention of many researchers who have conducted bibliometric analyses to understand the impact of freely available scientific information on scholarly communication. Borgman and Furner (2002) note that bibliometrics constitutes a powerful set of measures for the study of scholarly communication processes. Citation analysis can be used to indicate the impact of a work on scientific thinking, the assumption being that the more frequently a work is cited, the greater its impact. When interpreting the results of citation analyses of the open access literature, one must attend to the definition of open access used by the bibliometricians carrying out the analyses. The Budapest Open Access Initiative (www.soros.org/openaccess) considers the openly accessible literature to be comprised of both for-cost, copyrighted, peer-reviewed journal articles and also no-cost, copyright free, non-reviewed eprints (Chan, Cuplinskas, Eisen, Friend, Genova, Guédon, et al., 2002). Harnad and Brody (2004, online) additionally categorize journals according to their open access policies, with "gold" journals making all of their content freely available and "green" journals allowing some form of self-archiving. They estimate that only 5 percent of the world's journals are gold and 90 percent are green. Investigation of the accessibility of 284 titles claiming open accessibility indicates a substantial blurring between the two categories (Sotudeh & Horri, 2007b).

This is likely due to the struggle producers and consumers of the scientific literature have had during the last ten years in finding a balance between toll-free access and sustainability. Even though the term "open access" connotes free, unfettered availability and use, the cost of an open scientific article archive must be borne at some point by someone along the publication continuum; several of the current models require scientists to assume the financial burden. A range of influential producers of scientific information—including Elsevier, the Public Library of Science, Britain's Royal Society, and the American Chemical Society—have adopted a hybrid mode of open access where authors have the option of paying a fee to make their articles freely available online to nonsubscribers as soon as the article is accepted for publication (Rover, 2006). Consequently, it is possible that a single issue of a journal is a mixture of unrestricted and subscriber-only accessible works. Citation analysis of journals such as the *Proceedings of the National Academy of Sciences* (*PNAS*) is complicated by this hybrid mode of open access and further complicated by *PNAS*'s policy of depositing the final version of an article in the National Library of Medicine's *PubMed Central*, as well as making it freely available on their website, within six months of publication (National Academy of Sciences, 2008).

In addition to the definitions that are being used, the types of bibliometric data collected also influence the conclusions that are drawn. The Impact Factor (IF) and Immediacy Index (II) from the Institute for Scientific Information (ISI, now Thomson Reuters) have been used to study the usage of open access journals in scientific communication. The IF identifies the frequency with which an average article from a journal is cited in a particular year; the II measures how frequently the average article is cited within the same year it is published (Thomson Scientific, 2005). The IF is calculated by dividing the number of current year citations by the total number of items published in that journal during the previous two years. Garfield and Sher created the IF in 1960 to remove biases in citation data caused by a journal's age, frequency of publication, or number of articles published (Garfield, 1998). The II gives a measure of how quickly articles are cited after they are published, making it particularly helpful for judging the impact of journals that publish cutting edge research as well as for assessing the impact of open access titles with their virtually instantaneous availability. In spite of their widespread use, the IF and II are not without flaws, in particular their lack of consideration of different citing practices in different fields (van Raan, 2003) and the variations in the quality of citing journals. Consequently, interpretation of these data should be made with caution and ideally in conjunction with other indicators of scientists' communication practices. Glänzel and Moed (2002) provide a comprehensive overview of the advantages and limitations of the IF and II. Although the assortment of open access rubrics and the ranges of data collected complicate interpretation of bibliometric data, several citation analyses point to a steady climb in the use of the open access literature by scientists. What is less clear, however, is whether open access is fundamentally changing the ways in, rather than just the means by, which scientists communicate.

One of the earliest studies of open access publications and citation rates was conducted a decade ago on 39 peer-reviewed journals in several fields including computer science, mathematics, medicine, and psychology using IFs and IIs as indices of influence (Harter, 1998). The results indicate little citation advantage for open access, peer-reviewed journals. Although Harter carefully restricts the analysis to only the years for which the journal is freely available online, if a title is available both openly and via subscription during a given year, it is impossible to determine which version is cited, thereby clouding the interpretation of the data. By way of contrast, it is possible to conclude that open access does have an effect on scientific communication from a study conducted by Fosmire and Yu (2000). They excluded titles providing free online access with a subscription from their analysis. The 47 journals analyzed, 34 of which were electronic-only titles with no print-based counterpart, in the fields of agriculture, biological sciences, computer science, engineering, mathematics, medicine, and physics, scored well in terms of IF and II. However, in addition to complications in interpreting IFs and IIs, especially as regards to subject-specific citation practices, the reasons for the success of the open access titles may also have been influenced by the multiplicity of fields included in the analysis. Harter's study may also have been confounded because scientists' areas of study have been shown to shape their communication patterns (Kling & McKim, 2000).

To further address the issue of whether open access publications result in a citation advantage, Eysenbach (2006) compared the citation impact of articles published between June and December of 2004 in the multidisciplinary *PNAS*. The time frame studied followed *PNAS*'s launching of the option for authors to pay $1,000 to have their submission available online immediately upon acceptance. As a result, the article population is a mixture of 212 openly available, and 1,280 subscription only, articles. Analysis of Thomson Reuters' Web of Science data shows that, although the mean number of citations is equal in December 2004, the open access group garners significantly more citations than those not available openly both at four and 10 months following electronic posting. Eysenbach concludes there is a definite citation advantage associated with open access and therefore suggests that, to advance scientific discovery and accelerate the translation of research into practice, scientific communities should invest in early dissemination of articles. Eysenbach plans to continue to follow the same articles over a number of years to provide a more thorough depiction of the long-term citation impact of open access. However, because the *PNAS* is a multidisciplinary journal, disciplinary differences in communication behaviors among the *PNAS* audience may cloud the results (Kling & McKim, 2000).

McVeigh's (2004) examination of 219 electronically available, peer-reviewed, open access journals in life sciences, medicine, chemistry, and also physics, engineering, and mathematics begins to separate any field-dependent influences on the citation impact of open access journals on scientific communication. She considers a journal to be openly accessible if it does not charge for the right to access, download, copy, print, distribute, or search the most recent content. Additionally, McVeigh acknowledges that the variations in accessibility of the journals studied remains quite complex because each field has at least one journal where 20 or more years of issues are available to readers at no cost, while some titles started within the past 10 years have always been openly available. Still other titles in the sample have only the most recent one or two years freely available. The majority of the open access journals McVeigh studied are consistently among the lower-ranking journals regardless of field, as indicated by IF and II. The openly accessible journals in chemistry have even lower IFs and IIs compared to those in physics, engineering, and mathematics. Consistent among the four subject areas, however, is a higher II than IF. Examining this further, McVeigh (2004, online) finds that recent articles in open access journals receive more citations than do recent articles in traditionally accessible titles, suggesting an "early view" advantage due to the immediate availability of open access journals. Even though McVeigh has begun to differentiate the variety of scientific fields, it is possible that the results remain complicated by the combined analysis of the titles in physics, engineering, and mathematics (Kling & McKim, 2000). However the open citation advantage is likely to be real, in that mathematicians and physicists both use openly accessible works in their communication activities (Antelman, 2004; Brown, 1999; Ginsparg, 1996; Youngen, 1998).

Antelman (2004) reports articles appearing in ten leading mathematics journals, as defined by 2002 *Journal Citation Reports*, with any openly accessible full-text content to gain over 91 percent more citations than those not available freely online. Physicists, particularly those studying high-energy physics, have employed an open access mode of communication for over four decades first using paper preprints and more recently eprints. An eprint is the precursor to an article that may eventually be published in a peer-reviewed journal of record. Eprints are used to facilitate large international collaborations, to avoid duplication of effort, and to bypass lengthy journal publication schedules (Kreitz, Addis, Galic, & Johnson, 1997). In August 1991 Paul Ginsparg launched the pioneering online preprint repository, arXiv.org, to facilitate and enhance communication among high-energy physicists. The digital archive now houses over half a million papers in astronomy, physics, mathematics, nonlinear sciences, computer science, quantitative biology, and statistics and is accessed around the world over half a million times per day (arXiv.org, 2008). Enumeration of the citations made to the works in the physics section of arXiv.org indicates that the eprints have become an established and vital component of communication among physicists in spite of not having first passed through the traditional peer review process (Brown, 1999; Ginsparg, 1996; Youngen, 1998). Scientists in other disciplines have been slower to adopt eprints. The absence of peer review and its consequent unknown effects on scientific communication are provided as reasons for the lack of acceptance (Butler, 1999; Glaze, 1999; Koenig, 2000; Marshall, 1999a, 1999b; Wilkinson, 1998). Direct tallying of the citations to the eprints in Elsevier's Chemistry Preprint Server (CPS) shows that chemists haven not adopted eprints to the same extent as physicists (Brown, 2003b). The CPS, initiated in August 2000 with 20 eprints, provided a unique microcosm of chemical communication in which users could interact by commenting upon the articles posted. Even though authors depositing their work in the CPS believed the eprints posted to be of high quality and appreciated the forum provided for open discussion of current chemical research, they expressed concern over the lack of peer review and the uncertain permanence of eprint storage (Brown, 2003b). This skepticism, combined with the refusal of editors of the top chemistry journals subsequently to publish papers previously posted on the server, essentially caused the CPS to fail after a brief existence, from 2000 to 2004. Elsevier, nonetheless, maintains a permanent, free online archive housing the chemistry eprints deposited during the CPS's four-year life (www.sciencedirect.com/preprintarchive).

Similar to McVeigh (2004), Moed (2007) suggests that the accelerated rate of citation to articles deposited in arXiv.org demonstrates an "early view" effect, which allows scientists to read and cite a paper sooner than those appearing only in a published journal. Moed uses Web of Science to collect citation data, excluding author self-citations, for over 74,000 articles appearing in the arXiv.org section devoted to the sub-field of condensed matter from 1992 to 2005 and the articles in 24 journals in which the papers subsequently appeared. He reports that articles appearing in arXiv.org are cited earlier than articles published in the journals but were not deposited in the openly accessible archive. He points to the early view effect as evidence of the success of arXiv.org in fulfilling the primary function of an eprint depository, to make research available rapidly, and therefore suggests that future work should examine the early view influence in other publication models. One possible method offered is comparison of the citation rates of articles that are available electronically to subscribers on the publisher's website several months before their appearance in print.

As observed with mathematicians and physicists, there is a trend among astrophysicists toward citation of openly accessible works. Schwarz and Kennicutt (2004), editors of the *Astrophysical Journal,* studied the citation patterns for papers published in their journal from 1999 to 2002. Citation analysis reveals that papers posted prior to publication as eprints in arXiv.org's astrophysics (astro-ph) archive are cited twice as frequently as papers that are not posted on astro-ph, regardless of the sub-discipline within astrophysics. Metcalfe (2005) confirms the factor-of-two influence with a study of the citation rate of eprints posted in astro-ph from 13 international journals including major titles such as *Astrophysical Journal, Monthly Notices of the Royal Astronomical Society,* and *Astronomy and Astrophysics.* In contrast, a study of the influence of free availability and early dissemination using a dataset consisting of all the references from articles published in one of seven core astronomy journals to another article published in the same journals since 1970 finds no citation advantage attributable to open access (Kurtz, Eichhorn, Accomazzi, Grant, Demleitner, Henneken, et al., 2005). However, Kurtz and colleagues did observe the strong influence of early dissemination where citations were shifted toward more recent publications. This is similar to the results reported by McVeigh (2004) for life sciences, medicine, chemistry, physics, engineering, and mathematics and by Moed (2007) for the more specialized field of condensed matter physics. Kurtz and colleagues (2005) argue that the issue of open access and citation effect may be overstated for disciplines such as astronomy where other factors, such as access to equipment and funds, are greater barriers to scientific progress than is access to the literature. For more on this subject see the chapter by Kurtz and Bollen in the present volume.

In another study, Sotedeh and Horri (2007b) restrict their analysis to 99 open access titles with policies that met, for at least five years, their four criteria of free, immediate, full, and constant open access (Sotedeh & Horri, 2007a). The study is similar to McVeigh's (2004) in examining several disciplines but Sotedeh and Horri collected the citations at the article level rather than for the entire journal. Five years of citations to articles published in 2001 and three years of citations for those published in 2003 were gathered using *Web of Science.* The majority of the articles selected for analysis were life science journals (20,554), followed by multidisciplinary sciences

(7,917), natural sciences (2,111), and finally engineering and materials science (3,281) titles. Sotedeh and Horri (2007a) reported that almost 50 percent of the articles in engineering and materials science had not been cited while only 24 percent of the life sciences articles remain uncited. Almost 40 percent of the multidisciplinary and 31 percent of the natural sciences articles received no citations. The uncitedness of the engineering and materials science articles does not surprise the authors because publishing research in peer-reviewed journals is not highly valued in strongly practice-oriented scientific disciplines such as engineering (Yitzhaki & Hammershlag, 2004). The citation data suggest that researchers in the life sciences, including medicine, allied health, biology, and agriculture, are using works that are openly accessible at, or above, the level expected for all articles in the field, whereas in the natural sciences (chemistry, geology, physics, and mathematics) the open access articles are used less frequently than would be expected. When considering each field individually, open access chemistry articles are cited more than those in physics; the highest citation performance is in research and experimental medicine. These findings are at odds with those discussed earlier, which show that open access physics articles are an integral component of communication among physicists. Unfortunately, Sotedeh and Horri (2007a) do not suggest a reason for this discrepancy nor do they suggest any reason for the difference between the chemistry and physics data beyond different citing behaviors. The medical research community's use of open access articles is not unexpected by Sotedeh and Horri, who contend that this group has a long tradition of supporting open access initiatives. This contention may seem somewhat surprising in light of the debate on the wisdom of making medical research that has not undergone peer review openly accessible because it could negatively affect public well-being or diminish the quality of scientific publications (Weller, 2005). However, Sotedeh and Horri (2007a) exercised special care in selecting only journals with sufficient prestige to be included in the *Journal Citation Reports* and therefore the citation advantage of the articles is likely also to be a reflection of the high ranking journals they analyzed.

To understand clearly the influence of open access on science communication through citation analysis, not only is it necessary to study science fields separately but, as Harnad and Brody (2004) assert, it is also essential to compare individual open access articles to those that are not openly accessible within the same publication venue rather than to compare openly accessible journals to those that are not. Such comparisons remove the effect of irregular modes of open accessibility within one journal over time. Lawrence's (2001) analysis of the impact of freely available online conference papers in computer science versus those not online is the earliest citation study of this kind. Online conference papers in computer science gather an average of 336 percent more citations than papers not available online even when published via the same outlet. Lawrence selected conference papers for analysis because computer scientists consider these to be more prestigious than journal articles; conference paper acceptance rates are as low as 10 percent. The data presented by Lawrence are not distorted by discipline-specific communication differences and open accessibility mode variability, nor do the limitations of the IF and II complicate them. Instead, Lawrence uses direct citation counts, minus self-citations, gathered via the openly accessible citation database, *CiteSeer*, which employs a citation indexing system that automatically links references in research articles (Giles,

Bollacker, & Lawrence, 1998). Because computer scientists make extensive use of electronic information in their daily work (Shen, 2006), the high citation rate of freely available online papers is not entirely surprising. Also predictable are the results of the similarly pure citation analyses comparing the references from 14 million articles in 7,000 physics journals to those of 260,000 openly accessible self-archived physics articles in arXiv.org from 1991 to 2001 conducted by Brody, Stamerjohanns, Harnad, Gingras, Vallieres, and Oppenheim (2004). Brody and Harnad are strong proponents of open accessibility for the enhancement of scientific communication and have maintained a dynamic and comprehensive openly accessible online bibliography of studies on the effect of open access on citation impact since 2004 (Harnad, 2008).

Twenty years after the first citation analysis of openly accessible scientific journal articles, the initial citation advantage of open accessibility is diminishing (Davis, 2008). Davis suggests the decrease is due to the increasing ease of distributing and accessing articles beyond publishers' websites, eprint servers, and other easily traceable open access fora. As scientists disseminate and retrieve information using a range of electronic modes such as laboratory websites, digital repositories, listservs, and blogs, it becomes difficult to attribute citation influences to one means of open distribution. The citation rate to open access articles versus those not openly available in 11 biological and medical journals published from 2003 to 2007 is shrinking (Davis, 2008). Davis argues that the higher citation rates previously observed for openly accessible biological and biomedical articles are due to an early-adopter effect that is now being eroded by the normalization of the practice of making articles freely available online in a range of locations. This shifting and melding of digital access modes has created the opportunity for the development of additional indicators of scientific communication beyond traditional bibliometrics. Scientists' article downloading and posting activities, as well as the creation of hyperlinks within and among works posted on the Internet, are providing new insights into the shaping effects of the digital infrastructure on scientific communication.

## Communication by Downloading

Antelman's (2004) study of the citation impact of open access mathematics papers suggests that an understanding of the effects of open access on scientific communication can be achieved by using "hit-counts," or downloads, as additional measures of use. This idea was pursued by Davis and Fromerth (2007) who found that articles deposited in arXiv.org's mathematics section and subsequently published in four London Mathematical Society journals between 1997 and 2005 were downloaded from the publisher's (Cambridge University Press) website less frequently, yet received more citations than articles in the same four titles not available via arXiv.org. The citation data were gathered from the American Mathematical Society's online index of the mathematics literature, *MathSciNet*, rather than from ISI, because *MathSciNet* traces citations to the eprints in arXiv.org as well as those to the original article. Davis and Fromerth also assert that *MathSciNet* provides more complete coverage than ISI, yet they caution against generalizing too broadly from the results due to the small sample size. Nonetheless these findings are not affected by the biases and publication delays that complicate the use of citation data (Bollen & Van de Sompel, 2006).

The download patterns of the approximately 20,000 journals available to scientists at Los Alamos National Laboratory's research library show the value of online usage data in the depiction of scientific communication patterns (Bollen, Van de Sompel, Smith, & Luce, 2005). Comparison of journal impacts determined from locally collected journal download data (40,847 full-text articles downloaded between June and November of 2001 by 1,858 unique users from 1,892 journals) and the journals' IFs show no correlation. The authors caution that this may be a reflection of the unique electronic journal access habits of Los Alamos's community of physicists and nuclear scientists. Also noteworthy is the observation that only slightly less than 10 percent of the titles available at Los Alamos were downloaded during the six-month period. This would seem to suggest that a limited number of journals is of importance in the routine communication practices of the scientists working at Los Alamos National Laboratory.

Duy and Vaughan (2006) similarly find citation data collected locally to be more reliable than impact factors as an index of biochemistry and chemistry journal usage at Concordia University Libraries. The study is distinctive in that it combines a full year of print usage data gathered through shelving studies of titles published by the American Chemical Society, the Royal Society of Chemistry, Elsevier, and Wiley with two kinds of citation-based data: IFs and Library Journal Utilization Reports. The Utilization Reports, purchased from ISI, provide a measure of how many times Concordia's researchers published in each journal plus how often they were cited in each journal. Electronic delivery has little influence on the journal preferences of Concordia's chemists and biochemists because the most frequently read print titles are also those that are most often downloaded and cited. This is indicated by strong correlations between the electronic journal usage data and both the local shelving and the ISI Utilization Report data. Journal quality has little influence as no significant correlations were found between the journals' IFs and intensity of use. Taken together, these studies of researchers' downloading habits at Los Alamos National Laboratory and those of the biochemists and chemists at Concordia University suggest that downloading is a new facet of scientific communication, in addition to reading and citing practices.

Kurtz, Eichhorn, Accomazzi, Grant, Demleitner, and Murray (2005) explore the concept of electronic "reads" by comparing downloading data to citations for all the articles available through the U.S. National Aeronautic and Space Administrations' Astrophysics Data System (NASA-ADS) for the year 2000. A "read" is defined as every time a user selects the option to access more information, including the abstract, whole text, and references, from the full text online version; a "cite" refers to citations made in published papers. With seven times as many articles being read as cited, characteristics of an article—age, type, and content—were examined as possible factors responsible for the difference. Foremost is article age, with 95 percent of all articles that were read 256 or more times, yet cited fewer than four times, having been published within eighteen months of December 2000. However, older articles also are read more often than they are cited, presumably for their historical value. Type of publication is also important, as indicated by the similar frequency of citing and reading of full-length peer-reviewed articles; of the 1,272 non-peer-reviewed abstracts studied, 91 percent are read but only 22 percent cited. Finally, content differentiates reads from cites: The most cited article and second most highly read article during 2000 is Landolt's (1992) description of the basic calibration data for a fundamental measurement technique. In contrast, the most highly read article during 2000 is Trimble and Aschwanden's (2000) review of the previous year's literature in astrophysics, but it did not garner any citations. Also noted is the very small subset of articles that is actually read and cited, with 78 percent of the articles within NASA-ADS being neither read nor cited during 2000.

A study of the use of electronic chemistry journals by Davis and Solla (2003) also shows that most users download very few articles and that only a small number of users are responsible for the majority of the retrieval activity. Full-text article downloading statistics using unique IP (Internet Protocol) addresses to represent users of Cornell University Library were collected for 29 American Chemical Society titles. The majority of users retrieve articles from a small number of journals; 56 percent of downloading is associated with just one journal. The journals *Biochemistry* and the *Journal of Agricultural and Food Chemistry* were the most highly used during the study's three-month window of July to September of 2002. The results show the critical importance of these titles to scientists at Cornell. This is corroborated by ISI data for the *Journal of Agricultural and Food Chemistry*, which was reported in the 2001 *Journal Citation Reports* (Institute for Scientific Information, 2001) to be the most highly cited title of the 40 Food Science and Technology titles ranked. Unfortunately, Davis and Solla did not give similar consideration to the ISI ranking for the journal *Biochemistry*, which is also highly cited: third among 308 Biochemistry and Molecular Biology titles. Although the 2001 IFs for the *Journal of Agricultural and Food Chemistry* (9th) and *Biochemistry* (66th) are within the top quartile of their subject areas, they are not in the top tier. It appears that use of these titles by scientists at Cornell University is mirrored in ISI's citation data; yet once again, downloading activity does not directly reflect their IFs, suggesting that motivations for citing and downloading may be different. Also observed by Davis and Solla are field-specific differences in downloading activity, with the Chemistry and Chemical Engineering Department leading in the number of articles retrieved (42 percent) followed by Civil, Biological and Environmental, Materials, and Theoretical Engineering (12 percent); Medicine (6 percent); Food Science (4 percent); and Molecular Biology and Genetics (3 percent). The Cornell chemists also access electronic journals to the greatest extent, with 82 percent of the IP addresses downloading more than two articles. Finally, a very strong relationship ($r^2 = 0.92$) was found between the number of articles downloaded and the number of unique IP addresses, causing Davis and Solla to suggest that the size of a user population can be estimated by enumerating the total number of downloads per title. This notion seems to oversimplify the metrics of online journal usage but merits further study because the downloading of data brings another dimension to our understanding of scientists' communication behaviors.

Bollen and Van de Sompel (2006) tried to map the structure of science through usage statistics gathered at Los Alamos National Laboratory. Earlier mapping studies used a variety of techniques and data sets to represent relationships among journal articles including: content and co-citation data for agriculture-related biochemistry and chemoreception research (Braam, Mocd, & van Raan, 1991a,

1991b), co-authorship data from the digital library community (Liu, Bollen, Nelson, & Van de Sompel, 2005), and connections among the *Journal Citation Reports* information for 5,748 journals included in the 2001 science edition (Leydesdorff, 2004). Drawing on these studies, Bollen and Van de Sompel's analysis assumes that two journals are related if their articles are frequently accessed together in a particular sequence. A network of journals was constructed for a set of Los Alamos National Laboratory usage logs from February 2004 to April 2005. Their network depicts the usage of 330,109 articles published in 10,696 journals by 5,866 library users. These data were then used to chart journal relationships as they occurred in the usage network. To validate the method, the authors applied it to the more encompassing *Journal Citation Reports* subject information. Bollen and Van de Sompel consider the maps generated to depict accurately the interests of the scientists at Los Alamos; moreover the subject groupings in the mappings correspond to those delineated by ISI. The success of this local mapping of the usage of electronic journals by Los Alamos scientists indicates that the method could be applied to the usage of digital collections by the larger community of scientists and serve as a viable and novel indicator of current trends in scientific communication.

Brown (2007) also examined the relationship between citations and downloads in a study of the role of Web-based information in the communication behavior of chemists. Although the exact number of downloads is not made publicly available by the American Chemical Society, there is a list of the most frequently downloaded articles on the ACS Web Editions website (American Chemical Society, 2006). Analysis of eight journals representing a range of fields as well as IFs from 2004 reveals that articles attracting the highest levels of citation according to *Web of Science* are also those accessed most frequently from the subscription-only ACS Web Editions website. This is partially true for articles that are methodological in nature. Methodological articles have traditionally been among those most highly cited in chemistry, with the article describing the Lowry Method for protein assay published over 50 years ago in the *Journal of Biological Chemistry* (Lowry, Rosebrough, Farr, & Randall, 1951) having gathered over 65,500 citations to date (Thomson Reuters, 2008). Kurtz, Eichhorn, Accomazzi, Demleitner, and Murray (2005) also note a relationship between the downloading and citing of methodological articles by astronomers, suggesting that the content of an online article influences how often it will be read and cited by others.

## Communicating by Posting Articles Online

The studies of scientists' citing and reading behaviors indicate that they actively access and use information that is posted online and that these activities may be influenced by the content of the articles. If content influences use, one of the reasons for the citation success of open access articles may be that authors post their best work online. Kurtz, Eichhorn, Accomazzi, Demleitner, and Murray's (2005) study of the per article citation for the 2,592 articles published in the 2003 *Astrophysical Journal* in comparison with those posted as eprints in arXiv.org indicates a strong quality bias in the determination of the articles submitted. Moed (2007) also suggests a strong quality bias among physics papers deposited in arXiv.org as papers authored by well known scientists are overrepresented in the condensed matter physics section of the archive.

Using a range of IFs as a guide, Wren (2005) also finds a quality bias in the life sciences open access literature. Comparison of the posting trends between 13 subscription-based and four open access titles in the life sciences shows that life science journals with high IFs are more likely to be open access than those with a lower citation impact (Wren, 2005). The subscription-based titles studied include the *New England Journal of Medicine* with the highest IF (32), the midrange *EMBO Journal* (11), and *Nutrition Reviews* with the lowest IF (2). The four openly accessible titles studied include the *PNAS* with the highest (11) and the *Journal of Biological Chemistry* with the lowest (7) IF. Among the over 48,000 articles appearing in the 13 subscription based titles published between January 1994 and July 2004, those with the highest IFs have a larger fraction of papers posted online at non-journal sites than those with lower IFs. Wren's results suggest that articles published in higher impact life sciences journals are more likely to be freely available online at unidentified locations beyond the publisher's website than articles from journals with lower impacts.

Open availability may be more indicative of the value of conference papers in the communication processes of astronomers than the quality stamp of peer review (Schwarz & Kennicutt, 2004). Assessment of the impact of preprint posting on non-reviewed papers from conference proceedings published in 1999 that were deposited in the astrophysics section of arXiv.org (astro-ph) versus that of the papers that were not deposited, finds a doubling in citation rate due to posting in the online archive independent of peer review. In spite of the citation advantage of open accessibility for conference papers, Schwarz and Kennicutt caution that online posting in arXiv.org alone is not sufficient to ensure a high citation impact. They found the citation rates to papers appearing in the *Astrophysical Journal*, the American Astronomical Society's premier peer-reviewed journal, to be 20 times greater than those to conference papers published during the same time period, regardless of posting on astro-ph. Schwartz and Kennicutt conclude that in astronomy, publication in a peer-reviewed journal remains the primary determinant of the impact of a work.

Although there appears to be a relationship between citation and the quality of the materials posted online in some scientific fields, it is not clear from the bibliometric analyses conducted by Kurtz and colleagues (Kurtz, Eichhorn, Accomazzi, Grant, Demleitner, Henneken, et al., 2005), Moed (2007), Wren (2005), Schwarz and Kennicutt (2004), or Metcalfe (2005) if scientists are consciously posting only their best works online. To discover if scientists are selective in what they post in the open access portion of the *PNAS*, Eysenbach (2006) distributed a survey asking 313 authors of both openly accessible and traditionally published articles to rate, on a five-point Likert scale, the relative urgency, importance, and quality of their *PNAS* articles compared to their articles published elsewhere. Respondents reported no qualitative differences between the two groups of *PNAS* articles. The results of Eysenbach's survey suggest that authors of the multidisciplinary *PNAS* articles do not selectively post only their most important works on the Internet; however, this may be an artifact of the multidiscipline nature, as well as the high status of the *PNAS*, rather than a function of author bias. Additional factors may also be influencing the perceived quality of the articles posted online, including the design of the online portal, which can detract from, or contribute to, article use (Davis & Price, 2006). Mueller, Murali, Cha, Erwin, and Ghosh (2006), having found that journals in the field of general and internal medicine had increased IFs after becoming freely available online, suggest that the increased impact may result from a citing author having overlooked a relevant article because it was not available online. Craig, Plume, McVeigh, Pringle, and Amin (2007) also note that the initial success of an open access article may be due simply to its online availability and that the quality, importance, and relevance of an article will be more determinative of its lifetime citation rate than its open availability.

Whether articles posted online are of higher quality or whether posting online enhances an article's perceived quality are issues to be unraveled. Nonetheless, posting online increases the use of a work in the scientific communication system as indicated by the reading, downloading, and citing behaviors of scientists. In spite of the advantages, many scientists are reluctant to self-archive their work (Swan & Brown, 2005). Only 5 percent of chemists and pathologists post articles on their institution's website. Even though 20 percent of physicists use eprint archives to disseminate their work, they also submit their manuscripts to journals (Kurata et al., 2007). Journals continue to be the de facto method of communication for the Japanese scientists surveyed because journal publications are the yardstick by which they are evaluated and because journal articles reach the largest readership (Kurata et al., 2007). When asked to envisage the state of journal publishing in the next five years, of greatest importance to the Japanese researchers are the maintenance of peer review, accessibility to back issues, and round-the-clock availability. About 40 percent of the scientists surveyed by Kurata and colleagues predict a continued co-existence of print and electronic journals with very few (less than 13 percent) believing that electronic journals will dominate within five years.

## Communicating Through Linkages

Although the journal article continues to be an integral component of scientific communication, the system is expanding to include the dissemination and citation of Web-based research-related data. Initiatives for mounting and sharing research-related data on the Internet, or e-Science, began in the 1990s in the fields of particle physics, astronomy, meteorology, and DNA research where large volumes of data are generated and maintained using high-speed computer processing (Jankowski, 2007). In the early days of molecular biology research, DNA and amino acid sequences were published in their entirety in peer-reviewed journals. This practice rapidly became obsolete as the effort to map the human genome, as well as the molecular structure of many other organisms and plants, resulted in quantities of data too large for publication in a print journal. Limited page space plus the growing emphasis on describing functional significance, rather than composition, of an organism's molecular makeup, in combination with the growing capabilities of electronic storage, have made it both necessary and possible for scientists to organize, disseminate, and archive their research-related data digitally. Many of the premier outlets for the publication of biology research articles, including the *Journal of Biological Chemistry* and the *PNAS*, require relevant sequence data to be deposited and an accession number obtained before a manuscript will be accepted for publication (Hilgartner, 1995; McCain, 1995).

Such mandatory data submission has not been entirely accepted within the genetics research community, where members have traditionally exhibited a lack of openness (Weinberg, 1993). Geneticists classically voice concern over intellectual property protection prior to completion of a project and/or acceptance for publication in a peer-reviewed journal (Marshall, 1990; McCain, 1991). Yet by 2003 a sense of responsibility became a motivating force for molecular biologists who believe that science is "not science until it is shared and until someone else repeats it" (Brown, 2003a). The molecular biologists in Brown's case study are not concerned about the accuracy of the data disseminated online prior to peer review because scientists would not risk their reputation by submitting poor or incorrect data. When surveyed, a majority of the scientists says that peer review would only complicate, and therefore slow, the scientific process. Also, the scientists interviewed contend that because the data were generated using tax dollars, they should be freely available.

This study of molecular biologists' use of online repositories led to a pair of additional studies examining the usage and acceptance of freely available Web-based information by a diverse group of authors publishing in Academic Press's prestigious *Annual Reviews* series (Brown, 2004) and by chemists publishing in a select group of American Chemical Society journals (Brown, 2007). A content analysis of the 24 *Annual Reviews* titles in the sciences published between 1997 and 2001 was conducted to locate the presence of Uniform Resource Locators (URLs) within the full text of the articles by searching for the terms "www" and "http." A five-fold increase in the total number of URLs is noted and the total number of articles referring to a website increased four fold, suggesting that websites are an accepted means of communicating scientific information by authors and editors of titles in the venerable *Annual Reviews* series. In contrast, citation and content analyses of eight ACS titles from 1996, 2000, and 2004 indicate that although growing, chemists' use of a range of Web-based resources is not as great as that of the diverse group of scientists publishing in the *Annual Reviews* series (Brown, 2007). This may be attributed to the convenience and stability of the ACS electronic archive, which has a long tradition of making supporting information available to its readers, first as microfilm and more recently as free, albeit copyrighted, online files. For six of the eight journals studied, representing a range of chemistry sub-fields, the number of articles pointing to supporting information made available through the ACS website has increased steadily since 1996. Very few articles in the review journals—*Chemical Reviews* and *Accounts of Chemical Research*—referred to the ACS supporting information archive; but articles appearing in journals publishing research reports—including *Journal of the American Chemical Society, Analytical Chemistry Biochemistry Inorganic Chemistry, Journal of Organic Chemistry,* and *Chemistry of Materials*—make consistent reference to the supporting information. These observations indicate the key role the ACS supporting materials archive plays in the communication of research results, although the supporting information is of less importance in a topical review of the chemical literature.

Less than half of the 85 cancer clinical trials published between 1999 and 2003 that were studied by Piwowar, Day, and Fridsma (2007) had accompanying open access data. The authors suggest that cancer researchers may choose not to post their data online because they could be subjected to re-analysis by other researchers that could perhaps result in a challenge to the validity of the data. Such disputes could interfere with the original investigators' research agenda or necessitate a time-consuming rebutting of the re-analyses. As a result, laboratories freely sharing their data could be competitively disadvantaged compared to those maintaining propri-etary control of theirs. This is in spite of the finding that the 41 cancer trials with research-related data openly posted in a variety of locations on the Internet are cited 70 percent more frequently than those that do not publicly disseminate data. Sixty-eight percent of the datasets are located on laboratory websites, with the remainder being found on publisher websites or public databases. Some datasets are found in more than one location. Although Piwowar, Day, and Fridsma warn that their find-ings do not imply causation, they speculate that dissemination of data on the Internet alerts scientists to the existence of the published article, which in turn increases the possibility of citation.

The practice of including links to Web-based information within research publi-cations led Egghe (2000) to suggest that resource linking may act as an indicator of scientific communication in the same way as traditional article-to-article citation. The application of citation analysis techniques to Web-based information using Internet search engines to collect the data, often termed "webometrics," was pio-neered by Almind and Ingwersen (1997) in their case study of the Danish scholarly presence on the Web. The extensive review of the quantitative study of Web-related phenomena by Thelwall, Vaughan, and Björneborn (2005) indicates that in spite of the rather chaotic nature of data collected from the Web, webometrics is a useful way of studying scholarly communication, especially as more and more informa-tion sharing occurs digitally.

Vaughan and Shaw (2005) used webometric techniques to illuminate the influ-ence of changing technologies on the communication behaviors of scientists by mea-suring text mentions of an article in a source on the Web, or Web citations, in four scientific areas: biology, genetics, medicine, and multidisciplinary sciences. The number of traditional citations to approximately 6,000 articles from 114 journals was determined using the *Science Citation Index*. The title of each article was then searched on the Internet using *Google*. When the title phrase failed to locate an arti-cle, the search was supplemented with the subtitle and authors' names. The searches were repeated at various time intervals and the results were found to be stable over time. The Web citations outnumber and show a greater geographic diversity than the ISI citations, and correlate with the citation data in respect of the number of refer-ences to review journals, journals with high IFs, and works categorized as possess-ing intellectual impact. However, not all Web citations are of equal intellectual import: Only 30 percent of the citations are from research articles or class readings. The webometric data suggest that scientists are using Web-based resources in much the same way they use journal articles. Vaughan and Shaw note that Garfield (2001) expressed the hope that Web citation practices would become standardized. However they also suggest that the phenomenon may change with time, especially as it becomes easier to use the Internet as a way to cite and publish one's own work.

The citation feature provided by Google Scholar is a promising new bibliometric tool that has the potential to become a standard for measuring the influence of digital technologies on scientific communication (Kousha & Thelwall, 2007). Google Scholar provides citation data for a wide array of not only traditionally published scientific items but also openly accessible works for which citation data is not offered by ISI. In a pair of recent studies, Kousha and Thelwall (2007, 2008) explore the impact of the Web on the scholarly communication practices of scientists by using Google Scholar to trace Web-based citations. In both studies, 882 research articles from 39 English language open access journals indexed by ISI from four scientific disciplines (biology, physics, chemistry, and computer science) form the pool of articles selected for analysis. Articles published in 2001 were used to allow sufficient time for citations to accumulate. Like Vaughan and Shaw (2005), Kousha and Thelwall (2007) found a significant correlation between citations from Google Scholar and ISI, with biology and computer science showing the strongest, and chemistry the weakest, correlations. The data once again indicate similarities between traditional and Web-based citing practices, suggesting that the citation information collected from the Web could serve as an alternative to ISI's data for calculating citation impacts. However, citing Kling and McKim's (2000) observation that scientists in different fields communicate via the Web for a variety of purposes and to varying degrees, Kousha and Thelwall (2008) set out to explore the characteristics of the sources of the citations that are unique to Google Scholar; that is, those that don't overlap with ISI citations. This is an interesting approach as Google Scholar may illuminate works that are not indexed by traditional commercial bibliographic databases such as SciFinder Scholar and Web of Science, and hence provide access to potentially valuable research information that was previously hidden.

To reveal these works, first the number of citations was recorded for each article by selecting the "times cited" option in Web of Science. Then, for the Google Scholar citations, the article titles were searched as a phrase in Google Scholar and the number of citing sources, when available, was displayed by selecting the "cited by" link posted below each record. Although there are 3,202 unique citations from Google Scholar, the sample size was restricted to 1,950 by selecting all the unique citations to the biology, chemistry, and physics articles and 1,000 randomly selected unique citations from computer science. Although journal papers (34 percent) prevail overall among the unique Google Scholar citations, followed by conference and workshop papers (25 percent) and e-prints/preprints (23 percent), there are disciplinary differences by type of citing document. Biology and chemistry journal articles cite primarily other journal articles. Preprints and eprints dominate the physics citing sources and conference and workshop papers are the major citing sources of the computer science papers. These citing sources reflect the venues by which scientists in the different disciplines traditionally communicate their research results, with chemists relying on journal articles (Brown, 2003b), physicists on eprints (Brown, 2001), and computer scientists on conference proceedings (Lawrence, 2001). The results indicate that Google Scholar broadens access to citing sources beyond those indexed by ISI, yet, because the types of sources utilized are not inherently different, it appears that scientists' scholarly communication habits persist in the digital domain.

Kousha and Thelwall (2008) note, however, that because little is known about the quality of the content provided by Google Scholar, caution should be exercised when using its citation data in evaluating the impact of scientific research. The authority of Web-based citations could be improved by adding a level of quality control to Google Scholar and its online counterparts through a community-wide effort capitalizing on emerging online social bookmarking and collaborative tagging technologies such as those enabled by Connotea (Nature Publishing Group, www.connotea.org). Connotea is a freely available webspace designed to help scientists manage their references using tags assigned by each scientist. The tags can subsequently be made openly accessible to other scientists. Such informal evaluation from the research community could enhance the authority of Web-based information and hence increase its impact. Although little research has been conducted concerning the impact of online annotations on the use and subsequent citation of articles, Zemke (2007) finds, using adapted webometric techniques to identify coupled bookmarks, that 46 percent of scientists annotating their articles in Connotea with the term *apoptosis* also share at least one other bookmark. Zemke concludes that scientists using the term *apoptosis* form a unique community of scientists linked by their interest in programmed cell death. Although this innovative study does not directly indicate such an association, it does point to a different way of thinking about how scientists communicate as they use informally assigned tags. It seems possible that, if one scientist tags a paper with a particular term, a colleague might then be stimulated to read and cite the article as well as annotate it with similar, or perhaps additional, richer, terms. Thus a chain reaction is initiated where other scientists see the annotation, read the article, cite the work, and add further qualitative comments, all the while fostering a new community of scientists who may not have previously been afforded the opportunity to share their thoughts and ideas. This has the potential to vastly expand Price's (1963, p. 85) original concept of the "invisible college" as it gives scientists the ability to communicate and collaborate with a wide body of colleagues without leaving the laboratory or office.

Digital sharing initiatives have been given a mixed reception, yet the removal of physical, temporal, and geographical boundaries from scientific communication provides all scientists the opportunity to interact and discuss research results as they unfold. Originally, interpersonal communications among scientists were confined to letters, telephone conversations, and yearly conferences that in effect restricted the number of individuals capable of collaborating within a particular network. Also known as invisible colleges, these groups of scientists influence the course of research in their particular disciplines by presenting a united front in decision and policy making, including distribution of research funding and vetting of new streams of research (Price & Beaver, 1966). As a result, each scientific area's invisible college has been responsible for the majority of papers published and hence the flow of information within the scientific community. However, the ability of digital information-sharing tools to broaden the scope of scientific communication may require a reconsideration of the original concept of invisible colleges and how they intersect with the traditional models of scientific communication (Lievrouw & Carley, 1990).

## Invisible Colleges and Communication

Invisible colleges sustain the flow of information for the achievement of common scientific goals (Price & Beaver, 1966; Zuccala, 2006). Early ethnographic studies of scientific knowledge production conducted by Latour and Woolgar (1979) and Knorr-Cetina (1981) illustrate that the ongoing cycle of scientific communication involves not only texts, but also the scientific instruments used, the data gathered, and the people directly and indirectly involved in the research. It seems likely, as Lievrouw and Carley (1990) suggested almost twenty years ago, that the digital infrastructure can serve to increase interpersonal interactions and to expand communication beyond the elite groups forming each discipline's invisible colleges. However, Finholt (2002) suggests that such expansion has yet to be realized. He describes 15 instances of Web-based collaborations developed between 1980 and 2000 that connect scientists to each other, to instruments, and to data, outside their own laboratory walls. Finholt acknowledges that digitally facilitated collaborations have become an important aspect of the ways scientists interact, yet from the collaboratories examined, it does not appear that digital collaboration has changed fundamentally the way science is conducted. Since Finholt's *ARIST* review was published, communication among collaborating scientists has been explored by Hara, Solomon, Kim, and Sonnenwald (2003); Erdelez and Means (2005); Blake and Pratt (2007a, 2007b); and Palmer, Cragin, and Hogan (2007). These studies support Finholt's suggestions that digital communication technologies are facilitating, but are not altering, scientific communication, which depends greatly on intellectual and social ties.

Hara, Solomon, Kim, and Sonnenwald (2003) explore the social dimensions of scientific work to identify factors that facilitate or impede scientific collaboration within a newly formed multidisciplinary, geographically dispersed chemistry and chemical engineering research center comprised of 89 members and spanning four universities. Traditionally, chemists work in individual laboratories in close association with their own group of students, postdoctoral fellows, and technicians, and rarely venture beyond this network. The research center studied by Hara and colleagues gives chemists the opportunity to communicate with geographically dispersed colleagues using weekly teleconferences. However, once a connection is made and a level of collaboration established via teleconferencing, the scientists prefer to communicate via e-mail, in person, or by telephone rather than by a video connection. Using interviews, surveys, and observations, Hara and colleagues conclude that although the socio-technical infrastructure plays a role in collaborative work, three additional factors of note are involved: compatibility, research work connections, and incentives.

The case study by Erdelez and Means (2005) of the information sharing of life scientists working in a newly established life sciences research center at the University of Missouri-Columbia also shows the positive effects of a research center on information sharing that is not confined to the digital infrastructure. Erdelez and Means' study was initiated when the research center, built with the goal of creating a physical environment that would stimulate collaboration among life scientists, was in its formative stages with 22 faculty members distributed over seven research areas and a total membership of 150. The study is to be continued for four to five years, during which time the center is expected to reach its capacity of 37 research teams. Erdelez plans to collect comparative data over time using several techniques including: online surveys; focus groups; extensive, semi-structured, critical incident interviews; and observations of researchers from selected research teams. As these promisingly rich longitudinal data are awaited, the initial case study shows the research center as a catalyst for forging new contacts and exchanging ideas. However, at this early point in the research, only three of the 20 researchers surveyed spend more than a quarter of their time in collaborative efforts. When asked what types of interactions participants had with others in the center, formal types, including writing and research projects, are reported among those belonging to the same sub-field, while informal interactions, such as eating lunch together, were found across specialties. The primary sources of information for the survey respondents were electronic journals, online databases, and people, as well as conference attendance and the Internet. It will be interesting to monitor the results of subsequent iterations of this study as the research center expands in tandem with developments in the design and delivery of digital communication media.

Blake and Pratt's (2007a, 2007b) ethnographic study of medical and public health researchers writing a systematic literature review sheds further light on how scientists communicate as they work collaboratively. The interviews, direct observations, examination of meeting minutes and e-mail communications, and analyses of worksheets, spreadsheets, and final manuscripts capture four essential tasks needed to produce the article, including: retrieval, extraction, verification, and analysis. These processes are carried out both iteratively and collaboratively, with the medical researchers engaging in more collaboration than their public health peers. To craft their reviews the medical group conducts multiple searches, using several online bibliographic databases as well as manual searching of important journals and the references in each article. They also solicit contributions from experts in the field. Most of the medical group's consensus building occurs during their methodology meetings in which all group members participate. Although e-mail is used to disseminate meeting minutes, it is rarely used to reach a consensus. Less collaboration is seen among the public health researchers, which Blake and Pratt attribute to the diverse qualifications of the group; they are less homogenous than medical scientists. Hara and colleagues (2003) also note that corresponding work interests, skills, and expertise are critical to success in scientific collaboration. These three studies of collaborative work in the sciences (Blake & Pratt, 2007a, 2007b; Erdelez & Means, 2005; Hara et al., 2003) highlight the importance of person-to-person communication, with some assistance from electronic communication technologies, as scientists work together to carry out the activities needed to create the end product of their research, the journal article.

Palmer and colleagues' (2007) several-pronged ethnographic approach takes our understanding of the role of communication in the process of scientific discovery a step further with their extensive study of the information work involved in the practice of brain research. Palmer, Cragin, and Hogan use Herbert Simon's distinction between weak and strong research approaches to frame their study. Weak problem solving is associated with less than ideal circumstances, such as an ill-structured research problem, indistinct procedures, or a lack of domain knowledge; strong problem solving is consistent with a well defined research problem, systematic processes, and a high level of domain knowledge. Data collected by Palmer and colleagues from interviews, observations, online search diaries, and project documents focus on factors that make information important, useful, or difficult to find or use, as well as the social networks through which scientific information flows. A total of 25 brain researchers participated, from four distinct laboratories located at three research universities across the U.S. The key informants are the eleven project leaders; the remaining participants are senior and junior biological and computer scientists, postdoctoral researchers, graduate students, and laboratory technicians and managers. Analyses of the multifaceted data highlight the integral role of information in every task conducted by the neuroscientists from assessing their own and others' work, to integrating background knowledge, to solving instrument problems, to talking formally and informally, and to wrestling with the vast body of neuroscience research literature. Although the integral role of information is not unexpected, the results produced by Palmer, Cragin, and Hogan provide a detailed insider's look at laboratory life similar to that described by Latour and Woolgar 30 years ago. An updated description of the points along the continuum of scientific communication is presented where scientists employ footnote chasing, browsing of texts and bibliographic databases, data mining, and consultation with others in person and via email, both fruitfully and futilely depending on the strength of their research problem, scientific procedures, and subject expertise. It is interesting that these authors pay scant attention to digital modes of scientific communication, concentrating rather on the information behaviors of scientists, regardless of format and delivery mode.

## Concluding Comments

The study of scientific communication has captivated information scientists for over 80 years and continues to fascinate us as we move deeper into the digital era. Awareness of changes in the scientific communication system is critically important to information professionals in their mission to provide the products and services scientists want and need for the creation and dissemination of scientific knowledge. The peer-reviewed journal article has long been the gold standard of scientific communication and although it is common in some fields to disseminate manuscripts online, the peer-reviewed journal article continues to be the lynchpin of the scientific communication process. The studies reviewed here have shown the role of open access journal articles, eprints, conference papers, and data repositories in enhancing the visibility and use of a scientific work by extending accessibility beyond time and space boundaries, but not as a replacement for the peer-reviewed journal article.

Digital information-sharing technologies are thought to hold the potential to alter scientific communication significantly by enabling scientists to participate in worldwide virtual scientific communities. Several initiatives that capitalize on digital sharing tools are worthy of mention, including NIH's mandate to share funded research openly on the Internet as well as Nature Publishing Group's online reference management tool, Connotea. Also of interest for future study is the impact of Create Change, a cooperative educational initiative supported by the Association of Research Libraries and SPARC (Scholarly Publishing and Academic Resources Coalition), which encourages researchers to leverage the digital environment to their advantage (Association of Research Libraries, 2008). Additionally, several institutions are following the lead of Paul Ginsparg's arXiv.org in establishing their own online repositories of scholarly materials produced by their scientists, including e-Scholar (Purdue University, escholar.lib.purdue.edu), Digital Resource Commons (OhioLINK, drc-dev.ohiolink.edu), and MIT OpenCourseWare (web.mit.edu/ocw). The influence of institutional and subject repositories on scientific communication is still uncertain. Harvard University's requirement that their Arts and Science faculty members grant permission for their articles to be available freely online is another interesting development (Lawler, 2008). Possibly the most pervasive influence on scientific communication in the digital era is Google Scholar, which provides scientists around the globe with unprecedented open access to millions of journal articles through a single easy to use portal (scholar.google. com/schhp?hl=en&q=&tab=is). However, how and why scientists use Google Scholar, and how it may be altering their communication practices, has not been fully studied. Two additional innovative digital communication tools, the *Journal of Visualized Experiments* (JoVE, www.jove.com/?sn=BID21) and SciVee (www.scivee.tv), lift scientific research off the printed page and present it in an openly accessible video format. The ability to disseminate and access video-based experimental protocols, lectures, and conferences anytime, anywhere may transform scientific communication in ways the digitization of text alone has not.

The model of scientific communication proposed by Garvey and Griffith (1972) and updated by Hurd (1996, 2000) still holds in the current digital environment. The adoption of digital information sharing technologies by scientists has facilitated but not fundamentally altered communication processes within scientific collaborations and invisible colleges. Nonetheless, the highly volatile nature of the digital infrastructure does not preclude future change.

# References

Almind, T. C., & Ingwersen, P. (1997). Infometric analyses on the World Wide Web: Methodological approaches to "webometrics." *Journal of Documentation*, *53*(4), 404–426.

American Chemical Society. (2006). Publications. Retrieved October 29, 2008, from pubs.acs.org/about.html

Antelman, K. (2004). Do open-access articles have a greater research impact? *College & Research Libraries*, *65*, 372–382.

arXiv.org. (2008). *arXiv monthly submission rate statistics*. Retrieved October 29, 2008, from arxiv.org/show_monthly_submissions

Association of Research Libraries. (2008). Create change. Retrieved June 7, 2008, from www.create change.org

Atkins, D. E., Droegemeier, K. K., Stuart I., Feldman, S. I., Garcia-Molina, H., Klein, M. L., et al. (2003). *Revolutionizing science and engineering through cyberinfrastructure: Report of the National Science Foundation Blue Ribbon Advisory Panel on Cyberinfrastructure*. Arlington, VA: National Science Foundation. Retrieved October 29, 2008 from www.nsf.gov/cise/sci/reports/atkins.pdf

Bar-Ilan, J., & Fink, N. (2005). Preference for electronic format of scientific journals: A case study of the science library users at the Hebrew University. *Library & Information Science Research*, *27*, 363–376.

Blake, C., & Pratt, W. (2007a). Collaborative information synthesis I: A model of information behaviors of scientists in medicine and public health. *Journal of the American Society for Information Science and Technology, 57*(13), 1740–1749.

Blake, C., & Pratt, W. (2007b). Collaborative information synthesis II: Recommendations for information systems to support synthesis activities. *Journal of the American Society for Information Science and Technology, 57*(14), 1888–1895.

Bollen, J., & Van de Sompel, H. (2006). Mapping the structure of science through usage. *Scientiometrics, 69*(2), 227–258.

Bollen, J., Van de Sompel, H., Smith, J. A., & Luce, R. (2005). Toward alternative metrics of journal impact: A comparison of download and citation data. *Information Processing & Management, 41*(6), 1419–1440.

Borgman, C. L., & Furner, J. (2002). Scholarly communication and bibliometrics. *Annual Review of Information Science and Technology, 36*, 2–72.

Braam, R. R., Moed, H. F., & van Raan, A. F. J. (1991a). Mapping of science by combined co-citation and word analysis 1: Structural aspects. *Journal of the American Society for Information Science, 42*(4), 233–251.

Braam, R. R., Moed, H. F., & van Raan, A. F. J. (1991b). Mapping of science by combined co-citation and word analysis 2: Dynamical aspects. *Journal of the American Society for Information Science, 42*(4), 252–266.

Brody, T., Stamerjohanns, H., Harnad, S., Gingras, Y., Vallieres, F., & Oppenheim, C. (2004). *The effect of open access on citation impact.* Paper presented at the meeting of the National Policies on Open Access (OA) Provision for University Research Output: An International Meeting, Southampton University, Southampton UK. Retrieved June 9, 2008, from opcit.eprints.org/feb19oa/brody-impact.pdf

Brown, C. M. (1999). Information seeking behavior of scientists in the electronic information age: Astronomers, chemists, mathematicians, and physicists. *Journal of the American Society for Information Science, 50*(10), 929–943.

Brown, C. M. (2001). The e-volution of preprints in the scholarly communication of physicists and astronomers. *Journal of the American Society for Information Science and Technology, 52*(3), 187–200.

Brown, C. M. (2003a). The changing face of scientific discourse: Analysis of genomic and proteomic database usage and acceptance. *Journal of the American Society for Information Science and Technology, 54*(10), 926–938.

Brown, C. M. (2003b). The role of electronic preprints in chemical communication: Analysis of citation, usage, and acceptance in the journal literature. *Journal of the American Society for Information Science and Technology, 54*(5), 262–271.

Brown, C. M. (2004). The Matthew effect of the annual reviews of series and the flow of scientific communication through the World Wide Web. *Scientometrics, 60*(1), 25–30.

Brown, C. M. (2007). The role of Web based information in the scholarly communication of chemists: Citation and content analyses of American Chemical Society journals. *Journal of the American Society for Information Science and Technology, 58*(13), 2055–2065.

Bush, V. (1945a, July). As we may think. *Atlantic Monthly, 176*, 101–108.

Bush, V. (1945b). As we may think: A top scientist foresees a future world in which man-made machines will start to think. *Life, 19*(11), 112–114, 116, 121, 123–124.

Bush, V. (1945c). Summary of the report to the President on a program for postwar scientific research. *Science, 102*(2639), 79–81.

Butler, D. (1999). US biologists propose launch of electronic preprint archive. *Nature, 397*(6715), 91.

Chan, L., Cuplinskas, D., Eisen, M., Friend, F., Genova, Y., Guédon, J-C., et al. (2002). *The Budapest Open Access Initiative*. Retrieved June 6, 2008, from www.soros.org/openaccess/read.shtml

Covi, L. M. (2000). Debunking the myth of the Nintendo generation: How doctoral students introduce new electronic communication practices into university research. *Journal of the American Society for Information Science, 51*(14), 1284–1294.

Craig, I. D., Plume, A. M., McVeigh, M. E., Pringle, J., & Amin, M. (2007). Do open access articles have greater citation impact? A critical review of the literature. *Journal of Infometrics, 1*, 239–248.

Davis, P. M. (2008). Author-choice open access publishing in the biological and medical literature: A citation analysis. *Journal of the American Society for Information Science and Technology, 59*(14), 1–6.

Davis, P. M., & Fromerth, M. J. (2007). Does the arXiv lead to higher citations and reduced publisher downloads for mathematics articles? *Scientometrics, 71*(2), 203–215.

Davis, P. M., & Price, J. S. (2006). eJournal interface can influence usage statistics: Implications for libraries, publishers, and Project COUNTER. *Journal of the American Society for Information Science and Technology, 57*(9), 1243–1248.

Davis, P. M., & Solla, L. R. (2003). An IP-level analysis of usage statistics for electronic journals in chemistry: Making inferences about user behavior. *Journal of the American Society for Information Science and Technology, 54*(11), 1062–1068.

Drott, M. C. (2006). Open access. *Annual Review of Information Science and Technology, 40*, 79–109.

Duy, J., & Vaughan, L. (2006). Can electronic journal usage data replace citation data as a measure of journal use? An empirical examination. *Journal of Academic Librarianship, 32*, 512–517.

Egghe, L. (2000). New informetric aspects of the Internet: Some reflections—Many problems. *Journal of Information Science, 26*(5), 329–335.

Erdelez, S., & Means, T. (2005). Measuring changes in information sharing among life science researchers. *Proceedings of the 2005 International Conference on Knowledge Management*, 29–40.

Eysenbach, G. (2006). Citation advantage of open access articles. *PLoS Biology, 4*(5), 692–698. Retrieved October 29, 2008, from biology.plosjournals.org/perlserv/?request=get-document&doi=10.1371 %2Fjournal.pbio.0040157

Finholt, T. (2002). Collaboratories. *Annual Review of Information Science and Technology, 36*, 73–107.

Fosmire, M., & Yu, S. (2000). Free scholarly electronic journals: How good are they? *Issues in Science and Technology Librarianship, 27*. Retrieved October 29, 2008, from www.istl.org/00-summer/refereed.html

Garfield, E. (1998, May). *The use of journal impact factors and citation analysis for evaluation of science*. Paper presented at the 41st Annual Meeting of the Council of Biology Editors, Salt Lake City, UT. Retrieved October 29, 2008, from www.garfield.library.upenn.edu/papers/eval_of_science_CBE(Utah).html

Garfield, E. (2001). Impact factors, and why they won't go away. *Nature, 411*, 522.

Garvey, W. D., & Griffith, B. C. (1972). Communication and information processing within scientific disciplines: Empirical findings for psychology. *Information Storage and Retrieval, 8*(3), 123–136.

Giles, C. L., Bollacker, K. D., & Lawrence, S. (1998). CiteSeer: An automatic citation indexing system. *Proceedings of the Third ACM Conference on Digital Libraries*, 89–98.

Ginsparg, P. (1996). *Winners and losers in the global research village*. Paper presented at a conference held at UNESCO Headquarters. Retrieved October 29, 2008, from people.ccmr.cornell.edu/~ginsparg/blurb/pg96unesco.html

Glänzel, W., & Moed, H. F. (2002). Journal impact measures in bibliometric research. *Scientometrics, 53*(2), 171–193.

Glaze, W. H. (1999). Electronic preprint publications. *Environmental Science & Technology, 33*(13), 265a.

Hara, N., Solomon, P., Kim, S. L., & Sonnenwald, D. H. (2003). An emerging view of scientific collaboration: Scientists' perspectives on collaboration and factors that impact collaboration. *Journal of the American Society for Information Science and Technology, 54*(10), 952–965.

Harnad, S. (2008). *The effect of open access and downloads ('hits') on citation impact: A bibliography of studies*. Retrieved October 29, 2008, from opcit.eprints.org/oacitation-biblio.html#brody-harnad04

Harnad, S., & Brody, T. (2004). Comparing the impact of open access (OA) vs. non-OA articles in the same journals. *D-Lib Magazine, 10*(6). Retrieved October 29, 2008, from www.dlib.org/dlib/june04/harnad/06harnad.html

Harter, S. P. (1998). Scholarly communication and electronic journals: An impact study. *Journal of the American Society for Information Science, 49*(6), 507–516.

Hey, T., & Hey, J. (2006). e-Science and its implications for the library community. *Library Hi Tech, 24*(4), 515–528.

Hilgartner, S. (1995). Biomolecular databases: New communication regimes for biology? *Science Communication, 17*(2), 240–263.

Hurd, J. M. (1996). Models of scientific communication systems. In S. Y. Crawford, J. M. Hurd, & A. C. Weller (Eds.), *From print to electronic: The transformation of scientific communication* (pp. 9–33). Medford, NJ: Information Today.

Hurd, J. M. (2000). The transformation of scientific communication: A model for 2020. *Journal of the American Society for Information Science, 51*(4), 1279–1283.

Hyland, K., & Salager-Meyer, F. (2008). Scientific writing. *Annual Review of Information Science and Technology, 42*, 297–338.

Institute for Scientific Information. (2001). *Journal citation reports*. New York: Thomson Scientific.

Jankowski, N. W. (2007). Exploring e-science: An introduction. *Journal of Computer-Mediated Communication, 12*, 549–562.

King, D. W., & Tenopir, C. (1999). Using and reading scholarly literature. *Annual Review of Information Science and Technology, 34*, 423–477.

Kling, R. (2004). The Internet and unrefereed scholarly publishing. *Annual Review of Information Science and Technology, 38*, 591–631.

Kling, R., & Callahan, E. (2003). Electronic journals, the Internet, and scholarly communication. *Annual Review of Information Science and Technology, 37*, 127–177.

Kling, R., & McKim, G. (2000). Not just a matter of time: Field differences and the shaping of electronic media in supporting scientific communication. *Journal of the American Society for Information Science, 51*(14), 1306–1320.

Knorr-Cetina, K. D. (1981). *The manufacture of knowledge: An essay on the constructivist and contextual nature of science*. New York: Pergamon Press.

Koenig, R. (2000). Publishers discuss European e-print site. *Science, 287*(5453), 563–564.

Kousha, K., & Thelwall, M. (2007). Google Scholar citations and Google Web/URL citations: A multi-discipline exploratory analysis. *Journal of the American Society for Information Science and Technology, 58*(7), 1055–1065.

Kousha, K., & Thelwall, M. (2008). Sources of Google Scholar citations outside the *Science Citation Index*: A comparison between four science disciplines. *Scientometrics, 74*(2), 273–294.

Kreitz, P. A., Addis, L., Galic, H., & Johnson, T. (1997). The virtual library in action: Collaborative international control of high-energy physics pre-prints. *Publishing Research Quarterly, 13*(2), 24–32.

Kurata, K., Matsubayashi, M., Mine, S., Muranushi, T., & Ueda, S. (2007). Electronic journals and their unbundled functions in scholarly communication: Views and utilization by scientific, technological and medical researchers in Japan. *Information Processing & Management, 43*(5), 1402–1415.

Kurtz, M. J., Eichhorn, G., Accomazzi, A., Grant, C., Demleitner, M., Henneken, E., et al. (2005). The effect of use and access on citations. *Information Processing & Management, 41*(6), 1395–1402.

Kurtz, M. J., Eichhorn, G., Accomazzi, A., Grant, C., Demleitner, M., & Murray, S. S. (2005). Worldwide use and impact of the NASA Astrophysics Data System digital library. *Journal of the American Society for Information Science and Technology, 56*(1), 36–45.

Lancaster, F. W. (1978). *Toward paperless information systems.* New York: Academic Press.

Landolt, A. U. (1992). UBVRI photometric standard stars in the magnitude range 11.5–16.0 around the celestial equator. *Astronomical Journal, 104,* 340–371.

Latour, B. (1987). *Science in action: How to follow scientists and engineers through society.* Cambridge, MA: Harvard University Press.

Latour, B., & Woolgar, S. (1979). *Laboratory life: The social construction of scientific facts.* Beverly Hills, CA: Sage.

Lawler, A. (2008). Harvard faculty votes to make open access its default mode. *Science, 319*(5866), 1025.

Lawrence, S. (2001). Online or invisible? *Nature, 411*(6837), 521.

Leydesdorff, L. (2004). Clusters and maps of science journals based on bi-connected graphs in journal citation reports. *Journal of Documentation, 60*(4), 371–427.

Lievrouw, L. A., & Carley, K. (1990). Changing patterns of communication among scientists in an era of "telescience." *Technology in Society, 12,* 457–477.

Liu, X., Bollen, J., Nelson, M. L., & Van de Sompel, H. (2005). Co-authorship networks in the digital library research community. *Information Processing & Management, 41*(6), 1462–1480.

Lowry, O. H., Rosebrough, N. J., Farr, A. L., & Randall, R. J. (1951). Protein measurement with the folin phenol reagent. *Journal of Biological Chemistry, 193*(1), 265–275.

Lynch, C. A. (2008). e-Research crosses the pond: Contrasting transformations in the United States and United Kingdom. *Proceedings of the Annual Meeting of the American Society for Information Science and Technology, 45,* NA.

Marshall, E. (1990). Data sharing: A declining ethic? *Science, 248*(4958), 952–957.

Marshall, E. (1999a). NIH weighs bold plan for online preprint publishing. *Science, 283*(5408), 1610–1611.

Marshall, E. (1999b). Researchers plan free global preprint archive. *Science, 286*(5441), 887.

McCain, K. W. (1991). Communication, competition, and secrecy: The production and dissemination of research-related information in genetics. *Science, Technology, & Human Values, 16*(4), 491–516.

McCain, K. W. (1995). Mandating sharing: Journal policies in the natural sciences. *Science Communication, 16*(4), 403–432.

McVeigh, M. E. (2004). *Open access journals in the ISI citation databases: Analysis of impact factors and citation patterns: A citation study from Thomson Scientific.* Retrieved October 29, 2008, from science. thomsonreuters.com/m/pdfs/openaccesscitations2.pdf

Metcalfe, T. S. (2005). The rise and citation impact of astro-ph in major journals. Retrieved October 29, 2008, from arxiv.org/pdf/astro-ph/0503519v1"http://arxiv.org/pdf/astro-ph/0503519v1

Moed, H. F. (2007). The effect of "Open Access" on citation impact: An analysis of arXiv's condensed matter section. *Journal of the American Society for Information Science and Technology, 58*(13), 2047–2054.

Mueller, P. S., Murali, N. S., Cha, S. S., Erwin, P. J., & Ghosh, A. K. (2006). The effect of online status on the impact factors of general internal medicine journals. *Netherlands Journal of Medicine, 64*(2), 39–44.

National Academy of Sciences. (2008). *PNAS open access option*. Retrieved October 29, 2008, from www.pnas.org/site/subscriptions/open-access.shtml

Palmer, C. L., Cragin, M. H., & Hogan, T. P. (2007). Weak information work in scientific discovery. *Information Processing & Management, 43*(3), 808–820.

Peek, R. P., & Pomerantz, J. P. (1998). Electronic scholarly journal publishing. *Annual Review of Information Science and Technology, 33*, 321–356.

Piwowar, H. A., Day, R. S., & Fridsma D. B. (2007). Sharing detailed research data is associated with increased citation rate. *PLoS ONE, 2*(3), e308. Retrieved October 29, 2008, from www.plosone.org/article/info%3Adoi%2F10.1371%2Fjournal.pone.0000308

Price, D. J. D. (1963). *Little science, big science*. New York: Columbia University Press.

Price, D. J. D., & Beaver, D. D. (1966). Collaboration in an invisible college. *American Psychologist, 21*(11), 1011–1018.

Rover, S. (2006). Evolving access: Publishers experiment with immediate open access to articles if author pays. *Chemical & Engineering News, 84*(7), 8.

Schwarz, G. J., & Kennicutt, R. C. (2004). Demographic and citation trends in astrophysical journal papers and preprints. *Bulletin of the American Astronomical Society, 36*, 1654–1663. Retrieved October 29, 2008, from arxiv.org/pdf/astro-ph/0411275v1

Shen, Y. (2006). Scholarly communication in scientific research practice: A study of computer sciences faculty. *Libri, 56*, 239–251.

Smith, E. T. (2003). Changes in faculty reading behaviors: The impact of electronic journals on the University of Georgia. *Journal of Academic Librarianship, 29*(3), 162–168.

Sonnenwald, D. H. (2007). Scientific collaboration: Challenges and solutions. *Annual Review of Information Science and Technology, 41*, 643–682.

Sotudeh, H., & Horri, A. (2007a). The citation performance of open access journals: A disciplinary investigation of citation distribution models. *Journal of the American Society for Information Science and Technology, 58*(13), 2145–2156.

Sotudeh, H., & Horri, A. (2007b). Tracking open access journals evolution: Some considerations in open access data collection validation. *Journal of the American Society for Information Science and Technology, 58*(11), 1578–1585.

Suber, P. (2008). An Open Access mandate for the NIH. *SPARC Open Access Newsletter, 117*. Retrieved October 29, 2008, from www.earlham.edu/~peters/fos/newsletter/01-02-08.htm

Swan, A., & Brown, S. (2005). *Open access self-archiving: An author study*. Retrieved October 29, 2008, from eprints.ecs.soton.ac.uk/10999/01/jisc2.pdf

Tenopir, C., & King, D. W. (2000). *Towards electronic journals: Realities for scientists, librarians, and publishers*. Washington, DC: Special Libraries Association.

Tenopir, C., King, D. W., Boyce, P., Grayson, M., & Paulson, K. L. (2005). Relying on electronic journals: Reading patterns of astronomers. *Journal of the American Society for Information Science and Technology, 56*(8), 786–802.

Tenopir, C., King, D. W., Boyce, P., Grayson, M., Zhang, Y., & Ebuen, M. (2003). Patterns of journal use by scientists through three evolutionary phases. *D-Lib Magazine, 9*(5). Retrieved October 29, 2008, from www.dlib.org/dlib/may03/king/05king.html

Thelwall, M., Vaughan, L., & Björneborn, L. (2005). Webometrics. *Annual Review of Information Science and Technology, 39*, 81–135.

Thomson Reuters. (2008). *Web of science*. New York: Thomson Reuters.

Thomson Scientific. (2005). *Journal Citation Reports quick reference card*. Retrieved October 29, 2008, from scientific.thomson.com/media/scpdf/jcr_0805_q.pdf

Trager, R. (2008, January). NIH battles publishers over open access. *Chemistry World*. Retrieved October 29, 2008, from www.rsc.org/chemistryworld/News/2008/January/22010801.asp

Trimble, V., & Aschwanden, M. J. (2000). Astrophysics in 1999. *Publications of the Astronomical Society of the Pacific, 112*, 434–503.

Van House, N. A. (2004). Science and technology studies and information studies. *Annual Review of Information Science and Technology, 38*, 1–86.

van Raan, A. F. J. (2003). The use of bibliometric analysis in research performance assessment and monitoring of interdisciplinary scientific developments. *Technikfolgenabschätzung: Theorie und Praxis, 1*(12), 20–29. Retrieved October 29, 2008, from www.itas.fzk.de/tatup/031/raan03a.pdf

Vaughan L., & Shaw, D. (2005). Web citation data for impact assessment: A comparison of four science disciplines. *Journal of the American Society for Information Science and Technology, 56*(10), 1075–1087.

Voorbij, H., & Ongering, H. (2006). The use of electronic journals by Dutch researchers: A descriptive and exploratory study. *Journal of Academic Librarianship, 32*, 223–237.

Weinberg, R. A. (1993). Reflections on the current state of data and reagent exchange among biomedical researchers. In National Academy of Sciences, Committee on Science, Engineering and Public Policy, Panel on Scientific Responsibility and the Conduct of Research, *Responsible science: Ensuring the integrity of the research process* (Vol. 2, pp. 66–78). Washington, DC: The Academy.

Weller, A. C. (2005). Electronic scientific information, open access, and editorial peer review: Changes on the horizon? *Science & Technology Libraries, 26*(1), 89–108.

Wilkinson, S. (1998). Web continues to raise publishing issues. *Chemical & Engineering News, 77*(36), 11.

Wren, J. D. (2005). Open access and openly accessible: A study of scientific publications shared via the Internet. *British Medical Journal, 330*, 1128–1132. Retrieved October 29, 2008, from bmj.bmj journals.com/cgi/content/full/330/7500/1128

Yitzhaki, M., & Hammerslag, G. (2004). Accessibility and use of information sources among computer scientists and software engineers in Israel: Academy versus industry. *Journal of the American Society for Information Science and Technology, 55*(9), 832–842.

Youngen, G. K. (1998). Citation patterns to traditional and electronic preprints in the published literature. *College & Research Libraries, 59*(5), 448–456.

Zemke, S. L. (2007). *Academic knowledge sharing on the Web: Webometric analysis of bookmark and tag clustering trends in Connotea.* (Unpublished master's thesis, University of Oklahoma).

Zuccala, A. (2006). Modeling the invisible college. *Journal of the American Society for Information Science and Technology, 57*(2), 152–168.

# CHAPTER 8

# Digital Government

*Scott P. Robertson*
*University of Hawaii at Manoa*

*Ravi K. Vatrapu*
*Copenhagen Business School, Denmark*

## Introduction

> This I hope will be the age of experiments in government, and that
> their basis will be founded in principles of honesty, not of mere force.
> —Thomas Jefferson to John Adams, 1796

"The age of experiments in government" continues apace and is now undergoing dramatic changes that would have fascinated Jefferson and his contemporaries. Digital government, also often called e-government, refers to the application of information and communication technology (ICT) to the practice of government and to research in this area. In the long run, the impact of digital government might be to increase civic participation and revolutionize democratic practice, or it might be to create greater inequity among citizens and increase the power of police states, or it might be simply to streamline existing processes and practices. Of course, it will be all of these things and more. As in Jefferson's time, the possibilities of revolutionary practices, the ideas that they engender, and the threats that they pose are tremendous. It is an exciting time to be involved with digital government, and the goal of this chapter is to communicate the issues and the challenges, and perhaps to engender in small measure the thrill and trepidation that Jefferson, Adams, and their contemporaries must have felt as they embarked on their "experiment."

The chapter is organized into six sections. We begin with a discussion of information in government because in the context of government the role of ICT is to support the dissemination of information and the exchange of knowledge among citizens, between citizens and their government, and among government entities. We next make an attempt to explain what "digital government" encompasses. A single definition of digital government is impossible; therefore, this section contrasts various definitions in the literature, examines goals and purposes of digital government applications, and identifies stakeholders and scope. We also explore what distinguishes e-government applications from, for example, e-commerce applications or the ICT needs of other large organizations (e.g., streamlining interoffice operations or computerizing records). The next section argues that current digital government efforts originated in early attempts, now largely abandoned, to build "digital cities" online. This section also looks at the dramatic growth in the use of ICT for interaction with government entities and politicians. The next section is a wide-ranging treatment of "e-participation," covering digital citizenship, political campaigning online, electronic voting, e-rulemaking, political information seeking, blogging, social networking, and the possibility of virtual public spheres inhabited by non-co-located "netizens." After briefly examining the digital government-related technologies of geographic information systems and urban simulation, we conclude by looking at challenges such as access inequities, trust, power, and civic identity.

## Information and Government

Bimber (2003) describes the central role of "information" in Alexander Hamilton's *The Federalist*, a pre-constitution treatise meant to convince the public about the merits of a federal republic for the emerging United States. He points out that the word "information" appears "about three dozen times in *The Federalist*" (p. 35) and that the importance of information is emphasized in a wide variety of areas including manufacturing, commerce, taxation, the distribution of citizens across large distances, the power of factions, and politics. The concept of a single democratic polity distributed over such a vast geographical expanse as was envisioned by the Founding Fathers (more vast than they imagined, as it turned out) was novel and problematic. The structure of the federal government, particularly the Electoral College, can be seen in part as an information and knowledge management solution of the time, in addition to its role as a process for implementing representative democracy in a geographically sprawling country.

In the next century, the United States introduced systems of relatively inexpensive daily newspapers and universal, flat-rate mail service that greatly expanded the information environment (Fang, 1997; Schudson, 1998). Some scholars argue that these early information technologies deeply influenced citizens' feeling of common identity and sense of democratic purpose (Bimber, 2003; Schudson, 1998). In modern times, of course, radio and then television have been the dominant communication technologies. Their influence on government and politics has been widely studied (Ansolabehere, Iyengar, & Behr, 1993; Norris, 1996; Patterson, 1993; Putnam, 1995) and will not be discussed further here except to note that these technologies are non-collaborative, one-way, broadcast technologies. The information and communication technology that concerns us in this chapter is digital technology: the Internet and all of its manifestations (email, the World Wide Web, instant messaging, social networking, and virtual worlds) and mobile information and communication technologies such as cell phones and global positioning systems. There is no question that these technologies are becoming more central to the way governments work now and will work in the future (Agre, 2002; Alvarez & Hall, 2004; Fountain, 2001, 2006; Jaeger, 2005).

Digital technologies have had an impact on all of the issues that Hamilton described in *The Federalist* (manufacturing, commerce, taxation, distance, social cohesion, and politics) and more; their influence only underscores the Founding Fathers' prescience with regard to information dissemination and equitable knowledge distribution. Before beginning our exploration, however, we should note that the rosy picture just presented is the utopian dimension of a multi-dimensional value space for digital government. The dystopian analysis of digital government includes issues such as mass surveillance, privacy and security, trustworthiness, information warfare, and information equity. Many digital government applications, particularly after the September 11th attacks in the United States, have both a bright side and a dark side. Familiar examples might include the REAL ID program (Egelman & Cranor, 2005) or face recognition and government terrorist watch lists (Bowyer, 2004). Many of these problems currently hinder the progress of digital government while restraining the potential for coercion and disruption.

# What Is Digital Government?

## Definitions

Digital government, often called e-government (with no standardized use of hyphens or capitals), encompasses the use of information and communication technologies to enable citizens, politicians, government agencies, and other organizations to work with each other and to carry out activities that support civic life. This seems simple enough but disagreements have emerged.

The broadest definitions of digital government tend to emphasize the stakeholders and desirable outcomes of technology deployment:

> E-government is the use of information technology to support government operations, engage citizens, and provide government services.
> —Center for Technology in Government (2008, online)

> eGovernment is defined … as the use of information and communication technologies in public administrations combined with organisational change and new skills in order to improve public services and democratic processes and strengthen support to public policies.
> —The Commission of the European Communities (2003, online)

> "E-Government" refers to the use by government agencies of information technologies (such as wide area networks, the Internet, and mobile computing) that have the ability to transform relations with citizens, businesses, and other arms of government. These technologies can serve a variety of different ends: better delivery of government services to citizens, improved interactions with business and industry, citizen empowerment through access to information, or more efficient government management. The resulting benefits can be less corruption, increased transparency, greater convenience, revenue growth, and/or cost reductions.
> —World Bank (2009, online)

From these definitions we can deduce that the major stakeholders for digital government are citizens, administrative bodies within government, and businesses. The aims are typical for ICT deployment: streamlining and simplifying administrative processes, cost cutting, improving services, and generally improving efficiency.

Some unique items appear in these definitions as well, such as improving democratic processes, decreasing corruption, and engaging citizens. These latter goals for digital government are widely studied and will be a focus of this chapter.

## An Interdisciplinary Endeavor

Digital government is a highly interdisciplinary field. A glance at the references for this chapter (and any of their bibliographies) will show that the research is being conducted in the social sciences, political science, psychology, library science, information science, and other areas (see also Heeks & Bailur, 2007). It is a mix of basic and applied research. A serious study of digital government also requires inspection of many nontraditional publication venues for academics, including consultant reports, marketing surveys, and popular media. The field is concerned with basic questions such as how people process political information; applied questions such as how to integrate disparate information sources; political questions about how e-government might change democratic processes; philosophical questions about ethics and values; public policy questions such as how to encourage acceptance and increase awareness; and sociological questions about privacy, trustworthiness, and equity. A large part of the field is technical and legislative, encompassing questions such as how to integrate diverse data centers or how to modify laws. The methods employed in understanding and advancing digital government include surveys, empirical experimentation, prototype development and iterative testing, human factors engineering, focus groups and questionnaires, policy planning and enactment, legislative action, statistical modeling, persuasive rhetoric, action research, and actual deployment and usage of systems.

Some definitions of digital government stress the interdisciplinary nature of applications. For example, Dawes, Gregg, and Agouris (2004, p. 5) describe digital government as involving the "intersections of computer and information sciences, related social, political, and behavioral sciences, and the problems and missions of government agencies." Heeks and Bailur (2007, p. 252) say that "e-government can be seen as sitting at the crossroads between a number of other research domains, particularly computer science, information systems, public administration, and political science"; their examination of a large sample of research papers in e-government demonstrates that researchers come from many academic departments and non-academic entities as shown in Table 8.1.

Being interdisciplinary is often considered a sign of vibrancy and topicality; however, it can also be a source of confusion and, because of distributed and non-overlapping publication venues, a path to disconnected and redundant research and theory (Dawes, et al., 2004; Flak, Sein, & Sæbø, 2007; Scholl, 2006). Only recently has e-government begun to be recognized as a field in itself, as evidenced by the establishment of refereed journals, annual conferences, guides, and case studies (Bhatnagar, 2004; Gil-Garcia & Pardo, 2005; Jong & Lentz, 2005), overviews (McIver & Elmagarmid, 2001; West, 2005), and attempts at scoping problems (Dawes, Bloniarz, Kelly, & Fletcher, 2002; Dawes & Préfontaine, 2003; Schorr & Stolfo, 2000).

Table 8.1  Sources of research papers on digital government (from Heeks & Bailur, 2007)

| | |
|---|---|
| Business/management | 15% |
| Public administration | 13% |
| Political science | 11% |
| Computer science | 11% |
| Library and information studies | 8% |
| E-government | 8% |
| Information systems | 7% |
| Government/governance | 5% |
| Non-academic research institutions | 4% |
| Other | 18% |

## *Evolution*

Many analyses of digital government identify dimensions that can also be seen as evolutionary steps or developmental stages (Gil-Garcia & Martinez-Moyano, 2007; Hiller & Bélanger, 2001; Layne & Lee, 2001; Moon, 2002; Holden, Norris, & Fletcher, 2003). For example, focusing on citizens and government agencies, Elmagarmid and McIver (2001) characterize four stages in the evolution of services provided to clients:

- One-way communication with citizens to information about an agency or aspect of government

- Two-way communication for uncomplicated data collection such as gathering public comments

- More complex transactional services that have binding legal repercussions such as voter registration or motor vehicle licensing

- Integrated services across a whole government administration

With an interest in benchmarking the development of e-government initiatives, the U.N. identifies five stages of development (Ronaghan, 2002; United Nations, 2008):

- Emerging: Limited and static information; departmental webpages with no interaction

- Enhanced: Regularly updated information on public policy and governance; links provided to archives of documents, forms, reports, laws, etc.

- Interactive: Online services, form downloading, communication and limited transactions are supported

- Transactional: True two-way G2C [government-to-citizen] and C2G [citizen-to-government] communication and services such as passport and license renewals, paying taxes, and many payment-for-service transactions

- Connected: Total integration of all services across administrative and departmental boundaries; backoffice integration of departments and cross-unit information sharing

Marchionini, Samet, and Brandt (2003) distinguished among three broad categories of digital government activities:

- Access to information

- Transaction services

- Citizen participation

The first two reflect services similar to those described by Elmagarmid and McIver (2001), but the third is a new type of activity that includes citizen deliberation and characterizes many of the newest, Web 2.0-style applications of information technology to government (see also H. Chen, 2002; Eggers, 2005).

Layne and Lee (2001) see the development of e-government as evolutionary, with an increasingly complex dimension of technical capability and an increasingly complete dimension of inter-organizational integration. They describe four stages of growth for e-government of increasing technical complexity and integration:

- Catalogue: Online presence, catalogue presentation, downloadable forms

- Transaction: Services and forms online, working database supporting online transactions

- Vertical integration: Local systems linked to higher level systems within similar functionalities

- Horizontal integration: Systems integrated across different functions, real one-stop shopping for citizens

All of these stage analyses start with the provision of documents and static information. In some ways this is the "low hanging fruit" of digital government, the transfer of information between government agencies and from government agencies to citizens and to businesses in a more efficient manner. Closely related is enabling citizens to conduct basic transactions with government agencies. These applications closely resemble traditional enterprise architecture and e-commerce applications: Their purpose is to streamline the processes of information provision and service transaction and make them less costly through automation. Governments have lagged behind business in the transition from informational to transactional services. Digital information provision is mature in many national and state government sectors but transactional services vary considerably across federal agencies and are found less reliably at state and local levels (Holden, Norris, & Fletcher, 2003; Reddick, 2004a, 2004b).

## Applications and Purpose

The contexts of use of digital government services are as broad as the range of users. Digital government applications are relevant to local, national, and international government entities. In addition, governance is important to a host of private and commercial entities, some of which are quasi-official (e.g., community watch) or community-like (e.g., condominium associations), and some of which are purely commercial (e.g., company boards).

In addition to stages of development, several definitions offer a catalogue of application areas or aspects of government involvement that are affected by digital government. For example, the Center for Technology in Government identifies the following four dimensions of digital government (Dawes, 2002, p. 2):

- E-services: The electronic delivery of government information, programs, and services often (but not exclusively) over the Internet

- E-democracy: The use of electronic communications to increase citizen participation in the public decision-making process

- E-commerce: The electronic exchange of money for goods and services such as citizens paying taxes and utility bills, renewing vehicle registrations, and paying for recreation programs, or government buying supplies and auctioning surplus equipment

- E-management: The use of information technology to improve the management of government, from streamlining business processes to maintaining electronic records, to improving the flow and integration of information

The Center for Digital Government (www.centerdigitalgov.com), a consultancy that rates states and municipalities on their capabilities, uses several categories that illuminate the breadth of digital government applications:

- Social services: Availability of online information regarding program eligibility and applications procedures; application of digital technologies, such as electronic benefit transfer systems

- Law enforcement and the courts: Availability of online information regarding digital technologies by the judicial system, including online access to court opinions and the use of digital communications by police agencies

- Digital democracy: Application of digital technologies to permit Internet access to laws, candidate information, and electronic voting technologies

- Electronic commerce and business regulation: Availability of regulations, forms, and online assistance; the ability to submit required paperwork and payments; and the status of portals and e-procurement systems

- Management and administration: Adoption of new information technologies with applicability across programs and agencies; investment in long-term information technology infrastructure

- Taxation and revenue: Ability of taxpayers to obtain information, submit returns and payments online; ability of states to use digital technologies to store and retrieve taxpayer information

- Education: Utilization of digital technologies for educational purposes, including the provision of online access for administrative functions such as student admissions, financial aid and course registration, access to the Internet, and access to school performance measures; also utilization of distance education programs

- Geographic information system (GIS) and transportation: Utilization of digital technologies for mapping and management tools for storing and analyzing data for economic development, law enforcement, fire and transportation, and intelligent transportation and transportation systems

Categories not included here, but which should be considered parts of digital government, include:

- Emergency management: Utilization of digital technologies to monitor activities and situations, provide services, obtain and disseminate information, control and track resources, and maintain communications and coordination during large-scale emergencies

- Transparency: Providing citizens the means to learn what actions are being taken, considered, or scrutinized by politicians and legislators; citizens' ability to find and track the history of legislation and other deliberative matters and to find positions and votes of law makers and other government entities

- Community and neighborhood support: Supporting citizens to self-organize at local levels using common platforms that are easy to understand, provide Internet working capabilities, and promote a sense of local civic life

- Military or paramilitary

- Medical and healthcare

- Urban planning and development

- Land and resource management

## Unique Aspects of Digital Government

Many issues and problems encountered in digital government applications are similar to those encountered in other IT contexts. However, digital government has several unique properties. A report from the National Research Council Committee on Computing and Communications Research to Enable Better Use of Information

Technology in Government (2002) suggests the following areas in which e-government applications differ from commercial applications:

- Ubiquity: The need to provide services to all citizens.

- Trustworthiness: Confidentiality, privacy, and trust are important to gaining citizen compliance (e.g., taxes, census) and central to some aspects of government (e.g., intelligence, military).

- Information heterogeneity and semantic interoperability: This is an issue for all large-scale IT adopters, but in government there is often a need for ad-hoc cooperation (e.g., local, state, and federal response to emergencies) and long-standing agency independence and resistance to cooperation.

- Providing software interfaces to services: Agreed-upon and public APIs (application programming interfaces) and structured data representation.

- Building large-scale systems: Governmental systems are usually extremely large and must work correctly the first time.

To this list, we might add:

- Legislative and constitutional relevance: Government systems are subject to complex legal and constitutional guidelines and constraints, which are subject to change (Cresswell & Pardo, 2001; Olbrich & Simon, 2008).

- Public-private boundary spanning: Information technologies for use in the government sphere are often developed by private companies (e.g., tax software, voting machines) and thus become subject to public scrutiny.

## Users and Stakeholders

Digital government involves many stakeholders and several levels of application complexity. Some problems and the applications being developed to solve them, such as use of electronic mail within Congress or the digitization of government documents, are essentially the same as those encountered in large businesses. However, many applications are unique to the domain of government and citizenship, for example, electronic voting, digitally mediated political discourse, and electronic defense and large-scale emergency response.

The stakeholder analysis presented in Figure 8.1 comes from a RAND corporation benchmarking study of e-government initiatives in the U.S. and Europe (Graafland-Essers & Ettedgui, 2003). The three major stakeholders identified in this study, common to many analyses, are citizens, businesses, and government entities. Communication flows are identified between the pairings relevant to e-government. Graafland-Essers & Ettedgui (2003, p. 15) describe illustrative applications as follows:

- GtG (government-to-government): Back office, intra- and intergovernmental exchange, government networks, standards, expertise

- GtB (government-to-business): Delivery of business services and information, e-procurement (tendering), sales of government-owned business-relevant information

- BtG (business-to-government): Filing of business registration information, taxes, regulatory information, etc.

- CtG (citizen-to-government): Citizen information provision, tax filing, citizen reporting, electronic voting (e-democracy), vehicle licensing

- GtC (government-to-citizen): Provision of public information and transparency of information (both passive and active) about government workings and performance, electronic service delivery (including "one-stop shops")

An immediate question arises from the RAND analysis: What about the missing links, specifically BtB (business-to-business), BtC (business-to-citizen), and CtC (citizen-to-citizen)? BtB and BtC are arguably private matters in the domain of e-commerce. However, CtC is a rich area for digital government activity. Governments will not necessarily seek to support citizen-to-citizen political involvement within their own systems (hence the absence of this linkage in the RAND study); however, it is evolving within more general purpose social networking and other forms of ICT.

Within the various stakeholder groups, we may make several distinctions with regard to information needs. Citizens have administrative needs such as licensing and permitting; they receive social services from government and pay taxes; they require information and transactional processes to participate in governance through elections. Businesses have similar licensing and permitting, taxing, and benefit needs. Government is actually a diverse set of stakeholders, including government offices and agencies, elected representatives, and political candidates. Although we

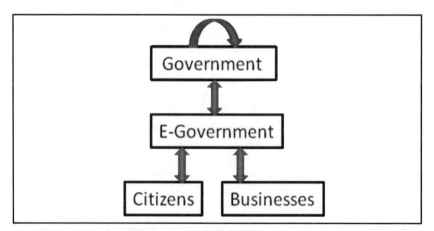

Figure 8.1   USA.gov, the Internet portal for the U.S. government, is organized by stakeholders and tasks.

do not focus on them in this chapter, the judicial, legislative, and military aspects of government have their own various information needs and stakeholders.

Flak and colleagues (2007) provide a more nuanced analysis of e-government stakeholders by subcategorizing the entities of *government* and *citizen*. Government stakeholders are categorized as *politicians, administrators,* and *service administrators.* Citizens are categorized as [information] *consumers, activists,* and *direct decision makers.* The authors point out that the demands for digital government services will differ depending on the communication pathways between these entities. For example, a politician addressing citizen activists is engaged in a very different activity from an administrator addressing information consumers, even though these both count as G2C pathways in many stakeholder analyses. Understanding the nature of all combinations of transactions leads to different practical and theoretical considerations for e-government applications.

To citizens, government, and business we should add non-governmental entities that have considerable interaction with government, or which serve as liaisons between citizen or business interests and the government. These include non-governmental organizations (NGOs), think tanks and academic entities with political purpose, and a growing number of intermediaries such as lobbyists and what we might call political information intermediaries such as the League of Women Voters or VoteSmart.com. Non-citizens may also be stakeholders in digital government sites. Visitors have many information and transaction needs as tourists or temporary visa holders.

The USA.gov portal (Figure 8.2) uses stakeholders as a primary organizational tool. Tabs along the top of the website identify four primary stakeholder groups and submenus activated by each tab further specify these groups as follows:

- Citizens
  - Kids
  - Teens
  - Parents
  - Seniors
  - Military and veterans
  - Americans abroad
  - Media
  - More (includes 27 subcategories)
- Businesses and nonprofits
  - Self-employed
  - Nonprofits
  - Corporations
  - Foreign businesses in the U.S.

- More (includes 10 subcategories)
- Government employees
  - Federal employees
  - Military and veterans
  - State and local employees
  - Tribal governments
- Visitors to the U.S.

The content available on a page, in particular the forms available and the tasks supported, differs with the stakeholder tab and subcategory selected.

## A Young, International Field

Digital government as a coherent area of research and development is relatively new. Although seriously envisioned as far back as 1978 (Nora & Minc,

**Figure 8.2   Stakeholder analysis of digital government systems (after Graafland-Essers & Ettedgui, 2003)**

1980), governments have been slow to adopt information and communication technologies. In 1993, the United States embarked on a project known as the National Information Infrastructure (NII) which was designed to achieve "the integration of hardware, software, and skills that will make it easy and affordable to connect people with each other, with computers, and with a vast array of services and information resources" (Clinton, 1993, online). The NII was often described as an enabling infrastructure on the order of the interstate highway or telephone system (Moeller, 1993; Simons, 1994; Weingarten, 1994). The needs of information users were described as (Malhotra, Al-Shehri, & Jones, 1995, online, section 3):

- Searching, discovering, updating, transforming, and retrieving useful information

- Building and maintaining electronic repositories of information

- Creating and distributing information electronically

- Executing and recording commercial, legal, financial, and other business transactions

- Supporting collaborative work efforts among collocated or remote individuals

In the United States, many local and state government websites and Internet-based information and service portals were developed throughout the 1990s. At the federal level, the United States enacted the Paperwork Reduction Act (1995), a major step toward digitization of government documents. The Government Paperwork Elimination Act (1998, Section 3504(a)(1)(B)(vi)) required, among other things, that government agencies develop "alternative information technologies that provide for electronic submission, maintenance, or disclosure of information as a substitute for paper" and that within five years all executive agencies "provide for the option of electronic maintenance, submission, or disclosure of information as a substitute for paper and for the use and acceptance of electronic signatures."

These acts were technology neutral but the overwhelming interpretation was that agencies should make documents and forms available on the Internet in familiar digital forms (e.g., pdf, html) and that they should be searchable with traditional search tools. In 1998, the Clinton administration instructed all executive departments and agencies to "make available online ... the forms needed for the top 500 government services used by the public" and further directed that "transactions with the Federal Government should be available online for online processing services." In a surprising recognition of the issue of usability, the same memorandum said that the data should be "identified and organized in a way that makes it easier for the public to find the information it seeks" and even specified that government information should be "organized not by agency, but by the type of service or information that people may be seeking" (Clinton, 1999, online).

In 1999, the Computer Science and Telecommunications Board (CSTB) of the National Academies of Science convened a Committee on Computing and Communications Research to Enable Better Use of Information Technology in Government (National Research Council, Computer Science and Telecommunications

Board, 1999, 2000). In 1998, the National Science Foundation recognized the importance of digital government as a research priority by establishing the Digital Government Research Program and funding the creation of the Digital Government Research Center (DGRC), a series of annual conferences, and a set of research projects in various areas of digital government. In 2006 the Digital Government Society of North America was established as an independent entity to continue the digital government annual conferences and serve as a professional society for researchers and practitioners in this area.

In September, 2000, the U.S. federal government launched FirstGov (www.first gov.gov), which at the time of launch provided integrated access to 47 million federal government Web pages in addition to links for many state, local, tribal, and District of Columbia pages (Garson, 2006). The E-Government Act of 2002 (H.R. 2458/S. 803) contained directives involving cross-agency initiatives: E-Rulemaking, Geospatial One-Stop, E-Records Management, E-Authentication, and FirstGov. The act also directed federal agencies to seek integration and interoperability with e-government efforts at state, local, and tribal levels.

The member states of the European Union (EU) have approached the development of e-government as a cooperative undertaking (Chadwick & May, 2003), addressing problems of interoperability and common vision at the outset. However, it adds a layer of complexity involving different languages, cultural practices, and even forms of government. In 1999, the European Commission of the EU launched an initiative to "bring the benefits of the Information Society to all Europeans" (European Union, 1999, online). The resulting *eEurope 2002 Action Plan* targeted three main objectives relevant to e-government (European Union, 2000, 2003):

- Cheaper, faster, and secure Internet

- Investing in people and skills

- Stimulating the use of the Internet

The plan was revised and updated for 2005 (European Union, 2002) and again for 2010 (European Union, 2005). Current research and development in the area of e-government is occurring under a strategy known as "i2020," with the following goals (European Union, 2005):

- Create a single European information space, which promotes an open and competitive internal market for information society and media services

- Strengthen innovation and investment in ICT research

- Support inclusion, better public services, and quality of life through the use of ICT

European digital government initiatives place a strong emphasis on supporting citizen participation (Coleman & Blumler, 2008; Coleman & Gøtze, 2001; Westholm, 2002), often referred to as "e-participation" or "e-democracy." In 2006, the Commission funded an ongoing effort, DEMO-net (www.demo-net.org), to promote and coordinate research and practice in the area of digital government throughout the European Union (Wimmer, 2007).

Other regions, specifically Asia, Africa, the Middle East, and Latin America, have no overarching digital government efforts similar to those in North America or the European Union; many countries do, however, have their own independent efforts (Forlano, 2004). Also, although North America and the EU are composed of liberal democracies that share common views about the fundamentals of government, the same cannot be said of the other regions mentioned, and it is therefore impossible to make generalizations about "Asian e-government" or "Latin American e-government," or even to say that one country's efforts are a model for another country in the area. However, Brown University's annual survey of e-government websites in 198 countries (West, 2007) ranks South Korea, Singapore, and Taiwan as the top three in terms of a range of features (the United States and Great Britain were fourth and fifth).

In Asia, Singapore was an early adopter of e-government technology. Singapore's eCitizen portal, launched in 1999, grew out of the Ministry of Finance's interest in e-commerce (Devadoss, Pan, & Huang, 2002). Singapore's eCitizen was one of the first to adopt the organizational concept of a "life event portal" (Vintar & Leben, 2002, p. 383; see also Lips, 2001) in which sections are organized by important actions in a citizen's life that might involve the government, such as getting married, becoming a parent, setting up a business, buying and selling property, or moving. Figure 8.3 shows the "Citizens & Residents" page of eCitizen. Note that the site is organized by stakeholders, represented by tabs along the top of the page, and life events, represented as links in the "Government Services" subsections.

In anticipation of the 2008 Olympics, and in a general push to modernize, China has moved aggressively since 2000 to develop "Digital Beijing" in particular and more generally to develop digital government initiatives across the country (X. Chen, 2002). The primary goal of these initiatives is economic development (Yuan, Zhang, & Zheng, 2004). Ma, Chung, and Thorson (2004) argue that China is pursuing seemingly contradictory goals: administrative decentralization and streamlining and also increased monitoring and control on the other.

India's National e-Governance Plan was launched in 2006. In contrast to China's and Singapore's efforts—which are aimed primarily at educated, literate, and technically sophisticated citizens—India's vision includes the goal of bringing digital government to illiterate, rural areas (Goswami, 2002) as well as to cities.

The United Nations (2008, p. 18) has developed an e-government readiness index, which assesses 189 countries in terms of "1. Their institutional capacity, leadership role, and willingness to engage their citizens by supporting and marketing participatory decision-making for public policy; and 2. The structures that are in place which facilitate citizens' access to public policy dialogue." The United States led in this ranking among the 189 countries until 2008, when Sweden, Denmark, and Norway took the top three positions (followed by the United States). Europe leads other regions in e-government readiness by a wide margin, followed by the Americas, Asia, Oceana, and Africa. The *UN E-Government Survey 2008* (United Nations, 2008) provides an excellent overview of the status of many international e-government efforts.

Figure 8.3 eCitizen, the Internet portal for the government of Singapore, is organized by stakeholders and life events.

# Origins and Growth

## Digital Cities and Community Networks as Origins

The evolution of digital government in the United States has been very much bottom-up. Before large-scale initiatives such as the NII, cities and municipalities had begun to experiment with electronic government and digital communities. Regional information networks (as opposed to community networks, construed more generally) are digital communities tied to a physical location, usually a town or city. The early 1970s Community Memory project in Berkeley, California, was the first regional electronic bulletin board (Farrington & Pine, 1997). In the 1980s, the Free Net project in Cleveland, Ohio, became the progenitor of a multifaceted regional information network in the United States (Ishida, Aurigi, Yasuoka, 2003). The network was not tied to government services in any way, but was intended as a local public space for citizens to meet. The advent of the World Wide Web changed everything for regional information networks and, according to Ishida and colleagues, over 300 Web-based city networks had developed by 1998. Political discourse emerged early on the Internet and researchers quickly imagined what the emergence of a new, more egalitarian, electronic public sphere might mean for politics (Abramson, Arterton, & Orren, 1988; Downing, 1989; Garramone, Harris, & Anderson, 1986; Meadow, 1986; Myers, 1993; O'Sullivan, 1995).

The Blacksburg Electronic Village (BEV) serves as an excellent (and extensively studied) example of a community-level regional information network that developed as the Web matured and Internet access began to spread more broadly throughout the population (Carroll & Rosson, 1996; Shuler, 1996). Early "digital cities" typically consisted of a Web portal offering access to community information such as bus schedules or library hours, administrative information such as license application forms, and tourist and shopping information such as downtown maps and local business promotions. More successful digital city applications included interactive components such as bulletin boards and e-mail.

In Europe and Asia, digital city applications usually involved government entities from the outset. *De Digitale Stad* (DDS) of Amsterdam was launched in 1994 and served as Europe's paradigm for a regional information network (Ishida, 2000; Ishida et al., 2003). The city government and the Dutch Ministry of Economic Affairs provided initial funding for the project; its goals from the beginning included the involvement of citizens in public dialogue and debate. Each user of DDS had an individual homepage and DDS used a physical metaphor of a city (not a real city!) as an interface. The developers were engaged to some degree in political activism; one of their explicit goals was to encourage more widespread political participation using new media and ICTs.

Helsinki, Finland, developed a virtual city application in 1995, modeling the actual city and using it as an interface metaphor. The City Hall of 1805, which was no longer in existence, was created as a virtual space online at the center of Helsinki's digital city.

In an effort to prevent the wheel from being reinvented, the European Commission supported the formation of "Telecities" to collect best practices and serve as a common forum for developers of digital cities across Europe. Miller (1996, online) summarized the goal of Telecities:

> Telecities is based on the familiar premise that telematics, as information technology applications are called in Europe, can play a key role in improving administration, health care, economic development, and other government functions. Local European political leaders are also realizing that technology can facilitate dialogue between the government and the governed.

This goal statement highlights differences between European digital cities and American ones. The European sense of government's scope is much broader and often includes issues and institutions such as health care, education, transportation, parks and public squares, art, and museums. Local economic development and well being, although important to European digital cities, were integrated with these many other facets of the urban fabric. This makes European digital cities more interesting and perhaps vibrant, but also more complicated to develop and maintain.

By the end of the 1990s, the regional information network movement, especially in America, had been overshadowed by large commercial information providers such as America Online (AOL) (which trademarked the term "Digital City" for its enterprise) and Microsoft ("Sidewalk") and its "cityguide" emphasis on recreational, tourist, and commercial activities. Aurigi (2000, p. 43) warned that the fate of the digital city could well be to become "a civic database, a glossy brochure to promote bits of the real town, [or] a nice exercise of 3D modeling." (In Europe and Asia, digital city applications usually involved government entities from the outset [see Aurigi (2005) for an excellent history of European digital cities].) However, these types of regional commercial portals now integrate community information with user-generated comments and recommendations in a mash-up of social network and community network technologies and are working toward migration to mobile applications. The e-mail and bulletin board functions that these networks provided have also been "outgrown" now that personal e-mail and various forms of social networking systems are ubiquitous. The extent to which "cityguide" applications still have anything to do with digital government is questionable, although they clearly stand at the beginning of the digital government movement and provide many best-practice guidelines and lessons.

Van den Besselaar and Beckers (1998, p. 108) sum up the fate of digital cities: "use of the Digital City is mainly recreational, and not yet integrated with other aspects of daily life" (see also van den Besselaar, 2001). The fate of digital cities may be tied to the different needs of governments at the local level versus those at the state and federal levels. Local governments have more concerns about economic and recreational outreach, neighborhood awareness and community building, and day-to-day activities of citizens than state or national governments. Social networking applications that integrate these local government issues with the rest of citizens' lives have made more progress than the planned communities of the digital cities era. At the same time that digital cities' Internet presence was diminishing, national and state governments were committing increasing resources to develop digital applications for their own needs. It is at these levels that we currently see the most growth in e-government applications supported by government resources. It would be a mistake, however, to ignore the use of new social networking technologies that are not specifically aimed at e-government.

## Adoption of Digital Government Applications

Adoption of digital government applications, particularly the early phases of information and transaction provision, can be measured from the supply side and the demand side (Reddick, 2004b; Thomas & Streib, 2003). The supply side refers to the governments and municipalities that have adopted digital government technologies. Moon (2002) examined data from a survey of 2,899 municipal governments conducted in 2000 by International City/County Management Association and Public Technology, Inc., which asked about e-government adoption. He found that 85 percent of municipal governments had websites but that only 8 percent actually had a strategic e-government plan. In this survey, only 97 municipal governments (3 percent) had moved from information dissemination to transaction services, and many of those did not offer transactions that required processing of financial information.

In the arena of G2C communications, West (2005, 2008) has tracked the websites of 198 nations around the world since 2001. West documents tremendous growth in both online information provision (Figure 8.4), including most recently multimedia content, and online booking services, passport ordering, change of address, benefits applications, and tax services. Growth is most pronounced in North America, followed in order by Asia, Pacific Ocean Islands, Western Europe, South America, the Middle East, Central America, Russia and Central Asia, Eastern Europe, and Africa.

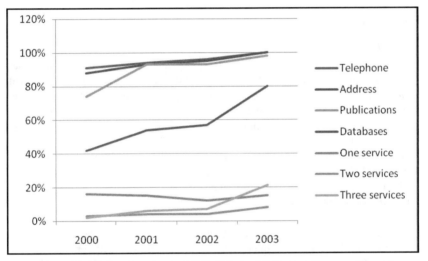

**Figure 8.4    Growth in percentage of U.S. state and federal online provision of different types of information and services over four years (data from West, 2008)**

In terms of C2G communications, a comprehensive 2004 survey of how Americans contacted government (Horrigan, 2004) showed that 29 percent had utilized websites in contrast to 42 percent who used the telephone. Some 54 percent of all Americans contact a government agency (for reasons other than taxes) in a typical year, the number of regular "Internet users" who contact government or search for information from government agencies was 77 percent, up 50 percent from one year earlier. The increase is due in part to increased communication of citizens' opinions to policy makers, suggesting that the availability of C2G e-government technologies increases political involvement. The following activities were listed as most frequent:

- 66 percent are looking for information from federal, state, or local government websites.

- 41 percent are doing research using government documents or statistics.

- 34 percent are finding recreational or tourist information.

- 28 percent are getting advice about health or safety issues.

- 27 percent are sending an e-mail.

- 23 percent are applying for benefits.

According to the survey, use of e-government websites and e-mail was more prevalent for federal-level information, followed by state-level information, followed by local-level information. There is no analysis of the differential availability of information and services at these different levels, however.

# E-Participation

## Citizens

E-participation refers to the use of ICTs by citizens to influence government, usually through elections, and ICT use by politicians and candidates for political office to reach citizens. The Pew Internet and American Life Project has been tracking Americans' use of the Internet to obtain political news since 2000. Figure 8.5 depicts the percentage of all adults who reported using the Internet in this way across several surveys (from Smith & Raine, 2008). The upsurge in Internet use corresponds primarily with a decrease in use of newspapers (Raine, Cornfield, & Horrigan, 2005).

In their report on survey data from the 2004 U.S. Presidential campaign, Raine and colleagues (2005, p. i) say:

> Last year [2004] was a breakout year for the role of the Internet in politics. Fully 75 million Americans—37 percent of the adult population and 61 percent of online Americans—used the Internet to get political news and information, discuss candidates and debate issues in emails, or participate directly in the political process by volunteering or giving contributions to candidates. The online political news consumer population grew dramatically from previous election years (up from 18 percent of the U.S. population in 2000 to 29 percent in 2004), and there was an increase of more than 50 percent between 2000 and 2004 in the number of registered voters who cited the Internet as one of their *primary* sources of news about the presidential campaign.

The study found growth not only in Americans' use of the Internet for news about politics, but also growth in the number of people who obtained voting information (up 150 percent), gave campaign donations (up 80 percent), used political discussion forums and chats (up 57 percent), researched candidates' voting records (up 38 percent), completed online surveys about political issues (up 15 percent), and researched candidates' positions (up 14 percent). About half (49 percent) of online Americans agreed with the phrase: "The Internet has raised the

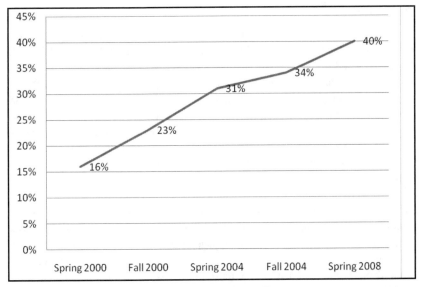

**Figure 8.5** **Percentage of Americans who said that they use the Internet to get political information across five campaign seasons (data from Pew Internet and American Life Project)**

overall quality of public debate," and 40 percent of Internet users reported that the Internet was "very important" or "somewhat important" in helping them decide how to vote.

One election cycle later, the latest Pew Internet and American Life Project report (Smith & Raine, 2008) found another dramatic jump in the use of the Internet by citizens for political purposes: 46 percent of all adult Americans were using the Internet to obtain information about the 2008 presidential election. In 2008, the increasing use of social networking sites and multimedia content (especially videos) was noted. Respondents to that survey, however, indicated that acceptance of the Internet is, to some extent, problematic. Sixty seven percent of Internet users disagreed with the statement "The Internet helps me feel more personally connected to my candidate or campaign of choice" and 74 percent disagreed with the statement "I would not be as involved in this campaign as much if it weren't for the Internet." Sixty percent agreed with the statement "The Internet is full of misinformation and propaganda that too many voters believe is accurate."

The adoption of e-government technologies from the citizens' side has repeatedly been found to depend on degree of trust (Warkentin, Gefen, Pavlou, & Rose, 2002; Otto, 2003), transparency (Marche & McNiven, 2003), and usability (Bertot & Jaeger, 2006; Choudrie & Ghinea, 2005; Warkentin et al., 2002; Wood, Siegel, LaCroix, Lyon, Benson, Cid, et al., 2003). Carter and Belanger (2004, 2006) applied a formal model of adoption from other technology contexts to e-government and found trust, perceived usefulness, and relative advantage to be important constructs (see also Kumar, Mukerji, Butt, & Persaud, 2007).

## Politicians

The increase in use of the Internet by citizens corresponds to an increased awareness and use of the Internet by politicians (Druckman, Kifer, & Parkin, 2007). U.S. Presidential and Congressional candidates had begun to use the Internet, primarily for website presences, by 1996 (D'Alessio, 1997; Kamarck, 1999). Dulio, Goff, and Thurber (1999) reported that more than two thirds of Congressional candidates had election websites in 1998; usage of websites for campaigns and as part of the presence of elected officials in the U.S. grew consistently in the following years (Puopolo, 2001; Stromer-Galley, Foot, Schneider, & Larsen, 2001) and expanded to a wide range of political actors by the beginning of the century (Foot & Schneider, 2006; Schneider & Foot, 2002).

In 2004, Democratic presidential candidate Howard Dean became the first major political candidate in America to use the Internet in a transactional manner. Dean's campaign manager, Joe Trippi, initially took the simple step of putting a link to a social networking website on the main page of the candidate's website. Later, the campaign added "Blog for America," a two-way channel that ultimately gave them what Trippi (2003) claimed to be a ten-fold increase in Internet-based supporters over John McCain in campaign contributions. Druckman and colleagues (2007) have shown that virtually all U.S. Congressional candidates and office holders utilize "publication" aspects of the Web (e.g., information) but that use of two-way, transactional features still lags behind, especially when races are heavily contested. They maintain that politicians still feel that their message is best conveyed and controlled by one-way, G2C communication.

In 2008, all presidential candidates had sophisticated websites with several interactive and transactional features, links to multimedia websites such as YouTube, and presence on social networking websites such as MySpace and Facebook. Figure 8.6 shows U.S. presidential candidate John McCain's Facebook top page with links to five other significant sites including YouTube, the candidate's website, and three social networking sites. Figure 8.7, composed of snips taken from U.S. presidential candidate Barack Obama's website, shows an online presence at 16 other sites, including several other social networking sites. It also shows the personalization feature available to Obama supporters (myBarackObama.com) and a link to "Obama Mobile." The Obama campaign's use of cell phone technology to collect voter information (from many young voters who did not have land line telephones and were therefore unavailable to the more traditional name collection methods) and to organize immediate political actions (e.g., call-ins to radio programs in progress) was one of the significant technology stories from the 2008 election.

Several days after the election, President-elect Obama's transition team established www.change.gov as an official (.gov extension) Web tool for communicating activities of the transition process and collecting input, in a variety of forms, from citizens. The press engaged in considerable speculation about the transition from use of ICTs exclusively for campaigning to their use for governance, engagement, and/or agenda setting by the White House.

**Figure 8.6   U.S. Presidential candidate (2008) John McCain's Facebook page**

## Electronic Voting

The turn of the century ushered in a new era of politics—one in which the voter took more control of elections, the ability to obtain information became more important to the average voter, the security and anonymity of the ballot box became paramount issues, political parties lost power as candidates were forced to speak more directly to a broader range of citizens, and new technology slowly being

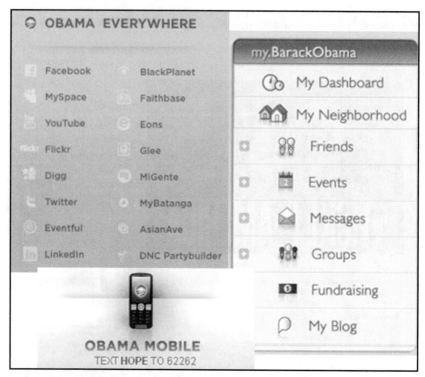

Figure 8.7   A montage of snips from Presidential candidate Barack Obama's
website in 2008 showing use of multiple Internet and ICT resources

adopted across the nation made voting easier. It also posed new challenges to voting equity by requiring greater literacy skills and access to technology.

It might be surprising to know that the preceding paragraph refers to the beginning of the twentieth century, not the twenty-first. In 1880, the "Australian ballot" was introduced in the United States and by 1910 was adopted by all states and municipalities. It was a revolutionary voting technology, in that all candidates and issues appeared on one ballot that the voter examined and marked in private. Unlike previous voting methods, no personal identifier was included on the ballot and voters obtained no record of how they voted. The Australian ballot allowed voters to use recognition memory rather than recall and allowed any choice to be made once a voter was in the privacy of the ballot booth. In theory, the Australian ballot reduced the coercive influence of earlier, more public voting, which was accomplished by obtaining and handing in a party ticket.

It is instructive that the new technology did not immediately change the voting landscape. Although the Fifteenth Amendment, adopted in 1870 as part of a series of "Reconstructionist Amendments," explicitly extended voting rights to African-Americans, the need to be better informed, literacy requirements, and poll taxes continued to suppress Black voters until the civil rights era of the 1960s. Suffragists argued that the Fifteenth Amendment also extended voting rights to women; a women's suffrage amendment was first introduced in Congress in 1872 but not passed until 1920.

Changes in the political landscape at the turn of the 20th century involved both technological and social innovations, unfolded over a period of many decades, and had both positive and negative consequences that are hard to untangle. At the turn of the 21st century we see another dramatic change in the technology of voting. Once again there is great optimism about the possibilities for broadening participation and access to government, but optimism is tempered by concern about equity, privacy, security, and other problems inherent in the technology and its deployment. Similarly, the advent of electronic voting (and digital government) is embedded in a larger social revolution brought on by ubiquitous computing and what we might call the "digitization of everything." The ubiquity of networked ICTs is arguably creating a new type of citizen with new expectations (Fountain, 2001).

The plebiscite is at the center of democracy and digital collection of votes is currently a very active area of development. The technology of voting has consistently evolved along with developments in recording and storage technology. In ancient Greece, citizens voted (on banishment of a citizen) by placing inscribed bits of tile into vessels. Paper was a significant improvement and paper balloting of one type or another was, and still is, widespread in all contemporary democracies. At the outset of the machine age, around the turn of the 20th century, lever balloting machines were introduced and many local governments in the United States spent large amounts of money to obtain them. The advantage of lever machines was in automation of counting, but it came at some cost to the voter in terms of usability.

The advent of the computer age toward the middle of the 20th century saw the introduction of the punch ballot and, ironically, the return of paper in the form of the punch cards that were inserted into punch ballot machines. Again, the advantage was in speed of tabulation, in this case the processing of cards by centralized, mainframe computers. The design of the interface for punch ballots was more flexible than for lever machines but, as the 2000 presidential election in Florida showed, this did not necessarily guarantee good interface design (the infamous "butterfly ballot" was an interface designed for a punch machine). As many Americans also learned during that election, the punch card is prone to errors in the form of incompletely punched holes, what we all know now as "hanging chads."

In the last decade or so, many municipalities have begun to move toward touch screen ballots. The general term for touch screen ballot devices that collect, store, and transmit ballot information is Direct Recording Electronic devices (DREs). DRE systems push virtually all of the technical issues into the realm of software, which is both their advantage and their disadvantage. Usability of information on the ballot interface is entirely a matter of graphical user interface (GUI) design and can be quite malleable. Some DRE devices have only a touch screen for all controls (e.g., selection, paging, vote submission) whereas others have navigation and/or vote recording hardware (e.g., a thumb wheel and paging, selection, and voting keys).

Table 8.2 shows statistics on voting technologies used in the 2006 U.S. elections (Election Data Services, 2006). As the table shows, 36.6 percent of counties and 38.4 percent of registered voters used DREs in 2006. The same report says that only

12.4 percent of voters used DREs in 2000, demonstrating a rapid change in voting technology. More than half of the DRE market in 2006 (in terms of registered voters) was dominated by two vendors: Diebold (27 percent) and Sequoia Systems (23 percent). The third-place vendor, Election Systems and Software, held 15 percent of the market. In general, private vendors have been unwilling to make their source code available for inspection, prompting many concerns and "unauthorized" testing.

**Table 8.2   Voting technologies used in the 2006 U.S. elections (from Election Data Services, 2006, online)**

| Type of voting equipment | Counties | | Registered voters | |
|---|---|---|---|---|
| | Number | Percent | Number | Percent |
| Punch cards | 13 | 0.42% | 414,027 | 0.24% |
| Lever machines | 62 | 1.99% | 11,627,385 | 6.77% |
| Hand-counted paper ballots | 57 | 1.83% | 330,912 | 0.19% |
| Optically scanned paper ballots | 1,752 | 56.19% | 84,026,447 | 48.94% |
| Electronic (DRE) equipment | 1,142 | 36.63% | 65,959,464 | 38.42% |
| Mixed (multiple types) | 92 | 2.95% | 9,341,055 | 5.44% |
| TOTAL | 3,118 | 100.00% | 171,699,290 | 100.00% |

Dill, Schneier, and Simons (2003) describe five basic attributes of voting technologies:

- Anonymity
- Scalability
- Speed
- Audit
- Accuracy

Some trade-off may be required. For example, anonymity, which refers to the need to separate voters' identities from their votes, limits the ability to audit. Auditing in the way that is common in commerce—checking records kept by the merchant (voting authority) against receipts kept by the customer (voter)—violates the anonymity of the voter and increases the chance of coercion by giving voters proof of how they voted, which they could then provide to someone else (who might pay them, for example).

The usability of DREs and screen-based ballots has also been studied extensively (Bederson, Lee, Sherman, Herrnson, & Niemi, 2003; Herrnson, Bederson, Lee, Francia, Sherman, Conrad, et al., 2005). Ballot usability is a well researched area; however, DREs and other forms of electronic voting introduce many new factors (Bederson et al., 2003; Herrnson, Niemi, Hanmer, Bederson, Conrad, &

Traugott, 2006; Herrnson, Niemi, Hanmer, Francia, Bederson, Conrad, et al., 2005; Traugott, Herrnson, & Niemi, 2006). Examples of new problems include signing on, navigating, error correction, ballot verification, and casting the ballot. Even "simple" acts such as how a checkbox behaves or how to complete a write-in become important design problems in the context of DREs. Legislation mandating usability analysis of electronic voting systems has been proposed to augment the Help America to Vote Act, and the National Institute of Standards and Technology has issued usability guidelines for summative testing of DREs (National Institute of Standards and Technology, 2007).

Robertson and his colleagues (Robertson, 2005, 2006, 2008; Robertson, Vatrapu, & Abraham, 2009; Robertson, Wania, & Park, 2007) have proposed formative analysis and participatory design of e-voting systems instead of summative analyses. They have investigated the feasibility of combining Internet search and browsing tools with online ballots, although initial findings suggest that users would prefer these tasks to be separate (Robertson, Achananuparp, Goldman, Park, Zhou, & Clare, 2005). Their research shows that small changes in the design of political search and browsing tools can result in dramatically varied voter information opportunities and exposure to very different materials about candidates and issues (Robertson, Wania, Abraham, & Park, 2008).

Concerns have been raised about issues of security, trust, and equity in the deployment of DREs (Ansolabehere, 2001; Ansolabehere & Stewart, 2004). Many researchers have challenged the security of DRE systems (Fischer, 2003; Kohno, Stubblefield, Rubin, & Wallach, 2004; Lauer, 2004; Mercuri, 2002; Mercuri & Neumann, 2002). "Stealth" studies of DRE equipment have found several security flaws in the code and the hardware of widely deployed systems (Herrnson, Bederson, & Abbe, 2002) and lack of trust in voting technology threatens to undermine their acceptance (Evans & Paul, 2004). Many municipalities now require that electronic voting machines supply a voter-verifiable piece of paper for audit purposes. Concerns that poorer municipalities are less likely to invest in new voting equipment are not, in general, supported by empirical evidence (Knack & Kropf, 2002) and, ironically, early adopters of DREs may be at a disadvantage because the technology is changing.

## E-Rulemaking

A significant direction in digital government research and practice is e-rulemaking, or the process of using digital technologies to produce, refine, and deliberate about legislation and rules promulgated by government agencies, especially regulatory bodies. Public input is an important part of the development of government regulations but the issues of how to communicate proposed regulations widely and equitably, collect and utilize often voluminous public comments, discover who is interested and affected, and refine regulations collaboratively have always been difficult. All of these issues are prime targets for technologically mediated solutions.

E-rulemaking is worthy of a chapter in its own right; here we highlight some major issues. According to Shulman, Callan, Hovy, and Zavestoski (2004), e-rulemaking systems should address the following issues:

- Basic information retrieval

- Text classification

- Overall text characterization using word frequency counts

- Duplicate detection

- Near-duplicate detection

- Text summarization

- Author typing (stakeholder analysis)

- Opinion/affect determination

- Document partitioning and cross indexing

Some of these issues aid in the process of directing documents in different stages of development to the appropriate offices or individuals. Others deal with the problem of characterizing voluminous comments and drafts.

Some states have established e-rulemaking portals designed to alert interested citizens and legislators to proposed rules relevant to them and allow them to comment and follow the rulemaking process. Florida's site (www.flrules.org) allows users to search for rules by agency, issue, department, division, and full text. The results list shows rule names, explanations, history, status, and other information. The site allows users to comment on rules and to set up alerts. The Virginia Regulatory Town Hall (www.townhall.virginia.gov) has a similar capability but allows for broader discussion of rules in public forums and lists all meetings (in real life) that are scheduled on regulatory items.

At the federal level in the United States a centralized portal for e-rulemaking has been established (www.regulations.gov). Federal agencies with regulatory authority use this portal as a common tool. It supports search, alerting through RSS, and e-mail notification. On the back end, the tool organizes and disseminates comments to stakeholders.

## Blogs and Social Networking: New Public Spheres

Habermas derived the notion of public spheres from a study of English salons, French cafés, and German table corners with an explicit focus on print media in the 18th and 19th centuries. He conceptualized the public sphere as a mediating space between the state and the civil society. Habermas (1991b, p. 398) defined "public sphere" as "a domain of our social life in which such a thing as public opinion can be formed."

A public sphere is a democratic space where public interests, opinions, agendas, and problems are formed, transformed, and exchanged by citizens' proactive participation. The relationship between citizens engaged in public discourse and communication is the critical feature of a public sphere. Critical rationality, equality, freedom of expression, and dissemination are the necessary conditions for the proper structuring and functioning of a Habermasian public sphere.

## Public Spheres and Social Imaginaries

ICTs and the Internet have radically altered our understanding of what is meant by a public and which kind of social formation can be termed public. Recent scholarship on social imaginaries is an effort to theorize and understand the newly forming and evolving social formations. *Social imaginary* refers broadly to the way a given people imagine their collective social life (Taylor, 2002). Taylor delineated three important social imaginaries: civil society, market economy, and public sphere. In Taylor's conception, public sphere occupies fluid middle ground between embodied practices and explicit doctrines. Writing on social imaginaries, Warner (2002) distinguishes "public" as:

- The Public

- The bounded public

- A Public

Habermas's ideal conception of a public sphere is that of "The Public," but in reality the English salons, French cafés, and German coffee tables constituted "a public." Warner lists seven features of "a public":

- A public is self-organized

- A public is a relation among strangers

- The address of public speech is both personal and impersonal

- A public is constituted through mere attention

- A public is the social space created by the reflexive circulation of discourse

- Publics act historically according to the temporality of their circulation

- A public is poetic world-making

## Public Spheres on the Internet

That the concept of public sphere has been theorized largely in terms of the nation state is a limitation. Congruence among the nation state, national citizenry, and the public sphere has been repeatedly pointed out in the writings of theorists of the public sphere (Habermas, 1991a; Hansen, 1993; Negt & Kluge, 1993). Recent empirical research has sought to underline the importance of the interconnections between the Internet and the public sphere, thereby enabling the public sphere to be understood productively within a transnational frame (Poor, 2005; Vatrapu, Robertson, & Dissanayake, 2008).

## Requirements for an Online Public Sphere

Habermas's conception of a traditional public sphere required the critical-rationality of the participants' communicative actions. Requirements for online public spheres have been a focus of inquiry: Dahlberg (2001) proposed six requirements for computer-mediated public spheres, Poor (2005) presented four criteria for online public spheres, and Vatrapu, Robertson, and Dissanayake (2008) drew attention to the sociological structures, political functions and technological features of virtual public spheres.

Dahlberg's (2001) six requirements are:

- Autonomy from state and economic power
- Thematization and critique of critizable, moral-practical, validity claims
- Reflexivity
- Ideal role-taking
- Sincerity
- Discursive equality and inclusion

Poor's (2005) four criteria are:

- Public spheres are spaces of discourse, often mediated
- Public spheres often allow for new, previously excluded, discussants
- Issues discussed are often political in nature
- Ideas are judged by their merit, not by the standing of the speaker

Recent empirical work has sought to document as public spheres various online spaces such as candidate websites (Foot & Schneider, 2006; Foot, Schneider, Dougherty, Xenos, & Larsen, 2003; Schneider & Foot, 2002), political blogs (Vatrapu et al., 2008), discussion forums (Poor, 2005; Schneider, 1996), and other political websites (Foot & Schneider, 2002). Fraser (1992) pointed out the actual limitations in realistic practices of the public sphere and drew attention to the exclusivity of the traditional public spheres. He argues that in Habermas's conception of a public sphere, communicative action is based on equality in the communication process, but he questions whether the prerequisite of equality can be met when participation requires representation of multiple interests and perspectives in, for example, multicultural societies. This criticism can be extended to civic participation and democratic deliberation in the Internet age (Hindman, 2009; Margolis & Resnick, 2000; Norris, 2001). The digital divide and digital literacy are significant factors in determining access to and engagement in online public spheres and discussion forums.

## Blogs

Blogs have proven to be a minefield for some politicians. At the late U.S. Senator Strom Thurmond's 100th birthday celebration in 2002, Senate majority leader Trent Lott said "When Strom Thurmond ran for President, we voted for him. We're proud of it. And if the rest of the country had followed our lead, we wouldn't have had all these problems over the years" (Edsall & Faler, 2002, p. A06). Thurmond ran in 1948 as a "Dixiecrat," a break-away party dedicated primarily to the preservation of racial segregation in the South, and his speeches (available online, of course) are shocking. Bloggers picked up the story, which the mainstream media largely ignored, and it became so significant that Lott was forced to resign his leadership position. Politicians have been paying attention to blogs ever since.

Blogs now share the spotlight with online videos in their ability to keep attention on politicians and issues. At a reelection campaign rally in 2006, Virginia Senator George Allen pointed to S. R. Sidarth, an audience member of Indian descent, and said "Let's give a welcome to macaca, here. Welcome to America and the real world of Virginia" (Craig & Shear, 2006, A01). Mr. Sidarth was videotaping the speech and the video was posted on YouTube (www.youtube.com/watch?v= r90z0PMnKwI). At the time of the remark, Senator Allen had a double digit lead in the polls and was being discussed as a 2008 presidential contender. The YouTube posting, however, was unstoppable and ultimately resulted in Senator Allen's defeat and disappearance from politics. In 2008, John Edwards and Barack Obama announced their candidacies for the presidency on YouTube and Hillary Clinton posted a video announcement on her website. YouTube had a dedicated election channel for the 2008 U.S. general election ("YouChoose 08") and election watchers compared numbers of YouTube subscriptions for various politicians' channels.

Proponents of the idea that blogs are a form of public sphere must contend with the fact that dialog in the political "blogosphere" is highly divided by political philosophy with very few interlinking references (Adamic & Glance, 2005). Sunstein (2002) notes that Internet users seek out information with which they already agree. In addition, a relatively few political blogs are read by political elites and journalists who, in turn, serve as gatekeepers to larger media exposure (Farrel & Drezner, 2007). Blogging networks focused on more local issues, however, may prove to be an important new form of citizen interaction (Kavanaugh, Schmitz, Zin, Perez-Quinones, Carroll, & Isenhour, 2006; Klein, 1999).

## Social Networks

Digital social networks such as Facebook and MySpace are so new that research is just beginning on their use in democratic discourse (Terranova & Library, 2004; van Dijk, 2005). Political candidates have populated these social sites in earnest and utilize many of their tools for collecting funds, disseminating messages, creating groups, and initiating collective activities. Many researchers have focused on the creation and maintenance of social capital in social networking environments and have noted that social networks tend to be homophilic (connecting people who are alike) (McPherson, Smith-Lovin, & Cook, 2001). Facebook users tend not to meet new people online but rather use the social networking tool to augment existing relationships (Lampe, Ellison, & Steinfield, 2006). Almost one third of U.S. Senate candidates and one in ten U.S. House of Representatives candidates in 2006 updated their Facebook pages (Williams & Gulati, 2008). Candidates were more likely to update their Facebook profiles when they were in competitive races, and their Facebook support was correlated with their final vote share (Williams & Gullati, 2008). Social networking sites such as Facebook are integrators of different aspects of network members' lives; as such, they might come closest to being like an online public sphere.

In many ways, some of the most exciting digital government phenomena occur in non-official systems that support C2C networking. Social movements and political interest groups form easily within online communities (Bimber, 1998) and their resulting power and influence on government action has yet to be fully realized or understood (Dianai, 2000; Sæbø, Rose, & Flak, 2008; Shuler, 1994).

# E-Government Related Technologies

Several fields of ICT research and practice are related to e-government even though they might not really be considered parts of e-government. These concern themselves with civic problem solving, utilize data that are collected and maintained by government entities, and often require collaboration among domain experts, government officials, politicians and policy makers, and citizens. Two important areas are geographic information systems (GIS) and urban simulation (UrbanSim).

## Geographic Information Systems

Geographic and geospatial information has always been a concern of governments. Historically, governments have made considerable investments to obtain, archive, and disseminate maps of new and existing territories and their characteristics. Government is interested in geospatial information for a host of reasons including security, resources, infrastructure, transportation and commerce, agriculture and weather, emergency response, and population and census studies. Digital geospatial data (Raper, 2009) is so important to the U.S. government that it has invested heavily in the development of a common spatial data infrastructure (SDI) (Mapping Sciences Committee, 1993; Maguire & Longley, 2004) and a one-stop Web portal (www.geodata.gov) for all users of that information. The quest for a spatial data standard that can be used by many governments has since become worldwide (Craglia & Masser, 2002; Maguire & Longley, 2004; Masser, 1999; Van Loenen & Kok, 2004).

The U.S. National Spatial Data Infrastructure initiative had three goals (Longley, Goodchild, Maguire, & Rhind, 2001; Maguire & Longley, 2004; Ryan, DeMulder, DeLoatch, Garie, & Sideralis, 2004):

- Develop standards for describing, accessing, and exchanging digital data

- Create a clearinghouse offering online access to spatial metadata

- Provide framework data sets (e.g., administrative boundaries, geology, atmosphere, elevation, water) that cover the whole country

GIS has proved useful for both planning and response purposes at Ground Zero (Cahan & Ball, 2002; Cutter, Richardson, & Wilbanks, 2003) and in other emergency situations (Cutter, 2003).

## Urban Simulation

Urban simulation, often referred to as "UrbanSim," is the use of complex modeling software and visualization techniques to address urban planning problems (Borning, Waddell, & Förster, 2008; Waddell, 2002; Waddell & Borning, 2004; Waddell & Ulfarsson, 2004). Issues addressed by UrbanSim techniques include:

- Household mobility
- Demographic trends
- Real estate development patterns and choices
- Transportation system planning
- Zoning and land-use decisions
- Regional economic forecasts

UrbanSim models a geographical region as a grid of interconnected cells containing objects such as households, automobiles, families, roads, businesses, and geological features. Each object has properties, derived from a plethora of data sources, that are used in the simulation; for example: income level, family size, number and value of automobiles, carbon emission. Modeling involves making assumptions about how these features interact with each other, creating a scenario about how one or more of the features might change (e.g., an influx of high income urban homesteaders), and then "running" the model through a series of time periods. Outputs of simulations can include demographic shifts and population density changes, economic movements, and traffic patterns. UrbanSim can be used by policymakers and citizens to make predictions about complex interacting systems and clarify assumptions (Borning, Friedman, Davis, & Lin, 2005; Borning & Waddell, 2006; Borning et al., 2008).

## Challenges

Jaeger (2003a) describes several broad areas in which e-government faces obstacles. These include:

- Security
- Privacy
- Homeland security
- Digital divide
- Economic disparities
- Education
- Accessibility
- Prioritization
- Citizen awareness and confidence

Jaeger and Thompson (2003) further suggest that all e-government systems must accomplish the following:

- Ensure ability to use required technologies
- Educate citizens about the value of e-government

- Ensure access to useful information and services

- Coordinate local, regional, and national e-government initiatives

- Develop methods and performance indicators to assess the services and standards of e-government

- Provide consistent and reliable electricity, telecommunications, and Internet access

- Address issues of language and communication

- Prevent e-government from lessening responsiveness of government officials

- Prevent e-government from lessening responsibility of government officials

- Include individuals with disabilities in e-government

## *Universal Access and Trust*

One of the most challenging issues for digital government systems is the need to serve all citizens (Sawhney & Jayakar, 2007). The many reasons that citizens might not be able to use e-government include:

- Lack of trust, which creates a barrier to engaging with e-government in the first place

- Lack of accessibility, which may frustrate users with disabilities in their early experience

- Lack of usability, which may frustrate users (with or without disabilities) in their early experience

Trust in information systems has been explored extensively (Marsh & Dibben, 2003). In the context of digital government, the trust issue arises from concerns about privacy, information sharing, and security. Digital government systems maintain data on citizens' health, employment and wealth, legal matters, and other issues that are sensitive and private. Legal barriers prohibit information sharing between some agencies, although there are frequent challenges to these barriers from within the government itself.

Political trust, or trust in government and politicians, also has a literature of its own (Citrin & Green, 1986; Easton, 1965; Hibbing & Theiss-Morse, 2001, 2002; Lawrence, 1997; Nye, 1997; Thomas, 1998). Considerable attention has been paid to the issues of how trust influences voting and other citizen activities (Hetherington, 1998, 1999) and how political factors such as the state of the economy influence trust (Citrin & Green, 1986; Hibbing & Theiss-Morse, 2001, 2002). Parent, Vandebeek, and Gemino (2004) propose that political self-efficacy, or citizens' feelings that they have some impact on political developments, is a mediating factor in trust in government. Welch and Hinnant (2003) maintain that transparency and interactivity are especially important determinants of trust in the context of e-government.

Data suggest that citizens do not necessarily trust digital government less than traditional government, but this may be due in part to very low overall trust in government (Hibbing & Theiss-Morse, 2001; Rosenstone & Hansen, 1993). Citizens with relatively positive trust in government are more willing to use e-government systems (Tolbert & Mossberger, 2006); perceived trustworthiness is a significant predictor of intention to use e-government services (Carter & Belanger, 2006). Positive experiences with e-government systems have been shown to build trust (Warkentin et al., 2002).

As with all information systems, accessibility and usability are critical for digital government applications. The barriers in this context are complex, however (Jaeger, 2006a, 2006b; West, 2004). Many accessibility issues are subject to legislation and linked to equity and civil rights (Anderson, Bohman, Burmeister, & Sampson-Wild, 2004; Jaeger & Bowman, 2005). In the United States, accessibility to federal government websites is mandated by law, as is also the case with many state and local government websites. Usually, accessibility requires alternative forms of content, such as auditory in place of visual content, but coverage of all types of disabilities is difficult (Jaeger, 2003b, 2006a, 2006b) and, unfortunately, compliance lags far behind targets (West, 2003, 2004).

Information equity refers to issues involving the digital divide, or asymmetries in the availability of information systems based on sociological and/or demographic variables such as income, race, gender, language, or religion (Doctor, 1992; Lievrouw & Farb, 2003). In some ways, the move to digital government will ease some equity issues by, for example, making it easier to provide content in many languages. There is concern that populations that lag behind technologically (e.g., urban poor) may be left out of digital government initiatives. The cost savings of digital applications to governments, and the greater penetration of information technology into homes, however, are trends that are mitigating issues of digital divide, at least in G2C systems. A fascinating research topic involves the degree to which equity issues are present in C2C systems in the context of politics and government.

## Priorities and Power

The development path for digital government systems is created as the consequence of a series of decisions by IT professionals and politicians about priorities. These decisions are themselves potential points for the introduction of systematic inequities. For example, should government favor the development of e-rulemaking systems as the result of pressure from businesses and contractors, while at the same time de-emphasizing the development of usability guidelines for voting technologies? The choices that governments make with regard to prioritization in the development of systems involve the exercise of power (Castells, 2007; Mahler & Regan, 2005, 2006).

In addition to development priorities, decisions about ownership of and commercial involvement in digital government systems also create power inequities. Some digital government applications are based on open source standards but others are proprietary (the most significant instance of the latter is electronic voting systems). Proprietary systems cede power to their commercial developers and rob citizens of their right to understand, probe, question, and ultimately change systems.

Digital systems create channels through which information and transactions flow between and among governments and citizens. Control of these tools, either in their design or administration, creates a potential for intrusion into democratic processes that have variously been called "infocracy" (Snellen, 2002; Zuurmond, 1998) or "Googlearchy/Googleocracy" issues (Hindman, 2009). Although transaction processing by digital systems can reduce arbitrary application of rules and enforce standards, it also reduces the power of street-level bureaucrats to understand and adapt to individual circumstances. Turning political dialog and civic interaction over to search and network algorithms has the potential to create elite information sources and de-emphasize unconnected voices (Hindman, 2009; Norris, 2001; Toregas, 2001).

### No Place

Finally, there is the challenge that results from the fact that virtual places are not real places (Augé, 1995; Fountain, 2006). Politics is personal and is linked to issues of identity and belonging. Development of so-called virtual states and the rise of transnational and trans-regional political interests on the Internet is proving to be a double-edged sword. On one hand, political activism on local, national, and international levels has been empowered by Internet tools (Ayers, 1999; Diani, 2000; Klein, 1999; Muhlberger, 2006). However, place-based issues related to a nation, state, city, neighborhood, or other regional political entity may be weakened by being less visible to participants in virtual communities (Ludlow, 2001). It remains to be seen whether civic engagement and a feeling of community will be a natural consequence of networked polities (Smith & Kollock, 1999; Terranova & Library, 2004; Tsagarousianou, Tambini, & Bryan, 1998; van Dijk, 2005).

## Conclusion

At the end of our discussion of digital government, it seems fitting to return to the Founding Fathers:

> Remember, democracy never lasts long. It soon wastes, exhausts, and murders itself. There never was a democracy yet that did not commit suicide. (John Adams letter to John Taylor, 1814)

It is reasonable to be excited about the changes now occurring in government, democracy, and international politics; but it is also prudent to be concerned and vigilant. The same technology that makes it possible to connect citizens internationally also brings the capability for surveillance of private dialogue (Strickland, Baldwin, & Justen, 2005). The same technology that makes it possible to vote more securely and with fewer errors also brings the specter of election rigging through malicious software. The development of digital government around the world, for all forms of government, is a trend that should be carefully followed by informed citizens.

# Acknowledgments

This material is based upon work supported by the National Science Foundation under Grant No. 0535036 to the first author. Opinions, findings, and conclusions or recommendations expressed in this material are those of the authors and do not necessarily reflect the views of the National Science Foundation.

# References

Abramson, J. B., Arterton, F. C., & Orren, G. R. (1988). *The electronic commonwealth: The impact of new media technologies on democratic politics*. New York: Basic Books.

Adamic, L.A., & Glance, N. (2005). The political blogosphere and the 2004 U.S. election: Divided they blog. *Proceedings of the 3rd International Workshop on Link Discovery* (pp. 36–43). New York: ACM Press.

Agre, P. E. (2002). Real-time politics: The Internet and the political process. *The Information Society, 18*(5), 311–331.

Alvarez, R. M., & Hall, T. E. (2004). *Point, click and vote: The future of Internet voting*. Washington, DC: Brookings Institution Press.

Anderson, S., Bohman, P. R., Burmeister, O. K., & Sampson-Wild, G. (2004). User needs and e-government accessibility: The future impact of WCAG 2.0. In C. Stary & C. Stephanidis (Eds.), *User-centered interaction paradigms for universal access in the information society: 8th ERCIM Workshop on User Interfaces for All: Revised selected papers* (Lecture Notes in Computer Science, 3196) (pp. 289–304). Berlin: Springer-Verlag.

Ansolabehere, S. (2001). Voting machines, race, and equal protection. *Election Law Journal, 1*(1), 61–70.

Ansolabehere, S., Iyengar, S., & Behr, R. (1993). *The media game: American politics in the television age*. New York: Macmillan.

Ansolabehere, S., & Stewart, C. (2004). Residual votes attributable to voting technologies. *Journal of Politics, 67*(2), 365–389.

Augé, M. (1995). *Non-places: Introduction to an anthropology of supermodernity*. London: Verso.

Aurigi, A. (2000). Digital city or urban simulator? In T. Ishida & K. Isbister (Eds.), *Digital cities: Technologies, experiences, and future perspectives* (Lecture Notes in Computer Science 1765) (pp. 33–44). Berlin, Germany: Springer-Verlag.

Aurigi, A. (2005). *Making the digital city: The early shaping of urban Internet space*. Burlington, VT: Ashgate.

Ayers, J. M. (1999). From the streets to the Internet: The cyber-diffusion of contention. *Annals of the American Academy of Political and Social Science, 566*(1), 132–143.

Bederson, B., Lee, B., Sherman, R. M., Herrnson, P. S., & Niemi, R. G. (2003). Electronic voting system usability issues. *Proceedings of the SIGCHI Conference on Human Factors in Computing Systems*, 145–152.

Bertot, J. C., & Jaeger, P. T. (2006). User centered e-government: Challenges and benefits of government Web sites. *Government Information Quarterly, 23*(2), 163–168.

Bhatnagar, S. (2004). *E-government: From vision to implementation: A practical guide with case studies*. London: Sage.

Bimber, B. (1998). The Internet and political transformation: Populism, community, accelerated pluralism. *Polity, 31*(1), 133–160.

Bimber, B. (2003). *Information and American democracy: Technology in the evolution of political power*. Cambridge, UK: Cambridge University Press.

Borning, A., Friedman, B., Davis, J., & Lin, P. (2005). Informing public deliberation: Value sensitive design of indicators for a large-scale urban simulation. *Proceedings of the 9th European Conference on Computer-Supported Cooperative Work*, 449–468.

Borning, A., & Waddell, P. (2006). UrbanSim: Interaction and participation in integrated urban land use, transportation, and environmental modeling. *Proceedings of the 7th Annual International Digital Government Research Conference* (pp. 133–134). New York: ACM Press.

Borning, A., Waddell, P., & Förster, R. (2008). Urbanism: Using simulation to inform public deliberation and decision-making. In H. Chen, L. Brandt, V. Gregg, R. Traunmüller, S. Dawes, E. Hovy, et al. (Eds.), *Digital government: E-Government research, case studies, and implementation* (pp. 440–465). Berlin: Springer-Verlag.

Bowyer, K. W. (2004). Face recognition technology: Security versus privacy. *IEEE Technology and Society Magazine, 23*(1), 9–19.

Cahan, B., & Ball, M. (2002). GIS at Groud Zero: Spatial technology bolsters World Trade Center response and recovery. *GEO World, 15*(1), 26–29.

Carroll, J. M., & Rosson, M. B. (1996). Developing the Blacksburg electronic village. *Communications of the ACM, 39*(12), 69–74.

Carter, L., & Belanger, F. (2004). Citizen adoption of electronic government initiatives. *Proceedings of the Hawaii International Conference on System Sciences*. Retrieved January 29, 2009, from doi.ieeecomputersociety.org/10.1109/HICSS.2004.1265306

Carter, L., & Belanger, F. (2006). The utilization of e-government services: Citizen trust, innovation, and acceptance factors. *Information Systems Journal, 15*(1), 5–25.

Castells, M. (2007). Communication, power and counter-power in the network society. *International Journal of Communication, 1*, 238–266.

Center for Technology in Government (2008). *Enabling e-government: Overview*. Albany, NY: The Center. Retrieved January 3, 2009, from www.ctg.albany.edu/themes/themes?chapter=egov

Chadwick, A., & May, C. (2003). Interaction between states and citizens in the age of the Internet: "E-government" in the United States, Britain, and the European Union, *Governance, 16*(2), 271–300.

Chen, H. (2002). Digital government: Technologies and practices. *Decision Support Systems, 34*, 223–227.

Chen, X. (2002). The E_GOV action plan in Beijing. In T. Ishida & K. Isbister (Eds.), *Digital cities: Technologies, experiences, and future perspectives* (Lecture Notes in Computer Science 1765) (pp. 69–74). Berlin: Springer-Verlag.

Choudrie, J., & Ghinea, G. (2005). Integrated views of e-government website usability: Perspectives from users and Web diagnostic tools. *Electronic Government, 2*(3), 318–333.

Citrin, J., & Green, D. P. (1986). Presidential leadership and the resurgence of trust in government. *British Journal of Political Science, 16*, 431–453.

Clinton, W. J. (1993). United States Advisory Council on the National Information Infrastructure (Executive Order 12864). *Federal Register, 58*(179). Retrieved March 30, 2009, from www.archives.gov/federal-register/executive-orders/pdf/12864.pdf

Clinton, W. J. (1999). *Presidential electronic commerce performance mandate*. Retrieved July 26, 2009, from www.gov.com/about_memo19991227.html

Coleman, S., & Blumler, J. (2008). *The Internet and democratic citizenship: Theory, practice and policy*. Cambridge, UK: Cambridge University Press.

Coleman, S., & Gøtze, J. (2001). *Bowling together: Online public engagement in policy deliberation*. London: Hansard Society.

Commission of the European Communities. (2003). *The role of eGovernment for Europe's future.* Brussels, Belgium: The Commission. Retrieved January 3, 2009, from ec.europa.eu/information_ society/eeurope/2005/doc/all_about/egov_communication_en.pdf

Craglia, M., & Masser, I. (2002). Geographic information and the enlargement of the European Union: Four national case studies. *Journal of the Urban and Regional Information Systems Association, 14*(2), 43–52.

Craig, T., & Shear, M. D. (2006, August 15). Allen quip provokes outrage, apology. *Washington Post*, A01.

Cresswell, A. M., & Pardo, T. (2001). Implications of legal and organizational issues for urban digital government development. *Government Information Quarterly, 18*(4), 269–278.

Cutter, S. L. (2003). GI science, disasters, and emergency management. *Transactions on GIS, 7*(4), 439–445.

Cutter, S. L., Richardson, D. B., & Wilbanks, T. J. (Eds.). (2003). *Geographical dimensions of terrorism.* New York: Routledge.

Dahlberg, L. (2001). Computer-mediated communication and the public sphere: A critical analysis. *Journal of Computer-Mediated Communication, 7*(1). Retrieved January 29, 2009, from jcmc. indiana.edu/vol7/issue1/dahlberg.html

D'Alessio, D. (1997). Use of the World Wide Web in the 1996 US election. *Electoral Studies, 16*(4), 489–500.

Dawes, S. S. (2002). *The future of e-government.* Albany, NY: Center for Technology in Government, University at Albany/SUNY. Retrieved March 30, 2009, from www.ctg.albany.edu/publications/ reports/future_of_egov/future_of_egov.pdf

Dawes, S. S., Bloniarz, P. A., Kelly, K. L., & Fletcher, P. D. (2002). Some assembly required: Building a digital government for the 21st century. *Proceedings of the 2002 Annual National Conference on Digital Government Research* (ACM International Conference Proceeding Series, vol. 129), 1–39.

Dawes, S. S., Gregg, V., & Agouris, P. (2004). Digital government research: Investigations at the crossroads of social and information science. *Social Science Computer Review, 22*(1), 5–10.

Dawes, S. S., & Préfontaine, L. (2003, January). Understanding new models of collaboration for delivering government services. *Communications of the ACM, 46*(1), 40–42.

Devadoss, P. R., Pan, S. L., & Huang, J. C. (2002). Structurational analysis of e-government initiatives: A case study of SCO. *Decision Support Systems, 34*, 253–269.

Diani, M. (2000). Social movement networks virtual and real. *Information, Communication & Society, 3*(3), 386–401.

Dill, D. L., Schneier, B., & Simons, B. (2003). Voting and technology: Who gets to count your vote? *Communications of the ACM, 46*(8), 29–31.

Doctor, R. (1992). Social equity and information technologies: Moving toward information democracy. *Annual Review of Information Science and Technology, 27*, 43–96.

Downing, J. (1989). Computers for political change: Peacenet and public data access. *Journal of Communication, 39*(3), 154–162.

Druckman, J., Kifer, M., & Parkin, M. (2007). The technological development of Congressional candidate websites: How and why candidates use Web innovations. *Social Science Computer Review, 25*(4), 425–442.

Dulio, D. A., Goff, D. L., & Thurber, J. A. (1999). Untangled Web: Internet use during the 1998 election. *PS: Political Science and Politics, 32*(1), 53–58.

Easton, D. (1965). *A systems analysis of political life.* New York: Wiley.

Edsall, T. B., & Faler, B. (2002, December 11). Lott remarks on Thurmond echoed 1980 words. *Washington Post*, A06.

Egelman, S., & Cranor, L. (2005). The Real ID Act: Fixing identity documents with duct tape. *I/S: A Journal of Law and Policy for the Information Society, 2*(1), 149–183.

Eggers, W. (2005). *Government 2.0: Using technology to improve education, cut red tape, reduce gridlock, and enhance democracy.* Lanham, MD: Rowman & Littlefield.

Election Data Services. (2006). *2006 voting equipment study.* Retrieved January 3, 2009, from www. electiondataservices.com/images/File/VotingEquipStudies%20/ve2006_news.pdf

Elmagarmid, A. K., & McIver, W. J., Jr. (2001). The ongoing march toward digital government. *IEEE Computer, 34*(2), 32–38.

European Union. (1999). *eEurope: An information society for all.* Communication on a Commission Initiative for the Special European Council of Lisbon. Brussels, Belgium: The Commission. March. Retrieved January 3, 2009, from ec.europa.eu/information_society/eeurope/i2010/docs/2002/english.pdf

European Union. (2000). *eEurope 2002: An information society for all: Action Plan.* Prepared by the Council and the European Commission for the Feira European Council. Brussels, Belgium: The Commission. Retrieved January 3, 2009, from ec.europa.eu/information_society/eeurope/i2010/docs/2002/action_plan/actionplan_en.pdf

European Union. (2002). *eEurope 2005: An information society for all: An Action Plan.* Communication from the Commission to the Council, the European Parliament, the Economic and Social Committee and the Committee of the Regions. Brussels, Belgium: The Commission. Retrieved January 3, 2009, from eur-lex.europa.eu/LexUriServ/LexUriServ.do?uri=CELEX:52002DC0263:EN:NOT

European Union. (2003). *eEurope 2002 Final Report.* Communication from the Commission to the Council, the European Parliament, the Economic and Social Committee and the Committee of the Regions. Brussels, Belgium: The Commission. Retrieved January 3, 2009, from eur-lex.europa.eu/LexUriServ/LexUriServ.do?uri=CELEX:52003DC0066:EN:NOT

European Union. (2005). *i2010: A European information society for growth and employment.* Communication from the Commission to the Council, the European Parliament, the European Economic and Social committee and the Committee of the Regions. Brussels, Belgium: The Commission.

Evans, D., & Paul, N. (2004). Election security: Perception and reality. *IEEE Security and Privacy, 2*(1), 24–31.

Fang, Z. (1997). E-government in digital era: Concept, practice and development. *International Journal of the Computer, the Internet and Management, 10*(2), 1–22.

Farrell, H., & Drezner, D. W. (2007). The power and politics of blogs. *Public Choice, 134*(1–2), 15–30.

Farrington, C., & Pine, E. (1997). Community memory: A case study in community communication. In P. E. Agre & D. Shuler (Eds.), *Reinventing technology, rediscovering community: Critical explorations of computing as a social practice* (pp. 219–228). Greenwich, CT: Ablex.

Fischer, E. A. (2003). *Election reform and electronic voting systems (DREs): Analysis of security issues* (Congressional Research Service Report RL32139). Washington, DC: The Library of Congress.

Flak, L. S., Sein, M. K., & Sæbø, Ø. (2007). Towards a cumulative tradition in e-government research: Going beyond the Gs and Cs. *Electronic Government: 6th International Conference, EGOV 2007, Proceedings* (Lecture Notes in Computer Science, 4656) (pp. 13–22). Berlin, Germany: Springer-Verlag.

Foot, K. A., & Schneider, S. M. (2002). Online action in campaign 2000: An exploratory analysis of the U.S. political Web sphere. *Journal of Broadcasting & Electronic Media, 46*(2), 222–244.

Foot, K. A., & Schneider, S. M. (2006). *Online campaigning.* Cambridge, MA: MIT Press.

Foot, K. A., Schneider, S. M., Dougherty, M., Xenos, M., & Larsen, E. (2003). Analyzing linking practices: Candidate sites in the 2002 US electoral Web sphere. *Journal of Computer Mediated Communication, 8*(4). Retrieved January 3, 2009, from jcmc.indiana.edu/vol8/issue4/foot.html

Forlano, L. (2004). The emergence of digital government: International perspectives. In A. Pavlichev & G. D. Garson (Eds.), *Digital government: Principles and best practices* (pp. 34–51). London: Idea Group.

Fountain, J. E. (2001). *Building the virtual state: Information technology and institutional change.* Washington, DC: Brookings Institution Press.

Fountain, J. E. (2006). Central issues in the political development of the virtual state. In M. Castells & G. Cardoso (Eds.), *The network society: From knowledge to policy.* Washington, DC: Brookings Institution Press.

Fraser, N. (1992). Rethinking the public sphere: A contribution to the critique of actually existing democracy. In C. Calhoun (Ed.), *Habermas and the public sphere* (pp. 109–142). Cambridge, MA: MIT Press.

Garramone, G. M., Harris, A. C., & Anderson, R. (1986). Uses of political computer bulletin boards. *Journal of Broadcasting and Electronic Media, 30*(3), 325–339.

Garson, D. (2006). *Public information technology and e-governance.* Boston: Jones & Bartlett.

Gil-Garcia, J. R., & Martinez-Moyano, I. J. (2007). Understanding the evolution of e-government: The influence of systems of rules on public sector dynamics. *Government Information Quarterly, 24*(2), 266–290.

Gil-Garcia, J. R., & Pardo, T. (2005). E-government success factors: Mapping practical tools to theoretical foundations. *Government Information Quarterly, 22*(2), 187–216.

Goswami, P. R. (2002). Literacy, information, and governance in the digital era: An Indian scenario. *International Information & Library Review, 34*(3), 255–270.

Government Paperwork Elimination Act of 1998, 44 U.S.C.A. § 3504 n. (West Supp. 1999).

Graafland-Essers, I., & Ettedgui, E. (2003). *Benchmarking e-Government in Europe and the US* (SIBUS Report IST-2000-26276). Leiden, The Netherlands: RAND Europe.

Grönlund, Ä., & Horan, T. (2005). Introducing e-GOV: History, definitions and issues. *Communications of the AIS, 15,* 713–729.

Habermas, J. (1991a). The public sphere. In C. Mukerji & M. Schudson (Eds.), *Rethinking popular culture: Contemporary perspectives in cultural studies* (pp. 398–404). Berkeley: University of California Press.

Habermas, J. (1991b). *The structural transformation of the public sphere: An inquiry into a category of bourgeois society* (T. Burger, Trans.). Cambridge, MA: MIT Press.

Hansen, M. (1993). Early cinema, late cinema: Permutations of the public sphere. *Screen, 34*(3), 197–210.

Heeks, R., & Bailur, S. (2007). Analyzing eGovernment research. *Government Information Quarterly, 22*(2), 243–265.

Herrnson, P., Bederson, B. B., & Abbe, O. (2002). An evaluation of Maryland's new voting machines. College Park, MD: University of Maryland Center for American Politics and Citizenship/Human Computer Interaction Lab. Retrieved January 3, 2009, from www.capc.umd.edu/rpts/MD_EVoteEval.pdf

Herrnson, P. S., Bederson, B. B., Lee, B., Francia, P. L., Sherman, R. M., Conrad, F. G., et al. (2005). Early appraisals of electronic voting. *Social Science Computer Review, 23*(3), 274–292.

Herrnson, P. S., Niemi, R. G., Hanmer, M. J., Bederson, B. B., Conrad, F. G., & Traugott, M. (2006). The importance of usability testing of voting systems. *Proceedings of the Usenix/Accurate Electronic Voting Technology Workshop* (August 1, 2006, Vancouver, B.C., Canada). Berkeley, CA: USENIX

Association. Retrieved January 3, 2009, from www.usenix.org/events/evt06/tech/full_papers/herrnson/herrnson.pdf

Herrnson, P. S., Niemi, R. G., Hanmer, M. J., Francia, P., Bederson, B., Conrad, F. G., et al. (2005, April). *The promise and pitfalls of electronic voting: Results from a usability field test*. Paper presented at the Annual Meeting of the Midwest Political Science Association, Chicago, IL.

Hetherington, M. J. (1998). The political relevance of political trust. *American Political Science Review*, 92(4), 791–808.

Hetherington, M. J. (1999). The effect of political trust on the presidential vote. *American Political Science Review*, 93, 311–326.

Hibbing, J. R., & Theiss-Morse, E. (Eds.). (2001). *What is it about government that Americans dislike?* Cambridge, UK: Cambridge University Press.

Hibbing, J. R., & Theiss-Morse, E. (2002). *Stealth democracy: Americans' beliefs about how government should work*. Cambridge, UK: Cambridge University Press.

Hiller, J. S., & Bélanger, F. (2001). Privacy strategies for electronic government. In M. A. Abramson & G. E. Means (Eds.), *E-government 2001* (pp. 162–198). Lanham, MD: Rowman & Littlefield.

Hindman, M. (2009). *The myth of digital democracy*. Princeton, NJ: Princeton University Press.

Holden, S. H., Norris, D. F., & Fletcher, P. D. (2003). Electronic government at the local level: Progress to date and future issues. *Public Performance and Management Review*, 26(4), 325–344.

Horrigan, J. (2004). *How Americans get in touch with government* (Pew Internet and American Life Project Report). Washington, DC: Pew Research Center. Retrieved January 3, 2009, from www.pewinternet.org/~/media//Files/Reports/2004/PIP_E-Gov_Report_0504.pdf.pdf

Ishida, T. (2000). Understanding digital cities. In T. Ishida & K. Isbister (Eds.), *Digital cities: Technologies, experiences, and future perspectives* (Lecture Notes in Computer Science 1765) (pp. 7–17). Berlin, Germany: Springer-Verlag.

Ishida, T., Aurigi, A., & Yasuoka, M. (2003). World digital cities: Beyond heterogeneity. In P. van den Besselaar & S. Koizumi (Eds.), *Digital Cities III: Information technologies for social capital: Cross-cultural perspectives: Third International Digital Cities Workshop, Revised Selected Papers* (Lecture Notes in Computer Science 3081) (pp. 184–198). Berlin, Germany: Springer-Verlag.

Jaeger, P. T. (2003a). The endless wire: E-government as global phenomenon. *Government Information Quarterly*, 20(4), 323–331.

Jaeger, P. T. (2003b). The importance of measuring the accessibility of the federal e-government: What studies are missing and how these issues can be addressed. *Information Technology and Disabilities*, 9(1). Retrieved January 29, 2009, from people.rit.edu/easi/itd/itdv09n1/jaeger.htm

Jaeger, P. T. (2005). Deliberative democracy and the conceptual foundations of electronic government. *Government Information Quarterly*, 22(4), 702–719.

Jaeger, P. T. (2006a). Assessing Section 508 compliance on federal e-government Web sites: A multi-method, user-centered evaluation of accessibility for persons with disabilities. *Government Information Quarterly*, 23(2), 169–190.

Jaeger, P. T. (2006b). Telecommunications policy and individuals with disabilities: Issues of accessibility and social inclusion in the policy and research agenda. *Telecommunications Policy*, 30, 112–124.

Jaeger, P. T., & Bowman, C. A. (2005). *Understanding disability: Inclusion, access, diversity, and civil rights*. Westport, CT: Praeger.

Jaeger, P. T., & Thompson, K. M. (2003). E-government around the world: Lessons, challenges, and new directions. *Government Information Quarterly*, 20(4), 389–394.

Jong, M., & Lentz, L. (2005). Scenario evaluation of municipal Web sites: Development and use of an expert-focused evaluation tool. *Government Information Quarterly*, 23(2), 191–206.

Kamarck, E. C. (1999). Campaigning on the Internet in the elections of 1998. In E. C. Kamarck & J. S. Nye (Eds.), *Democracy.com? Governance in the network world* (pp. 99–123). Hollis, NH: Hollis Publishing.

Kavanaugh, A., Schmitz, J., Zin, T. T., Perez-Quinones, M., Carroll, J. M., & Isenhour, P. (2006). When opinion leaders blog: New forms of citizen interaction. *Proceedings of the 7th Annual International Digital Government Research Conference*, 79–88.

Klein, H. K. (1999). Tocqueville in cyberspace: Using the Internet for citizen associations. *Information Society, 15*(4), 213–220.

Knack, K., & Kropf, M. (2002). Who uses inferior voting technology? *Political Science and Politics, 35,* 541–548.

Kohno, T., Stubblefield, A., Rubin, A., & Wallach, D. (2004). Analysis of an electronic voting system. *Proceedings of the IEEE Symposium on Security and Privacy*, 27–42.

Kumar, V., Mukerji, B., Butt, I., & Persaud, A. (2007). Factors for successful e-government adoption: A conceptual framework. *Electronic Journal of e-Government, 5*(1), 63–76.

Lampe, C., Ellison, N., & Steinfield, C. (2006). A face (book) in the crowd: Social searching and social browsing. *Proceedings of the 2006 Conference on Computer Supported Cooperative Work*, 167–170.

Lauer, T. W. (2004). The risk of e-voting. *Electronic Journal of E-Government, 2*(3), 177–186.

Lawrence, R. Z. (1997). Is it really the economy stupid? In J. S. Nye (Ed.), *Why people don't trust government* (pp. 111–132). Cambridge, MA: Harvard University Press.

Layne, K., & Lee, J. (2001). Developing fully functional e-government: A four stage model. *Government Information Quarterly, 18*(2), 122–136.

Lievrouw, L. A., & Farb, S. (2003). Information and equity. *Annual Review of Information Science and Technology, 37*, 499–540.

Lips, M. (2001). Designing electronic government around the world: Policy developments in the USA, Singapore, and Australia. In J. E. J. Prins (Ed.), *Designing e-government: On the crossroads of technological innovation and institutional change* (pp. 75–89). Boston, MA: Kluwer Law International.

Longley, P. A., Goodchild, M. F., Maguire, D. J., & Rhind, D. W. (2001). *Geographic information systems and science*. Chichester, UK: Wiley.

Ludlow, P. (Ed.). (2001). *Crypto anarchy, cyberstates, and pirate utopias*. Cambridge, MA: MIT Press.

Ma, L., Chung, J., & Thorson, S. (2004). E-government in China: Bringing economic development through administrative reform. *Government Information Quarterly, 22*(1), 20–37.

Maguire, D. J., & Longley, P. A. (2004). The emergence of geoportals and their role in spatial data infrastructures. *Computers, Environment and Urban Systems, 29*(1), 3–14.

Mahler, J., & Regan, P. M. (2005). Agency internets and changing dynamics of congressional oversight. *International Journal of Public Administration, 28*(7/8), 553–565.

Mahler, J., & Regan, P. M. (2006). Crafting the message: Controlling content on agency websites. *Government Information Quarterly, 24*(3), 505–521.

Malhotra, Y., Al-Shehri, A., & Jones, J. J. (1995). *National Information Infrastructure: Myths, metaphors and realities*. New York: BRINT Institute. Retrieved March 30, 2009, from www.brint.com/papers/nii

Mapping Sciences Committee. (1993). *Towards a coordinated spatial data infrastructure for the nation*. Washington, DC: National Academy Press.

Marche, S., & McNiven, J. D. (2003). E-government and e-governance: The future isn't what it used to be. *Canadian Journal of Administrative Sciences, 20*(1), 74–86.

Marchionini, G., Craig, A., Brandt, L., Klavans, J., & Chen, H. (2001). Digital libraries supporting digital government. *Proceedings of the 1st ACM/IEEE-CS Joint Conference on Digital Libraries*, 395–397. Retrieved January 3, 2009, from doi.acm.org/10.1145/379437.379733

Marchionini, G., Samet, H., & Brandt, L. (2003). Introduction to a special issue on digital government. *Communications of the ACM, 46*(1), 24–27.

Margolis, M., & Resnick, D. (2000). *Politics as usual: The cyberspace revolution.* Thousand Oaks, CA: Sage.

Marsh, S., & Dibben, M. (2003). The uses of trust in information science and technology. *Annual Review of Information Science and Technology, 37,* 465–498.

Masser, I. (1999). All shapes and sizes: The first generation of national spatial data infrastructures. *International Journal of Geographical Information Science, 13*(1), 67–84.

McIver, W. J., & Elmagarmid, A. K. (Eds.). (2001). *Advances in digital government: Technology, human factors, and policy.* Boston, MA: Kluwer Academic Publishers.

McPherson, M., Smith-Lovin, L., & Cook, J. M. (2001). Birds of a feather: Homophily in social networks. *Annual Review of Sociology, 27,* 415–444.

Meadow, R. G. (1986). The electronic machine: New technologies in political campaigns. *Election Politics, 3*(3), 26–31.

Mercuri, R. T. (2002). A better ballot box? *IEEE Spectrum, 39*(10), 46–50.

Mercuri, R. T., & Neumann, P. G. (2002). Verification for electronic balloting systems. In D. Gritzalis (Ed.), *Secure electronic voting: Advances in information security* (Vol. 7, pp. 31–42). Boston, MA: Kluwer Academic Publishers.

Miller, B. (1996, November). European cities link to improve quality of life. *Government Technology.* Retrieved January 3, 2009, from www.govtech.com/gt/95828

Moeller, M. (1993). Technology: Data superhighway. *Communications International, 20*(7), 16, 20.

Moon, M. J. (2002). The evolution of e-government among municipalities: Rhetoric or reality? *Public Administration Review, 62*(4), 424–433.

Muhlberger, P. (2006). Should e-government design for citizen participation? Stealth democracy and deliberation. *Proceedings of the 7th Annual International Digital Government Research Conference,* 53–61.

Myers, D. D. (1993). New technology and the 1992 Clinton presidential campaign. *American Behavioral Scientist, 37*(2), 181–187.

National Institute of Standards and Technology. (2007). *Usability performance benchmarks for the voluntary voting system guidelines.* Gaithersburg, MD: The Institute. Retrieved January 3, 2009, from vote.nist.gov/meeting-08172007/Usability-Benchmarks-080907.doc

National Research Council, Committee on Computing and Communications Research to Enable Better Use of Information Technology in Government. (2002). *Information technology research, innovation, and e-government.* Washington, DC: National Academy Press.

National Research Council, Computer Science and Telecommunications Board. (1999). *Summary of a workshop on information technology research for crisis management.* Washington, DC: National Academy Press.

National Research Council, Computer Science and Telecommunications Board. (2000). *Summary of a workshop on information technology research for federal statistics.* Washington, DC: National Academy Press.

Negt, O., & Kluge, A. (1993). *Public sphere and experience: Toward an analysis of the bourgeois and proletarian public sphere.* Minneapolis: University of Minnesota Press.

Nora, S., & Minc, A. (1980). *The computerization of society: A report to the president of France.* Cambridge, MA: MIT Press.

Norris, P. (1996). Does television erode social capital: A reply to Putnam. *PS: Political Science and Politics, 29*(3), 474–480.

Norris, P. (2001). *Digital divide: Civic engagement, information poverty, and the Internet worldwide.* Cambridge, UK: Cambridge University Press.

Nye, J. S. (Ed.). (1997). *Why people don't trust government.* Cambridge, MA: Harvard University Press.

Olbrich, S., & Simon, C. (2008). Process modelling towards e-government: Visualisation and semantic modelling of legal regulations as executable process sets. *Electronic Journal of e-Government, 6*(1), 43–54.

O'Sullivan, P. B. (1995). Computer networks and political participation: Santa Monica's teledemocracy project. *Journal of Applied Communication Research, 23*(2), 93–107.

Otto, P. (2003). New focus in e-government: From security to trust. In M. P. Gupta (Ed.), *Promises of e-governance: Management challenges, Proceedings of the International Conference on E-Governance* (pp. 6–16). New Delhi: Tata McGraw Hill.

Paperwork Reduction Act, 44 U.S.C. § 3501 (1995).

Parent, M., Vandebeek, C. A., & Gemino, A. C. (2004). Building citizen trust through e-government. *Proceedings of the 37th Hawaii International Conference on System Sciences.* Retrieved January 29, 2009, from doi.ieeecomputersociety.org/10.1109/HICSS.2004.1265304

Patterson, T. (1993). *Out of order.* New York: Vintage Books.

Poor, N. (2005). Mechanisms of an online public sphere: The website Slashdot. *Journal of Computer-Mediated Communication, 10*(2). Retrieved January 29, 2009, from jcmc.indiana.edu/vol10/issue2/poor.html

Puopolo, S. T. (2001). The Web and U.S. senatorial campaigns 2000. *American Behavioral Scientist, 44*(12), 2030–2047.

Putnam, R. (1995). Tuning in, tuning out: The strange disappearance of social capital in America. *PS: Political Science & Politics, 27*(4), 664–683.

Raine, J., Cornfield, M., & Horrigan, J. (2005). *The Internet and campaign 2004* (Pew Internet and American Life Project Report). Washington, DC: Pew Research Center. Retrieved January 3, 2009, from www.pewinternet.org/pdfs/PIP_2004_Campaign.pdf

Raine, J., & Horrigan, J. (2007). *Election 2006 online* (Pew Internet and American Life Project Report). Washington, DC: Pew Research Center. Retrieved January 3, 2009, from www.pewinternet.org/pdfs/PIP_Politics_2006.pdf

Raper, J. (2009). Geographical information science. *Annual Review of Information Science and Technology, 43*, 73–144.

Reddick, C. G. (2004a). A two-stage model of e-government growth: Theories and empirical evidence from U.S. cities, *Government Information Quarterly, 21*(1), 51–64.

Reddick, C. G. (2004b). Citizen interaction with e-government: From the streets to servers? *Government Information Quarterly, 22*(1), 38–57.

Robertson, S. (2005). Voter-centered design: Toward a voter decision support system. *ACM Transactions on Computer-Human Interaction, 12*(2), 263–292.

Robertson, S. (2006). Digital deliberation: Searching and deciding about how to vote. *Proceedings of the 7th Annual Conference on Digital Government Research*, 95–96.

Robertson, S. (2008). Design research in digital government: A query prosthesis for voters. *Proceedings of the 9th Annual Conference on Digital Government Research*, 73–88.

Robertson, S., Achananuparp, P., Goldman, J., Park, S. J., Zhou, N., & Clarc, M. (2005). Voting and political information gathering on paper and online. *Extended Abstracts of CHI '05: Human Factors in Computing Systems* (pp. 1753–1756). New York: ACM Press.

Robertson, S., Vatrapu, R., & Abraham, G. (2009). Note taking and note sharing while browsing campaign information. *Proceedings of the Hawaii International Conference on System Sciences.* Retrieved January 29, 2009, from doi.ieeecomputersociety.org/10.1109/HICSS.2009.326

Robertson, S., Wania, C., Abraham, G., & Park, S. J. (2008). Drop-down democracy: Internet portal design influences voters' search strategies. *Proceedings of the Hawaii International Conference on System Sciences.* Retrieved January 29, 2009, from doi.ieeecomputersociety.org/10.1109/HICSS.2008.131

Robertson, S., Wania, C., & Park, S. J. (2007). An observational study of voters on the Internet. *Proceedings of the Hawaii International Conference on System Sciences.* Retrieved January 29, 2009, from doi.ieeecomputersociety.org/10.1109/HICSS.2007.70

Ronaghan, S. A. (2002). *Benchmarking e-government: A global perspective.* New York: United Nations Division for Public Economics and Public Administration. Retrieved January 3, 2009, from unpan1.un.org/intradoc/groups/public/documents/UN/UNPAN021547.pdf

Rosenstone, S. J., & Hansen, M. (1993). *Mobilization, participation, and democracy in America.* New York: Macmillan.

Ryan, B. J., DeMulder, M. L., DeLoatch, I., Garie, H., & Sideralis, K. (2004, April 1). A clear vision of the NSDI, *Geospatial Solutions*, 30–31. Retrieved January 3, 2009, from www.geospatial-solutions.com/geospatialsolutions/article/articleDetail.jsp?id=89953

Sæbø, Ø., Rose, J., & Flak, S. (2008). The shape of eParticipation: Characterizing an emerging research area. *Government Information Quarterly, 25*(3), 400–428.

Sawhney, H., & Jayakar, K. (2007). Universal access. *Annual Review of Information Science and Technology, 41*, 159–221.

Schneider, S. M. (1996). Creating a democratic public sphere through political discussion: A case study of abortion conversation on the Internet. *Social Science Computer Review, 14*(4), 373–393.

Schneider, S. M., & Foot, K. A. (2002). Online structure for political action: Exploring presidential Web sites from the 2000 American election. *Javnost (The Public), 9*(2), 43–60.

Scholl, J. (2006). Is e-government research a flash in the pan or here for the long shot? *Electronic Government: 5th International Conference: Proceedings* (Lecture Notes in Computer Science, 4084) (pp. 13–24). Berlin, Germany: Springer-Verlag.

Schorr, H., & Stolfo, S. J. (2000). Towards the digital government of the 21st century: A report from the workshop on research and development opportunities in federal information services. *Proceedings of the 2000 Annual National Conference on Digital Government Research* (ACM International Conference Proceeding Series, vol. 128, pp. 1–40). Digital Government Research Center.

Schudson, M. (1998). *The good citizen: A history of American civic life.* Cambridge, MA: Harvard University Press.

Shuler, D. (1994). Community networks: Building a new participatory medium. *Communications of the ACM, 37*(1), 39–51.

Shuler, D. (1996). *New community networks: Wired for change.* Reading, MA: Addison Wesley.

Shulman, S., Callan, J., Hovy, E., & Zavestoski, S. (2004). SGER collaborative: A testbed for eRulemaking data. *Journal of E-Government, 1*(1), 123–127.

Simons, B. (1994). Questions about the NII. *Communications of the ACM, 37*(7), 170.

Smith, A., & Raine, L. (2008). *The Internet and the 2008 election* (Pew Internet and American Life Project Report). Washington, DC: Pew Research Center. Retrieved January 3, 2009, from www.pewinternet.org/pdfs/PIP_2008_election.pdf

Smith, M., & Kollock, P. (1999). *Communities in cyberspace.* New York: Routledge.

Snellen, I. (2002). Electronic governance: Implications for citizens, politicians, and public servants. *International Review of Administrative Sciences, 68*, 183–198.

Strickland, L. S., Baldwin, D. A., & Justen, M. (2005). Domestic security surveillance and civil liberties. *Annual Review of Information Science and Technology, 39*, 433–513.

Stromer-Galley, J., Foot, K. A., Schneider, S. M., & Larsen, E. (2001). What citizens want, where they went, and what they got online in the U.S. election 2000. In S. Coleman (Ed.), *Elections in the age of the Internet: Lessons from the United States* (pp. 26–35). London: Hansard Society.

Sunstein, C. (2002). *Republic.com*. Princeton, NJ: Princeton University Press.

Taylor, C. (2002). Modern social imaginaries. *Public Culture, 14*(1), 91–124.

Terranova, T., & Library, A. (2004). *Network culture: Politics for the information age*. London: Pluto Press.

Thomas, C. W. (1998). Maintaining and restoring public trust in government agencies and their employees. *Administration and Society, 30*(2), 166–193.

Thomas, J. C., & Streib, G. (2003). The new face of government: Citizen-initiated contacts in the era of e-government. *Journal of Public Administration Research and Theory, 13*(1), 83–102.

Tolbert, C., & Mossberger, K. (2006). The effects of e-government on trust and confidence in government. *Public Administration Review, 66*(3), 354–369.

Toregas, C. (2001). The politics of e-gov: The upcoming struggle for redefining civic engagement. *National Civic Review, 90*(3), 235–240.

Traugott, M. W., Herrnson, P. S., & Niemi, R. G. (2006). A project to assess voting technology and ballot design. *Proceedings of the 7th Annual International Digital Government Research Conference*, 38–39.

Trippi, J. (2003). *The revolution will not be televised*. New York: Harper Collins.

Tsagarousianou, R., Tambini, D., & Bryan, C. (1998). *Cyberdemocracy: Technology, cities and civic networks*. New York: Routledge.

United Nations (2008). *UN e-government survey: From e-government to connected governance*. New York: United Nations. Retrieved January 3, 2009, from unpan1.un.org/intradoc/groups/public/documents/UN/UNPAN028607.pdf

van den Besselaar, P. (2001). E-community versus e-commerce: The rise and decline of the Amsterdam digital city. *AI & Society, 15*(3), 280–288.

van den Besselaar, P., & Beckers, D. (1998). Demographics and sociographics of the digital city. In T. Ishida (Ed.), *Community computing and support systems: Social interaction in networked communities* (Lecture Notes in Computer Science 1519) (pp. 108–124). Berlin, Germany: Springer-Verlag.

van Dijk, J. (2005). *The network society: Social aspects of new media*. London: Sage.

Van Loenen, B., & Kok, B. C. (Eds.). (2004). *Spatial data infrastructure and policy development in Europe and the United States*. Delft, The Netherlands: DUP Science.

Vatrapu, R., Robertson, S., & Dissanayake, W. (2008). Are political weblogs public spheres or partisan spheres? *International Reports on Socio-Informatics, 5*(1), 7–26.

Vintar, M., & Leben, A. (2002). The concepts of an active life-event public portal. In K. Lenk & R. Traunmüller (Eds.), *Proceedings of the First International Conference on Electronic Government* (Lecture Notes in Computer Science, 2456) (pp. 383–390).

Waddell, P. (2002). UrbanSim: Modeling urban development for land use, transportation and environmental planning. *Journal of the American Planning Association, 68*(3), 297–314.

Waddell, P., & Borning, A. (2004). A case study in digital government: Developing and applying UrbanSim, a system for simulating urban land use, transportation, and environmental impacts. *Social Science Computing Review, 22*(1), 37–51.

Waddell, P., & Ulfarsson, G. F. (2004). Introduction to urban simulation: Design and development of operational models. In D. Stopher, K. J. Button, K. E. Kingsley, & P. R. Hensher (Eds.), *Handbook in Transport, Volume 5: Transport Geography and Spatial Systems* (pp. 203–236). Oxford, UK: Pergamon Press.

Warkentin, M., Gefen, D., Pavlou, P. A., & Rose, G. M. (2002). Encouraging citizen adoption of eGovernment by building trust. *Electronic Markets, 12*(3), 157–162.

Warner, M. (2002). Publics and counterpublics. *Public Culture, 14*(1) 49–90.

Weingarten, F. W. (1994). Public Interest and the NII. *Communications of the ACM, 37*(3), 17–19.

Welch, E. W., & Hinnant, C. C. (2003). Internet use, transparency, and interactivity effects on trust in government. *Proceedings of the Hawaii International Conference on Systems Sciences.* Retrieved January 29, 2009, from doi.ieeecomputersociety.org/10.1109/HICSS.2003.1174323

West, D. M. (2003). *Achieving e-government for all: Highlights from a national survey.* Washington, DC: Benton Foundation/Rockefeller Institute for Government.

West, D. M. (2004). Equity and accessibility in E-Government. *Journal of E-Government, 1*(2), 31–43.

West, D. M. (2005). *Digital government: Technology and public sector performance.* Princeton, NJ: Princeton University Press.

West, D. M. (2007). *Global e-government, 2007.* Providence, RI: Center for Public Policy, Brown University. Retrieved January 3, 2009, from www.insidepolitics.org/egovt07int.pdf

West, D. M. (2008). *Improving technology utilization in electronic government around the world, 2008.* Washington, DC: Brookings Institution. Retrieved January 3, 2009, from www.brookings.edu/~/media/Files/rc/reports/2008/0817_egovernment_west/0817_egovernment_west.pdf

Westholm, H. (2002). e-Democracy goes ahead. The Internet as a tool for improving deliberative policies? In R. Traunmüller & K. Lenk (Eds.), *Electronic Government First International Conference, EGOV 2002: Proceedings* (Lecture Notes in Computer Science, 2456) (pp. 237–244). Berlin, Germany: Springer-Verlag.

Williams, C. B., & Gulati, G. J. (2008). The political impact of Facebook: Evidence from the 2006 midterm elections and 2008 nomination contest. *Politics and Technology Review, 1*, 11–21.

Wimmer, M. A. (2007). Ontology for an e-participation virtual resource centre. *Proceedings of the 1st International Conference on Theory and Practice of Electronic Governance* (ACM International Conference Proceeding Series, Vol. 232), 89–98.

Wood, F. B., Siegel, E. R., Lacroix, E., Lyon, B. J., Benson, D. A., Cid, V., et al. (2003, May/June). A practical approach to e-government Web evaluation. *IEEE IT Professional Magazine,* 22–28.

World Bank. (2009). *Definition of e-government.* Washington, DC: World Bank Group. Retrieved January 3, 2009, from go.worldbank.org/M1JHE0Z280

Yuan, Y., Zhang, J., & Zheng, W. (2004). Can e-government help China meet the challenges of joining the World Trade Organization? *Electronic Government, an International Journal, 1*(1), 77–91.

Zuurmond, A. (1998). From bureaucracy to infocracy: Are democratic institutions lagging behind? In I. Snellen & W. B. H. J. van de Donk, (Eds.), *Public administration in an information age: A handbook* (pp. 259–272). Amsterdam: IOS Press.

# Economics

# CHAPTER 9

# The Knowledge-Based Economy and the Triple Helix Model

*Loet Leydesdorff*
*University of Amsterdam, The Netherlands*

## Introduction: The Metaphor of a Knowledge-Based Economy

Few concepts introduced by evolutionary economists have been politically more successful than the metaphor of a knowledge-based economy. For example, the European Summit of March 2000 was specifically held "to agree on a new strategic goal for the Union in order to strengthen employment, economic reform and social cohesion as part of a knowledge-based economy" (European Commission, 2000, online; 2005). Similarly and more recently, Barack Obama (2008, online) formulated in one of his campaign speeches: "This long-term agenda ... will require us first and foremost to train and educate our workforce with the skills necessary to compete in a knowledge-based economy. We'll also need to place a greater emphasis on areas like science and technology that will define the workforce of the 21st century, and invest in the research and innovation necessary to create the jobs and industries of the future right here in America."

Can such a large impact on the real economy be expected from something as poorly defined as the knowledge base of an economy? How can an economy be based on something as volatile as knowledge? In an introduction to a special issue on the topic, David and Foray (2002, p. 9) cautioned that the terminology was coined recently and noted that "as such, it marks a break in the continuity with earlier periods, more a 'sea-change' than a sharp discontinuity." However, these authors also warned against confusion because the transformations can be analyzed at a number of different levels. They concluded that *knowledge* and *information* should be more carefully distinguished by analyzing the development of a knowledge-based economy in terms of codification processes (Cowan, David, & Foray, 2000; Cowan & Foray, 1997).

Foray and Lundvall (1996) introduced the concept of a knowledge-based economy at a workshop of the Organisation for Economic Co-operation and Development (OECD) in 1994 (Organisation for Economic Co-operation and Development, 1996a). In that same workshop, Abramowitz and David (1996, p. 35) suggested that *codified* knowledge should be made central to the analysis:

Perhaps this single most salient characteristic of recent economic growth has been the secularly rising reliance upon *codified* knowledge as a basis for the organization and conduct of economic activities, including among the latter the purposive extension of the economically relevant knowledge base. While tacit knowledge continues to play critical roles, affecting individual and organizational competencies and the localization of scientific and technological advances, codification has been both the motive force and the favoured form taken by the expansion of the knowledge base.

Analytically, this focus on codified knowledge demarcated the new research program from the older concept of a knowledge economy, with its focus on knowledge workers and hence embodied knowledge (Cooke, 2002; Machlup, 1962; Penrose, 1959). Embodied and tacit knowledge are embedded in contexts (Bowker, 2005; Collins, 1974; Polanyi, 1961; Zuboff, 1988); codified knowledge can be decontextualized and therefore, among other things, traded in a market (Dasgupta & David, 1994). The metaphor of a knowledge-based economy appreciates the increased importance of organized research and development (R&D) in shaping systems of innovation. The knowledge production function has become a *structural* characteristic of the modern economy (Schumpeter, 1943, 1964).

Most economists have been more interested in the *effects* of codification on the economy than in the processes of codification itself. Social scientists have been more concerned with human knowledge than with knowledge as a social coordination mechanism; Daniel Bell (1973, p. 20) formulated the possibility of this new research program:

> Now, knowledge has of course been necessary in the functioning of any society. What is distinctive about the post-industrial society is the change in the character of knowledge itself. What has become decisive for the organization of decisions and the direction of change is the centrality of *theoretical* knowledge—the primacy of theory over empiricism and the codification of knowledge into abstract systems of symbols that, as in any axiomatic system, can be used to illustrate many different and varied areas of experience.

In other words, Bell (1968, p. 182) postulated "a new fusion between science and innovation." This fusion makes new institutional arrangements at the interfaces between systems possible (cf. Holzner & Marx, 1979; Whitley, 1984). The linear model of innovation in which basic research invents and industry applies with a one-directional arrow between them is replaced with an interactive and nonlinear model (Godin, 2006b; Rosenberg, 1994). In this context an improved understanding of the dynamic interplay among research, invention, innovation, and economic growth is required. In an age of changing practices of knowledge production and distribution, it is important to analyze how the communication of knowledge (e.g., discursive knowledge) and information relate and differ.

How do codifications within each sphere and knowledge transfer among institutional spheres interact? This project, in my opinion, requires an information-theoretical approach because of its focus on the relations between the production and distribution of both information and knowledge. National systems of innovation can be measured in terms of sectors and institutions, for example, by using national statistics; the ongoing globalization in a knowledge-based economy, however, strongly suggests a theoretically guided research agenda at a supra-national level (Foray, 2004). Codification adds dynamic complexity to the multivariate complexity in the relations. Note that this project can be considered as "infra-disciplinary"—that is, discipline and sector specific—unlike the "trans-disciplinary" project of Mode-2 (Gibbons, Limoges, Nowotny, Schwartzman, Scott, & Trow, 1994) (see section on The Restructuring of Knowledge in a Knowledge-Based Economy).

At the same OECD workshop, Carter (1996) noted immediately that the measurement of a knowledge-based economy would pose serious challenges. The OECD devoted considerable resources to developing indicators of the knowledge-based economy (David & Foray, 1995; Organisation for Economic Co-operation and Development, 1996b). This led to the yearly publication of the so-called *Science, Technology, and Industry Scoreboards* (e.g., Organisation for Economic Co-operation and Development, 1997) and the periodic summary of progress at the ministerial level in *Science and Technology Statistical Compendia* (e.g., Organisation for Economic Co-operation and Development, 2004). However, Godin (2006a, p. 24) believes that the metaphor of a knowledge-based economy has functioned, in this context, mainly as a label for reorganizing existing indicators—most of the time, assuming national systems of member states explicitly or implicitly as units of analysis. He warned again that "important methodological difficulties await anyone interested in measuring intangibles like knowledge" (p. 24).

## The Triple Helix as a Model of the Knowledge-Based Economy

The Triple Helix model of the knowledge-based economy defines the main institutions as university, industry, and government (Etzkowitz & Leydesdorff, 1995). However, these institutional carriers of an innovation system can be expected to entertain a dually layered network: One layer of institutional relations in which they constrain each other's behavior and another layer of functional relations in which they shape each other's expectations. For example, the function of university-industry relations can be performed by different institutional arrangements such as transfer offices, spin-off companies, and licensing agreements. The institutional relations provide us with network data, but the functions in a knowledge-based economy are to be analyzed in terms of the transformative dynamics. The knowledge base of an economy can be considered as a specific configuration in the structure of expectations, which feeds back as a transformation mechanism on the institutional arrangements.

How would a knowledge-based economy operate differently from a market-based or political economy? The market mechanism first equilibrates between supply and demand. Secondly, economic exchange relations can be regulated by political institutions. I shall argue that organized knowledge production has more recently added a third coordination mechanism to the social system in addition to economic exchange relations and political control (Gibbons et al., 1994; Schumpeter, 1964; Whitley, 1984).

Three subdynamics are reproduced as functions of a knowledge-based economy: (1) wealth generation in the economy, (2) novelty generation by organized science and technology, and (3) governance of the interactions among these two subdynamics by policy making in the public sphere and management in the private sphere. The economic system, the academic system, and the political system can be considered as relatively autonomous subsystems of society that operate with different mechanisms. However, in order to describe their mutual interdependence and interaction with respect to knowledge creation, one first needs to distinguish these mechanisms.

The three subdynamics are not given, but constructed and continuously reconstructed in social relations. They can be considered as three helices operating upon each other selectively. For example, a patent can be considered as an event in which the coordination mechanisms interact (Figure 9.1). The different mechanisms are integrated in the observable events (in this case, the patents) as co-variations among the latent dimensions. The dimensions are different in terms of their remaining variations. The variations in each dimension (that is, the covariation plus the remaining variations) develop over time recursively, that is, with reference to a previous state. The interactions among these functionally differentiated mechanisms drive a cultural evolution that requires a model more complex than the biological model of evolution (Luhmann, 1984, 1990, 1995b).

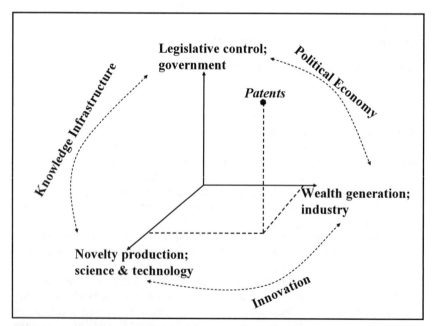

**Figure 9.1   Patents as events in the three-dimensional space of triple helix interactions**

Biological evolution assumes natural selection as a single selection mechanism. When selecting recursively upon each other, two selection mechanisms can be expected to develop into a co-evolution—as in a process of mutual shaping. The dynamics among three selection mechanisms, however, can be expected to lead to a higher degree of nonlinearity and therefore complexity (Li & Yorke, 1975; May, 1976; May & Leonard, 1975). The resulting complex dynamics evolve in terms of trajectories and regimes that change the system in which they emerge (Dosi, 1982).

Under such conditions, the independent (steering) variables at one moment of time may become dependent at the next moment. In other words, the dynamics can become self-organizing because the incentives for change can come from different sources and more than a single selection environment is operating. Consequently, the economic and political mechanisms no longer control, but function as selective feedback mechanisms that enable and constrain the development of scientific and technological knowledge. *Mutatis mutandis*, the development of scientific and technological knowledge has become a structural condition and a limiting factor on further socio-economic development.

The analytical function of the Triple Helix model is to unravel the complex dynamics of a knowledge-based economy in terms of its composing subdynamics. The formal model is not a grand super-theory: It builds on and remains dependent on appreciations of the phenomena at the level of the composing theories. Developments in the various discourses provide the data. Not incidentally, the Triple Helix model originated from the study of science and technology (Etzkowitz & Leydesdorff, 2000; Mirowski & Sent, 2007; Shinn, 2002; Slaughter & Rhodes, 2004).

The model is not first specified in terms of domains (e.g., national systems) or specific functions (e.g., knowledge production), but allows for interaction effects among domains and specific synergies among functions and institutions. The various subdynamics in the model can be considered from different analytical perspectives. These perspectives may be perpendicular and therefore develop as incommensurable discourses. Neo-classical economics, for example, has focused on the market as an equilibrating mechanism at each moment of time, whereas evolutionary economics focuses on innovations that upset the equilibria over time (Nelson & Winter, 1982). However, the different perspectives can be reconstructed in terms of their contributions to the specification of a Triple Helix model of the knowledge-based economy. Reflection on and abstraction from the specification of substantive mechanisms in favor of formalization enables us to understand the knowledge base of a social system as complex dynamics of expectations that are specified in variously coded communications.

Political discourse, for example, can be expected to operate differently from scientific discourse. Insofar as an overlay system of translations among these analytically different codes of communication can be shaped and reproduced, a next-order level of expectations may be stabilized and induce globalization as an additional feedback at the systems level. This feedback itself, however, remains a fallible expectation. The differentiations and translations among the variously codified expectations drive the development of the knowledge base in a social system.

In other words: Three interacting subdynamics can be expected to generate hypercycles on top of the cycles (e.g., business cycles, election cycles, paradigm changes) among the constitutive subdynamics. Structures in the data develop along trajectories, and the hypercycle provides us with a next-order regime. This regime may be more or less knowledge-based, depending on the configurations among the selection mechanisms on which it builds at the structural level.

For example, as long as economic exchanges and political control are not systematically affected by knowledge production and control, a political economy can be expected to prevail (Richta, Auerhan, Bareš, Bárta, Brenner, Cvekl, et al., 1968). In a knowledge-based economy, however, three levels can be distinguished: The level of the data where information is exchanged in (e.g., economic) relations, the level of (e.g., institutional) structures operating selectively—at this level specific meaning can be codified and selectively exchanged—and a third level at which configurations of meaning-exchanges can be knowledge based to varying extents.

In summary, this model is differentiated both horizontally and vertically. Horizontally, different coordination mechanisms operate upon one another. Vertically, the information is structured semantically and the structures can develop along trajectories, with the trajectories embedded in regimes that emerge from configurations among structures and trajectories. Luhmann (1984, 1995b, 1997) distinguished the horizontal differentiation as *functional* differentiation from the vertical one as *social* differentiation. Horizontal differentiation is based on differences among the codes of communication in the coordination systems and vertical differentiation corresponds with the distinction between institutional and functional dynamics in the Triple Helix model. Different subdynamics can be expected to operate in different layers, and to interact in the instantiations.

At the institutional level, functional dynamics are integrated historically in one arrangement or another and the various subsystems are thus instantiated (Giddens, 1984). These historical instantiations condition and enable the further development of functional subsystems, which develop in terms of flows of communication. Analytically, the instantiations enable us to specify the dynamics in terms of relevant parameters. The selection mechanisms, however, remain theoretical specifications with the epistemological status of an hypothesis. Entertaining the Triple Helix hypothesis that more than two selection environments need to be specified for the analysis of manifestations of the knowledge-based economy can enrich both the description and the analysis.

For example, in the context of a knowledge-intensive corporation, technological expectations have to be combined with market opportunities in planning cycles. Decisions in interactions at the organizational level shape the future orientation of the corporation, but have only localizable effects on the global market and the relevant technologies (Luhmann, 2000). These other two helices are instantiated by the decision in the third. However, the instantiations should not be confused with the dynamics.

In university-industry relations, for example, the institutional arrangements (e.g., transfer offices) can be evaluated in terms of how well they serve the transfer of new knowledge in exchange for university income. The knowledge transfer process may be enhanced or hindered by the institutional contexts. Thus, both the functions and the institutions remain contingent. Furthermore, the two layers can be coupled operationally; they may co-evolve or not. Co-evolution may lead to a dead end (lock-in) or provide a competitive advantage. These remain empirical questions.

In a pluriform society, the processes at different levels and in different dimensions develop concurrently, asynchronously, and in interaction with one another. The horizontal differentiation among the coordination mechanisms is based on the availability of different codes for communication. Because meanings are no longer given, but constructed and reproduced in discourses, the codes can also be translated into one another. For example, the political system can (attempt to) regulate the market because it first uses a code different from that of the market mechanism. However, the political system can, in addition to legislation, also reconstruct the market by creating market incentives. The codes are historically recombined by local agency, including institutional agency.

Insofar as the three (latent) functions resonate into a configuration, a knowledge-based economy can be generated. The various "horizons of meaning" (Husserl, 1973, p. 45) in the different dimensions resound in the communicative events that instantiate these systems. The observable instantiations can be expected to change the expectations in the next round. Note that there may be more than one configuration that is knowledge-based. In other words, the knowledge-basedness of a system poses an empirical question. The knowledge-based economy can be considered as a configuration among three leading coordination mechanisms such that a degree of freedom is added to the two previously leading mechanisms in a political economy (markets and political control).

Analytically, the market provides only a single selection mechanism, but two selection mechanisms can reinforce each other into the cycles of a political economy. A system with three selection mechanisms can additionally be globalized on top of the institutional stabilizations. Globalization, however, remains a meta-stable construct (with the theoretical status of a hypothesis about a hyper-cycle operating at a next-order level). The reproduction of this next-order system cannot be controlled by the constructing system because a self-organizing dynamic is supposedly generated.

In other words, globalization at the regime level remains a tendency in the historical systems (trajectories) that are globalizing. The two layers of institutional stabilization and retention versus functional restructuration are both needed and can be expected to feed back into each other, thus changing the institutional roles, the selection environments, and potentially the evolutionary functions of the various stakeholders in subsequent rounds of "creative destruction," transition, and change (Schumpeter, 1943, p. 81).

The observable networks function as infrastructures of the social system by constraining and enabling communication through them and among them.[1] Insofar as the fluxes of communication through these networks are guided by the different codes of communication, the system can self-organize a knowledge base in terms of a configuration among the functional subsystems of communication. Because the coordination mechanisms use different rules for the coding, a variety of meanings can be provided to the events from different perspectives. The more the codes of communication can be spanned orthogonally, the more complexity can be processed. This differentiation process is counterbalanced by processes of integration in the historical organization by instantiating agency. Thus, the two layers of the Triple Helix model support both differentiation and integration. Trade-offs between globalization and stabilization are endogenous to a knowledge-based economy. Knowledge-based systems remain in transition.

## Knowledge as a Social Coordination Mechanism

Knowledge enables us to codify the meaning of information. Information can be more or less meaningful given a perspective. However, meaning is provided from a system's perspective and with hindsight. Providing meaning to an uncertainty (that is, Shannon-type information) can be considered as a first codification. Knowledge enables us to discard some meanings and retain others in a (next-order) layer of discursive codifications. In other words, knowledge can be considered as a meaning that makes a difference.[2] Knowledge enables us to translate one meaning into another. Knowledge itself can also be codified; codified knowledge can, for example, be commercialized. Thus, a knowledge-based system operates in recursive loops of codification that one would expect to be increasingly specific in terms of the information to be retained.

Knowledge informs expectations in the present on the basis of previous operations of the system. Informed expectations orient the discourse toward future events and possible reconstructions. A knowledge-based economy is driven more by reflexively codified expectations than by its historical conditions (Lundvall & Borras, 1997). The knowledge base of a social system can be further developed over time by ongoing processes of theoretically informed deconstructions and reconstructions (Cowan et al., 2000; Foray, 2004).

In other words, science-based representations of possible futures (e.g., competitive advantages) feed back on historically manifest processes (Biggiero, 2001; Nonaka & Takeuchi, 1995). The manifestations, however, can be considered as the products of (interactions with) other subdynamics. The other subdynamics (markets, organizations) reflexively counteract upon and thus buffer against the transformative power of the knowledge base. Graham and Dickinson (2007), for example, noted that political discourse may be particularly resistant to the idea that it itself is only one among other subdynamics in a knowledge-based economy.

The reflexive orientation toward the future inverts the time axis locally (Figure 9.2). A movement against the axis of time is expected to reduce uncertainty. (It can be shown that the Second Law holds equally for probabilistic and thermodynamic entropy production [Theil, 1972].) However, a reflexive inversion of the arrow of time may change the dynamics in a historically stabilized system (cf. Giddens, 1990). Stabilization and destabilization can be considered historical processes (along the axis of time); reflexivity adds to the historical process an evolutionary dynamic that is based on selection in the present from the perspective of hindsight. By inverting the axis of time, stabilizing conditions can, under certain conditions, also be globalized (Coveney & Highfield, 1990; Mackenzie, 2001; Urry, 2000, 2003). Reflexivity, however, enables us to develop both perspectives as two sides of the same coin: The historical instantiations along trajectories and the evolutionary dynamics of expectations at the regime level.

Let us first follow the construction of a knowledge-based economy from the historical perspective. Codified knowledge has always been a relevant source of variance at the level of individual actions. Before the emergence of scientific and

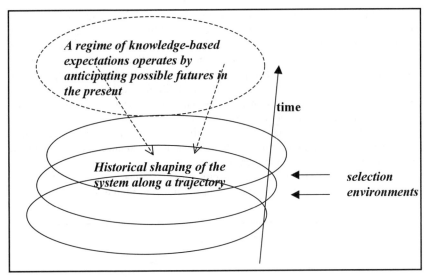

**Figure 9.2   A technological trajectory follows the axis of time; a knowledge-based regime operates within a system in terms of expectations, that is, against the axis of time.**

technological knowledge as another mechanism of social coordination, the economic exchange of knowledge was developed as distinct from the exchange of commodities within the context of the market economy.

For example, the patent system can be considered as a typical product of industrial competition. Patent legislation became crucial for regulating intellectual property in the late nineteenth century when knowledge markets emerged in chemistry and later in electrical engineering (Noble, 1977; Van den Belt & Rip, 1987). Patents package scientific knowledge so that new knowledge can function at the interface of science with the economy and be incorporated into knowledge-based innovations (Granstrand, 1999; Jaffe & Trajtenberg, 2002). Patents thus provide a format for codifying knowledge for purposes other than the internal requirements of quality control in scientific communication.

The organized production and control of knowledge for the purpose of industrial innovation increasingly emerged as a subdynamic of the socio-economic system in advanced capitalist societies by roughly 1870 (Braverman, 1974; Noble, 1977). Schumpeter (1964) is well known for his argument that the dynamics of innovation upset the market mechanism (Nelson & Winter, 1982). Market mechanisms seek equilibrium at each moment of time, but novelty production generates an orthogonal subdynamic along the time axis. In economics, this has been modeled as the difference between factor substitution (the change of input factors along the production function) and technological development (a shift in the production function toward the origin [Sahal, 1981a, 1981b]). Technological innovations enable enterprises to reduce factor costs in both labor and capital (Salter, 1960; cf. Rosenberg, 1976).

Improving a system innovatively presumes that one is able to handle the system purposefully. When this reflection is further refined by organizing knowledge, the innovative dynamics can be reinforced. This reinforcement will occur at some *places* more than at others. Thus, a third dimension pertinent to our subject can be specified: The geographical—and potentially national—distribution of whatever is invented, produced, traded, or retained. Nation-states, for example, can be expected to differ in terms of the relationship between their respective economy and its knowledge base (Lundvall, 1992; Nelson, 1993).

Geographically positioned units of analysis (e.g., firms, institutions), economic exchange relations, and novelty production cannot be reduced to one another. However, these independent dimensions can be expected to interact to varying extents (Storper, 1997). Given these specifications, one can create a model of the three dimensions and their interaction terms as shown in Figure 9.3.

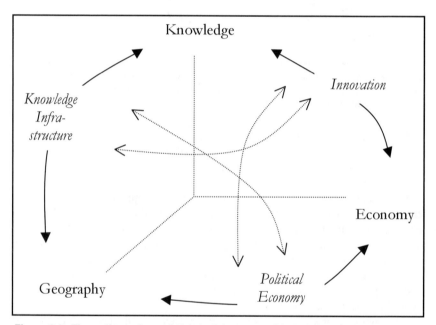

**Figure 9.3  Three dimensions of the social system with their interaction terms**

This distinction among the three dimensions will enable me in a later section to specify different micro-operations of the social system because agents (1) are geographically positioned and therefore locally embedded, (2) can maintain economic exchange relations across borders, and (3) learn from the resulting dynamics with reference to their positions and relations. The first micro-operation is considered in neo-classical economics as the micro-foundation of individual agency: Agents are considered as *endowed* with natural preferences. Lundvall (1988) proposed the second micro-operation of *interaction* as the alternative foundation of his program of national systems of innovation in evolutionary economics. I shall return to this proposal in more detail. The reflexive layer, however, adds a *third* micro-operation: Reflection can be both individual and relational. We shall see that this latter distinction also makes a difference: *Reflexive communications* can be expected to transform relations in an evolutionary mode (Beck, Giddens, & Lash, 1994; Bhaskar, 1979, 1998; Leydesdorff, 2009; Maturana, 1978).

Figure 9.3 elaborates the conceptualization by situating each of the interaction terms between two of the three dimensions. A political economy, for example, organizes markets within the context of a nation-state. The third coordination mechanism of knowledge and learning is more recently added and may change a political economy into a knowledge-based one (at some places more than others). In a pluriform and differentiated society, however, the various interaction terms are no longer synchronized *ex ante*, and thus they may begin to interact among themselves.

The developments are not coordinated and may thus develop in some dimensions at some places more than at others. For example, military anticipations that primarily developed in national contexts also shape non-market selection environments enabling firms to move forward in constructing competitive advantages in a relatively shielded environment (Rosenberg, 1976, 1990). Thus, the dynamics of the Triple Helix are not developed at a meta-level, but are endogenous once this model of subdynamics operating upon one another is available within a society. The social organization of knowledge-based expectations feeds back as a regime by transforming the trajectories from which it emerged.

# Neo-Evolutionary Dynamics in a Triple Helix of Coordination Mechanisms

During the formation of political economies in national systems during the nineteenth century, knowledge production was at first considered an exogenous given (List, 1904; Marx, 1971).[3] Under the condition of constitutional stability in the various nation states after approximately 1870,[4] *national systems of innovation* could gradually be developed among the axes of economic exchange and organized knowledge production and control (Noble, 1977; Rosenberg, 1976, 1982a). Globalization, however, restructures the relations among nations. The variation among nations provides another dimension to the global system. Interactions among three subdynamics, however, can be expected to generate a complex dynamics of transition.

It is less known that Schumpeter (1964, p. 175) himself signaled that the superposition of three cycles can be expected to generate chaotic patterns. In general, two interacting subdynamics can be expected to co-evolve along trajectories, as long as the third dynamic can be considered as relatively constant. Over time, two subdynamics can also lock into each other in a process of mutual shaping in a co-evolution (Arthur, 1994; McLuhan, 1964). However, stabilities or regular patterns developed between two subdynamics can be destabilized by a third. Historically, a hitherto stable context may begin to change under the pressure of an emerging subdynamic. For example, the erosion of relative stability in nation-states because of more recent globalization processes has changed the conditions of national innovation systems.

A political economy can be explained in terms of two subdynamics (for example, as a dialectic between production forces and production relations); more complex dynamics can be expected when three subdynamics are left free to operate upon one another. However, a configuration with three possible degrees of freedom—markets, governance, and knowledge production—can be modeled in terms of a Triple Helix of university-industry-government relations (Etzkowitz & Leydesdorff, 2000; cf. Lewontin, 2000). Governance can be considered as the variable that instantiates and organizes systems in the geographical dimension of the model, with industry as the main carrier of economic production and exchange, and universities playing a leading role in the organization of the knowledge-production function (Godin & Gingras, 2000).

In this (neo-)evolutionary model of interacting subdynamics, the institutional dimensions can no longer be expected to correspond one-to-one with the functions in the networks carried by and between the agencies. The analytical dimensions span a space in which the institutions operate. Each university and industry, for example, also has a geographical location and is therefore subject to regulation and legislation. In a knowledge-based system, however, functions no longer develop exclusively at the local level, that is, contained within institutional settings. Instead, the interactions generate evolutionary dynamics of change in relations at the network level. In other words, the functions provide a layer of development that is analytically different from, but historically coupled to, the institutional arrangements.

Two of the three functions (economy and science) can be considered as relatively open because they are universal (Luhmann, 1984, 1990, 1995b; Parsons, 1951). The function of control bends the space of possible interactions reflexively back to the *positions* of the operating units (e.g., the firms and the nations) in the marketplace and at the research front, respectively. In this dimension, the question of what can be retained locally during the reproduction of the innovation processes becomes crucial. The system of reference for this question about how to organize and interface the fluxes of communication remains the political economy.

Government policies and management strategies weave a reflexive layer with the private/public distinction as its specific degree of freedom. The advantages of entertaining a knowledge base can be incorporated only if the knowledge produced by the interacting fluxes can also be retained organizationally and reflexively by this network. In other words, the development of a knowledge base is dependent on the condition that knowledge production be socially organized into a knowledge infrastructure; for example, in R&D laboratories. The historical development of a regime of intellectual property rights reflects the function of government policies in securing the knowledge-based dynamics (Kingston, 2003).

As noted, the interfaces between institutions and functions can be expected to co-evolve in some configurations more than in others. However, these co-evolutions can be continuously disturbed by a third subdynamic. The knowledge-based economy cannot be developed without the consequent destabilizations and reconstructions, or, in Schumpeter's (1943, p. 81) terminology, "creative destruction." The destabilizing dynamics of innovation can be reinforced when they are knowledge-based because the dynamics of reconstruction are reinforced (Barras, 1990;

Freeman & Perez, 1988). Knowledge can make alternatives available; the more codified this knowledge is, the more globally this communication system can function as another selection context.

The expectations that are organized in a knowledge base can be further codified, as with scientific knowledge. The expectations can also be codified through the local use of knowledge and knowledge can be retained in textual practices. When increasingly organized by R&D management and policies for science and technology, the emerging structures in the expectations provide another selection environment. This global selection environment of scientific and technical knowledge remains pending as additional selection pressure upon the locally stabilized configurations. Thus, codification both stabilizes and globalizes discursive knowledge, and the third subdynamic of knowledge-based innovations can become increasingly a global driver of change by facilitating these changes of perspectives.

For example, Dosi (1982) distinguished between the stabilization of innovations and routines along technological *trajectories* and the knowledge base as a next-order *regime* that remains emergent as a paradigm. As innovations are further developed along trajectories, a knowledge base becomes reflexively available as an evolutionary mechanism for restructuring the historical trajectories on which it builds. This next-order perspective of the regime rests as an additional selection environment on the historical trajectories. In terms of Figure 9.3, this second-order system can be added as in Figure 9.4.

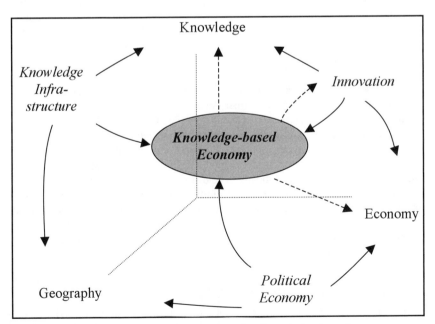

**Figure 9.4  The first-order interactions generate a knowledge-based economy as a next-order system.**

The construction of a knowledge base remains a bottom-up operation, but a control mechanism that tends to operate top-down is increasingly constructed at the systems level. DiMaggio and Powell (1983, p. 150) called this emerging control "coercive isomorphism" and Giddens (1979, p. 77) specified the mechanism as a "duality of structure," which would operate in a "virtual" dimension (p. 64). However, these specifications remained at the level of behavior and action, and did not specify the hypothesized dynamics as the evolutionary self-organization of expectations at a next-order level. Giddens (1984, p. xxxvii) deliberately abstained from the specification of next-order control mechanisms because it would, in his opinion, lead to reintroducing and potentially reifying a systems perspective in the manner of Parsons (cf. Merton, 1973).

From a systems perspective, Giddens's warning entails a non sequitur. Reification does not follow from an analytical distinction; the analytical distinction remains part of a discourse. However, the exclusive focus on observable variation in the action-oriented approaches and from the neo-institutional perspective prevents us from further developing an evolutionary and sociological theory of communications at more abstract levels. More abstract theorizing—for example, the specification of expectations about how expectations operate—is needed for understanding how the use of language and discursive knowledge can *change* structure/action contingency relations.

In my opinion, different selection mechanisms and levels can be distinguished. Note that the dynamics of selection environments are structural and therefore deterministic, although communication systems develop in terms of distributions and therefore uncertainties can be expected in the (distributions of) instantiations of the systems. The proposed change of perspective is analytical: The instantiations (observed values) can inform the expectations, but only insofar as the latter are specified. From this neo-evolutionary perspective, action can be considered as variation; the focus remains on the specification of the hypothesized selection mechanisms and their interactions.

The codes of communication in these coordination mechanisms provide different meanings to the distributions. A further development of the knowledge base of an economy as a construct can be expected under the condition that the various coordination mechanisms develop specific resonances in interactions among recurring variations, that is, in a self-organizing mode. However, this *self-organization* among the coordination mechanisms of society exhibits an evolutionary dynamics among the flows of communications analytically to be distinguished from the historical *organization* of relations among the carrying institutions (Luhmann, 1975, 1997). The neo-institutional perspective focused on networks of relations; a knowledge-based economy can be specified only from this neo-evolutionary perspective. The dynamics are based on changes in both the relations and the (potentially meaningful) organization of relations.

## The Operation of the Knowledge Base

Interacting expectations can provide a basis for changes in the behavior of the carrying agents. These behavioral changes differ from the institutional imperatives and market incentives that have driven the system previously (e.g., in terms of profit-maximizing behavior). Institutions and markets develop historically, that is, with the arrow of time; the knowledge-based structures of expectations drive the system in an anticipatory mode. Future-oriented planning cycles can be expected to become (in some places) more important than current prices on the market. Thus, informed anticipations increasingly change the dynamics of the system from an agent-based perspective toward a more abstract, knowledge-based one.

The knowledge-based subdynamic operates by reconstructing the past in the present on the basis of representations that contain informed expectations (e.g., curves and functions displayed on computer screens). As the intensity and speed of communication among the carrying agencies increases (e.g., because of the further developments of information and communication technology; see, for example, Kaufer & Carley [1993]; Luhmann [1997]), the codification of knowledge becomes increasingly a functional means to reduce complexity in inter-human communication. The emerging order of expectations remains accessible to reflexive agents with a capacity to learn. The expectations can be refined as they become more theoretically informed. The communicative competencies of the agents involved can be considered as rate-limiting factors.

Both participants and analysts are able to improve their understanding of the restructuring of the expectations at interfaces within the systems under study, and one is able to switch roles, albeit to variable extents (Giddens, 1976). As these communicative competencies are further developed among the carriers of the communications, the codifications in the expectations can be further developed. For example, in a knowledge-based economy the already abstract price-mechanism of a market-based economy can increasingly be reconstructed in terms of price/performance ratios based on expectations about the life-cycles of technologies (Galbraith, 1967; Heertje, 1973). No educated consumer nowadays buys a computer, for example, using only price comparisons. Thus, more abstract and knowledge-intensive criteria are increasingly guiding economic decision making. These more abstract criteria have been central to government (e.g., procurement) policies in advanced industrial nations since the early 1980s, in response to the second oil crisis (Freeman, 1982; Rothwell & Zegveld, 1981).

The dynamics of a complex system of knowledge-based innovations are nonlinear (Allen, 1994; Krugman, 1996). This nonlinearity is a consequence of interaction terms among the subsystems and the recursive processes operating within each of them simultaneously. In the long run, the nonlinear (interaction) terms can be expected to outweigh the linear (action) terms because of the higher exponents in the equations. For example, the *interaction* effects between demand pull and technology push can be expected to become more important, over time, for the systemic development of innovations than the sum of the linear action terms (Kline & Rosenberg, 1986; Mowery & Rosenberg, 1979, 1989). The nonlinear interaction terms can be expected to lead to unintended consequences.

For example, when a sector undergoes technological innovation, a lock-in to a market segment may first shape a specific trajectory of innovations (Arthur, 1994; David, 1985; cf. Liebowitz & Margolis, 1999). Learning curves can be steep following such a breakthrough and the stabilization of a trajectory in the marketplace (Arrow, 1962; Rosenberg, 1982b). Analogously, when a science-based technology locks into a nation-state (e.g., in the energy or health sector), a monopoly can be immunized against the third helix of market forces for considerable periods of time. Over longer periods of time, however, these lock-ins can be expected to erode because of the ongoing processes of creative destruction (Schumpeter, 1943). Such creative destruction is based on recombinations of market forces with new insights. For example, the monopolies of national telephone companies in Western Europe disappeared under the pressure of new (neo-liberal) industrial policies and the emergence of the cell phone. Corporations may have to disinvest in their own competencies in order to make room for new technologies.

For example, when the DC-3 airplane was introduced in the 1930s, it took Boeing two years to construct a competing airplane (the 307 Stratoliner) on the basis of adopting the "textbook" of its main competitor. When in a next revolution Boeing took the lead with the introduction of wide-body airplanes (the 707-series) in 1957, it took the company almost 25 years to establish its model as the dominate paradigm because in the meantime competition had become global and the old paradigm of propeller airplanes was well established. Only when Airbus adopted the new paradigm in 1981 did the textbook of the jet-engine powered airplane become fully established (Frenken, 2005; Frenken & Leydesdorff, 2000). Old trajectories can survive in niche markets and this may postpone crises. Interaction effects among negative feedbacks, however, may lead to global crises that require the restructuring of the carrying layer of institutions (Freeman & Perez, 1988).

Historically, interactions among the relevant (sub)dynamics were first enhanced by geographical proximity (for example, within a national context or the context of a single industry), but as the economic and technological dimensions of the systems globalized, dynamic scale effects became more important than static ones for the retention of wealth. Such dynamic scale effects through innovation were first realized by multinational corporations (Brusoni, Prencipe, & Pavitt., 2000; Galbraith, 1967; Granstrand, Patel, & Pavitt, 1997). They became a concern of governments in advanced, industrialized countries after the (global) oil crises of the 1970s (Organisation for Economic Cooperation and Development, 1980). Improving the knowledge base in the economies of these nations became a priority as science-based innovations were increasingly recognized as providing the main stimulus to growth (Freeman, 1982; Irvine & Martin, 1984; Porter, 1990; Rothwell & Zegveld, 1981).

In other words, the relatively stabilized arrangements of a political economy endogenously generate the meta-stability of a knowledge-based system when the geographical units begin to interact and exchange more intensively in the economic and technological dimensions. Under the pressure of globalization, the institutional make-up of national systems must be restructured: The national and international perspectives induce an oscillation in a system between its stabilized and globalized states. The oscillating system uses its institutional resources (among which are its innovative capacities) for the continuation of an endless transition.

# The Restructuring of Knowledge Production in a Knowledge-Based Economy

The knowledge base emerges by recursively codifying the expected information content of the underlying arrangements (Fujigaki, 1998; Luhmann, 1984, 1995b;

Maturana & Varela, 1980). A cultural reality of expectations is constructed piece-meal on top of a reality that seems naturally given (Berger & Luckmann, 1966). For example, what is natural or sustainable in a Dutch polder landscape can be defined differently with reference to different centuries in the past. "Nature" is no longer a given, but can be specified as one of the previous states of a technology. However, the technological expectations change with time. In a knowledge-based economy, this reconstruction of expectations has itself become the systemic consequence of industrial production.

Wide-body airplanes, for example, make possible mass tourism to destinations that were previously out of reach for large parts of the population. The regime level of expectations ("a winter break on a tropical island") emerges from the previous trajectories (e.g., of wide-body airplanes), but as a socially unintended consequence and a new market. A previously stabilized system globalizes with reference to its next-order or regime level as an order of expectations.

Innovations can be considered as the historical carriers of this transformative regime because they reconstruct, reorganize, and thus recontextualize the relevant interfaces among the relevant selection environments. Innovations instantiate the globalizing dynamics in the present and potentially restructure existing interfaces in a competitive mode. In an innovative environment, the existing arrangements must be reassessed continuously. For example, if one introduces high-speed trains, the standards and materials for constructing railways and rails may need to be reconsidered.

Once in place, a knowledge-based system thus feeds back on the terms of its construction by offering comparative improvements and advantages to the solutions found hitherto, that is, on the basis of previous crafts and skills. Knowledge intensity drives differentiation at the global level by providing us with alternatives. However, the emerging system continues to operate locally in terms of institutions and solutions that organize and produce observable integration across interfaces. The production facilities provide the historical basis—that is, the knowledge infra-structure—for further developing the knowledge-based operations within it.

Because of this historical shaping under interacting selection pressures of highly codified systems of communication, the expectations remain heavily structured and invested with interests. Finding solutions to puzzles requires investments of time and money. Some authors (Gibbons et al., 1994; Nowotny, Scott, & Gibbons, 2001) have claimed that the contemporary system exhibits de-differentiation among pol-icy making, economic transactions, and scientific insights due to the mutual con-textualization of these processes. These authors posit that a new mode of operation (Mode-2) has emerged at the level of the social system because of the dynamics of incorporating scientific knowledge.

Indeed, the perpetual restructuring of the system that is guided by the knowledge base (of interacting structures of expectations) can be expected to induce new insti-tutional arrangements. Such rearrangements may include the (perhaps temporary) reversal of traditional roles between industry and the university, for example, in interdisciplinary research centers (Etzkowitz, Webster, Gebhardt, & Terra, 2000). Among codified expectations, however, exchanges can be expected to remain highly structured and continue to reproduce differentiation for evolutionary rea-sons: A differentiated system of communications can process more complexity than an integrated one (Shinn, 2002; Shinn & Lamy, 2006). The integration in the instantiations ("de-differentiation") can be made fully compatible with a model that assumes functional differentiation among the codes of communications that flow through the instantiations.

Complex systems need both the local *integration* of the various subdynamics into organizational formats and global *differentiation* among the codes of communication in order to enhance further developments. This tension allows for meta-stabilization as a transitory state that can sustain both innovation and retention. In such systems, functions develop both in interactions with one another and along their own axes, and thirdly in interaction with the exchanges among the institutions. An integrated perspective such as Mode-2 provides a specific combination of perspectives among other possibilities.

At the interfaces between the economics of the market and the heuristics in R&D processes, different translation mechanisms can be further developed that structure and codify these interactions over time. I cited the example of developing the price mechanism into the (bivariate) price/performance criterion, but in innovative environments one can expect criteria to become multivariate. For example, knowledge-based corporations organize sophisticated interfaces between strategic (long-term) and operational (medium-term) planning cycles in order to appreciate and update the different perspectives (Galbraith & Nathanson, 1978).

Because communications in a knowledge-based system are no longer controlled by a single coordination mechanism, integration and differentiation can be expected to operate concurrently at the various interfaces, and without a priori synchronization. In terms of the dynamics of the system, differentiation and integration can thus be considered as two sides of the same coin: Integration may take different forms, and differentiations can be relatively integrated (as subsystems). From an evolutionary perspective, the question becomes: Where in the network can the relevant puzzles be solved and hence competitive edges be maintained? Thus, one can expect both geographically confined innovation systems and technological systems of innovation (Carlsson, 2002, 2006; Carlsson & Stankiewicz, 1991; Edqvist, 1997). The horizontal and vertical overlapping of systems and subsystems of innovation can be considered a hallmark of the knowledge-based economy.

In other words, the definition of a system of innovations becomes itself increasingly knowledge-based—that is, a research question!—in a knowledge-based economy, because the subsystems are differently codified, yet interacting (at different speeds) in the reproduction of the system. Governance of a knowledge-based economy can be based only on a set of informed assumptions about the relevant systems (Weiss, 1979). These hypotheses are predictably in need of more informed revisions because one expects new formats to be invented at the hitherto stabilized interfaces.

## The Knowledge-Based Economy and the Systems-of-Innovation Approach

When Lundvall (1988, p. 362) proposed that the nation be considered as the first candidate for the *integration* of innovation systems, he formulated this claim carefully in terms of a heuristic:

> The interdependency between production and innovation goes both ways. ... This interdependency between production and innovation makes it legitimate to take the national system of production as a starting point when defining a system of innovation.

The idea of integrating innovation into production at the *national* level has the analytical advantage of providing the analyst with an institutionally demarcated system of reference. If the market is continuously upset by innovation, can the nation then perhaps be considered as another, albeit institutionally organized, (quasi-)equilibrium (Aoki, 2001)?

The specification of the nation as a well defined system of reference enabled evolutionary economists to study, for example, the so-called "differential productivity growth puzzle" that is generated by the different speeds of development among the various industrial sectors (Nelson & Winter, 1975, p. 338). The problem of the relative rates of innovation cannot be defined properly without the specification of a system of reference that integrates different sectors of an economy (Nelson, 1982, 1994). The solutions to this puzzle can accordingly be expected to differ among nation states (Lundvall, 1992; Nelson, 1993).

The emergence of transnational levels of government, such as the European Union, together with an increased awareness of regional differences within and across nations have changed the functions of national governments (Braczyk, Cooke, & Heidenreich, 1998). The historical progression varies among countries; integration at the national level still plays a major role in systems of innovation (Skolnikoff, 1993). However, "government" has evolved from a hierarchically fixed point of reference into the variable "governance," which spans a variety of sub- and supranational levels. Larédo (2003) argued that this polycentric environment of stimulation has become a condition for effective innovation policies in the European Union.

Innovations are generated and incubated by locally producing units such as scientific laboratories, artisan workshops, and communities of instrument makers, but in interaction with market forces. The market can be considered in a first approximation as a global and relatively open network seeking equilibrium; innovation requires closure of the network in terms of the relevant stakeholders (Callon, 1998). This provides innovation with both a market dimension and a technological dimension. The two dimensions are traded off at interfaces: What can be produced in terms of technical characteristics encounters what can be diffused into relevant markets in terms of service characteristics (Frenken, 2005; Lancaster, 1979; Saviotti, 1996). Thus, a competitive edge can be shaped locally. Such a locally shielded network density can also be considered as a *niche* (Kemp, Schot, & Hoogma, 1998; Schot & Geels, 2007). Systems of innovation can be considered as complex systems because they are based on maintaining interfaces in a variety of dimensions.

Problems at interfaces may lead to costs, but they can be solved more easily within niches than in their surroundings. Unlike organizations, niches have no fixed delineations. They can be considered as densities of interfaces in an environment that is otherwise more loosely connected. Within a niche, competitive advantages are achieved by reducing transaction costs (Biggiero, 1998; Williamson, 1985). Niches can thus be shaped, for example, within the context of a multinational and diversified corporation or within a regional economy. In another context, Porter (1990) proposed analyzing national economies in terms of *clusters* of innovations. Clusters may span vertical and horizontal integrations along business columns or across different types of markets. They can be expected to act as systems of innovation that proceed more rapidly than their relevant environments and thus are able to maintain a competitive edge.

National systems of innovation can be expected to vary in terms of their strengths and weaknesses in different dimensions. In the case of Japan (Freeman, 1988), or in comparisons among Latin American countries (Cimoli, 2000), such a delineation may provide heuristics more than in the case of nations participating in the common frameworks of the European Union. Sometimes, the geographical delineation of systems of innovation in niches is straightforward, as in the case of the Italian industrial districts. These often comprise only a few valleys (Beccatini, Bellandi, Ottati, & Sforzi, 2003; Biggiero, 1998). The evaluation of a system of innovation can also vary according to the different perspectives of policy making. The OECD, for example, has focused on comparing national statistics; but the EU has had a tendency to focus on changes in the interactions among the member states, for example, in trans-border regions.[5]

For political reasons one may wish to define a system of innovation as national or regional (Cooke, 2002). However, an innovation system evolves and its shape is therefore not fixed (Bathelt, 2003). One may entertain the *hypothesis* of an innovation system, but the operationalization and the measurement remain crucial for the validation (Cooke & Leydesdorff, 2006). For example, Riba-Vilanova and Leydesdorff (2001) were *not* able to identify a Catalonian system of innovation in terms of knowledge-intensive indicators such as patents and publications despite references to this regional system of innovation prevalent in the literature on the basis of employment statistics (Braczyk et al., 1998).

Belgium provides an obvious example of regional differentiation. The country has been regionalized to such an extent that one can no longer expect the innovation dynamics of Flanders to be highly integrated with the francophone parts of the country. In a study of Hungary's national innovation system, Lengyel and Leydesdorff (2008) found that three different regimes were generated during the transition period with very different dynamics: (1) Budapest and its agglomeration emerged as a knowledge-based innovation system on every indicator; (2) in the northwestern part of the country, foreign-owned companies and foreign direct investment induced a shift in knowledge-organization; and (3) the system in the eastern and southern part of the country has remained organized in accordance with government expenditures. In the Hungarian case, the national level no longer adds to the synergy among these regional innovation systems. When Hungary entered its transition period after the demise of the Soviet Union it was probably too late to shape a national system of innovations given the concurrent aspiration of Hungary to join the European Union.

One would expect a system of innovations in the Cambridge (U.K.) region to be science-based (Etzkowitz et al., 2000) and the system of innovations in the Basque country to be industrially based and reliant on technology centers that focus on applied research rather than on universities for their knowledge base (Moso & Olazaran, 2002). In general, the question of which dimensions are relevant to the circumstances of a given innovation system requires empirical specification and research (Carlsson, 2006). However, in order to draw conclusions from such research efforts, a theoretical framework is needed. This framework should enable us to compare across innovation systems and in terms of relevant dimensions, but without an a priori identification of specific innovation systems. The systems under study provide the evidence; the analytical frameworks have to carry the explanation of the differences.

As has been argued, the emergence of a knowledge base requires the specification of at least three systems of reference. Innovations take place at interfaces, and the study of innovation therefore requires the specification of at least two systems of reference (e.g., knowledge production and economic exchanges). In my opinion, the Triple Helix can be elaborated into a neo-evolutionary model that integrates the Mode-2 thesis of the new production of scientific knowledge, the study of systems of innovation in evolutionary economics, *and* the neo-classical perspective on the dynamics of the market. In order to specify this model, the three relevant micro-operations have first to be distinguished analytically and in relation to the most relevant theories of innovation and technological development.

# The Knowledge-Based Economy and Neo-Evolutionary Theories of Innovation

## The Construction of the Evolving Unit

Nelson and Winter's (1982) trajectory approach has been central to evolutionary economics. In their seminal study entitled "In Search of Useful Theory of Innovation," Nelson and Winter (1977, pp. 48–49) formulated their research program:

> Our objective is to develop a class of models based on the following premises. First, in contrast with the production function oriented studies discussed earlier, we posit that almost any nontrivial change in product or process, if there has been no prior experience, is an innovation. That is, we abandon the sharp distinction between moving along a production function and shift to a new one that characterizes the studies surveyed earlier. Second, we treat any innovation as involving considerable uncertainty both before it is ready for introduction to the economy, and even after it is introduced, and thus we view the innovation process as involving a continuing disequilibrium. … We are attempting to build conformable sub-theories of the processes that lead to a new technology ready for trial use, and of what we call the selection environment that takes the flow of innovations as given. (Of course, there are important feedbacks.)

These two premises led these authors to a programmatic shift in the analysis from a focus on the specification of expectations to observable firm *behavior* and the development of industries along historical trajectories (Andersen, 1994). Thus, evolutionary economics could increasingly be shaped as a heterodox paradigm (Casson, 1997; Storper, 1997).

This shift in perspective from economic (and mathematically formulated) models to a focus on observable firm behavior has epistemological consequences. Both the neo-classical hypothesis of profit maximization by the operation of the market and Schumpeter's hypothesis of the upsetting dynamics of innovations were formulated as analytical perspectives. These theories specify expectations. However, the theory of the firm focuses on observable variation. The status of the model thus changed: Analytical idealizations such as factor substitution and technological development cannot be expected to develop historically in their ideal-typical forms.

Nelson and Winter's first premise proposed focusing on the observables not as an *explanandum*, but as *variation* to be selected in selection environments (second premise). Innovation is then no longer to be explained, but trajectory formation among innovations serves as the *explanandum* of the first of the two conformable theories. Trajectories enable enterprises to retain competences in terms of routines. Under evolutionary conditions of competition, one can expect the variation to be organized by firms along trajectories. From this perspective, however, the knowledge base is considered as completely embedded in the *institutional* contexts of the firm. (I would prefer to consider this institutional environment as providing a knowledge infrastructure.) The relations between the evolutionary and the institutional perspective were thus firmly engraved in this research program (Nelson, 1994).

Nelson and Winter (1977, 1982) consider the supra- and inter-institutional aspects of organized knowledge production and control (e.g., within scientific communities) as part of the selection environment. However, science and technology develop and interact at a global level with a dynamics different from institutional contexts. In the Nelson and Winter model, the economic and technological uncertainty cannot be distinguished other than in institutional terms (e.g., market versus non-market environments). These otherwise undifferentiated selection environments generate uncertainty in both the market introduction and the R&D phases. Thus, the two sources of uncertainty are not considered as a consequence of qualitatively different selection mechanisms that use different codes for the selections. The potentially different selection environments—markets, politics, and knowledge—are not specified as selective subdynamics that may interact in a nonlinear dynamics.

In other words, Nelson and Winter's models are formulated in terms of the biological metaphor of variation and selection (Nelson, 1995). From this perspective, selection is expected to operate blindly. Dosi (1982, p. 151) added the distinction between "technological trajectories" and "technological regimes," but his theory otherwise remained within the paradigm of Nelson and Winter's theory due to its focus on innovative firm behavior, that is, variation. Others have elaborated these models by using aggregates of firms, for example, in terms of sectors (e.g., Pavitt, 1984).

The models in this tradition have in common that the units of analysis (e.g., an industry) are institutionally defined and variation is organized along trajectories using a set of principles that is—for analytical reasons—kept completely separate from selection. The selection environments are not considered as differentiated (and thus at variance). Therefore, interactions among the various selection environments cannot be specified. Technological innovation is considered as endogenous to firm *behavior*; trajectories are conceptualized as routines of firms. Consequently, the technological component in the selection environments cannot be appreciated as a global effect of the networked interactions among firms, universities, and governments.

In a thorough reflection on this neo-Schumpterian model, Andersen (1994, p. 144) noted that firms (and their aggregates in industries) cannot be considered as the evolving units of an economy:

> The limitations of Nelson and Winter's (and similar) models of evolutionary-economic processes are most clearly seen when they are confronted with the major alternative in evolutionary modeling which may be called "evolutionary games." ... This difference is based on different answers to the question of "What evolves?" Nelson and Winter's answer is apparently "organisational routines in general" but a closer look reveals that only a certain kind of routine is taken into account. Their firms only interact in anonymous markets which do not suggest the playing of strategic games—even if the supply side may be quite concentrated.

An institutional model can legitimately begin with studying observables (and is thus "history friendly" [Malerba, Nelson, Orsenigo, & Winter, 1999, p. 26]); studies about evolutionary games begin with highly stylized starting points (Andersen, 1994). These abstract assumptions can be made comparable with and traded off against alternative hypotheses, such as the hypothesis of profit maximization prevailing in neo-classical economics. For example, one can ask to what extent an innovation trajectory can be explained in terms of the operation of market forces, in terms of its own internal dynamics of innovation, and/or in terms of interactions among the various subdynamics.

If selection mechanisms other than market choices can be specified—for example, in the case of organized knowledge production and control—the interactions among these different selection mechanisms can also be made the subject of simulation studies. In other words, the selection mechanisms span a space of possible events. The coordination mechanisms (or selection environments) cannot be observed directly, but they can be hypothesized. The model thus becomes more abstract than an institutional one. From this perspective, the observable trajectories can be considered as the historically stabilized results of selective structures operating upon one another, for example, in processes of mutual shaping. The evolutionary progression is a result of continually solving puzzles at the interfaces among the subdynamics. Thus, the routines and the trajectories can be explained from a systems-theoretical perspective as potentially special cases among other possible solutions. This next-order perspective, however, is necessarily knowledge-based because it is based on a reflexive turn (Kaufer & Carley, 1993).

## User-Producer Relations in Systems of Innovation

In an evolutionary model one can expect mechanisms to operate along a time axis different from the one prompted by the neo-classical assumption of profit maximization prevailing at each moment of time. Profit maximization by agency remains pervasive at the systems level, but this principle cannot explain the development of rigidities in the market like trajectories along the time axis (Rosenberg, 1976). In an evolutionary model, however, the (potentially stabilizing) subdynamic along the time axis has to be specified in addition to market clearing at each moment. Thus, a second selection environment over time was defined in this neo-evolutionary model. The comparison among different states (e.g., using different years) can be used for comparative static analysis, but the dynamics along the time axis are then not yet specified. In a later section, I shall specify a third selection mechanism as operating against the axis of time.

In his study of national systems of innovation, Lundvall (1988, p. 349) argued that the learning process in interactions between users and producers provides a *second micro-foundation* for the economy different from the neo-classical basis of profit maximization by individual agents:

> The kind of "microeconomics" to be presented here is quite different. While traditional microeconomics tends to focus upon decisions, made on the basis of a given amount of information, we shall focus upon a *process of learning*, permanently changing the amount and kind of information at the disposal of the actors. While standard economics tends to regard optimality in the allocation of a given set of use values as the economic problem, *par préférence*, we shall focus on the capability of an economy to produce and diffuse *use values with new characteristics*. And while standard economics takes an atomistic view of the economy, we shall focus upon the *systemic interdependence* between formally independent economic subjects.

After arguing—with a reference to Williamson's (1975, 1985) theory of transaction costs in organizations—that interactions between users and producers belonging to the same national system may work more efficiently for reasons of language and culture, Lundvall (1988) proceeded by proposing the nation as the main system of reference for innovations. Optimal interactions in user-producer relations enable developers to reduce uncertainties in the market more rapidly and over longer stretches of time than in the case of less coordinated economies (Hall & Soskice, 2001; Teubal, 1979). This was discussed in defining the function of niches (see the section on the Systems-of-Innovation Approach).

Lundvall's theory about user-producer interactions as another micro-foundation of economic wealth production at the network level can be considered as an epistemological contribution beyond his empirical focus on national systems. The relational system of reference for the micro-foundation is different from individual agents with preferences. From this perspective, the concept of systems of innovation could also be generalized to cross-sectoral innovation patterns and their institutional connections (Carlsson & Stankiewicz, 1991; Edqvist, 1997; Whitley, 2001). Because of this variety of possible relations, however, user-producer relations contribute to the creation and maintenance of a system as only one of the possible subdynamics. Other relations may also be relevant. For example, the relation between the user (in this case, the adopter) to the innovation itself—rather than to its producer—has been explored by Rogers (1962) and others who have conducted research into the diffusion of innovations.

In an early stage of the development of a technology, a close relation between technical specifications and market characteristics in user-producer interactions can provide a specific design with a competitive advantage (Rabeharisoa & Callon, 2002; Saviotti, 1996). In other words, proximity can be expected to serve the incubation of new technologies. However, the regions of origin do not necessarily coincide with the systems that profit from these technologies at a later stage of development. As has been noted, various Italian industrial districts provide examples of this flux. As local companies develop a competitive edge, they have tended to move out of the region, generating a threat of deindustrialization. This threat has to be countered continuously by these industrial districts (Dei Ottati, 2003; Sforzi, 2003).

Analogously, this mechanism is demonstrated by the four regions designated by the EU as "motors of innovation" in 1988 (Viale & Campodall'Orto, 2002, p. 162). The four regions—Catalonia, Lombardia, Baden-Württemberg, and Rhône-Alpes—were no longer the main loci of innovation in the late 1990s (Krauss & Wolff, 2002; Viale & Campodall'Orto, 2002). Such observations indicate the occurrence of unintended consequences: Bifurcations are generated when the diffusion dynamics of the market become more important than the local production dynamics. Diffusion may reach the level of the global market, and thereafter the globalized dimension can increasingly feed back on local production processes, for example, in terms of deindustrialization (Beccatini et al., 2003). Given the globalization of a dominant design, firms may even compete in their capacity to destroy knowledge bases from a previous period (Frenken & Leydesdorff, 2000).

In summary, a system of innovation defined as a localized nation or a region can be analyzed in terms of user-producer relations or aggregated in terms of institutional networks and the stocks and flows contained in this system. However, control and the consequent possibility of appropriation of competitive edges emerge from a recombination of institutional opportunities and functional requirements. In some cases and at certain stages of the innovation process, local stabilization in a geographic area may prove beneficial, for example, because of the increased puzzle-solving capacity in a niche. However, at a subsequent stage this advantage may turn into a disadvantage because the innovations may become increasingly locked into the local conditions. As various subdynamics compete and interact, the expectation is that a more complex dynamic will emerge. Therefore, the institutional perspective on a system of innovation has to be complemented with a functional analysis. A focus on the geographical perspective of national systems without this awareness of changing boundaries can be counterproductive (Bathelt, 2003).

## Mode-2 and the Production of Scientific Knowledge

The Mode-2 thesis of the production of scientific knowledge (Gibbons et al., 1994) implies that the contemporary system has more recently gained a degree of freedom as a result of globalization and the new communication technologies. What seemed institutionally rigid under a previous regime (e.g., nation states) can be made flexible under the globalizing regime of communications. In a follow-up study, Nowotny and colleagues (2001, p. 121) specified that the new flexibility is not to be considered only as "weak contextualization." They argue that a system of innovation is a construct that is continuously undergoing reconstruction and can be reconstructed even *in the core of its operations*. This "strong contextualization" (p. 131) affects not only instantaneous decisions, but also the longer-term structures in the selection processes over time. The possibilities for novelty and change are limited more in terms of our current capacity to reconstruct expectations than in terms of historical constraints.

How does one allocate the capacities for puzzle-solving and innovation across the system when the system boundaries become so fluid? The authors of the Mode-2 thesis answer as follows:

> There is no longer only one scientifically "correct" way, if there ever was only one, especially when—as is the case, for instance, with mapping the human genome—constraints of cost-efficiency and of time limits must be taken into account. There certainly is not only one scientifically "correct" way to discover an effective vaccine against AIDS or only one "correct" design configuration to solve problems in a particular industry. Instead, choices emerge in the course of a project because of many different factors, scientific, economic, political, and even cultural. These choices then suggest further choices in a dynamic and interactive process, opening the way for strategies of variation upon whose further development ultimately the selection through success will decide. (Nowotny et al., 2001, p. 115)

The perspective, consequently, is changed from interdisciplinary—that is, based on careful translations among different discourses—to *transdisciplinary*—that is, based on an external management perspective. The global perspective provides us with more choices than were realized hitherto. This global perspective emerges from reflexive communications. Reflexive communications add another dimension to (the sum of) agency-based reflections and thus can generate a dynamics of "reflexive" or "radical" modernization (Beck, Bonns, & Lau, 2003, pp. 1–3; see also Beck et al., 1994).

Lundvall (1988) had focused on interaction and argued that communications can stabilize the local innovation environment for agents. The authors of the Mode-2 thesis, however, argued that reflexive communications can provide us with a global perspective on the relevant environments. This global perspective enables us to assess the historically grown opportunities with the benefit of hindsight. In other words, the global perspective adds a dynamic that is different from the historical one that follows the time axis. The latter focuses on the opportunities and constraints of a given unit (e.g., a firm or region) in its historical context, but the reflexive discourse enables us to redefine the systems of reference by contextualizing and analyzing the subjects under study with hindsight. Thus, the focus shifts from the historical reconstruction of a system by following the actors (Latour, 1987) to the analysis of an innovation system operating in the present. The robustness of a construct would no longer depend on its historical generation, but on the present level of support that can be mobilized in terms of expectations from the various subsystems of society (e.g., the economy or the regulatory systems involved).

Proponents of the Mode-2 thesis focus on this reflexive subdynamic and claim its priority over the other subdynamics including the market. The knowledge-based subdynamic of innovations is integrated with the political subdynamic of control into a transdisciplinary perspective and the complex system under study is analyzed on the basis of an a priori priority of this reflexive perspective over social development. In other words, the complexity is reduced from the perspective of choosing the specific window of learning on the complex dynamics. The claim of this encompassing perspective among a variety of perspectives has appealed to policy makers (Hessels & Van Lente, 2008). From the Triple Helix perspective, this reduction of uncertainty by choosing a single perspective—on the basis of the assumption of a prevailing process of de-differentiation—means unnecessarily sacrificing explanatory power. What needs to be explained are the interactions among the different perspectives.

The transformation of the political system under Mode-2 conditions does not entail, in my opinion, that this subdynamic can be expected to develop hierarchical control. Indeed, this might reify an analytical perspective. The Mode-2 thesis focuses on a reflexive turn. The political subdynamic, however, remains part of the system which is supposedly to be steered from this perspective. Because of the nested dynamics, the political subsystem can function in some instances as the steering variable and at other times as a dependent variable; for example, in the case of unintended consequences. In the complex dynamics of communication, unintended consequences of specifically coded communications can be expected to prevail because each communication is part of a distribution of communications necessarily containing uncertainty. The complex dynamics consists of subdynamics that select upon each other; therefore, the system can also be resilient against steering, and in some phases more than in others (Van den Daele, Krohn, & Weingart, 1979; Weingart, 1997). Thus, the question of an empirical study (modeling and simulation) of systems of innovation remains crucial.

The optimism of the Mode-2 thesis—which did not imply the need to do systematic research beyond the telling of success stories (best practices)—resonated with aspirations at the level of the European Commission. Confronted with stubborn national rigidities, especially in the arena of science policy, a theory that legitimated a perspective of transnationality and transdisciplinarity could count on a warm welcome. Because the subsidiarity principle in the EU specifies that the Union should leave to national governments what does not require harmonization at the transnational levels, science policy initiatives had been successfully defended by national scientific elites against European intervention during the 1980s (Mulkay, 1976). The European Commission had circumvented this blockage by focusing on *innovation* policies—as distinct from science and technology policies—in the successive Framework Programs. In addition to demanding that two or more nationalities be represented in the bids for these programs, collaborations among universities, industries, and public research centers were required before one could qualify for a grant. From the perspective of pure science, this focus on development further legitimated a divide between the national systems of research councils—which are controlled by national scientific elites—and the gray and allegedly bureaucratic procedures of the European Commission.

Within this context, the Mode-2 thesis provided further legitimacy to the aspirations of the European Science Foundation and a European system of research councils that would balance U.S. systems such as the National Science Foundation and the National Institutes of Health. In the U.S., however, these systems are both federal and national, and therefore traditionally controlled by scientific elites at the national level (Brockman, 1995). In the European configuration, a transnational system of quality control would also require the construction of a transdisciplinary frame of reference. Citation analysis cannot provide this frame of reference because this would reproduce traditional differences among disciplines and national cultures in Europe. For example, the more internationally oriented countries such as Scandinavia, the U.K., Ireland, and The Netherlands would then dominate the framework.

In this context, the Mode-2 thesis provided a promising perspective: All systems can be deconstructed as specific constructs using reflexive policy analysis, and then the margins for deliberate intervention in the reconstruction would depend on the decomposing power of the reflexive discourse. However, this underestimates the problems involved in proceeding from discursive reconstruction to deliberate action. The latter presumes informed choices among and decisions about ranges of options that reproduce the complexity under study according to a complex dynamic that is different from its politically controlled subdynamic.

What did the Mode-2 model add to the model of national innovation systems? Lundvall's micro-economics were grounded in terms of interactions between users and producers rather than in terms of the individual preferences of agents. The authors of the Mode-2 thesis defined another communication dynamic relevant to the systems of innovation. This other perspective is possible because a network contains a dynamic both at the level of the nodes and at the level of the links. Although agency can be considered as a source or recipient of communication—and can be expected to be reflexive, for example, in terms of learning and entertaining preferences—an agent has a contingent position at a node in the network (Burt, 1982). The links of a communication system, however, operate differently from the nodes in the network. Links can be replaced for functional reasons and densities in the networks can thus migrate as an unintended consequence.

Concepts such as reflexivity and knowledge have different meanings from one layer of the network to another and these different layers can be made the subject of other discourses. For example, agents entertain preferences, but the structure of the network of communications provides some agents with more access than others. In addition to actions that generate the variations, the dynamics of communications, that is, at the level of the links, are transformative (Bhaskar, 1979; 1998) and therefore change (and may innovate!) the structural mechanisms of selection and coordination. These changes are endogenous to the network because they can be the result of nonlinear interactions among previously stabilized aggregates of actions. Recursions and interactions add nonlinear terms to the results of micro-actions.

Luhmann (1984) was the first to propose that communication *among* agents be considered as a system of reference different from agency. More specifically, one can expect the dynamics of inter-human coordination by communication to be different from the reflexive consciousness of agents' perceptions (e.g., Luhmann, 1996). Using the terminology of Maturana and Varela (1980, 1984), consciousness at the level of agency and communication can be considered as structurally coupled in the events. An interaction can be attributed as an action to an actor but it can be expected to function as a communication within a communication system (Leydesdorff, 2001; Maturana, 1978). However, the reflection by a social system operates differently from reflection at the level of individual consciousness. Human language enables us not only to provide meaning to the communication of information, but also to communicate meaning on top of the first-order dynamics of information.

Each coordination mechanism provides its own meaning to information by invoking its specific code of communication (Malone & Crowston, 1994). Words may have different meanings in different contexts. For example, in scientific communications *energy* has a meaning different from its meaning in political discourse. Economists and politicians may worry about shortages of energy, but energy is defined as a conserved quantity in physics. The evolutionary dynamics of social communication can add another layer of complexity to the first-order dynamics of information exchanges among agents.

The self-organization of communication into various (functionally different) coordination mechanisms on top of the institutional organization of society in a national system enables the social system to process more complexity than in an organizationally controlled mode. However, under this condition one can expect to lose increasingly the notion of accountable centers of coordination; central coordination is replaced with a number of more abstract and interacting coordination mechanisms. The interacting (sub)systems of communication can become increasingly differentiated in terms of their potential functions for the self-organization of the social system. This communication regime reshapes the existing communication structures as in a cultural evolution. In other words, selection mechanisms other than "natural" ones begin to reconstruct the system from the various perspectives of the respective coordination mechanisms.

In summary, the communicative layer provides society with a set of selection environments for historical institutions. In the case of communication systems, however, selections operate probabilistically, that is, with uncertainty. Translations among the differently coded communication may reduce the uncertainty. Thus, these selection mechanisms can be specified only as hypotheses. The specification of these expectations, however, guides the observations in terms of specifiable uncertainties (e.g., Leydesdorff & Fritsch, 2006). Furthermore, these communication dynamics of the social system are complex because the codes of the communication have been differentiated historically (Strydom, 1999).

Communications develop along the functionally different axes, but they can additionally be translated into each other by using the different codes at interfaces reflexively. Thus, systems of translation are generated. For example, interaction terms among codes of communication emerged as a matter of concern within knowledge-based corporations when interfaces between R&D and marketing had increasingly to be managed (Galbraith, 1967). In university-industry-government relations three types of communications are interfaced.

Let me now turn to my thesis that the utilization of the degrees of freedom between institutions and functions among the three subsystems interacting in a Triple Helix enables us to understand these processes of innovation.

## A Triple Helix Model of Innovations

The systems-of-innovation approach defined innovation systems in terms of institutional units of analysis. Mode-2 analysis defined innovations exclusively in terms of reconstructions on the basis of emerging perspectives in communication. The Triple Helix approach combines these two perspectives as different subdynamics of the systems under study. However, this model enables us to include the dynamics of the market as a third perspective. As noted, the perspective of neo-classical economics is micro-founded in the natural preferences of agents. Thus, one can assume that innovation systems are driven by various subdynamics to varying extents. Consequently, the discussion shifts from a philosophical one about what an innovation system "is," or the question of how it should be defined, to the methodological question of how one can study innovation systems in terms of their different dimensions and subdynamics.

Within this complex dynamic, the two mechanisms—user-producer interactions and reflexive communications—can be considered as complementary to the micro-foundation of neo-classical economics. First, each agent or aggregate of agencies is positioned differently in terms of preferences and other attributes. Second, the agents interact, for example, in economic exchange relations. This generates the network perspective. Third, the arrangements of positions (nodes) and relations (links) can be expected to contain information because not all network positions are held equally and links are selectively generated and maintained. The expected information content of the distributions can be *recognized* by relevant agents at local nodes. These recognitions provide meaning to the events and these meanings can also be communicated. The recognition thus generates knowledge bases both at the addresses of the agents, in their organizations, and at the level of society. Knowledge can also be processed as discursive knowledge in the network of exchange relations. Figure 9.5 summarizes this configuration.

With this visualization I intend to make my argument epistemologically consistent by relating these reflections to the underlying dimensions of the Triple Helix model. The three analytically independent dimensions of an innovation system were first distinguished in Figure 9.3 as (1) the geography, which organizes the positions of agents and their aggregates; (2) the economy, which organizes their exchange relations; and (3) the knowledge content, which emerges with reference to either of these dimensions (Archer, 1995). Given these specifications, we were able to add the relevant interaction terms. The second-order interaction among these interactions then provides us with the hypothesis of the development of a knowledge base endogenous to the system under study.

Figure 9.5 specifies the knowledge base as an interaction between discursive and tacit knowledge. The three micro-operations are represented along the three axes. Each agency (agents, institutions, nations) has a position in the network and can be considered as naturally gifted with a set of preferences. This assumption accords with the micro-foundation of neo-classical economics. The network dynamics are first micro-founded in terms of natural preferences. Learning in relations, however, can change both the agents and their institutions by embedding them in specific (e.g., non-market) contexts. The second (horizontal) axis thus corresponds with Lundvall's micro-foundation in user-producer interactions. National systems of innovation can then be considered as specific forms of organization that reduce

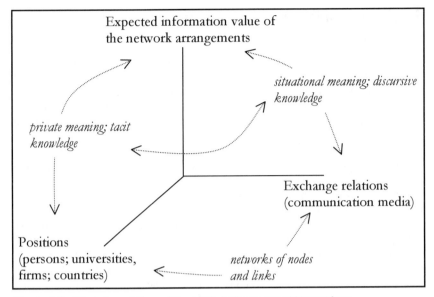

**Figure 9.5 Micro-foundation of the triple helix model of innovations**

transaction costs (Williamson, 1975, 1985). For example, the Scandinavian environment might generate an institutional framework that changes transaction costs to such an extent that a second independent dynamic, in addition to the market mechanism, can be sustained.

Mode-2 can be considered as the third axis: The interacting dynamics can be made the subject of reflexive analysis. I drew this third axis as vertical in Figure 9.5 because the emergence of a *meta*-perspective is the implicit assumption of the Mode-2 thesis. However, one can rotate the figure and change the order of the axes without any loss of explanatory power: Three micro-mechanisms are involved—one based on positions, a second based on the possibility of exchange, and a third based on the possibility for agent-based and discursive learning.

When the learning is grounded in agency, (social) psychological mechanisms and categories can be used for the analysis. However, when the learning is carried by distributions in networks, the socio-psychological categories provide us with only metaphors but the operations have to be specified differently because networks can be expected to contain dynamics different from agency. For example, agency tends to integrate conflicting perspectives by making trade-offs. Networks allow for other solutions, such as differentiation when different control mechanisms are available. For example, normative and analytical considerations can be entertained, distinguished, and traded-off at different positions in the network. The second-order interaction between learning in individuals and networks generates configurational knowledge as a next-order regime of expectations.

# Empirical Studies and Simulations Using the Triple Helix Model

Unlike biological models that focus on variation with reference to natural selection mechanisms, the Triple Helix model focuses primarily on the specification of different selection mechanisms. Selection is structural. Three helices are sufficiently complex to understand the social reproduction of the dynamics of innovation (Leydesdorff, 2009; cf. Lewontin, 2000). What is observable can be specified as relative equilibria at interfaces between two selection mechanisms operating upon each other. When repeated over time, each co-variation can be developed into a co-evolution, and a next-order, that is, more complex, system can be generated in a process of mutual shaping among the interactions.

I have argued that the Triple Helix can be elaborated into a neo-evolutionary model that enables us to recombine sociological notions of meaning processing, economic theorizing about exchange relations, and insights from science and technology studies regarding the organization and control of knowledge production. The further codification of meaning in scientific knowledge production can add value to the economic exchange relations (Foray, 2004; Frenken, 2005). The model can serve as a heuristic. Its abstract and analytical character enables us to explain current transitions toward a knowledge-based economy as a new regime of operations. The Triple Helix model thus substantiates and operationalizes the general notion of a knowledge-based economy as a self-organizing system (Krugman, 1996).

The differentiation in terms of selection mechanisms can be both horizontal and vertical. Vertically, the fluxes of communications are constrained by the institutional arrangements that are shaped in terms of stabilizations of previous communications. Horizontally, the coordination mechanisms can be of a different nature because they can be expected to use different codes. For example, market transactions are different from scientific communications. Market transactions can also be cross-tabulated with organizational hierarchies (Lundvall, 1988; Williamson, 1985). The control mechanisms at interfaces can be considered as functional for the differentiation among communications, but the hierarchy in the organization may help to reduce the problem of coordination between functions to a multi-level problem within the institutional dimension.

In summary, the functional perspective is different from the institutional one. Functional communications evolve; institutional relations function as retention mechanisms that respond to functional incentives. The specification of functions in the socio-economic analysis requires reflexivity. All reflections can again be made the subject of communication. Thus, one can study a Triple Helix at different levels and from different perspectives. For example, one can study university-industry-government relations from a (neo-)institutional perspective (e.g., da Rosa Pires & de Castro, 1997; Etzkowitz et al., 2000; Gunasekara, 2006) or one can focus on the relations between university science and the economy in terms of communications (e.g., Langford, Burch, & Langford, 1997). Different interpretations of the Triple Helix model can be at odds with each other and nevertheless inform the model. Each metaphor stabilizes a geometrical representation of otherwise more complex dynamics.

Competing hypotheses derived from different versions of the Triple Helix can be explored through formal modeling and appreciated through institutional analysis. The case studies inform the modeling efforts about contingencies and boundary conditions; simulation models enable us to relate the various perspectives. Such translations have the potential to reinforce the research process by raising new questions, for example, by comparing across different contexts and/or with reference to emerging phenomena. From this perspective, innovation can be considered as the reflexive recombination at an interface, such as between a technological option and a market perspective. Specification of the different contexts, however, requires theorizing. For the purpose of innovation, the perspectives have to be combined, for example, in terms of a plan.

The three strands of the Triple Helix are treated as formally equivalent in the model, but they are substantially very different. The selection mechanisms are expected to operate asymmetrically. One strand (university) is institutionally less powerful than the other two strands. Furthermore, the other two strands (government and industry) are increasingly and indirectly co-opting the university in a variety of ways, even if one disregards the direct influence of the so-called military-industrial complex. However, the university has specific strengths: First, it provides the other two systems with a continuous flow of new discursive knowledge (e.g., papers and patents) and new knowledge carriers (students). From this perspective, the university can be considered the main carrier of the knowledge-based innovation system (Godin & Gingras, 2000). Knowledge-based fluxes continually upset and reform the dynamic equilibria sought by the two other strands of the political economy.

The Triple Helix model is sufficiently complex to encompass the different perspectives of participant observers (e.g., case histories) and to guide us heuristically in searching for options newly emerging from the interactions. What is the contribution of this model in terms of providing heuristics to empirical research? First, the neo-institutional model of arrangements among different stakeholders can be used in case study analysis. Given the new mode of knowledge production, case studies can be enriched by addressing the relevance of the *three* major dimensions of the model. This is not to discount the value of studying, for example, bi-lateral academic-industry relations or government-university policies, but one can expect more interesting results by observing the interactions among the three subdynamics. Secondly, the model can be informed by the increasing understanding of complex dynamics and simulation studies from evolutionary economics (e.g., Malerba et al., 1999; Windrum, 1999). Thirdly, the Triple Helix model adds to the meta-biological models of evolutionary economics the sociological notion of meaning being exchanged among the institutional agents (Habermas, 1987; Leydesdorff, 2001; Luhmann, 1984, 1995b).

Finally, on the normative side of developing options for innovation policies, the Triple Helix model provides an incentive to search for *mismatches* between the institutional dimensions in the arrangements and the social functions carried by these arrangements. The frictions between the two layers (knowledge-based expectations and institutional interests), and among the three domains (economy, science, and policy) provide a wealth of opportunities for puzzle solving and innovation. The evolutionary regimes are expected to remain in transition because they are shaped along historical trajectories. A knowledge-based regime continuously upsets the political economy and the market equilibria because three subdynamics are now interacting. Conflicts of interest can be deconstructed and reconstructed, first analytically and then perhaps also in practice in the search for solutions to problems of economic productivity, wealth retention, and knowledge growth.

The rich semantics of partially conflicting models reinforces a focus on solving puzzles among differently codified communications reflexively. The lock-ins and the bifurcations are systemic, that is, largely beyond control; further developments are based on the self-organization of the interactions among the subdynamics. The subdynamics can also be considered as different sources of variance that disturb and select from one another. Resonances among selections can shape trajectories in co-evolutions, and the latter may recursively drive the system into new regimes. This neo-evolutionary framework assumes that the processes of both integration and differentiation remain under reconstruction.

## The Knowledge-Based Economy and Measurement

From the perspective of the information sciences, this discussion of innovation theory and theories of technological change needs to be complemented with a further specification about operationalization and measurement. Can a measurement theory for the communication of meaning and knowledge in a Triple Helix model also be specified? How does the communication of knowledge differ from the communication of information and meaning, and how can these differences be operationalized? How do the communication of information, meaning, and knowledge as layers in communication systems relate and potentially operate upon one another? How does this vertical differentiation in the codification relate to the horizontal differentiation among the three (or more) coordination mechanisms in a Triple Helix model?

### The Communication of Meaning and Information

The idea that human beings not only provide meaning to events, but are able to communicate meaning in addition to the communication of information, emerged gradually during the 20th century with the development of sociology as a discipline. According to Weber (e.g., 1968a, 1968b), values were to be considered as the crucial domain of human encounter and social development. As is well known, Weber advocated adopting value freeness as a methodological principle in sociological analysis, at the same time paying proper attention to the value-ladenness of the subject matter (Watkins, 1952). From Weber's (1968c) perspective, values govern human history as givens.

Durkheim (1912) noted in this same period that values can also be considered as collective consciousness. Parsons (1968) emphasized that this concept of *another dynamic at the supra-individual level* can, with hindsight, be considered as constitutive for the new science of sociology. He traced it—that is, the idea that *social interaction* bestows events with qualitatively different meanings—back to American pragmatism (Mead, 1934) on one hand, and on the other hand to Freud's (1911) and Durkheim's (1912) independent discoveries of the reality principle and collective consciousness, respectively. (According to Parsons's [1952] reading of Freud, the social environment is internalized at the level of the super-ego.) This new sociological program clashed with positivism—which also finds its origins in sociology (e.g., Auguste Comte), in opposition, however, to the idealistic philosophies of the 19th century—because the focus was no longer on empirical data, but rather on what the data mean and how the subjects under study can sometimes reach consensus or not in conflicts about such meaning. The ensuing *Positivismusstreit* in German sociology had its origins in the 1930s but was exported to the United States by German emigrants in the prewar period (Adorno, Albert, Dahrendorf, Habermas, Pilot, & Popper, 1969).

In his 1971 debates with Habermas (who, as a neo-Marxist, sided with the anti-positivists in the *Positivismusstreit*), Luhmann (1971) proposed that the communication of meaning be considered as the core subject of sociology: Coordination among human beings is not brought about by information transfer, but rather by the communication of meaning (Habermas & Luhmann, 1971). Unlike information, meaning cannot be transferred over a cable but it can be communicated in interactions among reflexive agents. According to Luhmann (1984), sociologists should focus on the dynamics of meaning in communication (Luhmann, 2002). Habermas (1981, 1987), however, wished to focus on communicative action and communicative competence as attributes of human beings.

In these exchanges, both Habermas and Luhmann made references to Husserl's reflections on intersubjectivity as a common base, but they provided Husserl's philosophy with another interpretation (Derrida, 1974; Husserl, 1962, 1973). Habermas (1981) followed Schutz (1952) in arguing that Husserl had failed to ground his concept of intersubjectivity in interhuman communication (cf. Luhmann, 1995a). This grounding would require the concept of a life-world in which communication is embedded. In my opinion, Luhmann remained closer to Husserl's so-called transcendental phenomenology by considering social relations as instantiations that are embedded in virtual, yet structured, communication fluxes. The communication dynamics explain the social relations instead of vice versa analyzing communication structures as a consequence of social relations in a "life-world" (Schutz, 1975, p. 72).

The approach that considers communications not as attributes of organizations and agency, but organizations and agency as constructed in and by inter-human communications, finds its philosophical origins in the *Cartesian Mediations,* which Husserl (1973) wrote in 1929. Husserl followed Descartes by questioning not only what it means to be human, but also the referent of human intentionality. The first question refers back to Descartes's (1637) *"cogito ergo sum,"* the latter addresses the subject of doubt, that is, the *cogitatum*: the external referent of one's doubting. For Descartes this *cogitatum* could be distinguished only negatively from the *cogito* as that which transcends the contingency of one's *cogito*. From this perspective, the other in the act of doubting is defined as God. God transcends the contingency of the *cogito*, and therefore one can expect this Other to be eternal.

Husserl proposed to consider the *cogitatum* no longer as a personal God, but as the intentional substance *among* human beings, which provides the *cogito* with an horizon of meanings. We—as *cogitantes*—are uncertain about what things mean, and the communication of this uncertainty generates an intersubjectivity that transcends our individual subjectivities. Although meanings are structured at the supra-individual level, these structures are no longer identified with a personal God. On the contrary, meaning can be constructed, enriched, and reproduced among human beings by using language. Husserl (1973, p. 40) acknowledged this function of language in the generation of meaning when he formulated, for example: "The beginning is the pure and one might say still mute experience which first has to be brought into the articulation of its meaning."

By using language one is able to relate meanings to one another. However, within language the world is resurrected as an architecture in which the words can be provided with meaning at the supra-individual level. This meaning is not provided by the words or their concatenations in sentences or networks of co-occurrences. Language organizes the concepts by providing specific meaning to the words at specific instances (e.g., in sentences). The instantiations refer to what could have been differently constructed and understood. In other words, the *cogitata* are not specific; they remain uncertain.

Husserl emphasized that this substance of the social system (intersubjective intentionality) is different from subjective intentionality because one knows it *ex ante* as beyond the domain of the individual. The study of this new domain—Husserl (1973, p. 159) used Leibniz's word *monade*—might provide us with "a concrete ontology and a theory of science." However, Husserl conceded that he had no instruments beyond the transcendental apperception of this domain and therefore he had to refrain from empirical investigations: "We must forgo a more precise investigation of the layer of meaning that provides the human world and culture, as such, with a specific meaning and therewith provides this world with specifically 'mental' predicates" (Husserl, 1973, p. 138; my translation).

In my opinion, two important developments in applied mathematics have made it possible to address the questions that Husserl felt to be beyond his reach: First, Shannon's mathematical theory of communication provides categories for analyzing communications in terms of uncertainties (Abramson, 1963; Leydesdorff, 1995; Theil, 1972), and, second, Rosen's (1985) mathematical theory of anticipatory system and Dubois's (1998) elaboration of this theory into the computation of anticipatory systems provide categories for studying the evolution of systems that are based on expectations and their potential functions for further developing codified communications (Leydesdorff, 2008, 2009).

## The Expectation of Social Structure

In addition to these methodological advances, some theoretical steps in sociology were crucial. First, Parsons (1951, p. 94; 1968, p. 436) elaborated the communication of meaning in terms of what he called a "double contingency" in inter-human relations. *Ego* relates to *Alter* not only in terms of observable relations, but also in terms of expectations. *Ego* expects *Alter* to entertain expectations like those *Ego* finds in her own mind. The two systems (*Ego* and *Alter*) expect each other to operate in terms of expectations. *Ego* and *Alter* are defined at the level of individual consciousness; Luhmann (1984, 1986) generalized this as the model of communication between and among meaning-processing systems (Vanderstraeten, 2002). From this perspective, the Triple Helix model can also be considered as representing a triple contingency among three communication systems (Leydesdorff, 2008; Strydom, 1999).

In addition to the model of double contingency, Luhmann used Parsons's (1963a, 1963b, 1968) further elaboration of mediation in terms of symbolically generalized codes of communication. For example, money enables us to make economic transactions without having to discuss the price. Using Maturana and Varela's (1980, 1984) theory of *autopoiesis,* Luhmann (1984, 1990, 1995b, 1997) elaborated a sociological theory of the dynamics of codified communications (Leydesdorff, 2001). Crucially, meaning can be communicated among human beings and the coordination of this communication can become self-organizing—that is, beyond the control of the communicating agents—under the condition of modernity, that is, under the pressure of the functional differentiation of the codes of communication in the various coordination mechanisms.

The differentiation in the codification (e.g., among economic exchange relations, political communication, and scientific communication) generates feedback that changes the organization and dynamics of the social system. However, Luhmann (1990, p. 340) added that "developing this perspective is only possible if an accordingly complex systems-theoretical arrangement is specified." In my opinion, this requires an information-theoretical elaboration of this sociological theory of communication. Information theory provides us with a mathematical apparatus to study communication systems at a more abstract level in terms of both composition and dynamic developments (Bar-Hillel, 1955; Brooks & Wiley, 1986; Leydesdorff, 1995; Theil, 1972; Yeung, 2008). One can distinguish layers and dimensions at different moments of time, for example, by using subscripts and superscripts as indices.

Structure in the data provides meaning to the uncertainty. Structure can be analyzed in observed data by using multivariate statistics, for example, factor analysis. Factor analysis reduces the data by focusing on the latent dimensions (eigenvectors) of the networks of relations among observable vectors. The eigenvectors, in other words, provide us with a second-order dynamics in terms of which changes at the level of relations among vectors—that is, the first-order dynamics in terms of observable data—can be provided with meaning.

Note that meaning can be provided both by an analyst and by a participant-observer within the system under study. In both cases, the relational data are positioned in a vector space with a topology very different from the relational space in which the network is constructed. For example, the vector space is based on continuous coordinates, but graph-theoretical network analysis is based on discrete events. The different topology of the vector space enables us to formalize the concepts of meaning and meaning-processing. This constructed space can be considered as a *cogitatum*. It remains a construct that cannot be observed directly. The function of this constructed space is to enable us to communicate intersubjectively the meaning of what one is able to observe in the first contingency of a relational space. Social structure is thus created as a cultural order of expectations.

Changes in the relational space communicate Shannon-type information. Meaning is communicated within a vector space. For example, proximity in terms of positions may make a difference in terms of how easily meaning can be communicated across relations (Burt, 1995; Freeman, 1978/1979). The distinction between a first- and a second-order dynamics of communicating information and meaning, respectively, enables us also to specify the mutual information between these two dynamics as meaningful information in the sense of Bateson's (1972, p. 453) dictum of "a difference which makes a difference."

A difference in the data can make a difference in terms of the organization of the data, and thus be meaningful. In other words, the organization of the data provides the (Shannon-type) information with meaning. However, not all uncertainty is meaningful, and thus a selection is involved. Selection is structural, but operates as a *cogitatum*. The Darwinian notion of natural selection is replaced with the hypothesis of different selection environments. Neither the selection environments as structures nor their dynamic functions should be reified from this perspective; they remain constructs and orders of expectations. The function of specifying these selection environments is to enable theoretical discourse to enrich the development by providing it with relevant distinctions in the knowledge base. For example, the distinction between market and non-market selection environments induced the emergence of evolutionary economics as a theoretical discourse in the 1980s (Nelson & Winter, 1977, 1982; Pavitt, 1984).

## Configurations in a Knowledge-Based Economy

This operationalization of the communication of meaning in a space with different characteristics provides us with a next step in the full specification of the Triple Helix model. Meaning-providing subsystems can be considered as carried by the eigenvectors of the networks, that is, as densities in the structures of communications. In the static model the eigenvectors can be spanned orthogonally. Dynamically, they represent selective structures. The observable variation at the first-order level provides the co-variation among these selective structures. For example, in Figure 9.1, patents were positioned as observable events in a vector space spanned by the three dimensions of the Triple Helix.

When three or more dimensions can operate upon one another, mutual information or co-variation in more than two dimensions can also be computed. The resulting information or more-dimensional co-variance can be either positive or negative (McGill & Quastler, 1955; Yeung, 2008). A negative expected information value of this measure would reduce uncertainty and can therefore be considered as configurational information (McGill, 1954). Configurational information provides us with an indicator of the interaction among different (and potentially orthogonal) dimensions.[6] Because this reduction of uncertainty can be attributed to the developments in and interactions among the (sub)systems under study, it can be considered as an indicator of self-organization, that is, the local production of negative entropy.

Note that this reduction of uncertainty at the level of a configuration among functions is analytically different from reduction of uncertainty provided by the factor analysis. The factor analysis reduces the data by capturing the common variances among the variables. This first-order reduction of uncertainty can be considered as a structure in the data to which one can ascribe a semantic meaning (for example, by designating the factors). The reduction of uncertainty because of the configuration among the main dimensions (eigenvectors of the data matrix) distinguishes in a next-order process among meanings that make a difference, and thus indicates the extent to which knowledge as codified meaning can be expected to operate within a system.

Figure 9.6 summarizes the model; it includes both horizontal and vertical differentiation. The horizontal differentiation among latent coordination mechanisms was considered by Luhmann (1997) as functional differentiation and is operationalized as the orthogonal dimensions that result from the factor analysis. Vertically, the model distinguishes between interactions at the bottom level, potential self-organization of the communications in different configurations at the top level, and structuration by organization at the level in between.

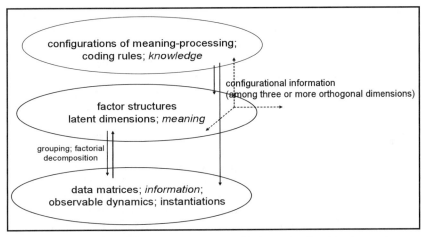

**Figure 9.6** A layered process of codification of information by meaning and codification of meaning in terms of a knowledge base

In summary, the evolving networks of relations among agents can be considered as the retention mechanisms of flows of communication through these networks. The flows are structured by functionally different codes of communication (Luhmann, 1984, 1995b) and enabled and constrained by structures in the data at each moment in time (Giddens, 1984). For example, a network of scientific communications may carry a flow of publications and/or patents. In a network of political communications, power and legitimacy provide the communications with differently codified meanings.

The functions of flows of communication develop evolutionarily in terms of the eigenvectors of the networks, but the networks of relations develop historically in terms of (aggregates of) actions. The functions can be operationalized as the latent dimensions (eigenvectors) of the networks of relations among the agents. However, the eigenvectors develop in a vector space with a topology and dynamics different from those of the relational space among the agents. For example, relations develop within a space, whereas the vector space can develop as a space, for example, by adding new dimensions.

The relations (and the nodes) are positioned in a vector space (Burt, 1982); positions reflect the meanings of relations (events) in the various dimensions. Reflexive agents are not only embedded in the relational space which they span, but also able to provide meaning to the positions and relations. This can be considered first-order reflexivity. When this reflexivity is made the subject of theoretical reflections, next-order reflexivity is added as an overlay to this dually layered system of relations and positions. The increased availability of this more abstract (because codified) type of communication changes the systems in which it emerges and on which it rests as another selection environment. The processes of reflexive change in such systems are enhanced by adding a knowledge base to the communication. This so-called radicalized or reflexive modernization (Beck et al., 1994, 2003; Giddens, 1990) can be expected to operate in some configurations more than in others. However, it tends to remain beyond the control of agents interacting in terms of relations (that is, generating uncertainty) and positions (that is, providing meaning to uncertainty).

The knowledge-base of an economy can be considered as this evolving *configuration* among the functions of coordination mechanisms. Using the Triple Helix model of university-industry-government relations, the carrying functions of a knowledge-based economy were specified as (1) economic wealth generation, (2) knowledge-based novelty production, and (3) normative (e.g., political) control (Etzkowitz & Leydesdorff, 2000). Over time, the knowledge base thus generated—indicated as the reduction of uncertainty contained in a configuration—can be stabilized, meta-stabilized, or globalized.

Configurations can thus be distinguished in terms of the extent to which a synergy is self-organized among the main subdynamics of a knowledge-based economy. Note that with the opposite sign, configurations may also frustrate the further development of a knowledge base at the systems level by generating more uncertainty than can be absorbed by the relevant subsystems in their current configuration. This empirical research program remains necessarily a piecemeal enterprise (e.g., Leydesdorff & Sun, 2009).

The information sciences are crucially positioned in a configuration at a crossroad among the other relevant sciences such as economics, policy analysis, and innovation studies because of their emphasis on operationalization and measurement. The envisaged research program entails the further specification of these complex (because nonlinear) relations among the processing of uncertainty, expectations/intentions/meaning, and knowledge in communication systems, so that the knowledge base of an economy can be further measured, modeled, and explained.

## Acknowledgments

I am grateful for the comments of Diana Lucio-Arias, Andrea Scharnhorst, Wilfred Dolfsma, and a number of anonymous reviewers on drafts of this review, which is based in part on Leydesdorff (2006).

## Endnotes

1. Whereas the networks of institutional relations can be analyzed by using multivariate statistics, the functions develop over time. The flows of communication change the networks of communication and a calculus is needed for the analysis of such complex dynamics. Bar-Hillel (1955) noted that Shannon's information theory provides us with such a calculus. This calculus can be elaborated into

a nonlinear dynamics of probabilistic entropy (Abramson, 1963; Brooks & Wiley, 1986; Jakulin & Bratko, 2004; Leydesdorff, 1995, 2008; Theil, 1972; Ulanowicz, 1997; Yeung, 2008), which enables us to decompose the complex dynamics in terms of different subdynamics and to specify the various contributions to the prevailing uncertainty in terms of bits of information. Eventually, this information-theoretical approach enables us to measure the knowledge-base of an economy in terms of the Triple Helix model (e.g., Leydesdorff & Fritsch, 2006).

2. Bateson (1972, p. 453) defined information as "a difference which makes a difference." From the perspective of this paper, one can consider this as the definition of "meaningful information," whereas Shannon-type information can be considered as a series of differences (Hayles, 1990).

3. Marx closely observed the *technological* condition of industrial capitalism, noting, for example, that:

> Nature does not build machines, locomotives, railways, electric telegraphs, self-acting mules, etc. These are the products of human industry; natural resources which are transformed into organs of the human control over nature or one's practices in nature. ... The development of fixed assets shows the extent to which knowledge available at the level of society is transformed into immediate productive force, and therefore, the extent to which the conditions of social life have themselves been brought under the control of the general intellect and have been transformed accordingly. Crucial is the degree to which the socially productive forces are produced not only as knowledge, but as immediate organs of social practice, that is, of the real process of living" (Marx, 1974, p. 594; my translation).

Although reflexively aware of the potential dynamics in organized knowledge production and control, Marx remained focused on the historical state of the development of science and technology, and on the integration of this condition into the political economy.

4. In 1870, Germany and Italy were unified; France had gone through a revolution leading to the establishment of a modern (third) republic. The Meji Restoration of 1869 had made Japan a player in the industrial competition, and the U.S.A. had emerged from the Civil War in 1865. Around 1870, the economic system had been reshaped into a system of nations with their respective political economies.

5. The Maastricht Treaty (1991) assigned an advisory role to the European Commission of Regions with regard to economic and social cohesion, trans-European infrastructure networks, health, education, and culture (Council and Commission of the European Communities, 1992). This role was further strengthened by the Treaty of Amsterdam in 1997, which envisaged direct consultations between this Committee of Regions and the European Parliament and extended its advisory role to employment policy, social policy, the environment, vocational training, and transport.

6. Reduction of uncertainty at the systems level contradicts the Second Law, which holds equally for probabilistic entropy $H$ (Theil, 1972). According to Gibbs entropy formula $S = k_B H$, the Boltzmann constant $k_B$ is multiplied by $H = - \sum_i p_i \log p_i$. Multiplication by the Boltzmann constant provides the otherwise dimensionless Shannon-entropy $H$ (expressed in bits) with the dimension of Joule/Kelvin. However, the dynamics of the Second Law are not caused by the Boltzmann constant for the very reason that this is a constant that remains external to the development of the probabilistic entropy $H$.

# References

Abramowitz, M., & David, P. A. (1996). Measuring performance of knowledge-based economy. In *Employment and growth in the knowledge-based economy* (pp. 35–60). Paris: Organisation for Economic Co-operation and Development.

Abramson, N. (1963). *Information theory and coding*. New York: McGraw-Hill.

Adorno, T. W., Albert, H., Dahrendorf, R., Habermas, J., Pilot, H., & Popper, K. R. (1969). *Positivismusstreit in der deutschen Soziologie*. Frankfurt am Main, Germany: Luchterhand.

Allen, P. M. (1994). Evolutionary complex systems: Models of technology change. In L. Leydesdorff & P. van den Besselaar (Eds.), *Evolutionary economics and chaos theory: New directions for technology studies* (pp. 1–18). London: Pinter.

Andersen, E. S. (1994). *Evolutionary economics: Post-Schumpeterian contributions*. London: Pinter.

Aoki, M. (2001). *Toward a comparative institutional analysis*. Cambridge, MA: MIT Press.

Archer, M. S. (1995). *Realist social theory: The morphogenetic approach*. Cambridge, UK: Cambridge University Press.

Arrow, K. J. (1962). The economic implications of learning by doing. *Review of Economic Studies, 29*, 155–173.

Arthur, W. B. (1994). *Increasing returns and path dependence in the economy*. Ann Arbor: University of Michigan Press.

Bar-Hillel, Y. (1955). An examination of information theory. *Philosophy of Science, 22*, 86–105.

Barras, R. (1990). Interactive innovation in financial and business services: The vanguard of the service revolution. *Research Policy, 19*, 215–237.

Bateson, G. (1972). *Steps to an ecology of mind*. New York: Ballantine.

Bathelt, H. (2003). Growth regimes in spatial perspective 1: Innovation, institutions and social systems. *Progress in Human Geography, 27*(6), 789–804.

Beccatini, G., Bellandi, M., Ottati, G. D., & Sforzi, F. (2003). *From industrial districts to local development: An itinerary of research*. Cheltenham, UK: Edward Elgar.

Beck, U., Bonns, W., & Lau, C. (2003). The theory of reflexive modernization: Problematic, hypotheses and research program. *Theory, Culture & Society, 20*(2), 1–33.

Beck, U., Giddens, A., & Lash, S. (1994). *Reflexive modernization: Politics, tradition, and aesthetics in the modern social order*. Stanford, CA: Stanford University Press.

Bell, D. (1968). The measurement of knowledge and technology. In E. B. Sheldon & W. E. Moore (Eds.), *Indicators of social change: Concepts and measurements* (pp. 145–246). Hartford, CT: Russell Sage Foundation.

Bell, D. (1973). *The coming of the post-industrial society*. New York: Basic Books.

Berger, P. L., & Luckmann, T. (1966). *The social construction of reality: A treatise in the sociology of knowledge*. Garden City, NY: Doubleday.

Bhaskar, R. (1979). *The possibility of naturalism: A philosophical critique of the human sciences*. Brighton, UK: Harvester Press.

Bhaskar, R. (1998). Societies. In M. Archer, R. Bhaskar, A. Collier, T. Lawson, & A. Norrie (Eds.), *Critical realism: Essential readings* (pp. 206–257). London: Routledge.

Biggiero, L. (1998). Italian industrial districts: A Triple Helix pattern of problem solving. *Industry and Higher Education, 12*(4), 227–234.

Biggiero, L. (2001). Self-organizing processes in building entrepreneurial networks: A theoretical and empirical investigation. *Human Systems Management, 20*(3), 209–222.

Bowker, G. C. (2005). *Memory practices in the sciences*. Cambridge, MA: MIT Press.

Braczyk, H.-J., Cooke, P., & Heidenreich, M. (Eds.). (1998). *Regional innovation systems*. London: University College London Press.

Braverman, H. (1974). *Labor and monopoly capital: The degradation of work in the twentieth century*. New York: Monthly Review Press.

Brockman, J. (Ed.). (1995). *The third culture*. New York: Simon & Schuster.

Brooks, D. R., & Wiley, E. O. (1986). *Evolution as entropy*. Chicago: University of Chicago Press.

Brusoni, S., Prencipe, A., & Pavitt, K. (2000). Knowledge specialization and the boundaries of the firm: Why do firms know more than they make? *Administrative Science Quarterly, 46*, 597–621.

Burt, R. S. (1982). *Toward a structural theory of action*. New York: Academic Press.

Burt, R. S. (1995). *Structural holes: The social structure of competition*. Cambridge, MA: Harvard University Press.

Callon, M. (1998). *The laws of the market*. Oxford, UK: Blackwell.

Callon, M., Méadel, C., & Rabeharisoa, V. (2002). The economy of qualities. *Economy and Society, 31*(2), 194–217.

Carlsson, B. (Ed.). (2002). *New technological systems in the bio industries: An international study*. Boston: Kluwer Academic Publishers.

Carlsson, B. (2006). Internationalization of innovation systems: A survey of the literature. *Research Policy, 35*(1), 56–67.

Carlsson, B., & Stankiewicz, R. (1991). On the nature, function, and composition of technological systems. *Journal of Evolutionary Economics, 1*(2), 93–118.

Carter, A. P. (1996). Measuring the performance of a knowledge-based economy. In D. Foray & B. A. Lundvall (Eds.), *Employment and growth in the knowledge-based economy* (pp. 61–68). Paris: Organisation for Economic Co-operation and Development.

Casson, M. (1997). *Information and organization: A new perspective on the theory of the firm*. Oxford, UK: Clarendon Press.

Cimoli, M. (Ed.). (2000). *Developing innovation systems: Mexico in a global context*. London: Continuum.

Collins, H. M. (1974). The TEA set: Tacit knowledge and scientific networks. *Science Studies, 4*(2), 165–185.

Cooke, P. (2002). *Knowledge economies*. London: Routledge.

Cooke, P., & Leydesdorff, L. (2006). Regional development in the knowledge-based economy: The construction of advantages. *Journal of Technology Transfer, 31*(1), 5–15.

Council and Commission of the European Communities. (1992). *The Maastricht Treaty on European Union*. Luxembourg, Belgium: Office for Official Publications of the European Communities.

Coveney, P., & Highfield, R. (1990). *The arrow of time*. London: Allen.

Cowan, R., David, P., & Foray, D. (2000). The explicit economics of knowledge codification and tacitness. *Industrial and Corporate Change, 9*(2), 211–253.

Cowan, R., & Foray, D. (1997). The economics of codification and the diffusion of knowledge. *Industrial and Corporate Change, 6*, 595–622.

da Rosa Pires, A., & de Castro, E. A. (1997). Can a strategic project for a university be strategic to regional development? *Science and Public Policy, 24*(1), 15–20.

Dasgupta, P., & David, P. (1994). Toward a new economics of science. *Research Policy, 23*(5), 487–522.

David, P. A. (1985). Clio and the economics of QWERTY. *American Economic Review, 75*, 332–337.

David, P. A., & Foray, D. (1995). Assessing and expanding the science and technology knowledge base. *STI Review, 16*, 13–68.

David, P. A., & Foray, D. (2002). An introduction to the economy of the knowledge society. *International Social Science Journal, 54*(171), 9–23.

Dei Ottati, G. (2003). Local governance and industrial districts' competitive advantage. In G. Beccatini, M. Bellandi, G. D. Ottati, & F. Sforzi (Eds.), *From industrial districts to local development: An itinerary of research* (pp. 184–209). Cheltenham, UK: Edward Elgar.

Derrida, J. (1974). *Edmund Husserl's origine de la géometrie*. Paris: Presses Universitaires de France.

Descartes, R. (1637). *Discours de la méthode pour bien conduire sa raison, et chercher la verité dans les sciences.* Leiden: Jan Maire.

DiMaggio, P. J., & Powell, W. W. (1983). The iron cage revisited. *American Sociological Review, 48*(2), 147–160.

Dosi, G. (1982). Technological paradigms and technological trajectories: A suggested interpretation of the determinants and directions of technical change. *Research Policy, 11*, 147–162.

Dubois, D. M. (1998). Computing anticipatory systems with incursion and hyperincursion. In D. M. Dubois (Ed.), *Computing anticipatory systems, CASYS-First International Conference* (Vol. 437, pp. 3–29). Woodbury, NY: American Institute of Physics.

Durkheim, E. (1912). *Les formes élémentaires de la vie religieuse.* Paris: F. Alcan.

Edqvist, C. (Ed.). (1997). *Systems of innovation: Technologies, institutions and organizations.* London: Pinter.

Etzkowitz, H., & Leydesdorff, L. (1995). The Triple Helix: University-industry-government relations: A laboratory for knowledge based economic development. *EASST Review, 14*, 14–19.

Etzkowitz, H., & Leydesdorff, L. (2000). The dynamics of innovation: From national systems and Mode-2 to a Triple Helix of university-industry-government relations. *Research Policy, 29*(2), 109–123.

Etzkowitz, H., Webster, A., Gebhardt, C., & Terra, B. R. C. (2000). The future of the university and the university of the future: Evolution of ivory tower to entrepreneurial paradigm. *Research Policy, 29*(2), 313–330.

European Commission. (2000). *Towards a European research area.* Brussels, Belgium: The Commission. Retrieved January 18, 2009, from europa.eu/research/era/pdf/com2000-6-en.pdf

European Commission. (2005). *Working together for growth and jobs: A new start for the Lisbon strategy.* Brussels, Belgium: The Commission. Retrieved January 18, 2009, from europa.eu/growthandjobs/pdf/comm_spring_en.pdf

Foray, D. (2004). *The economics of knowledge.* Cambridge, MA: MIT Press.

Foray, D., & Lundvall, B.-A. (1996). The knowledge-based economy: From the economics of knowledge to the learning economy. In *Employment and growth in the knowledge-based economy* (pp. 11–32). Paris: Organisation for Economic Co-operation and Development.

Freeman, C. (1982). *The economics of industrial innovation.* Harmondsworth, UK: Penguin.

Freeman, C. (1988). Japan, a new system of innovation. In G. Dosi, C. Freeman, R. R. Nelson, G. Silverberg, & L. Soete (Eds.), *Technical change and economic theory* (pp. 330–348). London: Pinter.

Freeman, C., & Perez, C. (1988). Structural crises of adjustment, business cycles and investment behaviour. In G. Dosi, C. Freeman, R. Nelson, G. Silverberg, & L. Soete (Eds.), *Technical change and economic theory* (pp. 38–66). London: Pinter.

Freeman, L. C. (1978/1979). Centrality in social networks: Conceptual clarification. *Social Networks, 1*, 215–239.

Frenken, K. (2005). *Innovation, evolution and complexity theory.* Cheltenham, UK: Edward Elgar.

Frenken, K., & Leydesdorff, L. (2000). Scaling trajectories in civil aircraft (1913–1970). *Research Policy, 29*(3), 331–348.

Freud, S. (1911). Formulations on the two principles of mental functioning. *Standard Edition, 12*, 213–226.

Fujigaki, Y. (1998). Filling the gap between discussions on science and scientists' everyday activities: Applying the autopoiesis system theory to scientific knowledge. *Social Science Information, 37*(1), 5–22.

Galbraith, J. K. (1967). *The new industrial state.* Harmondsworth, UK: Penguin.

Galbraith, J. R., & Nathanson, D. A. (1978). *Strategy implementation: The role of structure and process.* St. Paul, MN: West Publishing Company.

Gibbons, M., Limoges, C., Nowotny, H., Schwartzman, S., Scott, P., & Trow, M. (1994). *The new production of knowledge: The dynamics of science and research in contemporary societies.* London: Sage.

Giddens, A. (1976). *New rules of sociological method.* London: Hutchinson.

Giddens, A. (1979). *Central problems in social theory.* London: Macmillan.

Giddens, A. (1984). *The constitution of society.* Cambridge, UK: Polity Press.

Giddens, A. (1990). *The consequences of modernity.* Cambridge, UK: Polity Press.

Godin, B. (2006a). The knowledge-based economy: Conceptual framework or buzzword? *Journal of Technology Transfer, 31*(1), 17–30.

Godin, B. (2006b). The linear model of innovation: The historical construction of an analytical framework. *Science, Technology & Human Values, 31*(6), 639–667.

Godin, B., & Gingras, Y. (2000). The place of universities in the system of knowledge production. *Research Policy, 29*(2), 273–278.

Graham, P. J., & Dickinson, H. D. (2007). Knowledge-system theory in society: Charting the growth of knowledge-system models over a decade, 1994–2003. *Journal of the American Society for Information Science and Technology, 58*(14), 2372–2381.

Granstrand, O. (1999). *The economics and management of intellectual property: Towards intellectual capitalism.* Cheltenham, UK: Edward Elgar.

Granstrand, O., Patel, P., & Pavitt, K. (1997). Multitechnology corporations: Why they have 'distributed' rather than 'distinctive' core capabilities. *California Management Review, 39,* 8–25.

Gunasekara, C. (2006). Reframing the role of universities in the development of regional innovation systems. *Journal of Technology Transfer, 30*(3), 101–111.

Habermas, J. (1981). *Theorie des kommunikativen Handelns.* Frankfurt am Main, Germany: Suhrkamp.

Habermas, J. (1987). Excursus on Luhmann's appropriation of the philosophy of the subject through systems theory. In *The philosophical discourse of modernity: Twelve lectures* (pp. 368–385). Cambridge, MA: MIT Press.

Habermas, J., & Luhmann, N. (1971). *Theorie der Gesellschaft oder Sozialtechnologie.* Frankfurt am Main, Germany: Suhrkamp.

Hall, P. A., & Soskice, D. W. (Eds.). (2001). *Varieties of capitalism: The institutional foundations of comparative advantage.* Oxford, UK: Oxford University Press.

Hayles, N. K. (1990). *Chaos bound: Orderly disorder in contemporary literature and science.* Ithaca, NY: Cornell University Press.

Heertje, A. (1973). *Economie en Technische Ontwikkeling.* Leiden, The Netherlands: Stenfert Kroese.

Hessels, L. K., & van Lente, H. (2008). Re-thinking new knowledge production: A literature review and a research agenda. *Research Policy, 37*(4), 740–760.

Holzner, B., & Marx, J. H. (1979). *Knowledge application: The knowledge system in society.* Boston: Allyn and Bacon.

Husserl, E. (1962). *Die Krisis der Europäischen Wissenschaften und die Transzendentale Phänomenologie.* The Hague, The Netherlands: Martinus Nijhoff. (Original work published 1935/1936).

Husserl, E. (1973). *Cartesianische Meditationen und Pariser Vorträge [Cartesian meditations and the Paris lectures].* The Hague, The Netherlands: Martinus Nijhoff. (Original work published in 1929)

Irvine, J., & Martin, B. R. (1984). *Foresight in science: Picking the winners.* London: Pinter.

Jakulin, A., & Bratko, I. (2004). *Quantifying and visualizing attribute interactions: An approach based on entropy.* Retrieved January 20, 2009, from arxiv.org/abs/cs.AI/0308002

Jaffe, A. B., & Trajtenberg, M. (2002). *Patents, citations, and innovations: A window on the knowledge economy.* Cambridge, MA: MIT Press.

Kaufer, D. S., & Carley, K. M. (1993). *Communication at a distance.* Hillsdale, NJ: Erlbaum.

Kemp, R., Schot, J., & Hoogma, R. (1998). Regime shifts to sustainability through processes of niche formation: The approach of strategic niche management. *Technology Analysis and Strategic Management, 10*(2), 175–195.

Kingston, W. (2003). *Innovation: The creative impulse in human progress.* Washington, DC: Leonard R. Sugerman Press.

Kline, S., & Rosenberg, N. (1986). An overview of innovation. In R. Landau & N. Rosenberg (Eds.), *The positive sum strategy: Harnessing technology for economic growth* (pp. 275–306). Washington, DC: National Academy Press.

Krauss, G., & Wolff, H.-G. (2002). Technological strengths in mature sectors: An impediment of an asset of regional economic restructuring? The case of multimedia and biotechnology in Baden-Württemberg. *Journal of Technology Transfer, 27*(1), 39–50.

Krugman, P. (1996). *The self-organizing economy.* Malden, MA: Blackwell.

Lancaster, K. J. (1979). *Variety, equity and efficiency.* New York: Columbia University Press.

Langford, C. H., Burch, R. D., & Langford, M. W. (1997). The "well-stirred reactor": Evolution of industry-government-university relations in Canada. *Science and Public Policy, 24*(1), 21–27.

Larédo, P. (2003). Six major challenges facing public intervention in higher education, science, technology and innovation. *Science and Public Policy, 30*(1), 4–12.

Latour, B. (1987). *Science in action: How to follow scientists and engineers through society.* Milton Keynes, UK: Open University Press.

Lengyel, B., & Leydesdorff, L. (2008). A magyar gazdaság tudás-alapú szervezŒdésének mérése: Az innovációs rendszerek szinergiáinak térbelisége. *Közgazdasági Szemle [Economic Review], 55*, 522–547.

Lewontin, R. (2000). *The Triple Helix: Gene, organism, and environment.* Cambridge, MA: Harvard University Press.

Leydesdorff, L. (1995). *The challenge of scientometrics: The development, measurement, and self-organization of scientific communications.* Leiden, The Netherlands: DSWO Press, Leiden University.

Leydesdorff, L. (2001). *A sociological theory of communication: The self-organization of the knowledge-based society.* Parkland, FL: Universal Publishers.

Leydesdorff, L. (2006). *The knowledge-based economy: Modeled, measured, simulated.* Boca Raton, FL: Universal Publishers.

Leydesdorff, L. (2008). The communication of meaning in anticipatory systems: A simulation study of the dynamics of intentionality in social interactions. *Proceedings of the 8th International Conference on Computing Anticipatory Systems, 1051*, 33–49.

Leydesdorff, L. (2009). The non-linear dynamics of meaning-processing in social systems. *Social Science Information, 48*(1), 5–33.

Leydesdorff, L., & Fritsch, M. (2006). Measuring the knowledge base of regional innovation systems in Germany in terms of a Triple Helix dynamics. *Research Policy, 35*(10), 1538–1553.

Leydesdorff, L., & Sun, Y. (2009). National and international dimensions of the Triple Helix in Japan: University-industry-government versus international co-authorship relations. *Journal of the American Society for Information Science and Technology, 60*(4), 778–788.

Li, T.-Y., & Yorke, J. A. (1975). Period three implies chaos. *American Mathematical Monthly, 82*(10), 985–992.

Liebowitz, S. J., & Margolis, S. E. (1999). *Winners, losers & Microsoft: Competition and antitrust in high technology.* Oakland, CA: The Independent Institute.

List, F. (1904). *The national systems of political economy.* London: Longman. (Original work published 1841)

Luhmann, N. (1971). Sinn als Grundbegriff der Soziologie. In J. Habermas & N. Luhmann (Eds.), *Theorie der Gesellschaft oder Sozialtechnologie* (pp. 25–100). Frankfurt am Main, Germany: Suhrkamp.

Luhmann, N. (1975). Interaktion, Organisation, Gesellschaft: Anwendungen der Systemtheorie. In M. Gerhardt (Ed.), *Die Zukunft der Philosophie* (pp. 85–107). München, Germany: List.

Luhmann, N. (1984). *Soziale Systeme. Grundriß einer allgemeinen Theorie.* Frankfurt am Main, Germany: Suhrkamp.

Luhmann, N. (1986). The autopoiesis of social systems. In F. Geyer & J. v. d. Zouwen (Eds.), *Sociocybernetic paradoxes* (pp. 172–192). London: Sage.

Luhmann, N. (1990). *Die Wissenschaft der Gesellschaft.* Frankfurt am Main, Germany: Suhrkamp.

Luhmann, N. (1995a). Intersubjektivität oder Kommunkation: Unterschiedliche Ausgangspunkte soziologischer Theoriebildung. In *Soziologische Aufklärung 6* (pp. 169–188). Opladen, Germany: Westdeutscher Verlag.

Luhmann, N. (1995b). *Social systems.* Stanford, CA: Stanford University Press.

Luhmann, N. (1996). On the scientific context of the concept of communication. *Social Science Information, 35*(2), 257–267.

Luhmann, N. (1997). *Die Gesellschaft der Gesellschaft.* Frankfurt am Main, Germany: Surhkamp.

Luhmann, N. (2000). *Organisation und Entscheidung.* Opladen, Germany: Westdeutscher Verlag.

Luhmann, N. (2002). How can the mind participate in communication? In W. Rasch (Ed.), *Theories of distinction: Redescribing the descriptions of modernity* (pp. 169–184). Stanford, CA: Stanford University Press.

Lundvall, B.-Å. (1988). Innovation as an interactive process: From user-producer interaction to the national system of innovation. In G. Dosi, C. Freeman, R. Nelson, G. Silverberg, & L. Soete (Eds.), *Technical change and economic theory* (pp. 349–369). London: Pinter.

Lundvall, B.-Å. (Ed.). (1992). *National systems of innovation.* London: Pinter.

Lundvall, B.-Å., & Borras, S. (1997). *The globalising learning economy: Implication for innovation policy.* Brussels, Luxembourg: European Commission.

Machlup, F. (1962). *The production and distribution of knowledge in the United States.* Princeton, NJ: Princeton University Press.

Mackenzie, A. (2001). The technicity of time. *Time & Society, 10*(2/3), 235–257.

Malerba, F., Nelson, R., Orsenigo, L., & Winter, S. (1999). "History-friendly" models of industry evolution: The computer industry. *Industrial and Corporate Change, 8*(1), 3–35.

Malone, T. W., & Crowston, K. (1994). The interdisciplinary study of coordination. *ACM Computing Surveys, 26*(1), 87–119.

Marx, K. (1971). *Das Kapital I.* Berlin: Dietz. (Original work published 1867)

Marx, K. (1974). *Grundriße der Kritik der politischen Oekonomie.* Berlin: Dietz. (Original work published 1857)

Maturana, H. R. (1978). Biology of language: The epistemology of reality. In G. A. Miller & E. Lenneberg (Eds.), *Psychology and biology of language and thought: Essays in honor of Eric Lenneberg* (pp. 27–63). New York: Academic Press.

Maturana, H. R., & Varela, F. (1980). *Autopoiesis and cognition: The realization of the living*. Boston: Reidel.

Maturana, H. R., & Varela, F. J. (1984). *The tree of knowledge*. Boston: New Science Library.

May, R. M. (1976). Simple mathematical models with very complicated dynamics. *Nature, 261*, 459–467.

May, R. M., & Leonard, W. J. (1975). Nonlinear aspects of competition between three species. *SIAM Journal of Applied Mathematics, 29*(2), 243–253.

McGill, W. J. (1954). Multivariate information transmission. *Psychometrika, 19*, 97–116.

McGill, W. J., & Quastler, H. (1955). Standardized nomenclature: An attempt. In H. Quastler (Ed.), *Information theory in psychology: Problems and methods* (pp. 83–92). Woodbury, NY: The Free Press.

McLuhan, M. (1964). *Understanding media: The extension of man*. New York: McGraw-Hill.

Mead, G. H. (1934). The point of view of social behaviourism. In C. H. Morris (Ed.), *Mind, self, & society from the standpoint of a social behaviourist: Works of G. H. Mead* (Vol. 1, pp. 1–41). Chicago: University of Chicago Press.

Merton, R. K. (1973). *The sociology of science: Theoretical and empirical investigations*. Chicago: University of Chicago Press.

Mirowski, P., & Sent, E. M. (2007). The commercialization of science, and the response of STS. In E. J. Hackett, O. Amsterdamska, M. Lynch, & J. Wajcman (Eds.), *Handbook of science, technology and society studies* (pp. 635–689). Cambridge, MA: MIT Press.

Moso, M., & Olazaran, M. (2002). Regional technology policy and the emergence of an R&D system in the Basque country. *Journal of Technology Transfer, 27*(1), 61–75.

Mowery, D. C., & Rosenberg, N. (1979). The influence of market demand upon innovation: A critical review of some empirical studies. *Research Policy, 8*, 102–153.

Mowery, D. C., & Rosenberg, N. (1989). *Technology and the pursuit of economic growth*. Cambridge, UK: Cambridge University Press.

Mulkay, M. J. (1976). The mediating role of the scientific elite. *Social Studies of Science, 6*, 445–470.

Nelson, R. R. (Ed.). (1982). *Government and technical progress: A cross-industry analysis*. New York: Pergamon.

Nelson, R. R. (Ed.). (1993). *National innovation systems: A comparative analysis*. New York: Oxford University Press.

Nelson, R. R. (1994). Economic growth via the coevolution of technology and institutions. In L. Leydesdorff & P. van den Besselaar (Eds.), *Evolutionary economic and chaos theory: New directions in technology studies* (pp. 21–32). London: Pinter.

Nelson, R. R. (1995). Recent evolutionary theorizing about economic change. *Journal of Economic Literature, 33*(1), 48–90.

Nelson, R. R., & Winter, S. G. (1975). Growth theory from an evolutionary perspective: The differential productivity growth puzzle. *American Economic Review, 65*, 338–344.

Nelson, R. R., & Winter, S. G. (1977). In search of useful theory of innovation. *Research Policy, 6*, 35–76.

Nelson, R. R., & Winter, S. G. (1982). *An evolutionary theory of economic change*. Cambridge, MA: Belknap Press of Harvard University Press.

Noble, D. (1977). *America by design*. New York: Knopf.

Nonaka, I., & Takeuchi, H. (1995). *The knowledge creating company*. Oxford, UK: Oxford University Press.

Nowotny, H., Scott, P., & Gibbons, M. (2001). *Re-thinking science: Knowledge and the public in an age of uncertainty*. Cambridge, UK: Polity.

Obama, B. (2008, June 9). *Remarks of Senator Barack Obama: Change that works for you.* Retrieved January 28, 2009, from www.barackobama.com/2008/06/09/remarks_of_senator_barack_obam_76.php

Organisation for Economic Co-operation and Development. (1980). *Technical change and economic policy.* Paris: the Organisation.

Organisation for Economic Co-operation and Development. (1996a). *The knowledge-based economy.* Paris: The Organisation. Retrieved January 28, 2009, from www.oecd.org/dataoecd/51/8/1913021.pdf

Organisation for Economic Co-operation and Development. (1996b). *New indicators for the knowledge-based economy: Proposals for future work,* DSTI/STP/NESTI/GSS/TIP (96)6. Paris: The Organisation.

Organisation for Economic Co-operation and Development. (1997). *OECD science, technology, and industry scoreboard 2007.* Retrieved January 28, 2009, from www.oecd.org/document/10/0,3343,en_2649_33703_39493962_1_1_1_1,00.html

Organisation for Economic Co-operation and Development. (2004). *Science and technology statistical compendium 2004.* Retrieved January 28, 2009, from www.oecd.org/document/8/0,2340,en_2649_33703_23654472_1_1_1_1,00.html

Parsons, T. (1951). *The social system.* New York: The Free Press.

Parsons, T. (1952). Superego and the theory of social systems. In T. Parsons (Ed.), *Social structure and personality* (pp. 17–33). London: Routledge.

Parsons, T. (1963a). On the concept of influence. *Public Opinion Quarterly, 27,* 37–62.

Parsons, T. (1963b). On the concept of political power. *Proceedings of the American Philosophical Society, 107*(3), 232–262.

Parsons, T. (1968). Interaction: I. Social Interaction. In D. L. Sills (Ed.), *The international encyclopedia of the social sciences* (Vol. 7, pp. 429–441). New York: McGraw-Hill.

Pavitt, K. (1984). Sectoral patterns of technical change: Towards a theory and a taxonomy. *Research Policy, 13*(6), 343–373.

Penrose, E. T. (1959). *The theory of the growth of the firm.* New York: John Wiley.

Polanyi, M. (1961). Knowing and being. *Mind, 70*(280), 458–470.

Porter, M. E. (1990). *The competitive advantage of nations.* London: Macmillan.

Rabeharisoa, V., & Callon, M. (2002). The involvement of patients' associations in research. *International Social Science Journal, 54*(171), 57–65.

Riba-Vilanova, M., & Leydesdorff, L. (2001). Why Catalonia cannot be considered as a regional innovation system. *Scientometrics, 50*(2), 215–240.

Richta, R., Auerhan, J., Bareš, G., Bárta, D., Brenner, V., Cvekl, J., et al. (1968). *Politische Oekonomie des 20. Jahrhunderts.* Prague, Czechoslovakia: Makol.

Rogers, E. M. (1962). *Diffusion of innovations.* New York: The Free Press.

Rosen, R. (1985). *Anticipatory systems: Philosophical, mathematical and methodological foundations.* Oxford, UK: Pergamon Press.

Rosenberg, N. (1976). The direction of technological change: Inducement mechanisms and focusing devices. In N. Rosenberg (Ed.), *Perspectives on technology* (pp. 108–125). Cambridge, UK: Cambridge University Press.

Rosenberg, N. (1982a). *Inside the black box: Technology and economics.* Cambridge, UK: Cambridge University Press.

Rosenberg, N. (1982b). Learning by using. In N. Rosenberg (Ed.), *Inside the black box: Technology and economics* (pp. 120–140). Cambridge, UK: Cambridge University Press.

Rosenberg, N. (1990). Why do firms do basic research (with their own money)? *Research Policy, 19,* 165–174.

Rosenberg, N. (1994). *Exploring the black box: Technology, economics, and history.* Cambridge, UK: Cambridge University Press.

Rothwell, R., & Zegveld, W. (1981). *Industrial innovation and public policy.* London: Pinter.

Sahal, D. (1981a). Alternative conceptions of technology. *Research Policy, 10,* 2–24.

Sahal, D. (1981b). *Patterns of technological innovation.* Reading, MA: Addison Wesley.

Salter, W. E. G. (1960). *Productivity and technical change.* New York: Cambridge University Press.

Saviotti, P. P. (1996). *Technological evolution, variety and the economy.* Cheltenham, UK: Edward Elgar.

Scharnhorst, A. (1998). Citation-networks, science landscapes and evolutionary strategies. *Scientometrics, 43*(1), 95–106.

Schot, J., & Geels, F. W. (2007). Niches in evolutionary theories of technical change. *Journal of Evolutionary Economics, 17*(5), 605–622.

Schumpeter, J. (1943). *Socialism, capitalism and democracy.* London: Allen & Unwin.

Schumpeter, J. (1964). *Business cycles: A theoretical, historical and statistical analysis of capitalist process.* New York: McGraw-Hill. (Original work published 1939)

Schutz, A. (1952). Das Problem der transzendentalen Intersubjectivität bei Husserl. *Philosophische Rundschau, 5*(2), 81–107.

Schutz, A. (1975). *Collected papers III: Studies in phenomenological philosophy.* The Hague, The Netherlands: Martinus Nijhoff.

Sforzi, F. (2003). The "Tuscan model" and recent trends. In G. Beccatini, M. Bellandi, G. d. Ottati & F. Sforzi (Eds.), *From industrial districts to local developments: An itinerary of research* (pp. 29–61). Cheltenham, UK: Edward Elgar.

Shinn, T. (2002). The Triple Helix and new production of knowledge: Prepackaged thinking on science and technology. *Social Studies of Science, 32*(4), 599–614.

Shinn, T., & Lamy, E. (2006). Paths of commercial knowledge: Forms and consequences of university-enterprise synergy in scientist-sponsored firms. *Research Policy, 35*(10), 1465–1476.

Skolnikoff, E. B. (1993). *The elusive transformation: Science, technology and the evolution of international politics.* Princeton, NJ: Princeton University Press.

Slaughter, S., & Rhoades, G. (2004). *Academic capitalism and the new economy: Markets, state, and higher education.* Baltimore, MD: Johns Hopkins University Press.

Storper, M. (1997). *The regional world: Territorial development in a global economy.* New York: Guilford Press.

Strydom, P. (1999). Triple contingency: The theoretical problem of the public in communication societies. *Philosophy & Social Criticism, 25*(2), 1–25.

Teubal, M. (1979). On user needs and need determination: Aspects of a theory of technological innovation. In M. J. Baker (Ed.), *Industrial innovation: Technology, policy and diffusion* (pp. 266–289). London: Macmillan Press.

Theil, H. (1972). *Statistical Decomposition Analysis.* Amsterdam/ London: North-Holland.

Ulanowicz, R. E. (1997). *Ecology, the ascendent perspective.* New York: Columbia University Press.

Urry, J. (2000). *Sociology beyond societies: Mobilities for the twenty-first century.* London: Routledge.

Urry, J. (2003). *Global complexity.* Cambridge, UK: Polity.

Van den Belt, H., & Rip, A. (1987). The Nelson-Winter-Dosi model and synthetic dye chemistry. In W. E. Bijker, T. P. Hughes, & T. J. Pinch (Eds.), *The social construction of technological systems: New directions in the sociology and history of technology* (pp. 135–158.). Cambridge MA: MIT Press.

Van den Daele, W., Krohn, W., & Weingart, P. (Eds.). (1979). *Geplante Forschung: Vergleichende Studien über den Einfluss politischer Programme auf die Wissenschaftsentwicklung.* Frankfurt am Main, Germany: Suhrkamp.

Vanderstraeten, R. (2002). Parsons, Luhmann and the theorem of double contingency. *Journal of Classical Sociology, 2*(1), 77–92.

Viale, R., & Campodall'Orto, S. (2002). An evolutionary Triple Helix to strengthen academy-industry relations: Suggestions from European regions. *Science and Public Policy, 29*(3), 154–168.

Watkins, J. W. N. (1952). Ideal types and historical explanation. *British Journal for the Philosophy of Science, 3*(9), 22–43.

Weber, M. (1968a). Die Objektivität sozialwissenschaftlicher und sozialpolitischer Erkenntnis. In *Gesammelte Aufsätze zur Wissenschaftslehre* (pp. 146–214). Tübingen, Germany: Mohr. (Original work published 1904)

Weber, M. (1968b). Der Sinn der Wertfreiheit der soziologischen und ökonomischen Wissenschaften. In *Gesammelte Aufsätze zur Wissenschaftslehre* (pp. 489–540). Tübingen, Germany: Mohr. (Original work published 1917)

Weber, M. (1968c). Wissenschaft als Beruf [Science as a vocation]. In *Gesammelte Aufsätze zur Wissenschaftslehre* (pp. 582–613). Tübingen, Germany: Mohr. (Original work published 1919)

Weingart, P. (1997). From "finalization" to "Mode 2": Old wine in new bottles? *Social Science Information, 36*, 591–613.

Weiss, C. (1979). The many meanings of research utilization. *Public Administration Review, 39*(5), 426–431.

Whitley, R. D. (1984). *The intellectual and social organization of the sciences.* Oxford, UK: Oxford University Press.

Whitley, R. D. (2001). National innovation systems. In N. J. Smelser & P. B. Baltes (Eds.), *International encyclopedia of the social and behavioral sciences* (pp. 10303–10309). Oxford, UK: Elsevier.

Williamson, O. E. (1975). *Markets and hierarchies: Analysis and antitrust implications. A study in the economics of internal organization.* New York: Free Press.

Williamson, O. E. (1985). *The economic institutions of capitalism.* New York: Free Press.

Windrum, P. (1999). Simulation models of technological innovation: A review. *American Behavioral Scientist, 42*(10), 1531–1550.

Yeung, R. W. (2008). *Information theory and network coding.* New York: Springer.

Zuboff, S. (1988). *In the age of the smart machine: The future of work and power.* New York: Basic Books.

# CHAPTER 10

# Economic Theory as It Applies to Public Sector Information

*Kirsti Nilsen*
*University of Western Ontario, London, Canada*

## Introduction

This chapter[1] reviews the economics literature pertaining to public sector information. In addition, the economic arguments put forward in government studies and policy documents are reviewed, focusing on the current push for harmonization of public sector information policy across the European Union and the debate as to which model of information dissemination is preferable (i.e., the U.S. open access model versus the more restrictive European model). Some works by economists that appeared in the library and information science (LIS) and other literatures are covered, but the LIS literature in general is not reviewed.

The term "public sector information" (PSI) is used here rather than "government information" or "official information." The terms are synonymous, although PSI can be construed more broadly, to include any information produced by public sector bodies, including cultural and educational institutions. Public sector information (and content) is any kind of information that is produced and/or collected by a public body as part of the institution's mandated role. It is directly generated by, and associated with, the functioning of the public sector and is readily useable in commercial applications (Organisation for Economic Co-operation and Development, Directorate for Science, Technology and Industry, Working Party on the Economy, 2006). As will be discussed, the economic value of its commercial use is the focus of much recent attention in Europe.

The chapter begins with a brief summary of neoclassical economic theory, including the concepts of market failure and public goods, to lay the groundwork for the review. Readers familiar with these concepts may wish to move directly to the section on the economics of information. The literature on the history of information economics; the definitions of information used by economists; and their concepts of information as a public good, as a commodity, and as a contributor to social value are addressed. The review then focuses on the economic arguments and rationalization for public sector versus private sector supply of information, the impact of PSI on general economic efficiency, commercial re-use, value adding, and revenue generation. Then the literature on the pricing of information and the arguments around the imposition of user fees for PSI, and, finally, the arguments for and against copyrighting PSI are reviewed. The vast literature on the economics of e-government and of privatization is not addressed.

## Neoclassical Economic Theory

Neoclassical economic theory and social welfare theory are of particular interest for this review because both underlie the development of the economics of information. As Nobel economist Donald Lamberton pointed out (1994a), neoclassical economics provided a base and a language for information economics, which was necessary in order to keep an open dialogue with the economics profession, as well as with international and national decision makers in industry and government.

According to the neoclassical paradigm, individuals are assumed to have wants, desires, and preferences and to have freedom of choice as to how they will go about achieving these goals. Individuals themselves will determine the value (utility) of consuming goods and services that help them fulfill their goals. They do so through the process of exchange of goods, services, money, or time, which occurs when both parties perceive a benefit because of the different values they place on the resources in question (Babe, 1995; McKenzie, 1979).

The interaction of demand and supply determines the value of items to both parties of an exchange. "Underlying demand is the added 'utility' or the usefulness of the item in satisfying wants or needs; underlying supply is the cost (or foregone utility) in losing the item through sale" (Babe, 1995, p. 14). In order to produce goods and services for sale, the producer must purchase factor inputs (land, labor, capital, energy) and such purchases represent costs (foregone utility) to the firm. "Production will be undertaken only if it is anticipated that costs can be recouped through the sale of outputs over the long term" (p. 14). The result will be "market equilibrium": When the price and quantity are such that the amount supplied by the producer is set at a price that consumers are willing to pay (Kingma, 2001). When there is not market equilibrium, there is "market failure." Market equilibrium underlies the concept of "general equilibrium," which posits that interdependent economic forces are balanced by individual decisions based on self interest. General equilibrium is thought to lead to the greatest social welfare. Friedrich von Hayek (1937, 1945), one of the first information economists, argued that perfect equilibrium is impossible if there is a disturbance in knowledge creation or change in individual knowledge (i.e., imperfect information).

Definitions of economics indicate that the field is concerned not only with production and consumption, but also with distribution. Distribution, in this context, refers to the allocation of income and social welfare across the population. Social welfare is the focus of welfare economics, which evaluates the effects of economic policy on the well being of individuals. Of interest to welfare economists is society's attitude toward different distributions of income and welfare; that is, whether a society cares about inequality or not. Nobel economist Joseph Stiglitz (1994) wrote that the rationale for government redistribution programs lies in the fact that the market's distribution of income might not be socially desirable.

Neoclassical economists believe that the greatest social efficiency is achieved when supply equals demand: When prices are such that those goods and services that are produced do change hands (in economic terms, the market "clears"). This avoids wasteful overproduction and satisfies the wants, desires or preferences of consumers. When this occurs, it is believed that the "Pareto optimum" is achieved. A position is Pareto optimal if it would be impossible to improve the well being of one individual without harming at least one other individual. A producer may be better off if prices are raised, but if one consumer is made worse off—no longer able to afford the product or service—there would be no Pareto optimality. In addition there would be a socially inefficient level of production because of unsold products or unused services. A Pareto improvement leaves everyone better off because it makes at least one person better off and no one worse off, improving social welfare (Stiglitz, 2000b). Sandler (2001) illustrates the problem of relying on Pareto optimality: If a millionaire gives a penny to a poor man, the poor man is better off but the millionaire is not, therefore this action is not Pareto optimal.

Today it is argued that neoclassical economists focused on Pareto efficiency to the detriment of other considerations. Having assumed that consumers make choices in an attempt to maximize their individual well being (their utility), economists came "to the doctrinaire conclusion that the existing pattern of consumer choices must represent the highest possible attainable level of consumer welfare" (Adams & Brock, 1994, p. 129).

# Market Failure

Neoclassical economics is also criticized because it fails to address persistent conditions under which markets are not Pareto efficient. Rather than explaining these conditions through economic theory, neoclassical economists simply labeled them as "market failures" and set them aside. Stiglitz (2000b) identified six conditions of market failure: (1) failure of competition; (2) public goods; (3) externalities; (4) incomplete markets; (5) imperfect information; and (6) unemployment, inflation, and disequilibrium. He argued that each of these failures provides a rationale for government activity. Of particular interest for this chapter are (in the order covered), the failure of competition, externalities, imperfect information, and public goods. Addressing these considerations led some economists to develop the theories underlying information economics.

## *Failure of Competition*

Competition is seen as desirable in market economies because competitive pressures encourage change in companies and force them to increase productivity—benefits that are lost in the absence of competition. Thus government's role is to ensure effective competition in private markets. Pareto efficiency requires that markets have perfect competition; and competition fails where there is a monopoly or when there is imperfect information. Although monopolists are efficient, they charge too high a price and accordingly produce too little. Patents and copyrights can lead to failure of competition because monopolistic control is created over some information goods (Kingma, 2001; Stiglitz, 2000b; Stiglitz, Orszag, & Orszag, 2000).

## Externalities

Externalities occur when actions undertaken by one individual or firm affect another entity even though the latter did not pay or is not paid. Externalities may be negative (one individual's actions impose a cost on others, e.g., pollution) or they may be positive (one individual's actions impose a benefit on others, e.g., knowledge enhancement). The consequence of externalities is over-production of goods that generate negative externalities and under-supply of goods that generate positive externalities. Individuals and firms do not pay the full cost of activities that generate negative externalities and so will continue to engage in these activities. Conversely, they will engage in too few activities generating positive externalities because they do not enjoy the full benefits. Government policy may be able to correct market failures caused by externalities—in the case of negative externalities, government regulation, taxes, or educational programs can be used to promote a reduction in the consumption of a good or service to the socially efficient level; with positive externalities, government subsidies, regulation, or educational programs can be used to increase the level of output of a good or service to a socially efficient level (Kingma, 2001; Stiglitz, 2000b).

## Imperfect Information

When consumers and producers do not have perfect information, when they are misinformed or uninformed, they may not be able to judge a product's value. They may be reluctant to buy or sell goods and services, and then efficient markets cannot occur. Imperfect information (also known as asymmetric information) can result in inefficiencies, but market corrections for these inefficiencies can reassure the consumer of the quality of the good, such as name branding, warranties, and guarantees. Governments typically believe that the market, by itself, will supply too little information to consumers, and thus are motivated to enact or regulate a number of measures such as truth in lending, labeling, and disclosure of contents. Imperfect information problems are often identified as "transparency" problems. Transparency enables individuals to see clearly what they need and what is for sale. Imperfect information or lack of transparency contributes to the failure of competition discussed previously. Because neoclassical economists based all of their models on the assumption of perfect information, little attention was paid to the problem of imperfect information until the 1960s, when it became obvious that the neoclassical paradigm insufficiently recognized common information problems (DeLong & Froomkin, 2000; Kingma, 2001; Stiglitz, 2000b).

## Public Goods

In an economist's world, public goods are goods consumed by more than one person (e.g., books in a library, a television broadcast). In other words, more than one person enjoys the benefits of the good, without significantly detracting from the benefits enjoyed by others. Public goods need not necessarily be produced by the public sector. It is noted that the definition economists offer for a public good runs counter to its commonsense meaning. Although for most people "public" suggests government involvement and universal accessibility, for economists a good's availability and allocation determine whether it is a public or a private good (Gazier & Touffut, 2006; Kingma, 2001).

Paul A. Samuelson (1954, 1957) is credited with advancing the theory of public goods that identified two of their critical properties: (1) These goods usually will not be provided by the private sector because they cannot be provided exclusively to paying customers, and (2) non-paying customers cannot be prevented from benefiting from them. These properties explain why the public sector produces many public goods. These properties mean that: (1) it costs nothing for an additional individual to enjoy their benefits, and (2) it is, in general, difficult or impossible to exclude individuals from a public good. Hence economists say that these goods are "non-rivalrous" and "non-excludable." Non-rivalrous means that one person's consumption does not detract from another person's consumption; non-excludable means that no one can be excluded from benefitting from the good (without incurring great costs). Some public goods can be non-rivalrous but made excludable by various mechanisms such as prices and intellectual property legislation. Because of their non-rivalrous and non-exclusionary characteristics, public goods either will not be supplied by the market or, if supplied, will be supplied in insufficient quantity, therefore leading to market failure (Stiglitz, 2000b).

The absence of excludability, rivalry, and transparency is bad for private markets. Non-rivalry has been the basis of the theory of natural monopolies and of the production of public goods through government programs. The "solution has been to try to find a regulatory regime that will mimic the decisions that the competitive market ought to make, or to accept that the public provision of the good by the government is the best that can be done" (DeLong & Froomkin, 2000, p. 17).

A distinction is made between public goods that are "pure" and those that are "non-pure." Many goods are not pure public goods but have one or the other property (rivalrousness or excludability) to some degree. With a pure public good, there is zero marginal cost (that is, it does not cost more to provide it to an additional person and it is impossible to exclude people from receiving the good). Most public goods that government provides are not pure public goods in this sense. The cost of an additional person using the good may be very low but not zero (Stiglitz, 2000b). National defense is the classic example of a pure public good (one cannot choose not to benefit from it), but this and other frequently cited examples (e.g., lighthouses, street lighting) are contested (Gazier & Touffut, 2006). According to Stiglitz (2006), one of the reasons that pure public goods are typically provided in the public sector is that unless there is public sector provision, there will be under-supply.

Part of the market failure exemplified by public goods is the "free rider" problem. Individuals are reluctant to support public goods because they believe that they would benefit from the goods regardless of whether they contributed to them. There is no incentive to pay for the services voluntarily, so individuals must be forced to support these goods through taxation. Governments can collect taxes to pay for public goods but it is difficult to determine how much of the public good to provide, how much benefit citizens get from these public goods, and how much to tax each citizen for them (Kingma, 2001; Stiglitz, 2000b).

Inge Kaul (2006) explores the concept of global public goods, explaining that all countries, peoples, and generations share the benefits or costs of these public goods,

Claude Henry (2006) described them as both worldwide and intergenerational. Kaul and Henry provide the examples of the natural world, climate, international communication and transport networks, and freely circulating knowledge. Henry (2006) made an argument for knowledge as a global public good, but noted that it can be appropriated through intellectual property regimes (his example is patents), thus raising the social costs.

The term "collective goods" is sometimes used by economists to refer to public goods. Fritz Machlup (1980) argued that collective goods are public goods and/or goods whose production and consumption have external effects. Information is described as a classic example of a collective good because it is the type of commodity for which private market incentives lead to under-provision rather than over-provision (Hirshleifer, 1971). Others describe information as an "experience good" because one must experience it to know its value (Herings & Schinkel, 2005; Raban, 2003).

In contrast with public goods, a "private good" is one that only one person consumes and its benefits accrue to that person. Thus private goods are rivalrous and excludable and generally provided by the private sector. Some economists argue that public goods can provide private benefits. An example frequently noted is higher education—recipients of higher education gain private benefits in that their income is likely to be greater than those without college or university degrees. Bates (1988) argued, however, that education has ancillary social value and the fact that it is heavily subsidized by the public sector suggests that education's creation of ancillary value to society (and to industry) is widely recognized. Private goods and public goods are generally considered to be opposites, with the market mechanism seen as appropriate for private goods and government (or some other non-market mechanism) appropriate for public goods (Mandeville, 1999). Kaul (2006) argued that the concept of public goods is a social construct—some private goods are kept public by design (such as education), some non-rivalrous goods are made exclusive (by patents, for example). She noted that goods that are private one day can be public the next, and therefore one should not assume, based on its basic properties, that a good actually is private or public in consumption.

## Failure of Neoclassical Economic Theory to Account for Information

Throughout the 20th century, some economists argued that the neoclassical theory did not sufficiently address the role of information in the economy. This neglect is not surprising because information and knowledge are often free and economists generally ignore things that have no value (Lamberton, 1994b). The avoidance of informational problems resulted in "inconsistencies, paradoxes and failures" that led some neoclassical economists to acknowledge that they could not ignore the importance of availability and access to different kinds and amounts of information (Braman, 2006, p. 6). George Stigler (1961, p. 213) commented that information "occupies a slum dwelling in the town of economics." Stiglitz (2003) wrote, however, that although Stigler recognized the importance of information, he, like other neoclassical economists, considered information to be just a transaction cost, and that the standard results of economics would hold when those costs were incorporated into their economic models. Stiglitz argued that the "neoclassical synthesis" overlooked the process of information acquisition; it failed to explain certain problems of risk and capital markets and related phenomena that had been anticipated by Adam Smith and other 18th and 19th century economists. The competitive paradigm, Stiglitz (1985, p. 26) wrote, is an "artfully constructed structure: When one of the central pieces (the assumption of perfect information) is removed, the structure collapses." He argued that research and analysis over the last century turned out not to be sufficiently robust even when only slight imperfections of information are considered (Stiglitz, 2000a). Stiglitz recognized that information posed a challenge to the conventional notion of the market, forcing economists to reconsider central concepts and principles (Braman, 2006). This led to a "fundamental change in the prevailing paradigm in economics" (Stiglitz, 2003, p. 569).

## Economics of Information

Economics of information is an "umbrella term" that refers to issues raised by information at every level of analysis; it specifically deals with the problem of understanding information creation, processing, flows, and use from an economic perspective (Braman, 2006). Its emergence is described as a response to: (1) the deficiencies of economic theory that assumed perfect information; (2) the failure of policy; and (3) the emergence of intelligent electronics that enhanced the capacity for communication, computation, and control (Lamberton, 1984b).

Some 22 reviews covering the information economics literature have appeared in the *Annual Review of Information Science and Technology* (*ARIST*). The first of these was by later Nobel laureate Michael Spence (1974), reviewing the literature on the importance of information in non-information markets and other sectors of the economy. The most recent was by Sandra Braman (2006), covering the literature on the micro- and macroeconomics of information, a literature that she describes as now vast, noting that attempts to create online databases of the literature have fallen by the wayside. Harmeet Sawhney and Krishna Jayakar's (2007) review of the literature on universal access and Nancy Kranich and Jorge Reina Schement's (2008) review of the information commons literature provide recent coverage of aspects of the topic. Other *ARIST* reviews of particular value to this chapter are Lamberton's (1984a) review of the milestones in the literature up to the early 1980s, Aatto Repo's (1987) review of the literature from the viewpoint of information services, Michael Koenig's (1990) review of information services and productivity, and Sheila Webber's (1998) review of the pricing of online information services. Although it does not specifically focus on the economics literature, Karen Sy and Alice Robbins's (1990) review looked at U.S. federal statistical policies and programs in light of the budget restrictions of the 1980s. Other useful reviews include Badenoch, Reid, Burton, Gibbs, and Oppenheim's (1994) chapter on the value of information, Cronin and Gudim's (1986) review of research on information and productivity, and Eaton's (1987) review of literature on information as a resource.

Among the authors whom Lamberton (1994b) identified as most important to the emergence of information economics in its first half century (which he defines as 1921 to 1971), are Kenneth Arrow, Kenneth Boulding, Friedrich von Hayek, Fritz Machlup, and Herbert Simon. He explained that around 1973 there was a major assessment of information economics, placing heavy emphasis on the role of information in improving the efficiency of markets (Lamberton, 1994a). Twelve years later Braman (2006) observed that the focus has shifted to organizations rather than markets.

Eaton argued that economic analysis of information divided into two main tendencies: one leading to theoretical investigations of information as a commodity, which can be further divided into micro- and macroeconomic approaches, and another focusing on the role of knowledge or information in the economy. Eaton (1987) traced the microeconomic approach back to the work of Stigler (1961) and Jacob Marschak (1974a). Braman (2006) noted several strands of work at the microeconomic level that dealt with problems ranging from decision making under uncertainty to the nature of risk. For example, asymmetries of information are a focus of economic interest because they lead to the imperfect information market failure. Many authors have explored information asymmetries in risk, insurance, job hunting, and other specific topics. George Akerlof's (1970) paper on information asymmetries in the used car market is often cited as the most important information economics paper ever published.

Eaton (1987) provided a microeconomic analysis of information centers in individual decision making. In this model, the primary function and value of information lie in reducing uncertainty: An individual or a firm requires specific information to assist in making a decision and the cost and benefit of acquiring the information are calculated in order to define the "value" to the user. For example, Arrow (1985a) showed that those who have information can gain greater profits than would otherwise be the case. The microeconomic approaches focused on the individual or firm; the macroeconomics of information conceives of information (and knowledge in general) as a resource or commodity with singular characteristics that require differentiation from other kinds of material resources (Eaton, 1987).

The second tendency of the information economics literature that Eaton (1987) identified focused on the role of knowledge or information in the economy. Early research by Machlup (1962, 1980, 1982) and Marc Porat (1977) led to the development of the concept of an information economy. Eaton credits Machlup as the first (in 1962) to formulate this idea specifically and to attempt quantification and analysis of this new economy. The literature on information economics is intertwined with the literature on the information economy, which was influential in demonstrating the importance of information production, processing, storage, and distribution for the macroeconomy (Babe, 1995).

In recent years, Stiglitz (1999, 2000a, 2003) has published perhaps the clearest and most readable articles on the history and development of the economics of information. In particular, his 2003 article (a revised version of his 2001 Nobel speech) is highly recommended. In summarizing the influence of information economics, he argued (2000a) that it changed the way economists think, noting that the "key question is one of dynamics: How the economy adapts to new information, creates new knowledge and how the knowledge is disseminated, absorbed, and used throughout the economy" (p. 1469), and concluded that "information economics has gone beyond simply destroying the old results: It has provided explanations for phenomena and institutions for which the standard theory provides no explanation" (p. 1470).

There has been very little literature published relating specifically to the economics of public sector information. In the U.K. in 2004, an advisory panel concluded that academic and theoretical thinking about the economics of PSI was still at an early stage, with few scholarly articles and "no well established schools of thought or neat, standard models upon which to rely" (UK. Advisory Panel on Crown Copyright, 2004, online; note this panel is now the Advisory Panel on Public Sector Information). Accordingly, it cautions against dogmatic views that seek to suggest that the issue is straightforward.

## *How Economists Define Information*

The meaning that economists assign to the word "information" has always been ambiguous. Some define knowledge and information synonymously; others seek to make a distinction. A close and firm link between the two has always existed, according to Machlup (1983), who filled several pages in a semantic examination of these and other related terms. Hayek (1937) first identified the connection between economics and information/knowledge in a 1936 speech, where he argued that economists had overlooked this relationship. Assuming perfect knowledge, they ignored the general problem of how knowledge is acquired and communicated and how much of it is needed to achieve equilibrium. He argued that knowledge is divided among the minds of all humanity and that market order overcomes the division of knowledge (Ebenstein, 2003). Hayek (1937) equated the problem of division of knowledge with the division of labor. In what is described as his greatest work, Hayek (1945, p. 522) expanded on the problem of the division of knowledge, wrote of the different kinds of knowledge (expert, scientific, theoretical, technical, practical, unorganized), and noted that, in their economic models, economists overlooked practical, unorganized, or fleeting knowledge; for them "all such knowledge is supposed to be 'given.'" He believed that the utilization and communication of information and knowledge are critical for optimal economic productivity (Ebenstein, 2003).

In his various studies of the economics of knowledge production, Machlup progressed from stating (1962) that all information is knowledge to arguing (1979) that a distinction should be made between the information transmission process and the message content. He used (Machlup, 1980) the word "information" to refer to process and the word "knowledge" to refer specifically to content. Arrow (1985a), who broadly interpreted the word "invention" to mean production of knowledge, said that both invention and research are devoted to the production of information. Kenneth Boulding (1984, p. ix) argued that information is the enemy of knowledge and asserted that knowledge is often gained "by the orderly loss of information and by restructuring it, filtering it," and that "piling information on information merely produces noise." Graciela Chichilnisky (1999) described information as the medium in which knowledge is processed, stored, and communicated.

The terms are still often conflated and used interchangeably. In her study of the economics of knowledge, Foray (2004) stated that all the economists she cited saw no real difference between knowledge and information, which means that the economics of knowledge is defined very broadly. She tried to disentangle the concepts, noting that "the reproduction of knowledge and the reproduction of information are clearly different phenomena" (p. 4). The literature on the economics of information and that on the economics of knowledge are not substantially different, with both citing many of the same theorists. However, the literature on the economics of knowledge looks more deeply at the role of education, research, and development, and, as Foray (p. 5) puts it, "the mobilization of cognitive processes."

Other economists, such as Noll (1993), use a broad definition of information incorporating three concepts. Information can be: (1) Facts or natural laws about reality, recognizing that much of human knowledge is not accurately characterized as a fact or natural law; (2) some objective fact or conceptual model that reduces uncertainty about how the world works, thus improving decision making; and (3) communication. The concept of information as objective facts or conceptual models that remove uncertainty has been the focus of much writing. In 1973 Arrow (reprinted in 1984) was first to define information as something that reduces uncertainty. He wrote that defining information qualitatively was more useful for economic analysis than any quantitative definition, such as appears in information theory. A quantitative definition is of limited value because different bits of information that might be equal from the viewpoint of information theory will usually have very different benefits or costs (Arrow, 1974).

Noll (1993) argued that information is simply communication that is valued by the sender and receiver, perhaps exclusively as an end in itself. Rather than being a means for making better decisions, information in containers and conduits (such as books, music, television, the Internet) is a form of consumption. This concept of information is increasingly a focus of the information economics literature. Along these lines, Babe (1995) noted that the means whereby information is encoded (e.g., the physical book) is not the information itself. He argued that although information emanates from its source, it does not inhere in the originator or source alone. Information, he wrote (pp. 12–13), "comprises symbols or signs that represent or point to something else; does not stand alone but is inevitably in reference to something else;" it entails an interaction between source and recipient, but is "immaterial in destination, often in origin, and always in transmission." Further he noted that it is "inevitably processed by the mind, and only in being processed is meaning or significance constructed."

With the advent of information and computer technologies (ICTs) and the growth of information markets, some economists have conflated information with the technology, focusing narrowly on the format of information, arguing that anything that can be digitized is information, and an "information good" is one that can be distributed in digital form (Herings & Schinkel, 2005; Shapiro & Varian, 1999; Varian, 2000a). Information, as Braman (2006) observed, is often treated simultaneously as something that is free, complete, instantaneous, and universally available and as a commodity that is costly, partial, and deliberately restricted in availability.

Economists do not spend much time distinguishing between the concepts of information and knowledge and disentangling them is not essential for this review of the economics literature. As Stiglitz (2006) argued, the content of information is indivisible from knowledge, which he described as the most important example of a public good.

## Information as a Public Good

As has been explained, "pure" public goods are those goods that are non-rivalrous and non-excludable. "Non-pure" public goods may be excludable or rivalrous to some extent, but are still public goods because they can be consumed by more than one person. If someone buys a newspaper and benefits from that purchase through reading it, the paper itself or the news within it can be shared with others without detracting from the purchaser's benefit. Although the newspaper is produced by a private firm and there is a small cost to the original purchaser, the private producer cannot prevent non-paying individuals from benefiting from its content and its use by the original purchaser does not keep others from purchasing it. It is non-rivalrous and non-excludable in consumption and therefore a public good. Because the firm producing the newspaper gains most of its revenue from advertisements, the public good character is, in fact, a positive externality because more people will see the advertisements.

Information cannot be destroyed by its recipient and is diffused and enriched by interactivity (Herzog, 2006). It is usually *impossible* to exclude others from enjoying all of the benefits of information, and impossible to convert those benefits into property. Boulding (1971) conceded that intellectual property (he cited trade secrets and patents) is an example where knowledge (information) can be property. But others argue that information is intrinsically resistant to absolute appropriation (Eaton, 1987). When information is used, it is revealed (at least in part), and "no amount of legal protection can make a thoroughly appropriable commodity of something so intangible as information" (Arrow, 1985a, p. 110).

Because information is very difficult to appropriate, its production will be sub-optimal in a competitive market—firms will under-invest in information production because they cannot recoup costs from all who use it. Consumers have no incentive to pay for non-excludable goods and services. Hence, information does not automatically conform to the market mechanism of resource allocation and the private market will often provide an inadequate supply of information, just as it supplies an inadequate amount of other public goods (Arrow, 1984; Eaton, 1987; Stiglitz, 1994, 2000a, 2000b).

Although information content is identifiable as a pure public good, several common mechanisms are used to try to make information goods and services excludable such as copyright, pricing, the refusal of content owners to make it accessible by paper or electronic publishing, and (for public sector information) refusal to allow commercial re-use. In addition, some rivalry can be imposed by mechanisms such as failure to print or reprint sufficient quantities. Information goods in libraries can be made rivalrous by such practices as failing to purchase sufficient quantities of materials (best sellers for example) or by imposing time limits on Internet access. Such rivalry (a congestion problem) is not significant for most library patrons who are willing to wait and, in general, libraries provide non-rivalrous access to information. Information is neither a pure public good nor a pure private good. This fact has been overlooked by those who seek to commodify information goods and services (Kranich & Schement, 2008).

## Information as a Commodity

Central to the price-based economic theory of neoclassical economists is the notion that the ultimate end of economic activity is consumption. To measure economic activity they must focus on the consumption of *commoditized* or marketed goods and services. Commodities are goods or services that can be owned and consumed, either as articles of final consumption or as inputs in the production of other goods and services, and they can be exchanged for money or other commodities (Parker, 1994).

The problems of viewing information as a commodity have been much discussed (see, for example, Herings & Schinkel, 2005). Conceiving information as a commodity leads to the concept of information (and knowledge) as a resource that can be managed. The literature on the management of information and knowledge is not reviewed here. For a discussion of the qualities of information and knowledge that make their management difficult, see Eaton and Bawden (1991) and Yates-Mercer and Bawden (2002). Although information can be produced and consumed, created and destroyed, categorizing it as a commodity is problematic for economists because of the difficulty of quantifying, enumerating, and valuing information and its public good characteristics.

How to measure and value information remain challenges. Perhaps the first person to grapple with this problem was Boulding, whose 1966 paper (reprinted in 1971) on the economics of knowledge raised problems in commodifying knowledge that are equally applicable to the commodifying of information. He argued that knowledge cannot be appropriated, noting that if a thing cannot be property, it cannot be a commodity. Boulding lamented the absence of a "unit" of knowledge, which makes it difficult to think of a price for knowledge, and argued that a measure is needed that takes account of the significance of specific knowledge exchanges. New information is produced as older information is consumed. The consumption of new information does not merely add to one's existing stock of knowledge, but can qualitatively reconfigure and evaluate it. The consumption of new knowledge "raises basic and intractable difficulties for economic theories where *additivity* of commodities is assumed" (Parker, 1994, p. 83).

Information is indivisible in its use (i.e., the cost of an information product does not depend on its use). Attempting to sell information as a commodity is challenging because it cannot be evaluated by the purchaser until he or she knows what it is, and once it is known there is no need to purchase it. It is claimed that information's value is reduced or destroyed when it is used. Once information is purchased, a buyer in turn can sell it very cheaply. Nevertheless, an individual who has information can never lose it by transmitting it. Hence, information can be a commodity only to a limited extent (Arrow, 1984).

Information is unlike other economic commodities that are the basis of traditional economic thinking. Defining information as an economic commodity violates many standard assumptions of microeconomic theory (Aislabie, 1972; Allen, 1990; Arrow, 1984; Eaton, 1987; Koenig, 1990). Recognizing that information is fundamentally different from other commodities was a major breakthrough in the economics of information according to Stiglitz (2000a, pp. 1448–1449), who suggested that, because purchasers have imperfect information about information, "mechanisms like reputation —which played no role at all in traditional competitive theory—are central." Babe (1996) concluded that any attempt to commoditize information by restricting access to it through copyright, signal scrambling, or user fees, is economically dubious.

### Social Value of Information

The social value of information relates to the extent to which it is provided efficiently and maximizes social welfare. Although the social value of information is often mentioned in the literature, there has been relatively little work among economists focusing specifically on this question, probably because of the difficulty of measuring the effects of information. Attempts to determine the value of information (and knowledge) to society were made in the 1960s and 1970s by Machlup and by Porat, whose works quantified the expansion of the information workforce and led to the "information economy" and "information society" concepts much touted in recent years. These concepts presuppose that information has value to society at large.

Hirshleifer (1971) argued that information has value only if it can affect action. He found that private information makes possible large private profit without necessarily leading to socially useful activity. Public information, on the other hand, *has* social utility; it is "socially valuable in redirecting productive decisions, and [so] individuals will rationally combine (through government and other instruments) to generate public information" (p. 570). A similar comparison can be made between private and open source software. The latter ensures greater social welfare than private software because any user can access it (Lerner & Tirole, 2006).

Although it is recognized that users of information receive some value from its use, the principle that the use of a good by one individual can create value for others is less obvious. The use of information by one individual can create ancillary value to society at large, increasing social welfare. Bates (1988) explained that this ancillary social value tends to be diffuse and indirect and thus not apparent or recognizable to individuals. He concluded that ancillary social value created through the use of information goods is generally ignored in theoretical and real considerations of value.

# Economic Rationale for Public versus Private Sector Supply of Information

Noting that views regarding the role of government have fluctuated over time and across countries, Stiglitz and colleagues (2000) explained that the laissez-faire framework originating in the works of Adam Smith stressed that the government's role should be limited to correcting market failures that arise out of private production. Government activity is not automatically justified by such imperfections but does offer the potential for a social gain. Government itself may be subject to "governmental failure" as economic agents, government, and government agencies may suffer from failures such as lack of bankruptcy threat, lack of real incentives for workers, skewed incentives for managers, risk aversion, and dynamic inconsistency (failure to enforce public contracts while at the same time enforcing private contracts). Government intervention can take the form of governmental production or provision of public goods and services, but it need not. Government can finance production by contracting to private firms. Government can also tax private firms to achieve social objectives, such as pollution abatement.

Stiglitz and colleagues (2000) believe that government should provide private goods only under limited circumstances, even if private-sector firms are not providing them. They noted that government might sometimes be able to "jump start" new markets or provide universal access to a private good that is deemed sufficiently important that all citizens should have access to it. Government should exercise caution in entering such markets, however, and whenever possible work in conjunction with the private sector. In particular, government should be extremely cautious about entering markets in which private-sector firms are active. They argue that if private-sector firms are active, there is "a *prima facie* case against the existence of a public good" (p. 71). Furthermore, government should not generally enter markets to provide more competition to existing firms. Stiglitz and his colleagues explain that if the government is concerned that there is insufficient private-sector activity or that the activity is excessive relative to some social optimum, it should generally encourage or discourage such activity through other incentives (e.g., taxes and subsidies) rather than direct provision itself. However, if the private-sector activity results purely from governmental inefficiencies, then government is justified in entering these markets because it is a proper role of government to improve the efficiency with which its services are provided.

Although both public and private markets produce information goods, only the public market seems to recognize their social value and to incorporate that value into its production and consumption actions (Bates, 1988). Economic reasons justifying government involvement are:

1. Information's public good characteristics mean the market is unlikely to provide these products adequately.

2. Information products can generate positive benefits to other parties (externalities/spillovers) such that the market is unlikely to provide these products adequately.

3. Economies of scale and scope allow information agencies to supply information products and set their price. (Australia. Productivity Commission, 2001)

Motivation for government intervention is likely to be absent if there is an active private-sector presence. Information goods provided by the private sector are not pure public goods: They have been made rivalrous and/or excludable in some manner.

Herbert Burkert (2004) suggested that beginning in the 1970s, three forces drove policy decisions regarding PSI: (1) Developments in information and computer technologies, (2) the changing view of the state's role and financing, and (3) the public's demand for access to this information. The value of PSI has always been associated with specific qualities, for example, it is usually collected over a long period of time by what is seen as a neutral guardian, and its production is assumed to be reliable and sustainable. These qualities were increasingly seen by the private sector as essential for the future of the information market and it argued that PSI could not be left *only* to the public sector to exploit. As a result, at the same time that citizens challenged public administrations to make these information resources generally accessible at low or no cost, these same administrations were also under pressure either to exploit them more economically themselves or to lessen the burden on taxpayers by letting the private sector manage them in a profitable manner. Burkert observed that once the public sector understood the political and economic value of PSI, and the fact that the information's commercial value relied on the administrative structure in which the information was collected, the public sector became reluctant to relinquish it. Two strategies emerged to address these various pressures: (1) moving from an administrative fee structure to a market-oriented price structure (sometimes using new public or private sector companies controlled by the public sector) and/or (2) using contractual arrangements to ensure that the information industry added value to the raw information it received from the public sector. The outcome was that more comprehensive information policies emerged in many countries. Noll (1993) remarked that public policy about government-provided information (in the 1980s) did not reflect an informed consideration of the economics of information.

Asked to provide an independent analysis of the appropriate role of government in an information economy, Stiglitz and colleagues (2000) came up with a comprehensive and thoughtful analysis. They looked at the factors influencing the choices facing governments that must decide whether and how to intervene in markets in the digital economy. At the outset, they wrote that "on one hand, the public good nature of production in a digital economy ... may suggest a larger role [for government] than in the bricks-and-mortar economy ... , on the other hand, an information-based economy may also improve the quality and reduce the cost of obtaining information, which makes private markets work better than before" (p. 4).

Stiglitz and colleagues (2000, p. 44) explained that the digital economy succeeds because of "network externalities" (the value of using a specific type of product, such as a fax machine, depends on how many other people are using it) and of positive feedback (the more people who use the network the more valuable it is, and therefore more people use it). In addition, there is a winner-take-all potential in the digital economy because of low marginal costs and the possibility of exclusion; the reduction in communication costs creates a superstar phenomenon (e.g., Microsoft). Where there are network externalities and positive feedback, private markets can be inefficient. At the same time, in the attempt to become the best in a specific field, the superstar phenomenon generates substantial income inequality and excessive investment, the outcome of which can be inefficient from a social perspective. "The high fixed costs and low marginal costs of producing information and the impact of network externalities are both associated with significant dangers of limited competition," and network externalities and winner-take-all markets "may remove the automatic preference for private rather than public production" (p. 44). Stiglitz and his colleagues believe that in an information-based digital economy, the theoretical underpinning behind private versus public production shifts toward an expansion of public goods. Along with network externalities, this expansion suggests a larger public role in the digital economy, "which may be inconsistent with a laissez-faire approach to economic activity" (p. 40). They argue equally vigorously that private markets might work better than before, improving the quality and reducing the costs of obtaining information.

The Organisation for Economic Co-operation and Development (OECD) (Organisation for Economic Co-operation and Development, Directorate for Science, Technology and Industry, Working Party on the Economy, 2006) reiterated that governments generate information and data as part of their mandated role to fulfill their public tasks. It identified a "PSI value chain" that begins with the creation or collection of the data as raw material. The second step is the aggregation and organization of the raw material—creating more comprehensive data sets and permitting joint storage and retrieval. The OECD supported the notion that it is the government's role to produce and supply raw material, which can then be made available for re-use by the private sector that can, but need not, add value. It is argued, however, that when their information is made available for re-use, government bodies should also maintain a presence in the market because, if users are not aware of government's role in collecting and developing the data, their support for government's role may erode (Duncan, 1987).

Stiglitz and colleagues (2000) emphasized that providing public information and data is a *public* function and a proper government role. Because there was little theoretical guidance regarding the separation of government and business in a digital economy, they devised a set of twelve principles regarding government's role in the digital age. The first three principles are identified as "green light" activities that raise few concerns; principles four through nine are "yellow light" government activities that raise increasing levels of concern; and the remaining three are "red light" activities that raise significant concern. The Principles for On-Line and Informational Government Activity are:

1. Providing public data and information is a proper government role.

2. Improving the efficiency with which governmental services are provided is a proper government role.

3. The support of basic research is a proper governmental role.

4. The government should exercise caution in adding specialized value to public data and information.

5. The government should only provide private goods, even if private-sector firms are not providing them, under limited circumstances.

6. The government should only provide a service online if private provision with regulation or appropriate taxation would not be more efficient.

7. The government should ensure that mechanisms exist to protect privacy, security, and consumer protection online.

8. The government should promote network externalities only with great deliberation and care.

9. The government should be allowed to maintain proprietary information or exercise rights under patents and/or copyrights only under special conditions.

10. The government should exercise *substantial* caution in entering markets in which private-sector firms are active.

11. The government (including government corporations) should generally not aim to maximize net revenues or take actions that would reduce competition.

12. The government should only be allowed to provide goods and services for which appropriate privacy and conflict-of-interest protections have been created. (Stiglitz et al., 2000, p. 5)

## *Economic Arguments for Government Provision of Online Information*

Stiglitz and colleagues (2000) argued that government provision of information online is justified by their first principle (providing public data and information is a proper government role) and they urged governments to make as much public information available online as possible. Their second principle (improving the efficiency with which governmental services are provided is a proper governmental role) provides further justification for Internet provision of public sector information. Improving efficiency is socially beneficial and therefore governments should be encouraged to shift activities online, thus improving access to information and improving the efficiency of internal government activities. The authors provided the example of the online publication of public filings with the Securities and Exchange Commission (which had previously been difficult to obtain) on the EDGAR system. These filings are required by statute and it is sound public policy to allow online access to them. Such improvements should be undertaken, Stiglitz and colleagues (p. 55) argued, "despite any potential displacement or reduction in revenue of private firms." Nevertheless, their sixth principle means that, assuming there is appropriate regulation or taxation, government might be able to achieve its social objectives more efficiently by using private firms rather than by providing the good or service directly. Stiglitz and colleagues cite the example of telephone service. The benefit of direct (government) provision relative to private provision with regulation/taxation depends on many factors. Noting that government employees often have less incentive to innovate and reduce costs than do private sector employees, the authors noted such factors as (1) the internal efficiency of the government relative to the private sector in providing the good, (2) principal-agent and other information problems in regulating a private-sector entity, and (3) the potential for innovation and dynamic benefits from private provision. They referred to literature that suggests that public provision is preferable only "when innovation is relatively unimportant, competition is weak, information problems are substantial, or private sector concerns regarding reputation are inconsequential" (p. 64).

Governments have begun to examine the possibility of moving to free/libre and open source software (FLOSS) rather than proprietary software for ICT projects. A report to the European Commission on the economic impact of FLOSS on the European ICT sector noted continuously increasing use by the public sector both within Europe and around the world (Ghosh, 2006). A second report looked at the effect on the development of the information society of government organizations making their own software available as open source. Like the discussion around the free release of PSI for use and re-use, the cases studied indicated that release of public sector software is unlikely to have any negative economic impact on the economy as a whole and is likely to expand skills and participation in the information society (Ghosh, Glott, Gerloff, Schmitz, Aisola, & Boujraf, 2007). The use of FLOSS by PSI providers is expanding. For example, the Australian Bureau of Statistics noted successful FLOSS use for developing and sharing ICT capabilities (Australia. Parliament of Victoria, Economic Development and Infrastructure Committee, 2008). There is no readily available information on the economic impact on PSI itself of expanding the use of FLOSS in public sector agencies. It is likely to improve online access at lower costs, but the evidence is not yet available. Although the provision of PSI on the Internet appears to increase efficiency and equitable distribution, the European Commission (1999) raised the digital divide issue, noting the substantial differences that exist regarding access to the tools of the information society and citizens' ability to use them. Although the digital divide has narrowed since 1999, the problem still exists.

## Cost-Benefit Analysis for Public Sector Information Production

Because publicly produced public goods and services are generally not subject to market forces, the decision as to whether to produce them is often based on cost-benefit analysis, which tries to determine whether the total benefits will exceed the resources used to produce them. Individuals or groups who will incur costs or receive benefits are the stakeholders with an interest in the decision—taxpayers, clients, patrons, employees, volunteers, or government agencies. Cost-benefit analysis takes into consideration the demand, supply, costs, and benefits for each stakeholder group, leading, presumably, to better decisions (Kingma, 2001; Stiglitz, 2000b).

The problem of cost-benefit analysis is that both costs and benefits must be calculated on a monetary basis. It is thought that costs are easier to measure than benefits because we tend to dismiss those costs that cannot be measured in dollars. But a valid and comprehensive measure of costs is not just the sum of dollar estimates; one cannot ignore non-measurable costs, just as one cannot ignore non-measurable benefits. Using only financial prices to be paid for goods and services undervalues both the costs incurred by consumers and the benefits they receive (Bickner, 1983; Kingma, 2001). The costs and benefits of information projects are not usually known at the same time; benefits are diffuse and take longer to accrue than with more concrete endeavors. Assessing benefits depends on subjective judgments and attempting to assign a monetary figure to those benefits is suspect (Badenoch et al., 1994; Menou, 1994).

To economists, a market that is economically efficient is one in which benefits are greater than costs and the difference between benefits and costs is as large as possible. It is argued that a public project should be undertaken if total benefits exceed total costs. Total benefits include consumer surplus—which is the difference between what an individual is willing to pay and what he has to pay. Consumer surplus measures the entire amount that all consumers would be willing to pay, including theoretical payments in time spent. In public sector cost-benefit analysis, the amount individuals would pay (if they had to) for an information good is calculated as a benefit to them (Kingma, 2001; Stiglitz, 2000b).

The failure to include in cost-benefit analysis the value to users of time spent or saved using information can result in serious mistakes in the valuation of information systems or services. Other potential pitfalls of using cost-benefit analysis include: (1) Benefits or costs may be counted more than once, (2) items that seem to be costs and benefits to one group are not seen as such by another group, and (3) the costs and benefits of a program can occur over several years. In addition, a common error occurs when the wages and salaries of employees are counted as benefits rather than costs (salaries and wages are expenditures resulting from a project; the individual recipient provides services in exchange for payment). When advertising the benefits of a government project, government analysts frequently make this mistake (Kingma, 2001).

It is possible to calculate benefits in terms that are not monetary. Statistics on the use of public goods (such as libraries, computer services, public concerts) can be collected to determine if the value to users is greater than the cost of providing them. Information can produce both quantitative and qualitative benefits and the final appraisal or decision must take into account social and political aspects as well as economic ones (Badenoch et al., 1994; Hill, 1994; Kingma, 1996).

## Impact of Information on General Economic Efficiency

Many economists have focused on the value of information products rather than their content, assessing the value of information based on its being unavailable to competitors (Badenoch et al., 1994). Nevertheless, some early information economists were quick to note a more holistic contribution of information to the economy. Knowledge is described as the greatest source of wealth in a post-industrial society, as the force driving change in the world economy. It is an economic good and a factor of production because there is a positive return to an increase in knowledge. (See, for example, Arrow, 1965, reprinted in 1985b.) Knowledge is seen as the engine of economic progress, with information fueling that engine, and the generation of new knowledge is linked to innovation, wealth creation, and economic growth. Most economists do not deny that the handling of information contributes to a large part of the national economy. They ask what determines the demand and supply of the goods and services used to handle information and how social welfare is affected by the way resources are allocated to these goods and services (Chichilnisky, 1999; Kahin, 2006; Koenig, 1990; Marschak, 1974a). Furthermore, differences in information and even the lack of information play a key role in how the economic system operates, according to Arrow (quoted in Lamberton, 1998).

Gathering and processing information is time-consuming and costly, its communication imperfect, and the capacity and time to absorb it are limited. Supply exceeds demand and information quickly becomes obsolete. It is becoming cheaper and easier to reproduce and harder to charge for information (Stiglitz, 1985; Sveiby, 1997). These characteristics mean that the ways that individuals are organized to gather information, how it is communicated, and how decisions are made are critical to the performance of the economic system. In her review of the literature, Braman (2006, p. 17) noted that economists were aware of the butterfly effect, that "isolated pieces of information, even distributed to only a few actors, can have a profound impact on the economy" and they began to consider the disequilibrious effects of information on the nature and structure of the economy. In particular, they noted the influence of knowledge production, the role of information in global competition, and how events change the availability of information.

## Productivity of Information

Arrow (1985b) argued that the productivity differences among nations reflect differences in the states of their knowledge. Much of the literature on the contribution of information to productivity, however, focuses not on information or knowledge itself but on the impact of information and communication technology, which is implicitly valued as increasing productivity. It is argued that the productivity of information technology can be quantified because technology is capital; its contribution to the creation of a product can be measured (Brinberg, 1989). Many debated actual productivity effects of ICTs (see Brynjolfsson, 1993), but it is now recognized that because impact depends on network externalities and positive feedback, it comes late and is spread over time. Furthermore, the positive link between ICT investment and economic growth applies not only to various sub-sectors of the economy but also to human capital formation (Foray, 2006; Meijers, 2005; van Zon & Muyksen, 2005).

Reluctance to view information itself as a productive resource arises because assessing its productivity requires quantifiable measures. But information content is an unquantifiable abstraction that is not measurable by traditional methodologies (Taylor, 1980). Reviewers of the literature on productivity in the information sector, including Cronin and Gudim (1986) and Koenig (1990), also observed this problem. Taylor (1982) provided a framework for measuring the output of information activities but it did not address the intangibility of information. Koenig (1990) noted that citation analysis (used to judge productivity of organizations or individuals who publish) is not useful for determining how information services influence productivity within organizations. He observed that the conventional indicators of workers (typically either some measure of transactions processed, billable hours, or sales volume per employee) are not very useful for measuring the productivity of knowledge workers.

Cronin and Gudin (1986) argued that assessing whether the benefits of information to productivity outweigh the costs requires using indirect measures, such as the value of the time spent obtaining the information. Koenig (1990) found evidence that easy access to information by individuals and free flow of information were conducive to technological innovation.

Koenig (1990) concluded that, just as there are not good measures of information, there are not robust measures for the outputs of information services. In determining the productivity value of information and information services, "we depend primarily on the user's necessarily subjective assessment of the worth of reading an item or using an information service" (p. 75). He observed that, for the most part, what knowledge there is about information effects on productivity is limited almost entirely to the research and development area. Measuring information's value cannot be done with traditional productivity equations, but only through some type of aggregate analysis (Brinberg, 1989).

Information content has value to the economy because it functions as a catalyst, enhancing the productivity, effectiveness, and quality of other factors of production. Its value lies in its potential to lead to better decisions, provide for the best combination of other resources, speed the movement of goods and services through the economy, reduce waste, avoid crises, and enhance competitive advantage (Brinberg, 1989).

### Distributional versus Efficiency Impacts of Information

Neoclassical economics tried to separate equity and efficiency. Equity is measured by looking at some overall measure of inequality in society; efficiency is measured by summing up the gains or losses for each individual. Economists who focus on Pareto efficiency tend to overlook equity considerations but if a country cares about distribution (the share of income and social welfare among the population), efficiency/equity trade-offs must be considered. There will be some efficiency loss when attempting to make the distributional impact of a program's benefits more progressive. The question is how much loss of efficiency is acceptable (Stiglitz, 2000b).

Inequity is seen as a rationale for government intervention. Because income distribution will never be ideal from a social viewpoint, public goods have to be provided by the government sector (Sandler, 2001). Stiglitz (1994, p. 29) claimed that a government seeking to enhance equity through redistributive measures, particularly taxation, can be "unambiguously welfare improving."

Information, in and of itself, has distributional benefits whether it is produced by the private or public sector. Because of information's intrinsic public good characteristics, however, the private sector is likely to avoid producing unprofitable information even if it has great potential benefit to society. Kingma (1996) explained that a public good's units of output provide benefits to many consumers simultaneously, with each consumer sharing the benefit of each unit of the good. Therefore, the social benefit of each unit of a public good is not the benefit provided to one individual but the collective benefit that consumers or individuals receive. The advantage of public over private provision of information goods, Bates (1988) suggested, is that private markets are more likely to be suboptimal than public markets because the ancillary social value of the information is unlikely to be incorporated into private market considerations.

# Impact of Public Sector Information on General Economic Efficiency

Economists have not addressed the contribution of PSI to general economic efficiency to any extent. An early example illustrates the problem. When Machlup

(1962) categorized the knowledge-producing industries and occupations, he did not include government or government workers. He did attempt to assess the total value of (U.S.) government publications but focused on the value of government and commercially contracted printing plants, costs of distribution, cataloging, and indexing. None of his work considered the value of the content of government publications, and when he looked at value of knowledge conveyed by books, he deliberately excluded government publications: This kind of approach is typical of the literature—public sector information is seen as a given. Although public sector data have been used by economists in their analyses, little attempt was made to step back and look at the economic impact of this information. The situation has not improved.

There is a general lack of data about the economic significance of public sector information (Dekkers, Polman, te Velde, & de Vries, 2006), and an "absence of robust quantitative data on the economics of cost, pricing, and distribution models of PSI and the socio-economic gains of improved access to public cultural, educational, and other content" (Organisation for Economic Co-operation and Development, Directorate for Science, Technology and Industry, Working Party on the Economy, 2006, p. 8). A variety of economic actors makes different uses of public sector information, which means that estimating value is difficult—its importance differs across industries and its re-use is sometimes merely a secondary or ancillary activity. These re-uses are not readily identified in standard classifications: "Consequently it is hard to identify the shares of production, value added, and employment, which can be attributed to PSI" (p. 19).

Since 1989, The European Council has sought to harmonize access to public sector information across the European Union and to improve competitive market conditions by making such information openly accessible for re-use by the private sector. Moving to set up a Europe-wide information service market, the Council published guidelines for member countries designed to promote public sector support for private sector initiatives (European Commission, 1989). Action progressed more quickly following publication of the European Commission's 1999 Green Paper, *Public Sector Information: A Key Resource for Europe*, which argued that the ready and timely availability of public information is "an absolute prerequisite" for the competitiveness of European industry, furthering the economic potential of the networked economy, and, in particular, supporting small and medium enterprises (p. 1). This Green Paper noted that the bulk of commercial information services in the EU relied on PSI as their key resource. Arguing that its exploitation would lead to job creation, the Commission called for clear and consistent principles for the exploitation of this information across the European Union. It pointed out that EU companies were at a competitive disadvantage to American counterparts, "which benefit from a highly developed, efficient public information system at all levels of administration" (European Commission, 1999, Chapter 1).

The Commission then contracted with PIRA International to report on the potential for commercial exploitation of Europe's public sector information. The 2000 report provided the first comprehensive attempt to quantify the economic value of PSI, estimating both its investment value and economic value. With respect to investment value (what governments invest in the acquisition of public sector information), the European Commission (2000) calculated that across the EU as a whole, governments invest in PSI to the tune of €9.5 billion per year, and compared this to the U.S. investment, which was estimated at €19 billion per year. PIRA found that in every EU country the largest single component of PSI investment total is the geographical sector (mapping, land registration, meteorological services, environmental data, and hydrographical services), which takes over 37 percent of total investment in France and 57 percent in the United Kingdom.

With respect to economic value (that part of the national income attributable to industries and activities built on the exploitation of PSI; the value added by it to the economy as a whole), the central estimate of economic value for the European economy was €68 billion per annum, nearly 1 percent of EU gross domestic product (GDP), which it argued makes the PSI sector as important as several other established industries. Although it was described as a substantial slice of Europe's total economic activity, the European Commission (2000) noted that this percentage was considerably less than the corresponding figures for the U.S. A more recent study, *Measuring European Public Sector Information Resources*, using a different methodology and varying definitions of investment and economic value, estimated the overall market size for PSI in the European Union ranged from €10 to €48 billion with a mean value of around €27 billion (Dekkers et al., 2006).

Addressing the question of economic impact, the OECD Working Party on the Information Economy concluded that PSI is an important economic asset. It argued that because knowledge is a source of competitive advantage in the information economy, wide diffusion of this information is economically important. It observed that public sector information is economically valuable for two reasons: First, because it provides the "raw material" for value-added products and services across a wide range of industries, and, secondly, it has "indirect economic potential" as inputs into economic activities to improve efficient decision making and production (Organisation for Economic Co-operation and Development, Directorate for Science, Technology and Industry, Working Party on the Economy, 2006, online). Second, PSI's indirect benefits accrue to public sector bodies as well as to the private sector—given the impacts of public decision making, governments and ministries are the most powerful users of public sector information.

## Economic Impact of PSI Access Models

The distributional versus efficiency impact of public sector information depends on the prevailing model of access. Access models range from relatively open access in the United States to more restricted regimes that charge prices higher than marginal costs, impose copyright restrictions, hold PSI for their own use, employ cost-recovery strategies, or allow only limited and potentially expensive access (Organisation for Economic Co-operation and Development, Directorate for Science, Technology and Industry, Working Party on the Economy, 2006). Pull and push models exist as well. The pull model emphasizes disseminating information in response to individual requests, such as in freedom of information (FOI) requests, whereas the push model emphasizes proactive publication of information by governments. Most countries have a mixture of models, but increasing the amount of push is likely to decrease the cost of processing FOI requests (Australia. Parliament of Victoria, Economic Development and Infrastructure Committee, 2008).

Because of its attempts to harness PSI for economic purposes, the European Union grappled with the question of which access model best contributes to information's economic value. European countries have multiple access models, and the differences among them are seen as explaining differences in economic value of PSI in the U.S. and the EU as a whole. In the U.S., the private sector benefits from federal government information because there are no copyright restrictions on it; information collected at public expense is seen as belonging to the people, including the private sector, and open access is the norm. This argument is increasingly made in other countries as well (for example, see Australia. Parliament of Victoria, Economic Development and Infrastructure Committee, 2008).

The most important constitutional and statutory foundations for U.S. government information policy are the First Amendment to the U.S. Constitution, the Freedom of Information Act, the 1995 Paperwork Reduction Act, the Copyright Act, and the Office of Management and Budget (OMB) Circular A-130 (US. Office of Management and Budget, 2003), which provides guidance on the management of federal information resources. The 1995 Paperwork Reduction Act Amendments prevent an agency from establishing an exclusive, restrictive, or other distribution arrangement that interferes with timely and equitable availability of public information to the public, which means there can be no government monopolies operated by an agency or by a private sector entity on behalf of an agency (Gellman, 2004). U.S. federal information policy is based on the premise that government information is a valuable national resource and that the "economic benefits to society are maximized when taxpayer-funded information is made available inexpensively and as widely as possible" (Weiss, 2004b, p. 137). Gellman (2004) observed that the open access policies that make federal government information available to all without copyright, without high prices, and without restrictions have served the U.S. public well and contributed to the vibrant U.S. information marketplace. Those who support the U.S. model believe that public sector information's positive externalities are realized both at a social level and an economic level. At the social level, individuals can freely access information they need and at the economic level, PSI can be made available for re-use by the private sector to create information products that can be sold in the marketplace (De Saulles, 2007). (A similar economic argument is made for free and open source software [Lerner & Tirole, 2006].)

The European Commission (1999) reported that the European information industry claimed to be at a competitive disadvantage vis-à-vis its counterparts. More recent data cited in the OECD report support this conclusion (Organisation for Economic Co-operation and Development, Directorate for Science, Technology and Industry, Working Party on the Economy, 2006). With respect to the database industry, the OECD remarked that liberalized access to public information in the U.S. fosters growth of database publishers. Weiss (2004a, p. 70) argued that the U.S. database and information retrieval industries grew exponentially since the beginning of the Internet revolution and that this growth depended "to a great extent on free, unrestricted taxpayer-funded government information."

With respect to meteorological data, Stiglitz and colleagues (2000) explained that although the (U.S.) National Weather Service is the single "official" voice in times of weather emergencies, a significant more specialized private-sector weather forecasting industry exists. Weiss (2003, 2004b) provided further data on the U.S.

commercial meteorology sector and stated that in Europe the equivalent sector was a factor of ten smaller. He argued that the primary reason for the European lag was the restrictive data policies of European national meteorological services.

Lack of harmonization across European countries is seen as having created obstacles to success. In particular, an unfair trading environment created by public sector bodies raised a number of fair trade barriers (i.e., reluctance by public sector bodies to jeopardize revenue, over-pricing, lack of pricing transparency, mirroring [in which public sector bodies mirror private sector products creating unfair competition], exclusive deals, and copyright restrictions placed under the guise of preventing fraudulent use and protecting quality). Limited awareness (in public institutions) of the potential economic value of PSI prohibits efficient dissemination methods. PIRA recommended that the EU maximize the value of PSI to government, citizens, and business by adopting strong freedom of information regimes, eliminating government copyright, limiting cost recovery to marginal costs, requiring non-exclusive licensing, explicitly removing restrictions on re-use of licensed public sector information, and adopting marginal cost recovery (European Commission, 2000).

The OECD (Organisation for Economic Co-operation and Development, Directorate for Science, Technology and Industry, Working Party on the Economy, 2006) raised the question as to which access model better serves citizens, industry, and overall welfare. If an access regime provides only limited or expensive access to publicly collected information, it will be more costly for the consumer and for the taxpayer. Furthermore, the potential economic gains from new commercial activities based on re-use of the information will be foregone. Overall, the U.S. open access regime is seen as improving competitive market conditions for public sector re-use, stimulating economic growth, and creating jobs.

## Economic Arguments Regarding Re-Use of PSI

The European Commission (2001) is committed to making PSI available for re-use by the private sector because of its large economic potential. Economies of scale mean that the cost to government of collecting information is lower than it would be in the private sector. Allowing for commercial use of this information would result in positive economic and social benefits, with a wider spread of information, increased dissemination, and preservation of public content. Furthermore, unlike private firms in a competitive environment, government agencies are seen as doing a poor job of marketing and responding to customer needs and are often unable or unwilling to adapt quickly to the marketplace. Nevertheless, public institutions can be model producers and users of information (Organisation for Economic Co-operation and Development, Directorate for Science, Technology and Industry, Working Party on the Economy, 2006). Thus it is seen as most efficient if governments do the collecting and distribution, and make the "raw material" accessible to commercial re-users. A number of studies in Australia have found a positive economic return from improved access and re-use of PSI, particularly publicly funded research data (cited in Australia. Parliament of Victoria, Economic Development and Infrastructure Committee, 2008).

Because PSI policies in the U.S. leave the commercial re-use of data primarily to the private sector, its value is maximized as a diversity of entities become involved in its dissemination (Weiss & Backlund, 1997). Because this information is not copyrighted in the U.S., it is readily available to private entrepreneurs, who can repackage it for sale with or without added value. The U.S. model has the advantage of making government data available to redistributors outside the government, increasing the likelihood that "someone will meet public needs" (Gellman, 2004, p. 129). The European Commission (2001) argued that it is the re-use of federal information that gives American firms a competitive advantage over their European counterparts.

ICTs allow the private sector to combine data taken from different sources into added value products and services (European Commission, 2001). For example, Euromonitor PLC (based in the U.K.) provides specialized value-added products such as consumer market intelligence and international market research. Its products require information inputs from many countries, mainly from public institutions such as national statistics offices and Eurostat, the EU's statistical body. Euromonitor adds value to public information by identifying all relevant sources of statistical information and by aggregating and producing comparative data on the basis of heterogeneous basic statistics. Increasing standardization across Europe weakens the company's importance, however, because its business model is in part based on continually adding more value and more specifics (Organisation for Economic Co-operation and Development, Directorate for Science, Technology and Industry, Working Party on the Economy, 2006). It seems that increasing standardization and harmonization across Europe have both benefits and hazards for private sector information providers.

Rather than promoting re-use, the U.K. Office of Fair Trading (OFT) (2006) claimed that the public sector, itself, could contribute up to £1 billion annually to the economy by producing a wider range of competitively priced goods and services. Earlier, Weiss (2003, p. 132) commented on this kind of thinking by noting that the concept of government commercialization and the idea of the "entrepreneurial bureaucrat" (which he claimed was an oxymoron) "do not succeed in the face of economic realities under open competition policies."

The mandates of public bodies that provide information might not coincide with the mission of commercial ventures that exploit it (European Commission, 2000). Safeguarding public access to PSI raises a concern—once private interests enter the market, it becomes more difficult to ensure access for all citizens (European Commission, 1999). One outcome is that information formerly public can become proprietary (Starr & Corson, 1987). Private sector suppliers need to find a way to impose rivalry and exclusion in order to compete with other suppliers, and claiming copyright is a logical move. This can occur in non-PSI environments as well. For example, when proprietary products are built on public domain open source resources, copyright is used even when the original material is not copyrightable, a phenomenon that Ciffolilli (2004, online) identifies as "hijacking."

Commercial re-use is also challenged by those who believe that if re-users have low-cost access to the data collected at public expense, then taxpayers will have to pay twice for public sector information content, first as taxpayers, and secondly if they want to access the commercially available content. This same argument is made when a government charges user fees for access to its information. Paying twice is inefficient and inequitable. Others who challenge commercial PSI re-use are concerned about loss of revenue to the government, that a limited pool of re-users can gain fiscal advantage from it, and that re-users in other jurisdictions might make substantial profits from PSI which they have not supported as taxpayers (Australia. Parliament of Victoria, Economic Development and Infrastructure Committee, 2008). The problem is exacerbated if the re-user is given exclusive access to the information. Even when it is made available for re-use, the greatest efficiency is achieved when the public sector producer also disseminates its own information at marginal cost. Commenting on developments in Europe and the frequent comparisons with the American model, Pas and De Vuyst (2004) noted that theories of PSI commercialization originate in countries that have different views on commercial exploitation. They concluded that although PSI might be an important market, economic factors are not the only considerations that must be taken into account.

## Should Public Sector Agencies Add Value?

Whereas in the U.S. it is generally the private sector that adds value by producing information services out of public raw data, in Europe there is much more involvement by public administrations in producing value-added services. The issues raised over whether the government should add value to its own information or leave value-adding activities to the private sector are apparent in the European debate. There is no consensus in the economic literature about public provision of value-added services (Davies & Slivinski, 2005).

The first and second steps of the OECD's (Organisation for Economic Co-operation and Development, Directorate for Science, Technology and Industry, Working Party on the Economy, 2006) PSI value chain (creation or collection of the data and aggregation and organization of the data) occur naturally as public bodies fulfill the tasks inherent in their mandated roles. The third step in the value chain includes a variety of value-adding activities that depend on the end product or service (such as data processing, editing, repackaging, and remodeling). Marketing, distribution, and delivery of the information products and services are the final functions of the value chain. Although ICTs allow public sector information to be provided directly to end users, these same technologies provide opportunities for new value-adding entities (i.e., private sector firms that could handle steps three and four of the value chain). ICTs have also made it possible for public bodies to integrate the value chain vertically within government (Organisation for Economic Co-operation and Development, Directorate for Science, Technology and Industry, Working Party on the Economy, 2006).

While nominally supporting the direction in which the EU is moving, some initial resistance was evident in the U.K. The Review of Government Information conducted in the United Kingdom in 2000 agreed that the largest single information resource in a developed country is derived from the statutory and normal workings of governments and urged the government to contribute to the growth of the U.K. information sector by modifying its pricing and licensing policies. However, it did not recommend that government agencies turn information resources over to the private sector for the development of value-added services, as in the U.S. model, but encouraged government agencies to develop such services themselves in partnership with the private sector (UK. H. M. Treasury, 2000b, 2000d).

Stiglitz and colleagues (2000) addressed the issue in their fourth principle (government should exercise caution in adding specialized value to public data and information). They identified adding specialized value as a "yellow light" activity that raises concerns and argued that the "more specialized the benefit of a government information service ... the more cautious the government should be in providing it" (p. 57). For example, the government should provide statistics on macroeconomic activity but should be cautious about producing market studies of specific industries. This example raises more complicated questions, such as, should the government attempt to forecast growth in online sales? They argued that government projections of aggregate online sales serve a legitimate public purpose and are covered by their first principle. Just as the government produces forecasts of GDP growth and inflation, it could produce forecasts for other areas. However, the government's role does not need to be exclusive. They noted that in spite of official GDP forecasts from both the administration and the Congressional Budget Office, private firms also issue GDP forecasts based on their own projections. The question arises, at what point does the government go beyond providing a public good such as basic information and data that serves a direct public purpose. Stiglitz and colleagues (p. 59) argued, for example, that providing detailed projections of online sales in specific markets (e.g., forecasts of online book sales) "would seem to go too far." Such projections represent market research that can be provided by the private sector. Furthermore, although the government should provide search engines and "ferret" tools to assemble data, more specialized tasks (such as linking official information to related academic articles) should generally be left to non-government entities (p. 59). They explained that such case-specific or individual-specific tasks have "less of a public good nature than the underlying data" (p. 59).

Before the advent of ICTs, the division of tasks between government agencies and the private sector was reasonably clear: The public sector could make the raw data it produced available free of charge or at marginal price, whereas the private sector's task was to add value to the raw data, thus satisfying market needs (Pas & De Vuyst, 2004). Information technology made the information more attractive for the private sector, but at the same time the difference between raw data and sellable information became less clear. ICTs led to wide availability of high quality data, undercutting simple commercial redistribution with no or little value added, hence publishing activities with little added value were made redundant (Organisation for Economic Co-operation and Development, Directorate for Science, Technology and Industry, Working Party on the Economy, 2006). Today it takes little effort to combine different data and obtain commercially valuable information. From the end-user's perspective, there is less need for the added value that private firms might provide for raw government data. Such raw information has high value to start with, and government agencies themselves bring together data from different sources and distribute them in immediately useful formats. Pas and De Vuyst suggested that the private sector might have an interest in allowing the public sector to do so because the value adding effort may be too great for the private sector, or the public sector itself might discontinue production of PSI that has little public value without value-added components.

Because of economies of scope, it is efficient for a public agency to provide value-added information where it can be done more cheaply than by private firms (Davies & Slivinski, 2005). Nevertheless, Stiglitz and colleagues (2000) stressed that government should exercise increasing caution as it adds more and more value to raw data or information or as it provides more and more specialized services. They explained that one indication of specialized service is high marginal costs, arguing that the "higher the marginal cost of providing the service or information to a specific user, the more specialized the benefit of the service would appear to be" (p. 60).

## Economic Arguments Regarding Generating Revenue from PSI

In the United Kingdom, potential revenue to the government has been seen as trumping all other economic and social arguments regarding public sector information. Government guidelines encouraged public bodies to generate revenue (UK. Department of Trade and Industry, 1990; UK. H. M. Treasury, 2002). Serious consideration of public sector information trading dates back to 1983; and a tradable information initiative was launched to make as much government-held information as possible available on a commercial basis in order to promote the growth of the U.K. information services market. In the U.K., a distinction is made between "tradable" information and raw or "unrefined" information and the recommended access models differ accordingly. The term "tradable information" is used to cover Crown copyright-protected works produced within government, often as a by-product of core government activities. It is seen as incidental that the material was created by government (UK. Cabinet Office, 1999). Generally, tradable information has value-added components and is distributed through various nominally autonomous trading funds, which are required to recover their costs. The trading fund structure that was established provided greater certainty and autonomy in that PSI producers no longer had to rely on only variable subsidy from government and could keep revenues they generated. As a result, many government departments began publishing commercially priced information because they could retain the benefits of sales (Aichholzer & Tang, 2004; De Saulles, 2007; Hadi & McBride, 2000; Newbery, Bently, & Pollock, 2008). For Europe as a whole, seeing information as a source of revenue might raise questions in the field of competition, creating market distortions between companies in different member states that wanted to re-use the information (European Commission, 1999).

A commonly voiced argument for maximizing revenue generation is that "profits" can be used to cross-subsidize other governmental activities. Davies and Slivinski (2005, p. 23) countered that, according to standard economic analysis, "most of the commercial profits should flow through to support the operations of other areas of government rather than staying with the unit that produced them." They conceded, however, that retaining profits in the units producing them might provide incentives to public managers. On the other hand, Stiglitz and colleagues (2000, p. 74, no. 151) argued that "even if the activities that are being cross-subsidized are important policy objectives, it is not clear that the best source of revenue for them is profit-maximizing behavior." They concluded that one arm of government should generally not engage in profit-maximizing behavior merely to cross-subsidize another arm.

In their eleventh principle Stiglitz and colleagues (2000) stated that government should not take actions that would reduce competition (such as imposing higher costs on existing rivals, erecting entry barriers, or circumventing restrictions on below-cost pricing). Entities that seek to maximize revenue "may have a *stronger* incentive to engage in such anti-competitive behavior than profit-maximizing entities" (p. 73). Concern over revenue maximization can lead public-sector enterprises "to engage in costly activities that reduce profits but raise revenue" (p. 73).

Stiglitz and colleagues (2000, p. 70) argue that "a governmental entity should generally not be allowed to withhold information from the public solely because it believes such withholding increases its net revenue." Their eleventh principle clearly states that the government (including governmental corporations) should not aim to maximize net revenues. Revenue-maximizing activity is an inappropriate objective for public sector entities because if a governmental role is warranted, seeking to generate revenue means that the public-sector entity is not appropriately fulfilling its mission. On the other hand, if no governmental role is warranted, such activity should be undertaken by the private sector.

## Economic Theory with Respect to Pricing

Price is an accepted measure of value, but information economists have long argued that price also is a mechanism for communicating information. Hayek (1945) described price as abbreviated information. Simon (1991) argued that prices are only one mechanism for understanding behavior, explaining that quantities of goods sold and inventories convey as much information as prices. To most economists, prices allocate the supply of goods and services and finance their production—they are simply an allocation mechanism that determines who can purchase certain goods and services. Prices serve to encourage production at the same time that they ration demand; and those whose benefit exceeds the price will be the only consumers willing to purchase the good (Kahin & Varian, 2000; Kingma, 2001).

In economic terms, cost to the producer is the main element of supply and price to the consumer is the main element of demand; the interaction of supply and demand determines the price. This relationship between the price of a good and the quantity demanded is expressed in the law of demand (i.e., the inverse relationship between the price a consumer pays for a good and the quantity demanded) (Badenoch et al., 1994; Varian, Farrell, & Shapiro, 2004).

Market demand and supply determine the equilibrium market price and the market price allocates the production and consumption of the good. The allocation role of prices requires that they be set equal to marginal cost to achieve economic efficiency. Prices above or below marginal costs will result in "deadweight loss" (the reduction in consumer surplus or producer surplus that society would have received if the price were equal to the cost). Producers weigh the marginal costs against the marginal benefits to determine the number of units to be produced and will make and sell a good until the marginal cost just equals the market price (Kingma, 1996, 2001).

## Costing Mechanisms

Cost calculations are usually based on monetary expenditures, but these do not take into account social costs (which include the various cost functions of producing and disseminating products, but also the cost to society as a whole, including positive and negative externalities of production and consumption). The economist's concept of cost relates not necessarily to monetary payments but to the cost in foregone opportunity. What else might an individual, a firm, a society do with the money? What is the value of the time and effort expended? Thus, economists speak of "economic costs," which take into consideration both monetary expenditures and opportunity or alternative costs. Economic costs are costs of benefits lost—if we choose to use our resources for one thing, then these resources are not available for something else (Bickner, 1983; Noll, 1993).

Bickner (1983) explained the various kinds of costs to be considered in estimating the costs of a decision. Some, such as past costs, are irrelevant; relevant costs are in the future. Costs that have already been incurred are costs resulting from past decisions—economists identify them as sunk costs and, because they no longer represent meaningful alternatives, they are no longer real costs. Future or incremental costs are important but without a free, competitive, well-informed market for a good, the future value, or cost, of an item is difficult to estimate meaningfully in monetary terms.

Fixed costs (which do not change as the level of output increases within a specified period of time, such as overhead) and variable costs (which increase as the level of output increases within a given period of time) are both defined by the output and the period of time chosen (Kingma, 2001). According to Bickner (1983, p. 22), one should not include "even a pro rata share of estimate of fixed costs in an estimate of costs. Only the increase in variable costs is relevant to [a] decision."

Marginal cost is the change in the total cost that results when the quantity produced changes by one unit. They are the costs of increasing output within a given period of time; the costs of the variable inputs which must be employed to increase output (Kingma, 2001). Because of capacity restraint in the production processes of physical products, constant fixed costs and zero marginal costs are rarely observed. For information goods, however, Varian and colleagues (2004, p. 3) explained that this is a common cost structure, true not only for information goods, but even for physical goods such as silicon chips; it is "rare to find cost structures this extreme outside of technology and information industries."

## Pricing Mechanisms

"Marginal cost pricing" is based on the marginal cost of producing one additional unit after the first copy has been produced. Economists usually consider a marginal cost pricing to be the policy that maximizes net social benefit. Nevertheless, King and McDonald (1980, p. 48) argued that when there are scale economies and high fixed costs, "it is often preferable (in terms of net social benefit) to set prices slightly above marginal costs so that all costs are recovered." They did not indicate what they would include in "all costs." "Marginal social cost pricing" considers the social costs along with the marginal costs.

"Average cost pricing" (price per unit of output necessary for the producer to break even) "yields less value to society than marginal cost pricing since the price is always greater" (King & McDonald, 1980, p. 50). A real challenge in average cost pricing is that unless the producer knows the price/demand curve, it is very difficult to establish the break-even point. This is particularly true for information products or services with high fixed costs, such as those requiring database compilation and development. "The risk may be very great and an excessive loss is incurred or profit made (either of which achieves less net value for society). With low fixed costs or with marginal cost pricing, the risk is not as great because the prices can be chosen from relatively small range of prices" (p. 50).

"Monopoly pricing" raises different issues. A natural monopoly occurs when a firm must make a large fixed investment to enter the industry and marginal costs are low compared with the fixed investment. Failure of competition can result from the existence of a monopoly. This market failure occurs because monopolists charge too high a price and produce too little. Under-production and over-pricing result because, absent competition, the monopolist has exclusive control over price and supply and may be able to increase profit by charging exorbitantly high prices. The monopolist's pricing policy prevents the market from achieving the socially efficient level of output; the market fails to reach the Pareto optimum because of the higher monopoly price. This social loss is a deadweight loss (the deadweight burden of monopoly). To increase monopoly profits, consumers with lower marginal willingness to pay will be excluded from the market. As a natural monopoly raises its prices, it does not lose all its customers, but the demand curve will slope downward (Kingma, 2001; Stiglitz, 2000b).

Monopolies are pervasive in information markets because producers of information commodities have a strong incentive to avoid price competition and seek to protect commodity positions by copyright, product differentiation, and lock-in of existing customers (lock-in occurs when a customer chooses a particular information product and switching costs are high). Monopolists will raise the price of every copy above the negligible costs of reproduction, excluding users and wasting resources (David, 2005; Herings & Schinkel, 2005; Kingma, 2001).

Using any pricing mechanism or model entails costs to the seller. The time spent and the wages and costs of collecting payments are opportunity costs to the seller, who might be able to use those expenses in another way. Ronald Coase (1937) first identified such costs as transaction costs, which, it is argued, should be the primary consideration in determining whether to price a good for individual or group purchase (Shapiro & Varian, 1999). The transaction costs of pricing public goods were noted by Stiglitz (2000b), who wrote that although for most private goods the costs of exclusion are relatively small, for some publicly provided goods the administrative costs may be prohibitively large. Charging fees for access to government information and other services requires recording and collecting fees for individual transactions, which can add a significant pricing cost in addition to the cost of producing and providing the information. Because information products have low marginal costs of production, implementing user fees may not be worthwhile (Kingma, 2001).

# Pricing of Public Goods

Pricing of public goods (whether pure or non-pure) hinges on rivalrousness and excludability, which brings most economists to accept "that no pricing scheme for a public good is consistent with efficiency" (Lee, 1982, p. 99). Samuelson (1954) is generally credited with identifying the first-best conditions for pricing of what he called collective consumption goods (i.e., public goods). Samuelson's conditions for public good pricing "require that the marginal price for each consumer be equal to his marginal valuation (in money terms) of the good" (Lee, 1977, p. 404). Inefficiencies will result if there is deviation from the marginal price. Lowering the price below marginal cost increases the quantity desired, which reduces the marginal revenue below marginal cost, resulting in suboptimal output. On the other hand, raising the price discourages consumption. According to Samuelson, the optimal output of a public good occurs when the sum of all marginal values equals marginal cost (Lee, 1977). (Marginal value is the change in value associated with a unit increase, e.g., the extent to which printing one more copy of a book changes the value of that copy for the consumer—if only ten additional copies are to be printed they will each have higher marginal values than if a thousand are printed.) Determining the sum of all marginal values is difficult because, as Samuelson (1957, p. 199) commented wryly, one needs to know the value to each person and, "only God knows them for all men, I do not; the government does not; monopolists and competitors do not."

## Pricing Non-Rivalrous Goods

Because most commodities on the market are rivalrous, cost structures mandate that two cannot partake as cheaply as one (De Long & Froomkin, 2000). When a price is charged for non-rivalrous goods, however, some people are prevented from enjoying the good, even though their consumption of the good would have no marginal cost (Stiglitz, 2000b). Thus, charging for non-rivalrous goods results in underconsumption. Under-consumption is a form of inefficiency. Economists argue that in the "first-best" world, "people should not be excluded from the enjoyment of a good that exhibits non-rivalry and whose use involves no externalities from crowding or from mutual annoyance of participants" (Hellwig, 2005, pp. 1981–1982). Because it does not cost anything to provide an additional person with the opportunity to enjoy the public good, providers should not resort to exclusion. Sören Blomquist and Vidar Christiansen (2005) questioned the optimality of charging fees when there are no congestion problems. There is no efficiency argument to be made for imposing a fee on a non-rivalrous information good. However, if there is no charge for a non-rival good, there will be no incentive to supply it. In this case, inefficiency takes the form of undersupply (Stiglitz, 2000b). Thus, there are two basic forms of market failure associated with public goods: under-consumption and under-supply.

## Pricing Excludable Goods

Blomquist and Christiansen (2005) noted that there is a vast literature on the public and/or private provision of non-excludable public goods, but public provision and pricing of excludable public goods have not been much studied. There is, however, a considerable economic literature devoted to arguing for user fees on efficiency grounds. This is because "economists are first and foremost price theorists" and because prices are relatively efficient rationing devices; "it is not surprising that where feasible, economists tend to favour 'price-like' user fees over taxes" (Anderson, 1991, pp. 15–16).

When public goods are excludable (but still non-rivalrous) it is possible to impose a price beyond the marginal cost. At this point, the "first-best" Samuelson rules do not apply and one is in a "second-best" setting. Blomquist and Christiansen (2005, p. 74) stated that second-best theory has demonstrated that a case can be made "for positive prices and taxes that are not valid in a first-best regime." However, it is very difficult to achieve an optimum price because of the heavy information requirement (to establish an optimum price one needs to have information on consumer preferences, which consumers are not necessarily willing to reveal). They concluded that, from a policy perspective, there is "in practice at best an uneasy case for a positive price for an excludable public good" (p. 74).

Justification for pricing of public goods is usually based on the "benefit principle," which sanctions placing the costs of public services upon those who use them, so that those who benefit more pay more. When efficiency (and not redistribution) is the primary object, this principle is generally seen as applicable (Wagner, 1991). It is argued that the benefit principle has both economic and equity dimensions. Presumably it encourages those who benefit to recognize that government costs have been involved in production of the good or service and, furthermore, that the taxation burden on those who do not benefit has been reduced. The problem of externalities weakens the case for the benefit principle; there are many difficulties in identifying beneficiaries and charging them accordingly (Australia. Productivity Commission, 2001). Information is inherently subject to this weakness.

Claiming to argue on equity grounds, Martin Hellwig (2005) stated that when individual preferences are not known, equity concerns can justify use of exclusion to a public good (through pricing, for example) in spite of the efficiency loss. When information about individual preferences is private (i.e., the supplier does not know those preferences), people with different preferences will end up with different payoffs. By paying for admission to a public museum, for example, those who care for the museum will pay more for its provision than those who do not care and do not use it. Therefore, the payoff for those who do not use it is money saved and presumably fewer of their tax dollars going to its support (because of the admission fees). Those who do care may be willing to pay even more to use the museum, thus their payoff is increased consumer surplus and whatever private (personal) benefit they get from visiting the museum. Hellwig (pp. 1982–1983) argued (without noting his evidence) that people who care "always dissimulate" their preferences; hence "their contributions towards the provision of the public good cannot be made commensurate with the benefits they obtain" and he cited authors who claimed that "admission fees are the only way to obtain voluntary distributions towards the financing of the public good at all." He ignored the tremendous voluntary fund-raising and time given to assisting museums and other public institutions.

Hellwig (2005) also argued that the loss of efficiency that arises from excluding people who care a little but not enough to pay for a public good is outweighed by the equity gain from the payoffs, as has been noted. He assumed that people who are unwilling to pay do not care for the good, when, in fact, they may care a great deal but be unable to pay. In that case, efficiency decreases because of under-consumption. However, even if exclusion is possible, "when a good is non-rival, there is no impetus for exclusion from the standpoint of economic efficiency" (Stiglitz, 2000b, p. 129).

Although recognizing that "interim participation constraints" (admission fees) may be problematical on efficiency grounds, Hellwig (2005, p. 1984) argued that they "can be seen as a crude device for protecting those participants who are least well off against the imposition of a mechanism that worsens their position even further." Presumably this mechanism is higher taxation, but it could also be argued that charging admission fees worsens their position. He believes that taxation hurts those who do not care for the public good at all and assumes that these are the people in the economy who are worst off. Inequality, he argued, is exacerbated if those who do not care for public goods have to pay lump-sum taxes to contribute to their financing. His argument was based on the assumption that the less well off are not interested in public goods (such as museums), which cannot be proven using economic models. Further, he overlooked the economic arguments that taxation is instituted not only for public funding purposes but also for distributional purposes (Blomquist & Christiansen, 2005; Stiglitz, 1994).

In spite of his assertions, Hellwig's own analysis of the equity/efficiency trade-off when imposing admission fees did not show that optimal admission fees are positive. He concluded that pricing is not appropriate for such things as hospital services needed by people who are worse off than people who do not need them. Nevertheless, he argued that fees are appropriate for such things as sports facilities, opera productions, and university education, "the enjoyment of which provides a net [private] benefit rather than a compensation for disadvantages" (p. 1995), and ultimately that public funding of such facilities benefits the rich. He stated that pricing should take into account distributive concerns in relations between the people who use them and the people who do not. One of many counter-arguments would suggest that such facilities have positive externalities and ancillary social value for society as a whole.

Blomquist and Christiansen (2005) came to a different conclusion from Hellwig, finding that even a small price for excludable public goods is always welfare decreasing. They explained that this does not imply that a price for an excludable public good is never warranted, but even when it is, one can guarantee a welfare improvement only if an optimum, or very close to optimum, price is set. They suggested that whether an excludable public good is a final consumer good or an intermediate one can affect the rules for pricing and provision. Modeling final consumer goods in various ways, they explained that because the marginal cost of providing the public good consumed by an individual is zero, the price in their model resembled a tax. They found that under some conditions the price is arbitrary, but that the administrative cost of collecting a price will rule out neutrality between a zero and a non-zero price. In order for a strictly positive price to be optimal, they explained that a price increase above zero must strongly discourage consumption "without inflicting a too heavy loss of utility on the consumers" and that developing the conditions that are conducive to a strictly positive price "turns out to be an extremely cumbersome exercise" (p. 70).

Intermediate public goods are used in producing other goods that may themselves be private or public goods. The use of the public good makes production more efficient or use of labor more economical. Information is a perfect example. Blomquist and Christiansen (2005, p. 73) argued that charging a price for the intermediate, excludable public good distorts production: "We decrease the use of the public good although there is a zero social marginal cost of using it." The basic message of their analyses was that the sole effect of a positive price is to distort consumption of a public good. Stiglitz (2000b) agreed, noting that user fees are often thought of as an equitable way of raising revenues, but he argued that user fees introduce an inefficiency when consumption is non-rival.

## *User Fees and Charges*

For excludable public goods, if beneficiaries can be easily identified and charged directly, adherence to the benefit principle leads directly to user charges. Whereas taxes are presumed to be compulsory, user charges involve a direct connection between making a payment and receiving a service from government, and are assumed to be largely voluntary (Wagner, 1991). Dwight Lee (1991) called user fees "political pricing," which is imposed because market prices are not available. Wagner (1991, pp. xiii–xiv, 7) agreed, noting that governmental choices concerning user charges have little to do with promoting economic efficiency; they "promote the political interests of dominant interest groups pertinent to the issue at hand, and the resulting consequences of these policies may often be inequitable and inefficient as judged by the standards of the benefit principle."

Anderson (1991, p. 13) described user fees as the "fiscal panacea of the 1990s" that became popular as a means to raise revenue without raising taxes. User fees are said to be efficient if they closely resemble the market price and equal the marginal cost of providing the services to the consumer. Proponents believe that they promote economic efficiency because they are thought to induce appropriate marginal decisions by consumers of public goods. Some marginal cost pricing can be justified when externalities are present. However, Anderson argued that estimating externalities presents enormous problems and relies on guesswork. He noted that governments typically sidestep the issue, failing to make any calculation of the actual extent of externalities. Like taxes, real-world user fees are determined as the result of a political process.

Supporting the imposition of user fees, Bird and Tsiopoulos (1997) argued that the main economic rationale for them is not to produce revenue, but to promote economic efficiency by providing information to public sector suppliers on how much clients are actually willing to pay for particular services, thus ensuring that the public sector is valued at least at (marginal) cost by citizens. Like market prices, user fees can ration goods and services among competing users and, like market prices, they can provide information on the relative value consumers place on the good or service under consideration. In spite of these general advantages, "the circumstances under which user charges are efficiency enhancing are more restrictive than most economists realize" (Lee, 1991, p. 60). Blomquist and Christiansen (2005) conceded that there is a potential gain from charging a price, which is that it can improve efficiency by alleviating the effects of asymmetric information (consumer preferences could be determined by their response to the price). However, they explained that because consumer taxes are imposed on the final consumer products, consumer preferences are revealed by the taxes paid. Thus "we already have instruments available to set consumer prices," hence, they argued, "the use of a price for an intermediate excludable public good only has costs and no gains beyond those already attainable" (p. 73).

Government decisions as to whether to provide a good or service are more complicated than are private sector decisions (Stiglitz, 2000b). The private sector monopoly owner of a bridge, for example, would build the bridge only if his revenues equaled or exceeded the cost of the bridge. In the case of a publicly provided bridge, a toll fee might be charged but consumption would be reduced and some uses of the bridge whose benefits exceed the social cost would not be undertaken. The government must weigh equity considerations—the principle that those who benefit from the bridge should bear its costs—with efficiency considerations. "The distortions arising from the underutilization of the bridge would need to be compared with the distortions associated with alternative ways of raising revenues (for example, taxes) to finance the bridge" (pp. 129–130).

The government is often a monopoly supplier, and demand for public goods produced by the public sector can be inelastic. Thus user charges cannot truly reflect demand. Research has shown that increasing prices or fees will not change PSI use patterns significantly when there is a monopoly supplier and demand is inelastic (Nilsen, 2001). On the other hand, eliminating user fees can result in elasticity of demand. Newbery and colleagues (2008) provided data on the growth rate of use of official statistics and data in Australia and New Zealand following withdrawal of user charges.

Anderson (1991, p. 17) suggested that when the government charges a consumer a user fee, "in many cases it is simply making an offer the consumer cannot refuse." Furthermore, even if the government charges a user fee limited to the amount of the marginal cost of providing the service, this marginal cost might be much higher than would have been the case if the service ware privately provided. The issue, according to Yandle (1991), is how to set a price appropriately and collect revenues sufficient to cover costs. Without competition, there is a risk that public sector managers will never find the efficient price and instead seek to maximize revenues. During times of fiscal stress, the search for additional sources of revenue provides a rationale for applying new fees or raising old ones. He also noted that in debates about fees, efficiency economists generally dismiss the question of what is to be done with the revenues received. The efficiency argument for levying user fees, Yandle argued, is made in order to fund special interest programs and, once instituted, efforts will be made to increase demand for the fee-generating activity.

Lee (1991) found no efficiency in user charging. When goods and services are being charged for by politically imposed user fees, the efficiency of the response to consumers' preferences bears little relationship to the amount of revenue received, even if the charges are set at an efficient level. When the information for setting efficient charges is not available, "there may be little motivation for a budget-maximizing government bureau to set the user charges at the efficient level given the political incentives that will often dominate the pricing decision" (p. 61). In some instances, the public agency will prefer to keep user fees low in order to build up demand, thus keeping the agency well funded. If a bureau is operating efficiently to maximize its budget before the user charge is imposed, the imposition of the charge will result in smaller output. Imposing user charges on the bureau's output will result in little or no efficiency gain, even when the charges equal the marginal cost of production. Lee (pp. 68–69) argued that "if the user charge is set at the revenue-maximizing level it may reduce, or distort, consumption to such an extent that efficiency is reduced even if the bureau makes the appropriate supply response to the change."

Basing his work on the Niskanen (1971) model of bureaucratic behavior, Lee (1991) concluded that efficiency arguments for user pricing are based on the assumption that government bureaus respond to consequences of increasing the per-unit charge on their product in the same way a private firm does. This assumption, he wrote, is not warranted because "imposing a user charge cannot be expected to increase efficiency. The bureau will respond to the decrease in consumption that results from the imposition of a user charge by some combination of failing adequately to reduce output and increasing per unit cost" (p. 73).

User fees are often instituted when there are high marginal costs to a government activity, but the presence of a large user fee for a user-specific activity should raise questions about whether, instead, the activity should be undertaken by the private sector (Stiglitz et al., 2000, p. 61): "If the government *does* undertake activities with substantial marginal costs, government user fees should be imposed," however, "government should generally not be undertaking such tasks." Anderson (1991, p. 29) concluded that in practice, a user fee is a source of government revenue, "which is claimed to have some, perhaps only vague, relationship to the cost of providing the 'service' to the 'user.'" But, he added, "many 'users' required to pay fees would object to being classified as 'beneficiaries' at all, and would most certainly regard themselves as 'victims' instead" (p. 29).

## The Pricing of Information and Information Goods

Information pricing has been discussed in the literature since at least 1962, when Arrow wrote that if a price is charged for information, the demand is likely to be suboptimal. Creating a market for information is difficult because it is so resistant to appropriation, and this difficulty is seen as an advantage "from the standpoint of efficiently distributing an existing stock of information" (reprinted in Arrow, 1985a, p. 111). He argued that when there is no cost to distributing information, the optimal allocation calls for it to be distributed free of charge. Efficiency "requires that information be freely disseminated, or more accurately, that the only charge be for the actual cost of transmitting the information" (Stiglitz, 2000b, p. 84).

The theory suggesting that price depends on supply and demand breaks down in practice for information firms because, when setting prices, the data needed to distinguish costs clearly enough to construct actual demand and revenue curves are rarely available. Thus, there are no guidelines on how to arrive at acceptable or reasonable prices, and prices are invariably arbitrary. Because the marginal costs of information products and services are quite low, very little value is lost to society by marginal cost pricing (Badenoch et al., 1994; King & McDonald, 1980).

## *Valuing Information in Order to Price It*

Earlier in this chapter, along with a discussion of information's economic and social value, there was discussion of the general questions raised when attempting to value information as an economic commodity. Here value is considered specifically with respect to the pricing of information and information goods. The problem is that standard economic methods cannot be used to determine the value of information because the true and total benefits of using information can never be known (Raban, 2003). The U.K. Advisory Panel found that "no one has any concrete sense of the actual or potential value of PSI, nor indeed how it can or should be measured," and determining who the beneficiaries are can influence perceptions of value (UK. Advisory Panel on Public Sector Information, 2004–2007, online). The value of information will vary from user to user, which complicates attempts at economic calculations of costs and prices. Furthermore, the amount of information is not related to its value, as a small amount may have great value and vice versa (Marschak, 1974b, 1974c).

Its characteristics create problems for those attempting to value information in order to price it or buy it. Content, certainty, extent of diffusion, applicability, and decision relevance, along with price, quality, individual tastes, and resources are among the attributes that affect the value of information (Hirshleifer, 1973). Furthermore, information can be used to make better use of other valuable resources (Noll, 1993). Therefore, information that saves time or leads to better decisions increases the opportunities available to a user, thereby reducing economic costs. But the price of information tends to be linked to the medium of distribution (the information good rather than the quality or intrinsic utility of the information itself). The basic problem is that the value of information goods to buyers is determined by the information content, but the costs experienced by suppliers are determined by information form (Bates, 1988).

Some economists believe that the value of a datum is not primarily economic, but has to do with how "useful" it is to the recipient. Informational value, according to this view, relates to information's relative utility to a decision maker, its interest to a user, or its potential future use. Economists have tried to model this use-value approach but, because it excludes marketplace considerations, these analyses do not help with pricing decisions. Exchange value and use value are not necessarily the same—some information will lose exchange value through use, but the potential exchange value of other information will increase with use (Bellin, 1993). Eaton (1987) concluded that the value of information eludes precise calculation, noting that it is entirely dependent upon context, use, and outcome.

Many economists suggest that the value of information is related to its use, but Bates (1988) stressed that the value of information derives from its future usefulness; its value is influenced by the circumstances of that future use. He noted that because concrete value cannot be given to information goods prior to their use, some economists claim that information goods are beyond the scope of economic analysis. But Bates also argued that when economists model the value of information goods, value can be expressed "as the average of all possible values deriving from the use of that information, weighted by the probability that such a use will occur" (pp. 77–78). Determining "all possible values" appears to be a Herculean task.

Monetizing the value of information is necessary if one wants to calculate its costs and benefits in order to determine a price. Some public sector information providers have attempted to determine value to consumers by asking what they would be willing to pay for the information if they had to—seeking to calculate their hypothetical willingness-to-pay. This method of calculating value is often seen as too subjective; when actually asked to pay the amount they have indicated as acceptable, many consumers will balk, especially in the case of public goods for which they previously paid nothing or only marginal costs.

Willingness to pay must include calculation of the value of time spent finding and using information and the value of time saved by using the information or information service (Kingma, 2001). In fact, Stiglitz (2000b) noted that in valuing non-monetized costs and benefits, economists usually resort to valuing time, which is often determined by using an individual's hourly wage. The hourly wage is a good approximation of the value of an hour of an employee and to an employer, but there are problems with this simple evaluation because the value of an hour spent on a good or service is not always equal to the wage the individual earns; an individual might do more than one thing in an hour (Kingma, 2001).

Time spent can have positive or negative externalities on other consumers because of congestion. As public goods, information goods and services are sometimes subject to congestion because they can be shared among several users. "With a limited number of consumers, the service may be non-rival; however, as the number of consumers exceeds capacity, the service becomes congested. This congestion imposes a negative externality on users who must wait" (Kingma, 2001, p. 133).

## Costs of Information

In a much quoted statement, Shapiro and Varian (1999, p. 3) wrote that information is "costly to *produce* and cheap to *reproduce*." They explained that production of information goods involves high fixed costs but low marginal costs, in other words, the fixed costs of production are large but the variable costs of reproduction are small. This cost structure leads to substantial economies of scale—the more you produce, the lower your average cost of production. The dominant component of the fixed costs of information production, are *sunk costs*—costs that are not recoverable if production is halted.

The cost of creating an information product (the "first-copy cost") and the amount of work involved are independent of how many people use the product or of how extensively it is used (Noll, 1993). Therefore, the variable costs of information production are unusual in that the cost of producing an additional copy typically does not increase, even if a great many copies are made. Because there are normally no natural limits to the production of additional copies of information, if one copy can be produced, then millions of copies can be produced at roughly the same unit cost (Shapiro & Varian, 1999).

For paper products, once the first copy is produced there are additional dissemination costs associated with printing and distribution, and these depend on how many copies are actually sold. A large number of purchasers raises production and distribution costs but additional copies do not increase first-copy costs. Hence, economies of scale, in addition to natural monopolies, are created for some producers (Noll, 1993).

Technology lowers first-copy costs of both paper and electronic products, resulting in price reductions because first copy costs are spread over more users (Noll, 1993). Information delivered electronically "exhibits the first-copy problem in an extreme way," because once the first copy of the information is produced, additional copies cost essentially nothing (Shapiro & Varian, 1999, pp. 21–22). Thus it is generally agreed, as Babe (1996) observed, there is little or no incremental cost in diffusing information widely.

Some literature has focused on the costs to individuals of using information, as its use almost always involves other economic resources. The time spent in using information is seen as an opportunity cost to users because it always requires time and individual resources that could be devoted to other activities. The total cost to users increases if they must spend time assessing, evaluating, and aggregating information. The value of time spent is an opportunity cost to consumers. The value of time saved is a benefit that consumers receive from use of the information or information service, and that benefit can be compared with the cost of the good or service in cost-benefit analysis (Kingma, 2001; Koenig, 1990; Noll, 1993; Webber, 1998).

## Models of Public Good and Information Pricing

In two articles, Lee (1977, 1982) explained that to achieve an efficient pricing scheme, much depends on the likelihood of attaining perfect price discrimination among consumers. He argued that although public good pricing is generally considered to be inefficient, efficiency might be achieved by using fixed "all or none" entry pricing. Whereas in most discussions of public good pricing it is implicitly assumed that consumers can choose any number of units at the price charged, Lee argued that for a monopoly supplier "all or none" entry pricing lessens the degree of price discrimination needed for consumption efficiency. In this model, once individuals avail themselves of the benefits provided by a public good, they receive the benefits provided by the entire supply (Lee, 1977). Individuals who refuse to pay the entry price may be completely excluded, but once admitted they have no marginal control over the benefits provided, which, he noted, is a natural feature of public goods (Lee, 1977). Fixed entry pricing can reflect the quantity of the good provided and the time the consumer spends consuming it. An efficient pricing scheme imposes a marginal cost on each consumer, reflecting his or her marginal evaluation of the public good. By increasing the quantity of the good made available, the marginal benefit to the consumer may be increased. If unlimited time is allowed in consuming the good, the consumption value is also increased without adding to costs (other than opportunity cost to the consumer, which is not priced) (Lee, 1982).

Public goods can be priced by level of detail or amount of time spent using the good in question. For example, the units can be measured in terms of detail (e.g., an art gallery can be divided into sections with extra admission fees for access beyond the basic exhibition). One example is of a statistical agency with a detailed database in which access to more or less information in the database depends upon how much one is willing to pay (Blomquist & Christiansen, 2005).

Private and public information providers can use various pricing options (although, as explained earlier, pricing by public sector information providers is considered to be economically inefficient). Because production of information goods entails large fixed costs of production, high first-copy costs, and small variable costs of reproduction, there is little sense in basing prices on costs. Value-based pricing is seen as a much more effective way to cover the high first-copy costs because one can sell to a broad audience. People have widely different values for a particular piece of information; therefore, value-based pricing leads naturally to differential pricing, an option that allows different consumers to express their different valuations of a particular information good (Shapiro & Varian, 1999; Varian, 2000a; 2000b).

Differential pricing requires the seller to set prices at different levels for different consumers. Babe (1995) stated that differentiating among information products is a primary consideration in marketing them, but doing so raises the fundamental problem of setting prices so that "purchasers who are able and willing to pay high prices do so" (Varian, 2000b, p. 190).

Three degrees of price discrimination have been identified. The first allows for a market of one (allowing a retailer to direct particular items to individual clients, perhaps at a better price). Tailor-made information commodities can be offered to customers based on their previous sales records or search behaviors (Herings & Schinkel, 2005). First degree pricing requires knowledge of customers and raises privacy and trust issues. In second degree pricing everyone faces the same menu of prices for a set of related products (also known as market segmentation, versioning, or bundling, in which sellers are essentially competing against themselves and consumers self-select among the available choices, which Varian argued is often welfare enhancing). Third degree price discrimination is accomplished by selling at different prices for different groups, a classic form of price discrimination widely used by monopolies (Shapiro & Varian, 1999; Varian, 2000b; Varian et al., 2004). If public good monopolists do seek to price discriminate, it is in their interest to identify the most homogeneous sub-groups of consumers (if such exist) because the monopolist thereby can come closer to capturing all the net value generated by the private good (Lee, 1977).

In order to price discriminate, many information providers often use second degree aggregation and/or bundling. In aggregation, a group of information goods is made available over a period of time to a range of customers (for example, libraries) through site licensing or subscription. Aggregation of electronic information goods is expedited by the low costs of networking, digital processing, and storage of information. It allows sellers to increase and extract the value from a set of goods because production, distribution, and consumption are technologically complementary. The near-zero costs of reproduction for electronic goods makes aggregation attractive because, in addition to enhanced profitability, economic efficiency is increased—the maximum number of such goods can be provided to the maximum number of people for the maximum amount of time. Although aggregation often maximizes societal welfare and the sellers' profits, it is less attractive when marginal costs are high or when consumers are heterogeneous.

Bundling involves selling two or more distinct goods for a single price and is seen as a particularly attractive option for information goods because one can add an extra good to a bundle at a negligible marginal cost. Two distinct economic effects are involved: There is a reduced dispersion of willingness to pay, and there are increased barriers to entry. Buyers might be willing to buy each good separately, but can be induced to pay a slightly higher combined price for the same goods in a bundle (e.g., a book with an accompanying CD, or Microsoft Office). The seller's revenue is enhanced because bundling reduces the dispersion of willingness to pay. The other economic effect described, barriers to entry, causes competitors of the original seller to bundle their own product(s) with the original product in order to attract customers, which becomes very expensive (Varian et al., 2004). Research shows that "bundling significantly enhances firm profit and overall efficiency but at the cost of a reduction in consumer surplus [and] these effects are much stronger for information goods than for physical goods, due to the zero marginal cost of information goods" (pp. 19–20).

When consumers are heterogeneous, information goods can also be unbundled or disaggregated, that is, items formerly bundled together are taken apart (e.g., stories in a newspaper). In highly heterogeneous markets, disaggregation allows sellers to maximize their profits (by using pay-per-use or micropayment schemes). Thus, although sellers find that lower marginal costs of production tend to make bundling/aggregation attractive, they find that unbundling/disaggregation is also attractive because of lower transaction and distribution costs (Bakos & Brynjolfsson, 2000).

Price-discrimination maximizes the seller's profits and eliminates deadweight loss. Unfortunately it also eliminates the consumer's surplus. If the seller cannot price-discriminate, however, "the only single price that would eliminate the inefficiency from deadweight loss would be a price equal to the marginal cost, which is close to zero. [Such a low price] would not generate sufficient revenues to cover the fixed cost of production and is unlikely to be the profit-maximizing price. Yet any significant positive price will inefficiently exclude some consumers" (Bakos & Brynjolfsson, 2000, p. 118).

Whereas the economic arguments based on utility theory strongly support the concept of bundling, the same arguments are not so strong for pay-per-use pricing. Moreover, if consumers value a particular information good and know how much of it they are likely to consume, monopolists (such as many information producers) can obtain more revenue from a fixed-fee pricing plan because consumers are willing to pay a premium to avoid per-use pricing. Consumers appear to derive a positive utility from fixed-fee pricing and have a general preference for simple and predictable pricing. It is unlikely that à la carte pricing will remain the dominant mode of commerce in information goods (Fishburn, Odlyzko, & Siders, 2000).

## Pricing of Public Sector Information

Almost no economics literature addresses the question of PSI pricing. On the other hand, there was considerable discussion in the library and information science literature in the 1980s and 1990s in North America and the United Kingdom. Noteworthy was Thelma Freides's (1986) article providing the economic perspective on the controversy that arose when the U.S. federal government sought to impose controls on government information dissemination, described by Kranich and Schement (2008, p. 557) as an "enclosure movement." Some literature was also generated by political scientists and other information users (see, for example, William Alonso and Paul Starr's [1987] book on statistical information). All of this literature was a response to the commodification of public information and the various privatizing, revenue generating, and cost-recovery initiatives of governments of the time. The discussion centered around whether PSI should be priced at all, and if so, how to price it. Starr and Corson (1987) argued that it would be reasonable and fair to adjust prices for government-produced information to take account of its non-market value. In their critique of 1980s government statistical policy, they wrote that policies of treating information as a commodity diminish access to public data, and the public is denied the broader advantages for which public resources have been invested. They argued that profits made from public data are an incidental by-product and "not the reason we have given government authority to conduct statistical inquiries" (pp. 444–445).

The European Commission Green Paper on PSI described various pricing models: The French model that distinguishes between types of information and types of use, the U.K.'s market approach, and the U.S. model of open access. It noted that in the long run, the trend to make public sector information increasingly available free of charge on the Internet would likely affect prices and pricing models (European Commission, 1999, Chapter 3; Annex 1; Annex 3). Gellman (2004) noted evidence of these effects and explained that when Internet access to the U.S. Government Printing Office documents became a practical reality, the agency decided to ignore a 1993 law suggesting that it recover costs from users, noting the economic and political unsustainability of any attempt to charge public users.

It is occasionally argued that use of public sector information provides a "private benefit," and therefore should be charged for at "private good" prices. Information can indeed provide private benefits (as can education), but information is, by definition, a public good with ancillary social value.

## Cost-Recovery Pricing of PSI

Cost recovery was much espoused in the 1980s and 1990s. The Organisation for Economic Co-operation and Development's (1998) best practice guidelines for user charging for government services recommended that pricing should be based on full cost recovery or, when relevant, on competitive market prices. This strong statement was tempered by the recognition that equity considerations need to be addressed; the guidelines noted that reduced charges should be considered where an excessive financial burden might be imposed on individual users by full cost recovery. The guidelines suggested that tax and benefit measures might be more efficient means of ensuring equity than reduced charges.

The standard economic arguments for cost recovery are laid out in the Australia Productivity Commission's (2001) report, which noted that the benefit principle is a major rationale for developing and implementing cost recovery. The report included the arguments noted previously for imposition of user fees and claimed that cost recovery can be a means of improving efficiency and equity. It argued that cost recovery causes users to recognize the resource costs involved in production and asserted that "the cost of resources used in producing a product includes foregone opportunity of using those resources elsewhere, so pricing based on costs helps to ensure resources are allocated more efficiently within the economy" (p. 14). Further, the report suggested that by charging for their products, government agencies receive "signals" about which products are or are not in demand. Finally, it claimed that when goods are free, users demand more of them than they would otherwise. In spite of all of these claims, the Australian report admitted that because of political and financial pressures to increase revenues, cost recovery may have been imposed where it was not warranted on economic efficiency grounds.

Cost recovery assumes that the benefit of a government information program can be measured by its revenue and none of the broader benefits or positive externalities of public information are given any weight (Starr & Corson, 1987). Nevertheless, using a cost-recovery model for PSI pricing became accepted policy as public administrations were subjected to government cost-recovery initiatives. It quickly became apparent, however, that determining the cost-recovery price for information products and services was problematic, if not impossible, without knowing the price elasticity of demand. If demand is elastic, high prices may depress demand, reducing volume and raising unit costs, whereas low prices might yield a better return because a high volume of production will mean lower costs (Starr & Corson, 1987). The Australian Productivity Commission claimed that consumption of information products is usually discretionary, not mandatory, and that cost recovery might have an immediate impact on demand for and supply of information products. It argued that this characteristic leads agencies to use pricing to manage demand and to gain some indication of consumer preferences. The Commission did not indicate how it came to the conclusion that use is usually discretionary (which belies the uses to which PSI is put and the fact that governments are often monopoly suppliers), nor why it was necessary to manage demand. In spite of its pro-cost-recovery stand, the Commission conceded that where there are positive externalities from the use of PSI, subsidies to decrease costs to users may be appropriate, and agreed that because the costs of disseminating the information can be very low, inappropriate charges can impede the desirable use of information (Australia. Productivity Commission, 2001). Colin Hookham (1994) concluded that cost recovery was not devised with the specific characteristics of information in mind, noting that the practice is not used in the private sector. Whereas cost recovery seems to be an obvious way for governments to minimize costs related to PSI, Newbery and colleagues (2008, p. 117) found that the incentive to minimize costs was lost: PSI producers sought instead "to match costs to revenue."

In the U.K., cost recovery was described as "fundamental" to the maintenance and development of the high quality mapping and navigational charting activities of the Ordnance Survey and the U.K. Hydrographic Office (UK. Cabinet Office, 1999, Chapter 9). These same departments have been much criticized by industry, economists, and other commentators who argue that government should not be competing with the private sector (Aichholzer & Tang, 2004; Weiss & Backlund, 1997). Hookham (1994, p. 8.2.2) maintained that pricing geographic data beyond affordability results in the public sector "busily creating a largely stagnant pond of digital geographic information which neither the public sector nor the private sector has reasonable access to."

One of the effects of cost-recovery programs is that government agencies are required to pay each other for data, thus churning government funds without any added revenue to the government as a whole. In the U.K., government trading funds established to generate revenue from PSI make over 50 percent of their sales to other U.K. government customers (Newbery et al., 2008). Michael Cross (2006, online) argued in the *Guardian* that this policy has a wide cost in that "it generates an absurd bureaucracy in which one government agency has to negotiate contracts with another government agency for permission to use information which the government already owns."

Commercialized European government agencies generally overstated the benefits of cost recovery according to Weiss (2003), who cited several examples supporting his arguments. Noting that a number of countries in Europe were reconsidering whether the cost-recovery policy is good for the economy as a whole, the European Commission (2000) argued that it is not at all clear that cost recovery is the best approach for government finances in general, nor for maximizing the economic value of PSI to society. Comparing the EU and U.S. PSI markets, the Commission claimed that the U.S. marketplace is almost five times the size of the EU market. Furthermore, the EU PSI market "would not even have to double in size for government to recoup in extra tax receipts what they would lose by removing all charges for PSI" (p. 10).

The vogue for cost-recovery pricing for PSI seems to be passing, particularly in Europe where the thrust is to encourage private sector re-use of this information, in line with the American open access model. In the U.S., section 7 (c) of OMB Circular A-130 requires agencies to set user charges at a level sufficient to recover the cost of dissemination but not higher. In calculating costs, agencies are instructed to exclude costs associated with original collection and processing of information. Agencies may charge less than the cost of dissemination if they determine that "higher charges would constitute a significant barrier to properly performing the agency's functions, including reaching members of the public who the agency has a responsibility to inform" (US. Office of Management and Budget, 2003, section 7 [c]).

## Marginal Cost Pricing of PSI

As has been noted, economists believe that marginal cost pricing is the price that maximizes net social benefit. The need for the private sector to recover first copy costs through prices that exceed dissemination costs is a disadvantage, not an advantage, of private information production (Noll, 1993). Because government already pays the first-copy cost of collecting the information in order to carry out its own functions, it is clearly optimal for government to provide the information at the cost of dissemination. By adopting a policy that leads to a price for information that substantially exceeds its dissemination costs, the federal government undermines the effectiveness of its own programs. In so doing, "the government is ignoring a principal lesson of information economics" (p. 50).

In the U.K., up until 2000, PSI pricing was set at average costs (except for tradable information, for which there were no limits). In 2000, the Review of Government Information argued that average cost pricing creates a significant barrier to the re-use of information. In order to achieve an efficient allocation of resources, it recommended that prices be set equal to "long-run marginal costs" (i.e., all inputs including capital costs can be taken into consideration when calculating the marginal cost). The Review argued that when prices are set above (short-run) marginal costs "both the producer and the consumer of the incremental unit would benefit from the unit being sold; willingness to pay exceeds the costs of supply so there must be a social gain" (UK. H. M. Treasury, 2000b, p. 2). This argument ignored the standard economic concern with deadweight loss, which states that if prices are greater than short-run marginal costs, units that have benefits greater than their costs are not purchased. There is no social gain if the units are not purchased.

The U.K. information industry argued that information produced for the public benefit should be priced at marginal cost to all other users. The Review's authors replied that a "price which covers only the variable cost of supplying a few more units (short-run marginal cost pricing) would be insufficient to cover the total costs," implying that total cost recovery was preferred by H. M. Treasury. It unconvincingly argued that because information is an experience good, consumers may be unwilling to pay at first, but once information is used, consumers learn the true benefit to be gained from the information. The Review suggested, however, that prices "must be very low if these benefits are to be reaped" (UK. H. M. Treasury, 2000c, p. 1)

The Review also claimed that imposing marginal cost pricing on agencies that are required to generate revenue (such as trading funds in the U.K.) may reduce incentives to develop new products; but Newbery and colleagues (2008, p. 112) counter-argued that supplementing marginal cost pricing with some kind of per-unit output subsidy "could result in over-investment in quality and capacity improvements," which can stimulate demand and, hence, a larger subsidy. They stressed that a move to a marginal cost regime by trading funds would be welfare improving and recommended that these funds set a zero price when distributing raw or unrefined information.

Arguments in support of charging above marginal costs for public sector information tend to assert that those who benefit from the information should pay for it (benefit principle). For example, the European Commission (1999, Chapter 3) claimed that the population at large should not subsidize the small section of the public who wish to use a particular public sector information product. It claimed that people are willing "in certain circumstances" to pay for the services offered (p. 14). The paper did not explain what these circumstances are.

The U.K. Review presented arguments against short-run marginal cost pricing, noting that not all demands for government information are price sensitive. Therefore, government is able to use pricing strategies to recoup some of the fixed costs of production of its information without abusing its dominant position in particular markets. In addition, the Review argued that if the government had to bear the costs of information collection and price it at short-term marginal costs, then the resulting public expenditure would need to be funded from taxation (UK. H. M.

Treasury, 2000c). All of these arguments, and others put forward in the Review's appended "Economic Paper" (UK. H. M. Treasury, 2000b), suggest a mind-set that sees public sector information as an exploitable asset that benefits the government rather than seeing the benefits to society as a whole. The U.K. Advisory Panel on Public Sector Information noted that the Cabinet Office wanted PSI exploitation to enhance the government services and the knowledge economy in general, but the Treasury was keen on leveraging PSI to reduce the cost of government or to create new sources of revenue (UK. Advisory Panel on Public Sector Information, 2004–2007).

Discussing government provision of scientific information in Canada (particularly meteorological information) Davies and Slivinski (2005) distinguished between basic and value-added products and services, and between intermediate and final goods. They noted their agreement with the argument that basic information (e.g., raw weather data) is a public good and that although a fee set at marginal cost might be appropriate, the collection costs are often too large to make this advisable. When basic scientific information has positive externalities, the public sector should do *more* than make it freely available—in some cases "it should take steps to reduce the private costs individuals bear in accessing information even when no charge is levied for it" (p. 2). On the other hand, if it is socially efficient for the government to provide value-added information (defined as usually of interest not to the general public but to a single user or user group), Davies and Slivinski argued that charging above marginal cost is justified. Final information goods go directly to individuals (consumers and householders) and these, they maintain, should be provided freely. They agree essentially with Stiglitz and colleagues (2000).

Many of the arguments against charging above marginal costs for public sector information acknowledge that marginal prices should equal marginal cost and that public information is publicly funded. Hence it is argued that taxpayers have a right to access this information and should not have to pay twice for it. Furthermore, the European Commission (1999, Chapter 3) suggested that because public information is produced by taxpayers, public organizations might not have a right to charge for the provision of such information.

The economic arguments against charging above marginal costs for PSI suggest that due to its public good nature PSI can never raise revenue in a socially beneficial manner and that the transaction costs make it even less financially worthwhile to impose user charges. Weiss and Backlund (1997) argued that the fundamental characteristics of the economics of information preclude any realistic ability to use government information as a significant revenue generator. Specific examples are provided in several works by Weiss (2002, 2003, 2004a, 2004b). He (Weiss, 2004b) noted that due to negligible revenues from data sales and a growing recognition of the benefits of open access policies, the U.K. Meteorological Office decided to make significant categories of basic observations (surface) data available for free.

The OECD concluded that more research is needed. "While models based on marginal cost pricing, as opposed to cost recovery, have been frequently defended there is still need for further analyses to clearly understand comparative economic, political and social gains from different pricing" (Organisation for Economic Co-operation and Development, Directorate for Science, Technology and Industry, Working Party on the Economy, 2006, p. 46).

## PSI Licensing

In the U.K., the Review of Government Information noted the importance of government information to the growth of its private sector information market and supported the continuation of the existing policy of providing government information to this sector through licensing. It recommended the licensing of Crown copyrighted information for reproduction and re-use by the information industry using simpler licensing mechanisms, but called for high annual fees (UK. H. M. Treasury, 2000d, List of Recommendations). A background paper on licensing provided arguments supporting commercialization of government information by government agencies and covered the various licensing options available (UK. H. M. Treasury, 2000a).

The transaction costs of administering licenses need to be considered as opportunity costs for government agencies. Based on government records, Michael Geist (2008) noted that licensing of Crown copyrighted materials in Canada generates less than 3.5 percent of the cost of administering the federal government's Crown copyright system. The European Commission (2000) pointed out that revenue-based PSI licensing operates against the financial interests of governments. Although there will be some growth in income from commercial license fees, the Commission projected that by eliminating these fees the market size would more than double, resulting in additional employment and taxation revenues that would more than offset the income lost from public sector information charges. The PIRA report recommended that the EU maximize the value of PSI to government, citizens, and business by requiring non-exclusive licensing, explicitly removing restrictions on re-use of licensed public sector information. Where licensing is applied, the OECD has called for open content online licensing systems (Organisation for Economic Co-operation and Development, Directorate for Science, Technology and Industry, Committee for Information, Computer and Communications Policy, 2008b). Some countries that impose copyright on PSI have begun to look at the open content licensing model that allows for access and re-use of copyrighted materials with minimal transactions (see Australia. Parliament of Victoria, Economic Development and Infrastructure Committee, 2008). Such licenses are readily available and eliminate the need for governments to draft their own licensing systems, saving time and money (economic costs). Creative Commons is the most recognized open content licensing model, and a Dutch analysis found it well suited to facilitating implementation of the EU PSI re-use directive (European Parliament and Council of the European Union, 2003). However, where governments insist on cost recovery, the Creative Commons license cannot be used (van Eechoud & van der Waal, 2008, pp. 74–75, 79). Some critics argue that, rather than licensing copyrighted PSI, it would be more cost effective and supportive of public access simply to eliminate the copyright, moving PSI into the public domain (Australia. Parliament of Victoria, Economic Development and Infrastructure Committee, 2008).

## Competitive Pricing

As has been noted, in the U.S. PSI is readily available for re-use by the private sector, which may disseminate the information with or without value-added components.

In other countries, some PSI may be licensed to private sector firms for value-added dissemination. Governments may also develop value-added versions of their information in competition with private sector re-users. In these cases, how the public sector prices its information is a persistent concern and source of friction. Noting that tales of unfair practices abound, Cross (2006) argued that such competitive activity stifles the knowledge economy because any start-up business based on government data is liable to find itself in direct commercial competition with the producer of those data.

Weiss (2004b) noted that the public policy issue with respect to competition is whether it is proper for taxpayer-funded government agencies to compete with the private sector. In the U.S, where it is generally accepted that the government should not do so, competition arises when public sector agencies charge less than the private sector firms that are providing the same data. Defending such under-charging twenty years ago, U.S. federal government agencies maintained that their information generation activities were integral to the purposes for which the agencies were established, and therefore the associated costs should be borne by the agencies themselves and not recovered from users. The response of the private sector was to argue that development of private information initiatives would be stifled by this line of reasoning because the resulting low prices would be anti-competitive (Duncan, 1987). In order to keep private sector entities from competing with them, in 1995 the European national meteorological agencies prevailed on the World Meteorological Organization to replace its earlier policy of free and open exchange of meteorological information with a policy that sanctioned charging and use restrictions. Later these practices were found to be anti-competitive and in some countries the national services were completely privatized, so that they would be forced to compete against the private sector entities on a "level playing field" (Weiss, 2004b, pp. 145–146).

Public good information services can find themselves under conflicting pressures from commercial services concerned that their prices will be undercut and from customers concerned about loss of freedom of access and inappropriate use of public funds. If, for public good reasons, PSI producers set a low price for high-value information, potential customers of for-profit companies might be unwilling to pay high commercial prices for similar information even when they value it highly. On the other hand, competition from a free source might have the beneficial effect of encouraging database producers to add value to their products in order to differentiate them (Webber, 1998).

Weiss (2004b) pointed out that commercialized government agencies believe that they should be able to offer information products at market prices, and this should be done in a transparent manner on a level playing field shared by all market participants. He argued, however, that in the case of government agencies providing both commercial and public interest services, a level playing field without unfair competition and cross-subsidization is impossible.

## Copyrighting Public Sector Information

Public sector information is subject to copyright in some jurisdictions and not in others. There is no copyright on federal information in the U.S., whereas in the

U.K., Canada, and other Commonwealth countries the government interest in PSI is protected by Crown copyright. Elizabeth Judge (2005) provides a comparison of Crown copyright in several jurisdictions. Other countries have mixed systems. The reason for this diversity of approaches lies in Article 2, Section 4 of the Berne Convention, which permits the signatory states to determine for themselves whether to impose copyright on government information (Weiss & Backlund, 1997). The economic arguments around copyright in general are of relevance to any discussion of PSI copyrighting. These arguments are reviewed next, followed by a specific focus on copyrighting of PSI.

The role of copyright is to protect the creators and allow markets to emerge in which sellers and buyers can interact. It is generally recognized that intellectual property rights, including copyright, make public goods excludable, thus increasing their value to producers. In particular, those who hold intellectual property rights in digital information have a strong incentive to introduce rivalry and exclusion into information markets. Because patent and copyright laws enable the owners of intellectual property to be the sole suppliers of that property, these laws allow suppliers of intellectual property to behave like monopolists and charge socially inefficient prices (Boyer, 2004; DeLong & Froomkin, 2000; Kingma, 2001).

When the economics literature considers intellectual property rights, it tends to focus on the economic impact of patents in encouraging or discouraging innovation. Although the economic role of copyright is less frequently examined, William Landes and Richard Posner's (1989) article provides a solid exposition of the topic. Dimiter Gantchev (2004) claimed that a growing number of researchers has been finding a link between copyright and the economic performance of nations. This interest has arisen as international trade agreements such as the World Trade Organization's Trade Related Aspects of Intellectual Property Rights (TRIPS) agreement and the World Intellectual Property Organization (WIPO) Copyright Treaty have encouraged reform of the copyright regimes of many countries.

In contrast to government enthusiasm for strengthening copyright protection, Ronald Hirshhorn (2003) argued that *weakening* copyright protection can provide benefits such as improved access to works for consumers, lower costs of creating new works that draw upon earlier intellectual products, and savings in public sector administrative and private sector transactions costs. The efficiency of copyright rules depends on a balance between static efficiency and dynamic efficiency. Static efficiency calls for the maximization of the use of copyrighted material whose reproduction can be done at marginal cost; dynamic efficiency calls for ensuring the optimal production of new works—the production level that equalizes marginal cost to marginal social value. This means that unless the creator can appropriate the value of the creation, dynamic efficiency "supports all or most of the cost but cannot reap any or all or most of the benefits and [therefore] a sub-optimal level of production of information goods is likely to emerge" (Boyer, 2004, p. 38). The economic research shows that strengthening copyright protection may be economically inefficient if it emphasizes production over use.

## Does Private Copying Harm Copyright Owners?

Early analyses of the economics of private copying (e.g., photocopying) had shown that such copying has negative effects on information goods publishers, but later analyses demonstrated that by adjusting pricing of the original, publishers are able to appropriate the value that copy users place on these copies. The early analyses were based on the assumption of "direct appropriability" in which the direct purchasers bear the entire cost of originals, whereas copiers pay only the costs of making copies. This contrasted with later analyses using the "indirect appropriability" assumption in which "the demand for originals is assumed to reflect the value that is placed on originals both by direct purchasers and by all those who use originals indirectly through copying" (Besen & Kirby, 1989, p. 257). The ability to copy makes works more valuable to users and consumers are willing to pay more for information goods that they can share and trade with others. As a result, producers can increase their prices; they are likely to sell fewer units of each work but these units can be sold at higher prices. The seller will increase profit by allowing copying if the reduction in sales is exceeded by the willingness to pay for the right to copy. Hence, journal publishers were able indirectly to appropriate value from photocopying by charging institutional subscribers (who made journals available for photocopying) at a higher rate than they charged individual subscribers. Where there is indirect appropriability there is a congruence of interest between producers and consumers of intellectual property—consumer welfare increases along with producer profit as long as the marginal cost of copying is lower than the marginal cost of the original. Thus, the advent of photocopying was profitable to publishers, in spite of their claims to the contrary. It should be noted, also, that the same technology advances that make copying inexpensive also reduce the producer's fixed costs of content creation. Nevertheless, content producers continue to claim that sharing "devastates profit" and legislators continue to propose and enact protective legislation (Bakos, Brynjolfsson, & Lichtman, 1999, p. 119). If the amount of copying can be restricted, publishers will have an incentive to restrict the number of copies more severely than is optimal from the viewpoint of social welfare (see also David, 2005; Kinokuni, 2003; Liebowitz, 1985; Varian, 2005).

Copyright violations may be uneconomical for the publisher to pursue, incurring opportunity costs. Thus, the money spent in monitoring and possibly litigating such violations can be better spent producing new works. Varian (2005, p. 5) stressed the importance of recognizing that "works are not only outputs of the creative process but are also inputs. Increasing the number of creative works presumably stimulates the production of yet more works."

## Term of Copyright

The term of copyright tries to address the trade-off between encouraging creation and reducing restriction on consumption (Yuan, 2005). Legislators choose the duration of copyright to maximize social welfare but creators set prices above the marginal cost of reproduction and distribution during the copyright protection period in order to maximize profits. Doing so results in a loss of consumer surplus and a deadweight loss in social welfare. If longer copyright terms allow creators to produce more first-copies, then consumer welfare increases but existing products that are not generating profits increase the deadweight loss. Varian (2005) discussed the optimal term of copyright and compared the benefits that accrue to consumers under monopoly pricing with benefits under competitive pricing (after copyright has expired); he concluded that once the work has been created, total welfare in the competitive regime exceeds that of the monopoly regime.

The economic benefit of copyright term extensions (as in the U.S. 1998 Sonny Bono Copyright Term Extension Act, which extended author copyright from life plus 50 to life plus 70 years) is considered by many economists to be trivial. The twenty year extension on new works will generate very few royalties seventy years in the future for most authors or their heirs (most works will be out of print). Varian (2005) explained that the purpose of the Bono act was to make extension retroactive so that existing works near copyright expiration (such as Disney characters) would have a new lease on life. Economically, however, what matters is the value at the time a work is created. Furthermore, allowing older works to go into the public domain creates substantial social benefits. One argument for longer copyright duration is that new media enhance the marketable life of information products. Investigating this argument, Yuan (2005, p. 489) concluded that "a decrease in reproduction and distribution cost and an increase in demand for information products may call for shorter copyright duration."

## Database Protection

In 1996, in Directive 96/9/EC, the European Parliament and Council adopted a database protection right that aimed to harmonize the rules protecting databases across EU member countries, thus "safeguarding the investment of database makers" (European Parliament and Council of the European Union, 1996). Proponents argued that the differences in standards of originality required for database copyright protection impeded the free movement of database products across the region. The directive gave a high level of copyright protection to certain "original" databases under a new form of *sui generis* protection for compilations that are original not in the sense of intellectual creation, but in the sense that they require a substantial investment of skill, labor, or judgment in gathering together and/or checking ("sweat of the brow" as opposed to "creativity"). This right is much stronger than copyright because it disallows extraction or reutilization of even insubstantial portions of the database if such activity unreasonably prejudices the interests of the database maker.

Introduced to stimulate the production of databases in Europe, member countries were required to pass *sui generis* database legislation. Concerns about access prompted the Netherlands to specifically exempt PSI from its national legislation. Canada and the United States are under pressure to adopt a similar right but there is much opposition and case law does not support it. In 1991, the U.S. Supreme Court had already drawn a line between original and non-original works (in Feist Publications Inc. vs. Rural Telephone Service Co.), confirming that facts are not copyrightable. In 1996, the Canadian Federal Court of Appeals (Tele-Direct Publications Inc. vs. American Business Information Inc.) held that Canadian law contained a creativity requirement similar to Feist. Nevertheless, private sector database producers are likely to continue to urge legislators to pass such legislation (David, 2005; Maurer, 2001; Sanders, 2006; Trosow, 2005).

In 2005, the European Commission's Internal Market and Services Directorate General evaluated the database protection directive. The empirical findings cast doubt on the need for *sui generis* protection for the database industry (although the industry argued that this protection was "crucial" to its continued success) (p. 20). The evaluation found the economic impact of the directive to be "unproven" (p. 5). The database industry in Europe had declined, while the U.S. database industry (without *sui generis* protection) had grown and database protection had not reduced the economic gap with the U.S. (David, 2005; European Commission, 2005; Sanders, 2006).

## Economic Arguments for PSI Copyright

The European Commission's Green Paper, *Public Sector Information: A Key Resource for Europe*, suggested that the government may assert copyright for two reasons: (1) because the information is seen as a source of income and/or (2) in order to maintain the integrity of the content (European Commission, 1999, Chapter 3). The initial justification for Crown copyright in the United Kingdom lay neither in protecting integrity nor in guaranteeing revenue, but appears to have been a bureaucratic response to private sector initiatives. Crown copyright was first asserted in the 1911 Copyright Act in response to the authorized reproduction of official publications by private publishers in the last decades of the nineteenth century to protect the general taxpayer "against commercial interests of the few, who would obtain a private profit by unrestricted freedom to reproduce official matter" (UK. Cabinet Office, 1998, Chapter 2). Even today, this argument is raised without consideration of potential tax revenues from private sector activities or of the positive economic and social welfare externalities of disseminating information more widely.

A review of Crown copyright policy in the United Kingdom was launched in 1996, and a consultation paper, the 1998 Green Paper, *Crown Copyright in the Information Age*, used both the integrity and revenue arguments to justify continued copyright protection of PSI. The paper described Crown copyright as reflecting the "integrity, accuracy, and authenticity" of the information, while citing revenue generated as an argument for retention of the right (section 4.3). Loss of revenue, it was argued, would "have a marked impact on departments' ability to meet their aims and objectives" and divert resources from other priorities (UK. Cabinet Office, 1998, Chapter 4).

Following up on its Green Paper, the U.K. government published a White Paper, *Future Management of Crown Copyright*, in which integrity and authority remained an underlying justification for maintenance of Crown copyright (UK. Cabinet Office, 1999, Chapter 2). It allowed for the waiver of copyright, however, to ensure "light touch management" when it was in the government's interest (section 5.1). The White Paper allowed various options for charging (including free distribution to the public) and no longer required licensing for various categories of material (Aichholzer & Tang, 2004).

With respect to integrity, the European Commission raised the valid point that using copyright to maintain integrity of the content is relevant from the perspective of liability issues (European Commission, 1999, Chapter 3). Commercial information providers who called for the abolition of Crown copyright counter-argued that market discipline would ensure the accuracy of the material (UK. Cabinet Office, 1999, Chapter 2). The European Commission (2000, p. 21) report noted that the private sector "often feels that copyright restrictions, under the guise of preventing fraudulent use and protecting quality can be used by the public sector to restrict the reuse of PSI."

The arguments regarding integrity and accuracy are no longer relevant, Judge (2005) explained, because any re-publisher's reputation is linked to the quality of its published works. With legal information, for example, people can "easily cross-reference non-official to official versions" and they can also communicate inaccuracies to others; "word travels fast through e-mail and blogs" (p. 573). She concluded that ensuring accuracy and integrity can be achieved by other legal and technological mechanisms that are better suited to the task and will at the same time facilitate public access to those materials.

With respect to revenue, Judge (2005) noted that early commentators on English law downplayed its importance, believing that Crown copyright is of public benefit because it provided publications at a *lower* cost than commercial private publishers could. Since the 1980s, this argument has been seen as a quaint anachronism and revenue generation is the most frequent economic rationalization for copyrighting PSI. The U.K. White Paper argued that "any financial return to government reduces the burden on the future collection and maintenance of [tradable information] and benefits all taxpayers" (UK. Cabinet Office, 1999, section 9.2). The 1998 U.K Green Paper had noted the argument that without copyright there "would be less incentive for departments to develop products and services of an optional or discretionary nature [i.e., tradable information] derived from their internal skill and knowledge base to the greater benefit of all" (UK. Cabinet Office, 1998, Chapter 4). The various arguments that are made as to why copyright should exist in government works include the assertion that government copyright can be used to advance general economic welfare. David Vaver (1995, p. 6) responded that the general rule (that permission must be sought to use Crown copyright materials, permission can be denied, and royalties are payable) "does nothing to maximize use of government material or help the economy or society."

## Economic Arguments Against PSI Copyright

Stiglitz and colleagues (2000) explained that the principal purpose of copyright protection is to provide a financial incentive to private innovators. They argued that because public entities are not governed by the same profit incentives that apply in the private sector, copyright should not generally be necessary as an inducement for research or creative work within public-sector bodies. They believe that government should be allowed to maintain proprietary information or exercise rights under patents and/or copyrights only under special conditions. Holding such rights does not mean that they must be enforced, so although the public sector should be entitled to hold patents and copyrights, it should generally not exercise these rights.

They wrote that the public sector should not restrict the use of copyrighted material or charge for its use, despite holding the rights.

The 1998 U.K. Green Paper listed the arguments against copyrighting PSI. These included: (1) taxpayers have paid for the information through their taxes and it should be freely available; (2) the information market may grow and increased revenues would boost tax revenues; (3) administering copyright across many agencies is time-consuming, incoherent, inefficient (and therefore expensive); (4) government should not compete with the private sector; and (5) policing copyright is impractical in the information age (UK. Cabinet Office, 1998, Chapter 4). Aichholzer and Tang (2004) suggested that the *idea* of copyright was not a problem but its management had prompted many to regard U.K. information policy as a business strategy of government. Changes brought about by the 1999 U.K. White Paper have not dispelled criticism. Arthur and Cross (2006, online) described the *Guardian* newspaper's "Free Our Data" campaign as having the "simple" aim of persuading the government "to abandon copyright on essential national data, making it freely available to anyone, while keeping the crucial task of collecting the data in the hands of taxpayer-funded agencies."

Weiss and Backlund (1997) argued that copyrighting PSI permits the exclusion of the private sector and/or the maintenance of exclusive arrangements with preferred franchisees. The European Commission (2000) observed that the public sector often grants exclusive deals with private sector firms that it commissions to help with its information dissemination. It noted that these deals do not generally cause problems, providing the arrangements are transparent. When the aim of licensing is to add value and develop a commercial product, however, exclusive deals mean that one player in the market has an unfair advantage.

In the United States, federally produced information is expressly prohibited from copyright protection by the Copyright Act (17 USC 105). The act states that a work of the United States Government "is a work prepared by an officer or employee of the United States Government as part of that person's official duties" (s. 101) and that "copyright protection under this title is not available for any work of the United States Government, but the United States Government is not precluded from receiving and holding copyrights transferred to it by assignment, bequest, or otherwise" (s. 105). Individual states and cities can—and some do—impose copyright on their information.

In many countries, government agencies provide value-added products. Because copyright does not protect facts, ideas, concepts, or methods of operation (Varian, 2005), it has been suggested that those governments that copyright PSI will often add value in order to assert copyright on facts or data that they could not otherwise. When private sector re-users of PSI add value to the information, they, too, are likely to seek to copyright the added value. This measure can limit public access, especially when the government licenses access and re-use of the information to a single firm or when the government no longer provides access by allowing the information to go out of print or removing it from its websites. In the U.S., the migration of data from non-copyright government control to private sector copyright control has been a concern. Vaver (1995) noted that where government contractors can acquire copyrights, private owners may charge or even suppress information that was previously freely accessible and reproducible. Where government reorganization leads to contracting and privatizing of government information and services, policy objectives can be undercut.

As noted earlier in this chapter, the lack of copyright controls is seen as a powerful underpinning for the American information industry and a contributor to economic growth. For example, it is argued that the reason for differences between the U.S. and European weather risk management industries results from the assertion of copyright by European government agencies as well as the *sui generis* database protection right on taxpayer-funded information, neither of which is available in the United States (Weiss, 2003).

## *PSI Copyright Reform*

Judge (2005) described copyright as a blunt instrument for facilitating access to accurate and timely public information and not the best way to achieve the public purposes for which the PSI was designed. The guarantee of integrity and authority, she argued, could be maintained by use of "credentialing markers" on official versions of government information. Such markers would indicate that these versions have the status and authority of being published by the government-designated printer (p. 555). She concluded that for those who are still enamored of Crown copyright, "the Crown can retain the moral rights-type interests in works to ensure accuracy and integrity" (pp. 573–574).

Arguments in favor of Crown copyright reform in Canada were enhanced by the 2004 decision of the Supreme Court of Canada (in CCH vs. Law Society of Upper Canada) that found that copyright is a balance between two objectives: The incentive to create and the beneficial rewards of that creation. Rationalizing these objectives with the content protected by Crown copyright is difficult because neither the incentives nor rewards apply to Crown copyright. The mechanism does not result in greater quantity or quality of government information and is "as likely to keep information from circulating as to provide incentives to publish" (Judge, 2005, p. 572).

Increasing pressure to eliminate Crown copyright is evident throughout the Commonwealth countries. A 2005 review of Crown copyright in Australia recommended its abolition (cited in Australia. Parliament of Victoria, Economic Development and Infrastructure Committee, 2008). Pressure from the European Union might lead to revision or rescinding of the law in the United Kingdom. In Canada, the arguments against maintenance of Crown copyright were noted in an Industry Canada (2002) report on the Canadian copyright act. It agreed that eliminating Crown copyright might hamper the ability of government to provide material on a cost-recovery basis but noted that the absence of copyright protection does not hamper the U.S. government's publication of a large amount of material. It further argued that licensing the use of work subject to Crown copyright may result in a substantial burden for the user and concluded that unless user-friendly licensing is put in place, there is likely to be increasing pressure to remove Crown copyright protection entirely. In addition, the costs of administering Crown copyright, although not large in total budget terms, can raise concerns. As one Canadian copyright scholar wrote, "The urgency associated with eliminating the outdated notion of government control over work product bought and paid for by the public has never been greater" (Geist, 2005, online). There is little economic justification for public taxpayer investment in a system that limits access to PSI.

## Current Pricing and Re-Use Discussions in Europe and Elsewhere

The debate continues as to whether countries should make public sector information freely available for re-use by the private sector, as in the United States, or whether government agencies can exploit the information for their own revenue purposes, as in the United Kingdom. Comparisons of EU PSI policies with those of the U.S. led observers to see European restrictions on access (in freedom of information terms, as well as in private sector re-use) as a trade barrier (Burkert, 2004). The OECD identified a number of PSI pricing models in its member countries, including free dissemination, marginal cost dissemination, and various levels of cost-recovery pricing up to production cost-recovery plus profit (i.e., average cost plus a reasonable return) (Organisation for Economic Co-operation and Development, Directorate for Science, Technology and Industry, Working Party on the Economy, 2006). It stated that profit pricing was relatively rare and in Europe prices were commonly charged only to recover production costs partially. The report noted, however, that the pricing of public sector information is undergoing changes due to the recommendations of a 2003 European Parliament and Council of Europe *Directive on the Re-use of Public Sector Information.* This directive (European Parliament and Council of the European Union, 2003) was an outcome of the process begun by the European Commission Green Paper (European Commission, 1999).

The directive sought to bring about changes in some national policies on the re-use of PSI. When defining the principles relevant to charging and pricing, the directive avoided imposing on the right of member states to charge (or not to charge). Where individual member states wish to impose charges, it advised that the upper limit for charges should not exceed the total cost of collecting, producing, reproducing, and disseminating information, together with a reasonable investment return. At the same time, it urged member states to encourage public sector bodies to make documents available at charges that do not exceed the marginal costs for reproducing and disseminating the documents (European Parliament and Council of the European Union, 2003, Section 14). Critiquing a draft of the directive, Weiss (2003, p. 131) argued that it did not address the issue of "dissemination cost pricing versus cost-recovery pricing." Pas and De Vuyst (2004) concluded that the final version of the directive was vague, conceded too much to national rules and practices, and refrained from deciding upon pricing. They suggested that the directive might do more harm than good.

EU member countries are required to pass legislation or regulations adopting the re-use directive. In the U.K., regulations that came into effect in 2005 continue to allow PSI producers, including trading funds, to impose significant charges for their output (De Saulles, 2007; UK. Statutory Instruments, 2005). In response to the U.K. government's continued support of charging, the *Guardian* newspaper started its "Free Our Data" campaign in 2006. The data sets of such agencies as the Ordnance

Survey, the Hydrographic Office, and the Land Registry were described as "modern crown jewels" that should be used to boost national wealth, rather than restricting access to those who pay (Arthur & Cross, 2006, online). The counter-argument was made that such critics overlooked the costs of producing and maintaining reliable, quality data and that in other countries (read U.S.) where data are made available at no cost, they are often "out-of-date and inaccurate" (UK. Advisory Panel on Public Sector Information, 2006, p. 4). The Ordnance Survey's specific response can be found on the campaign's website, where discussion continues on an active blog (www.freeourdata.org.uk).

An assessment conducted in 2008 for the European Commission on the effect of the PSI re-use directive examined three public information sectors (geographical, legal, and meteorological) and found the strongest impact in the geographical information sector and almost none in the meteorological. Re-users in all sectors continue to complain about restrictive licensing and high prices. Many re-users compared the European dissemination model with the free dissemination and unrestrictive licenses provided in the United States. Potential re-users noted that PSI holders justified high prices and restrictive licensing by referring to their mandated public tasks. Although the assessment concluded that the impact of the directive was largely positive in encouraging re-use of PSI, it appears that many public bodies define their tasks in such a way as to lead them to carry out commercial activity in competition with the private sector (Fornefeld, Boele-Keimer, Recher, & Fanning, 2008). The EU debate has percolated to other countries as well. The Parliament of the state of Victoria in Australia has conducted an inquiry into improving access to PSI. It concluded that there is an emerging consensus that "access at no or marginal cost is the best approach to ensure the greatest re-use of PSI within the public domain" (Australia. Parliament of Victoria, Economic Development and Infrastructure Committee, 2008, p. 33).

In 2008 OECD ministers met and issued a declaration on the future of the digital economy (Organisation for Economic Co-operation and Development, Directorate for Science, Technology and Industry, Committee for Information, Computer and Communications Policy, 2008a). Among the many recommendations that emerged from the ministerial meeting were several encouraging enhanced access and effective use of PSI. Member countries should take due account, and implement policies of openness and access to maximize PSI availability for use and re-use. Availability should be "based upon the assumption of openness as the default rule," and this rule should apply "no matter what the model of funding is for the development and maintenance of the information" (Organisation for Economic Co-operation and Development, Directorate for Science, Technology and Industry, Committee for Information, Computer and Communications Policy, 2008b, p. 35). The recommendations further called for transparent conditions for re-use, elimination of exclusive arrangements, and the waiving or exercising of copyright in such a way as to encourage re-use. With respect to pricing, the declaration recommended that costs charged to users not exceed the marginal costs of maintenance and distribution (Annex F). It remains to be seen how the member countries respond, particularly those with onerous copyright restrictions.

## Summary

This chapter reviewed the information economics literature, with a particular focus on public sector information. The economic arguments for public sector versus private sector supply of information, the economic impact of PSI, its commercial re-use by the public or private sector, value adding and revenue generation by PSI producers, the pricing of information, and the arguments for and against copyright were reviewed. Underlying this review is the current push to harmonize PSI accessibility across the European Union and the debate as to which dissemination model is preferable, the U.S. open access model or the more restrictive European approach.

The economics literature recognizes that information is a public good, with ancillary social value and positive externalities. Pricing of non-rivalrous and non-excludable public goods is considered economically dubious. Costing and pricing of information are always difficult because of information's inherent characteristics (it is difficult to measure, value, or appropriate, and its benefits cannot be easily determined). Information production has high fixed costs and low variable costs; the marginal cost of producing additional copies is low or zero. Economists argue that the greatest social benefit is achieved when information is priced at marginal cost. When information is priced more highly there is no social net benefit because some people are prevented from enjoying the good even though their consumption of it would have no marginal cost. Items that are not purchased represent wasteful overproduction and provide no benefit to society.

Public sector information producers are subject to the cost recovery or revenue generation goals of their governments. The difficulty of determining costs of PSI production means that cost-recovery pricing cannot be established in an objective manner—user fees are invariably arbitrary; they are described as political pricing. Research suggests that cost-recovery pricing may not be the best approach for maximizing the economic value of public sector information, nor for government finances in general. Nevertheless, some governments claim that user fees are justifiable or necessary in order to avoid increases in taxation. Economists argue that support for government activities by taxation alone is justifiable because taxation can be unambiguously welfare improving. Any pricing of PSI above marginal cost is economically inefficient.

The arguments for copyrighting public sector information are based on maintaining the integrity and authority of the information and on generating revenues from it. Economists argue that if a government role is warranted in any given activity, then seeking to generate revenue means that a government entity is not fulfilling its mission. If a government role is not warranted, then the activity should be undertaken by the private sector. Although the economics literature reveals that there is no economic justification for copyrighting PSI, there may be some argument for maintaining copyright to protect the integrity and authority of this information. However, other mechanisms can be used to provide such protection.

There is no economic efficiency argument to be made for making information excludable by price or by copyright. Research comparing the U.S. and the EU information markets supports the argument that adoption of the American open access model for PSI across the European Union and elsewhere would have a positive economic impact and contribute to economic growth.

# Endnote

1. An earlier version of this chapter was prepared under a research contract for Statistics Canada (Nilsen, 2007): *Economic Theory as It Applies to Statistics Canada: A Review of the Literature.* This earlier version also includes a review of the economic literature in relation to official statistics and an analysis of the agency's production and dissemination program.

# References

Adams, W. J., & Brock, J. W. (1994). Economic theory: Rhetoric, reality, rationalization. In R. E. Babe (Ed.), *Information and communication in economics* (pp. 125–145). Boston: Kluwer.

Aichholzer, G., & Tang, P. (2004). Harnessing public sector information for general accessibility: Austria and the UK. In G. Aichholzer & H. Burkert (Eds.), *Public sector information in the digital age: Between markets, public management and citizens' rights* (pp. 287–326). Cheltenham, UK: Edward Elgar.

Aislabie, C. (1972). The economic efficiency of information producing activities. *Economic Record, 48*(124), 575–583.

Akerlof, G. (1970). The market for lemons. *Quarterly Journal of Economics, 84*(3), 488–500.

Allen, B. (1990). Information as an economic commodity. *American Economic Review, 80,* 268–273.

Alonso, W., & Starr, P. (Eds.). (1987). *The politics of numbers.* New York: Russell Sage.

Anderson, G. M. (1991). The fiscal significance of user charges and earmarked taxes: A survey. In R. E. Wagner (Ed.), *Charging for government: User charges and earmarked taxes in principle and practice* (pp. 13–33). London: Routledge.

Arrow, K. J. (1974). *The limits of organization.* New York: Norton.

Arrow, K. J. (1984). Information and economic behavior [Lecture presented to the Federation of Swedish Industries, Stockholm, 1973]. In *Collected Papers of Kenneth J. Arrow* (Vol. 4., pp. 136–152). Cambridge, MA: Harvard University Press.

Arrow, K. J. (1985a). Economic welfare and the allocation of resources for invention. In *Collected papers of Kenneth J. Arrow* (Vol. 5, pp. 104–119). Cambridge MA: Harvard University Press. (Originally published in *The Rate and Direction of Inventive Activity: Economic and Social Factors,* pp. 609–625). Princeton NJ: Princeton University Press, 1962)

Arrow, K. J. (1985b). Knowledge, productivity, and practice. *Collected Papers of Kenneth J. Arrow,* Vol. 5 (pp. 191–199). Cambridge, MA: Harvard University Press. (Originally published in *Bulletin SEDEIS* Étude no. 909 suppl., 1965)

Arthur, C., & Cross, M. (2006, March 9). Give us back our crown jewels. *Guardian Unlimited.* Retrieved January 26, 2009, from technology.guardian.co.uk/weekly/story/0,,1726229,00.html

Australia. Parliament of Victoria. Economic Development and Infrastructure Committee. (2008). *Inquiry into improving access to Victoria's public sector information and data: Discussion paper.* Melbourne, Australia: Victorian Government Printer. Retrieved January 28, 2009, from www.parliament.vic. gov.au/edic/inquiries/access_to_PSI/EDIC_PSI_Discussion_Paper.pdf

Australia. Productivity Commission. (2001). Economics of cost recovery. In *Cost Recovery by Government Agencies* (Chapter 2, pp. 11–34). Canberra, Australia: AusInfo. Retrieved January 26, 2009, from www.pc.gov.au/__data/assets/pdf_file/0004/36877/costrecovery1.pdf

Babe, R. E. (1995). *Communication and the transformation of economics.* Boulder, CO: Westview.

Babe, R. E. (1996). Economics and information: Toward a new (and more sustainable) world view. *Canadian Journal of Communication, 21,* 161–178.

Badenoch, D., Reid, C., Burton, P., Gibbs, F., & Oppenheim, C. (1994). The value of information. In M. Feeney & M. Grieves (Eds.), *The value and impact of information* (pp. 9–77). London: Bowker-Saur.

Bakos, Y., & Brynjolfsson, E. (2000). Aggregation and disaggregation of information goods: Implication for bundling, site licensing, and micropayment systems. In B. Kahin & H. R. Varian (Eds.), *Internet publishing and beyond: The economics of digital information and intellectual property* (pp. 114–137). Cambridge, MA: MIT Press.

Bakos, Y., Brynjolfsson, E., & Lichtman, D. (1999). Shared information goods. *Journal of Law and Economics, 42,* 117–155.

Bates, B. J. (1988). Information as an economic good: Sources of individual and social value. In V. Mosco & J. Wasco (Eds.), *The political economy of information* (pp. 76–94). Madison: University of Wisconsin Press.

Bellin, D. (1993). The economic value of information. *Knowledge: Creation, Diffusion, Utilization, 15*(2), 233–240.

Besen, S. M., & Kirby, S, N. (1989). Private copying, appropriability, and optimal copying royalties. *Journal of Law and Economics, 32,* 255–273.

Bickner, R. E. (1983). Concepts of economic cost. In D. W. King, N. K. Roderer, & H. A. Olsen (Eds.), *Key papers in the economics of information* (pp. 10–49). White Plains, NY: Knowledge Industry Publications. (Originally published in G. H. Fisher (Ed.), *Cost considerations in systems analysis* (pp. 24–63). New York: American Elsevier, 1971)

Bird, R. M., & Tsiopoulos, T. (1997). *User charging in the federal government: A background document.* Ottawa, Canada: Treasury Board. Retrieved January 26, 2009, from www.tbs-sct.gc.ca/pubs_pol/opepubs/TB_H/UCFG_e.asp

Blomquist, S., & Christiansen, V. (2005). The role of prices for excludable public goods. *International Tax and Public Finance, 12,* 61–79.

Boulding, K. E. (1971). The economics of knowledge and the knowledge of economics. *Collected Papers* (Vol. 2, pp. 367–379). Boulder, CO: Associated University Press.

Boulding, K. E. (1984). A note on information, knowledge, and production. In M. Jussawalla & H. Benfield (Eds.), *Communication and information economics: New perspectives* (pp. vii–ix). New York: North Holland.

Boyer, M. (2004). *Assessing the economic impact of copyright reform.* Project report for Industry Canada. Montreal: CIRANO [Centre interuniversitaire de recherche et analyse des organizations]. Retrieved January 26, 2009, from www.cirano.qc.ca/pdf/publication/2004RP-01.pdf

Braman, S. (2006). Micro- and macroeconomics of information. *Annual Review of Information Science and Technology, 40,* 3–52.

Brinberg, H. R. (1989). Information economics: Valuing information. *Information Management Review,* 4(3), 59–63.

Brynjolfsson, E. (1993). The productivity paradox of information technology. *Communications of the ACM, 36*(12), 66–77.

Burkert, H. (2004). The mechanics of public sector information. In G. Aichholzer & H. Burkert (Eds.), *Public sector information in the digital age: Between markets, public management and citizens' rights* (pp. 3–19). Cheltenham, UK: Edward Elgar.

Chichilnisky, G. (1999). Introduction. In G. Chichilnisky (Ed.), *Markets, information and uncertainty: Essays in economic theory in honor of Kenneth J. Arrow* (pp. 13–18). New York: Cambridge University Press.

Ciffolilli, A. (2004). The economics of open source hijacking and the declining quality of digital information resources: A case for copyleft. *First Monday, 9*(9). Retrieved January 26, 2009, from first monday.org/htbin/cgiwrap/bin/ojs/index.php/fm/article/view/1173/1093

Coase, R. H. (1937). The nature of the firm. *Economica*, (New Series) *4*(16), 386–405.

Cronin, B., & Gudim, M. (1986). Information and productivity: A review of research. *International Journal of Information Management, 6*(2), 84–101.

Cross, M. (2006, May 29). One small step on a long-haul journey. *Guardian Unlimited*. Retrieved January 26, 2009, from technology.guardian.co.uk/weekly/story/0,,1781888,00.html

David, P. A. (2005). Does the new economy need all the old IPR institutions and still more?" In L. Soete & B. ter Weel (Eds.), *The economics of the digital society* (pp. 113–151). Cheltenham, UK: Edward Elgar.

Davies, J. B., & Slivinski, A. (2005). *The public role in provision of scientific information: An economic approach* (Economic Policy Research Institute Working Paper no. 2005-1). London: Department of Economics, The University of Western Ontario. Retrieved January 26, 2009, from economics.uwo.ca/centres/epri/wp2005/Davies_Slivinski_01.pdf

DeLong, J. B., & Froomkin, M. (2000). Speculative macroeconomics for tomorrow's economy. In B. Kahin & H. R. Varian (Eds.), *Internet publishing and beyond: The economics of digital information and intellectual property* (pp. 6–44). Cambridge, MA: MIT Press.

Dekkers, M., Polman, F., te Velde, R., & de Vries, M. (2006). *MEPSIR: Measuring European Public Sector Information Resources: Executive Summary*. Retrieved January 26, 2009, from europa.eu.int/information_society/policy/psi/docs/pdfs/mepsir/executive_summary.pdf

De Saulles, M. (2007). When public meets private: Conflicts in information policy. *Info, 9*(6), 10–16.

Duncan, J. W. (1987). Technology, costs, and the new economics of statistics. In W. Alonso & P. Starr (Eds.), *The politics of numbers* (pp. 395–413). New York: Russell Sage.

Eaton, J. J. (1987). *Is information a "resource"? A review of the literature relating to the economic significance of information* (Occasional Paper No. 4). Sheffield, UK: Dept. of Information Studies, University of Sheffield.

Eaton, J. J., & Bawden, D. D. (1991). What kind of a resource is information? *International Journal of Information Management, 11*, 156–165.

Ebenstein, A. (2003). *Hayek's journey: The mind of Friedrich Hayek*. New York: Palgrave Macmillan.

European Commission. (1989). *Guidelines for improving the synergy between the public and private sectors in the information market*. Brussels, Belgium: The Commission. Retrieved January 26, 2009, from europa.eu.int/information_society/policy/psi/library/index_en.htm

European Commission. (1999). *Public sector information: A key resource for Europe* (Green paper on public sector information in the information society). Brussels, Belgium: The Commission. Retrieved January 26, 2009, from aei.pitt.edu/1168/01/public_sector_information_gp_COM_98_585.pdf

European Commission. (2000). *Commercial exploitation of Europe's public sector information: Executive summary*. Prepared by Pira International Ltd. Luxembourg: Office for Official Publications of the European Communities. Retrieved January 26, 2009, from ftp://ftp.cordis.europa.eu/pub/econtent/docs/2000_1558_en.pdf

European Commission. (2001). eEurope 2002: Creating a EU framework for the exploitation of public sector information. Brussels, Belgium: The Commission. Retrieved January 26, 2009, from ftp://ftp.cordis.europa.eu/pub/econtent/docs/2001_607_en.pdf

European Commission. (2005). *First evaluation of the 96/9/EC on the legal protection of databases* (DG Internal Market and Services working paper). Brussels, Belgium: The Commission. Retrieved January 26, 2009, from ec.europa.eu/internal_market/copyright/docs/databases/evaluation_report_en.pdf

European Parliament and Council of the European Union. (1996). Directive 96/9/EC on the legal protection of databases. *Official Journal of the European Union, L 077*, 0020–0028. Retrieved January 26, 2009, from eur-lex.europa.eu/LexUriServ/LexUriServ.do?uri=CELEX:31996L0009:EN:HTML

European Parliament and Council of the European Union. (2003). Directive 2003/98/EC on the re-use of public information. *Official Journal of the European Union, I 345*, 90–96. Retrieved January 26, 2009, from ec.europa.eu/information_society/policy/psi/docs/pdfs/directive/psi_directive_en.pdf

Fishburn, P. C., Odlyzko, A. M., & Siders, R. C. (2000). Fixed-fee versus unit pricing for information goods: Competition, equilibrium, and price wars. In B. Kahin & H. R. Varian (Eds.), *Internet publishing and beyond: The economics of digital information and intellectual property* (pp. 167–189). Cambridge, MA: MIT Press.

Foray, D. (2004). *Economics of knowledge*. Cambridge, MA: MIT Press.

Foray, D. (2006). Optimizing the use of knowledge. In B. Kahin & D. Foray (Eds.), *Advancing knowledge and the knowledge economy* (pp. 9–15). Cambridge, MA: MIT Press.

Fornefeld, M., Boele-Keimer, G., Recher, S., & Fanning, M. (2008). *Assessment of the re-use of public sector information in the geographical information, meteorological information and legal information sectors: Final report*. Düsseldorf, Germany: MICUS Management Consulting GmbH. (Prepared for the European Commission). Retrieved January 26, 2009, from ec.europa.eu/information_society/policy/psi/docs/pdfs/micus_report_december2008.pdf

Freides, T. (1986). The federal information controversy from an economic perspective. *College & Research Libraries, 47*, 425–437.

Gantchev, D. (2004). The WIPO guide on surveying the economic contribution of the copyright industries. *Review of Economic Research on Copyright Issues, 1*, 5–16. Retrieved January 26, 2009, from www.serci.org/docs/gantchev.pdf

Gazier, B., & Touffut, J.-P. (2006). Introduction: Public goods and social enactions. In J.-P. Touffut (Ed.), *Advancing public goods: Papers from 6th Conference of the Cournot Centre for Economic Studies (Paris, 2003)* (pp. 1–12). Cheltenham, UK: Edward Elgar.

Geist, M. (2005, March 14). Keeping an eye on a Canadian prize. *Toronto Star*. Retrieved January 26, 2009, from www.michaelgeist.ca/resc/html_bkup/mar142005.html

Geist, M. (2008, May 12). *Records indicate government is misusing crown copyright*. Michael Geist's blog. Retrieved January 25, 2009, from www.michaelgeist.ca/content/view/2920/135

Gellman, R. (2004). The foundations of United States government information dissemination policy. In G. Aichholzer & H. Burkert (Eds.), *Public sector information in the digital age: Between markets, public management and citizens' rights* (pp. 123–136). Cheltenham, UK: Edward Elgar.

Ghosh, R. A. (2006). *Study on the economic impact of open source software on innovation and competitiveness of the information and communication technologies* (ICT Sector in the EU Final report. Prepared for the European Commission). Retrieved January 29, 2009, from cc.europa.eu/enterprise/ict/policy/doc/2006-11-20-flossimpact.pdf

Ghosh, R. A., Glott, R., Gerloff, K., Schmitz, P.-E., Aisola, K., & Boujraf, A. (2007). *Study of the effect on the development of the information society of European public bodies making their own software available as open source* (Prepared for the European Commission). Retrieved January 29, 2009, from www.publicsectoross.info/images/resources/15_154_file.pdf

Hadi, Z. A., & McBride, N. (2000). The commercialisation of public sector information within UK government departments. *International Journal of Public Management, 13*(7), 552–570.

Hayek, F. A. v. (1937). Economics and knowledge. *Economica*, (New Series), *4*(13), 33–54.

Hayek, F. A. v. (1945). The use of knowledge in society. *American Economic Review, 35*(4), 519–530.

Hellwig, M. F. (2005). A utilitarian approach to the provision and pricing of excludable public goods. *Journal of Public Economics, 89*, 1981–2003.

Henry, C. (2006). Knowledge as global public good: Production conditions and preconditions. In J.-P. Touffut (Ed.), *Advancing public goods: Papers from 6th Conference of the Cournot Centre for Economic Studies (Paris, 2003)* (pp. 137–148). Cheltenham, UK: Edward Elgar.

Herings, P. J.-J., & Schinkel, M. P. (2005). World-wide-welfare: A micro-analysis of "the new economy." In L. Soete & B. ter Weel (Eds.), *The economics of the digital society* (pp. 14–53). Cheltenham, UK: Edward Elgar.

Herzog, P. (2006). Services of general interest in a competitive multinational space. In J.-P. Touffut (Ed.), *Advancing public goods: Papers from 6th Conference of the Cournot Centre for Economic Studies, (Paris, 2003)* (pp. 69–103). Cheltenham, UK: Edward Elgar.

Hill, M. W. (1994). The economics of information: General overview. In M. Feeney & M. Grieves (Eds.), *Changing Information Technologies: Research Challenges in the Economics of Information: The Third International Information Research Conference* (pp. 3–17). London: Bowker Saur.

Hirshhorn, R. (2003). *Assessing the impact of copyright reform in the area of technology-enhanced learning.* Ottawa, Canada: Marketplace Framework Policy Branch, Industry Canada. Retrieved January 26, 2009, from strategis.ic.gc.ca/epic/site/ippd-dppi.nsf/vwapj/hirshhorn_final_e.pdf/$FILE/hirshhorn_final_e.pdf

Hirshleifer, J. (1971). The private and social value of information and the reward to inventive activity. *American Economic Review, 61,* 561–574.

Hirshleifer, J. (1973). Where are we in the theory of information? *American Economic Review, 63*(2), 31–39.

Hookham, C. (1994). The need for public sector policies for information availability & pricing. *Association for Geographic Information Conference Proceedings,* 8.2.1–8.2.5.

Industry Canada. (2002). *Supporting culture and innovation: Report on the provisions and operation of the copyright act.* Ottawa, Canada: The author. Retrieved January 26, 2009, from strategis.ic.gc.ca/epic/site/crp-prda.nsf/en/rp00866e.html

Judge, E. F. (2005). Crown copyright and copyright reform in Canada. In M. Geist (Ed.), *In the public interest: The future of Canadian copyright law* (pp. 550–594). Toronto: Irwin Law.

Kahin, B. (2006). Prospects for knowledge policy. In B. Kahin & D. Foray (Eds.), *Advancing knowledge and the knowledge economy* (pp. 1–8). Cambridge, MA: MIT Press.

Kahin, B., & Varian, H. R. (Eds.). (2000). *Internet publishing and beyond: The economics of digital information and intellectual property.* Cambridge, MA: MIT Press.

Kaul, I. (2006). Public goods, a positive analysis. In J.-P. Touffut (Ed.), *Advancing public goods: Papers from 6th Conference of the Cournot Centre for Economic Studies (Paris, 2003)* (pp. 13–39). Cheltenham, UK: Edward Elgar.

King, D., & McDonald, D. D. (1980). *Federal and non-federal relationships in providing scientific and technical information: Policies, arrangements, flow of funds and user charges.* Rockville, MD: King Research, Inc.

Kingma, B. R. (1996). *The economics of information: A guide to economic and cost-benefit analysis for information professionals.* Englewood, CO: Libraries Unlimited.

Kingma, B. R. (2001). *The economics of information: A guide to economic and cost-benefit analysis for information professionals* (2nd ed.). Englewood, CO: Libraries Unlimited.

Kinokuni, H. (2003). Copy-protection policies and profitability. *Information Economics and Policy, 15*(4), 521–536.

Koenig, M. (1990). Information services and downstream productivity. *Annual Review of Information Science and Technology, 25,* 55–86.

Kranich, N., & Schement, J. R. (2008). Information commons. *Annual Review of Information Science and Technology, 42*, 547–591.

Lamberton, D. M. (1984a). The economics of information and organization. *Annual Review of Information Science and Technology, 19*, 3–30.

Lamberton, D. M. (1984b). The emergence of information economics. In M. Jussawalla & H. Benfield (Eds.), *Communication and information economics: New perspectives* (pp. 7–22). New York: North Holland.

Lamberton, D. M. (1994a). Information and organization: Questions and clues. In M. Feeney & M. Grieves (Eds.), *Changing information technologies: Research challenges in the economics of information: The Third International Information Research Conference* (pp. 293–302). London: Bowker Saur.

Lamberton, D. M. (1994b). The information economy revisited. In R. E. Babe (Ed.), *Information and communication in economics* (pp. 1–33). Boston: Kluwer.

Lamberton, D. M. (1998). Information economics research: Points of departure. *Information Economics and Policy, 10*(3), 325–330.

Landes, W. M., & Posner, R. A. (1989). An economic analysis of copyright law. *Journal of Legal Studies, 18*, 325–363.

Lee, D. R. (1977). Discrimination and efficiency in the pricing of public goods. *Journals of Law and Economics, 20*(2), 403–420.

Lee, D. R. (1982). On the pricing of public goods. *Southern Economic Journal, 49*(1), 99–105.

Lee, D. R. (1991). The political economy of user charges: Some bureaucratic implications. In R. E. Wagner (Ed.), *Charging for government: User charges and earmarked taxes in principle and practice* (pp. 60–74). London: Routledge.

Lerner, J., & Tirole, J. (2006). The economics of technology sharing: Open source and beyond. In B. Kahin & D. Foray (Eds.), *Advancing knowledge and the knowledge economy* (pp. 169–189). Cambridge, MA: MIT Press.

Liebowitz, S. J. (1985). Copying and indirect appropriability: Photocopying of journals. *Journal of Political Economy, 93*(5), 945–957.

Machlup, F. (1962). *The production and distribution of knowledge in the United States*. Princeton, NJ: Princeton University Press.

Machlup, F. (1979). Uses, value and benefits of knowledge. *Knowledge: Creation, Diffusion, Utilization, 1*(1), 62–81.

Machlup, F. (1980). *Knowledge: Its creation, distribution, and economic significance.* Vol. 1: *Knowledge and knowledge production*. Princeton, NJ: Princeton University Press.

Machlup, F. (1982). *Knowledge: Its creation, distribution, and economic significance.* Vol. II: *The branches of learning*. Princeton, NJ: Princeton University Press.

Machlup, F. (1983). Semantic quirks in studies of information. In F. Machlup & U. Mansfield (Eds.), *The study of information: Interdisciplinary messages* (pp. 641–671). New York: Wiley.

Mandeville, T. (1999). Codified knowledge and information. In S. Macdonald & J. Nightingale (Eds.), *Information and organization: A tribute to the work of Don Lamberton* (pp. 157–166). Amsterdam, The Netherlands: Elsevier.

Marschak, J. (1974a). Economics of information systems. *Economic information, decision and prediction: Selected essays* (Vol. II, pp. 270–341). Boston: Reidel.

Marschak, J. (1974b). Economics of inquiring, communicating, deciding. *Economic information, decision and prediction: Selected essays* (Vol. II, pp. 250–269). Boston: Reidel.

Marschak, J. (1974c). Remarks on the economics of information. *Economic information, decision and prediction: Selected essays* (Vol. II, pp. 91–117). Boston: Reidel.

Maurer, S. M. (2001, May). *Between two worlds: Database protection in the US and Europe*. Prepared for Industry Canada's Conference on Intellectual Property and Innovation in the Knowledge Based Economy. Retrieved January 26, 2009, from strategis.ic.gc.ca/epic/internet/inippd-dppi.nsf/vwapj/13-EN2%20Maurer.pdf/$file/13-EN2%20Maurer.pdf

McKenzie, R. B. (1979). The economist's paradigm. *Library Trends, 28*, 1–24.

Meijers, H. (2005). Adoption and diffusion of e-business and the role of network effects. In L. Soete & B. ter Weel (Eds.), *The economics of the digital society* (pp. 64–88). Cheltenham, UK: Edward Elgar.

Menou, M. (1994). The impact of information on development: Results of a preliminary investigation. In M. Feeney & M. Grieves (Eds.), *Changing information technologies: Research challenges in the economics of information: The Third International Information Research Conference* (pp. 123–155). London: Bowker Saur.

Newbery, D., Bently, L., & Pollock, R. (2008). *Models of public sector information provision via trading funds* (Report commissioned by Department of Business Enterprise and Regulatory Reform and H. M. Treasury). London: The Department. Retrieved January 26, 2009, from www.berr.gov.uk/files/file45136.pdf

Nilsen, K. (2001). *The impact of information policy: Measuring the effects of the commercialization of Canadian government statistics*. Westport, CT: Ablex.

Nilsen, K. (2007). *Economic theory as it applies to Statistics Canada: A review of the literature*. Toronto, Canada. Retrieved January 26, 2009, from www.chass.utoronto.ca/datalib/misc/Nilsen%20Economics%20Paper%202007%20final%20version.pdf

Niskanen, W. A. (1971). *Bureaucracy and representative government*. Chicago: Aldine, Atherton.

Noll, R. G. (1993). The economics of information: A user's guide. In *The knowledge economy: The nature of information in the 21st century: Fifth annual review of the Institute for Information Studies* (pp. 25–52). Nashville, TN: The Institute.

Organisation for Economic Co-operation and Development. (1998). *User charging for government services: Best practice guidelines and case studies*. Paris: The Organisation.

Organisation for Economic Co-operation and Development. Directorate for Science, Technology and Industry. Committee for Information, Computer and Communications Policy. (2008a). *Seoul declaration for the future of the Internet economy*. Retrieved January 28, 2009, from www.oecd.org/dataoecd/49/28/40839436.pdf

Organisation for Economic Co-operation and Development. Directorate for Science, Technology and Industry. Committee for Information, Computer and Communications Policy. (2008b). *Shaping policies for the future of the Internet economy: Annexes*. Retrieved January 28, 2009, from www.oecd.org/dataoecd/1/28/40821729.pdf

Organisation for Economic Co-operation and Development. Directorate for Science, Technology and Industry. Working Party on the Information Economy. (2006). *Digital broadband content: Public sector information and content*. Paris: The Organisation. Retrieved January 26, 2009, from www.oecd.org/dataoecd/10/22/36481524.pdf

Parker, I. (1994). Commodities as sign systems. In R. E. Babe (Ed.), *Information and communication in economics* (pp. 69–91). Boston: Kluwer.

Pas, J., & De Vuyst, B. (2004). Re-establishing the balance between the public and private sector: Regulating public sector information commercialization in Europe. *Journal of Information Law and Technology, 2*. Retrieved January 26, 2009, from www2.warwick.ac.uk/fac/soc/law/elj/jilt/2004_2/pasanddevuyst

Porat, M. U. (1977). *The information economy.* 8 vols. Washington, DC: Office of Telecommunications, Department of Commerce.

Raban, D. (2003). A primer in information economics. *Searcher, 11*(2), 54–58.

Repo, A. J. (1987). Economics of information. *Annual Review of Information Science and Technology, 22,* 3–25.

Samuelson, P. A. (1954). The pure theory of public expenditure. *Review of Economics and Statistics, 36*(4), 387–389.

Samuelson, P. A. (1957). Pitfalls in the analysis of public goods. *Journal of Law and Economics, 19,* 199–204.

Sanders, A. K. (2006). Limits to database protection: Fair use and scientific research exceptions. *Research Policy, 25,* 854–874.

Sandler, T. (2001). *Economic concepts for the social sciences.* Cambridge, UK: Cambridge University Press.

Sawhney, H., & Jayakar, K. (2007). Universal access. *Annual Review of Information Science and Technology, 41,* 159–221.

Shapiro, C., & Varian, H. R. (1999). *Information rules: A strategic guide to the network economy.* Boston: Harvard Business School Press.

Simon, H. A. (1991). Organization and markets. *Journal of Economic Perspectives, 5*(2), 25–44.

Spence, A. M. (1974). An economist's view of information. *Annual Review of Information Science and Technology, 9,* 57–78.

Starr, P., & Corson, R. (1987). Who will have the numbers? The rise of the statistical services industry and the politics of public data. In W. Alonso & P. Starr (Eds.), *The politics of numbers* (pp. 413–447). New York: Russell Sage.

Stigler, G. J. (1961). The economics of information. *Journal of Political Economy, 69*(3), 213–225.

Stiglitz, J. E. (1985). Information and economic analysis: A perspective. *Economic Journal, 95,* (Supplement: Conference Papers), 21–41.

Stiglitz, J. E. (1994). *Whither socialism?* Cambridge, MA: MIT Press.

Stiglitz, J. E. (1999). *Knowledge as a global public good.* Washington, DC: World Bank. Retrieved January 26, 2009, from www.worldbank.org/knowledge/chiefecon/articles/undpk2/index.htm

Stiglitz, J. E. (2000a). The contributions of the economics of information to twentieth century economics. *Quarterly Journal of Economics, 115*(4), 1441–1478.

Stiglitz, J. E. (2000b). *Economics of the public sector* (3rd ed.). New York: W. W. Norton.

Stiglitz, J. E. (2003). Information and the change in the paradigm in economics. In R. Arnott, B. Greenwald, R. Kanbur, & B. Nalebuff (Eds.), *Economics for an imperfect world: Essays in honor of Joseph E. Stiglitz* (pp. 569–639). Cambridge MA: MIT Press.

Stiglitz, J. E. (2006). Global public goods and global finance: Does global governance ensure that the global public interest is served? In J.-P. Touffut (Ed.), *Advancing public goods: Papers from 6th Conference of the Cournot Centre for Economic Studies (Paris, 2003)* (pp. 149–164). Cheltenham, UK: Edward Elgar.

Stiglitz, J. E., Orszag, P. R., & Orszag, J. M. ( 2000). *The role of government in a digital age.* Washington, DC: Computer and Communications Industry Association. Retrieved January 26, 2009, from archive. epinet.org/real_media/010111/materials/stiglitz.pdf

Sveiby, K. E. (1997). *The new organizational wealth: Managing and measuring knowledge-based assets.* San Francisco: Berrett-Koehler.

Sy, K., & Robbin, A. (1990). Federal statistical policies and programs: How good are the numbers? *Annual Review of Information Science and Technology, 25*, 3–54.

Taylor, R. S. (1980). Information and productivity: Definition and relationship. *Proceedings of the Annual Meeting of the American Society for Information Science*, 236–238.

Taylor, R. S. (1982). Information and productivity: Defining information output. *Social Science Information Studies, 2*(5), 131–138.

Trosow, S. E. (2005). *Sui generis* database legislation: A critical analysis. *Yale Journal of Law and Technology*, 534–642. Retrieved January 26, 2009, from www.yjolt.org/files/trosow-7-YJOLT-534.pdf

UK. Advisory Panel on Crown Copyright. (2004, March). *First Annual Seminar: The Economics of Public Sector Information*. London: HMSO. Retrieved January 26, 2009, from www.appsi.gov.uk/minutes/2004-03-18.pdf

UK. Advisory Panel on Public Sector Information. (2004–2007). *Annual report*. Richmond, UK: The Panel. Retrieved January 26, 2009, from www.appsi.gov.uk/archive/index.htm

UK. Advisory Panel on Public Sector Information. (2006). *Taking Public Sector Information Seriously: Minutes of the 3rd Annual Seminar*. Oxford Internet Institute. Richmond, UK: The Panel. Retrieved January 26, 2009, from www.appsi.gov.uk/minutes/2006-03-16.pdf

UK. Cabinet Office. (1998). *Crown copyright in the information age* [Green Paper]. London: Stationery Office. Retrieved January 26, 2009, from www.opsi.gov.uk/advice/crown-copyright/crown-copyright-in-the-information-age.pdf

UK. Cabinet Office. (1999). *Future management of crown copyright*. [White Paper]. London: Stationery Office. Retrieved January 26, 2009, from www.opsi.gov.uk/advice/crown-copyright/future-management-of-crown-copyright.pdf

UK. Department of Trade and Industry. (1990). *Government held tradable information: Guidelines for government departments in dealing with the private sector*. London: The Department.

UK. H. M. Treasury. (2000a). Background paper on licensing: Appendix E of the economics of government information. In *Cross-cutting review of the knowledge economy*. London: H.M. Treasury. Retrieved January 26, 2009, from www.hm-treasury.gov.uk/spend_sr00_ad_ccrappe.htm

UK. H. M. Treasury. (2000b). Economic paper: How can the government improve the dissemination of its resources? Appendix C of the economics of government information. In *Cross-cutting review of the knowledge economy*. London: H. M. Treasury. Retrieved January 26, 2009, from www.hm-treasury.gov.uk/spend_sr00_ad_ccrpart5.htm

UK. H. M. Treasury. (2000c). The economics of government information: Part 5: Review of government information. In *Cross-cutting review of the knowledge economy*. London: H. M. Treasury. Retrieved January 26, 2009, from www.hm-treasury.gov.uk/spend_sr00_ad_ccrpart5.htm

UK. H. M. Treasury. (2000d). Review of government information: Final report. In *Cross-cutting review of the knowledge economy*. London: H. M. Treasury. Retrieved January 26, 2009, from www.hm-treasury.gov.uk/spend_sr00_ccr.htm

UK. H. M. Treasury. (2002). *Selling into wider markets: A policy note for public bodies*. London: H. M. Treasury. Retrieved January 26, 2009, from www.hm-treasury.gov.uk/d/New_WM_Guidance.pdf

UK. Office of Fair Trading. (2006). *The commercial use of public information*. London: The Office. Retrieved January 26, 2009, from www.oft.gov.uk/shared_oft/reports/consumer_protection/oft861.pdf

UK. Statutory Instruments. (2005). *Re-use of public sector information regulations*. London: The Stationary Office. Retrieved January 26, 2009, from www.opsi.gov.uk/si/si2005/20051515

US. Office of Management and Budget. (2003). *Management of federal information resources* (Circular A-130. Revised). Washington, DC: The Office. Retrieved January 26, 2009, from www.white house.gov/omb/circulars/a130/a130trans4.html

van Eechoud, M., & van der Waal, B. (2008). *Creative commons licensing for public sector information.* Amsterdam: Institute for Information Law, University of Amsterdam. Retrieved January 28, 2009, from learn.creativecommons.org/wp-content/uploads/2008/03/cc_publicsectorinformation_report_ v3.pdf

van Zon, A., & Muyksen, J. (2005). The impact of ICT investment on knowledge accumulation and economic growth. In L. Soete & B. ter Weel (Eds.), *The economics of the digital society* (pp. 305–329). Cheltenham, UK: Edward Elgar.

Varian, H. R. (2000a). Market structure in the network age. In E. Brynjolfsson & B. Kahin (Eds.), *Understanding the digital economy: Data, tools and research* (pp. 137–150). Cambridge, MA: MIT Press.

Varian, H. R. (2000b). Versioning information goods. In B. Kahin & H. R. Varian (Eds.), *Internet publishing and beyond: The economics of digital information and intellectual property* (pp. 190–202). Cambridge, MA: MIT Press.

Varian, H. R. (2005). *Copying and copyright.* Berkeley: University of California. Retrieved January 26, 2009, from www.ischool.berkeley.edu/~hal/Papers/2004/copying-and-copyright.pdf

Varian, H. R., Farrell, J., & Shapiro, C. (2004). *The economics of information technology: An introduction.* New York: Cambridge University Press.

Vaver, D. (1995). *Copyright and the state in Canada and the United States.* Montreal, Canada: Centre de recherche en droit public, Faculté de droit, Université de Montréal. Retrieved January 26, 2009, from www.lexum.umontreal.ca/conf/dac/en/vaver/vaver.html

Wagner, R. E. (1991). *Charging for government: User charges and earmarked taxes in principle and practice.* London: Routledge.

Webber, S. A. E. (1998). Pricing and marketing online information services. *Annual Review of Information Science and Technology, 33,* 39–83.

Weiss, P. (2002). *Borders in cyberspace: Conflicting public sector information policies and their economic impact: Summary report.* Washington, DC: National Weather Service, Department of Commerce. Retrieved January 26, 2009, from www.nws.noaa.gov/iao/pdf/Borders%20report% 202.pdf

Weiss, P. (2003). Conflicting international public sector information policies and their effects on the public domain and the economy. In J. M. Esanu & P. F. Uhlir (Eds.), *Role of scientific and technical data and information in the public domain* (pp. 129–132). Washington, DC: National Academies Press. Retrieved January 26, 2009, from www.nap.edu/openbook.php?record_id=10785&page=129

Weiss, P. (2004a). Borders in cyberspace: Conflicting government information policies and their economic impacts. In J. M. Esanu & P. F. Uhlir (Eds.), *Open access and the public domain in digital data and information for science* (pp. 69–73). Washington, DC: National Academies Press. Retrieved January 26, 2009, from www.nap.edu/openbook.php?record_id=11030&page=69

Weiss, P. (2004b). Borders in cyberspace: Conflicting public sector information policies and their economic impacts. In G. Aichholzer & H. Burkert (Eds.), *Public sector information in the digital age: Between markets, public management and citizens' rights* (pp. 137–159). Cheltenham, UK: Edward Elgar.

Weiss, P., & Backlund, P. (1997). International information policy and conflict: Open and unrestricted access versus government commercialization. In B. Kahin & C. Nesson (Eds.), *Borders in cyberspace: Information policy and the global information infrastructure* (pp. 300–321). Cambridge, MA: MIT Press.

Yandle, B. (1991). User charges, rent seeking, and public choice. In R. E. Wagner (Ed.), *Charging for government: User charges and earmarked taxes in principle and practice* (pp. 34–59). London: Routledge.

Yates-Mercer, P., & Bawden, D. (2002). Managing the paradox: The valuation of knowledge and knowledge management. *Journal of Information Science, 28*(1), 19–29.

Yuan, M. Y. (2005). Does decrease in copying cost support copyright term extension? *Information Economics and Policy, 17*, 471–494.

# Practice

# CHAPTER 11

# Information Practices of Immigrants

*Nadia Caidi*
*Danielle Allard*
*Lisa Quirke*
*University of Toronto, Canada*

## Introduction

International migrants are defined as people living outside their country of birth (International Organization for Migration, n.d.). International migration is one of the most vital global issues of our century; according to the International Organization for Migration (n.d.), more people are moving across international borders than ever before and close to 200 million people currently live outside their country of birth. This figure represents approximately three percent of the world's population, meaning that one in every thirty-five persons in the world is a migrant. The number of international migrants increased by 45 million between 1965 and 1990; it is currently growing at an annual rate of 2.9 percent (International Organization for Migration, n.d.). There are many reasons people migrate from one country to another. If well managed, migration can be beneficial for both individuals and societies. Yet, migration remains a complex issue that affects the economic and social fabric of many countries.

This chapter examines the roles that information resources, institutions, and technologies play in the everyday lives of international migrants. With millions of people migrating to another country and needing to settle and "integrate" in the host society, there are significant opportunities and challenges for the information professions in terms of understanding how immigrants seek information, what their needs are, what practices they have adopted and adapted, and the potential barriers they encounter along the way.

Because of the complexity of the immigration experience, we specifically address immigrant information needs and uses in the context of everyday life—with an eye toward information and information practices that help migrants in their settlement and inclusion into the new country. Research within library and information science (LIS) points to the importance that identifying information needs and barriers has on individual lives. When information about settlement services, housing, employment opportunities, health, or education is not easily available to newcomers, navigation through the information environment is daunting. Because immigrants often lack the basic information, as well as social, civic, and economic

493

capital to function fully in their new country, theirs is more often a matter of survival than full participation and inclusion (Omidvar & Richmond, 2003).

In this chapter we focus primarily on the experiences of immigrants in the United States and Canada, largely because this is primarily what appears in LIS literature. The scope of this research is large; our synthesis is therefore limited to studies that examine how the lived experiences of immigrants have an impact on their information behaviors (needs, sources, uses, and barriers). A scan of the LIS literature containing the terms immigrant, immigration, multicultural, or multilingual reveals thousands of articles. Most of this literature is beyond the scope of this review. For example, we do not address research in the following areas: multiculturalism in LIS schools or among library staff (Abdullahi, 2007; Alexander, 2008; Allard, Mehra, & Qayyym, 2007; Greiner, 2008; Hall-Ellis, 2007); specific service provision to immigrants at public libraries (Berry, 2007; Bober, 2008; Hammond-Todd, 2008; Winkel, 2007); multilingual service provision to international students in academic libraries (Zhuo, Emanuel, & Jiao, 2007); representations of multiculturalism in various media such as children's books (Bowen, 2007; Bradford & Huang, 2007); the merits or demerits of diversity, multiculturalism, or multilingual services in libraries (Cooper, 2008; Neely & Peterson, 2007); and technical systems issues such as multilingual searching or retrieval, interface design, or subject headings (Alpert, 2006; Beall, 2006; Bjorner, 2008; Booth, 2006; Daumke, Marku, Poprat, Schulz & Klar, 2007; Notess, 2008; Ravid, Bar-Ilan, Baruchson-Arbib, & Rafaeli, 2007). Exceptions are made to the extent that articles within any of these bodies of literature specifically address how immigrants, themselves, seek or use information in the contexts of their daily lives.

The studies in this review are, for the most part, academic or research-based. This stands in contrast to the fact that most of the literature within LIS on the topic of immigration is practitioner-based and focuses on the practicalities and debates that surround the provision of public library services to immigrants. The practitioner-based literature is often descriptive and does not always reveal a great deal about the day-to-day information practices of immigrants. However, the perspective of individuals serving and working with immigrants is invaluable. Wherever possible, we make use of this literature to complement the more research-oriented literature in the field that addresses how information fits within the lived experiences of immigrants.

The scope of this review is multidisciplinary and extends beyond the LIS domain. Within the immigration literature more generally, a great deal has been written that is relevant to this topic. Information practices are often not identified as such and are subsumed under other immigrant activities such as settlement or media consumption. Where relevant, we also examine research from communication and media studies, immigrant and refugee studies, cultural studies, and sociology.

The chapter is divided into three sections: the first defines key terms (i.e., what is an immigrant?) and issues vital to the study and understanding of immigration. In the second, we examine what is known about the information practices of immigrants, surveying the LIS literature as well as exploring literature in related fields that shed light on immigrants and their lived experiences. Finally, we propose a research agenda for future work in this area and outline gaps in the literature.

# The Immigrant Experience

International migration involves the movement of millions of people annually. This process, whether prompted by economic, political, or environmental concerns, has vast implications for both sending and receiving nations. Although this chapter focuses on the experiences, needs, and uses of information by immigrants, it is important to define a few key terms and issues essential to an understanding of immigration: (1) immigration policies, (2) the context of immigrant reception in the host society, (3) the heterogeneity of immigrants, and (4) the challenges of defining and studying the processes of immigrant settlement and integration.

## Who Is an Immigrant?

Immigrants are people who migrate "from one country to another on a permanent basis" (Li, 2003, p. 1). As such, immigrants are a subset of the hundreds of millions of individuals currently living outside their country of birth or citizenship. International migrants include anyone living outside their country of citizenship but the condition of permanence in the term immigrant excludes those living abroad temporarily, such as visitors, migrant workers, and international students. It should be noted that we have included several studies of temporary migrant groups, including migrant workers and international students, in this review. In addition to comprising a large portion of the literature, these groups have many commonalities with other immigrants and therefore their inclusion contributes to our overall understanding of the everyday life contexts of immigrants.

Refugees are a part of the immigrant population but differ in many ways from other immigrants as their migration is involuntary. Refugees are defined as international migrants who have been found to have a justified fear of persecution that makes them unwilling or unable to return to their country of origin (Castles & Miller, 1998). Unlike most immigrants, refugees may have experienced trauma, imprisonment, persecution, or lengthy residence in a refugee camp prior to resettlement. These experiences may provide additional challenges in their lives following migration and may result in unique information needs and uses. The criteria, procedures, and policies determining immigrant or refugee status vary among nations.

## Immigration Policies

Immigration policy is the "crucial element determining immigration patterns" (Meyers, 2004, p. 3). Although immigration policy has a significant impact on the settlement and integration of immigrants, no LIS research to date has examined how immigration policy affects the everyday life information seeking or information practices of immigrants.

In order to cope with vast numbers of potential immigrants, nations such as the United States and Canada have instituted policies designed to control the number as well as the qualifications and characteristics of immigrants permitted to settle permanently. A wide range of factors influences the formation of immigration policy by nations; these are too numerous to be discussed here in great detail. Examples include: economic concerns, birth rates, international political allegiances, humanitarian issues, and colonial histories. Falling birth rates and labor market shortages may prompt a country to increase the number of immigrants admitted annually; political and historical ties to other nations, as well as commitments to humanitarian initiatives in different regions, are factors that may determine the source countries from which immigrants are admitted. For a more complete discussion of the determinants of migration policy, see Meyers (2004) or Cornelius and Tsuda (2004).

Canadian immigration policy distinguishes three categories of immigrants eligible for admission: the family class, the economic class, and the refugee class. The family class includes close family members of Canadian citizens or permanent residents, such as spouses, children, parents, and common-law partners; the economic class includes skilled workers or investors selected on the basis of educational criteria or financial capacity to invest (Li, 2003). The refugee class includes individuals and families admitted on humanitarian grounds. Immigrants in the economic class are selected using a system that awards points based on criteria such as education, language ability, work experience, and age; this system is not applied to family class immigrants or to refugees (Li, 2003). Almost 55 percent of immigrants who entered Canada in 2007 belonged to the economic class; 28 percent were family class, and 12 percent were refugees (Citizenship and Immigration Canada, 2008) (see Table 11.1). These figures demonstrate the priority given to economic factors in determining Canada's immigration policy.

U.S. immigration policy shares common characteristics with the Canadian system. Family sponsorships comprise the vast majority (66 percent) of immigrants to the U.S. annually; economic immigrants, refugees, and diversity immigrants make up 15 percent, 13 percent, and 6 percent of the total, respectively (Jefferys & Monger, 2008) (see Table 11.1). As in Canada, methods of selection applied to economic migrants in the U.S. do not apply to family members or refugees (Meyers, 2004). Not all immigrants to the United States enter the country as immigrants, however; more than half arrive on non-permanent visas, such as the H-1B visa for skilled temporary foreign workers, and adjust their status at a later date while residing in the U.S. (Martin, 2004).

It should be noted that a tightening of restrictions has taken place since the 1980s, leading to a reduction in the number of refugees admitted to countries such as the U.S. and Canada, as well as many European nations (U.N. Department of Economic and Social Affairs, 2002). Only a small proportion of asylum seekers, people whose application for refugee status has yet to be approved, are eventually accepted as refugees (U.N. Department of Economic and Social Affairs, 2002).

Although immigration policy determines who can be considered an immigrant, individual nations cannot always fully control who migrates. This becomes evident when one examines the nature and scale of illegal or irregular migration. Undocumented migrants, also referred to as non-status, are those who either enter a country without permission to stay or enter legally but overstay their permits. The Department of Homeland Security estimates that, in 2007, 11.8 million undocumented migrants were living in the U.S., with an annual average increase of almost 500,000 people (Hoefer, Rytina, & Baker, 2008). Although the Canadian government does not publish estimates of the number of undocumented migrants currently living in Canada, an advocacy group places the figure at between 200,000 and 500,000 (No One is Illegal Vancouver, n.d.). Due to the paucity of

**Table 11.1   Annual immigrant admission by category (data from Citizenship and Immigration Canada, 2008; Jefferys & Monger, 2008)**

| Country (most recent year available) | Canada (2007) | United States (2007) |
|---|---|---|
| Approximate number of immigrants (annually) | 240,000 | 1,050,000 |
| Family class | 28% | 66% |
| Economic or employment | 55% | 15% |
| Refugees | 12% | 13% |
| Other (e.g., diversity immigrants in U.S.) (Martin, 2004) | 5% | 6% |

research on undocumented migrants, their information uses and needs are not discussed in this chapter.

## Context of Reception

Although immigration is a global phenomenon, it is also one that is greatly influenced by local contexts. Various country-specific structural factors influence the lives of immigrants and refugees before and upon arrival, including immigration policies (as has been noted), economic and labor market issues, public perception of and attitudes toward immigrants and refugees, and the degree of assistance provided by the government or other agencies to support resettlement.

Both the micro and macro aspects of the immigration experience can greatly affect the context of reception for immigrants and refugees and have important implications for the process of adjustment, settlement, and integration. These aspects, in turn, may significantly influence the informational needs and information-seeking behaviors of immigrants and refugees, as well as the nature of social networks and other resources at their disposal.

The institutional realities of the host country can shape the experiences of immigrants in a variety of ways, for instance, by offering support in settlement and citizenship acquisition (Bloemraad, 2006) or by permitting or restricting the sponsorship of family members by immigrants. Nations encourage immigrants to become citizens through various policies. In its most basic sense, citizenship is the possession of full membership in a community and articulates the relationship between the individual and the state (Joppke, 2007). In Canada, immigrants are understood by government as potential citizens and are encouraged to participate in civic life and become involved in their new communities through a number of programs and initiatives (Bloemraad, 2006). Resources such as information services, settlement services, support through ethnocultural community agencies, and language courses are made available to newcomers in Canada at no cost; these are funded by the federal government. In the U.S., the federal government does not provide immigrants with resources to acquire citizenship, a process that is left up to the individual newcomer (Bloemraad, 2006). Many nations are now actively encouraging not only immigrant citizenship but also permitting dual citizenship.

In some cases, financial assistance, housing, orientation programs, and other forms of support are provided by the government specifically for refugees following their arrival in the host country (Citizenship and Immigration Canada, 2005; U.S. Department of Health and Human Services, Administration for Children and Families, 2008).

## Heterogeneity of Immigrants

Relatively little is known about how immigrant communities locate and access information in forms that are understandable and usable to them. Little is known also about their attitudes toward awareness of and skills in utilizing various information institutions and related technologies. This situation is due in large extent to the heterogeneous nature of immigrants as a user group.

Immigrants and refugees are extremely diverse groups whose needs, experiences, and strengths vary significantly depending on various factors, including: education, age, sex, country of origin, family status, and their knowledge of English or the dominant language in their new country. Immigrants also arrive under a variety of immigration classes, have diverse backgrounds, and may or may not be familiar with the receiving country's institutions and values. For example, skilled workers or business class immigrants may have differing information needs and practices than sponsored family members or refugees.

## Challenges in the Field of Immigration Research

Some challenges to the study of immigration and the information practices of immigrants relate to the difficulty in defining key concepts such as "integration," "inclusion/exclusion," or settlement"; others relate to methodological issues having to do with conducting research on such a diverse and heterogeneous study population.

### Defining Concepts

Integration is a concept that is extremely difficult to define; its meaning depends greatly on the context of immigrant reception in each society and can change over time. Anthropologists define a related concept, acculturation, as the adoption of the norms, values, and behaviors of one group by another (Berry, 1997). Psychologists explore acculturation at the individual level by examining factors that influence the series of decisions made by individual immigrants in giving up or retaining different aspects of their culture of origin (Berry, 1997). In sociology, integration has been considered a one-way process of assimilation, in which the immigrant gives up his or her culture in favor of adopting that of the host society (Park & Burgess, 1921) or a two-way exchange through which both the immigrant and the institutions of the host society adapt as a result of their exposure to one another (Gordon, 1964). Alternate models of immigrant adaptation in psychology have called into question the linear nature of assimilation. The concept of biculturalism, for instance, proposes that immigrants may assume cultural characteristics of the host society while maintaining their culture of origin (LaFromboise, Coleman, & Gerton, 1993). Immigration researchers have not reached consensus and debates over the nature of immigrant adjustment are ongoing. It is evident, therefore, that a variety of challenges exist for LIS researchers attempting to both define this process and understand how it affects the everyday lives of immigrants and their information practices. For a more complete discussion of models of immigrant assimilation and integration and their evolution over time, see Gordon (1964) or Alba and Nee (2003).

Social inclusion is another concept that frames the experiences of immigrants and their reception in the host society. Primarily found in policy documents and research in Europe and more recently in Canada, the concept of social inclusion originated in Europe in the 1970s. Social inclusion is a multi-dimensional concept with economic, cultural, social, and political dimensions. It emphasizes the multiple interconnected ways exclusion occurs (i.e., on many levels and as a result of multiple inequalities and social, economic, and civic barriers). As used today in Canada, social inclusion is a tool for promoting social justice and inclusion for marginalized members of Canadian society (Frazee, 2003; Luxton, 2002; Mitchell & Shillington, 2002; Omidvar & Richmond, 2003). It argues that individuals have a voice into *what* they are and supports the rights of individuals to make meaningful decisions about themselves and their communities.

For immigrants and refugees, social inclusion refers to the realization of their "full and equal participation in the economic, social, cultural, and political dimensions of life" (Omidvar & Richmond, 2003, p. 1). Research examines how immigrants are at risk of exclusion (e.g., Omidvar & Richmond, 2003; Saloojee, 2005). Because immigrants often lack the basic information, as well as social, civic, and economic capital to function fully in their new country, Omidvar and Richmond (2003) argue that theirs is more often a matter of survival than full participation and inclusion. Caidi and Allard (2005) maintain that access to necessary information is also a fundamental component for achieving social inclusion for immigrants. Without adequate information access, immigrants will be unable to make informed choices and decisions. When immigrants do not have readily available information about settlement services, housing, employment opportunities, citizenship, health, or education, navigation through an unfamiliar information environment and inclusion into a new country becomes a difficult and frustrating process.

In addition to the concepts of integration and social inclusion, transnationalism is another useful framework that shapes the information practices and needs of immigrants. Transnationalism, a concept that emerged out of anthropology in the early 1990s, is defined as "the processes by which immigrants forge and sustain multi-stranded social relations that link together their societies of origin and settlement, and through which they create transnational social fields that cross national borders" (Basch, Glick Schiller, & Szanton Blanc, 1994, p. 6). It posits that immigrants do not enter a host nation and sever all links with their country of origin, being absorbed seamlessly into their new culture (as suggested by some theories of assimilation described previously). Instead, many immigrants retain ties with their home countries through "social, cultural, economic, and political linkages" (Faist, 2000, p. 210).

Indeed, many new immigrants maintain ongoing and sustained contact with their home nations in a variety of ways, including remaining politically active in their country of origin (Guarnizo, Portes, & Haller, 2003; Sampredo, 1998), sending remittances back to family members, and remaining in close and frequent contact with family and friends. Transnational processes have been enabled in our present historical context through the abundance of new technologies, such as the Internet, inexpensive telephone calls and airfares, and international financial institutions (Kelly, 2003). Of relevance to LIS, information seeking and exchange is a common transnational activity (Faist, 2000) occurring among immigrant social networks and via various technologies and media.

The term *immigrant settlement* represents another concept central to the study of immigration and the informational needs of newcomers. Settlement is the process by which immigrants adjust to their new homeland; it involves the search for housing, employment, schools for their children, healthcare, and the acquisition or improvement of English language skills. Although this term is used to refer to the short-term and practical experiences of immigrants (as opposed to integration, which refers to cultural and behavioral adaptation that could take a lifetime or multiple generations to achieve), there are aspects of the concept of settlement that have not yet been clearly defined.

It has been argued that adapting to life in a new country is best understood as a process, or a continuum, with various stages associated with specific needs and attitudes toward resources, institutions, and technologies. Mwarigha (2002) notes three overlapping stages in the settlement process of newcomers. In the first, needs include pressing matters such as food, shelter, orientation to a new city, language interpretation, and language instruction. In the intermediate stage, newcomers' needs include access to various local systems and institutions, such as municipal services, legal services, long-term housing, health services, and employment-specific language instruction. Lastly, immigrants "strive to become equal participants in the country's economic, cultural, social and political life" (Mwarigha, 2002, p. 9). At this stage immigrant needs are more diverse and individual in nature. Learning how to overcome systemic barriers to equal participation can be viewed as a common process for many immigrants at this stage. As they become accustomed to their adopted country, find their place in society, and actively contribute economically and socially to their communities, immigrants may experience, for example, the need to belong more fully and to become an active citizen through political participation, civic engagement, and cultural celebrations (Papillon, 2002).

Attempts to create a model of settlement, however, raise questions as to the linear nature of settlement and the concept's temporal limits. For instance, the search for employment could be considered a short- or long-term settlement need, as immigrants may find initial employment upon arrival but may spend years searching for, or even be ultimately unsuccessful in finding, employment suitable to their qualifications.

The ambiguity of immigrant settlement and integration as temporal processes can be seen in the lack of consistent or well-defined terminology with which to refer to and distinguish among groups of recently arrived or longer-settled immigrants.

The terms "newcomer" or "recent immigrant" are used without definition in policy documents; academics appear to take a longer view and often differentiate among groups based on generational status.

In academic studies of immigrant integration, authors refer to those who were born abroad as the first generation and their children born in the new homeland as the second generation. Studies of this nature attempt to identify differences between generational groups in terms of their educational status, income, employment levels, language ability, and other characteristics. This is done in order to trace the effects of immigration on different groups over time. For more detailed analyses of the experiences of the second generation and the 1.5 generation (a term which refers to youth who immigrated as children) see Zhou (1997), Boyd and Grieco (1998), Boyd (2002), Alba (2005), and Waldinger and Feliciano (2004).

Another challenge in immigration research is the practical difficulty of involving immigrants themselves. This issue is likely the cause of significant gaps in the literature on immigrant populations and recently arrived immigrants in particular. Difficulties in contacting and recruiting recently sarrived immigrants, as well as the costs of translation and interpretation services, pose barriers to researchers hoping to study the process of immigrant settlement and the information practices of immigrants (for examples, see Deri, 2005; Reitmanova & Gustafson, 2008).

It should be clear from this discussion of immigration policy and the challenges of immigration research that the issues facing both LIS researchers and service providers attempting to meet the informational needs of immigrants are complex. Immigrants, as both study populations and user groups, are extremely diverse and, as a result, their information practices and needs vary substantially.

## Information Practices of Immigrants

We now turn our attention to what the literature says about immigrants' everyday lives and the role played by information. We examine in particular the concept of information practices, which encompasses information seeking, information use, and information sharing (Savolainen, 2008).

### Some Key Concepts

For immigrants (particularly newcomers) who may not yet have established patterns or information practices, finding information to navigate everyday life can be a dauntingly complex process. Mehra and Papajohn (2007, p. 12) refer to this as a "culturally alien information environment." Both information needs and barriers to accessing adequate information are significant. During the immigration process individuals need to make sense of the values and patterns in their lives, which are generally in flux. New patterns and networks must be established; all of this has an impact on information practices and the ability to find relevant information. Srinivasan and Pyati (2007) coined the term "diasporic information environment" as a way to capture the complexity of immigrant lives that operate on both local and transnational planes.

The notion of everyday life information seeking (or ELIS) is useful in shedding light on the complexity of immigrants' quotidian information practices. ELIS holds that individuals seek information on a daily basis in complex ways and from a variety of sources in order to manage their lives (Savolainen, 1995, 2007, 2008). In other words, the everyday life context out of which an information need arises contributes significantly to how that need is made sense of and addressed. Personal attributes and societal structures and values shape the way individuals organize, prioritize, and live their lives. Thus ELIS is often habitual, non-rational, and has multiple goals.

A related concept, "information practices" (also referred to as "everyday information practices" as such activities are usually embedded in everyday contexts), is also particularly suited to the study of immigrants. Savolainen (2008, p. 2) defines it as "a set of socially and culturally established ways to identify, seek, use, and share the information available in various sources such as television, newspapers, and the Internet." Savolainen (and others) emphasize in particular the "habitual" nature of these practices, and their occurrence in work as well as non-work-related contexts. Moreover, as McKenzie (2003) notes, information practices captures active information seeking as well as less-directed activities. Active information practices include the recognition of an information need (or gap in one's knowledge about a subject) as well as information seeking (or the attempt to resolve that gap). Less-directed practices include browsing the Internet or gaining unanticipated but useful information from chatting with someone. Information practices capture subtle activities such as recognizing an information need but choosing to ignore it or not recognizing the need for information at all. Information practices also account for the myriad creative ways that individuals attempt to work around barriers that limit their information seeking. Information practices are not strictly strategic but are linked to our understandings of the world and everyday habits. The concepts of "information fields" (Johnson, Case, Andrews, Allard, & Johnson, 2006, p. 570), "information horizons" (Sonnenwald, 1999, p. 176) and "information source horizons" (Savolainen & Kari, 2004, p. 415) all suggest ways in which individuals make sense of, and navigate, their information worlds, along with their preferred information sources.

Information practices are structured along three modes: information seeking, information use, and information sharing (Savolainen, 2008, p. 4). The inclusion of information sharing is particularly useful for our understanding of the relationships among information and communication activities. Indeed, the social and communicative dimensions of information sharing among individuals are manifest through the establishment, maintenance, and extension of social networks; through transnational ties; as part of activities taking place in information grounds; and so on.

Using concepts that imply fluidity between the deliberate and less conscious or unconscious information practices of immigrants emphasizes the fact that immigrants are a population in transition struggling to deal with an unknown information environment. This is reflected in the academic LIS literature addressing the information practices of immigrants (Caidi, Allard, & Dechief, 2008; Caidi & MacDonald, 2008; Chu, 1999; Courtright, 2005; Fisher, Durrance, & Bouch Hinton, 2004; Fisher, Marcoux, Miller, Sanchez, & Ramirez, 2004; Flythe, 2001; Holroyd, Taylor-Piliae, & Twinn, 2003; Jeong, 2004; Liu & Redford, 1997; Mehra & Papajohn, 2007; Metoyer-Duran, 1993; Silvio, 2006; Sligo & Jameson, 2000; Su & Conaway, 1995).

Another useful concept for understanding immigrants' encounters with information is "information poverty" (Chatman, 1996, p. 197): Information seeking may be problematic for vulnerable populations in economic poverty as they also tend to suffer from information poverty. Information poverty is characterized as lacking necessary resources such as adequate social networks and information-finding skills that enable everyday life information seeking. It has been argued that among immigrant groups, new immigrants in particular can be characterized as information poor because they have not had time or opportunities to develop adequate local networks (in terms of both network size and access to resources), and they may not yet know how to navigate their new information environment.

There is, unfortunately, a lack of empirical studies that systematically explore how new immigrants seek and make use of information. The remainder of this section explores these issues: We first review the information needs of immigrants as outlined in the literature; we next explore the state of the research on how immigrants seek and use information (including pathways and sources accessed); then we discuss information sharing and other more expressive activities. We conclude with a discussion of the barriers and challenges to accessing information by this user group.[1]

## *Characterizing the Information Needs of Immigrants*

In his overview of ELIS, Savolainen (1995, 2008) distinguishes between orienting and practical (i.e., problem-specific) information seeking in everyday contexts. Orienting information refers to the daily habits that individuals engage in as a means of monitoring everyday events through various sources, particularly the media. By contrast, the seeking of problem-specific information relates to the solving of individual problems or performing specific tasks (Savolainen, 2008, p. 83). These tend to be more episodic in nature (albeit with a clear starting point), but may present variations in terms of time to completion (i.e., until a solution is found or a problem is solved).

In some cases, however, the two modes are intertwined. For instance, systematic seeking of orienting information may help to solve specific problems. This seems to ring true particularly for immigrants. Indeed, the information needs (or gap in one's knowledge about a particular subject) that immigrants (and especially newcomers) encounter and must resolve are numerous and complex and straddle orienting as well as problem-specific activities. The following examples are selected from studies that examine specific information needs of immigrants (all of which have also been identified as critical by the immigration and settlement literature).

### Orienting Information Seeking

- Monitoring the environment for information about the new culture as well as orientation on "life in the new country" (George & Mwarigha, 1999)

- Information about cultural or religious events (Jeong, 2004; Su & Conoway, 1995)

- Political information and current events (including news about the country of origin) (Caidi & MacDonald, 2008; Fisher, Marcoux, et al., 2004; Silvio, 2006)

- Information about broader societal contexts, including identity issues (Aizlewood & Doody, 2002; Caidi & MacDonald, 2008; Srinivasan & Pyati, 2007).

In the early stages of settlement, newcomers will attempt to establish ways of monitoring everyday events through various information sources. These activities will depend in part on what their habits were in the country of origin (such as reading newspapers daily, watching television or listening to the radio, speaking to one's doctor) or they may be specific to the new circumstances (e.g., they do not own a television yet, they may prefer to listen to radio or read the newspapers to familiarize themselves with the new environment, they may rely on informal support networks for understanding how things work or how to get things done). This process is not well documented in the LIS literature. Empirical and longitudinal studies can shed light on these processes and preferences for some information sources over others (e.g., print vs. online media, human sources, organizational sources) as well as how these preferences evolve over time as the immigrant becomes more established.

What is clear, however, is that barriers to seeking orienting information documented in previous studies also apply to immigrants, namely, struggling with information overload, difficulties in identifying where to gain access to information that is appropriate to their needs (and in this case, in a language that they can understand), and problems related to the credibility of information (Savolainen, 2008, p. 95). In addition, immigrants also face other specific difficulties such as emotional stress and social isolation stemming from being in a new environment, limited support networks, and/or a lack of financial stability.

## Problem-Specific Information Seeking

- Language information (including information about training, translation, and interpretation services) (Fisher, Marcoux, et al., 2004; George, Fong, Da, & Chang, 2004; George & Mwarigha, 1999; George & Tsang, 2000; Su & Conaway, 1995)

- Employment information (including job searching skills and special services to foreign trained professionals) (Chu, 1999; Jensen, 2002; Fisher, Marcoux, et al., 2004; George et al., 2004; George & Mwarigha, 1999; George & Tsang, 2000; Silvio, 2006)

- Information about making connections in the community (including connections to professional associations, volunteering opportunities, mentoring, and community organizations) (Caidi, Allard, Dechief, & Longford, 2008; Dechief, 2006; George et al., 2004)

- Housing information (George et al., 2004; George & Mwarigha, 1999; George & Tsang, 2000; Prock, 2003)

- Health information (Cortinois, 2008; Courtright, 2005; George & Tsang, 2000; Jensen, 2002; Prock, 2003; Silvio, 2006; Su & Conaway, 1995)

- Information about workplace safety (Jensen, 2002; Prock, 2003)

- Legal information (Chu, 1999; Jensen, 2002; Prock, 2003; Fisher, Marcoux, et al., 2004)

- Education-related information (Chu, 1999; Fisher, Marcoux, et al., 2004; George & Mwarigha,1999; Silvio, 2006)

- Information about recreation (Chu, 1999; Fisher, Marcoux, et al., 2004; Su & Conoway, 1995)

- Information about transportation (Chu, 1999; Su & Conaway, 1995)

- Information about banking (Shoham & Strauss, 2007)

In the case of problem-specific information seeking, some of the barriers specified in the literature include identifying and accessing relevant human sources (for instance, in public sector organizations), the slowness of bureaucratic processes (e.g., it may take a long time to obtain a health card, a driver's license, banking permissions) (Savolainen, 2008). These problems are compounded for immigrants, who are generally unfamiliar with the overall system in the new country (how things work) and may not know how or where to seek help in the new information environment.

Research that examines the information needs of immigrants tends to be conducted on particular ethno-cultural groups within particular settings. One reason, as has been suggested, is that it is difficult to generalize across immigrant groups (and even within them). However, we observe that in general the information needs of immigrants have remained relatively similar across immigrants' source countries. This point is reiterated by George and colleagues (2004), who suggest that the needs and barriers faced by newcomer immigrant groups in the process of settlement do not differ greatly (George, 2002; George et al., 2004; George & Mwarigha, 1999). Indeed, distinctions within ethno-cultural groups are often overlooked, resulting in the homogenization of diverse communities. Comparisons might usefully be drawn across such categories as age, gender, employment, socioeconomic conditions, and class of entry into source country. However, too few studies exist at this time to make such comparisons possible.

Another approach, advocated by Caidi, Allard, and Dechief (2008), is one that situates the information needs of immigrants along a continuum of settlement stages. Using Mwarigha's (2002) stages of settlement model combined with George and colleagues' (2004) work on pre-migration stages, the authors point out the usefulness of situating information needs along four (overlapping) stages: (1) the pre-migration stage (before the individual actually immigrates to the new country; information is then gathered from formal sources such as government agencies' publications and websites, immigration lawyers or agencies, as well as informal sources such as family and friends, blogs, and online listservs); (2) the immediate stage (e.g., information about pressing needs for survival such as shelter, orientation to the new city, language instruction); (3) the intermediate stage (information needed to access various local systems and institutions, such as municipal, legal, long-term housing, health, and employment services; and (4) the integrative stage (as immigrants become accustomed to their new country, their information needs are more diverse and may encompass the desire for increased political and civic participation).

Too few studies to date have examined information needs in the context of a settlement stages model; however, indications within current research suggest that this would be a beneficial approach. In a study of the pre-migration information flows of business migrants to New Zealand, Benson-Rea and Rawlinson (2003) suggest that pre-migration information is an essential component of the immigration and settlement process and that pre-migration information is often found to be insufficient in terms of both quantity and content, thus increasing difficulties during the settlement process. In their exploration of the information needs of new North American immigrants to Israel, Shoham and Strauss (2007) identified which channels of information were used by the immigrants before and after immigration to try to satisfy their needs. Many of these needs were satisfied either prior to immigration or during the absorption process; others were not, leaving the immigrants with gaps in their knowledge, feelings of uncertainty, and, at times, anxiety. According to the authors, during the preparations for immigration, the greatest source of information came from the Internet. After immigration, word-of-mouth and personal contacts were the main sources used by these immigrants to satisfy their information needs. Studies from social work that focus specifically on immigrant settlement also highlight specific information needs and their urgency during the settlement period (George, 2002; George, et al., 2004; George & Mwarigha, 1999).

A review of the literature suggests that settlement information (particularly at the pre-migration and immediate stages) generally tends to include more time-sensitive and critical information such as housing and employment information; non-settlement-related needs (at the intermediate and integrative stages) are broader in scope (Caidi, Allard, & Dechief, 2008). Access to leisure materials is an example. Cuesta (1990), To (1995), and Flythe (2001) all identify differences in reading patterns across the settlement process. Upon arrival, newcomers are significantly busier and are most likely to read instructional resources (e.g., language improvement; material about the local community or about finding and applying for employment) (To, 1995). At this stage, their reading practices are designed to help them settle in a new country. As they adjust to their new life, they are more likely to read more broadly (e.g., novels, "self-help," "how-to," and other leisure material) (Cuesta, 1990). In her examination of Hispanic populations' use of public library reading materials in the U.S., Cuesta (1990, p. 27) argues that immigrant reading needs become more varied "as their attention turns to enhancement of their daily lives." Magazines and newspapers from the source country and in their mother tongue are read at all stages of the immigrant process as are documents written in immigrants' first language.

### Pathways and Sources

Particularly important aspects of the information activities of immigrants are the identification and use of pathways (deliberate and happenstance) by which they find the sources they choose to consult in their information seeking process. The concept of information pathways was first proposed by Johnson and colleagues (2006) and may be understood as the route someone follows in the pursuit of answers to questions within one's information environment (what Johnson and colleagues [p. 571] refer to as "information fields"). Information pathways are a dynamic and active means of accessing information.

Immigrants commonly make use of multiple sources and pathways. The next section identifies a set of commonly identified sources, which we group in four categories: social networks, formal sources (organizations), information and communication technologies, and ethnic media.

## Social Networks

Researchers in the field of LIS and elsewhere have pointed to the importance of social networks as sources of information for so-called vulnerable or marginalized populations (Birkel & Repucci, 1983; Fisher, Marcoux, et al., 2004; Flythe, 2001; Gollop, 1997; Liu, 1995). Like most people, it appears that immigrants are most likely to ask other individuals for help as the first step when seeking information (Fisher, Durrance, et al., 2004; Shoham & Strauss, 2007; Silvio, 2006). Research indicates that they rely on strong ties or people with whom they have close personal relationships such as family, friends, neighbors, and co-workers (Fisher, Durrance, et al., 2004; Jeong, 2004). They also tend to rely on weak ties or people who are not particularly close to them such as settlement workers and government employees (Courtright, 2005). Likewise, studies in the immigration literature examine how strong ties in ethnic and immigrant communities within the receiving country contribute to social capital formation in the form of aid, social support, and reciprocity (Nee & Sanders, 2001; Portes & Bach, 1985; Salaff & Greve, 2004; Waters, 2003).

Courtright's (2005) study of the social networking practices of Latino newcomers in the U.S. seeking health information points to the use of both strong and weak social ties. She found that immigrant newcomers will initially rely on family, friends, and co-workers (their strong ties) for health information. The information that comes from these strong ties is often inadequate. However, family and friends are frequently able to put newcomers in contact with weak ties such as health care or settlement workers (within the family's or friend's network); these weak ties are often able to provide newcomers with adequate information.

Gatekeepers have also been identified as an important local source of information in ethnically diverse communities (Agada, 1999; Chatman, 1987; Chu, 1999; Metoyer-Duran, 1991, 1993; Stavri, 2001). Chu (1999) refers to ethnolinguistic gatekeepers as those individuals who are able to operate within two or more speech communities because they speak both the first language of the group and the official language(s) of the host country. Ethnolinguistic gatekeepers provide links between communities through their ability to access and disseminate information. These gatekeepers need not be professionals or linked to formal sources; rather they can play this gatekeeping role in an informal or personal capacity.

Metoyer-Duran's (1991, 1993) studies of the role that information gatekeepers play in various ethnolinguistic communities in California led her to develop a taxonomy of gatekeepers based on cognitive theoretical work, taking into account concept usage, data usage, and affect as key dimensions characterizing gatekeepers. Six gatekeeper profiles emerged from her work (impeder, broker, unaffiliated gatekeeper, affiliated gatekeeper, information professional, and leader-executive).

Metoyer-Duran's findings suggest that ethnolinguistic gatekeepers are generally knowledgeable about information access. They are often called upon to provide or find information for community members and are able to harness the power of information and communication technologies (ICTs) to facilitate this role. In her study of personal health information seeking, Stavri (2001) built on Metoyer-Duran's framework and incorporated another category of gatekeepers: those who act as translators of medical terminology into lay language for those individuals who are confused by the language and concepts used by an unfamiliar (and possibly intimidating) medical establishment.

Gatekeepers can also interfere with access to information and introduce bias. In his study of Korean international graduate students residing in the U.S., Jeong (2004) identifies a Korean clergyman as an information gatekeeper for students. At times the clergyman limits what information is made available to the students and also provides inaccurate information. Chu (1999) examines how immigrant children act as information mediators for their families, often information mediators for their parents, because they are likely to develop English language skills more quickly. Chu argues that when children become responsible for identifying and collecting information for family use, this may result in poor information choices and retrieval because children tend to have less sophisticated information seeking and evaluation techniques than do adults.

Some immigrant communities rely on social networks for information (particularly close ties such as well known community members, family, and friends) as trust appears to play a large role in information uptake and use. According to Silvio (2006), most Sudanese youth who immigrate to Canada with their families to escape civil war and find a better life prefer easily accessible informal sources such as trusted friends, relatives, and co-workers. Fisher, Marcoux, and colleagues' (2004) examination of low income Hispanic farm migrants reveals that they also prefer to use trusted informal sources for their information needs such as family and friends who emigrated to the region months or years earlier. If information is not readily available through these sources, they will not pursue it. Fisher and colleague's (2004, p. 9) findings suggest that, "in social networking terms, [immigrants] want to create strong ties from their invaluable weak ties." Strong ties are used for both information seeking and social support. In a study of female newcomers' access to primary mental health care, Hynie and colleagues also reported family and friends as being the principal sources of support for these women, along with community members who were often cited as the main sources of informational support (Crooks, Hynie, Killian, Giesbrecht, & Castleden, in press).

It is important, however, not to assume that trust issues apply only to so-called "vulnerable immigrants." For example, international university students, in Liu and Redfern's (1997) study, indicated that they were reluctant to use the reference desk at the university library because they were afraid that their English was not good enough either to ask a question or to understand the response. Reluctance to use the reference desk may indicate a mistrust of "outsiders" and their willingness to be tolerant or understanding of language difficulties. Because issues of trust play a significant role in preventing immigrants from accessing necessary information, it is evident that more research is needed on trust-building and related issues.

Immigrants are also known to retain social networks with individuals from the source country. Although immigrants may have difficulty accessing information sources within their new countries, they may have access to transnational network ties not available to non-immigrants. Examples of transnational ties include: collecting pre-migration information from family and friends who have migrated (Wong & Salaff, 1998), transnational entrepreneurship (Wong, 2004), providing or receiving employment and other referrals from individuals abroad (Kennedy, 2004), and locating health and other information from and for family and friends abroad (Faist, 2000). Additionally, transnational sources such as online language newspapers and websites are regularly consulted by immigrants (Aizlewood & Doody, 2002; Caidi & MacDonald, 2008).

Within LIS, there is little research that directly examines the transnational ties of immigrants. Srinivasan and Pyati (2007, p. 1734) acknowledge that there is much to be learned from "recognizing the place-based, lived realities of immigrant communities while also acknowledging the existence of complex, globalized, diasporic information environments." They propose a new model for dealing with these complexities called the Diasporic Information Environment Model (DIEM). This identifies several research methods that have the potential to advance our understanding of the relationships among the local context of immigrants' everyday lives (including their information practices) and their diasporic and transnational online activities as well as their identity practices. Because so little research exists in this area, it remains to be seen whether and how this model can shed light on the local and transnational information activities adopted by immigrants.

## Formal Sources

Formal organizations such as settlement agencies, government departments, community centers, ethno-cultural organizations, libraries, and other service providers (Flythe, 2001; George & Mwarigha, 1999; George & Tsang, 2000) are also important sources of information for immigrants. For instance, the LIS literature abounds with studies about how public and academic libraries act as spaces for both formal and informal information gathering by immigrants (Caidi & Allard, 2005; Chu, 1999; Dali, 2004, 2005; Dilevko & Dali, 2002; Fisher, Durrance, et al., 2004; Liu & Redfern, 1997; Luévano-Molina, 2001; Quirke, 2006; Shoham & Rabinovich, 2008). Indeed, libraries promote information sharing because information tends to travel informally in spaces where people meet, a phenomenon referred to as "information grounds." An information ground has been defined by Fisher (neé Pettigrew, 1999, p. 811) as "an environment temporarily created by the behavior of people who have come together to perform a given task, but from which emerges a social atmosphere that fosters the spontaneous and serendipitous sharing of information."

More research is needed into what types of information grounds exist for immigrants, or which venues become a de facto information ground for them, for example, bowling alleys, grocery stores, or churches. In their study of Hispanic migrant workers, Fisher, Marcoux, and colleagues (2004) identify church, school, and the workplace as sites where information spontaneously traveled among participants. Fisher, Durrance, and Bouch Hinton (2004) examine how literacy and coping skills programs at the Queen's Borough Public Library act as an information ground for immigrants by helping meet their psychological, social, and practical needs. They identify four building blocks in immigrants' perceptions of the public library: (1) discovery of the library and experience of its safe and accommodating environment, (2) awareness of the resources available and acquisition of library skills, (3) telling family and friends about how libraries can help them, and (4) learning to trust library staff (Fisher, Durrance, et al., 2004, p. 760). Immigrants experienced each of these steps as they incorporated the public library into their daily lives. Bordanaro (2006) describes how university libraries act as informal spaces for international students to develop their English language skills through self-directed learning and practice. Her study indicates that international students use the library as a practice space to engage in second language speaking, listening, reading, and writing.

Although most LIS research examines the contemporary role of the library in providing services to immigrants, a small body of literature documents and explores the historical role played by these services (Jones, 1999; Novotny, 2003; Pokorny, 2003). Scholarly research within LIS has also examined how the library, in particular, responds to immigrants' information needs (Chu, 1999; Fisher, Durrance, et al., 2004; Liu & Redfern, 1997; To, 1995). In addition, there is a vast body of practitioner-based literature that documents how libraries are currently serving or should serve immigrants (Cunningham, 2004; Dezarn, 2008; Hickok, 2005; Jang, 2004; Jensen, 2002; Jonsson-Lanevska, 2005; McGowen, 2008; Mylopoulos, 2004; Nedlina, 2007; Orange, 2004; O'Toole, 2005; Prock, 2003; Vander Kooy, 2004; Vang, 2003; Virgilio, 2003; Zhang, 2001).

Practitioner-based LIS literature deals primarily with issues relating to the design and delivery of library services to immigrant patrons and also identifies underserved populations and gaps in services. It consists of primarily descriptive articles, often written by practitioners based on an assessment of their library's services and/or user groups. For example, Prock (2003) describes the information needs of migrant farm workers and Jensen (2002) examines day laborers. Both of these groups are historically underserved library populations with very particular information needs. Cuesta (1990), on the other hand, explores the reading habits of Hispanic immigrants at the public library. In these and other examples, the challenge for libraries seems to be in striking the proper balance between the specific needs of immigrants and the library's mandate to serve the general population.

Libraries are but one of many organizations that provide formal information services targeted at immigrants; others include community organizations, social service agencies, government agencies, employment centers, settlement agencies, language training centres, ethno-cultural organizations, immigrant organizations, professional associations, and schools. For instance, Dechief (2006) explores the role that community networks play in the social and economic inclusion of immigrants. She argues that although newcomers initially go to community networks to make use of their publicly available ICT terminals and services, they often become volunteers at these organizations (in her study, the Vancouver Community Network). Through volunteering, immigrants acquire local work experience and increase local social networks that contribute to civic participation and finding employment.

In his study of 211 Toronto, a free information and referral service, Cortinois (2008) reports that the participants deemed the service extremely useful, although the majority of respondents did not learn about it immediately after arrival. For these immigrants, learning about 211 Toronto had been accidental, as for the most part, they had never before experienced anything similar and therefore could not even conceptualize the existence of such a service. Cortinois reports that even after learning about 211 Toronto, and sometimes even after using it several times, most participants did not know very much about the service, how it worked, and the types of information it offered. However, the respondents reported that 211 Toronto counsellors' friendly and respectful attitude, the fact that they spoke their language, and the precision and usefulness of the information they gave were the most important reasons for them to trust the service and keep returning to it (p. 219).

## Information and Communication Technologies

Information and communication technologies, such as computers and the Internet (Aizlewood & Doody, 2002; Mehra & Papajohn, 2007; Srinivasan & Pyati, 2007) but also mobile phones, radio, television, and satellite systems (Caidi & MacDonald, 2008; Lee, 2004; Naficy, 2003; Roald, 2004; Shoham & Stam, 2001; Shoham & Strauss, 2007), are significant information sources for immigrants. Indeed, they play a pivotal role in the shifts taking place within immigration by providing accessible cultural media such as online local newspapers in languages other than the official language, newsgroups, chat rooms, and home country Internet sites (Aizlewood & Doody, 2002).

Technology is one of the main facilitators of transnational practices because it allows for relatively easy and rapid communication across great distances. For example, Vertovec (2004) explores how the proliferation of inexpensive phone cards has contributed to transnational contact. Uy-Tioco (2007) describes how text messaging allows overseas Filipina workers to parent from abroad. Transnational entrepreneurial opportunities are also facilitated through ICTs (Chen & Wellman, 2007; Salaff & Greve, 2004; Wong, 2004). Additionally, immigrants often participate in the civic and political life of their home countries via online newspapers, the Internet, and telephone (Guarnizo et al., 2003).

Within the LIS literature, not much research examines how ICTs fit within the information behaviors of immigrants. In their study of international students, Mehra and Papajohn (2007) describe how ICTs are used as part of this group's information practices, spanning both local and transnational environments. They describe how International Teaching Assistants (ITAs) use the Internet for "glocal" (both local and global) information activities. Their study found that, among ITAs, e-mail and the telephone were the preferred means for both communication with the home country and finding information in the U.S. This study also indicated that students who spent more time engaging in social activities on campus also spent more time engaging in online activities, such as chatrooms, listservs, newsgroups, and audio/videoconferences (p. 26). Viewed from this perspective, the Internet is a potentially valuable tool for fostering both local and transnational networks.

Chien's research (2005) examines Settlement.Org, a Toronto based website produced by the Ontario Council of Agencies Serving Immigrants (OCASI) that provides settlement information to newcomers. She studied the uses of Settlement.Org's online bulletin board by immigrants and argues that, in addition to informing immigrants, the board helps involve them in Canadian life by connecting them to other individuals (both immigrants and Canadian-born) and by allowing them to contribute content, share opinions and stories, and give advice to others. She also observes that newcomers often have blogs in their first languages directed to others who are contemplating emigrating from a shared home country. Not only do immigrants find information from these sources but they are a significant locus of engagement and social networking for both content contributors and information seekers before and after arrival.

A report on the role played by ICTs in fostering social inclusion, commissioned by Human Resources and Social Development Canada (Caidi, Allard, Dechief, & Longford, 2008), documents how publicly available ICTs are used by immigrants at non-profit institutions such as community networks (CNs), settlement agencies, and public libraries. Their findings demonstrate that employment-related activities are among the main reasons immigrants use ICTs at these locations. Indeed, new immigrants are very busy making ends meet and have to make strategic use of their time in public settings where computers and other information and settlement resources are available. The report indicates that ICTs may be used for a variety of other purposes, such as for communicating with family and friends in the home country and accessing various online media in multiple languages. In addition to the fact that social networks are necessary for information seeking, information seeking itself (using a variety of pathways including ICTs, weak network ties, and formal organizations such as libraries and community networks) promotes the development of much needed local social networks for immigrants.

Caidi, Allard, Dechief, and Longford's (2008) findings also suggest that the prevalence of the Internet may not necessarily be beneficial to all immigrants because it creates barriers to access. Bureaucratic structures and online interfaces, for instance, may prove difficult to navigate for new users who are unfamiliar with the Canadian system or whose first language is not English. In other words, ICTs have the potential to create opportunities for immigrants (in terms of accessing information and media, and communicating locally and transnationally) but more research is needed to identify how ICTs act as both barrier and opportunity for immigrant communities.

## Ethnic Media

Computers and the Internet remain significant sources of information for immigrants but more traditional media, including ethnic media, are also heavily used. Satellite TV, local minority language newspapers and radio, and international websites are all examples of such media (Caidi & MacDonald, 2008; Cormack & Hourigan, 2007; Flythe, 2001; Joh, Yue, Hawkins, Pookong, & Fox, 2001; Karim, 2003; Moon & Park, 2007; Su & Conaway, 1995; Viswanath & Arora, 2000). Studies also highlight the use of non-English language print and broadcast media of both local and international origin. These resources appear to be a significant source of information for both newcomers and longer established immigrants (Karanfil, 2007; Lee, 2004; Lin & Song, 2006). Most of the research within this area emerges from communication studies as well as the immigration and settlement studies literature more generally.

Examples include how ethnic local newspapers are used to keep track of events in both the source country and the local neighborhood (Lin & Song, 2006). As such, they act to promote connections abroad and locally. Another example examines how the proliferation of satellite TV is contributing to transnational contact (Karanfil, 2007; Lee, 2004). In this instance, immigrants appear to prefer to watch news programs from their countries of origin, indicating a keen interest in what is going on in those countries (Karanfil, 2007; Lee, 2004).

Aizlewood and Doody (2002) found that immigrant Internet users can be divided into two categories: those who maintain and those who explore their ethno-cultural identity. The former tend to be immigrants, particularly recently-arrived immigrants. Maintenance occurs through frequent communication with others within their ethno-cultural group through newsgroups, chat rooms, and e-mail. Online newspapers and other Web-based media are also consumed. Among the latter are those "who have more indirect ties to their background, perhaps through a parent or grandparent" (p. 3), for example, first and second generation immigrants. They use the Internet to find information about their cultural heritage in an attempt to reclaim their roots and learn more about the associated traditions and practices.

Srinivasan and Pyati (2007, p. 1734) refer to the proliferation of ethnic media online as "e-diaspora," suggesting that immigrants' experience with transnational identities in an online environment has an effect on their (offline) lived realities and communities. Mitra (2006) and Wenjing (2005) both describe how virtual spaces such as websites are used to create unique immigrant identities. In both studies, the development and maintenance of identity motivates information practice. Mitra (2006) argues that immigrants of Indian origin use Indian websites as safe spaces where they can express themselves freely. Wenjing argues that Chinese diasporic websites allow Chinese immigrants to maintain their Chinese identities while creating new identities based on experiences in their new countries.

Caidi and MacDonald (2008) examine Canadian Muslims and how their information practices mediate and shape their experiences and sense of belonging in Canada. The findings point to an interesting—if not surprising—paradox between the respondents' lack of confidence in fair reporting on Islam and Muslims in the local media after 9/11, along with an increased awareness and consumption of media objects (both local and ethnic) by the population sampled. The users are depicted as avid consumers of information in various forms and in different languages, thus exposing them to a variety of perspectives on events that unfold in the world around them (p. 359). In addition to the more generic uses of the Internet and computers, there are specific uses, such as accessing websites in languages other than English or visiting sites that are tailored to groups belonging to a particular cultural group or religious affiliation (p. 360).

## *Information Sharing and Expressive Information Activities*

Most research on the information practices of immigrants tends to focus on the identification of task-based information activities (Chu, 1999; Flythe, 2001; Prock, 2003; Silvio, 2006; Su & Conaway, 1995). The social and communicative dimensions of information activities (including information sharing) have been described less often, or in the context of spaces or places where people meet formally or informally. In their study of Hispanic migrant workers, Fisher, Marcoux, and colleagues (2004) identify church, school, and the workplace as sites where information spontaneously circulated among participants. More research is needed into which venues become a de facto information ground—bowling alleys, grocery stores, churches.

As is evident from the previous sections, immigrants' information practices are not simply straightforward plans designed to acquire particular pieces of information. Indeed, when the term "information practices" is expanded to include non-directed activities such as media browsing or communication with the home country, it becomes obvious that information practices are about more than finding *instrumental* information—information with which to complete a task. Information practices also comprise more *expressive* or communicative activities. These activities, which often have a *phatic* function (i.e., small talk or informal activities that open up a social channel and can lead to more substantial or focused communication) are not often accounted for in discussions of immigrants' information practices. Indeed, expressive information activities are not as well documented although concepts such as informal support networks or information grounds acknowledge the conversational and serendipitous nature of information transfer and uptake.

Mehra and Papajohn (2007) argue that there is a significant link between emotional well-being, cultural understanding, and information practices. International students in their study use the Internet to maintain transnational contacts because they perceive the Internet as providing "significant social and psychological/emotional benefits in the process of maintaining communication to the home country" (p. 26). These authors interpret communicating with home as an information practice because the emotional support derived from transnational ties contributes (in terms of psychological comfort and overcoming isolation) to their ability to understand and function within U.S. culture, which is an alien information environment.

Caidi and MacDonald (2008) examine Canadian Muslims (the majority of whom had been in the country for an average of nine years) and how their information practices mediate and shape their experiences and sense of belonging in Canada. The authors note the keen interest in news items (world news, home country news, Canadian news, local news) and the strong transnational ties held and maintained by many respondents (e.g., they may have families living in other parts of the world, they may be newcomers themselves or foreign students, or seek information sources from other parts of the globe). The authors show that the information practices of their sample contribute to shaping their sense of belonging (or not) in Canadian society in the post-9/11 world. The authors also note a significant level of sophistication shown by the participants in their understanding of the importance of accessing multiple and varied sources of information and making sense of the content as well as the context of production of the information. The search for a variety of trusted information sources seems to be related to the needs of these individuals to question and negotiate their sense of identity and what it means to be a Muslim in Canada.

Apart from the LIS literature there is a growing body of research underway that sheds light on the relationship between information practices (although not always identified as such) and cultural identity formation and negotiation. For instance, Sampredo (1998) illustrates how immigrants use transnational ties to create connections or feelings of closeness with their home country. He observes that daily newspapers are read for reasons other than information collection; they are consumed to create symbolic closeness with the home country. Mitra (2006) and Wenjing (2005) both describe how virtual spaces such as websites are used to create unique immigrant identities. In both studies, the development and maintenance of identity practices motivate or underlie the information activities.

The use of ICTs has also emerged as a possible alternative in Cortinois's (2008) study of health information seeking by immigrants. He suggests that information and communication technologies could be used to support a virtual community of users, built on the Wikipedia model, aimed at maximizing the efficiency and impact of the casual "information chains" employed and described by his respondents (p. 225). In this way, informal support networks that are key to information sharing can benefit a broader range of individuals, provided these have access to ICTs and have the skills and know-how to access the resources.

## Barriers and Challenges to Information Practices

Multiple barriers prevent immigrants from finding information upon arrival in their new country. The literature identifies both structural and social barriers. Structural barriers include language proficiency, learning how systems work (i.e., the settlement and immigration process), and limitations arising from one's immigration status. Social barriers include, among other things, social isolation, differences in cultural values or understandings, and communication problems. We review these here:

### Structural Barriers to Accessing Information

#### Insufficient Language Proficiency

One of the most significant barriers that new immigrants appear to face is lack of language proficiency or insufficient language proficiency (Cortinois, 2008; Fisher, Marcoux, et al., 2004; George & Mwarigha, 1999; George & Tsang, 2000; Jeong, 2004; Silvio, 2006; Stavri, 2001; Su & Conaway, 1995). In studies by Cortinois (2008) as well as Crooks and colleagues (in press), language was confirmed as the most fundamental barrier experienced by participants when accessing health services. In addition to not being able to speak or understand the official language(s) of their new country, some immigrants are reluctant to speak English even when they understand it (Liu & Redfern, 1997). In a similar vein, Fisher, Marcoux, and colleagues' (2004) examination of low income Hispanic farm migrants reveals that respondents prefer to use trusted Spanish speaking sources for their information needs. Because language is the largest barrier for this group, Spanish language radio and community organizations are the preferred information sources. Other important information sources are family and friends who emigrated to the region months or years earlier.

#### Learning How the System Works

Learning how the system works includes lack of familiarity with receiving country information sources; lack of knowledge about how to navigate the local information environment; not knowing what services are available or how to ask for services; and literacy issues (Chu, 1999; Caidi & Allard, 2005; Caidi, Allard, Dechief, & Longford, 2008; Cortinois, 2008; Fisher, Durrance, et al., 2004; Prock, 2003; Shoham & Strauss, 2008; Stavri, 2001; Su & Conaway, 1995). Many immigrants face significant challenges in finding appropriate information after they enter the new country. In the case of personal health information seeking, the barriers include being too busy to take care of one's self, being unfamiliar with health information sources and the health care system in their new country, language barriers, dismissive attitudes on the part of some health care providers, and inadequate support networks (Cortinois, 2008; Courtright, 2005; Crooks et al., in press; Holroyd, Taylor-Piliae, & Twinn, 2003; Stavri, 2001). Courtright's (2005) study of Latino newcomers in the U.S. also indicates that they prefer human sources from which to acquire health information and do not use the Internet to locate health information. Cortinois (2008) reported that the immigrants in his sample arrived in Canada with expectations that in most cases clashed with the reality they encountered. In some cases they did not find what they were hoping for; in others they found resources and services with which they were not familiar. These included services that were conceptually so remote from what they had experienced in their countries of origin as to be virtually invisible. That was probably one of the reasons most participants had discovered 211 Toronto only late in the resettlement process (p. 224).

Several articles illustrate that in order to communicate information adequately to newcomers, it is necessary to be able to put it in their terms (Stavri, 2001). For example, Allen, Matthew, and Boland (2004) describe the relative lack of medical terminology in the Hmong language. Communicating medical concepts is therefore accomplished by translating Western biomedical models of health into the Hmong language using words and concepts of health, well-being, and death understood by the Hmong.

Another significant barrier to health information access is the language in which written health information is published. Immigrant groups in Ahmad, Shik, Vanza, Cheung, George, and Stewart's (2004) study stated that they wanted health information in their first language through ethnic newspapers, television, Internet, workshops, health workers, pamphlets, and displays at family physician clinics. Sun, Zang, Tsoh, Wong-Kim, and Chow (2007) determine that, because of the low English health literacy rates among Chinese immigrant women in San Francisco, media campaigns in both Cantonese and Mandarin using local Chinese media proved successful in promoting breast health to this demographic.

### Limitations Arising from One's Immigration Status

Depending on one's status, access to resources or services may not be possible. For instance, in Canada, even legally landed immigrants cannot obtain public health care for the first three months after their arrival. It has been well documented that on average, immigrants tend to be in better health than the average Canadian before they immigrate. However, their health usually deteriorates rapidly due in part to lack of social support, mental distress, social isolation, and lack of financial stability (Morrow, 2003; Pumariega, Rothe, & Pumariega, 2005). Being unable to access health care services in their first three months, these individuals have to seek alternative options and sources of information on health.

The problem is compounded for refugee claimants or undocumented immigrants. They cannot access many services because of their status (or lack thereof). There is also the problem of stigma that weighs on certain individuals. In their study of female newcomers' access to primary mental health care, Crooks and colleagues (in press) report that many of these women (many of whom were refugees) would refrain from seeking information and help for a variety of reasons having to do with hiding their true condition (being depressed or sad was not socially accepted) or out of fear that such information would jeopardize their immigration proceedings (if it were to be made publicly available or recorded on one's file). As Chatman (2000, p. 7) noted in her discussion of information poverty, "when concerns and problems present themselves and when information is recognized as potentially helpful but is ignored, individuals live in an impoverished information world." More formal support services, regardless of language or immigration status, are desirable but this can be achieved only if service providers receive adequate resources and training.

## Social Barriers to Accessing Information

### Social Isolation

Social isolation includes the sense of being an outsider, lack of support, and mistrust of others (Caidi & MacDonald, 2008; Chatman 1996; Fisher, Marcoux, et al., 2004; George & Tsang, 2000; Prock, 2003; Silvio, 2006; Sligo & Jameson, 2000). Resettlement in a new country can be a deeply traumatic experience, particularly in the case of forced migration (as is the case for many refugees). The reality of resettlement includes the emotional shock of relocation; linguistic and cultural barriers of all types; and the need to solve multiple, complex, and intertwined tasks while attempting to navigate an unfamiliar environment without any support networks along the way (Cortinois, 2008, p. 224). Hence the importance of having access to reliable, consistent, and comprehensive information on a broad spectrum of subjects (ranging from how to use the public transportation system, to the cardinal reference system for finding one's way across the city, to critical information such as health or employment-related information (Asanin & Wilson, 2008). Lack of social support and mistrust of others may lead immigrants to feel isolated and emotionally distressed (Morrow, 2003; Pumariega et al., 2005).

### Communication Problems

Negative experiences with a service provider or a system (e.g., health care) can have devastating consequences on an immigrant's settlement process and overall well-being. Examples of problems identified by Cortinois (2008, p. 233) in the context of immigrants' health information seeking include: the difficulty of finding a family physician; rushed consultations; providers' unfriendly, unsympathetic, dismissive attitudes; long waiting times at hospital emergency departments and in securing appointments with specialists; challenges in learning and understanding health care practices in Canada; and, more important than any other barrier, communication problems with providers.

Communication problems can occur at any point of the exchange and involve both parties: the user (patron, patient) may be frustrated with the (seemingly) impersonal nature of the transaction with the service provider. He/she may not feel that the person has probed enough or does not appear to care about the individual's concerns. By contrast, the provider may mistake the individual's aloofness and reserved attitude for passivity (he/she is not volunteering information). In some cases, a provider may only ask questions or probe deeper when there are resources or time to deal with the answer (Crooks et al., in press).

Moreover, research suggests that certain information (such as that about health) is often presented to immigrant groups in a way that can be significantly different from how these individuals envision the world and how they relate to such matters as health or illness—for instance, faith may not play a significant role in the mode of operating of the host country's health care model. Immigrants generally acquire less quality health care information and underutilize the health care system in their new country (Cortinois, 2008; Courtright, 2005; Holroyd et al., 2003). It is commonly thought that one of the main reasons for this state of affairs is that immigrants "experience clashes between their ethnocultural or religious beliefs and Western medical care" (Weerasinghe, 2000, p. 11). Different understandings of health, illness, and treatment often lead to communication problems and immigrant dissatisfaction with the health care system. In addition to varying beliefs about health and illness, cultural norms about appropriate behavior may play a large role in the health information practices of certain immigrant groups. For example, Sligo and Jameson (2000) argue that concern about what other community members will think of them prevents Pacific Island immigrants to New Zealand from getting cervical smears as reproductive health is a taboo area. They argue therefore that health information providers should take cultural differences into consideration when designing services. The use of insider endorsements may be employed to address cultural norms and taboos. Indeed, insiders have authority that outsiders do not because they are part of the group and are understood to share the same values and belief system as the group (Chatman, 1996; Sligo & Jameson, 2000).

There is a need to address ways in which communication can be facilitated between service providers and community members. In particular, the mistrust and alienation within communities needs to be addressed. One way is to work with gatekeepers or to facilitate foreign-trained professionals who can act as mediators because of their knowledge of the language, cultural systems, and communication practices of the new immigrants' country of origin as well as that of the host country. Rather than the occasional cross-cultural competencies workshops and one-time efforts to teach service providers about the importance of cross-cultural communication, there seems to be a need for a more holistic approach that takes into account how professionals in various sectors are trained to deal with the reality of cultural diversity in their local settings.

### Differences in Cultural Values or Understandings

Lack of cultural relevance may pose a significant barrier to information access for immigrants (George et al., 2004; Srinivasan, 2007). It is a topic that emerges in various areas related to this subject. As illustrated earlier, examining the health information practices of immigrants provides an excellent example of the need to identify cultural distinctions between and among immigrant groups and provide culturally relevant services, particularly where information may be sensitive. Indeed, lack of cultural relevance may represent a significant barrier to information uptake and retrieval. For example, cultural relevance may affect an individual's willingness to visit the library, use ICTs, or simply accept information provided from someone outside his or her cultural group. The development of information systems within the context of culturally differentiated communities has been researched by Srinivasan (2006, 2007) and Srinivasan and Pyati (2007) among others.

Srinivasan's (2007) research on Tribal Peace, a cultural information system designed by and for members of Native American reservations in California, illustrates how an information system can be developed to engage communities to develop their socioeconomic, educational, and cultural infrastructures. This and similar research illustrates how an analysis of communities' cultural practices (immigrant and otherwise) can be used as guiding points for designing an information system's architecture, particularly with respect to how it represents, categorizes, and disseminates the information it stores.

Lenhart, Horrigan, Rainie, Allen, Boyce, Madden, and colleagues' (2003) study of the barriers to Internet access shows that what a person thinks of the Internet affects use. Similarly, cross-cultural metaphors of ICTs have not been heavily studied, although much can be learned from them. Duncker's (2002) study of digital libraries and computing metaphors among the Maori in New Zealand suggests that metaphors are deeply rooted in cultural practices and, as such, should be an integral part of information systems design. Previous research on the use of Internet search tools (Iivonen & White, 2001) has shown differences in how users from different cultural groups search for information. These differences in behavior have implications for cross-cultural usability and the design of information resources and services for culturally diverse groups (Bilal & Bachir, 2007a, 2007b; Komlodi, Caidi, & Wheeler, 2004; Smith, 2006).

It should be noted, however, that most of the studies examined focused on the information practices of low-income groups. The barriers they identify may not be entirely representative of less vulnerable immigrants, such as those with financial means.

## Conclusions and Future Directions

This review has examined several key concepts drawn from the LIS literature and beyond that can be used to frame both current and future research on the needs and uses of information by immigrants. It becomes clear from this chapter that, in spite of numerous gaps, there is an increasingly rich and useful body of literature from a wide range of disciplines that examines (directly or indirectly) the information practices of immigrants.

From our review, it is clear that communication barriers, lack of knowledge of the host country, poor socioeconomic and family networks, and lack of recognition of foreign educational or professional credentials are some of the established causes of social exclusion by immigrants (Weerasinghe, 2000). All of these issues are, to some extent, problems caused by a lack of relevant information. We therefore conclude this overview of the literature by reiterating what we have suggested earlier: Social exclusion may well be an information problem, caused in part by the significant barriers immigrants face as they navigate an unknown information environment.

In order to understand better the information practices of immigrants, a holistic approach is advocated to encourage a closer examination of the relationships among social inclusion, the everyday life context of both new and longer established immigrants, and their information practices (Caidi & Allard, 2005). Indeed, assessing the contextual and situational factors constituting the information environments that define the information practices of immigrants is essential.

In spite of the importance of information for immigration and settlement purposes, studies on the information practices (including information seeking, use, and sharing) of immigrants tend to take a narrow approach, focusing on specific demographics or contexts. Although these approaches are extremely valuable, more research is needed that draws conclusions across the various small studies. We conclude this chapter by highlighting several research gaps; (and therefore research opportunities) identified in the literature and propose an agenda for future research.

## Examining Immigrant Demographics

More research is needed that compares the information practices of various types of immigrants, most notably differences between newcomers and longer established immigrants. Similarly, more research is needed that identifies the differences between immigrants and refugees, and between different classes of immigrants (skilled workers, family class, entrepreneurs, etc.). It should be noted that we found very few studies that examined the information practices of business or economic class immigrants (Chen & Wellman, 2007; Wong & Ng, 2002). Comparing immigrants living in urban and rural or isolated settings is also a much needed area of research. Furthermore, the effects of age (e.g., generational gaps, specific needs of seniors or youth), along with gender differences, socioeconomic status, and even race may also be factors to consider in order to obtain a more robust understanding of the immigration and settlement process.

## Research on Specific Information Needs

This review identified relatively few studies that focus on specific types of information needs (with the notable exception of health information). More research on information needs and uses in other settlement-related areas (e.g., employment, housing, leisure) along with comparisons between them is needed. One of the most significant information needs a newcomer faces has to do with finding employment (George et al., 2004). However, no studies within the information literature specifically address how immigrants find employment or make use of employment information to secure work.

Although we found some evidence that information needs do change across the settlement process, more empirical studies and longitudinal approaches (i.e., immigrants' information needs across stages of immigration or the life course lens) would contribute greatly to our understanding of how newcomers and longer-established immigrants find the information they need at different stages of settlement and in the context of their daily lives. Current studies might also make use of the data they collect differently. Most studies we examined did identify when newcomers arrived; however, they did not explore information practices in the light of these data.

### Research on Expressive Information Activities

Most LIS research examines the specific task-based information needs of immigrants. This is particularly important as instrumental information needs are especially crucial and numerous during the settlement process. However, there is an opportunity for those who wish to examine the information practices of immigrants to cast a wider net and explore the relationship between information and communication activities. The heavy reliance on informal sources by immigrants calls for more research on ways of supporting informal networks. Informal networks have proved crucial for information access, dissemination, and information sharing (although so much relies on luck, such as whom one meets, from whom one rents, how helpful and proactive people in one's immediate environment are). A better understanding of the role of these informal support networks, their dynamics, and their role in information sharing will have implications for how community agencies provide more active support and help in building such community networks and support groups.

Other expressive information activities include identity formation and negotiation by newcomers and longer established immigrants (including hybrid citizenship) and their conceptualization of inclusion and belonging in a new country.

### Research on ICTs

Little research exists about the use of information and communication technologies for information seeking and use. What we did find was largely based in a Canadian context. We simply do not have enough data about how immigrants make use of the Internet at home and in public spaces. More studies are needed to capture how it is used for both expressive (social) and instrumental functions. It is particularly important to interview immigrants themselves and hear their stories about how ICTs act as either barriers or opportunities, or both, in increasing inclusion and settlement. An example of a neighborhood ethnography of Internet usage was conducted by the Everyday Internet project (Viseu, Clement, & Aspinall, 2004) but the emphasis was not on immigrants per se, although data were collected about them in the course of the study.

Within the ICT literature, more research is needed on the relationship between Internet-based information practices and concepts such as social capital. For example, studies that examine employment-seeking practices using the Internet (Jansen & Spink, 2005; McQuaid, Lindsay, & Greig, 2004) indicate that, although Web-based job searching can be fruitful, it is important to recognize the overriding importance of local social networks for employment information sharing and referrals (McQuaid, et al., 2004).

### Research on Transnationalism

There are also many gaps to be filled in our understanding of the relationship between transnationalism and information practices, although research in this area is increasing. Research might examine how new immigrants, for instance, make use of their transnational network ties (individuals living outside of the host country and with whom they have contact) when seeking settlement information (e.g., employment, housing, citizenship information). Drawing upon the notion of social capital, one can explore how local and transnational network ties constrain and/or provide access to information resources. It would be useful to trace how local and transnational networks are mobilized by individuals, as well as the motivations individuals identify as they seek information through a variety of formats and pathways.

### Interdisciplinary Research

Another fruitful area of study would be to analyze systematically the means by which different bodies of literature approach and comprehend settlement or immigration "needs." What is brought into focus and what is obscured in each strand of literature (e.g., library and information studies, communication studies, community-based research, social work, immigrant studies) reveals telling differences about how the immigration process is understood by policymakers, service providers, researchers, and the immigrants themselves. Juxtaposing the research results could result in a dialogue among the various stakeholders and elicit rich findings about the assumptions made and the gaps between discourse and practice, between imagined lives and real needs. Finally, more research is needed on the most effective ways of engaging immigrant communities in disseminating knowledge about themselves.

### Information Environments

The notion of information environments is increasingly being used to describe the particular everyday life context in which immigrants find themselves upon arrival in the host country. For example, Mehra and Papajohn (2007, p. 13) use the term "culturally alien information environment" and Srinivasan and Pyati (2007, p. 1739) refer to the "diasporic information environment." Information environments have a profound effect on the daily information practices employed by immigrants. There are several other areas where the information environments of immigrants can be explored more fully. For example, what impact do immigration policies/practices by the state and/or community have on the trajectory of immigrants (e.g., integration or inclusion models)? How does the current politically charged post-9/11 environment (with its emphasis on national security) shape the discourse around multiculturalism and immigration?

As we mentioned at the beginning, this literature review is by no means exhaustive. Instead, this chapter's intent is to map out the general terrain that represents the information practices of immigrants. Its aim is to offer a snapshot of the current landscape and suggest areas for potential research with a view to generating new insights and contributions as well as the development of conceptual frameworks that can further our understanding of the vital issues in this interdisciplinary area of research.

## Acknowledgments

The authors wish to thank the anonymous reviewers and Reijo Sovolainen for their helpful comments.

# Endnote

1. Significant portions of the text in this section were adapted from an unpublished report: *Information Practices of Immigrants* (by Nadia Caidi, Danielle Allard, & Diane Dechief, 2008) for Citizenship and Immigration Canada.

# References

Abdullahi, I. (2007). Diversity and intercultural issues in library and information science (LIS) education. *New Library World, 108*(9–10), 453–459.

Agada, J. (1999). Intercity gatekeepers: An exploratory survey of their information use environment. *Journal of the American Society for Information Science, 50*(1), 74–85.

Ahmad, F., Shik, A., Vanza, R., Cheung, A., George, U., & Stewart, D. E. (2004). Popular health promotion strategies among Chinese and East Indian immigrant women. *Women & Health, 40*(1), 21–40.

Aizlewood, A., & Doody, M. (2002). *Seeking community on the Internet: Ethnocultural use of information communication technology.* Hull, Québec: Department of Heritage Canada.

Alba, R. (2005). Bright vs. blurred boundaries: Second generation assimilation and exclusion in France, Germany, and the United States. *Ethnic and Racial Studies, 28*(1), 20–49.

Alba, R., & Nee, V. (2003). *Remaking the American mainstream: Assimilation and contemporary immigration.* Cambridge, MA: Harvard University Press.

Alexander, L. B. (2008). An online course in multicultural materials for LIS graduate students at the University of South Florida. *Education Libraries, 31*(1), 32–37.

Allard, S., Mehra, B., & Qayyym, M. A. (2007). Intercultural leadership toolkit for librarians: Building awareness to effectively serve diverse multicultural populations. *Education Libraries, 30*(1), 5–51.

Allen, M., Matthew, S., & Boland, M. J. (2004). Working with immigrant and refugee populations: Issues and Hmong case study. *Library Trends, 53*(2), 301–328.

Alpert, P. S. (2006). Effect of multiculturalism and automation on public library collection development and technical services. *Public Library Quarterly, 25*(1/2), 91–98.

Asanin, J., & Wilson, K. (2008). "I spent nine years looking for a doctor": Exploring access to health care among immigrants in Mississauga, Ontario, Canada. *Social Science & Medicine, 66*(6), 1271–1283.

Basch, L., Glick Schiller, N., & Szanton Blanc, C. (1994). *Nations unbound: Transnational projects, post-colonial predicaments and deterritorialized nation-states.* New York: Gordon and Breach.

Beall, J. (2006). Ethnic groups and Library of Congress subject headings. *Colorado Libraries, 32*(4), 37–36.

Benson-Rea, M., & Rawlinson, S. (2003). Highly skilled and business migrants: Information processes and settlement outcomes. *International Migration, 4*(2), 59–77.

Berry, E. (2007). Family storytimes for new immigrants combine learning and fun. *Feliciter, 53*(1), 44–45.

Berry, J. W. (1997). Immigration, acculturation, and adaptation. *Applied Psychology, 46*(1), 5–34.

Bilal, D., & Bachir, I. (2007a). Children's interaction with cross-cultural and multilingual digital libraries I: Understanding interface design representations. *Information Processing & Management, 43*(1), 47–64.

Bilal, D., & Bachir, I. (2007b). Children's interaction with cross-cultural and multilingual digital libraries II: Information seeking, success, and affective experience. *Information Processing & Management, 43*(1), 65–80.

Birkel, R., & Repucci, N. (1983). Social networks, information-seeking, and utilization of services. *American Journal of Community Psychology, 11*(2), 185–205.

Bjorner, S. (2008). Diacritical issues for multilingual searching. *Searcher, 16*(1), 34–39.

Bloemraad, I. (2006). *Becoming a citizen: Incorporating immigrants and refugees in the United States and Canada.* Berkeley: University of California Press.

Bober, C. (2008). Evaluating and selecting multicultural children's literature. *Education Libraries, 31*(1), 77–79.

Booth, P. F. (2006). Translating and indexing: Some thoughts on their relationship. *The Indexer, 25*(2), 89–88.

Bordonaro, K. (2006). Language learning in the library: An exploratory study of ESL students. *Journal of Academic Librarianship, 32*(5), 518–526.

Bowen, D. N. (2007). Another look at African cultures through picture books. *School Library Media Activities Monthly, 23*(10), 22–24.

Boyd, M. (2002). Educational attainments of immigrant offspring: Success or segmented assimilation? *International Migration Review, 36*(4), 1037–1060.

Boyd, M., & Grieco, E. (1998). Triumphant transitions: Socioeconomic achievements of the second generation in Canada. *International Migration Review, 32*(4), 857–876.

Bradford, C., & Huang, H.-L. (2007). Exclusions and inclusions: Multiculturalism in contemporary Taiwanese and Australian picture books. *Bookbird, 45*(3), 5–12.

Caidi, N., & Allard, D. (2005). Social inclusion of newcomers to Canada: An information problem? *Library & Information Science Research, 27*(3), 302–324.

Caidi, N., Allard, D., & Dechief, D. (2008). *Information practices of immigrants to Canada: A review of the literature.* Unpublished Report to Citizenship and Immigration Canada.

Caidi, N., Allard, D., Dechief, D., & Longford, G. (2008). *Including immigrants in Canadian society: What role do ICTs play?* Unpublished Report to Human Resources and Social Development Canada.

Caidi, N., & MacDonald, S. (2008). Information practices of Canadian Muslims post 9/11. *Government Information Quarterly, 25*(3), 348–378.

Castles, S., & Miller, M. J. (1998). *The age of migration: International population movements in the modern world.* Hampshire, UK: Macmillan Press.

Chatman, E. A. (1987). The information world of low-skilled workers. *Library & Information Science Research, 9*(4), 265–283.

Chatman, E. A. (1996). The impoverished life world of outsiders. *Journal of the American Society for Information Science, 47*(3), 193–206.

Chatman, E. A. (2000). Framing social life in theory and research. *New Review of Information Behaviour Research, 1*, 3–17.

Chen, W., & Wellman, B. (2007). Doing business at home and away: Policy implications of Chinese-Canadian entrepreneurship. Asia Pacific Foundation of Canada. Retrieved December 10, 2008, from www.asiapacific.ca/analysis/pubs/pdfs/can_in_asia/cia_doing_business.pdf

Chien, E. (2005). *Informing and involving newcomers online: Users' perspectives of Settlement.Org.* Unpublished master's thesis, University of Toronto.

Chu, C. M. (1999). Immigrant children mediators (ICM): Bridging the literacy gap in immigrant communities. *New Review of Children's Literature and Librarianship, 5*, 85–94.

Citizenship and Immigration Canada. (2005). *Government-assisted refugee program.* Retrieved November 14, 2008, from www.cic.gc.ca/English/refugees/outside/resettle-gov.asp

Citizenship and Immigration Canada. (2008). *Facts and figures 2007: Immigration overview.* Retrieved November 14, 2008, from www.cic.gc.ca/english/resources/statistics/facts2007/permanent/01.asp

Cooper, D. (2008). Sustaining language diversity: The role of public libraries. *Australasian Public Libraries and Information Services, 21*(1), 28–32.

Cormack, M., & Hourigan, N. (Eds.). (2007). *Minority language media: Concepts, critiques and case studies.* Toronto: Multilingual Matters.

Cornelius, W. A., & Tsuda, T. (2004). Controlling immigration: The limits of government intervention. In W. A. Cornelius, T. Tsuda, P. L. Martin, & J. F. Hollifield (Eds.), *Controlling Immigration: A global perspective* (pp. 3–48). Stanford, CA: Stanford University Press.

Cortinois, A. (2008). *Supporting recent immigrants in their effort to access information on health and health-related services: The case of 211 Toronto.* Doctoral dissertation, University of Toronto.

Courtright, C. (2005). Health information-seeking among Latino newcomers: An exploratory study. *Information Research, 10*(2). Retrieved January 9, 2009, from informationr.net/ir/10-2/paper224.html

Crooks, V. A., Hynie, M., Killian, K., Giesbrecht, M., & Castleden, H. (in press). Female newcomers' adjustment to life in Toronto: Sources of mental stress and their implications for delivering primary mental health care. *Geojournal.*

Cuesta, Y. J. (1990). From survival to sophistication. *Library Journal, 115*(9), 26–28.

Cunningham, A. (2004). Global and local support dimensions for emerging community languages. *Australasian Public Libraries and Information Services, 17*(3), 113–124.

Dali, K. (2004). Reading by Russian-speaking immigrants in Toronto: Use of public libraries, bookstores, and home book collections. *The International Information & Library Review, 36*(4), 341–366.

Dali, K. (2005). Russian-language periodicals in Toronto: Information sources for immigrants and records for documenting community. *Slavic & East European Information Resources, 6*(1), 57–100.

Daumke, P., Marku, K., Poprat, M., Schulz, S., & Klar, R. (2007). Biomedical information retrieval across languages. *Medical Informatics & the Internet in Medicine, 32*(2), 131–147.

Dechief, D. (2006). *Recent immigrants as an "alternate civic core": Providing Internet services, gaining "Canadian experiences."* Unpublished master's thesis, Concordia University.

Deri, C. (2005). Social networks and health service utilization. *Journal of Health Economics, 24*(6), 1076–1107.

Dezarn, L. M. (2008). The challenge of Latino immigration for the rural library. *Bookmobile and Outreach Services, 11*(1), 25–45.

Dilevko, J., & Dali, K. (2002). The challenge of building multilingual collections in Canadian public libraries. *Library Resources & Technical Services, 46*(4), 116–137.

Duncker, E. (2002). Cross-cultural usability of the library metaphor. *Proceedings of the ACM-IEEE Joint Conference on Digital Libraries*, 223–230.

Faist, T. (2000). Transnationalization in international migration: Implications for the study of citizenship and culture. *Ethnic and Racial Studies, 23*(2), 189–222.

Fisher, K., Durrance, J. C., & Bouch Hinton, M. (2004). Information grounds and the use of needs-based services by immigrants in Queens, New York: A context-based, outcome evaluation approach. *Journal of the American Society for Information Science and Technology, 55*(8), 754–766.

Fisher, K., Marcoux, E., Miller, L. S., Sanchez, A., & Ramirez, E. (2004). Information behaviour of migrant farm workers and their families in the Pacific Northwest. *Information Research, 10*(1). Retrieved January 9, 2009, from informationr.net/ir/10-1/paper199.html

Flythe, F. H. (2001). *Identification of the information needs of newly arrived Hispanic/Latino immigrants in Durham County, North Carolina, and how the public library may address those needs.* Unpublished master's thesis, University of North Carolina at Chapel Hill.

Frazee, C. (2003). *Thumbs up: Inclusion, rights and equality as experienced by youth with disabilities.* Toronto: Laidlaw Foundation.

George, U. (2002). A needs-based model for settlement service delivery for newcomers to Canada. *International Social Work, 45*(4), 465–480.

George, U., Fong, E., Da, W. W., & Chang, R. (2004). *Citizenship and Immigration Canada, Ontario Region Settlement Directorate response to: Recommendations for the delivery of services to Mandarin speaking newcomers from Mainland China.* Toronto: Joint Centre of Excellence for Research on Immigration and Settlement.

George, U., & Mwarigha, M. S. (1999). *Consultation on settlement programming for African newcomers: Final report.* Toronto: Citizenship and Immigration Canada, Ontario Administration of Settlement and Immigration Services.

George, U., & Tsang, A. K. T. (2000). Newcomers to Canada from former Yugoslavia: Settlement issues. *International Social Work, 43*(3), 381–393.

Gollop, C. (1997). Health information-seeking behavior of older African-American women. *Bulletin of the Medical Library Association, 85*(2), 141–146.

Gordon, M. M. (1964). *Assimilation in American life: The role of race, religion, and national origins.* New York: Oxford University Press.

Greiner, T. (2008, May 1). Diversity and the MLS. *Library Journal, 133*(8), 36.

Guarnizo, L. E., Portes, A., & Haller, W. (2003). Assimilation and transnationalism: Determinants of transnational political action among contemporary migrants. *American Journal of Sociology, 108*(6), 1211–1248.

Hall-Ellis, S. D. (2007). Language proficiencies among catalogers and technical services librarians. *Technical Services Quarterly, 25*(2), 31–47.

Hammond-Todd, S. (2008). Immigrant services in public libraries. *Mississippi Libraries, 72*(2), 36–38.

Hickok, J. (2005). ESL (English as a Second Language) Web sites: Resources for library administrators, librarians, and ESL library users. *Journal of Library Administration, 43*(3/4), 247–262.

Hoefer, M., Rytina, N., & Baker, B. C. (2008). *Estimates of the unauthorized immigrant population residing in the United States: January 2007.* Washington, DC: Department of Homeland Security, Office of Immigration Statistics. Retrieved November 14, 2008, from www.dhs.gov/ximgtn/statistics

Holroyd, E. A., Taylor-Piliae, R. E., & Twinn, S. F. (2003). Investigating Hong Kong's Filipino domestic workers' healthcare behaviour, knowledge, beliefs and attitudes towards cervical cancer and cervical screening. *Women & Health, 38*(1), 69–82.

Iivonen, M., & White M. (2001). The choice of initial Web search strategies: A comparison between Finnish and American searchers. *Journal of Documentation, 57*(4), 465–491.

IOM. International Organization for Migration. (n.d.) *About migration.* Retrieved July 10, 2008, from www.iom.int/jahia/jsp/index.jsp

Jang, W. (2004). Richmond Public Library: Serving an increasingly diverse community. *Feliciter, 50*(1). Retrieved on July 10, 2008, from www.cla.ca/AM/Template.cfm?section=Vol_53_No_6

Jansen, B., & Spink, A. (2005). An analysis of Web searching by European AlltheWeb.com users. *Information Processing & Management, 41*(2), 361–381.

Jefferys, K., & Monger, R. (2008). *U.S. Legal Permanent Residents: 2007.* Washington, DC: Department of Homeland Security, Office of Immigration Statistics, Policy Directorate. Retrieved November 14, 2008, from www.dhs.gov/ximgtn/statistics

Jensen, B. (2002). Service to day laborers: A job libraries have left undone. *Reference & User Services Quarterly, 41*(3), 228–233.

Jeong, W. (2004). Unbreakable ethnic bonds: Information-seeking behaviour of Korean graduate students in the United States. *Library & Information Science Research, 26*(3), 384–400.

Joh, S., Yue, A., Hawkins, G., Pookong, K., & Fox, J. (2001). Chinese cosmopolitanism and media use. In S. Cunnigham & J. Sinclair (Eds.), *Floating lives: The media and the Asian diasporas* (pp. 35–90). New York: Rowman and Littlefield.

Johnson, J. D., Case, D. O., Andrews, J., Allard, S. L., & Johnson, N. E. (2006). Fields and pathways: Contrasting or complementary views of information seeking. *Information Processing & Management, 42*(2), 569–582.

Jones, P. A. (1999). *Libraries, immigrants, and the American experience.* Westport, CT: Greenwood Press.

Jonsson-Lanevska, Y. (2005). The gate to understanding: Swedish libraries and immigrants. *New Library World, 106*(3/4), 128–140.

Joppke, C. (2007). The transformation of citizenship: Status, rights, identity. *Citizenship Studies, 11*(1), 37–48.

Karanfil, G. (2007). Satellite television and its discontents: Reflections on the experiences of Turkish-Australian lives. *Continuum: Journal of Media and Cultural Studies, 21*(1), 59–69.

Karim, K. H. (Ed.). (2003). *The media of diaspora.* New York: Routledge.

Kelly, P. (2003). Canadian-Asian transnationalism. *Canadian Geographer, 47*(3), 209–218.

Kennedy, P. (2004). Making global society: Friendship networks among transnational professionals in the building design industry. *Global Networks, 4*(2), 157–179.

Komlodi, A., Caidi, N., & Wheeler, K. (2004). Cross-cultural usability of digital libraries. In Z. Chen, H. Chen, & Q. Miao (Eds.), *Digital libraries: International collaboration and cross-fertilization: 7th International Conference on Asian Digital Libraries* (pp. 584–593). Heidelberg, Germany: Springer-Verlag.

LaFromboise, T., Coleman, H. L. K., & Gerton, J. (1993). Psychological impact of biculturalism: Evidence and theory. *Psychological Bulletin, 114*(3): 395–412.

Lee, C. (2004). Korean immigrants' viewing patterns of Korean satellite television and its role in their lives. *Asian Journal of Communication, 14*(1), 68–90.

Lenhart, A., Horrigan, J., Rainie, L., Allen, K., Boyce, A., Madden, M., et al. (2003). *The ever-shifting Internet population: A new look at Internet access and the digital divide.* Washington, DC: Pew Internet & American Life Project.

Li, P. S. (2003). *Destination Canada: Immigration debates and issues.* Toronto: Oxford University Press.

Lin, W., & Song, H. (2006). Geo-ethnic storytelling: An examination of ethnic media content in contemporary immigrant communities. *Journalism, 7*(3), 362–388.

Liu, M. (1995). Ethnicity and information seeking. *Reference Librarian, 49/50,* 123–134.

Liu, M., & Redfern, B. (1997). Information-seeking behavior of multicultural students: A case study at San Jose State University. *College & Research Libraries,* 348–354.

Luévano-Molina, S. (2001). Mexican/Latino immigrants and the Santa Ana Public Library: An urban ethnography. In S. Luévano-Molina (Ed.), *Immigrant politics and the public library* (pp. 43–68). Westport, CT: Greenwood Press.

Luxton, M. (2002). *Feminist perspectives on social inclusion and children's well-being.* Toronto: Laidlaw Foundation.

Martin, P. L. (2004). The United States: The continuing immigration debate. In W. A. Cornelius, T. Tsuda, P. L. Martin, & J. F. Hollifield (Eds.), *Controlling immigration: A global perspective* (pp. 51–85). Stanford, CA: Stanford University Press.

McGowen, K. (2008). Serving migrant agricultural workers in the rural library. *Bookmobile and Outreach Services, 11*(1), 47–61.

McKenzie, P. J. (2003). A model of information practices in accounts of everyday-life information seeking. *Journal of Documentation, 59*(1), 19–40.

McQuaid, R., Lindsay, C., & Greig, M. (2004). "Reconnecting" the unemployed. *Information, Communication and Society*, *7*(3), 364–388.

Mehra, B., & Papajohn, D. (2007). "Glocal" patterns of communication-information convergences in Internet use: Cross cultural behaviour of international teaching assistants in a culturally alien information environment. *International Information & Library Review*, *39*(1), 12–30.

Metoyer-Duran, C. (1991). Information-seeking behavior of gatekeepers in ethnolinguistic communities: Overview of taxonomy. *Library & Information Science Research*, *13*(4), 319–346.

Metoyer-Duran, C. (1993). Information gatekeepers. *Annual Review of Information Science and Technology*, *28*, 111–150.

Meyers, E. (2004). *International immigration policy: A theoretical and comparative analysis*. New York: Palgrave Macmillan.

Mitchell, A., & Shillington, R. (2002). *Poverty, inequality, and social inclusion*. Toronto: Laidlaw Foundation.

Mitra, A. (2006). Towards finding a cybernetic safe place: Illustrations from people of Indian origin. *New Media & Society*, *8*(2), 251–268.

Moon, S., & Park, C. Y. (2007). Media effects on acculturation and biculturalism: A case study of Korean immigrants in Los Angeles' Koreatown. *Mass Communication and Society*, *10*(3), 319–343.

Morrow, M. (2003). *Mainstreaming women's mental health: Building a Canadian strategy*. Vancouver: British Columbia Centre of Excellence for Women's Health.

Mwarigha, M. S. (2002). *Towards a framework for local responsibility: Taking action to end the current limbo in immigrant settlement: Toronto*. Toronto: Maytree Foundation.

Mylopoulos, C. (2004). New faces on the block: Emerging immigrant communities and how to identify them. *Feliciter*, *50*(1), 12–13.

Naficy, H. (2003). Narrowcasting in diaspora: Middle Eastern television in Los Angeles. In K. H. Karim (Ed.), *The media of diaspora*. New York: Routledge.

Nedlina, Y. G. (2007). Public services to Russian-speaking patrons: The view of a bilingual librarian. *Bookmobile & Outreach Services*, *10*(1), 25–31.

Nee, V., & Sanders, J. (2001). Understanding the diversity of immigrant incorporation: A forms-of-capital model. *Ethnic & Racial Studies*, *24*(3), 386–411.

Neely, T. Y., & Peterson, L. (2007). Achieving racial and ethnic diversity among academic and research librarians: The recruitment, retention, and advancement of librarians of color: A white paper. *College & Research Libraries News*, *68*(9), 562–565.

No One is Illegal Vancouver. (n.d). *Regularization: Status for all*. Retrieved December 8, 2008, from noii-van.resist.ca/?page_id=89

Notess, G. R. (2008). Multilingual searching: Search engine language tools. *Online*, *32*(3), 40–42.

Novotny, E. (2003). Library services to immigrants: The debate in the library literature, 1900–1920, and a Chicago case study. *Reference & User Services Quarterly*, *42*(4), 342–352.

Omidvar, R., & Richmond, T. (2003). *Immigrant settlement and social inclusion in Canada*. Toronto: Law Foundation.

Orange, S. M. (2004). Reaching underserved populations [sessions at the 2003 Great American Bookmobile and Outreach Services Conference]. *Bookmobile & Outreach Services*, *7*(1), 55–60.

O'Toole, E. (2005). Reading America program fosters intergenerational understanding in Chinese immigrant families. *Public Libraries*, *44*(6), 355–359.

Papillon, M. (2002). *Immigration, diversity and social inclusion in Canada's cities*. Ottawa: Canadian Policy Research Networks.

Park, R. E., & Burgess, E. W. (1921). *Introduction to the science of sociology*. Chicago: University of Chicago Press.

Pettigrew, K. E. (1999). Waiting for chiropody: Contextual results from an ethnographic study of the information behaviour among attendees at community clinics. *Information Processing & Management*, *35*(6), 801–817.

Pokorny, R. E. (2003). Library services to immigrants and non-native speakers of English: From our past to our present. *Bookmobile & Outreach Services*, 6(2), 21–34.

Portes, A., & Bach, R. (1985). *Latin journey: Cuban and Mexican immigrants in the United States*. Berkeley: University of California Press.

Prock, A. (2003). Serving the invisible population: Library outreach for migrant farm workers. *Bookmobile & Outreach Services*, 6(1), 37–51.

Pumariega, A., Rothe, E., & Pumariega, J. (2005). Mental health of immigrants and refugees. *Community Mental Health Journal*, *41*(5), 581–597.

Quirke, L. C. (2006). Public libraries serving newcomers to Canada: A comparison of the Toronto and Windsor public libraries. Unpublished master's thesis, Ryerson University, Toronto.

Ravid, G., Bar-Ilan, J., Baruchson-Arbib, S., & Rafaeli, S. (2007). Popularity and findability through log analysis of search terms and queries: The case of a multilingual public service website. *Journal of Information Science*, *33*(5), 567–583.

Reitmanova, S., & Gustafson, D. L. (2008). "They can't understand it": Maternity health and care needs of immigrant Muslim women in St. John's, Newfoundland. *Maternal and Child Health Journal*, *12*(1), 101–111.

Roald, A. S. (2004). Arab satellite broadcasting: The immigrants' extended ear to their homelands. In J. Malik (Ed.), *Muslims in Europe: From the margin to the centre* (pp. 207–226). Münster, Germany: LIT Verlag.

Salaff, J. W., & Greve, A. (2004). Can women's social networks really migrate? *Women's Studies International Forum*, *27*(2), 149–162.

Saloojee, A. (2005). Social inclusion, anti-racism and democratic citizenship. *Policy Matters*, *14*, 1–6.

Sampredo, V. (1998). Grounding the displaced: Local media reception in a transnational context. *Journal of Communication*, *48*, 125–143.

Savolainen, R. (1995). Everyday life information seeking: Approaching information seeking in the context of "way of life." *Library & Information Science Research*, *17*(3), 259–294.

Savolainen, R. (2007). Information behavior and information practice: Reviewing the umbrella concepts of information-seeking studies. *Library Quarterly*, *77*(2), 109–132.

Savolainen, R. (2008). *Everyday information practices: A social phenomenological perspective*. Toronto: Scarecrow Press.

Savolainen, R., & Kari, J. (2004). Placing the Internet in information source horizons: A study of information seeking by Internet users in the context of self-development. *Library & Information Science Research*, *26*(4), 415–433.

Shoham, E., & Stam, R. (Eds.). (2001). *Multiculturalism, postcoloniality and transnational media*. New Brunswick, NJ: Rutgers University Press.

Shoham, S., & Rabinovich, R. (2008). Public library services to new immigrants in Israel: The case of immigrants from the former Soviet Union and Ethiopia. *International Information & Library Review*, *40*(1), 21–42.

Shoham, S., & Strauss, S. (2007). Information needs of North American immigrants to Israel. *Journal of Information, Communication & Ethics in Society*, *5*(2/3), 185–205.

Shoham, S., & Strauss, S. K. (2008). Immigrants' information needs: Their role in the absorption process. *Information Research*, *13*(4). Retrieved July 26, 2009, from informationr.net/ir/13-4/paper359.html

Silvio, D. H. (2006). The information needs and information seeking behaviour of immigrant southern Sudanese youth in the city of London, Ontario: An exploratory study. *Library Review*, *55*(4), 259–266.

Sligo, F., & Jameson, A. (2000). The knowledge-behaviour gap in use of health information: Cervical screen for Pacific immigrants living in New Zealand. *Journal of the American Society for Information Science and Technology*, *51*(9), 858–869.

Smith, C. (2006). Multiple cultures, multiple intelligences: Applying cognitive theory to usability of digital libraries. *Libri*, *56*(4), 227–238.

Sonnenwald, D. H. (1999). Evolving perspectives of human information behaviour: Contexts, situations, social networks and information horizons. *Proceedings of the 2nd International Conference on Research in Information Needs, Seeking and Use in Different Contexts*, 176–190.

Srinivasan, R. (2006). Indigenous, ethnic, and cultural articulations of new media. *International Journal of Cultural Studies*, *9*(4), 497–518.

Srinivasan, R. (2007). Ethnomethodological architectures: Information systems driven by cultural and community visions. *Journal of the American Society for Information Science and Technology*, *58*(5), 723–733.

Srinivasan, R., & Pyati, A. (2007). Diasporic information environments: Re-framing information behavior research. *Journal of the American Society for Information Science and Technology*, *58*(12), 1734–1744.

Stavri, P. Z. (2001). Personal health information-seeking: A qualitative review of the literature. *MEDINFO Proceedings of the 10th World Conference on Medical Informatics*, 1484–1488.

Su, S. S., & Conaway, C. W. (1995). Information and a forgotten minority: Elderly Chinese immigrants. *Library & Information Science Research*, *17*(1), 69–86.

Sun, A., Zang, J., Tsoh, J., Wong-Kim, E., & Chow, E. (2007). The effectiveness in utilizing Chinese media to promote breast health among Chinese women. *Journal of Health Communication*, *12*(2), 157–171.

To, T. (1995). Survey on the library needs of and library use by the Chinese language readers in Fairfield, New South Wales: Preliminary report. *Public Library Quarterly*, *14*(4), 27–50.

U.N. Department of Economic and Social Affairs. (2002). *International migration report 2002*. Retrieved November 12, 2008, from www.un.org/esa/population/publications/ittmig2002/2002ITTMIG TEXT22-11.pdf

U.S. Department of Health and Human Services, Administration for Children and Families. (2008). *Refugee assistance*. Retrieved November 14, 2008, from www.acf.hhs.gov/programs/orr/about/divisions.htm

Uy-Tioco, C. (2007). Overseas Filipino workers and text messaging: Reinventing transnational mothering. *Continuum: Journal of Media and Cultural Studies*, *21*(2), 253–265.

Vander Kooy, M. (2004). Toronto: The globe in the microcosm. *Feliciter*, *50*(1). Retrieved May 30, 2009, from www.cla.ca/docs/Vol_55_No_2.pdf

Vang, V. (2003). Public library services to the Hmong-American community: Much room for improvement. Retrieved July 10, 2008, from libres.curtin.edu.au/libres14n1/March%2004_Ess%20&%20Op_VangNov20_03.htm

Vertovec, S. (2004). Cheap calls: The social glue of migrant transnationalism. *Global Networks*, *4*(2), 219–224.

Virgilio, D. (2003). Service to the international community. *Bookmobile & Outreach Services*, *6*(2), 7–15.

Viseu, A., Clement, A., & Aspinall, J. (2004). Situating privacy online. *Information, Communication & Society, 7*(1), 92–114.

Viswanath, K., & Arora, P. (2000). Ethnic media in the United States: An essay on their role in integration, assimilation and social control. *Mass Communication and Society, 3*(1), 39–56.

Waldinger, R., & Feliciano, C. (2004). Will the new second generation experience "downward assimilation"? Segmented assimilation re-assessed. *Ethnic & Racial Studies, 27*(3), 376–402.

Waters, J. (2003). Flexible citizens? Transnationalism and citizenship amongst economic immigrants in Vancouver. *Canadian Geographer, 47*(3), 219–234.

Weerasinghe, S. (2000). *Equitable access to healthcare, health promotion, and disease prevention for recent immigrant women living in Nova Scotia, Canada: Report on phase 1.* Halifax, NS: Maritime Centre of Excellence for Women's Health.

Wenjing, X. (2005). Virtual space, real identity: Exploring cultural identity of Chinese diaspora in virtual community. *Telematics & Informatics, 22*(4), 395–404.

Winkel, A. (2007). Lessons on evaluating programs and collections for immigrant communities at the Queens Borough Public Library. *Colorado Libraries, 33*(1), 43–46.

Wong, L., & Ng, M. (2002). The emergence of small transnational enterprise in Vancouver: The case of Chinese entrepreneur immigrants. *International Journal of Urban and Regional Research, 26*(3), 508–530.

Wong, L. L. (2004). Taiwanese immigrant entrepreneurs in Canada and transnational social spaces. *International Migration, 42*(2), 113–150.

Wong, S., & Salaff, J. W. (1998). Network capital: Emigration from Hong Kong. *British Journal of Sociology, 49*(3), 358–374.

Zhang, X. (2001). The practice and politics of public library services to Asian immigrants. In S. Luévano-Molina (Ed.), *Immigrant politics and the public library* (pp. 141–150). Westport, CT: Greenwood Press.

Zhou, M. (1997). Segmented assimilation: Issues, controversies and recent research for the new second generation. *International Migration Review, 31*(4), 975–1008.

Zhuo, F., Emanuel, J., & Jiao, S. (2007). International students and language preferences in library database use. *Technical Services Quarterly, 24*(4), 1–13.

# CHAPTER 12

# Confessional Methods and Everyday Life Information Seeking

*Elisabeth Davenport*
*Edinburgh Napier University*

## Introduction

The American Library Association's Jesse H. Shera Award for Excellence in Published Research was given in 2008 to a group of researchers from the Information Behavior in Everyday Contexts (IBEC) group at the University of Washington iSchool. The winning paper by Meyers, Fisher, and Marcoux (2007, p. 311) presents a "holistic" approach to capturing the everyday information habits of pre-teen high school students in the United States. The authors use mixed methods—incentivized focus groups and paired and individual interviews, all undertaken with punctilious compliance with U.S. human subjects research regulations. The protocol for the interview uses a vocabulary that is standard in everyday life information seeking (ELIS) research—"user needs," "information seeking," and, a recent entrant, "information grounds." The award-winning paper focuses on methods, not full results (extensive empirical work had not been completed at the time when the paper was nominated) and it addresses a vogue topic: the everyday habits of "youth" (Agosto & Hughes-Hassell, 2005, 2006a, 2006b; Chelton & Cool, 2004, 2007). So what makes this paper a prize winner? The chapter that follows addresses this question by reviewing the methodological context of the paper—a corpus of work that draws on a common repertoire, the "confessional methods" of the title.

ELIS is part of broader domain in library and information science (LIS) that focuses on human information behavior (HIB) (Spink & Cole, 2006a, 2006b). Like their colleagues in the cognate domain of information seeking in context (ISIC) (Vakkari, Savolainen, & Dervin, 1997; Wilson & Allen, 1999), ELIS researchers are concerned with situated users; where ISIC explores task and work environments, ELIS focuses on non-work contexts. ELIS methods are an appropriate topic for a number of reasons. The domain is of interest to researchers, designers, vendors, and policy makers. Many researchers believe that methods that uncover private motivations, desires, feelings, and worldviews can explain patterns of information use; designers and vendors are confident that such research can enhance the allure of products and services; policy makers wish to understand the forms of life that are emerging from a widening range of media (ubiquitous, mobile, ambient) as individuals and groups become experts in managing information for themselves. ELIS studies, like those of HIB in general, have not delivered robust results (Case, 2006) and an explanatory analysis is timely. This chapter offers a critical review of three commonly used methods in ELIS research and suggests that methodological and theoretical confusion can explain the lack of robust results. Although these methods form the historic core, it may be noted that they are only part of the current ELIS repertoire, which embraces a wider set of methods including discourse analysis and ethnography (McKechnie, 2000; MacKenzie 2004, 2006; Talja, 1997, 1999; Talja & MacKenzie, 2007; Williamson, 2006).

The following methods are discussed in detail: critical incident technique (CI), focus groups, and the micro-moment time-line interview in sense-making methodology (SMM). The three share certain characteristics. First, they elicit accounts of activities and mental states that are not directly observed. Second, they involve a researcher (an authoritative figure or expert) and one or more subjects and thus are not interactions among peers. Third, the aim of the interaction is intervention that improves service or system design. These methods, common in qualitative social science, are designed to elicit hidden truths or meanings from participants; they are examples of "disciplinary technology" (Dreyfus & Rabinow, 1983, p. xxvii), a concept elaborated by Foucault in a series of works (e.g., Foucault, 1979, 1980). Two important techniques are associated with disciplinary technology: confession and examination. The latter focuses on the body and does its works through observation; confession focuses on desire and its revelation in confessional dialogue. Such "isolating, ordering, systematizing practices" support the exploration of subjectivity as a social science (Dreyfus & Rabinow, 1983, p. xxvii). A corollary of the confessional method is belief that one can, with the help of experts, tell the truth about oneself; this belief is integral to the line of ELIS work reviewed here. Paraphrasing Foucault, Dreyfus and Rabinow suggest that such "technologies of the self" are now perceived as so natural that it "seems unrealistic to posit that such self-examination is the outcome of a strategy of power" (p. 175) through which the state and its concomitant institutions "turn individuals into meaningful subjects and docile objects" (p. xvii).

Foucault's work underpins a number of critical analyses of library and information science (e.g., Frohmann, 1994, 2001, 2004, 2008). His explication of confessional talk can throw light on a number of tensions, pretensions, and paradoxes in ELIS methodology. These include tension over the participant's status as subject or object (or how to turn talk into data), tension over the researcher's status, and debate over whether ELIS studies should conform with the norms of modern or postmodern science. Most importantly, Foucault's focus on the historical and societal forces at work in the development and appropriation of "technologies of the self" (see Foucault, 1988, p. 16) draws attention to the historical contingency of confessional work. In LIS, for example, we can trace the shift in perceptions of the user (McKechnie, Julien, Pecoskie, & Dixon, 2006) from the docile object of formal systems testing (think Cranfield and the Text Retrieval Conference) to the meaningful subject, whose motivations, gratifications, fears, and desires can be recovered through talk. Current expressions of the meaningful subject can be found in recent edited monographs by Nahl and Bilal (2007, p. 1) ("the emergent affective paradigm"), and Chelton and Cool (2007, p. 1; also 2004) ("youth information-seeking behavior")—see, for example, the contribution to the latter by Hughes-Hassell and

Agosto (2007), which invokes technologies of the self quite overtly in a typology of adolescent selves that can be accommodated by means of intrapersonal management techniques at both system and personal levels.

For critical analysts (e.g., Radway, 1989; Schultze, 2000), the investigator is one of the many selves that must be accounted for in any research narrative. However, few ELIS researchers reflect on their role as producers of objects and subjects; the work of Dervin is an example. Dervin's (1992, p. 70) own pronouncement that "there is always the mandate to cope with self" has been little heeded by ELIS researchers who invoke her methods.

Frohmann (1990, p. 46) has drawn on Foucault's work to critique "mentalism" in LIS, and, more recently, to probe the concept of the ethical subject (Frohmann, 2008). His critical monograph, *Deflating Information* (Frohmann, 2004), characterizes methodological tensions in ELIS in terms of a struggle between nominalists and realists over the nature of information as a theoretical kind (e.g., Frohmann, 2004, pp. 55, 80–81, 120). For realists, information is a phenomenon whose attributes may be discovered through rigorous empirical observation and reporting by the researcher; the greater the number of studies, the more complete the understanding. For nominalists, information is in "the mind's eye of the user" (to use Dervin's [1992, p. 61] phrase) and the user is best qualified to report on it. Frohmann (2004, p. 66) notes that the "cognitive turn" coincided with a historical move (Dervin, 1976, 1989; Zweizig & Dervin, 1977) to explore everyday lifeworlds as sources for authentic accounts of information use. Dialogic methods that elicit internal states and everyday life studies have thus been tightly coupled for many years. But the protocols that are used in ELIS interviews are problematic research instruments in a number of ways—it is difficult, for example, to characterize "information" when studies are so localized and disparate and when they differ in their treatment of the data elicited in interviews, often in the form of retrospective narratives. Few researchers analyze narratives as specimens of informant discourse; many treat them as factual or "factist" accounts (Talja, 1999, pp. 471–472). Frohmann (2004, p. 79) suggests that ELIS studies are thus an arena where fundamental methodological issues are in play, although insouciance on the part of researchers (Pettigrew is named as an honorable exception) means that they are rarely addressed, let alone resolved.

## Sources

The approach in this chapter differs from recent *ARIST* reviews that otherwise appear to be cognate. What is reviewed here is a set of methods that has attracted a large number of adherents in the past thirty years or so. The chapter thus complements the comprehensive reviews of information behavior studies by Case (2007) and Fisher and Julien (2009). It draws on secondary texts that are seminal to the ISIC/ELIS confessional tradition: the monograph on sense-making methodology (Dervin & Foreman-Wernet, 2003); the proceedings of the Information Seeking in Context conferences (Vakkari et al., 1997; Wilson & Allen, 1999), and the issues of the *New Review of Information Behaviour Research* that replaced the ISIC conference publication; Case's (2007) monograph on information behavior research; and Fisher, Erdelez, and McKechnie's (2005) edited collection, *Theories of Information*

*Behavior.* In addition, the chapter draws on the discourse analytic tradition in LIS (Frohmann, 1991, 1994, 2004, 2008; Talja & MacKenzie, 2007; Tuominen, 1997; Tuominen & Savolainen, 1997) and more general work on historical ontology (Hacking, 1995, 2004, 2006) and the writing of science, specifically scientific nomenclature (Halliday & Martin, 1993). The chapter does not, however, attempt to provide a genealogy of user studies, which has been done elsewhere (see, for example, Savolainen, 2007; Talja & Hartel, 2007).

The overall aim is to provide a critical review of methods. The chapter is not intended as a comment on the *oeuvre* of individuals or on the entire corpus of ELIS research. It is shaped as follows. The confession is defined as a specific dialogue type and linked to an established dialogic tradition in library and information science research. Three frequently used dialogic methods are presented in detail. The chapter then explores the scientificity of confessional work and concludes with a brief review of alternative approaches to confessional methods. Individual papers are cited where a particular line of argument requires illustration.

## Confession and Dialogue

Dialogue as a means of eliciting real-time information needs is a long established technique in information science. The explication in this chapter starts with the work of Taylor (1962, 1968). Taylor's 1962 paper on the process of asking questions presents dialogue as a primary means of eliciting library patrons' needs. He develops a seminal model of information seeking that delineates a process whereby internal urges are elicited by means of dialogue, to produce a "compromised" need (that is, a need jointly articulated with a professional intermediary who is familiar with a relevant source); the need is then addressed by means of search expressions that have been negotiated in the dialogue between professional and client. In Taylor's version of reference work, confessional (revealing what is hidden to an appropriate authority) and professional (listening from a position of authority) activities are complementary and they intersect to produce information through the process of question negotiation. Taylor's (1962, p. 394) model is frequently invoked as a typology of needs; his own focus, however, is the answering of questions as a process, one that depends on the "state of mind at a specific moment in relation to a particular investigation" of the inquirer, which is "not, of course, a fixed position."

The process model is elaborated further in the second paper, where an inquiry is defined as "merely a micro-event in a shifting non-linear adaptive mechanism" (Taylor, 1968, p. 179). A number of studies (e.g., Fidel, 1985; Procter, Goldenberg, Davenport, & McKinlay, 1998) have analyzed the reference interview as a series of (more or less routine) moves in response to reference artifacts such as the on-screen list or printout of search results. One of Taylor's (1968, p. 186) respondents views the negotiation process as a "game of chess" wherein such moves refine a user's query and lead to a recognized closure. This type of analysis leads to classification either to improve the efficiency of the interaction—to identify the moves and refinements that are appropriate to a conclusion (e.g., Fidel, 1985) or to classify and sort queries into simple and more complex (Procter et al. [1998] suggest that documentary and genre analysis can help here).

An alternative process model emphasizes the evolution of inner states that drive or motivate observable moves. The interview elicits a narrative of the mind's journey; users' mental models or constructs (of problems, of the self, of acceptable resolutions) are invoked and compared and/or aligned with the conceptual models that underpin the structure and form of information sources/systems (Bates, 1999). Historically, elicitation has focused on "closed" encounters where "need" is articulated in terms of objectives and problem solving and elicitation of a user's model of the problem can guide alignment. Much of this work has been undertaken by ISIC researchers analyzing the search behavior of students working on class assignments (Kuhlthau, 1988, 1991, 1993). The "problem" is task or system focused and the models that have emerged are largely descriptive; few of them identify factors in a way that supports prediction (Frohmann, 2004). Bernier (2007) provides a critique of this line of work: It presents an impoverished image of young people and fails to capture the abundant pleasures, demands, strategies, media, and sources that characterize information activity in this group in the wild.

ELIS researchers have moved beyond the overtly disciplinary or institutional environment of the classroom or the library to explore information behavior in the world at large. Early formulations of this approach (e.g., Dervin, 1976, 1983; Zweizig & Dervin, 1977) suggest that the focus of researcher and management should not be "how citizens relate to sources" but "the reciprocal question of how sources relate to citizens" (Dervin, 1976, p. 30). Because lives in the everyday world cannot be observed in real time, interviews or dialogues must elicit retrospective accounts, supported at best with snapshots of real-time activity. These retrospective accounts allow researchers to establish the local and personal conditions that characterize a user's situation. Situation is both inner and outer (or mental/emotional and physical) and a resource in individual sense making. Everyday lives are less bounded by tasks and roles than lives in institutional contexts; thus, the confessional account is of necessity contingent. According to confessional ELIS research, people in everyday contexts do not so much seek information or knowledge as try to master a way of life or make sense of their worlds, worlds that are fragmented, dynamic, and gap laden (Savolainen, 1995a, 1995b).

The sense-making approach is fully consolidated as an LIS method (as distinct from a communication studies one) in Dervin and Nilan's (1986) *ARIST* chapter, where it is presented as a radical alternative to existing methods. Nevertheless, sense making can be seen as a continuation (to some extent) of established methods, as it combines elicitation and mental models. It differs, however, in its emphasis on retrospection and in its privileging of the informant as a source of authentic experience. Frohmann (2004, pp. 65–66) finds "epistemic continuity" between SMM and the approaches that it aspires to replace: "a striking feature of their 'alternative paradigm' is the continuity between the concept of information as a theoretical kind … a cognitivist one … with earlier cognitivist approaches; information is constituted inside the privacy of the mind, not outside, in the public realm, in shared practices." As SMM researchers resort to the fundamentals of the human condition to categorize mental processes, Frohmann (2004, p. 67) further observes that "it is an open question whether, once discovered, they render the information user significantly less 'robotic' than the information processors of the old paradigm."

## Confessional Methods in Detail

Three confessional methods are reviewed in this section: critical incident (CI) technique, focus groups, and the SMM micro-moment timeline interview, all selected because they are commonly used in ISIC/ELIS research. Where appropriate, reviews and critiques of these methods by LIS and communication studies researchers are summarized.

### Critical Incident Analysis

Critical incident analysis emerged in World War II (like many other techniques in social science) in studies of air crews and their competence in specific material environments; it diffused, post-war, into industry. It has been used by a number of ELIS researchers and a detailed reprise of the original technique is provided here to act as a validity benchmark—many studies that claim to use CI do not follow the procedures that are required (see Urquhart, Light, Thomas, Barker, Yeoman, Cooper, et al., 2003; Urquhart & Rowley, 2007). Flanagan (1954, p. 351) provides a detailed account of the history and procedures involved in this technique, which is locally situated and inductive: "The critical incident technique, rather than collecting opinions, hunches, and estimates, obtains a record of specific behaviors from those in the best position to make the necessary observations and evaluation." The aims of CI are to "solve practical problems" and "develop psychological principles" (p. 327). The second aim has proven (and continues to prove) to be problematic.

An incident is defined as "any observable human activity that is sufficiently complete in itself to permit inferences and predications to be made about the person performing the act" (Flanagan, 1954, p. 327)—CI is thus a fitting technique for analyzing the confessional phenomena that are the focus of this chapter. To be critical, an incident must "occur in a situation where the purpose or intent of the act seems fairly clear to the observers, and where its consequences are sufficiently defined to leave little doubt concerning its effects" (p. 327). The objective is to analyze and classify observations into "relationships for further testing"—for example, in one of the early studies using CI, "733 pilot behaviors were classified into 24 critical requirements" (p. 336). Numbers are important—for a robust analysis, thousands of incidents should be recorded, a requirement that is rarely met in ELIS work.

Data are to be gathered from "first-hand reports or reports from objective records" (Flanagan, 1954, p. 329); sometimes the two can be combined into triangulated accounts of satisfactory and unsatisfactory completion of tasks. Flanagan discusses in detail two issues that are likely to raise problems. The first is the difficulty of achieving immediacy because it is not always possible to provide a report "on the spot"; the second is proximity—how removed from the action can an observer be? Flanagan suggests that trained observers can provide valid accounts, although these may differ: In one of his case studies, separate reports by foremen and researchers focused on different aspects of incidents. More significant is the time lapse between incident and recall (whether recall is elicited in interviews or reports does not matter): "Foremen who reported only at the end of the week had forgotten approximately one half of the incidents they would have reported under a daily reporting plan" (p. 331). After two weeks, they appeared to have forgotten 80 percent of the incidents observed. The implications of this finding for inviting participants, as often happen in ELIS research, to "name an incident" in an act of unspecified retrospection are troubling. Flanagan also discusses a third problem: Even when asked to describe incidents that did not deviate greatly from the norm, respondents tended to offer substantially deviant incidents, thus offering sensationalist accounts.

For Flanagan, CI analysis is a method of establishing facts from qualitative data that is reliable only where safeguards are employed. These include member checking, triangulation, and mindful selection of data. Member checking (Flanagan, 1954, p. 335) is an important part of the technique (and one that is often missing in ELIS accounts). Classification is a particularly difficult area. Flanagan notes that, "In the absence of an adequate theory of human behavior this step is usually an inductive one and is relatively subjective" (p. 335) (and, one might add, in the context of ELIS studies, in the absence of an adequate theory of human information behavior). Classifications should be checked or triangulated with the "ideas of a number of well-qualified authorities" (p. 337): professionals, either on-the-ground experts or academics. According to Flanagan (p. 345), "The induction of categories from the basic data in the form of incidents is a task requiring insight, experience, and judgment." The freshness of the data ("evaluated, classified and recorded while the facts are still fresh in the mind of the observer" [p. 339]) is also important.

Flanagan describes in great detail the questioning technique that elicits accounts of critical incidents. For example, an early study of pilot vertigo (Flanagan, 1954, p. 328) required observers to comment on "what they say, heard, or felt that brought on the experience." The researcher's remarks should be "neutral and permissive and should show that he accepts the observer as an expert" (p. 342). The analyst must have information on place, persons, conditions, and activities; must consider the relevance of the account (p. 338) to the aim of the study (i.e., what it reveals about the activity and the person involved in that activity) and the extent of the effect of what is reported—some narratives may be excluded if the effects of the activity are not important. If suitable precautions are taken, recalled incidents can be relied upon to provide adequate data for a "fairly adequate first approximation to a statement of the requirements of the activity" (p. 340).

CI has been used in a number of confessional ELIS studies, although Flanagan's caveats are rarely discussed, let alone heeded. The difficulties are manifold. As has been noted, the fragmentation of the field (Case, 2007; Fisher et al., 2005) means that there is no commonly accepted theory of human information behavior. Second, the condition of direct or immediate observation is difficult to fulfill. Third, the issue of non-participant observers (the status of many of the researchers who use the technique) and their competence to comment on incidents is rarely addressed in ELIS work: Chatman's (1987) study of campus janitors is a notable exception here. ELIS applications of the method range from the perfunctory (Julien, 1999) to the extensively reflective (Savolainen, 1995a). As has been noted, Flanagan's (1954) original presentation of the method covers issues of reliability and validity at great length; ELIS studies show differing levels of compliance here. Niemela and Huotari (2008) use mixed methods, with informants keeping diaries that are matched against informant narratives. Fisher and Landry (2007) attempt triangulation. Respondents, however, are desultory in their diary-keeping, and the researchers find that "learning and adopting participants' language" greatly improves the trustworthiness of their data (p. 217). Savolainen (1995a) offers an honest, painstaking, and insightful account of CI analysis in an empirical study of middle and working-class urban information seekers. He finds that (p. 283) "description of critical incidents ... scattered on a wide area" and two informants "failed to report" any acceptable story. Savolainen suggests that CI technique in ELIS should focus on a few clear topics such as health or unemployment. A further problem is the contingency of the reported incidents: "if one happened to choose a relatively 'easy' critical incident with a happy end, one might have come to think that the informant acted rationally in problem solving"; reporting of a more complicated incident "might imply the informant had failed to benefit from the most useful information sources" (p. 284). The results of his study, based on single incidents, are thus "somewhat impressionistic" (p. 284).

## Focus Groups

The second dialogic technique reviewed here is the focus group interview. Like CI, focus group elicitation is a technique that emerged in World War II, in Lazerfeld and Merton's 1941 studies that elicited responses to public broadcasting campaigns. Merton (1987, p. 558), in a retrospective view of the method, observes: "For us, qualitative focused group interviews were taken as a source of new ideas and hypotheses, not as demonstrated findings with regard to the extent and distribution of the provisionally identified qualitative patterns of response." Lunt (1996, p. 81) in a review of historical and current applications of the method, observes that "contemporary uses of the focus group challenge Merton's approach and take more seriously the group nature of the discussion." Researchers who use focus groups must make a number of important decisions at every stage of a research project about design, sampling, and analysis. Will the group consist of friends ("naturally occurring groups of like-minded people" [p. 82]) or strangers? Where does the focus group fit—is it a part or the whole of data collection? Will there be one or many sessions? What is the status of the researcher—a participant in the group or an observer of the group?

The issue of individual versus group as a unit of analysis haunts the method. For Merton, as has been noted, focus groups offer a convenient way to collect aggregated individual opinion, revealing issues or outliers that might warrant further study in large-scale surveys. Here the group is primarily a vehicle. Analysts of discourse/conversation and other socially oriented researchers take a different view. As Lunt (1996, p. 85) observes, "focus groups can be understood not by analogy to the survey ... but as a simulation of those routine but inaccessible communicative contexts in which meaning is socially constructed in everyday talk." From this perspective, focus groups are an "admittedly approximate simulation of everyday talk/conversation" and may be used in conjunction with, and in order to overcome, the disadvantages of other qualitative methods (p. 85). Optimally, then, the researcher should try to create "social occasions in themselves that bear sufficient resemblance to the social occasions under study" (p. 85). Lunt (p. 86) calls this "quasi-ethnography" or "quasi-naturalistic research."

Theoretical choices are thus important. Different theoretical frameworks result in different conceptions of the group context with consequences for the design and conduct of the focus groups themselves. Each of the approaches to treating focus group material depends upon a different understanding of the personal-social-political relations among the participants (including the researcher). This raises the issue of moderation and control. Lunt (1996) suggests that if the purpose of the group is to listen to everyday conversation ("what people actually do or say when they come together for a discussion" [p. 87]) then the group should run itself—all conversation is inherently dialogic and focus groups are "an opportunity to observe informants conducting their own discursive tests, negotiating meaning, and confirming or disconfirming appropriate ways of speaking" (p. 88).

Lunt discusses two major criticisms of the method. The first states that focus groups fail to satisfy the validity and reliability conditions that characterize robust social science. Lunt offers two ways to rebut the criticism. The first is reliability through exhaustion, which takes two forms. Triangulation, he suggests (Lunt, 1996, p. 92), can be achieved through multiple comparative groups: "The exhaustion of the various things to be said (by repeat groups) on a given topic is part of the constant validity of the method, offering a notion of reliability related not to the identity of two runs of the method, but to the rate of information given." The second rebuttal involves internal validity in cases where the "group acts as if conducting an inquiry" (p. 93). In this situation, member checking is undertaken *within* rather than *across* groups. This raises a further issue of moderator training—moderators should be trained to "reduce the effects of false consensus or group polarization" (p. 94). A further criticism concerns the selection of material for analysis (pp. 94–95): "the local discursive context of an utterance or extract being analyzed has proven a particularly intractable problem for qualitative researchers ... the extent to which illustrative quotations represent broader themes is also problematic ... if the analysis of qualitative data is to be systematic, the presentation of extracts from the interviews is insufficient ... if the discussion is simulating the ethnographic process of talk and argumentation." The solution here is to avoid seductive quotes and undertake systematic content analysis of complete transcripts.

Focus groups have been used in a number of ELIS studies, although the rationale for this type of research design is rarely discussed. Dervin (2007) recently presented focus groups as a key technique in SMM. Far from taking the group interaction as "an admittedly approximate simulation of everyday talk/conversation" (Lunt, 1996, p. 85), Dervin admits only disciplined conversation that obeys house rules and advocates the use of a prescriptive protocol. In a recent empirical study (Dervin, 2006, p. 12), her team uses "smoothing" techniques to present the evidence and to categorize the material using "quotable quotes" as units of analysis, which runs counter to Lunt's caveat about using extracts out of their local discursive context. Meyers and colleagues (2007), in contrast, describe in detail the sampling, recruitment, physical conditions, and conduct of focus groups at two sites; comment on the development of peer discourse in the sessions; and offer advice on how to moderate when informants become uncooperative. Focus groups are a key component of the "Tween day" methodology (Meyers et al., 2007, pp. 317–318).

## Micro-Moment Time-Line Interviews

The third dialogic or confessional technique that is covered in this section is the interview as used in sense-making methodology. SMM covers a range of methodological issues (some of these are reprised in a later section); the focus at this point is interviewing. Although there is little acknowledgment of Flanagan's work in SMM research, micro-moment time line interviewing is similar to CI in a number of respects. Both require a re-construction of experience; and in both, the interviewer is required to take a neutral stance and treat the informant as the expert on the situation that is the focus of inquiry. But there are major differences, which are important to the critique on methods that is developed in this chapter. The first is the nature of the micro-events that are described by informants. For Flanagan, the micro-events that are of interest are physical or physiological. For SMM researchers, they are primarily "internal," evoked in the "why?" "what did you feel?" questions that play no part in CI protocols. Responses to "what helped?" and "what hindered?" questions in SMM are as likely to involve emotions as artifacts or actions. Crudely put, CI disciplines the body; SMM disciplines the soul. A second difference lies in the approach to triangulation of informants' accounts. This is an intrinsic part of CI analysis. But evocations of internal events are difficult to triangulate out of their documentary context—and SMM researchers differ in their levels of commitment to this activity.

A number of different types of dialogue are to be found in SMM, such as "the life-line, the micro-moment time-line, the helping chain and so on" (Dervin, 2003, p. 2). However, the "micro-moment time-line interview" is the "core method," according to Dervin (1992, p. 70). Sense making is "applicable to both formalized and extended interviews in research studies as well as to less formalized and often briefer interviews during which the institution interacts with its users or potential users to provide service" (p. 70). Micro-moment time lining can be adapted to different research contexts. The abbreviated interview is suited to routine behavior and respondents are asked to focus on only one incident in this approach. The help chain involves repeated queries to the respondent of the type "and how did that help you?" until the respondent feels the statement of help has been made "in the most personal and life-relevant terms" (p. 72). "Neutral questioning" is a refinement of the protocol to be applied in reference interviews (Dervin & Dewdney, 1986, p. 506). In all of the variants, information is conceptualized as "that sense created at a specific moment in time-space by one or more humans" (Dervin, 1992, p. 63) although it is not clear if the moment is that of the interview, or that of the recollected incident, or if the two are to be considered as the same. Dervin (p. 70) states that "the moments are seen as vehicles for examining gap-defining and gap-bridging, not representative of reality as it is." Somewhat confusingly, however, the experiences that are narrated are "real" (p. 72).

Each technique requires a participant to re-count (or "re-construct" [Dervin, 1992, p. 72]) the experience that has led him or her to enter into dialogue with others to solve a problem, either in the past, or in the case of reference interviews, in the current situation. The starting point is a single "moment" or event that is anatomized in terms of "who?" "where?" "why?" "what? "how?". According to proponents of the approach, participants can thus clarify or make sense of circumstances and actions that were formerly opaque or troubling. What was hidden or obscure is made visible to both participant and listener (for example, a service manager or a researcher)—the sense-making interview thus enacts the confessional/professional dynamic described in the introduction to this chapter. As "sense" is tightly coupled with "information" (see the previous paragraph), this appears to be a construction-ist account. The trained listener together with the trained respondent can classify the confessional narrative in terms of different effects (moving forward, getting help) and these may be the basis of professional intervention.

In a methods piece that focuses on feminist inquiry, Shields and Dervin (1993) further discuss the status of the researcher. Setting up the straw (wo)man of the over-engaged researcher, the authors take pains to distance sense making from overtly emancipatory experientialist techniques that can result in an unhealthy dependency of subject on researcher: "What sense-making has attempted to do, therefore, is develop a generalizable interviewing approach that, as much as possi-ble, gets the interviewer out of the interview while at the same time utilizes a qual-itatively powerful, systematic, and comparable set of queries to the respondent" (p. 74). This critique of experientialist accounts and promotion of SMM is somewhat specious. Flick (2000, and see 1994, 2002) discusses experientialist and other forms of episodic interviewing and suggests that sensitive use of techniques reduces the danger of over-engagement. Bates (2004), working in the ELIS domain, has demon-strated that experiential narrative techniques can be used without compromising the independence of the informant. Shields and Dervin (1993, p. 79) concede that com-plete transparency and neutrality are not possible; the aim, they say, is to guide the respondent's story "in such a way that the result is systematically illuminating both for researcher and researched." This echoes Dervin's (1992, p. 73) claim that "results suggest that there is, when sense-making interviews are at their best, a consciousness-raising, and therapeutic value in the process for respondents." Because the respondent is "conceptualized as a colleague," the interviewer has to learn "how to assist the respondents in re-constructing their sense-making" and respondents are "taught many aspects of the interviewing approach" (p. 73).

Sense-making narratives are constructed, situated, and thus idiosyncratic: "each specific study context can involve its own detailed set of content analytic cate-gories" (Dervin, 1992, p. 75). It is difficult, if not impossible, to generalize from the data. Dervin attempts to address this difficulty with a number of moves. The first move is to control both data collection and interpretation by introducing the manda-tory interview protocol previously described and its corollary, a limited repertoire of interpretive categories (Dervin, 1992, p. 75). This limits what is addressed in the research dialogue to the gap defining and gap bridging aspects of "situation facing" (p. 75) and also restricts the affordance of subsequent coding, which must elaborate a sequence of "situation stops," attempts to "bridge," and so on (p. 75). When texts of micro-moment time-line interviews are analyzed, such categories act as the moral anchors of the (albeit tendentious) story; stories can be cumulated into a sense-making corpus where the categories can be seen to be applicable across a wide range of contextual narratives. Dervin (1992, p. 66) asserts that any theory derived from them will "move research toward a new kind of generalizability"—a tautologous claim given the mandatory structure of the protocol for micro-moment time-line interviews. The categories "are universal in the sense that they pertain to gap-bridging and gap-defining across situations while at the same time they capture

important aspects of particular situations" (Dervin, 1992, p. 75). Dervin has sufficient confidence in these "universals" (Shields & Dervin, 1993, p. 74) to promote
their use in quantitative studies where respondents are asked to describe "which of
a series of gap-bridging and gap-defining categories describe their situations best"
(Dervin, 1992, p. 73); the result is an "approach with qualitative sensibility which
is amenable to the systematic power of quantitative analysis" (p. 81).

SMM attempts to address the problem of generalizability in a further move
whereby a "moment" or "step" (Dervin, 1992, p. 68) is translated into process. The
researcher elicits accounts of individual progress that are built up moment by
moment, step by step as the interview protocol is followed: The situated events or
moments are a necessary device as they allow the professional interviewer to evoke
a richer experiential account ("What did you feel about this?" "What did it mean?"
"What was the opportunity that was made available?" etc.). At the same time, the
micro-moment time-line interview provides the material for a process ontology that
supports exploration of human movement through space and time. The moments are
translated into process by means of a lexical move: verbing. In verbing (Dervin,
1993, p. 45), internal and external human behaviors that are discovered in interviews are labeled with gerundive verb forms "idea makings and idea repeatings,
thinkings, and emoting," "listening," and "arguing" (p. 51). Weick (1979, p. 44) had
made a similar point: "The process of moving requires time, it extends through
time, and it involves change. Without verbs, people would not see motion, change,
and flow; people would only see static displays." Dervin admits that verbing is
"clumsy" (1993, p. 49) but suggests that it is a necessary rhetorical move to force
researchers to think dynamically.

SMM's interview protocols have been widely adopted in HIB research (Olsson,
2008), and Dervin's website provides an inventory of illustrative studies. In some
situations (those pertinent to "the service mandate of an institution" [Dervin, 1992,
p. 71], for example), confessional methods undoubtedly provide a means to identify
areas where specific and local system and service design may be improved. Dervin
and other proponents of SMM (Dervin, 1992; Fisher, Durrance, & Hinton, 2004)
present a number of exemplar studies: a blood transfusion service, outreach service
in a library, cancer care services, an anti-smoking campaign targeted at adolescents—see Dervin, 1992, p. 73 ff. Corroborating Shields and Dervin's (1993) claim
that the approach has empowering and therapeutic value, Harris and Dewdney
(1994) apply SMM to explore the lifeworlds of battered women, to discredit prevailing models that present such women as victims, and to propose a radical reorganization of library services that are currently failing this population. Fisher,
Durrance, and Hinton (2004) have used confessional methods to explore the lifeworlds of immigrants and propose a model for their "information grounds." But
when the artifactual or institutional focus is removed from inquiry and unanchored
"information-in-the-lifeworld" becomes the focus, loosely attached to highly disparate sub-groups, empirical work can deliver only high level insights that have little purchasing power in either practical or theoretical terms.

The SMM approach has been subject to critique by ELIS scholars. Although a
strong supporter and advocate of Dervin's work at a programmatic level, Savolainen
(1992, 1993, 2006, 2007) raises a number of issues and challenges. Several points
from his 1993 discussion are pertinent here. He observes that "one may have good

reason to question the 'unquestioned postulate' that discontinuity is a constant of nature, with its metaphysical assumptions of constant features of reality" (Salvolanien, 1993, p. 16). In addition, Savolainen (p. 17) is not impressed by the universalist argument and observes that achieving generalizability "may not be an easy task because gap defining and gap bridging are contingent by nature depending on individual and situational factors." A further difficulty arises because "the core concepts of the theory have been defined metaphorically" and the theory has "focused on the individual and the individual's internal world ... the problems of constructing sense with other people through dialogue have thus remained secondary" (p. 26). Thirteen years on, Savolainen (2006) offers a further review and finds that the problems remain unresolved. "As to the study of the specific nature of information use/processes, the formulations of sensemaking so far have remained quite general" (p. 1122); "So far, we lack empirical studies focusing on the processes of information design from this perspective" (p. 1124).

Savolainen (2006) also notes that SMM's lexicon and categorization techniques are problematic. Tuominen and Savolainen (1997) and Tuominen (1997) have additional concerns about how SMM addresses the role of the researcher. Tuominen (1997, p. 367) observes that "user centered discourse does not necessarily liberate the user from the constraints of the system, and for both librarians and users, there is no easy way out of the web of discursive power and the subject positions of an expert and a client that the user-centered discourse offers to them." Such observations raise issues about the scientificity of confessional ELIS work that go beyond details of compliance or non-compliance with specific methodological protocols. These are discussed in the next section.

## Scientificity

The text so far has identified problems with the application of three core confessional methods that affect the quality of outcomes in ELIS research. These arise for a number of reasons. In the case of CI, for example, few current researchers comply with the protocols that have been so carefully described by Flanagan; these researchers appear to be unaware of the caveats that surround his accounts of empirical work. And few confessional ELIS researchers treat focus groups as probes or exploratory accounts, preferring to code their transcripts to support realist accounts of information attributes such as motivation (Meyers et al., 2007). The claims to authenticity of the third approach, SMM, require researchers to take a leap of faith and work with a number of postulates that underlie a strictly enforced protocol. In addition, all three methods are often used in mash-ups that result in studies that are conceptually and theoretically inconsistent.

The cheap and cheerful fusion of methods and models adds further problems. A recent edited monograph on *Theories of Information Behavior* (Fisher et al., 2005) offers over 70 short contributions, many of which in fact describe methods. And it may be noted that Dervin (1992, p. 70) has described SMM as "a theory of how to conduct interviews with respondents." The "off-the-shelf" approach is sustained in Fisher and Julien's recent (2009) *ARIST* chapter—this devotes a bare page (pp. 318–319) to methods, which are inventoried, with little discussion of what is appropriate where. This "ready to wear" approach is sustained by designer labels—a name ("Fisher," "Chatman," "Dervin") is invoked as a proxy for a method without discussion. Much of the muddle can be explained, as Frohmann (2004, pp. 60–61, 78) observes, in terms of tensions between realist and nominalist accounts. In seeking to discover the attributes of an underlying substance or phenomenon ("information" or "sense making"), ELIS studies are realist in intent. But in seeking to discover such attributes in populations that are defined by the elastic term "situation," with no control of sampling, they are nominalist in practice. The section that follows explores these tensions in four areas—authenticity, reflexivity, nomenclature, and positioning—focusing on how confessional researchers do their science.

## Authenticity

ELIS researchers acknowledge that any scholarly domain must establish the authenticity of the phenomena that are the focus of attention across a series of empirical studies that allow substantial attributes to emerge. Fisher, for example, states that a long program of research is needed to establish the attributes of information grounds (Fisher & Naumur, 2006), a point also made by Frohmann (2004, p. 80). Dervin also reminds readers frequently of the long research tradition that underpins SMM (see, for example, Dervin, 1999, 2006). But such programs require some level of consistency in the samples that are explored and ELIS researchers have not achieved this. Some analysts explore populations ("tweens," "activists," "seniors," "people who believe in UFOs"); others explore "situations," an elastic term as has been noted. In Dervin's (1992, p. 73) account of an earlier co-authored study of a California library, users are asked "what happened to them in the most recent troublesome situation they were in"; in Julien's (1999) study, the situation is that of a high school student seeking career advice; in Fisher and Landry's (2007) analysis of stay-at-home mothers (SAHMs) the situation is that of being a trained professional at home with young children. If any lifeworld context is a situation, the concept becomes bleached. A number of ELIS researchers fudge the sampling issue by declaring that their empirical work is exploratory.

Discussions of authenticity in ELIS studies often focus on establishing the veracity of the account, the realism of the setting, the appropriateness of the sample. The most common tactic is to triangulate confessional material with other types of evidence (diaries, logs) and to put subjects at their ease in familiar or naturalistic settings. Where triangulation across observers is not possible—in doctoral dissertation work, for example, only one researcher may be involved—ELIS researchers resolve the issue in different ways. Hersberger (2001) is confident that the accounts she presents are realistic because the behavior that she hears about in the second phase of her project is consistent with what she herself observed the earlier "volunteer" observer phase of her project. Fisher and Landry (2007) rely on multiple forms of triangulation in the SAHMs study. When mothers reveal that they cannot complete their diaries because of time constraints, the authors use the little that has been done as a starting point for conversation rather than a means of triangulation. But they then use observations of body language to corroborate the accounts of affective states that are offered by their subjects. All of the data are thus accommodated and some level of triangulation is achieved.

These issues are often addressed in discussions of access to subjects (Carey et al., 2001). Some researchers seek to achieve the elision of self by becoming naturalized actors in the situations they observe in a form of participant observation. Hersberger (2001, p. 125), for example, works in a homeless shelter as a volunteer before entering into dialogue with her participants; she then presents herself as a "student writing a book"; Carey (Carey et al., 2001) presents herself as a volunteer librarian and works with her subjects in a voluntary counseling group for cancer patients; McKechnie (2000, p. 69) becomes a familiar figure ("the lady") in the library where interviews are held with her pre-school informants; Fisher and Landry (2007) gather data in the homes and haunts of the stay-at-home mothers who are the participants in their study. An alternative approach is to simulate the habitat of informants. Meyers and colleagues (2007, pp. 313–314) attempt to achieve this by incorporating insights from developmental studies into their field site design, drawing on psychological and physiological research into the age group that is the focus of their study.

Having discussed access and triangulation (or paid their methodological dues, as it were), realist confessional ELIS researchers treat what they are told by respondents as a captured reality, although it may be noted that Meyers and colleagues (2007) offer a more nuanced account and discuss the weakness of their approach (p. 324).

In SMM, two main arguments are used to support claims to authenticity. The first is the argument from design. The micro-moment time-line interview (see previous section) elicits accounts of moves, and moves are irreducible facts of life, "at least in part designed" (Dervin, 1999, p. 733). Because they are "in part designed," moves are "practices that are in some way theorized even if that theorizing appears mute or inarticulate or dominated and constrained" (p. 733). It is not clear whether moves are hard-wired in the human brain or designed by the individual sense maker (Savolainen [2006] takes the latter view). Either way, the argument from design implies that in evoking accounts of moves, the SMM interview evokes accounts of the human condition that are unquestionably authentic. The second claim to authenticity rests on the argument from disintermediation: "The interviewer does not (in fact cannot) have a priori understanding of the respondent, but rather develops this understanding in communication, allowing the respondent to present self as unimpeded as possible by the reviewer" (Dervin, 1992, p. 76). SMM accepts that informants' memories are imperfect and that an interview or conversation may stimulate recollection—informants may telephone a researcher after a meeting with additional information or contribute to a focus group over a sustained period. Any inconsistencies, irregularities, gaps, deceits, and confusions are examples of the continuous micro-level theorizing that supports subjects as they navigate the world. There is no need for triangulation with "an interviewing approach that does not name the world for the actor, but rather mandates the actor to name the world for herself" (Dervin, 1999, p. 740).

But how authentic can these subjects be? As has been noted, their accounts are framed for them; they are examples of "systematic subjectivity" (Shields & Dervin, 1993, p. 74) (a thoroughly Foucauldian concept). The cognitive status of moves (and thus the authenticity of sense making) is assigned by fiat, not derived from empirical observation. Crabtree, Nichols, O'Brien, Rouncefield, and Twidale

(2000), working ethnographers, have criticized SMM and other ELIS methods on this ground (and see Frohmann, 2004, p. 77). Robust ethnomethodology offers accounts of social ordering as it is performed by situated actors; it does not impose external interpretations of that ordering. Although SMM purports to do the former (participants code their own transcripts, a point that will be discussed in more detail), it actually does the latter (the codes that participants use are prescribed attributes of a phenomenon whose ontological status is unquestioned). In addition, re-constructive techniques are problematic unless the concepts of "construction" and "re-construction" are fully clarified. If "reality" or "sense" or "worlds" are presented/constructed in stories or experiential narratives (Bates, 2004, pp. 16, 27), then re-presentation or re-construction by the experiencing subject acting alone or with a researcher enacts a different reality or sense—versions matter (Tuominen & Savolainen, 1997). The researcher, that additional actor, always complicates as much as explicates.

## Reflexivity

Savolainen (2007, pp. 119, 126), in a recent review of HIB research, comments on its lack of reflexivity and tendency to work with received ideas. ELIS researchers' failure to reflect adequately on the consistency and compatibility of methods has been discussed; the focus here is reflection on the position of the researcher in the many different power networks that constitute scholarly work.

Although Fisher and her colleagues (Carey, McKechnie, & MacKenzie, 2001; Fisher & Landry, 2007; Meyers et al., 2007) frequently comment on how they set about their projects—engaging subjects and so on—the emphasis is on compliance with social science norms rather than on issues of power. Discussion is thus confined to issues such as access, authenticity (see the previous section) with, at most, some comments on reducing observer effects. Much of this discussion is meliorist in tone, emphasizing empowerment of subjects (Fisher, Durrance, & Hinton, 2004; Fisher, Marcoux, Miller, Sanchez, & Cunningham, 2004; Hersberger, 2001; Julien, 1999) and improvement of services. Few researchers appear to be able to hold back; Chatman, in contrast, presents a phenomenon, such as information poverty, but does not prescribe a cure (Chatman, 2000, pp. 6–7; see also Chatman, 1987, 1996).

Relationships with sponsors are rarely discussed and are to be inferred for the most part from acknowledgments. Dervin's (e.g., 1999, p. 746) discussion of reflexivity is exceptional: "Sense-Making ... mandates that the researcher interview herself both as she would interview her informants/respondents and also in terms of her on-going relations to the project." But the methodology puts the researcher in a double bind. On one hand, the core method (time-lining) seeks to elide the individual interviewer from the dialogue (as s/he is simply the administrator of the S-M protocol). Under these circumstances, reflexivity must either be restricted to reflections on interviewer bias with a view to correction or put the interviewer in the position of a ventriloquist's dummy asked to reflect on its role in the performance. But even in the reduced role of protocol administrator, the researcher's role is ambivalent as the distinction between invention and discovery is blurred in the micro-moment time-line interview. The researcher is described as jointly constructing (or inventing) the sense-making narrative with the informant (an on-the-spot performance or achievement), but sense making is at the same time a universal "mandate for the human species" (Dervin, 1999, p. 738), which implies that it is merely invoked (discovered) by the researcher. The second element of the double bind lies in the "mandate" that the researcher treat him- or herself as a peer, on a par with other participants in the confessional act. This is not achievable by means of a declarative speech act of this kind (a point that will be discussed in more detail). Dervin (2006, pp. 26–27, and see footnote 3 in Dervin, 1999, p. 729) positions SMM in "the intersections of the writings of American and European theorists … in the fields of philosophy, sociology, psychology, education, cultural studies, communication, and feminist cultural and postmodern studies"; she can hardly be unaware of debates about the position of the researcher in narrative (and non-narrative) methods, which have not resolved the issue.

The elision of the researcher is amplified in a plea for the human species to "humble" its knowledge: "This implies that the researcher must be involved in a new order of research verbings to serve a mandate of self-conscious self-reflexivity. … It requires a positioning of self as a focus of investigation, as an exemplar of the human condition" (Dervin, 1999, p. 734). Researchers must avoid being complicit in the oppressive practices of experts and professionals who deal in "information" because these practices are partial, both in the sense of incomplete, and in the sense of biased (pp. 738–739). In the 1999 paper, information is defined as restrictive "factizing": "Factizing of course is not the only verbing that creates what we call knowledge. There are [*sic*] a host of other verbings involved (e.g., consensusing, negotiating, power-brokering, defining, hunching, muddling, suppressing)" (p. 732). Information also has to be defined as elitist: "Information is typically used to describe the observings of experts … which have been given the imprimatur of the consensus through the actions of empowered collectivities and enterprises (e.g., the professions or science). Most information seeking and use research constrains itself to this realm" (p. 738).

But of course confessional researchers (SMM adherents included) cannot achieve parity with participants. As Dreyfus and Rabinow (1983, p. 174) observe: "The cultural desire to know the truth about oneself prompts the telling of truth; in confession after confession, to oneself and to others, this *mise en discours* has placed the individual in a network of relations of power with those who claim to extract the truth of these confessions through their possession of the keys to interpretation." Giving participants the power to do their own coding with a prescribed set of codes is not the same as handing over the keys to interpretation—it is more akin to allowing them to insert the key into the lock. No matter how demotic the language that is used, the power of the academic apparatus lies behind the researcher, and relationships will always be asymmetric. Power relations are one of SMM's major concerns (Dervin indeed invokes Foucault in the footnote to the 1999 paper that has been mentioned [Dervin, 1999, p. 729; and see Dervin, 1999, p. 732]), but the treatment of power focuses on subjectivity. Dervin, like other confessional ELIS researchers, does not address "the forces and relations of production that shape … academic disciplines" (Day, 1996, p. 322). SMM researchers have also neglected the forces that shape the societal institutions that define much of everyday life identified by Frohmann (2008) as an appropriate focus for analysis of information ethics. Dervin (1994, p. 370) briefly considers financial institutions as an appropriate topic for information research but does not pursue the option, focusing on subjectivity instead and leaving SMM's account of power incomplete.

## Nomenclature

Nomenclature is an area of ELIS research where nominalist/realist tension runs high. The term "nomenclature" in this chapter denotes a linguistic system that describes phenomena in terms (both lexical and grammatical) that support systematic exploration and classification of attributes into scientific kinds. Some researchers, as Frohmann (2004, pp. 77–80) notes, strive "heroically" to reconcile the two positions. This finely honed apparatus evolves over time in a domain, as categories or codes are ratified and scientific kinds are consolidated; Fisher (2005, p. 188), for example, describes "information grounds" as a phenomenon that has always been there, but not identified in scientific terms, and acknowledges that the task of translation or conversion is at an early stage. She is aware that to establish information grounds as a "real" phenomenon (p. 187), she must establish a robust set of categories that can be consolidated and naturalized to support the evolving field. She thus has to both provide a typology (Fisher, 2005) and describe a series of empirical projects that validate that typology (Fisher & Naumer, 2006). It remains to be seen whether Fisher and others who are developing this approach (McKechnie & MacKenzie, 2004; Prigoda & MacKenzie, 2007) will be able to establish a robust nomenclature.

Savolainen (2007, p. 111) has recently reviewed the development of nomenclature ("umbrella concepts") in HIB; he suggests that this is a problematic area: "Researchers are often satisfied with proposing their own definition without reflecting on how it relates to definitions suggested previously." He continues, "theories and classifications such as these which indicate the power to name, are not necessarily without problems" (p. 112). In addition, the level at which coding is reported varies greatly across studies. Hersberger (2001)—she is not unique in this—simply indicates that interview transcripts were coded and analyzed using Nud.Ist (others use Atlas TI, Ethnograph, and so on) but does not give examples of the coding schedules. Fisher and Landry (2007, p. 221) provide an account of coding in their study of SAHMs, where multiple mini-situations ("What to do about diaper rash?" "Where to find organic blueberries?"), linked to the multiple roles that mothers perform in caring for young children, are categorized in terms of their affective burden. A standard psychological scale for emotion is used and a simple, if somewhat uninformative, triangular model derived.

Dervin is aware of the importance of robust nomenclature but seeks to establish this through tight control of the means (SMM) by which nomenclature is established. In the interests of democracy, however, SMM encourages informants to undertake their own coding of situational micro-narratives in a reversal of the professional/confessional dialectic. But coding is complicated by the fact that categories are both mandatory and evolving (how does one keep track of the evolving mandate?) and have changed as the methodology has developed—from the "5Ps" (Dervin, 1983), to the "Six H's" (Dervin, 2003a), to the "primitives" (Dervin, 2006, p. 26): "time, space, horizon, gap, bridge, movement, power, constancy, and change." In true nominalist fashion, as has been noted, Dervin (1999, p. 739) defines the "fodder" of sense making as "any realm of experiencing that actors define themselves as using in their sense-making. ... The patient who says 'my body told me' is making sense, so is the problem-solver who said 'God told me' or 'I listened to my feelings' as well as the one who said 'I looked it up on the Web' or 'I asked an expert.'" This is because "We work in a context where no matter how loud the protestations there is no longer one scientific method, and one acceptable approach to studying the human condition" (Dervin, 2003b, p. 136). Information as a privileged theoretical kind has been dismissed ("Sense-making mandates the disappearance of the term 'information' as an absolute ontological category" [Dervin, 1999, p. 738]), to be replaced not with an alternative theoretical kind, but with a fundamentalist kind—sense making.

As has been noted, verbing, the means by which micro-moment time-line interviews are converted into named processes, is a key technique in SMM. It is promoted as an anti-scientific method, an antidote to the systematic nomenclature of the social sciences. Weick (1979, 1995) suggests that verbing is an effective way of mobilizing colleagues and moving forward in organizational contexts and, it may be noted, Savolainen (1993) interprets SMM in this way, describing it as redolent of "can do" Americanism. But verbing in science is a very different proposition. According to Halliday (Halliday & Martin, 1993, p. 52) "the practice, the activity of 'doing science' ... is enacted in the forms of the language, and there has been a broad consensus about what constitutes scientific practice." Science works through a process of "objectification" (p. 52) that turns the world into nouns, terms for objects that may be further qualified, classified, and described in terms of shared relationships; it is achieved by the linguistic process of "grammatical metaphor, whereby a phenomenon of one kind is construed in a way that typically represents a phenomenon of some other kind (actions, events, qualities as if they were things)." Objectification is a parsimonious and effective device, honed over centuries, for making scientific realities: It backgrounds some objects (as given) and foregrounds others (as available for exploration).

Undoing nominalization by verbing and including "every verb of individual and collective sense-making" (Dervin, 1999, p. 732) as evidence does not produce alternative science; it simply removes the power to discriminate. SMM's pluralistic and post-modern stance, and tilting at scientific norms (e.g., Dervin, Reinhard, & Kerr, 2006, p. 245), is disingenuous, however, because, when it suits, SMM practitioners do work within the apparatus of traditional science. The 2007 study of affect and sense making (Dervin & Reinhard, 2007a, 2007b) can serve as an example. This involves an assessment of how academics at different professional levels use electronic and other sources and resources; it seeks to establish whether situation or emotion is a better predictor of information behavior. Informants (undergraduate students, graduate students, and faculty) provided data on six situation types in a mix of personal and institutional contexts—"everyday life" in this project involves both. Respondents (interviewed by telephone) code their situational mini-narratives themselves, using ten mandatory (or a priori) categories; these are in turn correlated with a set of a priori emotional categories, to produce affective profiles for factor analysis. The method involved "deep qualitative interviewing that incorporated some quantitative aspects, followed by systematic content analysis, and, for the report, statistical analysis" (Dervin & Reinhard, 2007a, p. 57) The project is unusual in the context of ELIS because of the relatively large numbers of incidents or situations that are analyzed and in the rigor of the sampling process. The results (given the premises) are banal: For example, the authors establish that "getting there in difficult situations can be a very hard thing to do" (p. 75). Such opportunistic recourse to standard methods is described by Dervin (2005, p. 29; 1999, p. 742) as "Rendering-unto-Caesar."

Although Dervin (e.g., 1999, p. 730) justifies SMM's methodological practices as a "third way" between "chaos" and "order" in science, the consequences of such linguistic sleights of hand as verbing are highly problematic for information science. Savolainen (1993, 2006) observes that studies based on the idiosyncratic SMM lexicon can be compared only with themselves, and not with mainstream LIS research. He suggests that "There may … be translation problems between the vocabularies of sense making and other approaches. These approaches may render it difficult to compare research findings obtained within alternative research frameworks because they may suggest different operationalizations of the phenomena of information use" (Savolainen, 2006, p. 1124). In addition, the categorization that is undertaken in sense making "may result in difficulties for researchers outside the sense making discourse community … relating to their understanding of the methodological tools provided by this approach. Certain concepts, for example, verbing, may not be found as easily approachable and they connote varying meanings" (p. 1124).

## Positioning

What is the position of confessional ELIS research within the larger domain of HIB studies and the field of LIS? A recent study of HIB citation habits by McKechnie, Julien, Goodall, and Lajoie-Paquete (2005) found that citation patterns are tightly knit. There is also a heavy degree of self-citation. The referencing habits of confessional ELIS researchers show the same pattern. They are parochial: As noted in the introduction, work is presented and cited in a restricted set of channels. And they are incestuous: There is a high level of self and mutual citation (see, for example, Fisher & Landry, 2007, pp. 211–214). Tightly bound citation within a group of this type serves a number of functions. It supports claims that a domain is consolidating and maturing (McKechnie et al., 2005; Wilson, 2008); it establishes the reputations of individuals (such as researchers in the universities of Washington, Western Ontario, and Tampere) and of institutions as hubs of significant activity; and it establishes a comfort zone where the uncritical and unadventurous researcher can find shelter.

According to Olsson (2008, p. 162), Dervin has been ranked among the most highly cited authors in the HIB domain. In a series of papers (Olsson, 2005, 2007, 2008) based on his doctoral thesis, Olsson attempts to deconstruct her authorial presence over time. The empirical component of his doctoral work consists of interviews with a number of LIS scholars to establish how they have engaged with SMM. Many SMM adherents enjoy a close personal relationship with Dervin, whose direct control (in the role of mentor and guide) of those who use her methods is unusual. This strong coupling of individual and method (Dervin [1999, p. 730] refers to herself as "Sense-Making's primary author") amplifies her citation footprint. A number of Olsson's respondents, in contrast, state that they have cited

Dervin opportunistically, in order to have work published in certain journals. That such citations have not been questioned by peer reviewers and editors suggests complicity on the part of the former and complaisance on the part of the latter. There is a danger that confessional ELIS research, like other such tight-knit communities of interest, has over time become exclusive, rather than inclusive, with selection criteria that are ritualistic. Lievrouw (2000, p. 100), in a review of the first issue of the *New Review of Information Behaviour Research,* raises this issue and warns the editors to keep their selection criteria transparent.

Outside HIB, ELIS confessional work has had little impact (McKechnie et al., 2005). It appears that the comments on user studies made by Menzel (1966, p. 42) are still valid: He describes "results of dubious reliability and validity, or else of barren superficiality." Ironically, Dervin (1999, p. 747) makes a similar critique of information studies, although her "third way" approach appears to have compounded the problem. As Case (2006, p. 323) observes: "Certainly we could say that information behavior research has become more 'scholarly' but perhaps also more pointless as well."

In terms of institutional and corporate reception, confessional researchers working on everyday life concerns have had some success in attracting funds from government agencies with an interest in the service economy—in Europe, the U.S., and Canada; Julien, Fisher, and Dervin are among the researchers cited here who have been sponsored by national funding bodies in North America; Savolainen and his colleagues have received considerable government support in Finland. And it may be noted that Fisher and Dervin are currently working on projects supported by Microsoft and OCLC, respectively.

## Conclusion

So what makes the paper by Meyers and colleagues (2007) a winner? It is deeply pertinent to the topic of this review as it is concerned with confessional talk; indeed the study has been funded as part of a program called "Talking with You." The authors engage with many of the issues relating to scientificity that are at the heart of the critique offered here, although the tension between realism and nominalism is not resolved: The worlds that are revealed in the two study communities are not readily amenable to common description. The authors do not dwell on these inconsistencies. These are not, however, points that the judges are likely to have considered in making the award. More pertinent are issues of reputation and the paper's focus on the social and material circumstances of the fieldwork. The authors come from a respectable stable, they are disarmingly frank about methods, and they provide procedural details that are often missing in ELIS studies (including a copy of the interview protocol). The paper provides an engaging experiential account of how to manage members of an age group who are difficult to pin down as research informants, and at a practical level, is exemplary. But in terms of output, and in terms of contribution to either realist or nominalist theory, the paper says little that is new (Fisher, Marcoux, Meyers, & Landry, 2007).

There are alternatives to the confessional approach in ELIS research, as we note in the introduction. One approach is to explore information practice (IP) (Talja & MacKenzie, 2007) rather than information behavior. Savolainen (2007) compares both approaches, and although he has serious methodological concerns about HIB, believes that there is unlikely to be an early counter-movement from information practice researchers. Talja and McKenzie (2007), however, observes that all dominant discourses produce counter discourses, although these take time to develop and gain adherents (sometimes when the old guard withdraws—many confessional researchers are long-standing academics and their retirement may alter the power dynamics of the ELIS domain). Studies based on discourse analysis and conversational analysis may be signs of a counter movement.

The IP line of work can be described in terms of two paths. The first focuses on language and what language does (Talja & MacKenzie, 2007); the study of public library discourse by Hedemark, Hedman, and Sundin (2005) is a recent example of such discursive work. The second approach is concerned with material practice, drawing on an existing tradition that treats artifacts and documents as agents rather than structures or constraints (Skare, Lund, & Vårheim, 2007). Dalrymple (2001), reviewing the legacy of Zweizig and Dervin, suggests that there will be a move toward a document-centered approach; Frohmann (2004) advocates such a shift. Recent ethnographic studies also engage with artifacts and institutions (McKechnie, 2000; MacKenzie, 2004, 2006); and Fisher and Julien (2009) conclude their *ARIST* chapter with the observation that HIB research will focus more on systems. A renewal of interest in "physical" (Ellis, 1992, p. 45) and material information will overcome a number of problems in confessional ELIS work by improving the specificity of the objects of research.

Web analysis offers a further alternative. The enactment of everyday life on Internet and mobile technology platforms offers ELIS researchers an environment where data are abundant rather than scarce (Abbott, 2001) and where data mining can complement dialogue as a means of eliciting hidden phenomena. Although there may be residual applications of confessional methods in this context (Kari & Hartel, 2007; Kari & Savolainen, 2007), the need for confessional/professional interaction has become less pressing as informants provide data for and by themselves—on social sites accessed with mobile technologies, for example, using social tagging. The resulting archive is a rich site for ELIS and other social science research (Thelwall & Wouters, 2005) into relationships (Thelwall, 2008) and content (Nicholas, Huntington, Williams, & Dobrowolski, 2006). Further content analysis pertinent to ELIS research has been undertaken by, for example, Buente and Robbin (2008) using large scale survey data from the Pew Institute.

More pressing is the need for reflexive analysis of such platforms. Frohmann (2008, p. 271), in an analysis of information ethics in a world of "autonomous and authorless information processes that bypass consciousness," suggests that "The ethical practices of Foucauldian 'criticism' can be directed to the specific 'historical ontologies' in which contemporary information systems, techniques, and technologies are implicated in 'making up people'" (Frohmann, 2008, p. 275; and see Hacking, 1995, 2004, 2006). Poster (2000, 2006) and others are undertaking such work but it has yet to be embraced by the ELIS domain.

## Acknowledgments

The author would like to thank the three anonymous reviewers for their helpful comments.

# References

Abbott, A. (2001). *Time matters: On theory and method.* Chicago: University of Chicago Press.

Agosto, D. E., & Hughes-Hassell, S. (2005). People, places, and questions: An investigation of the everyday life information-seeking behaviors of urban young adults. *Library & Information Science Research, 27,* 141–163.

Agosto, D. E., & Hughes-Hassell, S. (2006a). Toward a model of the everyday life information needs of urban teenagers, part 1: Theoretical model. *Journal of the American Society for Information Science and Technology, 57,* 1394–1403.

Agosto, D. E., & Hughes-Hassell, S. (2006b). Toward a model of the everyday life information needs of urban teenagers, part 2: Empirical model. *Journal of the American Society for Information Science and Technology, 57,* 1418–1426.

Bates, J. (2004). Use of narrative interviewing in everyday information behavior research. *Library & Information Science Research, 26,* 15–28.

Bates, M. (1999). The invisible substrate of information science. *Journal of the American Society for Information Science, 50*(12), 1043–1050.

Bernier, A. (2007). Introduction: Not broken by someone else's schedule: On joy and young adults information seeking. In M. K. Chelton & C. Cool (Eds.), *Youth information seeking behaviors II: Context, theories, models and issues* (pp. xiii–xxviii). Lanham, MD: Scarecrow Press.

Billig, M. (1992). *Talking of the royal family.* London: Routledge.

Buente, W., & Robbin, A. (2008). Trends in Internet information behavior. *Journal of the American Society for Information Science and Technology, 59*(11), 1743–1760.

Carey, R. F., McKechnie, L., & MacKenzie, P. (2001). Gaining access to everyday information seeking. *Library & Information Science Research, 23,* 319–334.

Case, D. (2006). Information behavior. *Annual Review of Information Science and Technology, 40,* 293–327.

Case, D. (2007). *Looking for information: A survey of research on information seeking, needs and behavior* (2nd ed.). Amsterdam; Elsevier.

Chatman, E. A. (1987). The information world of low-skilled workers. *Library & Information Science Research, 9,* 265–283.

Chatman, E. A. (1996). The impoverished life-world of outsiders. *Journal of the American Society for Information Science, 47,* 193–206.

Chatman, E. A. (2000). Framing social life in theory and research. *New Review of Information Behaviour Research, 1,* 3-17.

Chelton, M. K., & Cool, C. (Eds.). (2004). *Youth information seeking behaviors: Theories, models and issues.* Lanham, MD: Scarecrow Press.

Chelton, M. K., & Cool, C. (Eds.). (2007). *Youth information seeking behaviors II: Context, theories, models and issues.* Lanham, MD: Scarecrow Press.

Crabtree, A., Nichols, D. M., O'Brien, M., Rouncefield, M., & Twidale, M. B. (2000). Ethnomethodologically informed ethnography and information systems design. *Journal of the American Society for Information Science and Technology, 51*(7), 666–682.

Dalrymple, P. W. (2001). A quarter century's user-centered study. The impact of Zweizig and Dervin on LIS research. *Library & Information Science Research, 23,* 155–165.

Day, R. (1996). LIS, method, and postmodern science. *Journal of Education for Library and Information Science, 37*(4), 317–324.

Dervin, B. (1976). The everyday information needs of the average citizen: A taxonomy for analysis. In M. Kochen & J. P. Donohue (Eds.), *Information for the community* (pp. 19–38). Chicago: American Library Association.

Dervin, B. (1983, May). *An overview of sense-making research: Concepts, methods and results to date.* Paper presented at the International Communication Association Annual Meeting, Dallas, TX.

Dervin, B. (1989). Users of communication/information systems as research inventions: Perpetuating myths, reifying inequities. *Journal of Communication, 39*(3), 216–232.

Dervin, B. (1991/2001). *An example of a sense-making designed focus group: Design for focus groups for phone user constituencies.* Unpublished report.

Dervin, B. (1992). From the mind's eye of the user: The sense-making qualitative-quantitative methodology. In J. D. Glazier & R. R. Powell (Eds.), *Qualitative research in information management* (pp. 61–84). Englewood, CO: Libraries Unlimited.

Dervin, B. (1993). Verbing communication: Mandate for disciplinary invention. *Journal of Communication, 43*(3), 45–54.

Dervin, B. (1994). Information-democracy: An examination of underlying assumptions. *Journal of the American Society for Information Science, 45*(6), 369–385.

Dervin, B. (1999). On studying information seeking methodologically: The implications of connecting metatheory to method. *Information Processing & Management, 35*, 727–750.

Dervin, B. (2003a). A brief pictorial guide to Dervin's Sense-Making Methodology. Retrieved August 20, 2008, from communication.sbs.ohio-state.edu/sense-making

Dervin, B. (2003b). Sense-making's journey from meta theory to methodology to method: An example using information seeking and use as research focus. In B. Dervin & L. Foreman-Wernet (with E. Lauterbach) (Eds.). *Sense-making methodology reader: Selected writings of Brenda Dervin* (pp. 133–164). Cresskill, NJ: Hampton Press.

Dervin, B. (2005). What methodology does to theory: Sense-making methodology as exemplar. In K. E. Fisher, S. Erdelez, & E. F. McKechnie (Eds.), *Theories of information behavior* (pp. 25–30). Medford, NJ: Information Today.

Dervin, B. (2006). Project overview: Sense-making methodology as dialogic approach to communicating for research and practice. In B. Dervin, C. D. Reinhard, S. K. Adamson, T. T. Lu, N. M. Karnolt, & T. Berberick (Eds.), *Sense-making the information confluence: The whys and hows of college and university user satisficing of information needs. Phase I: Project overview, the Three-Field Dialogue Project, and state-of-the-art reviews* (Report on National Leadership Grant LG-02-03-0062-03, to Institute of Museum and Library Services, Washington, D.C.) Columbus: School of Communication, The Ohio State University. Retrieved August 20, 2008, from imlsproject.comm.ohio-state.edu/imls_reports/imls_PH_I_report_list.html

Dervin, B. (2007, May). *Applying sense-making methodology to focus group design: Addressing both collective and individual agency.* Paper presented at Non-Divisional Working Symposium on Making communication studies matter: Field relevance/irrelevance to media, library, electronic, communication system designs, policies, practices, San Francisco. Retrieved August 20, 2008, from communication. sbs.ohio-state.edu/sense-making/meet/2007/meet07_dervin.pdf

Dervin, B., & Dewdney, P. (1986). Neutral questioning: A new approach to the reference interview. *Reference Quarterly, 25*(4), 506–513.

Dervin, B., & Foreman-Wernet, L. (Eds.). (2003). *Sense-making methodology reader. Selected writings of Brenda Dervin.* Cresskill, NJ: Hampton Press.

Dervin, B., & Nilan, M. (1986). Information needs and uses. *Annual Review of Information Science and Technology, 21*, 3–33.

Dervin, B., & Reinhard, C. D. (2006a). Beyond communication: Research as communicating: Making user and audience studies matter, paper 2. *Information Research, 12*. Retrieved September 28, 2008, from informationR.net/ir/12-1/paper287.html

Dervin, B., & Reinhard, C. D. (2006b). Researchers and practitioners talk about users and each other: Making user and audience studies matter, paper 1. *Information Research, 12*. Retrieved September 28, 2008, from informationR.net/ir/12-1/paper286.html

Dervin, B., & Reinhard, C. (2007a). How emotional dimensions of situated information-seeking relate to user evaluations of help from source: An exemplar study informed by sense-making methodology. In D. Nahl & D. Bilal (Eds.), *Information and emotion: The emergent affective paradigm in information behavior research and theory* (pp. 51–84). Medford, NJ: Information Today.

Dervin, B., & Reinhard, C. (2007b, October). *Predicting library, Internet, and other source use: A comparison of the predictive power of two user-defined categorizations of information seeking situations: Nature of situation versus "emotions" assessments*. Poster presented at the Annual Meeting of the American Society for Information Science and Technology, Milwaukee, WI. Retrieved September 20, 2008, from imlsproject.comm.ohio-state.edu/imls_papers/asist07poster)_full.pdf

Dervin, B., Reinhard, C. D., & Kerr, Z. Y. (2006). The burden of being special: Adding clarity about communicating to researching and serving users, special and otherwise. *Advances in Librarianship, 30*, 241–277.

Dervin, B., Reinhard, C. D., Kerr, Z. Y., Connaway, L. S., Prabha, C., Normore, L., et al. (2006, November). *How libraries, Internet browsers and other sources help: A comparison of sense-making evaluations of sources used in recent college/university and personal life situations by faculty, graduate student, and undergraduate users*. Poster presented at Annual Meeting of the American Society for Information Science and Technology, Austin, TX. Retrieved August 31, 2008, from www.asis.org/Conferences/AM06/papers/273.html

Dervin, B., Zweizig, D., Banister, M., Gabriel, M., Hall. E. P., & Kwan, C. (1976). *The development of strategies for dealing with the information needs of urban residents: Phase 1: The citizen study*. Washington, DC: U.S Office of Education. (ERIC Document Reproduction Service No. ED 125640)

Dreyfus, H., & Rabinow, P. (1983). *Michel Foucault: Beyond structuralism and hermeneutics* (2nd ed.). Chicago: University of Chicago Press.

Ellis, D. (1992). The physical and cognitive paradigms in information retrieval research. *Journal of Documentation, 48*(1), 45–64.

Fidel, R. (1985). Moves in online searching. *Online Review, 9*, 91–74.

Fisher, K. (2005). Information grounds. In K. E. Fisher, S. Erdelez, & E. F. McKechnie (Eds.), *Theories of information behavior* (pp. 185–190). Medford, NJ: Information Today.

Fisher, K., & Julien, H. (2009). Information behavior. *Annual Review of Information Science and Technology, 43*, 317–358.

Fisher, K. E., Durrance, J. C., & Hinton, M. B. (2004). Information grounds and the use of need-based services by immigrants in Queens NY: A context-based, outcome evaluation approach. *Journal of the American Society for Information Science and Technology, 55*, 754–766.

Fisher, K. E., Erdelez, S., & McKechnie, E. F. (Eds.). (2005). *Theories of information behavior*. Medford, NJ: Information Today.

Fisher, K. E., & Landry, C. F. (2007). Understanding the information behavior of stay-at-home mothers through affect. In D. Nahl & D. Bilal (Eds.), *Information and emotion: The emergent affective paradigm in information behavior research* (pp. 211–234). Medford, NJ: Information Today.

Fisher, K. E., Marcoux, E., Meyers, E., & Landry, C. F. (2007). Tweens and everyday life: Preliminary findings from Seattle. In M. K. Chelton & C. Cool (Eds.), *Youth information seeking behaviors: Context, theories, models and issues* (Vol. 2, pp. 1–25). Lanham, MD: Scarecrow.

Fisher, K. E., Marcoux, E., Miller, L. S., Sanchez, A., & Cunningham, E. R. (2004). Information behavior of migrant Hispanic farm workers and their families in the Pacific Northwest. *Information Research, 10*(1). Retrieved September 12, 2008, from informationR.net/ir/10-1/paper199.html

Fisher, K. E., & Naumer, C. M. (2006). Information grounds: Theoretical basis and empirical findings on information flow in social settings. In A. Spink & C. Cole (Eds.), *New directions in human information behavior* (pp. 93–111). Dordrecht, The Netherlands: Springer.

Flanagan, J. C. (1954). The critical incident technique. *Psychological Bulletin, 51*, 327–358.

Flick, U. (1994). Social representations and the social construction of everyday knowledge: Theoretical and methodological queries. *Social Science Information, 2*, 179–197.

Flick, U. (2000). Episodic interviewing. In M. W. Bauer & G. Gaskell (Eds.), *Qualitative researching with text, image and sound* (pp. 75–92). London: Sage.

Flick, U. (2002). *Introduction to qualitative research* (2nd ed.). London: Sage.

Foucault, M. (1979). *Discipline and punish: The birth of the prison* (A. Sheridan, Trans.). New York: Vintage/Random House.

Foucault, M. (1980). *The history of sexuality. Volume 1. Introduction* (R. Hurley, Trans.). New York: Vintage/Random House.

Foucault, M. (1988). *Technologies of the self: A seminar with Michel Foucault* (L. H. Martin, H. Gutman, & P. H. Hutton, Eds.). London: Tavistock.

Frohmann, B. (1990). Rules of indexing: A critique of mentalism in information retrieval theory. *Journal of Documentation, 46*(2), 81–101.

Frohmann, B. (1991). Knowledge and power in library and information science: Towards a discourse analysis of the cognitive view point. In P. Vakkari & B. Cronin (Eds.), *Conceptions of library and information science: Historical, empirical and theoretical perspectives* (pp. 135–148). London: Taylor Graham.

Frohmann, B. (1994). Discourse analysis as a research method in library and information science. *Library & Information Science Research, 16*, 119–138.

Frohmann, B. (2001). Discourse and documentation: Some implications for pedagogy and research. *Journal of Education for Library and Information Science, 42*(1), 13–26.

Frohmann, B. (2004). *Deflating information: From science studies to documentation*. Toronto: University of Toronto Press.

Frohmann, B. (2008). Subjectivity and information ethics. *Journal of the American Society for Information Science and Technology, 59*(2), 267–277.

Hacking, I. (1995). *Rewriting the soul: Multiple personality and the sciences of memory*. Princeton, NJ: Princeton University Press.

Hacking, I. (2004). *Historical ontology*. Cambridge, MA: Harvard University Press.

Hacking, I. (2006, August 17). Making up people. *London Review of Books*, 23–26.

Halliday, M. A. K., & Martin, J. R. (1993). *Writing science: Literacy and discursive power*. London: The Falmer Press.

Harris, R. M., & Dewdney, P. (1994). *Barriers to information: How formal help systems fail battered women*. Westport, CT: Greenwood.

Hedemark, Å., Hedman, J., & Sundin, O. (2005). Speaking of users: On user discourses in the field of public libraries. *Information Research, 10*(2). Retrieved August 28, 2008, from informationR.net/ir/10-2/paper218.html

Hersberger, J. (2001). Everyday information needs and information sources of homeless parents. *New Review of Information Behaviour Research, 2*, 119–134.

Hughes-Hassell, S., & Agosto, D. (2007). Modeling the everyday life information needs of urban teenagers. In M. K. Chelton & C. Cool (Eds.), *Youth information seeking behaviors II: Context, theories, models and issues* (pp. 27–62). Lanham, MD: Scarecrow Press.

Information Behavior in Everyday Contexts. (2004). *Information grounds.* Retrieved September 20, 2008, from ibec.ischool.washington.edu/info_grounds.php

Julien. H. (1999). Barriers to adolescents' information seeking for career decision making. *Journal of the American Society for Information Science, 50*(1), 38–48.

Kari, J., & Hartel, J. (2007). Information and higher things in life: Addressing the pleasurable and the profound in information science. *Journal of the American Society for Information Science and Technology, 58*, 1131–1147.

Kari, J., & Savolainen, R. (2007). Relationships between information seeking and context: A qualitative study of Internet searching and the goals of personal development. *Library & Information Science Research, 29*, 47–69.

Kuhlthau, C. C. (1988). Developing a model of the library search process: Cognitive and affective aspects. *RQ, 28*(7), 232–242.

Kuhlthau, C. C. (1991). Inside the search process: Information seeking from the user's perspective. *Journal of the American Society for Information Science, 42*, 361–371.

Kuhlthau, C. C. (1993). *Seeking meaning: A process approach to library and information services.* Norwood, NJ: Ablex Publishing.

Lievrouw, L. (2000). The new review of information behaviour. *Library & Information Science Research, 24*, 99–100.

Lunt, P. (1996). Rethinking the focus group in media and communications research. *Journal of Communication, 46*(2), 79–98.

Martin, J. R. (1993). Life as a noun: Arresting the universe in science and humanities. In M. A. K. Halliday & J. R. Martin (Eds.), *Writing science: Literacy and discursive power* (pp. 221–267). London: Falmer Press.

McKechnie, L. (E. F.). (2000). Ethnographic observation of preschool children in the public library. *Library & Information Science Research, 22*, 61–76.

McKechnie, L., Baker, L., Greenwood, M., & Julien, H. (2002). Research methods trends in human information behavior literature. *New Review of Information Behaviour Research, 3*, 113–125.

McKechnie, L., & MacKenzie, P. J. (2004, October). *The young child/adult caregiver storytime program as information ground.* Paper presented at Library Research Seminar III, Kansas City, KS.

McKechnie, L. E. F., Julien, H., Goodall, G., & Lajoie-Paquette, D. (2005). How human information behaviour researchers use each other's work: A basic citation analysis study. *Information Research, 10*(2). Retrieved August 20, 2008, from informationR.net/ir/10-2/paper220.html

McKechnie, L. E. F., Julien, H., Pecoskie, J., & Dixon, C. (2006). The presentation of the user in reports of human information behaviour research. *Information Research, 12*(1). Retrieved August 20, 2008, from informationR.net/ir/12-1/paper278.html

MacKenzie, P. J. (2004). Positioning theory and the negotiation of information needs in a clinical midwifery setting. *Journal of the American Society for Information Science and Technology, 55*(8), 685–694.

MacKenzie, P. J. (2006). Mapping textually mediated information practice in clinical midwifery care. In A. Spink & C. Cole (Eds.), *New directions in human information behavior* (pp. 73–92). Dordrecht, The Netherlands: Springer.

Menzel, H. (1966). Information needs and uses in science and technology. *Annual Review of Information Science and Technology, 1*, 41–69.

Merton, R. K. (1987). Focussed interviews and focus groups: Continuities and discontinuities. *Public Opinion Quarterly, 51*(4), 550–566.

Meyers, E. M., Fisher, K. E., & Marcoux, E. (2007). Studying the everyday information behavior of tweens: Notes from the field. *Library & Information Science Research, 29,* 310–331.

Nahl, D., & Bilal, D. (Eds.). (2007). *Information and emotion: The emergent affective paradigm in information behavior research and theory.* Medford, NJ: Information Today.

Nicholas, D., Huntington, P., Williams, P., & Dobrowolski, T. (2006). The digital information consumer. In A. Spink & C. Cole (Eds.), *New directions in human information behavior* (pp. 203–228). Dordrecht, The Netherlands: Springer.

Niemela, R., & Huotari, M.-L. (2008). Everyday life information behavior. In M.-L. Huotari & E. Davenport (Eds.), *From information provision to knowledge production. Proceedings of the International Conference for the Celebration of the 20th Anniversary of Information Studies, Faculty of Humanities, University of Oulu* (pp. 141–160). Oulu, Finland: University of Oulu.

Olsson, M. (2005). Making sense of sense-making: Information behaviour researchers construct an "author." *Canadian Journal of Information & Library Science, 29,* 315–334.

Olsson, M. (2007). Power/knowledge: The discursive construction of an author. *Library Quarterly, 77,* 219–240.

Olsson, M. (2008). Academic citation as a strategic discursive practice. In M.-L. Huotari & E. Davenport (Eds.), *From information provision to knowledge production. Proceedings of the International Conference for the Celebration of the 20th Anniversary of Information Studies, Faculty of Humanities, University of Oulu* (pp. 161–173). Oulu, Finland: University of Oulu.

Poster, M. (2000). *The mode of information.* London: Polity Press.

Poster, M. (2006). *Information please.* Durham, NC: Duke University Press.

Prigoda, E., & MacKenzie, P. J. (2007). Purls of wisdom: A collectivist study of human information behaviour in a public library knitting group. *Journal of Documentation, 63*(1), 90–114.

Procter, R., Goldenberg, A., Davenport, E., & McKinlay, A. (1998). Genres in support of collaborative information retrieval in the virtual library. *Interacting with Computers, 10,* 157–175.

Radway, J. (1989). Ethnography among elites: Comparing discourses of power. *Journal of Communication Inquiry, 13*(2), 3–11.

Savolainen, R. (1992). The sense-making theory: An alternative to intermediary-centered approaches in library and information science? In P. Vakkari & B. Cronin (Eds.), *Conceptions of library and information science: Historical, empirical and theoretical perspectives* (pp. 149–164). London: Taylor Graham.

Savolainen, R. (1993). The sense-making theory: Reviewing the interests of a user-centred approach to information seeking and use. *Information Processing & Management, 29,* 13–28.

Savolainen, R (1995a). Everyday life information seeking: Approaching information seeking in the context of "way of life." *Library & Information Science Research, 17*(3), 259–294.

Savolainen, R. (1995b). Everyday life information seeking: Findings and methodological questions of an empirical study. In M. Hancock Beaulieu & N. O. Pors (Eds.), *Proceedings of the 1st Nordic-British Conference* (pp. 313–331). Copenhagen, Denmark: Royal School of Librarianship.

Savolainen, R. (2006). Information use as gap-bridging: The viewpoint of sense-making methodology. *Journal of the American Society for Information Science and Technology, 57*(8), 1116–1125.

Savolainen, R. (2007). Information behavior and information practice: Reviewing the "umbrella concepts" of information-seeking studies. *Library Quarterly, 77*(2), 109–132.

Schultze, U. (2000). A confessional account of an ethnography about knowledge work. *MIS Quarterly, 24*(1), 3–41.

Shields, V., & Dervin, B. (1993). Sense-making in feminist social science research: A call to enlarge the methodological options of feminist studies. *Women's Studies International Forum, 16*(1), 65–81.

Skare, R., Lund, N. W., & Vårheim, A. (Eds.). (2007). *A document (re)turn.* Frankfurt am Main, Germany: Peter Land.

Spink, A., & Cole, C. (2001). Introduction to the special issue: Everyday life information-seeking research. *Library & Information Science Research, 23*(4), 301–304.

Spink, A., & Cole, C. (2006a). Human information behavior: Integrating diverse approaches and information use. *Journal of the American Society for Information Science and Technology, 57*(1), 25–35.

Spink, A., & Cole, C. (Eds.). (2006b). *New directions in human information behavior.* Dordrecht, The Netherlands: Springer.

Talja, S. (1997). Constituting "information" and "user" as research objects: A theory of knowledge formations as an alternative to the information man-theory. *Information Seeking in Context: Proceedings of an International Conference on Research in Information Needs, Seeking and Use in Different Contexts,* 67–80.

Talja, S. (1999). Analyzing qualitative interview data: The discourse analytic method. *Library & Information Science Research, 21*(4), 459–477.

Talja, S., & Hartel, J. (2007, August). *Revisiting the user-centered turn in information science research: An intellectual history perspective.* Paper presented at CoLIS: Sixth International Conference on Conceptions of Library and Information Science, Borås, Sweden.

Talja, S., & MacKenzie, P. J. (2007). Editors' introduction: Special issue on discursive approaches to information seeking in context. *Library Quarterly, 77,* 97–107.

Taylor, R. S. (1962). The process of asking questions. *American Documentation, 13,* 391–396.

Taylor, R. S. (1968). Question-negotiation and information seeking in libraries. *College & Research Libraries, 29*(3), 178–194.

Thelwall, M. (2008). Social networks, gender and friending: An analysis of MySpace member profiles. *Journal of the American Society for Information Science and Technology, 59*(8), 1321–1330.

Thelwall, M., & Wouters, P. (2005). What's the deal with the Web/blogs/the next big technology: A key role for information science in e-social science research? *International Conference on Conceptions of Library and Information Science,* 187–199.

Tuominen, K. (1997). User-centered discourse: An analysis of the subject positions of the user and librarian. *Library Quarterly, 4,* 350–371.

Tuominen, K., & Savolainen, R. (1997). A social constructionist approach to the study of information use as discursive action. *Information Seeking in Context: Proceedings of an International Conference on Research in Information Needs, Seeking and Use in Different Contexts,* 81–96.

Urquhart, C., Light, A., Thomas, R., Barker, A., Yeoman, A., Cooper, J., et al. (2003). Critical incident technique and explicitation interviewing in studies of information behavior. *Library & Information Science Research, 25*(1), 63–88.

Urquhart, C., & Rowley, J. (2007). Understanding student information behavior in relation to electronic information services: Lessons from longitudinal monitoring and evaluation, Part 2. *Journal of the American Society for Information Science and Technology, 58,* 1188–1197.

Vakkari, P., Savolainen, R., & Dervin, B. (Eds.). (1997). *Information Seeking in Context: Proceedings of an International Conference on Research in Information Needs, Seeking and Use in Different Contexts.* London: Taylor Graham.

Williamson, K. (2006). Research in constructivist frameworks using ethnographic techniques. *Library Trends, 55*(1), 83–101.

Weick, K. (1979). *The social psychology of organizing* (2nd ed.). New York: McGraw-Hill.

Weick, K. (1995). *Sense-making in organizations*. London: Sage.

Wilson, T. D. (2008). The information user: Past, present and future. *Journal of Information Science*, *34*(4), 457–464.

Wilson, T. D., & Allen, D. K. (Eds.). (1999). *Exploring the Contexts of Information Behaviour: Proceedings of the Second International Conference on Research in Information Needs, Seeking and Use in Different Contexts*. London: Taylor Graham.

Zweizig, D., & Dervin, B. (1977). Public library use, users, uses: Advances in knowledge of the characteristics and needs of the adult clientele of American public libraries. *Advances in Librarianship*, *7*, 231–255.

# Index

82games, 124, 125, 133
211 Toronto website, 511, 516

## A

Aaron computer artist, 215–216
Abbe, O., 343
Abbott, A., 554
Abdullahi, I., 494
aboutness, concept of, 183–188
Abraham, G., 343
Abramowitz, M., 367–368
Abramson, J. B., 333
Abramson, N., 402
abstract symbolism, 215
Abt, H. A., 33–34
accessibility
  of digital government, 351
  of journals, 293
accessibility of information
  social barriers to, 517–519
  structural barriers to, 515–517
access models, and impact of public sector information, 441–443
access to subjects for ELIS studies, 547
Accomazzi, A., 3, 15–16, 17, 18, 19, 21, 22, 23, 25–26, 28, 29, 30, 31–32, 33–34, 35, 44, 45, 295, 298, 300, 301
acculturation of immigrants, 498–499
Achananuparp, P., 343
Ackoff, R., 120
AC Milan soccer club, 116, 135
Adamic, L. A., 347
Adams, F., 163
Adams, John, 352
Adams, W. J., 421
Addis, L., 294

Adelman, J., 53
adjusted line yards, in football, 131
adjusted plus/minus rating system, in basketball, 133–134
Adkisson, H., 243
Adler, J., 139
admission fees, and public goods, 453
Adorno, T. W., 401
Advanced Media, 147
Advanced Scout, 137–138
Aggarwal, C. C., 41
aggregation, and price discrimination, 460–461
Agosto, D., 534–535
Agosto, D. E., 533
Agouris, P., 320
Agre, P. E., 208, 209, 231, 318
Aguayo-Albasini, J. L., 80
Ah-Ki, E., 259
Ahmad, F., 516
AI, *see* Artificial Intelligence
Aichholzer, G., 447, 463, 472, 474
A-index, 74
Aislabie, C., 430
Aisola, K., 436
Aitchison, J., 251, 257, 258, 259, 265
Aizlewood, A., 504, 509, 511, 513
Akerlof, G., 426
Alavi, M., 120
Alba, R., 499, 501
Albert, H., 401
Albert, J., 129, 144
Alencastro, A. C. R., 80
Alexander, L. B., 494
Allard, D., 499, 502–503, 504, 505, 506, 509, 512, 516, 520
Allard, S., 494
Allard, S. L., 502, 506–507

# More Titles of Interest from Information Today, Inc.

## Digital Inclusion

### Measuring the Impact of Information and Community Technology

*Edited by Michael Crandall and Karen E. Fisher*

In this important book, Michael Crandall and Karen E. Fisher and a dozen contributors have made "Digital Inclusion" their rallying cry. They provide a framework for thinking about the effects of community technology on digital inclusion and present concrete examples of the impact successful community technology providers have had on individual users, communities, and society as a whole.

200 pp/hardbound/ISBN 978-1-57387-373-4
ASIST Members $47.60 • Nonmembers $59.50

## Theories of Information Behavior

*Edited by Karen E. Fisher, Sanda Erdelez, and Lynne (E. F.) McKechnie*

This unique book presents authoritative overviews of more than 70 conceptual frameworks for understanding how people seek, manage, share, and use information in different contexts. Covering both established and newly proposed theories of information behavior, the book includes contributions from 85 scholars from 10 countries. Theory descriptions cover origins, propositions, methodological implications, usage, and links to related theories.

456 pp/hardbound/ISBN 978-1-57387-230-0
ASIST Members $39.60 • Nonmembers $49.50

## Knowledge Management Lessons Learned
### *What Works and What Doesn't*

*Edited by Michael E. D. Koenig and T. Kanti Srikantaiah*

A follow-up to Srikantaiah and Koenig's ground-breaking *Knowledge Management for the Information Professional*, this new book surveys recent applications and innovations in KM. More than 30 experts describe KM in practice, revealing what has been learned, what works, and what doesn't. Includes projects undertaken by organizations at the forefront of KM, and coverage of KM strategy and implementation, cost analysis, education and training, content management, communities of practice, competitive intelligence, and much more.

**624 pp/hardbound/ISBN 978-1-57387-181-5**
**ASIST Members $35.60 • Nonmembers $44.50**


## Knowledge Management in Practice
### *Connections and Context*

*Edited by T. Kanti Srikantaiah and Michael E. D. Koenig*

This third entry in the ambitious, highly regarded KM series from editors Srikantaiah and Koenig features 26 chapters contributed by more than 20 experts from around the globe. The book not only looks at how KM is being implemented in organizations today, but is unique in surveying the efforts of KM professionals to extend knowledge beyond their organizations and in providing a framework for understanding user context. *Knowledge Management in Practice* is a must-read for any professional seeking to connect organizational KM systems with increasingly diverse and geographically dispersed user communities.

**544 pp/hardbound/ISBN 978-1-57387-312-3**
**ASIST Members $47.60 • Nonmembers $59.50**

# Information and Emotion

## *The Emergent Affective Paradigm in Information Behavior Research and Theory*

*Edited by Diane Nahl and Dania Bilal*

*Information and Emotion* introduces the new research areas of affective issues in information seeking and use and the affective paradigm applied to information behavior in a variety of populations, cultures, and contexts. The book's editors and authors are information behavior researchers at the forefront of charting the emotional quality of the information environment. Colletively, their contributions make *Information and Emotion* a unique source of research findings on the user perspective; the user experience; and how emotional aspects can be interpreted, mitigated, or enhanced through design that is informed by use, and by users who directly participate in information design.

392 pp/hardbound/ISBN 978-1-57387-310-9
ASIST Members $47.60 • Nonmembers $59.50

# Computerization Movements and Technology Diffusion

## *From Mainframes to Ubiquitous Computing*

*Edited by Margaret S. Elliott and Kenneth L. Kraemer*

"Computerization movement" (CM), as first articulated by Rob Kling, refers to a special kind of social and technological movement that promotes the adoption of computing within organizations and society. Here, editors Margaret S. Elliott and Kenneth L. Kraemer and more than two dozen noted scholars trace the successes and failures of CMs from the mainframe and PC eras to the emerging era of ubiquitous computing. The empirical studies presented here show the need for designers, users, and the media to be aware that CM rhetoric can propose grand visions that never become part of a reality and reinforce the need for critical and scholarly review of promising new technologies.

608 pp/hardbound/ISBN 978-1-57387-311-6
ASIST Members $47.60 • Nonmembers $59.50

# ARIST 43

*Edited by Blaise Cronin*

*ARIST*, published annually since 1966, is a landmark publication within the information science community. Contents of Volume 43 (2009) includes:

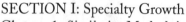

SECTION I: Specialty Growth
Chapter 1: *Similarity Methods in Chemoinformatics*, Peter Willett
Chapter 2: *Geographic Information Science*, Jonathan Raper

SECTION II: Information Organization and Discovery
Chapter 3: *Information Architecture*, Elin K. Jacob and Aaron Loehrlein
Chapter 4: *Collaborative Semantic Tagging and Annotation Systems*, Jane Hunter
Chapter 5: *Literature-Related Discovery*, Ronald N. Kostoff, Joel A. Block, Jeffrey L. Solka, Michael B. Briggs, Robert L. Rushenberg, Jesse A. Stump, Dustin Johnson, Terence J. Lyons, and Jeffrey R. Wyatt
Chapter 6: *Author Name Disambiguation*, Neil R. Smalheiser and Vetle I. Torvik

SECTION III: Information Use
Chapter 7: *Information Behavior*, Karen E. Fisher and Heidi Julien
Chapter 8: *The Layperson and Open Access*, Alesia Zuccala

SECTION IV: Theory Building
Chapter 9: *Document Theory*, Niels Windfeld Lund
Chapter 10: *Gatekeeping: A Critical Review*, Karine Barzilai-Nahon

**544 pp/hardbound/ISBN 978-1-57387-340-6**
**ASIST Members $99.95 • Nonmembers $124.95**

# TANZANIA, JOURNEY TO REPUBLIC

Randal Sadleir

Foreword by
Dr Julius Nyerere

The Radcliffe Press
London · New York

Published in 1999 by The Radcliffe Press
Reprinted with corrections 2000
Victoria House, Bloomsbury Square
London, WC1B 4DZ
175 Fifth Avenue, New York NY 10010

In the United States and Canada
distributed by St Martin's Press
175 Fifth Avenue, New York NY 10010

ISBN 1-86064-437-6

A full CIP record for this book is available from the British Library
A full CIP record for this book is available from the Library of Congress

Library of Congress Catalogue card: available

Typeset in Sabon by Oxford Publishing Services, Oxford
Printed and bound in Great Britain